JEFFERY A. COLE
Anoka–Ramsey Community College

GARY K. ROCKSWOLD
Mankato State University

INSTRUCTOR'S SOLUTIONS MANUAL
VOLUME 1

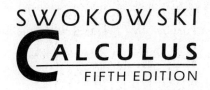

SWOKOWSKI
CALCULUS
FIFTH EDITION

PWS-KENT PUBLISHING COMPANY
Boston

PWS–KENT
Publishing Company

20 Park Plaza
Boston, Massachusetts 02116

PWS–KENT Publishing Company is a division of Wadsworth, Inc.

ISBN 0–534–92485–9

Printed in the United States of America

95 94 93 92   / 10 9 8 7 6 5 4 3 2

PREFACE

This manual contains answers to all exercises in Chapters 1 through 8 of the text, *Calculus, Fifth Edition,* by Earl W. Swokowski. For most problems, a reasonably detailed solution is included. We have tried to correlate the length of the solutions with their difficulty. It is our hope that by merely browsing through the solutions, the instructor will save time in determining appropriate assignments for their particular class.

All figures are new for this edition. Most function values have been plotted using computer software, and we are very happy with the high precision provided by this method. We would appreciate any feedback concerning errors, solution correctness, solution style, or manual style. These and any other comments may be sent directly to us or in care of the publisher.

We would like to thank: Editor Dave Geggis, for entrusting us with this project and continued support; Earl Swokowski, for his assistance; Sally Lifland and Gail Magin of Lifland et al., Bookmakers, for assembling the final manuscript; and George and Bryan Morris, for preparing the new figures. We dedicate this book to our wives, Joan and Wendy, and thank them for their support and understanding.

Jeffery A. Cole

Anoka-Ramsey Community College

11200 Mississippi Blvd. NW

Coon Rapids, MN 55433

Gary K. Rockswold

Mankato State University

P.O. Box 41

Mankato, MN 56002

Table of Contents

In the review sections, the solutions are abbreviated since more detailed solutions were given in sections. In easier groups of exercises, representative solutions are shown. When appropriate, only the answer is listed. When possible, we tried to make each piece of art with the same scale to show a realistic and consistent graph. This manual was done using EXP: *The Scientific Word Processor*.

The following <u>notations</u> are used in the manual.

Note: Notes to the instructor pertaining to hints on instruction or conventions to follow.

{ }	{ comments to the reader are in braces }
$\Rightarrow$	{ implies, next equation, logically follows }
$\Leftrightarrow$	{ if and only if, is equivalent to }
•	{ bullet, used to separate problem statement from solution or explanation }
★	{ used to identify the answer to the problem }
§	{ <u>section</u> references }
$\forall$	{ For all, i.e., $\forall x$ means "for all x". }
$\mathbb{R} - \{a\}$	{ The set of all real numbers except a. }
$\therefore$	{ therefore }

The following notations are defined in the manual, but also listed here for convenience.

DNE	{ Does Not Exist }
L, I	{ the original limit or integral }
T, S	{ the result is obtained from using the trapezoidal rule or Simpson's rule }
↑, ↓	{ increasing, decreasing }
CN	{ critical number(s) }
PI	{ point(s) of inflection }
CU, CD	{ concave up, concave down }
MAX, MIN	{ absolute maximum or minimum }
LMAX, LMIN	{ local maximum or minimum }
VA, HA, OA	{ vertical, horizontal, or oblique asymptote }
QI, QII, QIII, QIV	{ quadrants I, II, III, IV }

Chapter 1: Precalculus Review

1   (a) $(-5)|3 - 6| = -15$ (b) $|-6|/(-2) = -3$ (c) $|7| + |-4| = 11$

2   (a) $(4)|6 - 7| = 4$ (b) $5/|-2| = \frac{5}{2}$ (c) $|-1| + |-9| = 10$

3   (a) Since $(4 - \pi)$ is positive, $|4 - \pi| = 4 - \pi$.

     (b) Since $(\pi - 4)$ is negative, $|\pi - 4| = -(\pi - 4) = 4 - \pi$.

     (c) Since $(\sqrt{2} - 1.5)$ is negative, $|\sqrt{2} - 1.5| = -(\sqrt{2} - 1.5) = 1.5 - \sqrt{2}$.

4   (a) Since $(\sqrt{3} - 1.7)$ is positive, $|\sqrt{3} - 1.7| = \sqrt{3} - 1.7$.

     (b) Since $(1.7 - \sqrt{3})$ is negative, $|1.7 - \sqrt{3}| = -(1.7 - \sqrt{3}) = \sqrt{3} - 1.7$.

     (c) $\left|\frac{1}{5} - \frac{1}{3}\right| = \left|\frac{3}{15} - \frac{5}{15}\right| = \left|-\frac{2}{15}\right| = -(-\frac{2}{15}) = \frac{2}{15}$

Note: Have students substitute a value to test if the expression inside the absolute value symbol is positive or negative first, then generalize.

5   If $x < -3$, then $3 + x < 0$. Thus, $|3 + x| = -(3 + x) = -x - 3$.

6   If $x > 5$, then $5 - x < 0$. Thus, $|5 - x| = -(5 - x) = x - 5$.

7   If $x < 2$, then $2 - x > 0$. Thus, $|2 - x| = 2 - x$.

8   If $x \geq -7$, then $7 + x > 0$. Thus, $|7 + x| = 7 + x$.

9 $15x^2 - 12 = -8x \Rightarrow 15x^2 + 8x - 12 = 0 \Rightarrow (5x + 6)(3x - 2) = 0 \Rightarrow x = -\frac{6}{5}, \frac{2}{3}$

10 $15x^2 - 14 = 29x \Rightarrow 15x^2 - 29x - 14 = 0 \Rightarrow (5x + 2)(3x - 7) = 0 \Rightarrow x = -\frac{2}{5}, \frac{7}{3}$

11 $2x(4x + 15) = 27 \Rightarrow 8x^2 + 30x - 27 = 0 \Rightarrow (2x + 9)(4x - 3) = 0 \Rightarrow x = -\frac{9}{2}, \frac{3}{4}$

12 $x(3x + 10) = 77 \Rightarrow 3x^2 + 10x - 77 = 0 \Rightarrow (x + 7)(3x - 11) = 0 \Rightarrow x = -7, \frac{11}{3}$

13 $x^2 + 4x + 2 = 0 \Rightarrow x = \dfrac{-4 \pm \sqrt{8}}{2} = -2 \pm \sqrt{2}$

14 $x^2 - 6x - 3 = 0 \Rightarrow x = \dfrac{6 \pm \sqrt{48}}{2} = 3 \pm 2\sqrt{3}$

15 $2x^2 - 3x - 4 = 0 \Rightarrow x = \dfrac{3 \pm \sqrt{41}}{4} = \frac{3}{4} \pm \frac{1}{4}\sqrt{41}$

16 $3x^2 + 5x + 1 = 0 \Rightarrow x = \dfrac{-5 \pm \sqrt{13}}{6} = -\frac{5}{6} \pm \frac{1}{6}\sqrt{13}$

17 $2x + 5 < 3x - 7 \Rightarrow -x < -12 \Rightarrow x > 12 \Leftrightarrow (12, \infty)$

18 $x - 8 > 5x + 3 \Rightarrow -4x > 11 \Rightarrow x < -\frac{11}{4} \Leftrightarrow (-\infty, -\frac{11}{4})$

19 $3 \leq \dfrac{2x - 3}{5} < 7 \Rightarrow 15 \leq 2x - 3 < 35 \Rightarrow 18 \leq 2x < 38 \Rightarrow 9 \leq x < 19 \Leftrightarrow [9, 19)$

20 $-2 < \dfrac{4x + 1}{3} \leq 0 \Rightarrow -6 < 4x + 1 \leq 0 \Rightarrow -7 < 4x \leq -1 \Rightarrow$

$$-\tfrac{7}{4} < x \leq -\tfrac{1}{4} \Leftrightarrow (-\tfrac{7}{4}, -\tfrac{1}{4}]$$

Note: For the problems using sign charts the following procedure is used.

     1)   Factor the expression into linear and/or quadratic factors.

     2)   Construct the sign chart.

     3)   Determine the regions containing the desired sign. { The sign of the region is negative if the region contains an odd number of negative signs, positive if the region contains an even number of negative signs. }

21 $x^2 - x - 6 < 0 \Rightarrow (x-3)(x+2) < 0 \Rightarrow -2 < x < 3 \Leftrightarrow (-2, 3)$

Value of x:		-2		3	
Sign of $x - 3$:	$-$		$-$		$+$
Sign of $x + 2$:	$-$		$+$		$+$

Chart 21

Value of x:		-3		-1	
Sign of $x + 1$:	$-$		$-$		$+$
Sign of $x + 3$:	$-$		$+$		$+$

Chart 22

22 $x^2 + 4x + 3 \geq 0 \Rightarrow (x+1)(x+3) \geq 0 \Rightarrow$

$$x \leq -3 \text{ or } x \geq -1 \Leftrightarrow (-\infty, -3] \cup [-1, \infty)$$

23 $x^2 - 2x - 5 > 3 \Rightarrow x^2 - 2x - 8 > 0 \Rightarrow (x-4)(x+2) > 0 \Rightarrow$

$$x < -2 \text{ or } x > 4 \Leftrightarrow (-\infty, -2) \cup (4, \infty)$$

Value of x:		-2		4	
Sign of $x - 4$:	$-$		$-$		$+$
Sign of $x + 2$:	$-$		$+$		$+$

Chart 23

Value of x:		-3		7	
Sign of $x - 7$:	$-$		$-$		$+$
Sign of $x + 3$:	$-$		$+$		$+$

Chart 24

24 $x^2 - 4x - 17 \leq 4 \Rightarrow x^2 - 4x - 21 \leq 0 \Rightarrow (x-7)(x+3) \leq 0 \Rightarrow$

$$-3 \leq x \leq 7 \Leftrightarrow [-3, 7]$$

25 $x(2x + 3) \geq 5 \Rightarrow 2x^2 + 3x - 5 \geq 0 \Rightarrow (2x+5)(x-1) \geq 0 \Rightarrow$

$$x \leq -\tfrac{5}{2} \text{ or } x \geq 1 \Leftrightarrow (-\infty, -\tfrac{5}{2}] \cup [1, \infty)$$

Value of x:		$-5/2$		1	
Sign of $x - 1$:	$-$		$-$		$+$
Sign of $2x + 5$:	$-$		$+$		$+$

Chart 25

Value of x:		-1		$4/3$	
Sign of $3x - 4$:	$-$		$-$		$+$
Sign of $x + 1$:	$-$		$+$		$+$

Chart 26

26 $x(3x - 1) \leq 4 \Rightarrow 3x^2 - x - 4 \leq 0 \Rightarrow (3x-4)(x+1) \leq 0 \Rightarrow$

$$-1 \leq x \leq \tfrac{4}{3} \Leftrightarrow [-1, \tfrac{4}{3}]$$

27 $\dfrac{x + 1}{2x - 3} > 2 \Rightarrow \dfrac{x + 1 - 2(2x - 3)}{2x - 3} > 0 \Rightarrow \dfrac{-3x + 7}{2x - 3} > 0 \Rightarrow \tfrac{3}{2} < x < \tfrac{7}{3} \Leftrightarrow (\tfrac{3}{2}, \tfrac{7}{3})$

Value of x:		$3/2$		$7/3$	
Sign of $-3x + 7$:	$+$		$+$		$-$
Sign of $2x - 3$:	$-$		$+$		$+$

Chart 27

Value of x:		-2		$-5/3$	
Sign of $3x + 5$:	$-$		$-$		$+$
Sign of $-11x-22$:	$+$		$-$		$-$

Chart 28

28 $\dfrac{x - 2}{3x + 5} \leq 4 \Rightarrow \dfrac{x - 2 - 4(3x + 5)}{3x + 5} \leq 0 \Rightarrow \dfrac{-11x - 22}{3x + 5} \leq 0 \Rightarrow$

$$x < -2 \text{ or } x > -\tfrac{5}{3} \Leftrightarrow (-\infty, -2] \cup (-\tfrac{5}{3}, \infty)$$

29 $\dfrac{1}{x - 2} \geq \dfrac{3}{x + 1} \Rightarrow \dfrac{1(x + 1) - 3(x - 2)}{(x - 2)(x + 1)} \geq 0 \Rightarrow \dfrac{-2x + 7}{(x - 2)(x + 1)} \geq 0 \Leftrightarrow$

$$(-\infty, -1) \cup (2, \tfrac{7}{2}]$$

Value of x:		-1		2		$7/2$	
Sign of $-2x+7$:	$+$		$+$		$+$		$-$
Sign of $x - 2$:	$-$		$-$		$+$		$+$
Sign of $x + 1$:	$-$		$+$		$+$		$+$

Chart 29

x values:		-8		$-3/2$		5	
$x - 5$:	$-$		$-$		$-$		$+$
$2x + 3$:	$-$		$-$		$+$		$+$
$-2x - 16$:	$+$		$-$		$-$		$-$

Chart 30

30 $\dfrac{2}{2x + 3} \leq \dfrac{2}{x - 5} \Rightarrow \dfrac{2(x - 5) - 2(2x + 3)}{(2x + 3)(x - 5)} \leq 0 \Rightarrow \dfrac{-2x - 16}{(2x + 3)(x - 5)} \leq 0 \Leftrightarrow$

$$[-8, -\tfrac{3}{2}) \cup (5, \infty)$$

31 $|x + 3| < 0.01 \Rightarrow -0.01 < x + 3 < 0.01 \Rightarrow -3.01 < x < -2.99 \Leftrightarrow (-3.01 \; -2.99)$

32 $|x - 4| \leq 0.03 \Rightarrow -0.03 \leq x - 4 \leq 0.03 \Rightarrow 3.97 \leq x \leq 4.03 \Leftrightarrow [3.97, 4.03]$

33 $|x + 2| \geq 0.001 \Rightarrow x + 2 \geq 0.001 \text{ or } x + 2 \leq -0.001 \Rightarrow$

$$x \geq -1.999 \text{ or } x \leq -2.001 \Leftrightarrow (-\infty, -2.001] \cup [-1.999, \infty)$$

$\boxed{34}$ $|x - 3| > 0.002 \Rightarrow x - 3 > 0.002 \text{ or } x - 3 < -0.002 \Rightarrow$

$$x > 3.002 \text{ or } x < 2.998 \Leftrightarrow (-\infty, 2.998) \cup (3.002, \infty)$$

$\boxed{35}$ $|2x + 5| < 4 \Rightarrow -4 < 2x + 5 < 4 \Rightarrow -9 < 2x < -1 \Rightarrow$

$$-\tfrac{9}{2} < x < -\tfrac{1}{2} \Leftrightarrow \left(-\tfrac{9}{2}, -\tfrac{1}{2}\right)$$

$\boxed{36}$ $|3x - 7| \geq 5 \Rightarrow 3x - 7 \geq 5 \text{ or } 3x - 7 \leq -5 \Rightarrow$

$$x \geq 4 \text{ or } x \leq \tfrac{2}{3} \Leftrightarrow \left(-\infty, \tfrac{2}{3}\right] \cup [4, \infty)$$

$\boxed{37}$ $|6 - 5x| \leq 3 \Rightarrow -3 \leq 6 - 5x \leq 3 \Rightarrow -9 \leq -5x \leq -3 \Rightarrow \tfrac{3}{5} \leq x \leq \tfrac{9}{5} \Leftrightarrow \left[\tfrac{3}{5}, \tfrac{9}{5}\right]$

$\boxed{38}$ $|-11 - 7x| > 6 \Rightarrow -11 - 7x > 6 \text{ or } -11 - 7x < -6 \Rightarrow$

$$x < -\tfrac{17}{7} \text{ or } x > -\tfrac{5}{7} \Leftrightarrow \left(-\infty, -\tfrac{17}{7}\right) \cup \left(-\tfrac{5}{7}, \infty\right)$$

$\boxed{39}$ (a) $x = -2$ is the line parallel to the y-axis that intersects the x-axis at $(-2, 0)$.

(b) $y = 3$ is the line parallel to the x-axis that intersects the y-axis at $(0, 3)$.

(c) $x \geq 0$ is the set of all points to the right of and on the y-axis.

(d) $xy > 0$ is the set of all points in quadrants I and III.

(e) $y < 0$ is the set of all points below the x-axis.

(f) $|x| \leq 2$ and $|y| \leq 1$ is the set of all points within the rectangle such that
$$-2 \leq x \leq 2 \text{ and } -1 \leq y \leq 1.$$

$\boxed{40}$ (a) $y = -2$ is the line parallel to the x-axis that intersects the y-axis at $(0, -2)$.

(b) $x = -4$ is the line parallel to the y-axis that intersects the x-axis at $(-4, 0)$.

(c) $x/y < 0$ is the set of all points in quadrants II and IV.

(d) $xy = 0$ is the set of all points on the x-axis or y-axis.

(e) $y > 1$ is the set of all points above the line parallel to the x-axis
that intersects the y-axis at $(0, 1)$.

(f) $|x| \geq 2$ and $|y| \geq 3$ is the set of all points that are at least 2 units from the y-axis
and 3 units from the x-axis.

$\boxed{41}$ (a) $d(A, B) = \sqrt{(6 - 4)^2 + [2 - (-3)]^2} = \sqrt{4 + 25} = \sqrt{29}$

(b) $M(A, B) = \left(\dfrac{4 + 6}{2}, \dfrac{-3 + 2}{2}\right) = \left(5, -\tfrac{1}{2}\right)$

$\boxed{42}$ $A(-2, -5), \ B(4, 6)$ ●　　　　　　　★ (a) $\sqrt{157}$　(b) $\left(1, \tfrac{1}{2}\right)$

$\boxed{43}$ Show that $d(A, C)^2 = d(A, B)^2 + d(B, C)^2$, i.e., $(\sqrt{130})^2 = (\sqrt{98})^2 + (\sqrt{32})^2$.

$$\text{Area} = \tfrac{1}{2}bh = \tfrac{1}{2}(\sqrt{32})(\sqrt{98}) = 28$$

$\boxed{44}$ Show that $d(A, B) = d(B, C) = d(C, D) = d(D, A)$ {each is $\sqrt{29}$} and

$$d(A, C)^2 = d(A, B)^2 + d(B, C)^2 \ \{ d(A, C) = \sqrt{58} \}$$

$\boxed{45}$ $y = 2x^2 - 1$ ●　　　　　　　$\boxed{46}$ $y = -x^2 + 2$ ●

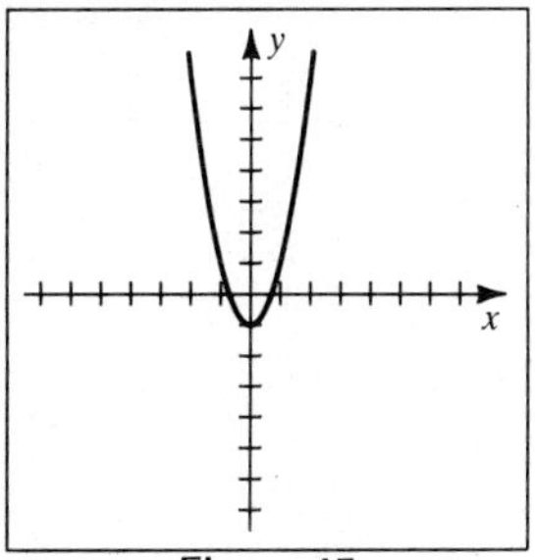

Figure 45

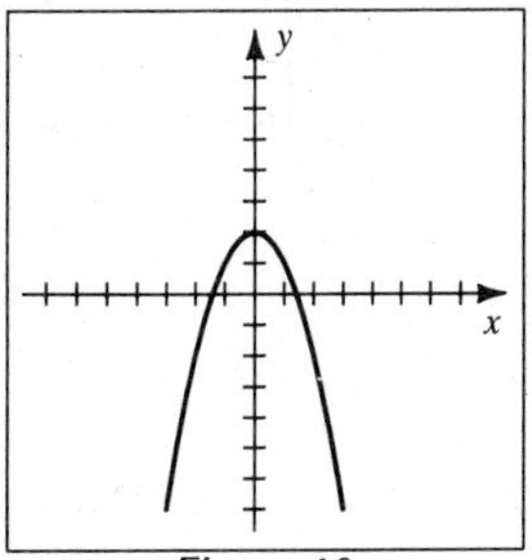

Figure 46

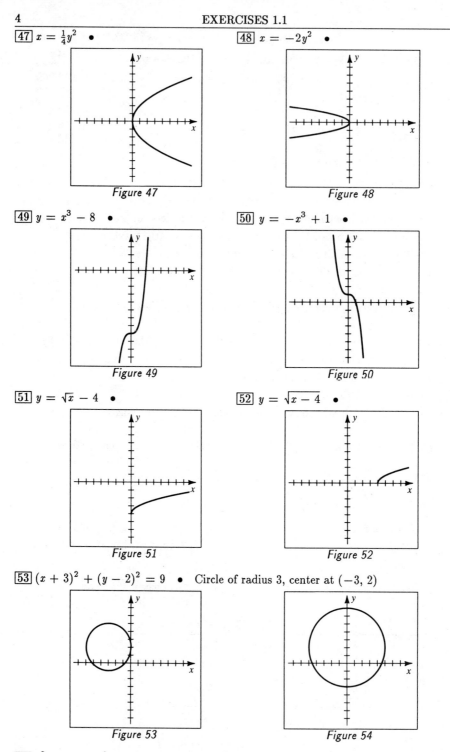

$\boxed{47}$ $x = \frac{1}{4}y^2$ •

Figure 47

$\boxed{48}$ $x = -2y^2$ •

Figure 48

$\boxed{49}$ $y = x^3 - 8$ •

Figure 49

$\boxed{50}$ $y = -x^3 + 1$ •

Figure 50

$\boxed{51}$ $y = \sqrt{x} - 4$ •

Figure 51

$\boxed{52}$ $y = \sqrt{x - 4}$ •

Figure 52

$\boxed{53}$ $(x + 3)^2 + (y - 2)^2 = 9$ •   Circle of radius 3, center at $(-3, 2)$

Figure 53

Figure 54

$\boxed{54}$ $x^2 + (y - 2)^2 = 25$ •   Circle of radius 5, center at $(0, 2)$

$\boxed{55}$ $y = -\sqrt{16 - x^2}$ • $\boxed{56}$ $y = \sqrt{4 - x^2}$ •

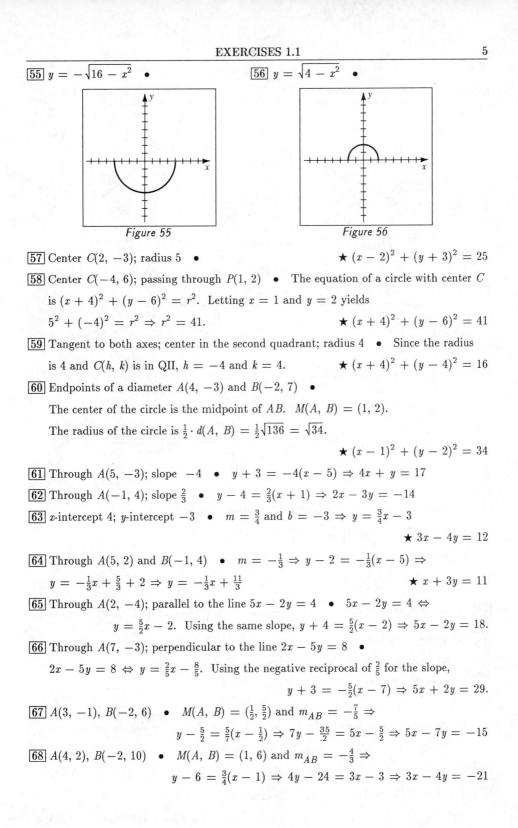

Figure 55   Figure 56

$\boxed{57}$ Center $C(2, -3)$; radius 5 • $\bigstar$ $(x - 2)^2 + (y + 3)^2 = 25$

$\boxed{58}$ Center $C(-4, 6)$; passing through $P(1, 2)$ •   The equation of a circle with center C
is $(x + 4)^2 + (y - 6)^2 = r^2$. Letting $x = 1$ and $y = 2$ yields
$5^2 + (-4)^2 = r^2 \Rightarrow r^2 = 41$. $\bigstar$ $(x + 4)^2 + (y - 6)^2 = 41$

$\boxed{59}$ Tangent to both axes; center in the second quadrant; radius 4 •   Since the radius
is 4 and $C(h, k)$ is in QII, $h = -4$ and $k = 4$. $\bigstar$ $(x + 4)^2 + (y - 4)^2 = 16$

$\boxed{60}$ Endpoints of a diameter $A(4, -3)$ and $B(-2, 7)$ •

The center of the circle is the midpoint of AB. $M(A, B) = (1, 2)$.

The radius of the circle is $\frac{1}{2} \cdot d(A, B) = \frac{1}{2}\sqrt{136} = \sqrt{34}$.

$\bigstar$ $(x - 1)^2 + (y - 2)^2 = 34$

$\boxed{61}$ Through $A(5, -3)$; slope -4 • $y + 3 = -4(x - 5) \Rightarrow 4x + y = 17$

$\boxed{62}$ Through $A(-1, 4)$; slope $\frac{2}{3}$ • $y - 4 = \frac{2}{3}(x + 1) \Rightarrow 2x - 3y = -14$

$\boxed{63}$ x-intercept 4; y-intercept -3 • $m = \frac{3}{4}$ and $b = -3 \Rightarrow y = \frac{3}{4}x - 3$

$\bigstar$ $3x - 4y = 12$

$\boxed{64}$ Through $A(5, 2)$ and $B(-1, 4)$ • $m = -\frac{1}{3} \Rightarrow y - 2 = -\frac{1}{3}(x - 5) \Rightarrow$
$y = -\frac{1}{3}x + \frac{5}{3} + 2 \Rightarrow y = -\frac{1}{3}x + \frac{11}{3}$ $\bigstar$ $x + 3y = 11$

$\boxed{65}$ Through $A(2, -4)$; parallel to the line $5x - 2y = 4$ • $5x - 2y = 4 \Leftrightarrow$
$y = \frac{5}{2}x - 2$. Using the same slope, $y + 4 = \frac{5}{2}(x - 2) \Rightarrow 5x - 2y = 18$.

$\boxed{66}$ Through $A(7, -3)$; perpendicular to the line $2x - 5y = 8$ •

$2x - 5y = 8 \Leftrightarrow y = \frac{2}{5}x - \frac{8}{5}$. Using the negative reciprocal of $\frac{2}{5}$ for the slope,
$y + 3 = -\frac{5}{2}(x - 7) \Rightarrow 5x + 2y = 29$.

$\boxed{67}$ $A(3, -1)$, $B(-2, 6)$ • $M(A, B) = (\frac{1}{2}, \frac{5}{2})$ and $m_{AB} = -\frac{7}{5} \Rightarrow$
$y - \frac{5}{2} = \frac{5}{7}(x - \frac{1}{2}) \Rightarrow 7y - \frac{35}{2} = 5x - \frac{5}{2} \Rightarrow 5x - 7y = -15$

$\boxed{68}$ $A(4, 2)$, $B(-2, 10)$ • $M(A, B) = (1, 6)$ and $m_{AB} = -\frac{4}{3} \Rightarrow$
$y - 6 = \frac{3}{4}(x - 1) \Rightarrow 4y - 24 = 3x - 3 \Rightarrow 3x - 4y = -21$

Note: The notation E_1 and E_2 refers to the first equation and the second equation.

69 $2x + 3y = 2$; $x - 2y = 8$ $\quad\bullet\quad$ $-2\,E_2 + E_1 \Rightarrow 7y = -14 \Rightarrow y = -2$; $x = 4$

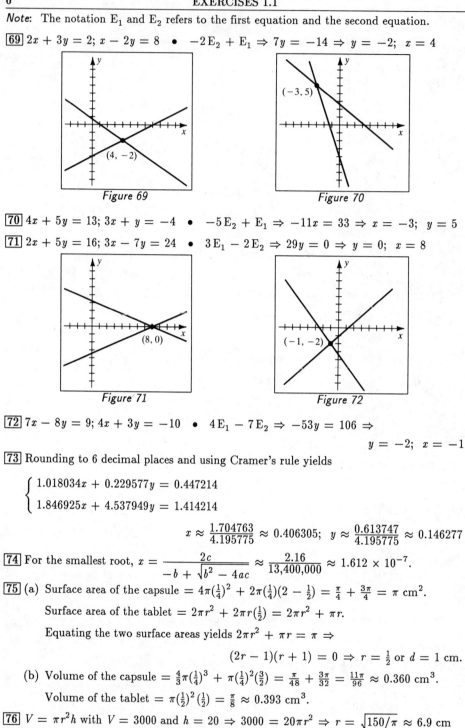

Figure 69   Figure 70

70 $4x + 5y = 13$; $3x + y = -4$ $\quad\bullet\quad$ $-5\,E_2 + E_1 \Rightarrow -11x = 33 \Rightarrow x = -3$; $y = 5$

71 $2x + 5y = 16$; $3x - 7y = 24$ $\quad\bullet\quad$ $3\,E_1 - 2\,E_2 \Rightarrow 29y = 0 \Rightarrow y = 0$; $x = 8$

Figure 71   Figure 72

72 $7x - 8y = 9$; $4x + 3y = -10$ $\quad\bullet\quad$ $4\,E_1 - 7\,E_2 \Rightarrow -53y = 106 \Rightarrow$
$$y = -2; \quad x = -1$$

73 Rounding to 6 decimal places and using Cramer's rule yields
$$\begin{cases} 1.018034x + 0.229577y = 0.447214 \\ 1.846925x + 4.537949y = 1.414214 \end{cases}$$
$$x \approx \frac{1.704763}{4.195775} \approx 0.406305; \quad y \approx \frac{0.613747}{4.195775} \approx 0.146277$$

74 For the smallest root, $x = \dfrac{2c}{-b + \sqrt{b^2 - 4ac}} \approx \dfrac{2.16}{13,400,000} \approx 1.612 \times 10^{-7}$.

75 (a) Surface area of the capsule $= 4\pi(\frac{1}{4})^2 + 2\pi(\frac{1}{4})(2 - \frac{1}{2}) = \frac{\pi}{4} + \frac{3\pi}{4} = \pi$ cm^2.

Surface area of the tablet $= 2\pi r^2 + 2\pi r(\frac{1}{2}) = 2\pi r^2 + \pi r$.

Equating the two surface areas yields $2\pi r^2 + \pi r = \pi \Rightarrow$
$$(2r - 1)(r + 1) = 0 \Rightarrow r = \tfrac{1}{2} \text{ or } d = 1 \text{ cm}.$$

(b) Volume of the capsule $= \frac{4}{3}\pi(\frac{1}{4})^3 + \pi(\frac{1}{4})^2(\frac{3}{2}) = \frac{\pi}{48} + \frac{3\pi}{32} = \frac{11\pi}{96} \approx 0.360$ cm^3.

Volume of the tablet $= \pi(\frac{1}{2})^2(\frac{1}{2}) = \frac{\pi}{8} \approx 0.393$ cm^3.

76 $V = \pi r^2 h$ with $V = 3000$ and $h = 20 \Rightarrow 3000 = 20\pi r^2 \Rightarrow r = \sqrt{150/\pi} \approx 6.9$ cm

77 $M \geq 3 \Rightarrow \dfrac{6}{6 - p} \geq 3 \Rightarrow 6 \geq 18 - 3p$ {since $6 - p > 0$} $\Rightarrow$
$$p \geq 4, \text{ but } p < 6 \text{ since } p < f. \text{ Thus, } 4 \leq p < 6.$$

78   $W < 5 \Rightarrow 125\left(\dfrac{6400}{6400 + x}\right)^2 < 5 \Rightarrow \left(\dfrac{6400}{6400 + x}\right)^2 < \left(\dfrac{1}{5}\right)^2 \Rightarrow$

$\dfrac{6400}{6400 + x} < \dfrac{1}{5}$ { since $\dfrac{6400}{6400 + x} > 0$ } $\Rightarrow x + 6400 > 32{,}000 \Rightarrow x > 25{,}600$ km

79   $d < 75 \Rightarrow v + \frac{1}{20}v^2 < 75 \Rightarrow v^2 + 20v - 1500 < 0 \Rightarrow$

$(v + 50)(v - 30) < 0 \Rightarrow -50 < v < 30$ and $v \geq 0 \Rightarrow 0 \leq v < 30$

80   $c > 4 \Rightarrow \dfrac{20t}{t^2 + 4} > 4 \Rightarrow 5t > t^2 + 4 \Rightarrow$

$t^2 - 5t + 4 < 0 \Rightarrow (t - 1)(t - 4) < 0 \Rightarrow 1 < t < 4$

81   (a) $R = R_0 \Rightarrow R_0 = R_0(1 + aT) \Rightarrow 1 = 1 + aT \Rightarrow aT = 0.$

Since $a > 0$, T must be $0\,°C$. Thus, R_0 is the resistance when $T = 0\,°C$.

(b) $R = 0$ and $T = -273 \Rightarrow 0 = R_0(1 - 273a) \Rightarrow$

{ since $R_0 > 0$ } $1 - 273a = 0 \Rightarrow a = \frac{1}{273}$.

(c) $R = 2$, $R_0 = 1.25 = \frac{5}{4}$, and $a = \frac{1}{273} \Rightarrow 2 = \frac{5}{4}\left(1 + \frac{1}{273}T\right) \Rightarrow$

$\frac{8}{5} = 1 + \frac{1}{273}T \Rightarrow \frac{3}{5} = \frac{1}{273}T \Rightarrow T = \frac{819}{5} \Rightarrow T = 163.8\,°C.$

82   (a)

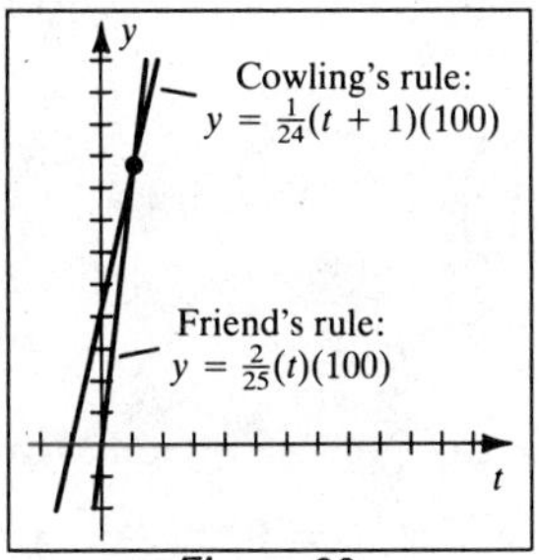

Cowling's rule:
$y = \frac{1}{24}(t + 1)(100)$

Friend's rule:
$y = \frac{2}{25}(t)(100)$

Figure 82

(b) $\dfrac{t + 1}{24}(a) = \frac{2}{25}(ta) \Rightarrow$

$25t + 25 = 48t \Rightarrow$

$t = \frac{25}{23}$ years ≈ 13 months

Exercises 1.2

1   If $f(x) = \sqrt{x - 4} - 3x$, find $f(4)$, $f(8)$, and $f(13)$. •   ★ -12; -22; -36

2   If $f(x) = \dfrac{x}{x - 3}$, find $f(-2)$, $f(0)$, and $f(3.01)$. •   ★ $\frac{2}{5}$; 0; 301

3   $f(x) = 5x - 2$ •   (a) $f(a) = 5(a) - 2 = 5a - 2$

(b) $f(-a) = 5(-a) - 2 = -5a - 2$ (c) $-f(a) = -1 \cdot (5a - 2) = -5a + 2$

(d) $f(a + h) = 5(a + h) - 2 = 5a + 5h - 2$

(e) $f(a) + f(h) = (5a - 2) + (5h - 2) = 5a + 5h - 4$

(f) $\dfrac{f(a + h) - f(a)}{h} = \dfrac{(5a + 5h - 2) - (5a - 2)}{h} = \dfrac{5h}{h} = 5$

4   (a) $3 - 4a$ (b) $3 + 4a$ (c) $4a - 3$ (d) $3 - 4a - 4h$ (e) $6 - 4a - 4h$ (f) -4

5   (a) $a^2 - a + 3$ (b) $a^2 + a + 3$ (c) $-a^2 + a - 3$

(d) $a^2 + 2ah + h^2 - a - h + 3$ (e) $a^2 + h^2 - a - h + 6$ (f) $2a + h - 1$

6   $f(x) = 2x^2 + 3x - 7$ •   (a) $f(a) = 2(a)^2 + 3(a) - 7 = 2a^2 + 3a - 7$

(b) $f(-a) = 2(-a)^2 + 3(-a) - 7 = 2a^2 - 3a - 7$

(c) $-f(a) = -1 \cdot (2a^2 + 3a - 7) = -2a^2 - 3a + 7$

(d) $f(a + h) = 2(a + h)^2 + 3(a + h) - 7 = 2(a^2 + 2ah + h^2) + 3a + 3h - 7 =$

$2a^2 + 4ah + 2h^2 + 3a + 3h - 7$

(e) $f(a) + f(h) = (2a^2 + 3a - 7) + (2h^2 + 3h - 7) = 2a^2 + 2h^2 + 3a + 3h - 14$

(f) $\dfrac{f(a + h) - f(a)}{h} = \dfrac{(2a^2 + 4ah + 2h^2 + 3a + 3h - 7) - (2a^2 + 3a - 7)}{h}$

$$= \dfrac{4ah + 2h^2 + 3h}{h} = \dfrac{h(4a + 2h + 3)}{h} = 4a + 2h + 3$$

7 $x^3 - 4x = 0 \Rightarrow x(x + 2)(x - 2) = 0$ ★ All real numbers except -2, 0, and 2

8 $6x^2 + 13x - 5 = 0 \Rightarrow (2x + 5)(3x - 1) = 0$ ★ All real numbers except $-\frac{5}{2}$ and $\frac{1}{3}$

9 $x^2 - 5x + 4 = 0 \Rightarrow x = 1, 4; \; 2x - 3 \geq 0 \Rightarrow x \geq \frac{3}{2}$ ★ $[\frac{3}{2}, 4) \cup (4, \infty)$

10 $x^2 - 4 = 0 \Rightarrow x = \pm 2; \; 4x - 3 \geq 0 \Rightarrow x \geq \frac{3}{4}$ ★ $[\frac{3}{4}, 2) \cup (2, \infty)$

11 (a) $f(-x) = 5(-x)^3 + 2(-x) = -5x^3 - 2x = -f(x)$

   (b) $f(-x) = |-x| - 3 = |x| - 3 = f(x)$

   (c) $f(-x) = \left[8(-x)^3 - 3(-x)^2\right]^3 = (-8x^3 - 3x^2)^3 = -(8x^3 + 3x^2)^3 \neq \pm f(x)$

                       ★ (a) Odd   (b) Even   (c) Neither

12 (a) $f(-x) = \sqrt{3(-x)^4 + 2(-x)^2 - 5} = \sqrt{3x^4 + 2x^2 - 5} = f(x)$

   (b) $f(-x) = 6(-x)^5 - 4(-x)^3 + 2(-x) = -6x^5 + 4x^3 - 2x =$

                                  $-(6x^5 - 4x^3 + 2x) = -f(x)$

   (c) $f(-x) = (-x)\left[(-x) - 5\right] = x(x + 5) \neq \pm f(x)$

                       ★ (a) Even   (b) Odd   (c) Neither

13 $f(x) = |x| + c; \; c = 0, 1, -3$ •

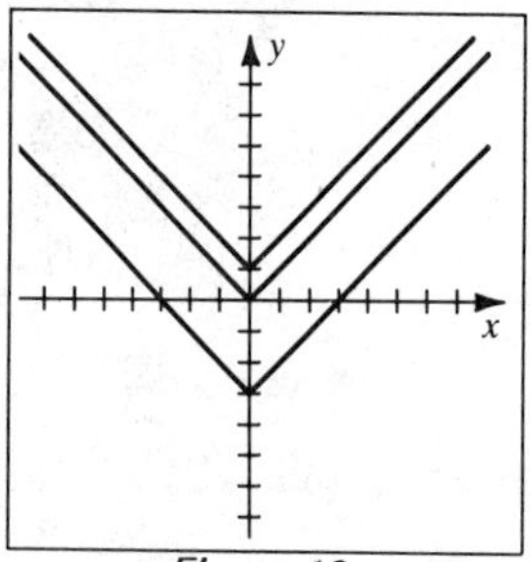

Figure 13

14 $f(x) = |x - c|; \; c = 0, 2, -3$ •

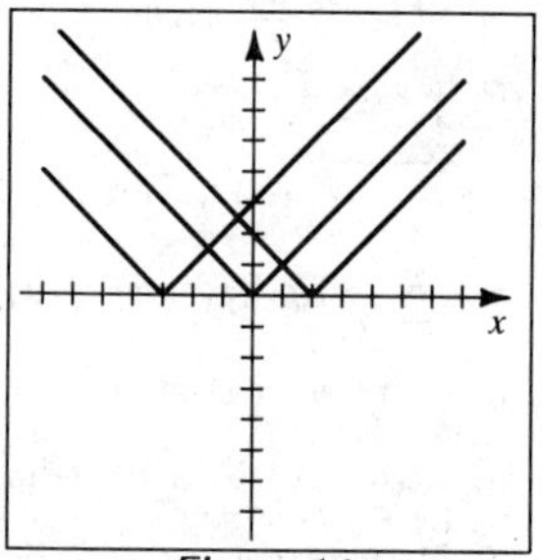

Figure 14

15 $f(x) = 2\sqrt{x} + c; \; c = 0, 3, -2$ •

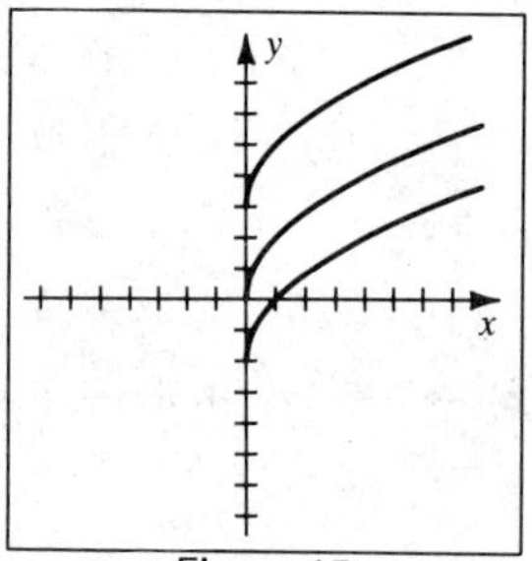

Figure 15

16 $f(x) = \sqrt{9 - x^2} + c; \; c = 0, 1, -3$ •

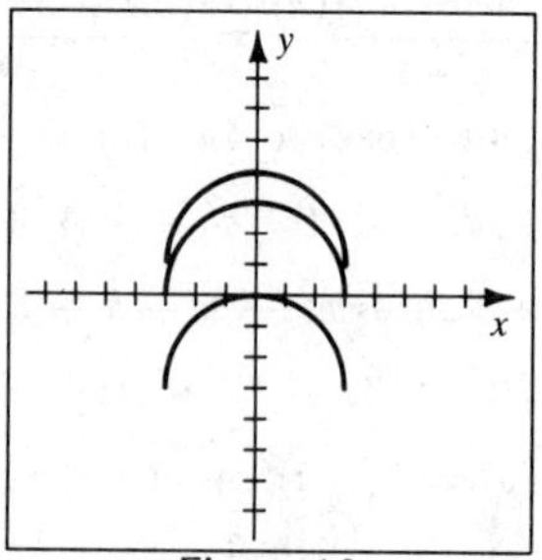

Figure 16

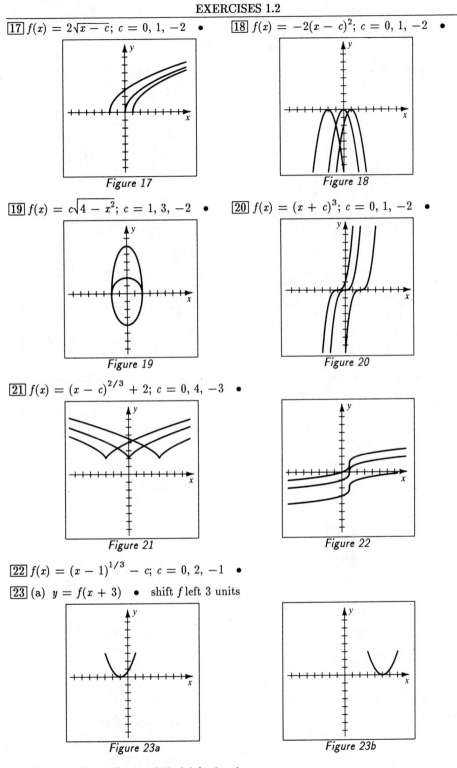

17 $f(x) = 2\sqrt{x - c}$; $c = 0, 1, -2$ •

Figure 17

18 $f(x) = -2(x - c)^2$; $c = 0, 1, -2$ •

Figure 18

19 $f(x) = c\sqrt{4 - x^2}$; $c = 1, 3, -2$ •

Figure 19

20 $f(x) = (x + c)^3$; $c = 0, 1, -2$ •

Figure 20

21 $f(x) = (x - c)^{2/3} + 2$; $c = 0, 4, -3$ •

Figure 21

Figure 22

22 $f(x) = (x - 1)^{1/3} - c$; $c = 0, 2, -1$ •

23 (a) $y = f(x + 3)$ • shift f left 3 units

Figure 23a

Figure 23b

(b) $y = f(x - 3)$ • shift f right 3 units

(c) $y = f(x) + 3$ • shift f up 3 units

(d) $y = f(x) - 3$ • shift f down 3 units

(e) $y = -3f(x)$ • stretch f by a factor of 3 and reflect through the x-axis

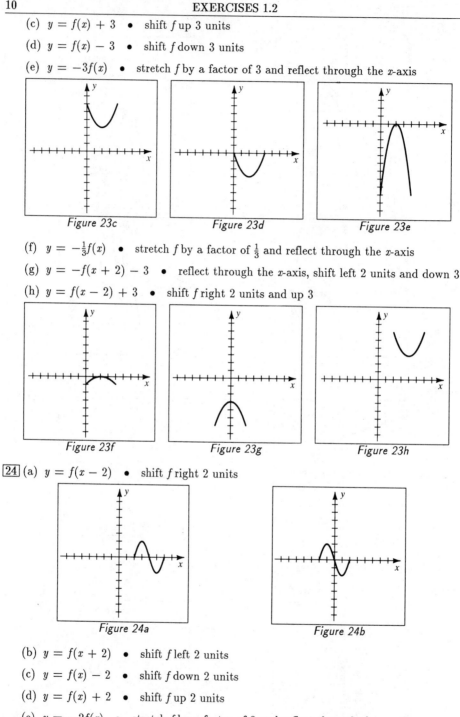

Figure 23c   Figure 23d   Figure 23e

(f) $y = -\frac{1}{3}f(x)$ • stretch f by a factor of $\frac{1}{3}$ and reflect through the x-axis

(g) $y = -f(x + 2) - 3$ • reflect through the x-axis, shift left 2 units and down 3

(h) $y = f(x - 2) + 3$ • shift f right 2 units and up 3

Figure 23f   Figure 23g   Figure 23h

24 (a) $y = f(x - 2)$ • shift f right 2 units

Figure 24a   Figure 24b

(b) $y = f(x + 2)$ • shift f left 2 units

(c) $y = f(x) - 2$ • shift f down 2 units

(d) $y = f(x) + 2$ • shift f up 2 units

(e) $y = -2f(x)$ • stretch f by a factor of 2 and reflect through the x-axis

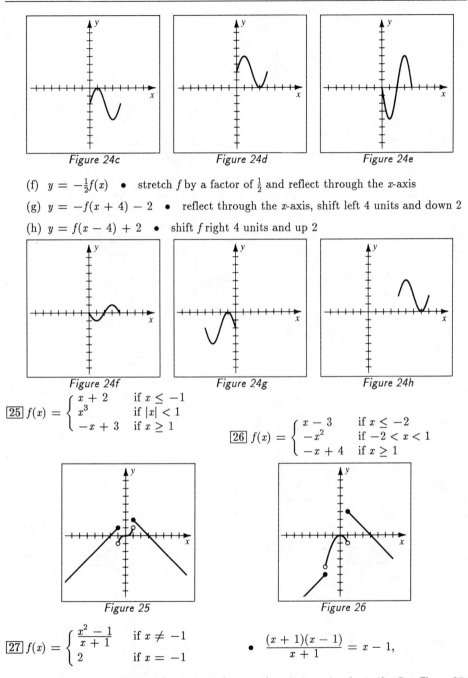

Figure 24c   Figure 24d   Figure 24e

(f) $y = -\frac{1}{2}f(x)$ • stretch f by a factor of $\frac{1}{2}$ and reflect through the x-axis

(g) $y = -f(x+4) - 2$ • reflect through the x-axis, shift left 4 units and down 2

(h) $y = f(x-4) + 2$ • shift f right 4 units and up 2

Figure 24f   Figure 24g   Figure 24h

25   $f(x) = \begin{cases} x+2 & \text{if } x \le -1 \\ x^3 & \text{if } |x| < 1 \\ -x+3 & \text{if } x \ge 1 \end{cases}$

26   $f(x) = \begin{cases} x-3 & \text{if } x \le -2 \\ -x^2 & \text{if } -2 < x < 1 \\ -x+4 & \text{if } x \ge 1 \end{cases}$

Figure 25   Figure 26

27   $f(x) = \begin{cases} \dfrac{x^2 - 1}{x + 1} & \text{if } x \ne -1 \\ 2 & \text{if } x = -1 \end{cases}$ • $\dfrac{(x+1)(x-1)}{x+1} = x - 1,$

f is a line with a hole at $(-1, -2)$ and the point $(-1, 2)$. See *Figure 27*.

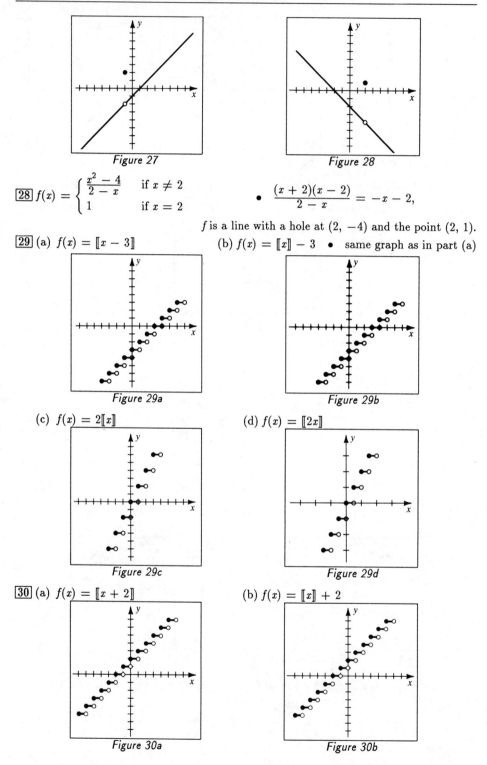

Figure 27

Figure 28

28 $f(x) = \begin{cases} \dfrac{x^2 - 4}{2 - x} & \text{if } x \neq 2 \\ 1 & \text{if } x = 2 \end{cases}$

• $\dfrac{(x + 2)(x - 2)}{2 - x} = -x - 2,$

f is a line with a hole at $(2, -4)$ and the point $(2, 1)$.

29 (a) $f(x) = [\![x - 3]\!]$ (b) $f(x) = [\![x]\!] - 3$ •   same graph as in part (a)

Figure 29a

Figure 29b

(c) $f(x) = 2[\![x]\!]$ (d) $f(x) = [\![2x]\!]$

Figure 29c

Figure 29d

30 (a) $f(x) = [\![x + 2]\!]$ (b) $f(x) = [\![x]\!] + 2$

Figure 30a

Figure 30b

(c) $f(x) = \frac{1}{2}[\![x]\!]$ (d) $f(x) = [\![\frac{1}{2}x]\!]$

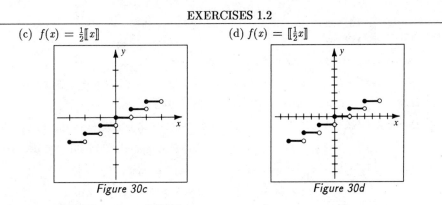

Figure 30c   Figure 30d

$\boxed{31}$ $f(x) = \sqrt{x+5}$; $g(x) = \sqrt{x+5}$ •

★ (a) $2\sqrt{x+5}$; 0; $x+5$; 1 (b) $[-5, \infty)$; $(-5, \infty)$

$\boxed{32}$ $f(x) = \sqrt{3-2x}$; $g(x) = \sqrt{x+4}$ •   ★ (a) $\sqrt{3-2x} + \sqrt{x+4}$;

$\sqrt{3-2x} - \sqrt{x+4}$; $\sqrt{(3-2x)(x+4)}$; $\sqrt{\dfrac{3-2x}{x+4}}$ (b) $[-4, \frac{3}{2}]$; $(-4, \frac{3}{2}]$

$\boxed{33}$ $f(x) = \dfrac{2x}{x-4}$; $g(x) = \dfrac{x}{x+5}$ •

★ (a) $\dfrac{3x^2+6x}{(x-4)(x+5)}$; $\dfrac{x^2+14x}{(x-4)(x+5)}$; $\dfrac{2x^2}{(x-4)(x+5)}$; $\dfrac{2x+10}{x-4}$

(b) All real numbers except -5 and 4; all real numbers except -5, 0, and 4

$\boxed{34}$ $f(x) = \dfrac{x}{x-2}$; $g(x) = \dfrac{3x}{x+4}$ •

(a) $(f+g)(x) = f(x) + g(x) = \dfrac{x}{x-2} + \dfrac{3x}{x+4} = \dfrac{4x^2-2x}{(x-2)(x+4)}$;

$(f-g)(x) = f(x) - g(x) = \dfrac{x}{x-2} - \dfrac{3x}{x+4} = \dfrac{-2x^2+10x}{(x-2)(x+4)}$;

$(fg)(x) = f(x) \cdot g(x) = \dfrac{x}{x-2} \cdot \dfrac{3x}{x+4} = \dfrac{3x^2}{(x-2)(x+4)}$;

$\left(\dfrac{f}{g}\right)(x) = \dfrac{f(x)}{g(x)} = \dfrac{x/(x-2)}{(3x)/(x+4)} = \dfrac{x+4}{3(x-2)}$

(b) All real numbers except -4 and 2; The domain of f/g also excludes the

zeros of g, and hence is all real numbers except -4, 0, and 2.

Note: Let $h(x) = (f \circ g)(x) = f(g(x))$ and $k(x) = (g \circ f)(x) = g(f(x))$.

$\boxed{35}$ (a) $h(x) = (\sqrt{x+2})^2 - 3(\sqrt{x+2}) = x + 2 - 3\sqrt{x+2}$.

The domain of $(f \circ g)(x)$ is the set of all x in the domain of g $(x \ge -2)$ such that

$g(x)$ (the range of g is $y \ge 0$) is in the domain of f. Since the domain of f is $\mathbb{R}$,

any value of $g(x)$ is in its domain. Thus, the domain is all x such that $x \ge -2$.

(b) $k(x) = \sqrt{(x^2-3x)+2} = \sqrt{x^2-3x+2}$.

The domain of $(g \circ f)(x)$ is the set of all x in the domain of f (all $\mathbb{R}$) such that

$f(x)$ (the range of f is $y \ge -\frac{9}{4}$) is in the domain of g. Since the domain of g is

$x \ge -2$, we must solve $f(x) \ge -2$. $x^2 - 3x \ge -2 \Rightarrow x^2 - 3x + 2 \ge 0 \Rightarrow$

$(x-1)(x-2) \ge 0 \Rightarrow x \in (-\infty, 1] \cup [2, \infty)$ { use a sign chart as before to

solve the quadratic inequality }. Thus, the domain is $(-\infty, 1] \cup [2, \infty)$.

---

36 (a) $h(x) = \sqrt{(x^2 + 2x) - 15} = \sqrt{x^2 + 2x - 15}$.

Domain of $g = \mathbb{R}$. Domain of $f = [15, \infty)$. $g(x) \geq 15 \Rightarrow x^2 + 2x \geq 15 \Rightarrow$

$x^2 + 2x - 15 \geq 0 \Rightarrow (x + 5)(x - 3) \geq 0 \Rightarrow x \in (-\infty, -5] \cup [3, \infty)$.

(b) $k(x) = (\sqrt{x - 15})^2 + 2(\sqrt{x - 15}) = x - 15 + 2\sqrt{x - 15}$.

Domain of $f = [15, \infty)$. Domain of $g = \mathbb{R}$. Since $f(x)$ is always in the domain

of g, the domain of $g \circ f$ is the same as the domain of f, $[15, \infty)$.

37 (a) $h(x) = \sqrt{\sqrt{x + 5} - 2}$. Domain of $g = [-5, \infty)$. Domain of $f = [2, \infty)$.

$g(x) \geq 2 \Rightarrow \sqrt{x + 5} \geq 2 \Rightarrow x + 5 \geq 4 \Rightarrow x \geq -1$ or $x \in [-1, \infty)$.

(b) $k(x) = \sqrt{\sqrt{x - 2} + 5}$. Domain of $f = [2, \infty)$. Domain of $g = [-5, \infty)$.

$f(x) \geq -5 \Rightarrow \sqrt{x - 2} \geq -5$. This is always true since the result of a square

root is nonnegative. The domain is $[2, \infty)$.

38 (a) $h(x) = \sqrt{3 - \sqrt{x + 2}}$. Domain of $g = [-2, \infty)$. Domain of $f = (-\infty, 3]$.

$g(x) \leq 3 \Rightarrow \sqrt{x + 2} \leq 3 \Rightarrow x + 2 \leq 9 \Rightarrow x \leq 7$.

We must remember that $x \geq -2$, hence, $-2 \leq x \leq 7$.

(b) $k(x) = \sqrt{\sqrt{3 - x} + 2}$. Domain of $f = (-\infty, 3]$. Domain of $g = [-2, \infty)$.

$f(x) \geq -2 \Rightarrow \sqrt{3 - x} \geq -2$. This is always true since the result of a square

root is nonnegative. The domain is $(-\infty, 3]$.

39 (a) $h(x) = \sqrt{25 - (\sqrt{x - 3})^2} = \sqrt{25 - (x - 3)} = \sqrt{28 - x}$. Domain of $g = [3, \infty)$.

Domain of $f = [-5, 5]$. $g(x) \leq 5$ { $g(x)$ cannot be less than 0 } $\Rightarrow$

$\sqrt{x - 3} \leq 5 \Rightarrow x - 3 \leq 25 \Rightarrow x \leq 28$. $[3, \infty) \cap (-\infty, 28] = [3, 28]$

(b) $k(x) = \sqrt{\sqrt{25 - x^2} - 3}$. Domain of $f = [-5, 5]$. Domain of $g = [3, \infty)$.

$f(x) \geq 3 \Rightarrow \sqrt{25 - x^2} \geq 3 \Rightarrow 25 - x^2 \geq 9 \Rightarrow x^2 \leq 16 \Rightarrow x \in [-4, 4]$.

40 (a) $h(x) = \sqrt{3 - \sqrt{x^2 - 16}}$. Domain of $g = (-\infty, -4] \cup [4, \infty)$.

Domain of $f = (-\infty, 3]$. $g(x) \leq 3 \Rightarrow \sqrt{x^2 - 16} \leq 3 \Rightarrow x^2 - 16 \leq 9 \Rightarrow$

$x^2 \leq 25 \Rightarrow x \in [-5, 5]$. But $|x| \geq 4$ from the domain of g.

Hence, the domain of $f \circ g$ is $[-5, -4] \cup [4, 5]$.

(b) $k(x) = \sqrt{(\sqrt{3 - x})^2 - 16} = \sqrt{3 - x - 16} = \sqrt{-x - 13}$.

Domain of $f = (-\infty, 3]$. Domain of $g = (-\infty, -4] \cup [4, \infty)$. $f(x) \geq 4$

{ $f(x)$ cannot be less than 0 } $\Rightarrow \sqrt{3 - x} \geq 4 \Rightarrow 3 - x \geq 16 \Rightarrow x \leq -13$.

41 (a) $h(x) = \dfrac{2/x}{3(2/x) + 2} = \dfrac{2}{6 + 2x} = \dfrac{1}{x + 3}$.

Domain of $g = \mathbb{R} - \{0\}$. Domain of $f = \mathbb{R} - \{-\frac{2}{3}\}$. $g(x) \neq -\frac{2}{3} \Rightarrow$

$\frac{2}{x} \neq -\frac{2}{3} \Rightarrow x \neq -3$. Hence, the domain of $f \circ g$ is $\mathbb{R} - \{-3, 0\}$.

(b) $k(x) = \dfrac{2}{x/(3x + 2)} = \dfrac{6x + 4}{x}$.

Domain of $f = \mathbb{R} - \{-\frac{2}{3}\}$. Domain of $g = \mathbb{R} - \{0\}$.

$f(x) \neq 0 \Rightarrow \dfrac{x}{3x + 2} \neq 0 \Rightarrow x \neq 0$. Hence, the domain of $g \circ f$ is $\mathbb{R} - \{-\frac{2}{3}, 0\}$.

$\boxed{42}$ (a) $h(x) = \dfrac{3/x}{(3/x) - 2} \cdot \dfrac{x}{x} = \dfrac{3}{3 - 2x}$. Domain of $g = \mathbb{R} - \{0\}$.

Domain of $f = \mathbb{R} - \{2\}$. $g(x) \neq 2 \Rightarrow \frac{3}{x} \neq 2 \Rightarrow x \neq \frac{3}{2}$.

Hence, the domain of $f \circ g$ is $\mathbb{R} - \{0, \frac{3}{2}\}$.

(b) $k(x) = \dfrac{3}{x/(x - 2)} = \dfrac{3x - 6}{x}$. Domain of $f = \mathbb{R} - \{2\}$.

Domain of $g = \mathbb{R} - \{0\}$. $f(x) \neq 0 \Rightarrow \frac{x}{x - 2} \neq 0 \Rightarrow x \neq 0$.

Hence, the domain of $g \circ f$ is $\mathbb{R} - \{0, 2\}$.

Note: In anticipation of using the chain rule, you may want to think of the <u>last</u>
calculator operation (if you were evaluating on a calculator) as your choice for y.

$\boxed{43}$ $y = (x^2 + 3x)^{1/3}$ •   ★ $u = x^2 + 3x,\ y = u^{1/3}$

$\boxed{44}$ $y = \sqrt[4]{x^4 - 16}$ •   ★ $u = x^4 - 16,\ y = \sqrt[4]{u}$

$\boxed{45}$ $y = \dfrac{1}{(x - 3)^4}$ •   ★ $u = x - 3,\ y = 1/u^4$

$\boxed{46}$ $y = 4 + \sqrt{x^2 + 1}$ •   ★ $u = x^2 + 1,\ y = 4 + \sqrt{u}$

$\boxed{47}$ $y = (x^4 - 2x^2 + 5)^5$ •   ★ $u = x^4 - 2x^2 + 5,\ y = u^5$

$\boxed{48}$ $y = \dfrac{1}{(x^2 + 3x - 5)^3}$ •   ★ $u = x^2 + 3x - 5,\ y = 1/u^3$

$\boxed{49}$ $y = \dfrac{\sqrt{x + 4} - 2}{\sqrt{x + 4} + 2}$ •   ★ $u = \sqrt{x + 4},\ y = \dfrac{u - 2}{u + 2}$

$\boxed{50}$ $y = \dfrac{\sqrt[3]{x}}{1 + \sqrt[3]{x}}$ •   ★ $u = \sqrt[3]{x},\ y = \dfrac{u}{1 + u}$

$\boxed{51}$ $(f \circ g)(2.4) = f(g(2.4)) \approx f(8.019658) \approx 7.91296$;

$(g \circ f)(2.4) = g(f(2.4)) \approx g(2.014944) \approx 5.04811$

$\boxed{52}$ $f(0.0001) \approx \dfrac{10^{-12}}{2} = 5 \times 10^{-13}$

$\boxed{53}$ $V = lwh = (30 - 2x)(20 - 2x)(x) = 4x^3 - 100x^2 + 600x$

$\boxed{54}$ (a) $V = lwh \Rightarrow 6 = xy(1.5) \Rightarrow xy = 4 \Rightarrow y = 4/x$

(b) $S = xy + 2(1.5)x + 2(1.5)y = x(4/x) + 3x + 3(4/x) = 4 + 3x + 12/x$

$\boxed{55}$ $d^2 = 100^2 + (2t)^2 \Rightarrow d = 2\sqrt{t^2 + 2500}$

$\boxed{56}$ $S = 2\pi r(10) + 2(2\pi r^2) = 20\pi r + 4\pi r^2 = 4\pi r(5 + r)$

$\boxed{57}$ (a) $r^2 + y^2 = (h + r)^2 \Rightarrow y^2 = h^2 + 2rh\ \{y > 0\} \Rightarrow y = \sqrt{h^2 + 2hr}$

(b) $y = \sqrt{(200)^2 + 2(200)(4000)} = \sqrt{(200)^2(1 + 40)} = 200\sqrt{41} \approx 1280.6$ mi.

$\boxed{58}$ (a) $x^2 + y^2 = 15^2 \Rightarrow y = \sqrt{225 - x^2}$;

domain for the function is $[-15, 15]$ and $(0, 15)$ will form triangles.

(b) $A = \frac{1}{2}bh = \frac{1}{2}x\sqrt{225 - x^2}$

$\boxed{59}$ Let y denote the distance from the control booth to the beginning of the runway.

Then $y^2 = 300^2 + 20^2$ and $d^2 = y^2 + x^2$, or solving for d, $d = \sqrt{90{,}400 + x^2}$.

60 $S = 2(4)(x) + (4)(y) = 8x + 4y; \quad C = 2(8x) + 5(4y) \Rightarrow 16x + 20y = 400$

    (a) $16x + 20y = 400 \Leftrightarrow y = 20 - \frac{4}{5}x$ (b) $V = 4xy = 4x(20 - \frac{4}{5}x)$

61 (a) $\frac{y}{b} = \frac{y+h}{a} \Rightarrow ay = by + bh \Rightarrow y(a - b) = bh \Rightarrow y = \frac{bh}{a-b}$

    (b) $V = \frac{1}{3}\pi a^2(y + h) - \frac{1}{3}\pi b^2 y = \frac{\pi}{3}\Big[(a^2 - b^2)y + a^2 h\Big] =$

$$\frac{\pi}{3}\Big[(a^2 - b^2)\frac{bh}{a-b} + a^2 h\Big] = \frac{\pi}{3}h\Big[(a + b)b + a^2\Big] = \frac{\pi}{3}h(a^2 + ab + b^2)$$

    (c) $600 = \frac{\pi}{3}h(6^2 + 6 \cdot 3 + 3^2) \Rightarrow h = \frac{1800}{63\pi} = \frac{200}{7\pi} \approx 9.1$ ft

62 (a) $\frac{12 - h}{r} = \frac{12}{4} = 3 \Leftrightarrow 12 - h = 3r \Rightarrow h = 12 - 3r = 3(4 - r)$

    (b) $V = \pi r^2 h = \pi r^2(12 - 3r) = 3\pi r^2(4 - r)$

Exercises 1.3

Note: Multiply each degree measure by $\frac{\pi}{180}$ to obtain the listed radian measure.

1 (a) $150° \cdot \frac{\pi}{180} = \frac{5 \cdot 30\pi}{6 \cdot 30} = \frac{5\pi}{6}$ (b) $120° \cdot \frac{\pi}{180} = \frac{2 \cdot 60\pi}{3 \cdot 60} = \frac{2\pi}{3}$

  (c) $450° \cdot \frac{\pi}{180} = \frac{5 \cdot 90\pi}{2 \cdot 90} = \frac{5\pi}{2}$ (d) $-60° \cdot \frac{\pi}{180} = -\frac{60\pi}{3 \cdot 60} = -\frac{\pi}{3}$

2 (a) $225° \cdot \frac{\pi}{180} = \frac{5 \cdot 45\pi}{4 \cdot 45} = \frac{5\pi}{4}$ (b) $210° \cdot \frac{\pi}{180} = \frac{7 \cdot 30\pi}{6 \cdot 30} = \frac{7\pi}{6}$

  (c) $630° \cdot \frac{\pi}{180} = \frac{7 \cdot 90\pi}{2 \cdot 90} = \frac{7\pi}{2}$ (d) $-135° \cdot \frac{\pi}{180} = -\frac{3 \cdot 45\pi}{4 \cdot 45} = -\frac{3\pi}{4}$

Note: Multiply each radian measure by $\frac{180}{\pi}$ to obtain the listed degree measure.

3 (a) $\frac{2\pi}{3} \cdot (\frac{180}{\pi})° = (\frac{2 \cdot 60 \cdot 3\pi}{3\pi})° = 120°$ (b) $\frac{5\pi}{6} \cdot (\frac{180}{\pi})° = (\frac{5 \cdot 30 \cdot 6\pi}{6\pi})° = 150°$

  (c) $\frac{3\pi}{4} \cdot (\frac{180}{\pi})° = (\frac{3 \cdot 45 \cdot 4\pi}{4\pi})° = 135°$ (d) $-\frac{7\pi}{2} \cdot (\frac{180}{\pi})° = -(\frac{7 \cdot 90 \cdot 2\pi}{2\pi})° = -630°$

4 (a) $\frac{11\pi}{6} \cdot (\frac{180}{\pi})° = (\frac{11 \cdot 30 \cdot 6\pi}{6\pi})° = 330°$ (b) $\frac{4\pi}{3} \cdot (\frac{180}{\pi})° = (\frac{4 \cdot 60 \cdot 3\pi}{3\pi})° = 240°$

  (c) $\frac{11\pi}{4} \cdot (\frac{180}{\pi})° = (\frac{11 \cdot 45 \cdot 4\pi}{4\pi})° = 495°$ (d) $-\frac{5\pi}{2} \cdot (\frac{180}{\pi})° = -(\frac{5 \cdot 90 \cdot 2\pi}{2\pi})° = -450°$

5 $s = r\theta = (\frac{1}{2} \cdot 16)(50 \cdot \frac{\pi}{180}) = \frac{20\pi}{9} \approx 6.98$

6 $s = r\theta = (\frac{1}{2} \cdot 120)(2.2) = 132$

7 $\sin 30° = \frac{4}{x} \Rightarrow \frac{1}{2} = \frac{4}{x} \Rightarrow x = 8; \quad \tan 30° = \frac{4}{y} \Rightarrow \frac{\sqrt{3}}{3} = \frac{4}{y} \Rightarrow y = 4\sqrt{3}$

8 $\sin 60° = \frac{3}{x} \Rightarrow \frac{\sqrt{3}}{2} = \frac{3}{x} \Rightarrow x = 2\sqrt{3}; \quad \tan 60° = \frac{3}{y} \Rightarrow \sqrt{3} = \frac{3}{y} \Rightarrow y = \sqrt{3}$

Note: Use the Pythagorean theorem to find the remaining side.

9 $\sin\theta = \frac{3}{5}$ • (adj)$^2 + 3^2 = 5^2 \Rightarrow$ adj $= 4$;   ★ $\frac{3}{5}, \frac{4}{5}, \frac{3}{4}, \frac{4}{3}, \frac{5}{4}, \frac{5}{3}$

10 $\cos\theta = \frac{8}{17}$ • $8^2 + (opp)^2 = 17^2 \Rightarrow$ opp $= 15$;   ★ $\frac{15}{17}, \frac{8}{17}, \frac{15}{8}, \frac{8}{15}, \frac{17}{8}, \frac{17}{15}$

11 $\tan\theta = \frac{5}{12}$ • $12^2 + 5^2 = (hyp)^2 \Rightarrow$ hyp $= 13$;   ★ $\frac{5}{13}, \frac{12}{13}, \frac{5}{12}, \frac{12}{5}, \frac{13}{12}, \frac{13}{5}$

12 $\cot\theta = 1$ • $1^2 + 1^2 = (hyp)^2 \Rightarrow$ hyp $= \sqrt{2}$;   ★ $\frac{\sqrt{2}}{2}, \frac{\sqrt{2}}{2}, 1, 1, \sqrt{2}, \sqrt{2}$

13 $x = 4$ and $y = -3 \Rightarrow r = \sqrt{4^2 + (-3)^2} = 5$.   ★ $-\frac{3}{5}, \frac{4}{5}, -\frac{3}{4}, -\frac{4}{3}, \frac{5}{4}, -\frac{5}{3}$

14 $x = -8$ and $y = -15 \Rightarrow r = \sqrt{(-8)^2 + (-15)^2} = 17$.

                                         ★ $-\frac{15}{17}, -\frac{8}{17}, \frac{15}{8}, \frac{8}{15}, -\frac{17}{8}, -\frac{17}{15}$

$\boxed{15}$ $2y - 7x + 2 = 0 \Leftrightarrow y = \frac{7}{2}x - 1$. Thus, the slope of the given line is $\frac{7}{2}$. The line through the origin with that slope is $y = \frac{7}{2}x$. If $x = -2$, then $y = -7$ and $(-2, -7)$ is a point on the terminal side of θ. $x = -2$ and $y = -7 \Rightarrow$
$r = \sqrt{(-2)^2 + (-7)^2} = \sqrt{53}$. $\bigstar$ $-\frac{7}{\sqrt{53}}, -\frac{2}{\sqrt{53}}, \frac{7}{2}, \frac{2}{7}, -\frac{\sqrt{53}}{2}, -\frac{\sqrt{53}}{7}$

$\boxed{16}$ $m_{AB} = \frac{-3 - 12}{-3 - 5} = \frac{15}{8}$. The line through the origin with slope $-\frac{8}{15}$ { the negative reciprocal of $\frac{15}{8}$} is $y = -\frac{8}{15}x$. If $x = 15$, then $y = -8$ and $(15, -8)$ is a point on the terminal side of θ. $x = 15$ and $y = -8 \Rightarrow r = \sqrt{15^2 + (-8)^2} = 17$;
$\bigstar$ $-\frac{8}{17}, \frac{15}{17}, -\frac{8}{15}, -\frac{15}{8}, \frac{17}{15}, -\frac{17}{8}$

$\boxed{17}$ (a) $\cot\theta = \frac{\cos\theta}{\sin\theta} = \frac{\sqrt{1 - \sin^2\theta}}{\sin\theta}$ (b) $\sec\theta = \frac{1}{\cos\theta} = \frac{1}{\sqrt{1 - \sin^2\theta}}$

$\boxed{18}$ (a) $\tan\theta = \frac{\sin\theta}{\cos\theta} = \frac{\sqrt{1 - \cos^2\theta}}{\cos\theta}$ (b) $\csc\theta = \frac{1}{\sin\theta} = \frac{1}{\sqrt{1 - \cos^2\theta}}$

$\boxed{19}$ (a) $1 + \tan^2\theta = \sec^2\theta \Rightarrow \tan^2\theta = \sec^2\theta - 1 \Rightarrow \tan\theta = \sqrt{\sec^2\theta - 1}$

(b) $\sin\theta = \sqrt{1 - \cos^2\theta} = \sqrt{1 - \frac{1}{\sec^2\theta}} = \frac{\sqrt{\sec^2\theta - 1}}{\sec\theta}$ or

$$\sin\theta = \frac{\sin\theta/\cos\theta}{1/\cos\theta} = \frac{\tan\theta}{\sec\theta} = \frac{\sqrt{\sec^2\theta - 1}}{\sec\theta}$$

$\boxed{20}$ (a) $1 + \cot^2\theta = \csc^2\theta \Rightarrow \cot^2\theta = \csc^2\theta - 1 \Rightarrow \cot\theta = \sqrt{\csc^2\theta - 1}$

(b) $\cos\theta = \frac{\cos\theta/\sin\theta}{1/\sin\theta} = \frac{\cot\theta}{\csc\theta} = \frac{\cot\theta}{\sqrt{1 + \cot^2\theta}}$

$\boxed{21}$ $\sqrt{16 - x^2} = \sqrt{16 - 16\sin^2\theta} = \sqrt{16(1 - \sin^2\theta)} = 4\sqrt{\cos^2\theta} =$
$4|\cos\theta| = 4\cos\theta$ since $\cos\theta \geq 0$ if $-\frac{\pi}{2} \leq \theta \leq \frac{\pi}{2}$

$\boxed{22}$ $\frac{x^2}{\sqrt{9 - x^2}} = \frac{9\sin^2\theta}{\sqrt{9 - 9\sin^2\theta}}$ { simplify as in Exercise 21 } $= \frac{9\sin^2\theta}{3\cos\theta} = 3\sin\theta\tan\theta$

$\boxed{23}$ $\frac{x}{\sqrt{25 + x^2}} = \frac{5\tan\theta}{\sqrt{25 + 25\tan^2\theta}} = \frac{5\tan\theta}{\sqrt{25(1 + \tan^2\theta)}} = \frac{5\tan\theta}{5\sqrt{\sec^2\theta}} = \frac{\tan\theta}{|\sec\theta|} = \frac{\tan\theta}{\sec\theta}$
{ since $\sec\theta > 0$ if $-\frac{\pi}{2} < \theta < \frac{\pi}{2}$ } $= \sin\theta$

$\boxed{24}$ $\frac{\sqrt{x^2 + 4}}{x^2} = \frac{\sqrt{4\tan^2\theta + 4}}{4\tan^2\theta}$ { simplify as in Exercise 23 } $= \frac{2\sec\theta}{4\tan^2\theta} = \frac{1}{2}\cot\theta\csc\theta$

$\boxed{25}$ $\frac{\sqrt{x^2 - 9}}{x} = \frac{\sqrt{9\sec^2\theta - 9}}{3\sec\theta} = \frac{\sqrt{9(\sec^2\theta - 1)}}{3\sec\theta} = \frac{3\sqrt{\tan^2\theta}}{3\sec\theta} = \frac{|\tan\theta|}{\sec\theta} = \frac{\tan\theta}{\sec\theta}$

{ since $\tan\theta > 0$ if $0 < \theta < \frac{\pi}{2}$ } $= \sin\theta$

$\boxed{26}$ $x^3\sqrt{x^2 - 25} = 125\sec^3\theta\sqrt{25\sec^2\theta - 25} =$
$125\sec^3\theta\,(5\tan\theta)$ { simplify as in Exercise 25 } $= 625\sec^3\theta\tan\theta$

Note: For the following problems, we use the formulas for negatives and then reference angles before evaluating.

$\boxed{27}$ (a) $\sin \frac{2\pi}{3} = \sin \frac{\pi}{3} = \frac{\sqrt{3}}{2}$ (b) $\sin\left(-\frac{5\pi}{4}\right) = -\sin \frac{5\pi}{4} = -\left(-\sin \frac{\pi}{4}\right) = \frac{\sqrt{2}}{2}$

$\boxed{28}$ (a) $\cos 150° = -\cos 30° = -\frac{\sqrt{3}}{2}$ (b) $\cos\left(-60°\right) = \cos 60° = \frac{1}{2}$

$\boxed{29}$ (a) $\tan \frac{5\pi}{6} = -\tan \frac{\pi}{6} = -\frac{\sqrt{3}}{3}$ (b) $\tan\left(-\frac{\pi}{3}\right) = -\tan \frac{\pi}{3} = -\sqrt{3}$

$\boxed{30}$ (a) $\cot 120° = -\cot 60° = -\frac{\sqrt{3}}{3}$

$\quad$ (b) $\cot\left(-150°\right) = -\cot 150° = -\left(-\cot 30°\right) = \sqrt{3}$

$\boxed{31}$ (a) $\sec \frac{2\pi}{3} = -\sec \frac{\pi}{3} = -2$ (b) $\sec\left(-\frac{\pi}{6}\right) = \sec \frac{\pi}{6} = \frac{2}{\sqrt{3}}$

$\boxed{32}$ (a) $\csc 240° = -\csc 60° = -\frac{2}{\sqrt{3}}$ (b) $\csc\left(-330°\right) = -\csc 330° = -\left(-\csc 30°\right) = 2$

Note: We will refer to $f(x) = \sin x$ as just $\sin x$ ($f(x) = \cos x$ as $\cos x$, etc.).

$\boxed{33}$ (a) $f(x) = \frac{1}{4}\sin x$ • vertically compress $\sin x$ by a factor of 4

$\quad$ (b) $f(x) = -4\sin x$ • reflect the graph of $\sin x$ through the x-axis and vertically

$\qquad\qquad\qquad\qquad\qquad\qquad\qquad\qquad\qquad\qquad$ stretch it by a factor of 4

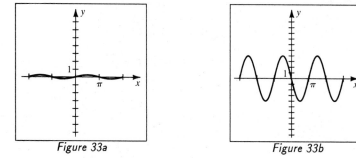

Figure 33a $\qquad\qquad\qquad\qquad\qquad$ Figure 33b

$\boxed{34}$ (a) $f(x) = \sin\left(x - \frac{\pi}{2}\right)$ • shift $\sin x$ to the right $\frac{\pi}{2}$ units

$\quad$ (b) $f(x) = \sin x - \frac{\pi}{2}$ • shift $\sin x$ down $\frac{\pi}{2}$ units

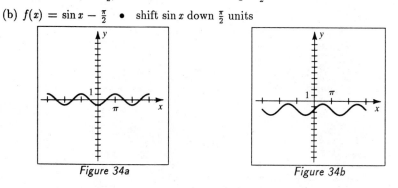

Figure 34a $\qquad\qquad\qquad\qquad\qquad$ Figure 34b

$\boxed{35}$ (a) $f(x) = 2\cos(x + \pi)$ •

shift $\cos x$ to the left π units and vertically stretch it by a factor of 2

(b) $f(x) = 2\cos x + \pi$ •

vertically stretch $\cos x$ by a factor of 2 and shift up π units

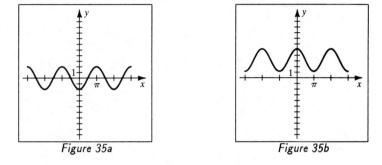

Figure 35a   Figure 35b

$\boxed{36}$ (a) $f(x) = \frac{1}{3}\cos x$ • vertically compress $\cos x$ by a factor of 3

(b) $f(x) = -3\cos x$ • reflect the graph of $\cos x$ through the x-axis and vertically

stretch it by a factor of 3

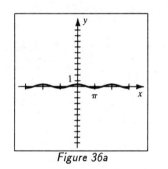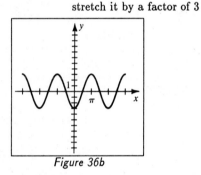

Figure 36a   Figure 36b

$\boxed{37}$ (a) $f(x) = 4\tan x$ • vertically stretch $\tan x$ by a factor of 4

(b) $f(x) = \tan\left(x - \frac{\pi}{4}\right)$ • shift $\tan x$ to the right $\frac{\pi}{4}$ units

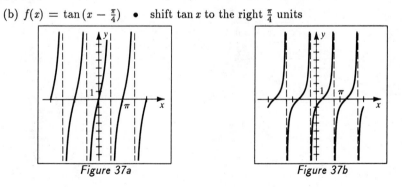

Figure 37a   Figure 37b

$\boxed{38}$ (a) $f(x) = \frac{1}{4}\tan x$ • vertically compress $\tan x$ by a factor of 4

(b) $f(x) = \tan\left(x + \frac{3\pi}{4}\right)$ • shift $\tan x$ to the left $\frac{3\pi}{4}$ units

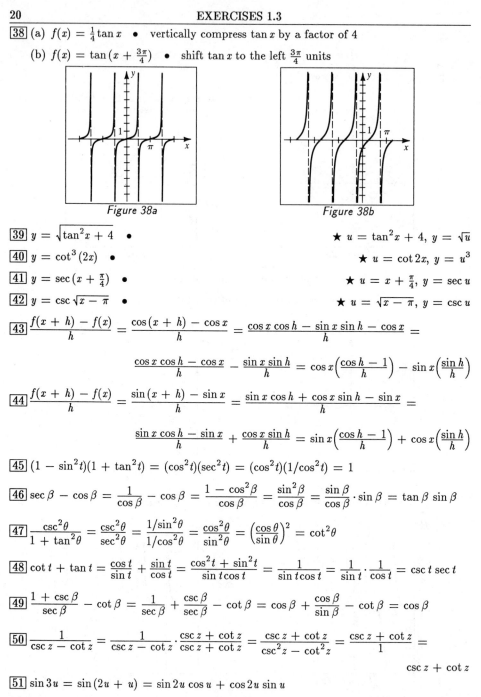

Figure 38a   Figure 38b

$\boxed{39}$ $y = \sqrt{\tan^2 x + 4}$ •   ★ $u = \tan^2 x + 4$, $y = \sqrt{u}$

$\boxed{40}$ $y = \cot^3(2x)$ •   ★ $u = \cot 2x$, $y = u^3$

$\boxed{41}$ $y = \sec\left(x + \frac{\pi}{4}\right)$ •   ★ $u = x + \frac{\pi}{4}$, $y = \sec u$

$\boxed{42}$ $y = \csc\sqrt{x - \pi}$ •   ★ $u = \sqrt{x - \pi}$, $y = \csc u$

$\boxed{43}$ $\dfrac{f(x+h) - f(x)}{h} = \dfrac{\cos(x+h) - \cos x}{h} = \dfrac{\cos x \cos h - \sin x \sin h - \cos x}{h} =$

$$\dfrac{\cos x \cos h - \cos x}{h} - \dfrac{\sin x \sin h}{h} = \cos x\left(\dfrac{\cos h - 1}{h}\right) - \sin x\left(\dfrac{\sin h}{h}\right)$$

$\boxed{44}$ $\dfrac{f(x+h) - f(x)}{h} = \dfrac{\sin(x+h) - \sin x}{h} = \dfrac{\sin x \cos h + \cos x \sin h - \sin x}{h} =$

$$\dfrac{\sin x \cos h - \sin x}{h} + \dfrac{\cos x \sin h}{h} = \sin x\left(\dfrac{\cos h - 1}{h}\right) + \cos x\left(\dfrac{\sin h}{h}\right)$$

$\boxed{45}$ $(1 - \sin^2 t)(1 + \tan^2 t) = (\cos^2 t)(\sec^2 t) = (\cos^2 t)(1/\cos^2 t) = 1$

$\boxed{46}$ $\sec\beta - \cos\beta = \dfrac{1}{\cos\beta} - \cos\beta = \dfrac{1 - \cos^2\beta}{\cos\beta} = \dfrac{\sin^2\beta}{\cos\beta} = \dfrac{\sin\beta}{\cos\beta}\cdot\sin\beta = \tan\beta\sin\beta$

$\boxed{47}$ $\dfrac{\csc^2\theta}{1 + \tan^2\theta} = \dfrac{\csc^2\theta}{\sec^2\theta} = \dfrac{1/\sin^2\theta}{1/\cos^2\theta} = \dfrac{\cos^2\theta}{\sin^2\theta} = \left(\dfrac{\cos\theta}{\sin\theta}\right)^2 = \cot^2\theta$

$\boxed{48}$ $\cot t + \tan t = \dfrac{\cos t}{\sin t} + \dfrac{\sin t}{\cos t} = \dfrac{\cos^2 t + \sin^2 t}{\sin t \cos t} = \dfrac{1}{\sin t \cos t} = \dfrac{1}{\sin t}\cdot\dfrac{1}{\cos t} = \csc t \sec t$

$\boxed{49}$ $\dfrac{1 + \csc\beta}{\sec\beta} - \cot\beta = \dfrac{1}{\sec\beta} + \dfrac{\csc\beta}{\sec\beta} - \cot\beta = \cos\beta + \dfrac{\cos\beta}{\sin\beta} - \cot\beta = \cos\beta$

$\boxed{50}$ $\dfrac{1}{\csc z - \cot z} = \dfrac{1}{\csc z - \cot z}\cdot\dfrac{\csc z + \cot z}{\csc z + \cot z} = \dfrac{\csc z + \cot z}{\csc^2 z - \cot^2 z} = \dfrac{\csc z + \cot z}{1} =$

$$\csc z + \cot z$$

$\boxed{51}$ $\sin 3u = \sin(2u + u) = \sin 2u \cos u + \cos 2u \sin u$

$$= (2\sin u \cos u)\cos u + (1 - 2\sin^2 u)\sin u = 2\sin u \cos^2 u + \sin u - 2\sin^3 u$$

$$= 2\sin u(1 - \sin^2 u) + \sin u - 2\sin^3 u = 2\sin u - 2\sin^3 u + \sin u - 2\sin^3 u$$

$$= 3\sin u - 4\sin^3 u = \sin u(3 - 4\sin^2 u)$$

$\boxed{52}$ $2\sin^2 2t + \cos 4t = 2\sin^2 2t + \cos(2\cdot 2t) = 2\sin^2 2t + (1 - 2\sin^2 2t) = 1$

$\boxed{53}$ $\cos^4 \frac{\theta}{2} = (\cos^2 \frac{\theta}{2})^2$

$$= \left(\frac{1 + \cos\theta}{2}\right)^2 = \frac{1 + 2\cos\theta + \cos^2\theta}{4} = \frac{1}{4} + \frac{1}{2}\cos\theta + \frac{1}{4}\left(\frac{1 + \cos 2\theta}{2}\right)$$

$$= \frac{1}{4} + \frac{1}{2}\cos\theta + \frac{1}{8} + \frac{1}{8}\cos 2\theta = \frac{3}{8} + \frac{1}{2}\cos\theta + \frac{1}{8}\cos 2\theta$$

$\boxed{54}$ $\sin^4 2x = (\sin^2 2x)^2$

$$= \left(\frac{1 - \cos 4x}{2}\right)^2 = \frac{1 - 2\cos 4x + \cos^2 4x}{4} = \frac{1}{4} - \frac{1}{2}\cos 4x + \frac{1}{4}\left(\frac{1 + \cos 8x}{2}\right)$$

$$= \frac{1}{4} - \frac{1}{2}\cos 4x + \frac{1}{8} + \frac{1}{8}\cos 8x = \frac{3}{8} - \frac{1}{2}\cos 4x + \frac{1}{8}\cos 8x$$

$\boxed{55}$ $2\cos 2\theta - \sqrt{3} = 0 \Rightarrow \cos 2\theta = \frac{\sqrt{3}}{2} \Rightarrow 2\theta = \frac{\pi}{6} + 2\pi n, \frac{11\pi}{6} + 2\pi n \Rightarrow$

$$\theta = \frac{\pi}{12} + \pi n, \frac{11\pi}{12} + \pi n, \text{ where } n \text{ denotes any integer}$$

$\boxed{56}$ $2\sin 3\theta + \sqrt{2} = 0 \Rightarrow \sin 3\theta = -\frac{\sqrt{2}}{2} \Rightarrow 3\theta = \frac{5\pi}{4} + 2\pi n, \frac{7\pi}{4} + 2\pi n \Rightarrow$

$$\theta = \frac{5\pi}{12} + \frac{2\pi}{3}n, \frac{7\pi}{12} + \frac{2\pi}{3}n$$

$\boxed{57}$ $2\sin^2 u = 1 - \sin u \Rightarrow 2\sin^2 u + \sin u - 1 = 0 \Rightarrow (2\sin u - 1)(\sin u + 1) = 0 \Rightarrow$

$$\sin u = \frac{1}{2}, -1 \Rightarrow u = \frac{\pi}{6}, \frac{5\pi}{6}, \frac{3\pi}{2}$$

$\boxed{58}$ $\cos\theta - \sin\theta = 1 \Rightarrow \cos\theta = 1 + \sin\theta$. Square both sides to obtain an equation in

either sin or cos. $\cos^2\theta = 1 + 2\sin\theta + \sin^2\theta \Rightarrow$

$1 - \sin^2\theta = 1 + 2\sin\theta + \sin^2\theta \Rightarrow 2\sin^2\theta + 2\sin\theta = 0 \Rightarrow$

$2\sin\theta(\sin\theta + 1) = 0 \Rightarrow \sin\theta = 0, -1 \Rightarrow \theta = 0, \pi, \frac{3\pi}{2}$.

Since each side of the equation was squared,

the solutions must be checked in the original equation. π is an extraneous solution.

$\boxed{59}$ $2\tan t - \sec^2 t = 0 \Rightarrow 2\tan t - (1 + \tan^2 t) = 0 \Rightarrow \tan^2 t - 2\tan t + 1 = 0 \Rightarrow$

$$(\tan t - 1)^2 = 0 \Rightarrow \tan t = 1 \Rightarrow t = \frac{\pi}{4}, \frac{5\pi}{4}$$

$\boxed{60}$ $\sin x + \cos x \cot x = \sin x + \cos x \cdot \frac{\cos x}{\sin x} = \frac{\sin^2 x + \cos^2 x}{\sin x} = \frac{1}{\sin x} = \csc x$.

This is an identity and is true for <u>all numbers in $[0, 2\pi)$ except 0 and π</u>

since these values make the original equation undefined.

$\boxed{61}$ $\sin 2t + \sin t = 0 \Rightarrow 2\sin t\cos t + \sin t = 0 \Rightarrow \sin t(2\cos t + 1) = 0 \Rightarrow$

$$\sin t = 0 \text{ or } \cos t = -\frac{1}{2} \Rightarrow t = 0, \pi \text{ or } \frac{2\pi}{3}, \frac{4\pi}{3}$$

$\boxed{62}$ $\cos u + \cos 2u = 0 \Rightarrow \cos u + 2\cos^2 u - 1 = 0 \Rightarrow (2\cos u - 1)(\cos u + 1) = 0 \Rightarrow$

$$\cos u = \frac{1}{2}, -1 \Rightarrow u = \frac{\pi}{3}, \frac{5\pi}{3}, \pi$$

$\boxed{63}$ $\tan 2x = \tan x \Rightarrow 2x = x + \pi n \Rightarrow x = \pi n \Rightarrow x = 0, \pi$. Another approach is:

$\tan 2x = \tan x \Rightarrow \frac{\sin 2x}{\cos 2x} = \frac{\sin x}{\cos x} \Rightarrow \sin 2x \cos x = \sin x \cos 2x \Rightarrow$

$\sin 2x \cos x - \sin x \cos 2x = 0 \Rightarrow \sin(2x - x) = 0 \Rightarrow \sin x = 0 \Rightarrow x = 0, \pi.$

$\boxed{64}$ $\sin\frac{1}{2}u + \cos u = 1 \Rightarrow \sin\frac{1}{2}u + \left[1 - 2\sin^2(\frac{1}{2}u)\right] = 1 \Rightarrow \sin\frac{1}{2}u - 2\sin^2(\frac{1}{2}u) = 0 \Rightarrow$

$\sin\frac{1}{2}u(1 - 2\sin\frac{1}{2}u) = 0 \Rightarrow \sin\frac{1}{2}u = 0, \frac{1}{2} \Rightarrow \frac{1}{2}u = 0, \frac{\pi}{6}, \frac{5\pi}{6} \Rightarrow u = 0, \frac{\pi}{3}, \frac{5\pi}{3}$

65 $\sin\theta = -0.5640$ • After pressing $\boxed{\text{INV}}$ $\boxed{\text{SIN}}$ and converting to degrees on a calculator, we obtain $-34°20'$. Since the sine is negative in QIII and QIV, we want the angles in those quadrants whose reference angle is $34°20'$.

$$180° + 34°20' = \underline{214°20'} \text{ and } 360° - 34°20' = \underline{325°40'}$$

66 $\cos\theta = 0.7490$ • Enter 0.7490 and then press $\boxed{\text{INV}}$ $\boxed{\text{COS}}$ to obtain $41.50°$ to two decimal places. $\theta_R = 41°30'$, QI: $41°30'$, QIV: $318°30'$

67 $\tan\theta = 2.798$ • $\theta_R = 70°20'$, QI: $70°20'$, QIII: $250°20'$

68 $\cot\theta = -0.9601$ • After entering -0.9601, use $\boxed{1/x}$ and then $\boxed{\text{INV}}$ $\boxed{\text{TAN}}$.

$$\theta_R = 46°10', \text{ QII: } 133°50', \text{ QIV: } 313°50'$$

69 $\sec\theta = -1.116$ • After entering -1.116, use $\boxed{1/x}$ and then $\boxed{\text{INV}}$ $\boxed{\text{COS}}$.

$$\theta_R = 26°20', \text{ QII: } 153°40', \text{ QIII: } 206°20'$$

70 $\csc\theta = 1.485$ • After entering 1.485, use $\boxed{1/x}$ and then $\boxed{\text{INV}}$ $\boxed{\text{SIN}}$.

$$\theta_R = 42°20', \text{ QI: } 42°20', \text{ QII: } 137°40'$$

71 The x-intercepts are approximately -0.73 and 0.38.

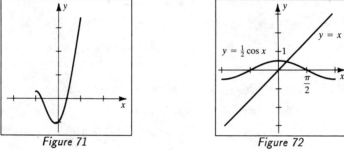

Figure 71   Figure 72

72 From *Figure 72*, a reasonable first approximation is $x_1 \approx 0.5$.

$x_2 = \frac{1}{2}\cos x_1 \approx 0.438791$ $\qquad$ $x_3 = \frac{1}{2}\cos x_2 \approx 0.452633$ $\qquad$ $x_4 = \frac{1}{2}\cos x_3 \approx 0.449649$

$x_5 = \frac{1}{2}\cos x_4 \approx 0.450300$ $\qquad$ $x_6 = \frac{1}{2}\cos x_5 \approx 0.450158$ $\qquad$ $x_7 = \frac{1}{2}\cos x_6 \approx 0.450189$

$x_8 = \frac{1}{2}\cos x_7 \approx 0.450182$ $\qquad$ $x_9 = \frac{1}{2}\cos x_8 \approx 0.450184$ $\qquad$ $x_{10} = \frac{1}{2}\cos x_9 \approx 0.450184$

Since x_9 and x_{10} agree to 6-decimal-places, $x \approx 0.450184$.

Chapter 2: Limits of Functions

Note: DNE denotes Does Not Exist.

1 $\lim_{x \to -2} (3x - 1) = 3(-2) - 1 = -7$ **2** $\lim_{x \to 3} (x^2 + 2) = 3^2 + 2 = 11$

3 $\lim_{x \to 4} x = 4$ **4** $\lim_{x \to -3} (-x) = -(-3) = 3$

5 $\lim_{x \to 100} 7 = 7$ **6** $\lim_{x \to 7} 100 = 100$

7 $\lim_{x \to -1} \pi = \pi$ **8** $\lim_{x \to \pi} (-1) = -1$

9 $\lim_{x \to -1} \dfrac{x + 4}{2x + 1} = \dfrac{-1 + 4}{2(-1) + 1} = \dfrac{3}{-1} = -3$

10 $\lim_{x \to 5} \dfrac{x + 2}{x - 4} = \dfrac{5 + 2}{5 - 4} = \dfrac{7}{1} = 7$

11 $\lim_{x \to -3} \dfrac{(x + 3)(x - 4)}{(x + 3)(x + 1)} = \lim_{x \to -3} \dfrac{x - 4}{x + 1} = \dfrac{-7}{-2} = \dfrac{7}{2}$

12 $\lim_{x \to -1} \dfrac{(x + 1)(x^2 + 3)}{x + 1} = \lim_{x \to -1} (x^2 + 3) = (-1)^2 + 3 = 4$

13 $\lim_{x \to 2} \dfrac{x^2 - 4}{x - 2} = \lim_{x \to 2} \dfrac{(x + 2)(x - 2)}{x - 2} = \lim_{x \to 2} (x + 2) = 4$

14 $\lim_{x \to 3} \dfrac{2x^3 - 6x^2 + x - 3}{x - 3} = \lim_{x \to 3} \dfrac{(2x^2 + 1)(x - 3)}{x - 3} = \lim_{x \to 3} (2x^2 + 1) = 19$

15 $\lim_{r \to 1} \dfrac{r^2 - r}{2r^2 + 5r - 7} = \lim_{r \to 1} \dfrac{r(r - 1)}{(2r + 7)(r - 1)} = \lim_{r \to 1} \dfrac{r}{2r + 7} = \dfrac{1}{9}$

16 $\lim_{r \to -3} \dfrac{r^2 + 2r - 3}{r^2 + 7r + 12} = \lim_{r \to -3} \dfrac{(r + 3)(r - 1)}{(r + 3)(r + 4)} = \lim_{r \to -3} \dfrac{r - 1}{r + 4} = \dfrac{-4}{1} = -4$

17 $\lim_{k \to 4} \dfrac{k^2 - 16}{\sqrt{k} - 2} = \lim_{k \to 4} \dfrac{(k + 4)(\sqrt{k} + 2)(\sqrt{k} - 2)}{\sqrt{k} - 2} = \lim_{k \to 4} (k + 4)(\sqrt{k} + 2) = 32$

18 $\lim_{x \to 25} \dfrac{\sqrt{x} - 5}{x - 25} = \lim_{x \to 25} \dfrac{\sqrt{x} - 5}{(\sqrt{x} - 5)(\sqrt{x} + 5)} = \lim_{x \to 25} \dfrac{1}{\sqrt{x} + 5} = \dfrac{1}{10}$

19 $\lim_{h \to 0} \dfrac{(x + h)^2 - x^2}{h} = \lim_{h \to 0} \dfrac{2xh + h^2}{h} = \lim_{h \to 0} (2x + h) = 2x$

20 $\lim_{h \to 0} \dfrac{(x + h)^3 - x^3}{h} = \lim_{h \to 0} \dfrac{3x^2 h + 3xh^2 + h^3}{h} = \lim_{h \to 0} (3x^2 + 3xh + h^2) = 3x^2$

21 $\lim_{h \to -2} \dfrac{h^3 + 8}{h + 2} = \lim_{h \to -2} \dfrac{(h + 2)(h^2 - 2h + 4)}{h + 2} = \lim_{h \to -2} (h^2 - 2h + 4) = 12$

22 $\lim_{h \to 2} \dfrac{h^3 - 8}{h^2 - 4} = \lim_{h \to 2} \dfrac{(h - 2)(h^2 + 2h + 4)}{(h + 2)(h - 2)} = \lim_{h \to 2} \dfrac{h^2 + 2h + 4}{h + 2} = \dfrac{12}{4} = 3$

23 $\lim_{z \to -2} \dfrac{z - 4}{z^2 - 2z - 8} = \lim_{z \to -2} \dfrac{1}{z + 2}$. Since $\dfrac{1}{z + 2}$

does not approach some real number L as z approaches -2, the limit DNE.

24 $\lim\limits_{z \to 5} \dfrac{z - 5}{z^2 - 10z + 25} = \lim\limits_{z \to 5} \dfrac{1}{z - 5}$. Since $\dfrac{1}{z - 5}$

         does not approach some real number L as z approaches 5, the limit DNE.

25 (a) $\lim\limits_{x \to 4^-} \dfrac{|x - 4|}{x - 4} = \lim\limits_{x \to 4^-} (-1) = -1$ (b) $\lim\limits_{x \to 4^+} \dfrac{|x - 4|}{x - 4} = \lim\limits_{x \to 4^+} (1) = 1$

   (c) Since the right-hand and left-hand limits are not equal, the limit DNE.

26 (a) $\lim\limits_{x \to -5^-} \dfrac{x + 5}{|x + 5|} = \lim\limits_{x \to -5^-} (-1) = -1$ (b) $\lim\limits_{x \to -5^+} \dfrac{x + 5}{|x + 5|} = \lim\limits_{x \to -5^+} (1) = 1$

   (c) Since the right-hand and left-hand limits are not equal, the limit DNE.

27 (a) $\lim\limits_{x \to -6^-} (\sqrt{x + 6} + x)$ DNE, since $\sqrt{x + 6}$ is undefined for $x < -6$.

   (b) $\lim\limits_{x \to -6^+} (\sqrt{x + 6} + x) = -6$, since $\sqrt{x + 6}$ is defined for $x > -6$.

   (c) The limit DNE,

            since $\sqrt{x + 6}$ is not defined throughout an open interval containing -6.

28 (a) $\lim\limits_{x \to 5/2^-} (\sqrt{5 - 2x} - x^2) = -\frac{25}{4}$, since $\sqrt{5 - 2x}$ is defined for $x < \frac{5}{2}$.

   (b) $\lim\limits_{x \to 5/2^+} (\sqrt{5 - 2x} - x^2)$ DNE, since $\sqrt{5 - 2x}$ is undefined for $x > \frac{5}{2}$.

   (c) The limit DNE,

            since $\sqrt{5 - 2x}$ is not defined throughout an open interval containing $\frac{5}{2}$.

29 (a) $\lim\limits_{x \to 0^-} (1/x^3)$ DNE, since the function becomes unbounded in the negative sense.

   (b) $\lim\limits_{x \to 0^+} (1/x^3)$ DNE, since the function becomes unbounded in the positive sense.

   (c) Since $1/x^3$ does not approach some real number L as x approaches 0,

                                                       the limit DNE.

30 (a) $\lim\limits_{x \to 8^-} \dfrac{1}{x - 8}$ DNE, since the function becomes unbounded in the negative sense.

   (b) $\lim\limits_{x \to 8^+} \dfrac{1}{x - 8}$ DNE, since the function becomes unbounded in the positive sense.

   (c) Since $\dfrac{1}{x - 8}$ does not approach some real number L as x approaches 8,

                                                       the limit DNE.

31 (a) 3	(b) 1	(c) DNE	(d) 2	(e) 2	(f) 2
32 (a) 4	(b) 4	(c) 4	(d) 1	(e) 1	(f) 1
33 (a) 1	(b) 1	(c) 1	(d) 3	(e) 3	(f) 3
34 (a) 1	(b) 2	(c) DNE	(d) -1	(e) -1	(f) -1
35 (a) 1	(b) 0	(c) DNE	(d) 1	(e) 0	(f) DNE
36 (a) -1	(b) -2	(c) DNE	(d) 1	(e) 0	(f) DNE
37 (a) DNE	(b) DNE	(c) DNE	(d) DNE	(e) 0	(f) DNE
38 (a) DNE	(b) DNE	(c) DNE	(d) 0	(e) 0	(f) 0
39 (a) -1	(b) -1	(c) -1	(d) DNE	(e) 1	(f) DNE
40 (a) 0	(b) DNE	(c) DNE	(d) 1	(e) 1	(f) 1

41 (a) $\lim_{x \to 1^-} f(x) = \lim_{x \to 1^-} (x^2 - 1) = 0$ (b) $\lim_{x \to 1^+} f(x) = \lim_{x \to 1^+} (4 - x) = 3$

(c) Since the left-hand and right-hand limits are not equal, $\lim_{x \to 1} f(x)$ DNE.

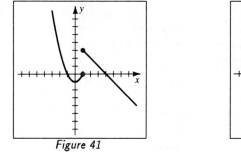

Figure 41   Figure 42

42 (a) $\lim_{x \to 1^-} f(x) = \lim_{x \to 1^-} x^3 = 1$ (b) $\lim_{x \to 1^+} f(x) = \lim_{x \to 1^+} (3 - x) = 2$

(c) Since the left-hand and right-hand limits are not equal, $\lim_{x \to 1} f(x)$ DNE.

43 (a) $\lim_{x \to 1^-} f(x) = \lim_{x \to 1^-} (3x - 1) = 2$ (b) $\lim_{x \to 1^+} f(x) = \lim_{x \to 1^+} (3 - x) = 2$

(c) Since the left-hand and right-hand limits both exist and are equal, $\lim_{x \to 1} f(x) = 2$.

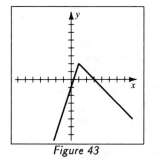 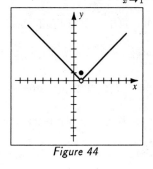

Figure 43   Figure 44

44 (a) $\lim_{x \to 1^-} f(x) = \lim_{x \to 1^-} (1 - x) = 0$ (b) $\lim_{x \to 1^+} f(x) = \lim_{x \to 1^+} (x - 1) = 0$

(c) Since the left-hand and right-hand limits both exist and are equal, $\lim_{x \to 1} f(x) = 0$.

45 (a) $\lim_{x \to 1^-} f(x) = \lim_{x \to 1^-} (x^2 + 1) = 2$ (b) $\lim_{x \to 1^+} f(x) = \lim_{x \to 1^+} (x + 1) = 2$

(c) Since the left-hand and right-hand limits both exist and are equal, $\lim_{x \to 1} f(x) = 2$.

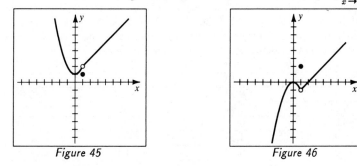

Figure 45   Figure 46

$\boxed{46}$ (a) $\lim\limits_{x \to 1^-} f(x) = \lim\limits_{x \to 1^-} (-x^2) = -1$ $\qquad$ (b) $\lim\limits_{x \to 1^+} f(x) = \lim\limits_{x \to 1^+} (x - 2) = -1$

(c) Since the left-hand and right-hand limits both exist and are equal,

$$\lim\limits_{x \to 1} f(x) = -1. \text{ See } Figure\ 46.$$

$\boxed{47}$ (a) $T(x) = \begin{cases} 0.15x & \text{if } x \leq 20{,}000 \\ 3000 + 0.20(x - 20{,}000) & \text{if } x > 20{,}000 \end{cases}$

$\qquad = \begin{cases} 0.15x & \text{if } x \leq 20{,}000 \\ 0.20x - 1000 & \text{if } x > 20{,}000 \end{cases}$

(b) $\lim\limits_{x \to 20{,}000^-} T(x) = \lim\limits_{x \to 20{,}000^-} (0.15x) = 3000$

$\qquad \lim\limits_{x \to 20{,}000^+} T(x) = \lim\limits_{x \to 20{,}000^+} (0.20x - 1000) = 3000$

$\boxed{48}$ (a) $C(x) = \begin{cases} 0.25 & \text{if } x \leq 1 \\ 0.25 + 0.15(x - 1) & \text{if } x > 1 \end{cases} = \begin{cases} 0.25 & \text{if } x \leq 1 \\ 0.10 + 0.15x & \text{if } x > 1 \end{cases}$

(b) $\lim\limits_{x \to n^-} C(x) = \lim\limits_{x \to n^-} (0.10 + 0.15x) = 0.10 + 0.15n$

$\qquad \lim\limits_{x \to n^+} C(x) = \lim\limits_{x \to n^+} \left[(0.10 + 0.15x) + 0.15 \right] = 0.25 + 0.15n$

$\boxed{49}$ (a) $\lim\limits_{t \to 0^+} F(t) = 2$; at liftoff there is a force of 2 g's.

(b) $\lim\limits_{t \to 3.5^-} F(t) = 8$; just before the second booster is released, the force is 8 g's.

$\qquad \lim\limits_{t \to 3.5^+} F(t) = 1$; just after the second booster is released, the force is 1 g.

(c) $\lim\limits_{x \to 5^-} F(t) = 3$; just before the spacecraft's engines shut off, the force is 3 g's.

$\qquad \lim\limits_{x \to 5^+} F(t) = 0$; just after the spacecraft's engines shut off, there is no force.

$\boxed{50}$ $\lim\limits_{t \to 8^-} f(t) = 200$; just before the second additional 100 mg dose,

$$\text{the patient has 200 mg of a drug in the bloodstream.}$$

$\qquad \lim\limits_{t \to 8^+} f(t) = 300$; just after the second additional 100 mg dose,

$$\text{the patient has 300 mg of a drug in the bloodstream.}$$

Note: In Exercises 51–56, answers may vary depending on the type of calculator used. Round-off will affect answers. The values in the tables were found using double precision. Since we cannot enter arbitrarily small values on a calculator, we cannot even begin to use a calculator to prove that a limit exists.

$\boxed{51}$

x	$1 + x$	$1/x$	$(1 + x)^{1/x}$
0.1	1.10	10	2.5937
-0.1	0.90	-10	2.8680
0.01	1.01	100	2.7048
-0.01	0.99	-100	2.7320
0.001	1.001	1000	2.7169
-0.001	0.999	-1000	2.7196

52

x	$1 + 2x$	$3/x$	$(1 + 2x)^{3/x}$
0.1	1.20	30	237.38
−0.1	0.80	−30	807.79
0.01	1.02	300	380.23
−0.01	0.98	−300	428.72
0.001	1.002	3000	401.02
−0.001	0.998	−3000	405.86
0.0001	1.0002	30,000	403.19
−0.0001	0.9998	−30,000	403.67
0.00001	1.00002	300,000	403.40
−0.00001	0.99998	−300,000	403.45

53

x	$x - 2$	$3^x - 9$	$(3^x - 9)/(x - 2)$
2.1	0.1	1.0451	10.451
1.9	−0.1	−0.9364	9.364
2.01	0.01	0.09942	9.942
1.99	−0.01	−0.09833	9.833
2.001	0.001	0.009893	9.893
1.999	−0.001	−0.009882	9.882

54

x	$x - 1$	$2^x - 2$	$(2^x - 2)/(x - 1)$
1.1	0.1	0.1435	1.435
0.9	−0.1	−0.1339	1.339
1.01	0.01	0.01391	1.391
0.99	−0.01	−0.01382	1.382
1.001	0.001	0.001387	1.387
0.999	−0.001	−0.001386	1.386

55

$x*$	$\dfrac{1}{\|x\|}$	$\dfrac{4^{\|x\|} + 9^{\|x\|}}{2}$	$\left(\dfrac{4^{\|x\|} + 9^{\|x\|}}{2}\right)^{1/\|x\|}$
0.1	10	1.1972146	6.0495
0.01	100	1.0180874	6.0049
0.001	1000	1.0017934	6.0005

* Only positive values for x were used since the sign of x does not affect the value of any of the expressions.

56

x	$\|x\|$	$\|x\|^x$
0.1	0.1	0.7943
−0.1	0.1	1.2589
0.01	0.01	0.9550
−0.01	0.01	1.0471
0.001	0.001	0.9931
−0.001	0.001	1.0069
0.0001	0.0001	0.9991
−0.0001	0.0001	1.0009

57 (a) Approximate values: 1.0000, 1.0000, 1.0000; −1.2802, 0.6290, −0.8913

(b) The limit does not exist.

58 (a) 0.04424; 0.02199; 0.00025   (b) The limit appears to be 0, but is actually −0.933.

1   (a) $\lim\limits_{t \to c} v(t) = K$ means that for every $\epsilon > 0$,

there is a $\delta > 0$ such that if $0 < |t - c| < \delta$, then $|v(t) - K| < \epsilon$.

  (b) $\lim\limits_{t \to c} v(t) = K$ means that for every $\epsilon > 0$,

there is a $\delta > 0$ such that if t is in the open interval $(c - \delta, c + \delta)$

and $t \neq c$, then $v(t)$ is in the open interval $(K - \epsilon, K + \epsilon)$.

2   (a) $\lim\limits_{t \to b} f(t) = M$ means that for every $\epsilon > 0$,

there is a $\delta > 0$ such that if $0 < |t - b| < \delta$, then $|f(t) - M| < \epsilon$.

  (b) $\lim\limits_{t \to b} f(t) = M$ means that for every $\epsilon > 0$,

there is a $\delta > 0$ such that if t is in the open interval $(b - \delta, b + \delta)$

and $t \neq b$, then $f(t)$ is in the open interval $(M - \epsilon, M + \epsilon)$.

3   (a) $\lim\limits_{x \to p-} g(x) = C$ means that for every $\epsilon > 0$,

there is a $\delta > 0$ such that if $p - \delta < x < p$, then $|g(x) - C| < \epsilon$.

  (b) $\lim\limits_{x \to p-} g(x) = C$ means that for every $\epsilon > 0$,

there is a $\delta > 0$ such that if x is in the open interval $(p - \delta, p)$,

then $g(x)$ is in the open interval $(C - \epsilon, C + \epsilon)$.

4   (a) $\lim\limits_{z \to a-} h(z) = L$ means that for every $\epsilon > 0$,

there is a $\delta > 0$ such that if $a - \delta < z < a$, then $|h(z) - L| < \epsilon$.

  (b) $\lim\limits_{z \to a-} h(z) = L$ means that for every $\epsilon > 0$,

there is a $\delta > 0$ such that if z is in the open interval $(a - \delta, a)$,

then $h(z)$ is in the open interval $(L - \epsilon, L + \epsilon)$.

5   (a) $\lim\limits_{z \to t+} f(z) = N$ means that for every $\epsilon > 0$,

there is a $\delta > 0$ such that if $t < z < t + \delta$, then $|f(z) - N| < \epsilon$.

  (b) $\lim\limits_{z \to t+} f(z) = N$ means that for every $\epsilon > 0$,

there is a $\delta > 0$ such that if z is in the open interval $(t, t + \delta)$,

then $f(z)$ is in the open interval $(N - \epsilon, N + \epsilon)$.

6   (a) $\lim\limits_{x \to c+} s(x) = D$ means that for every $\epsilon > 0$,

there is a $\delta > 0$ such that if $c < x < c + \delta$, then $|s(x) - D| < \epsilon$.

  (b) $\lim\limits_{x \to c+} s(x) = D$ means that for every $\epsilon > 0$,

there is a $\delta > 0$ such that if x is in the open interval $(c, c + \delta)$,

then $s(x)$ is in the open interval $(D - \epsilon, D + \epsilon)$.

$\boxed{7}$ $\frac{4x^2 - 9}{2x - 3} = 2x + 3$ if $x \neq \frac{3}{2}$. For $\epsilon = 0.01$, use the lines $y = 6 - 0.01$ and

$y = 6 + 0.01$. Hence, $5.99 < 2x + 3 < 6.01$, or, equivalently, $1.495 < x < 1.505$.

Thus, δ must be within $1.505 - \frac{3}{2} = \underline{0.005}$ units of $\frac{3}{2}$.

$\boxed{8}$ $\frac{9x^2 - 4}{3x + 2} = 3x - 2$ if $x \neq -\frac{2}{3}$. For $\epsilon = 0.1$, use the lines $y = -4 - 0.1$

and $y = -4 + 0.1$. Hence, $-4.1 < 3x - 2 < -3.9$, or, equivalently,

$-0.7 < x < -0.6\overline{3}$. Thus, δ must be within $-0.6\overline{3} - (-\frac{2}{3}) = \underline{0.0\overline{3}}$ units of $-\frac{2}{3}$.

$\boxed{9}$ Use the lines $y = 16 \pm 0.1$. In order to assure us that $15.9 < x^2 < 16.1$, we must

have δ less than or equal to the *minimum* of $\left|\sqrt{15.9} - 4\right| \approx |-0.01252|$ and

$$\left|\sqrt{16.1} - 4\right| \approx |0.01248|. \text{ Hence, } \delta = \sqrt{16.1} - 4 \approx 0.01248.$$

$\boxed{10}$ Use the lines $y = 27 \pm 0.01$. In order to assure us that $26.99 < x^3 < 27.01$, we must

have δ less than or equal to the *minimum* of $\left|\sqrt[3]{26.99} - 3\right| \approx |-0.000370416|$ and

$$\left|\sqrt[3]{27.01} - 3\right| \approx |0.000370325|. \text{ Hence, } \delta = \sqrt[3]{27.01} - 3 \approx 0.000370325.$$

$\boxed{11}$ Use the lines $y = 4 \pm 0.1$. In order to assure us that $3.9 < \sqrt{x} < 4.1$,

we must have δ less than or equal to the *minimum* of $\left|(3.9)^2 - 16\right| = |-0.79|$ and

$$\left|(4.1)^2 - 16\right| = |0.81|. \text{ Hence, } \delta = \left|(3.9)^2 - 16\right| = 0.79.$$

$\boxed{12}$ Use the lines $y = 3 \pm 0.1$. In order to assure us that $2.9 < \sqrt[3]{x} < 3.1$,

we must have δ less than or equal to the *minimum* of $\left|(2.9)^3 - 27\right| = |-2.611|$ and

$$\left|(3.1)^3 - 27\right| = |2.791|. \text{ Hence, } \delta = \left|(2.9)^2 - 27\right| = 2.611.$$

$\boxed{13}$ Here, $f(x) = 5x$, $L = 15$, and $a = 3$. Then $\left|f(x) - L\right| = \left|(5x) - 15\right| = 5\left|x - 3\right|$.

Thus, $\left|f(x) - L\right| < \epsilon \Leftrightarrow 5\left|x - 3\right| < \epsilon \Leftrightarrow \left|x - 3\right| < \frac{\epsilon}{5}$.

Hence, we may choose $\delta = \frac{\epsilon}{5}$. Now if $0 < \left|x - 3\right| < \delta$,

then $\left|f(x) - L\right| = 5\left|x - 3\right| < 5\delta = 5(\frac{\epsilon}{5}) = \epsilon$, as desired.

Note: We could have selected *any* positive $\delta < \frac{\epsilon}{5}$.

It is only required that we satisfy the definition with one particular value of δ.

$\boxed{14}$ Here, $f(x) = -4x$, $L = -20$, and $a = 5$. Then $\left|f(x) - L\right| = \left|(-4x) + 20\right| =$

$|-4\|x - 5| = 4\left|x - 5\right|$. Thus, $\left|f(x) - L\right| < \epsilon \Leftrightarrow 4\left|x - 5\right| < \epsilon \Leftrightarrow \left|x - 5\right| < \frac{\epsilon}{4}$.

Hence, we may choose $\delta = \frac{\epsilon}{4}$. Now if $0 < \left|x - 5\right| < \delta$,

then $\left|f(x) - L\right| = 4\left|x - 5\right| < 4\delta = 4(\frac{\epsilon}{4}) = \epsilon$, as desired.

$\boxed{15}$ Here, $f(x) = 2x + 1$, $L = -5$, and $a = -3$. Then $\left|f(x) - L\right| = \left|(2x + 1) + 5\right| =$

$|2x + 6| = 2\left|x + 3\right|$. Thus, $\left|f(x) - L\right| < \epsilon \Leftrightarrow 2\left|x + 3\right| < \epsilon \Leftrightarrow \left|x + 3\right| < \frac{\epsilon}{2}$.

Hence, we may choose $\delta = \frac{\epsilon}{2}$. Now if $0 < \left|x + 3\right| < \delta$,

then $\left|f(x) - L\right| = 2\left|x + 3\right| < 2\delta = 2(\frac{\epsilon}{2}) = \epsilon$, as desired.

$\boxed{16}$ Here, $f(x) = 5x - 3$, $L = 7$, and $a = 2$. Then $\left|f(x) - L\right| = \left|(5x - 3) - 7\right| =$

$|5x - 10| = 5\left|x - 2\right|$. Thus, $\left|f(x) - L\right| < \epsilon \Leftrightarrow 5\left|x - 2\right| < \epsilon \Leftrightarrow \left|x - 2\right| < \frac{\epsilon}{5}$.

Hence, we may choose $\delta = \frac{\epsilon}{5}$. Now if $0 < \left|x - 2\right| < \delta$,

then $\left|f(x) - L\right| = 5\left|x - 2\right| < 5\delta = 5(\frac{\epsilon}{5}) = \epsilon$, as desired.

$\boxed{17}$ Here, $f(x) = 10 - 9x$, $L = 64$, and $a = -6$. Then $|f(x) - L| = |(10 - 9x) - 64|$
$= |-9||x + 6| = 9|x + 6|$. Thus, $|f(x) - L| < \epsilon \Leftrightarrow 9|x + 6| < \epsilon \Leftrightarrow |x + 6| < \frac{\epsilon}{9}$.
Hence, we may choose $\delta = \frac{\epsilon}{9}$. Now if $0 < |x + 6| < \delta$,
$$\text{then } |f(x) - L| = 9|x + 6| < 9\delta = 9(\tfrac{\epsilon}{9}) = \epsilon, \text{ as desired.}$$

$\boxed{18}$ Here, $f(x) = 15 - 8x$, $L = -17$, and $a = 4$. Then $|f(x) - L| = |(15 - 8x) + 17|$
$= |-8||x - 4| = 8|x - 4|$. Thus, $|f(x) - L| < \epsilon \Leftrightarrow 8|x - 4| < \epsilon \Leftrightarrow |x - 4| < \frac{\epsilon}{8}$.
Hence, we may choose $\delta = \frac{\epsilon}{8}$. Now if $0 < |x - 4| < \delta$,
$$\text{then } |f(x) - L| = 8|x - 4| < 8\delta = 8(\tfrac{\epsilon}{8}) = \epsilon, \text{ as desired.}$$

$\boxed{19}$ Here, $f(x) = 3 - \frac{1}{2}x$, $L = 0$, and $a = 6$. Then $|f(x) - L| = |(3 - \frac{1}{2}x) - 0| =$
$|-\frac{1}{2}||x - 6| = \frac{1}{2}|x - 6|$. Thus, $|f(x) - L| < \epsilon \Leftrightarrow \frac{1}{2}|x - 6| < \epsilon \Leftrightarrow |x - 6| < 2\epsilon$.
Hence, we may choose $\delta = 2\epsilon$. Now if $0 < |x - 6| < \delta$,
$$\text{then } |f(x) - L| = \tfrac{1}{2}|x - 6| < \tfrac{1}{2}\delta = \tfrac{1}{2}(2\epsilon) = \epsilon, \text{ as desired.}$$

$\boxed{20}$ Here, $f(x) = 9 - \frac{1}{6}x$, $L = 8$, and $a = 6$. Then $|f(x) - L| = |(9 - \frac{1}{6}x) - 8| =$
$|-\frac{1}{6}||x - 6| = \frac{1}{6}|x - 6|$. Thus, $|f(x) - L| < \epsilon \Leftrightarrow \frac{1}{6}|x - 6| < \epsilon \Leftrightarrow |x - 6| < 6\epsilon$.
Hence, we may choose $\delta = 6\epsilon$. Now if $0 < |x - 6| < \delta$,
$$\text{then } |f(x) - L| = \tfrac{1}{6}|x - 6| < \tfrac{1}{6}\delta = \tfrac{1}{6}(6\epsilon) = \epsilon, \text{ as desired.}$$

$\boxed{21}$ Here, $f(x) = 5$, $L = 5$, and $a = 3$. Then $|f(x) - L| = |5 - 5| = 0 < \epsilon$ for all x
and any $\epsilon > 0$. So any $\delta > 0$ will satisfy (2.4), that is, δ can be chosen arbitrarily.

$\boxed{22}$ Here, $f(x) = 3$, $L = 3$, and $a = 5$. Then $|f(x) - L| = |3 - 3| = 0 < \epsilon$ for all x
and any $\epsilon > 0$. So any $\delta > 0$ will satisfy (2.4), that is, δ can be chosen arbitrarily.

$\boxed{23}$ Here, $f(x) = c$, $L = c$, and a is arbitrary. Then $|f(x) - L| = |c - c| = 0 < \epsilon \ \forall x$
and any $\epsilon > 0$. So any $\delta > 0$ will satisfy (2.4), that is, δ can be chosen arbitrarily.

$\boxed{24}$ Here, $f(x) = mx + b$, $L = ma + b$, and a is arbitrary. If $m \neq 0$,
then $|f(x) - L| = |(mx + b) - (ma + b)| = |m(x - a)| = |m||x - a|$.
Thus, $|f(x) - L| < \epsilon \Leftrightarrow |m||x - a| < \epsilon \Leftrightarrow |x - a| < \epsilon/|m|$.
Hence, we may choose $\delta = \epsilon/|m|$. Now if $0 < |x - a| < \delta$,
$$\text{then } |f(x) - L| = |m||x - a| < |m|\delta = |m|(\epsilon/|m|) = \epsilon, \text{ as desired.}$$
If $m = 0$, then $f(x) = b$ and any $\delta > 0$ may be chosen by Exercise 23.

$\boxed{25}$ Let $f(x) = x^2$. For any small positive ϵ consider the lines $y = a^2 + \epsilon$ and
$y = a^2 - \epsilon$ in *Figure 25*.   These lines intersect the graph of f at points with
x-coordinates $-\sqrt{a^2 + \epsilon}$ and $-\sqrt{a^2 - \epsilon}$. If $x \in (-\sqrt{a^2 + \epsilon}, -\sqrt{a^2 - \epsilon})$, then
$f(x) \in (a^2 - \epsilon, a^2 + \epsilon)$. Thus, if we choose δ less than or equal to the minimum of
$(-\sqrt{a^2 - \epsilon} + a)$ and $(-a + \sqrt{a^2 + \epsilon})$, it follows that $x \in (a - \delta, a + \delta) \Rightarrow$
$x \in (-\sqrt{a^2 + \epsilon}, -\sqrt{a^2 - \epsilon}) \Rightarrow f(x) \in (a^2 - \epsilon, a^2 + \epsilon)$. By (2.5), $\lim\limits_{x \to a} x^2 = a^2$.

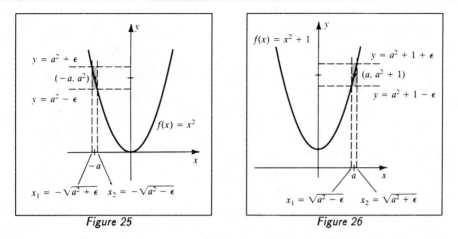

Figure 25   Figure 26

[26] Let $f(x) = x^2 + 1$. For any small positive ϵ consider the lines $y = a^2 + 1 + \epsilon$ and $y = a^2 + 1 - \epsilon$ in *Figure 26*. These lines intersect the graph of f at points with x-coordinates $\sqrt{a^2 + \epsilon}$ and $\sqrt{a^2 - \epsilon}$. If $x \in (\sqrt{a^2 - \epsilon}, \sqrt{a^2 + \epsilon})$, then $f(x) \in (a^2 + 1 - \epsilon, a^2 + 1 + \epsilon)$. Thus, if we choose δ less than or equal to the minimum of $(\sqrt{a^2 + \epsilon} - a)$ and $(a - \sqrt{a^2 - \epsilon})$, it follows that $x \in (a - \delta, a + \delta)$ $\Rightarrow x \in (\sqrt{a^2 - \epsilon}, \sqrt{a^2 + \epsilon}) \Rightarrow f(x) \in (a^2 + 1 - \epsilon, a^2 + 1 + \epsilon)$.

By (2.5), $\lim\limits_{x \to a} (x^2 + 1) = a^2 + 1$.

[27] Let $f(x) = x^3$. For any small positive ϵ consider the lines $y = a^3 + \epsilon$ and $y = a^3 - \epsilon$ in *Figure 27*. These lines intersect the graph of f at points with x-coordinates $\sqrt[3]{a^3 + \epsilon}$ and $\sqrt[3]{a^3 - \epsilon}$. If $x \in (\sqrt[3]{a^3 - \epsilon}, \sqrt[3]{a^3 + \epsilon})$, then $f(x) \in (a^3 - \epsilon, a^3 + \epsilon)$. Thus, if we choose δ less than or equal to the minimum of $(\sqrt[3]{a^3 + \epsilon} - a)$ and $(a - \sqrt[3]{a^3 - \epsilon})$, it follows that $x \in (a - \delta, a + \delta) \Rightarrow$ $x \in (\sqrt[3]{a^3 - \epsilon}, \sqrt[3]{a^3 + \epsilon}) \Rightarrow f(x) \in (a^3 - \epsilon, a^3 + \epsilon)$. By (2.5), $\lim\limits_{x \to a} x^3 = a^3$.

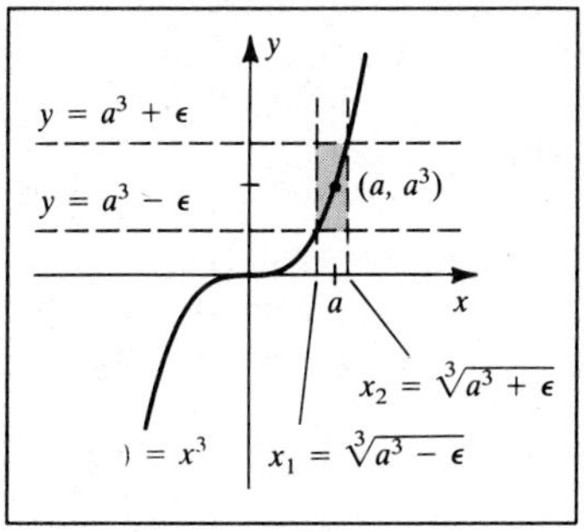

Figure 27 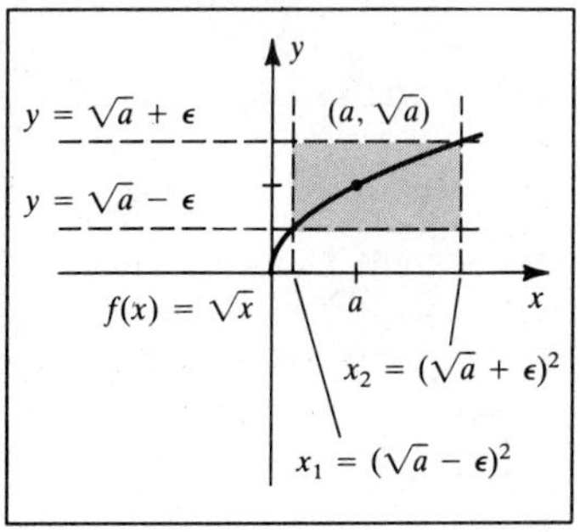   Figure 29

[28] This is similar to Example 2 except we replace a^2 with a^4, $\sqrt{}$ with $\sqrt[4]{}$, etc.

29 Let $f(x) = \sqrt{x}$. For any small positive ϵ consider the lines $y = \sqrt{a} + \epsilon$ and $y = \sqrt{a} - \epsilon$ in *Figure 29*. These lines intersect the graph of f at points with x-coordinates $(\sqrt{a} + \epsilon)^2$ and $(\sqrt{a} - \epsilon)^2$. If $x \in ((\sqrt{a} - \epsilon)^2, (\sqrt{a} + \epsilon)^2)$, then $f(x) \in (\sqrt{a} - \epsilon, \sqrt{a} + \epsilon)$. Thus, if we choose δ less than or equal to the minimum of $\left[(\sqrt{a} + \epsilon)^2 - a\right]$ and $\left[a - (\sqrt{a} - \epsilon)^2\right]$, it follows that $x \in (a - \delta, a + \delta) \Rightarrow$

$$x \in ((\sqrt{a} - \epsilon)^2, (\sqrt{a} + \epsilon)^2) \Rightarrow f(x) \in (\sqrt{a} - \epsilon, \sqrt{a} + \epsilon). \text{ By (2.5), } \lim_{x \to a} \sqrt{x} = \sqrt{a}.$$

30 This is similar to Exercise 29 except we replace $\sqrt{a}$ with $\sqrt[3]{a}$, etc.

31 Since $f(x) = 1$ for $x > 3$ and $f(x) = -1$ for $x < 3$, it is geometrically evident that no limit exists. Formally, assume the limit L exists. If $\epsilon = \frac{1}{2}$ then there is a δ that satisfies (2.4). Let $x_1 \in (3 - \delta, 3)$, $x_2 \in (3, 3 + \delta)$ so that $f(x_1) = -1$, $f(x_2) = 1$. Then $2 = |f(x_2) - f(x_1)| = \left\| \left[f(x_2) - L\right] - \left[f(x_1) - L\right] \right\| \le$

$$|f(x_2) - L| + |f(x_1) - L| < \epsilon + \epsilon = 1.$$

This is a contradiction and hence the limit does not exist.

32 The solution is like that of Exercise 31 except that the interval of width 2δ on the x-axis is centered at $x = -2$, $f(x) = 1$ for $x > -2$, and $f(x) = -1$ for $x < -2$.

33 Assume the limit L exists. For each $\epsilon \le 1$ there is a δ that satisfies (2.4). Let $x_1 \in (-1 - \delta, -1)$ and $x_2 \in (-1, -1 + \delta)$. Then $f(x_1) = -3$ and $f(x_2) = 3$. So

$$6 = |f(x_2) - f(x_1)| = \left\| \left[f(x_2) - L\right] - \left[f(x_1) - L\right] \right\| \le |f(x_2) - L| + |f(x_1) - L|$$

$$< \epsilon + \epsilon \le 2. \text{ This is a contradiction and hence the limit does not exist.}$$

34 Assume the limit L exists. For each $\epsilon \le 1$ there is a δ that satisfies (2.4). Let $x_1 \in (5 - \delta, 5)$ and $x_2 \in (5, 5 + \delta)$. Then $f(x_1) = -2$ and $f(x_2) = 2$. So

$$4 = |f(x_2) - f(x_1)| = \left\| \left[f(x_2) - L\right] - \left[f(x_1) - L\right] \right\| \le |f(x_2) - L| + |f(x_1) - L|$$

$$< \epsilon + \epsilon \le 2. \text{ This is a contradiction and hence the limit does not exist.}$$

35 Assume the limit L exists. Then by (2.4), there is a $\delta > 0$ such that

$x \in (-\delta, \delta)$, $x \ne 0 \Rightarrow 1/x^2 \in (L - \epsilon, L + \epsilon)$. But this is impossible since $1/x^2$ can be made arbitrarily large by picking $|x|$ small enough — that is, $0 < |x| < \dfrac{1}{\sqrt{|L + \epsilon|}}$

$$\Rightarrow 1/x^2 > L + \epsilon. \text{ This is a contradiction and the limit does not exist.}$$

36 Assume the limit L exists. Then by (2.4) there is a $\delta > 0$ such that if

$x \in (4 - \delta, 4 + \delta)$, $x \ne 4$, then $\dfrac{7}{x - 4} \in (L - \epsilon, L + \epsilon)$. But this is impossible since $\dfrac{7}{x - 4}$ can be made arbitrarily large by picking $x - 4 > 0$ small enough — that

$$\text{is, } \frac{7}{x - 4} > |L + \epsilon| \Leftrightarrow x - 4 < \frac{7}{|L + \epsilon|}.$$

[37] If $\lim\limits_{x \to -5} \dfrac{1}{x+5} = L$ exists, then given any $\epsilon > 0$, we could find $\delta > 0$ such that

if $-5 - \delta < x < -5 + \delta$, $x \neq -5$, then $L - \epsilon < \dfrac{1}{x+5} < L + \epsilon$ by (2.5).

But this is impossible since $\dfrac{1}{x+5}$ can be made larger than $L + \epsilon$ by

making $x + 5 > 0$ small enough.

[38] The solution is like that of Exercise 35. For $\epsilon > 0$, it is not possible to find a $\delta > 0$

such that $0 < |x - 1| < \delta \Rightarrow \left| \dfrac{1}{(x-1)^2} - L \right| < \epsilon$ for a fixed number L.

[39] There are many examples; one is $f(x) = (x^2 - 1)/(x - 1)$ if $x \neq 1$ and $f(1) = 3$.

Also, see Exercises 32, 33, 44, and 45 in §2.1.

[40] Informally, the right-hand limit of the function for every integer a is equal to a. The left-hand limit of the function for every integer a is equal to $a - 1$. Hence the limit does not exist. See Figure 1.19. Formally, we prove indirectly that no limit exists. If $\lim\limits_{x \to a} f(x) = \lim\limits_{x \to a} [\![x]\!] = L$ exists, where a is an integer, then given any positive $\epsilon \leq \frac{1}{2}$ we can find $\delta < 0$ such that, if $a - \delta < x < a + \delta$, $x \neq a$, then $|f(x) - L| < \epsilon < \frac{1}{2}$. Now let x_1 and x_2 satisfy $a - \delta < x_2 < a < x_1 < a + \delta$. Then, as in the first sentence, $f(x_1) = a$, $f(x_2) = a - 1$ and $|f(x_1) - f(x_2)| = |a - (a - 1)| = 1$. But, using the triangle inequality, we obtain $1 = |f(x_1) - f(x_2)| = \left| [f(x_1) - L] + [L - f(x_2)] \right| \leq |f(x_1) - L| + |f(x_2) - L| < \epsilon + \epsilon \leq \frac{1}{2} + \frac{1}{2} = 1$ and we have the result $1 < 1$, which is a contradiction.

[41] Assume L exists. Let $\epsilon \leq \frac{1}{4}$ and δ satisfy (2.4). The interval $(a - \delta, \ a + \delta)$ contains both rational and irrational numbers. Let x_1 and x_2 be rational and irrational numbers, respectively, in this interval. Then, $1 = |f(x_2) - f(x_1)| = \left| [f(x_2) - L] - [f(x_1) - L] \right| \leq |f(x_2) - L| + |f(x_1) - L| < \epsilon + \epsilon \leq \frac{1}{2}$.

This is a contradiction and so L does not exist.

[42] Definition (2.4) requires that the function be defined on an *open* interval containing a. But $f(x) = \sqrt{x}$ is not defined to the left of zero, and hence the definition does not apply at 0.

Exercises 2.3

Note: L denotes the original limit for the exercise.

[1] $\lim\limits_{x \to \sqrt{2}} 15 = 15$

[2] $\lim\limits_{x \to 15} \sqrt{2} = \sqrt{2}$

[3] $\lim\limits_{x \to -2} x = -2$

[4] $\lim\limits_{x \to 3} x = 3$

[5] $\lim\limits_{x \to 4} (3x - 4) = 3(4) - 4 = 8$

[6] $\lim\limits_{x \to -2} (-3x + 1) = -3(-2) + 1 = 7$

[7] $\lim\limits_{x \to -2} \dfrac{x - 5}{4x + 3} = \dfrac{-7}{-5} = \dfrac{7}{5}$

[8] $\lim\limits_{x \to 4} \dfrac{2x - 1}{3x + 1} = \dfrac{7}{13} = \dfrac{7}{13}$

9 $\lim\limits_{x \to 1} (-2x + 5)^4 = 3^4 = 81$ 10 $\lim\limits_{x \to -2} (3x - 1)^5 = (-7)^5 = -16{,}807$

11 $\lim\limits_{x \to 3} (3x - 9)^{100} = (0)^{100} = 0$ 12 $\lim\limits_{x \to 1/2} (4x - 1)^{50} = (1)^{50} = 1$

13 $\lim\limits_{x \to -2} (3x^3 - 2x + 7) = (-24 + 4 + 7) = -13$

14 $\lim\limits_{x \to 4} (5x^2 - 9x - 8) = (80 - 36 - 8) = 36$

15 $\lim\limits_{x \to \sqrt{2}} (x^2 + 3)(x - 4) = \lim\limits_{x \to \sqrt{2}} (x^2 + 3) \cdot \lim\limits_{x \to \sqrt{2}} (x - 4) = 5(\sqrt{2} - 4) = 5\sqrt{2} - 20$

16 $\lim\limits_{t \to -3} (3t + 4)(7t - 9) = \lim\limits_{t \to -3} (3t + 4) \cdot \lim\limits_{t \to -3} (7t - 9) = (-5)(-30) = 150$

17 $\lim\limits_{x \to \pi} (x - 3.1416) = \pi - 3.1416$ 18 $\lim\limits_{x \to \pi} (\tfrac{1}{2}x - \tfrac{11}{7}) = \tfrac{\pi}{2} - \tfrac{11}{7}$

19 $\lim\limits_{s \to 4} \dfrac{6s - 1}{2s - 9} = \dfrac{23}{-1} = -23$

20 $\lim\limits_{x \to 1/2} \dfrac{4x^2 - 6x + 3}{16x^3 + 8x - 7} = \dfrac{1 - 3 + 3}{2 + 4 - 7} = -1$

21 $\lim\limits_{x \to 1/2} \dfrac{2x^2 + 5x - 3}{6x^2 - 7x + 2} = \lim\limits_{x \to 1/2} \dfrac{(2x - 1)(x + 3)}{(2x - 1)(3x - 2)} = \lim\limits_{x \to 1/2} \dfrac{x + 3}{3x - 2} = -7$

22 $\lim\limits_{x \to 2} \dfrac{x - 2}{x^3 - 8} = \lim\limits_{x \to 2} \dfrac{x - 2}{(x - 2)(x^2 + 2x + 4)} = \lim\limits_{x \to 2} \dfrac{1}{x^2 + 2x + 4} = \dfrac{1}{12}$

23 $\lim\limits_{x \to 2} \dfrac{x^2 - x - 2}{(x - 2)^2} = \lim\limits_{x \to 2} \dfrac{(x - 2)(x + 1)}{(x - 2)(x - 2)} = \lim\limits_{x \to 2} \dfrac{x + 1}{x - 2}$, DNE

24 $\lim\limits_{x \to -2} \dfrac{x^2 + 2x - 3}{x^2 + 5x + 6} = \lim\limits_{x \to -2} \dfrac{(x + 3)(x - 1)}{(x + 3)(x + 2)} = \lim\limits_{x \to -2} \dfrac{x - 1}{x + 2}$, DNE

25 $\lim\limits_{x \to -2} \dfrac{x^3 + 8}{x^4 - 16} = \lim\limits_{x \to -2} \dfrac{(x + 2)(x^2 - 2x + 4)}{(x + 2)(x - 2)(x^2 + 4)} = \lim\limits_{x \to -2} \dfrac{x^2 - 2x + 4}{(x - 2)(x^2 + 4)} =$
$$\dfrac{12}{-32} = -\dfrac{3}{8}$$

26 $\lim\limits_{x \to 16} \dfrac{x - 16}{\sqrt{x} - 4} = \lim\limits_{x \to 16} \dfrac{(\sqrt{x} - 4)(\sqrt{x} + 4)}{\sqrt{x} - 4} = \lim\limits_{x \to 16} (\sqrt{x} + 4) = 8$

27 $\lim\limits_{x \to 2} \dfrac{(1/x) - (1/2)}{x - 2} = \lim\limits_{x \to 2} \dfrac{(2 - x)/(2x)}{x - 2} = \lim\limits_{x \to 2} \dfrac{-1}{2x} = -\dfrac{1}{4}$

28 $\lim\limits_{x \to -3} \dfrac{x + 3}{(1/x) + (1/3)} = \lim\limits_{x \to -3} \dfrac{x + 3}{(x + 3)/(3x)} = \lim\limits_{x \to -3} (3x) = -9$

29 $\lim\limits_{x \to 1} \left(\dfrac{x^2}{x - 1} - \dfrac{1}{x - 1} \right) = \lim\limits_{x \to 1} \dfrac{x^2 - 1}{x - 1} = \lim\limits_{x \to 1} (x + 1) = 2$

30 $\lim\limits_{x \to 1} \left(\sqrt{x} + \dfrac{1}{\sqrt{x}} \right)^6 = (1 + 1)^6 = 2^6 = 64$

31 $\lim\limits_{x \to 16} \dfrac{2\sqrt{x} + x^{3/2}}{\sqrt[4]{x} + 5} = \dfrac{8 + 64}{2 + 5} = \dfrac{72}{7}$ 32 $\lim\limits_{x \to -8} \dfrac{16x^{2/3}}{4 - x^{4/3}} = \dfrac{16(4)}{4 - 16} = -\dfrac{16}{3}$

33 $\lim\limits_{x \to 4} \sqrt[3]{x^2 - 5x - 4} = \sqrt[3]{\lim\limits_{x \to 4} (x^2 - 5x - 4)} = \sqrt[3]{-8} = -2$

34 $\lim\limits_{x \to -2} \sqrt{x^4 - 4x + 1} = \sqrt{\lim\limits_{x \to -2} (x^4 - 4x + 1)} = \sqrt{25} = 5$

$\boxed{35}$ $\lim\limits_{x \to 3} \sqrt[3]{\dfrac{2 + 5x - 3x^3}{x^2 - 1}} = \sqrt[3]{\lim\limits_{x \to 3} \dfrac{2 + 5x - 3x^3}{x^2 - 1}} = \sqrt[3]{\dfrac{2 + 15 - 81}{8}} = \sqrt[3]{-8} = -2$

$\boxed{36}$ $\lim\limits_{x \to \pi} \sqrt[5]{\dfrac{x - \pi}{x + \pi}} = \sqrt[5]{\lim\limits_{x \to \pi} \dfrac{x - \pi}{x + \pi}} = \sqrt[5]{\dfrac{0}{2\pi}} = 0$

$\boxed{37}$ $\lim\limits_{h \to 0} \dfrac{4 - \sqrt{16 + h}}{h} = \lim\limits_{h \to 0} \dfrac{4 - \sqrt{16 + h}}{h} \cdot \dfrac{4 + \sqrt{16 + h}}{4 + \sqrt{16 + h}} = \lim\limits_{h \to 0} \dfrac{-1}{4 + \sqrt{16 + h}} = -\dfrac{1}{8}$

$\boxed{38}$ $\lim\limits_{h \to 0} \left(\dfrac{1}{h}\right)\left(\dfrac{1}{\sqrt{1 + h}} - 1\right) = \lim\limits_{h \to 0} \dfrac{1 - \sqrt{1 + h}}{h\sqrt{1 + h}} \cdot \dfrac{1 + \sqrt{1 + h}}{1 + \sqrt{1 + h}} =$

$$\lim\limits_{h \to 0} \dfrac{-1}{(\sqrt{1 + h})(1 + \sqrt{1 + h})} = -\dfrac{1}{2}$$

$\boxed{39}$ $\lim\limits_{x \to 1} \dfrac{x^2 + x - 2}{x^5 - 1} = \lim\limits_{x \to 1} \dfrac{(x + 2)(x - 1)}{(x - 1)(x^4 + x^3 + x^2 + x + 1)} = \dfrac{3}{5}$

$\boxed{40}$ $\lim\limits_{x \to 2} \dfrac{x^2 - 7x + 10}{x^6 - 64} = \lim\limits_{x \to 2} \dfrac{(x - 2)(x - 5)}{(x - 2)(x^5 + 2x^4 + 4x^3 + 8x^2 + 16x + 32)} =$

$$\dfrac{-3}{6(32)} = -\dfrac{1}{64}$$

$\boxed{41}$ $\lim\limits_{v \to 3} v^2(3v - 4)(9 - v^3) = (9)(5)(-18) = -810$

$\boxed{42}$ $\lim\limits_{k \to 2} \sqrt{3k^2 + 4} \ \sqrt[3]{3k + 2} = \sqrt{16} \ \sqrt[3]{8} = 8$

$\boxed{43}$ $\lim\limits_{x \to 5^+} (\sqrt{x^2 - 25} + 3) = \sqrt{0} + 3 = 3$ $\boxed{44}$ $\lim\limits_{x \to 3^-} x\sqrt{9 - x^2} = 3\sqrt{0} = 0$

$\boxed{45}$ $\lim\limits_{x \to 3^+} \dfrac{\sqrt{(x - 3)^2}}{x - 3} = \lim\limits_{x \to 3^+} \dfrac{|x - 3|}{x - 3} = \lim\limits_{x \to 3^+} \dfrac{x - 3}{x - 3} \ (x - 3 > 0 \text{ if } x > 3) = 1$

$\boxed{46}$ $\lim\limits_{x \to -10^-} \dfrac{x + 10}{\sqrt{(x + 10)^2}} = \lim\limits_{x \to -10^-} \dfrac{x + 10}{|x + 10|} = \lim\limits_{x \to -10^-} \left[\dfrac{x + 10}{-(x + 10)}\right]$

$$(x + 10 < 0 \text{ if } x < -10) = -1$$

$\boxed{47}$ $\lim\limits_{x \to 5^+} \dfrac{1 + \sqrt{2x - 10}}{x + 3} = \dfrac{1 + 0}{5 + 3} = \dfrac{1}{8}$ $\boxed{48}$ $\lim\limits_{x \to 4^+} \dfrac{\sqrt[4]{x^2 - 16}}{x + 4} = \dfrac{\sqrt[4]{0}}{4 + 4} = 0$

$\boxed{49}$ (a) $\lim\limits_{x \to 5^-} \sqrt{5 - x} = \sqrt{5 - 5} = 0$

(b) $\lim\limits_{x \to 5^+} \sqrt{5 - x}$ DNE since $5 - x < 0$ for $x > 5$.

(c) $\lim\limits_{x \to 5} \sqrt{5 - x}$ DNE since the limit in (b) does not exist.

$\boxed{50}$ (a) $\lim\limits_{x \to 2^-} \sqrt{8 - x^3} = \sqrt{8 - 2^3} = 0$

(b) $\lim\limits_{x \to 2^+} \sqrt{8 - x^3}$ DNE since $8 - x^3 < 0$ if $x > 2$.

(c) $\lim\limits_{x \to 2} \sqrt{8 - x^3}$ DNE since the limit in (b) does not exist.

$\boxed{51}$ (a) $\lim\limits_{x \to 1^-} \sqrt[3]{x^3 - 1} = \sqrt[3]{1^3 - 1} = 0$

(b) $\lim\limits_{x \to 1^+} \sqrt[3]{x^3 - 1} = \sqrt[3]{1^3 - 1} = 0$

(c) $\lim\limits_{x \to 1} \sqrt[3]{x^3 - 1} = 0$ since the limits in (a) and (b) exist and are equal.

52 (a) $\lim_{x \to -8^-} x^{2/3} = (\sqrt[3]{-8})^2 = (-2)^2 = 4$

(b) $\lim_{x \to -8^+} x^{2/3} = (\sqrt[3]{-8})^2 = (-2)^2 = 4$

(c) $\lim_{x \to -8} x^{2/3} = 4$ since the limits in (a) and (b) exist and are equal.

53 If $x \to n^-$, then x is in the interval $[n - 1, n)$. Hence $\lim_{x \to n^-} f(x) = (-1)^{n-1}$.

If $x \to n^+$, then x is in the interval $[n, n + 1)$, and $\lim_{x \to n^+} f(x) = (-1)^n$.

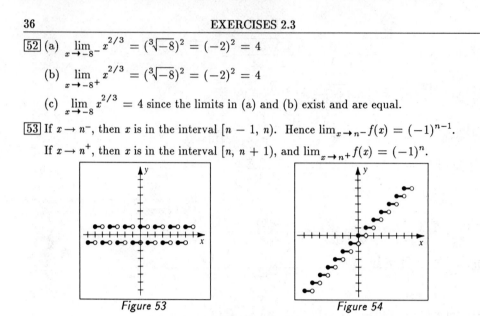

Figure 53   Figure 54

54 This is the greatest integer function and the solution is similar to that of Exercise 53.

Thus, $\lim_{x \to n^-} f(x) = n - 1$ and $\lim_{x \to n^+} f(x) = n$.

55 Since $x \neq n$, $\lim_{x \to n^-} f(x) = 0$ and $\lim_{x \to n^+} f(x) = 0$.

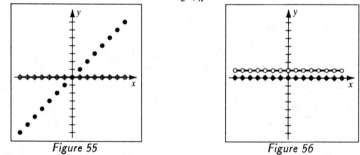

Figure 55   Figure 56

56 For $n < x < n + 1$, $f(x) = 1$ and, thus, $\lim_{x \to n^+} f(x) = \lim_{x \to n^+} 1 = 1$.

Similarly, if $n - 1 < x < n$, $f(x) = 1$ and $\lim_{x \to n^-} f(x) = \lim_{x \to n^-} 1 = 1$.

57 Recall that if $n < x < n + 1$, then $[\![x]\!] = n$ and $\lim_{x \to n^+} [\![x]\!] = n$.

Also, if $n - 1 < x < n$, then $[\![x]\!] = n - 1$ and $\lim_{x \to n^-} [\![x]\!] = n - 1$.

(a) $\lim_{x \to n^-} [\![x]\!] = n - 1$ (b) $\lim_{x \to n^+} [\![x]\!] = n$

58 (a) $\lim_{x \to n^-} (x - [\![x]\!]) = n - (n - 1) = 1$ (b) $\lim_{x \to n^+} (x - [\![x]\!]) = n - n = 0$

59 (a) $n - 1 < x < n \Rightarrow -n < -x < -(n - 1) \Rightarrow [\![-x]\!] = -n \Rightarrow$

$$\lim_{x \to n^-} (-[\![-x]\!]) = -\lim_{x \to n^-} [\![-x]\!] = -(-n) = n$$

(b) $n < x < n + 1 \Rightarrow -(n + 1) < -x < -n \Rightarrow [\![-x]\!] = -(n + 1) \Rightarrow$

$$\lim_{x \to n^+} (-[\![-x]\!]) = -\lim_{x \to n^+} [\![-x]\!] = -(-(n + 1)) = n + 1$$

$\boxed{60}$ (a) $\lim\limits_{x \to n^-} (\llbracket x \rrbracket - x^2) = (n-1) - n^2 = n - 1 - n^2$

(b) $\lim\limits_{x \to n^+} (\llbracket x \rrbracket - x^2) = n - n^2$

$\boxed{61}$ If $-1 \le x \le 1$, then $0 \le x^2 \le |x|$ and $1 \le x^2 + 1 \le |x| + 1$. But $\lim\limits_{x \to 0} 1 = 1$ and

$\lim\limits_{x \to 0} (|x| + 1) = 1$ as given. By the sandwich theorem, $\lim\limits_{x \to 0} (x^2 + 1) = 1$.

$\boxed{62}$ $\forall x \ne 0$, $\sqrt{x^4 + 4x^2 + 7} > \sqrt{7} > 1$. Hence, $0 \le \dfrac{|x|}{\sqrt{x^4 + 4x^2 + 7}} < |x|$.

$\lim\limits_{x \to 0} 0 = 0$ and $\lim\limits_{x \to 0} |x| = 0$. By the sandwich theorem, $L = 0$.

$\boxed{63}$ $\forall x \ne 0$, $0 \le |\sin(1/x)| \le 1 \Leftrightarrow 0 \le |x \sin(1/x)| \le |x| \Leftrightarrow -|x| \le x \sin(1/x) \le |x|$.

$\lim\limits_{x \to 0} (-|x|) = 0$ and $\lim\limits_{x \to 0} |x| = 0$. By the sandwich theorem, $L = 0$.

$\boxed{64}$ $\forall x \ne 0$, $-1 \le \sin(1/\sqrt[3]{x}) \le 1 \Leftrightarrow -x^4 \le x^4 \sin(1/\sqrt[3]{x}) \le x^4$.

$\lim\limits_{x \to 0} (-x^4) = 0$ and $\lim\limits_{x \to 0} x^4 = 0$. By the sandwich theorem, $L = 0$.

$\boxed{65}$ Since $0 \le f(x) \le c$ and $x^2 \ge 0$, $0 \le x^2 f(x) \le x^2 c$.

$\lim\limits_{x \to 0} 0 = 0$ and $\lim\limits_{x \to 0} cx^2 = 0$. By the sandwich theorem, $L = 0$.

$\boxed{66}$ Following the hint, $L = 0 \cdot M = 0$ by (2.8(ii)), which contradicts $L \ne 0$.

$\boxed{67}$ Because Theorem (2.8) is applicable only when the individual limits exist,

and $\lim\limits_{x \to 0} \sin \frac{1}{x}$ does not exist.

$\boxed{68}$ Because Theorem (2.8) is applicable only when the individual limits exist,

and $\lim\limits_{x \to 0} \frac{1}{x}$ does not exist.

$\boxed{69}$ (a) $\lim\limits_{T \to -273^+} V = \lim\limits_{T \to -273^+} \left[V_0 (1 + \frac{1}{273} T) \right] = V_0(1 + -1) = 0$

(b) If $T < -273\,°C$, the volume V is negative, an absurdity.

$\boxed{70}$ (a) $\lim\limits_{v \to c^-} m = \lim\limits_{v \to c^-} \dfrac{m_0}{\sqrt{1 - (v^2/c^2)}}$ does not exist since the ratio becomes unbounded

in the positive sense. As an object approaches the speed of light,

its apparent mass increases without bound.

(b) If $v \ge c$, the mass m does not exist.

$\boxed{71}$ (a) $\dfrac{1}{p} + \dfrac{1}{q} = \dfrac{1}{f} \Rightarrow \dfrac{1}{q} = \dfrac{1}{f} - \dfrac{1}{p} \Rightarrow q = \dfrac{pf}{p - f}$. $\lim\limits_{p \to f^+} q = \lim\limits_{p \to f^+} \dfrac{pf}{p - f}$ DNE

since the ratio becomes unbounded in the positive sense.

(b) The image is moving to the right and approaching an infinite distance from the lens.

$\boxed{72}$ (a) Since the lens equation still applies we have

$\lim\limits_{p \to 0^+} M = \lim\limits_{p \to 0^+} \dfrac{q}{p} = \lim\limits_{p \to 0^+} \dfrac{\left| \frac{pf}{p - f} \right|}{p} = \lim\limits_{p \to 0^+} \left| \dfrac{f}{p - f} \right| = 1.$ There   is   less

magnification as the object moves toward the lens. (*Note*: In the lens equation, q

is considered to be negative because the image is located on the *same* side of the lens as the object. The absolute value is necessary to make the magnification positive.) The right-hand limit is necessary because the object must be between the focus and the lens.

(b) $\lim\limits_{p \to f^-} M = \lim\limits_{p \to f^-} \left| \dfrac{f}{p-f} \right|$ DNE since the expression becomes unbounded in the

positive sense. The image size is increasing without bound.

Exercises 2.4

Note: Let LS denote $\lim\limits_{x \to a^-} f(x)$, RS denote $\lim\limits_{x \to a^+} f(x)$, and L denote $\lim\limits_{x \to a} f(x)$.

$\boxed{1}$ (a) As $x \to 4^-$, $(x - 4) \to 0^-$. Thus, LS $= -\infty$.

　(b) As $x \to 4^+$, $(x - 4) \to 0^+$. Thus, RS $= \infty$.　　　　　　(c) L DNE

$\boxed{2}$ (a) As $x \to 4^-$, $(4 - x) \to 0^+$. Thus, LS $= \infty$.

　(b) As $x \to 4^+$, $(4 - x) \to 0^-$. Thus, RS $= -\infty$.　　　　　　(c) L DNE

$\boxed{3}$ (a) As $x \to -\frac{5}{2}^-$, $(2x + 5)^3 \to 0^-$. Thus, LS $= -\infty$.

　(b) As $x \to -\frac{5}{2}^+$, $(2x + 5)^3 \to 0^+$. Thus, RS $= \infty$.　　　　(c) L DNE

$\boxed{4}$ (a) As $x \to -\frac{3}{7}^-$, $(7x + 3) \to 0^-$. Thus, LS $= \infty$.

　(b) As $x \to -\frac{3}{7}^+$, $(7x + 3) \to 0^+$. Thus, RS $= -\infty$.　　　　(c) L DNE

$\boxed{5}$ (a) As $x \to -8^-$, $3x \to -24$ and $(x + 8)^2 \to 0^+$. Thus, LS $= -\infty$.

　(b) As $x \to -8^+$, $3x \to -24$ and $(x + 8)^2 \to 0^+$. Thus, RS $= -\infty$.　　(c) L $= -\infty$

$\boxed{6}$ (a) As $x \to \frac{9}{2}^-$, $3x^2 \to \frac{27}{4}$ and $(2x - 9)^2 \to 0^+$. Thus, LS $= \infty$.

　(b) As $x \to \frac{9}{2}^+$, $3x^2 \to \frac{27}{4}$ and $(2x - 9)^2 \to 0^+$. Thus, RS $= \infty$.　　(c) L $= \infty$

$\boxed{7}$ (a) As $x \to -1^-$, $2x^2 \to 2$ and $(x^2 - x - 2) = (x - 2)(x + 1) \to 0^+$.

　　Thus, LS $= \infty$.

　(b) As $x \to -1^+$, $2x^2 \to 2$ and $(x^2 - x - 2) = (x - 2)(x + 1) \to 0^-$.

　　Thus, RS $= -\infty$.　　　　　　　　　　　　　　　　　　　(c) L DNE

$\boxed{8}$ (a) As $x \to 1^-$, $4x \to 4$ and $(x^2 - 4x + 3) = (x - 1)(x - 3) \to 0^+$. Thus, LS $= \infty$.

　(b) As $x \to 1^+$, $4x \to 4$ and $(x^2 - 4x + 3) = (x - 1)(x - 3) \to 0^-$.

　　Thus, RS $= -\infty$.　　　　　　　　　　　　　　　　　　　(c) L DNE

$\boxed{9}$ (a) As $x \to 3^-$, $x(x - 3)^2 \to 0^+$. Thus, LS $= \infty$.

　(b) As $x \to 3^+$, $x(x - 3)^2 \to 0^+$. Thus, RS $= \infty$.　　　　　　(c) L $= \infty$

$\boxed{10}$ (a) As $x \to -1^-$, $(x + 1)^2 \to 0^+$. Thus, LS $= -\infty$.

　(b) As $x \to -1^+$, $(x + 1)^2 \to 0^+$. Thus, RS $= -\infty$.　　　　　(c) L $= -\infty$

Note: The first step in 11–24 is the result of dividing the expression by the term containing the highest power of x in the denominator.

$\boxed{11}$ $\lim\limits_{x \to \infty} \dfrac{5x^2 - 3x + 1}{2x^2 + 4x - 7} = \lim\limits_{x \to \infty} \dfrac{5 - 3/x + 1/x^2}{2 + 4/x - 7/x^2} = \dfrac{5}{2}$

12 $\lim\limits_{x \to \infty} \dfrac{3x^3 - x + 1}{6x^3 + 2x^2 - 7} = \lim\limits_{x \to \infty} \dfrac{3 - 1/x^2 + 1/x^3}{6 + 2/x - 7/x^3} = \dfrac{3}{6} = \dfrac{1}{2}$

13 $\lim\limits_{x \to -\infty} \dfrac{4 - 7x}{2 + 3x} = \lim\limits_{x \to -\infty} \dfrac{4/x - 7}{2/x + 3} = -\dfrac{7}{3}$

14 $\lim\limits_{x \to -\infty} \dfrac{(3x + 4)(x - 1)}{(2x + 7)(x + 2)} = \lim\limits_{x \to -\infty} \dfrac{(3 + 4/x)(1 - 1/x)}{(2 + 7/x)(1 + 2/x)}$ { divide by x^2 } $= \dfrac{3}{2}$

15 $\lim\limits_{x \to -\infty} \dfrac{2x^2 - 3}{4x^3 + 5x} = \lim\limits_{x \to -\infty} \dfrac{2/x - 3/x^3}{4 + 5/x^2} = \dfrac{0}{4} = 0$

16 $\lim\limits_{x \to \infty} \dfrac{2x^2 - x + 3}{x^3 + 1} = \lim\limits_{x \to \infty} \dfrac{2/x - 1/x^2 + 3/x^3}{1 + 1/x^3} = \dfrac{0}{1} = 0$

17 $\lim\limits_{x \to \infty} \dfrac{-x^3 + 2x}{2x^2 - 3} = \lim\limits_{x \to \infty} \dfrac{-x + 2/x}{2 - 3/x^2} = \dfrac{-\infty}{2} = -\infty$

18 $\lim\limits_{x \to -\infty} \dfrac{x^2 + 2}{x - 1} = \lim\limits_{x \to -\infty} \dfrac{x + 2/x}{1 - 1/x} = \dfrac{-\infty}{1} = -\infty$

19 $\lim\limits_{x \to -\infty} \dfrac{2 - x^2}{x + 3} = \lim\limits_{x \to -\infty} \dfrac{2/x - x}{1 + 3/x} = \dfrac{-(-\infty)}{1} = \infty$

20 $\lim\limits_{x \to \infty} \dfrac{3x^4 + x + 1}{x^2 - 5} = \lim\limits_{x \to \infty} \dfrac{3x^2 + 1/x + 1/x^2}{1 - 5/x^2} = \dfrac{\infty}{1} = \infty$

21 $\lim\limits_{x \to \infty} \sqrt[3]{\dfrac{8 + x^2}{x(x + 1)}} = \lim\limits_{x \to \infty} \sqrt[3]{\dfrac{8/x^2 + 1}{1 + 1/x}} = \sqrt[3]{1} = 1$

22 $\lim\limits_{x \to -\infty} \dfrac{4x - 3}{\sqrt{x^2 + 1}} = \lim\limits_{x \to -\infty} \dfrac{4 - 3/x}{\sqrt{x^2 + 1}/(-\sqrt{x^2})}$ (if $x < 0$, $x = -\sqrt{x^2}$) $=$

$\lim\limits_{x \to -\infty} -\dfrac{4 - 3/x}{\sqrt{1 + 1/x^2}} = -4$

23 $\lim\limits_{x \to \infty} \sin x$ DNE since $\sin x$ does not approach a real number L,

but rather oscillates between -1 and 1 as x increases without bound.

24 $\lim\limits_{x \to \infty} \cos x$ DNE since $\cos x$ does not approach a real number L,

but rather oscillates between -1 and 1 as x increases without bound.

25 $n = 1, 2, 3, 4 \Rightarrow x = 10, 100, 1000, 10{,}000 \Rightarrow \frac{1}{x} \tan\left(\frac{\pi}{2} - \frac{1}{x}\right) = \frac{1}{x} \cot\left(\frac{1}{x}\right) \approx$

0.996664442, 0.999966666, 0.999999666, 0.999999996; the limit appears to be 1.

26 $n = 1, 2, 3, 4 \Rightarrow x = 10, 100, 1000, 10{,}000 \Rightarrow \lim\limits_{x \to \infty} \sqrt{x} \sin\frac{1}{x} \approx$

0.315700983, 0.099998333, 0.031622771, 0.009999999; the limit appears to be 0

Note: Let VA and HA denote vertical and horizontal asymptote, respectively. The

vertical asymptotes are found by finding the zeros of the denominator in the

reduced form of $f(x)$.

The horizontal asymptote is found by finding $\lim\limits_{x \to \infty} f(x)$ and $\lim\limits_{x \to -\infty} f(x)$.

27 $f(x) = \dfrac{1}{x^2 - 4} = \dfrac{1}{(x + 2)(x - 2)}$; VA: $x = -2$ and $x = 2$; HA: $y = 0$.

28 $f(x) = \dfrac{5x}{4 - x^2} = \dfrac{5x}{(2 + x)(2 - x)}$; VA: $x = -2$ and $x = 2$; HA: $y = 0$.

29 $f(x) = \dfrac{2x^2}{x^2 + 1}$; No VA; HA: $y = 2$.   **30** $f(x) = \dfrac{3x}{x^2 + 1}$; No VA; HA: $y = 0$.

31 $f(x) = \dfrac{1}{x^3 + x^2 - 6x} = \dfrac{1}{x(x + 3)(x - 2)}$; VA: $x = -3$, $x = 0$, and $x = 2$;

$$\text{HA: } y = 0.$$

32 $f(x) = \dfrac{x^2 - x}{16 - x^2} = \dfrac{x(x - 1)}{(4 + x)(4 - x)}$; VA: $x = -4$ and $x = 4$; HA: $y = -1$.

33 $f(x) = \dfrac{x^2 + 3x + 2}{x^2 + 2x - 3} = \dfrac{(x + 1)(x + 2)}{(x + 3)(x - 1)}$; VA: $x = -3$ and $x = 1$; HA: $y = 1$.

34 $f(x) = \dfrac{x^2 - 5x}{x^2 - 25} = \dfrac{x(x - 5)}{(x + 5)(x - 5)} = \dfrac{x}{x + 5}$ if $x \neq 5$; VA: $x = -5$; HA: $y = 1$.

35 $f(x) = \dfrac{x + 4}{x^2 - 16} = \dfrac{x + 4}{(x + 4)(x - 4)} = \dfrac{1}{x - 4}$ if $x \neq -4$; VA: $x = 4$; HA: $y = 0$.

36 $f(x) = \dfrac{\sqrt[3]{16 - x^2}}{4 - x} = \sqrt[3]{\dfrac{4 + x}{(4 - x)^2}}$; VA: $x = 4$; HA: $y = 0$.

Note: For Exercises 37–40, the figure was plotted using the listed function.

37 $f(x) = \dfrac{x - 2}{x - 3}$ **38** $f(x) = \dfrac{1 - x}{x - 2}$

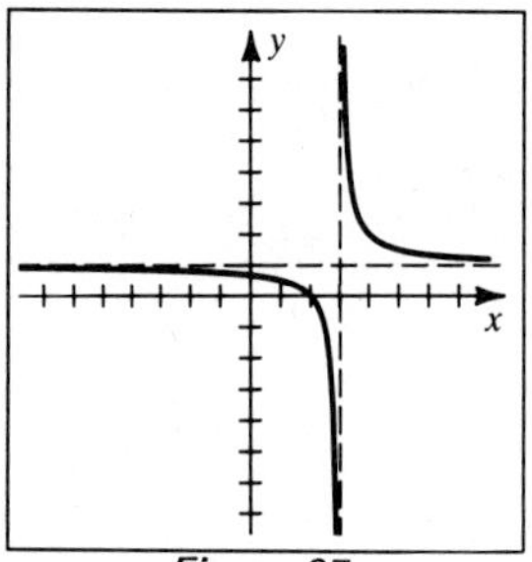

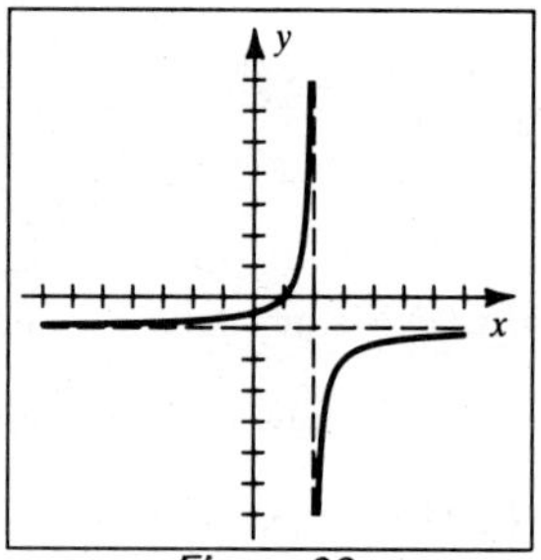

Figure 37   Figure 38

39 $f(x) = \dfrac{-2(x - 1)^2}{(x + 1)(x - 3)} = \dfrac{-2x^2 + 4x - 2}{x^2 - 2x - 3}$

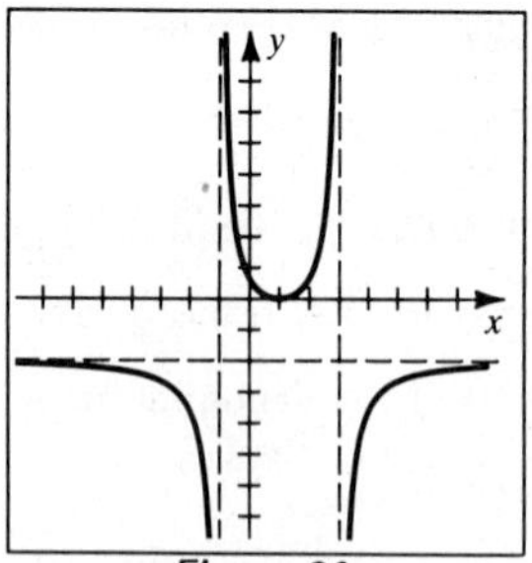

Figure 39   Figure 40

40 $f(x) = \dfrac{3(x + 3)(x - 2)}{(x + 2)(x - 1)} = \dfrac{3x^2 + 3x - 18}{x^2 + x - 2}$

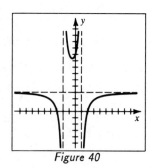

$\boxed{41}$ (a) Since 5 gallons of water flow into the tank each minute, $V(t) = 50 + 5t$. Since

each additional gallon of water contains 0.1 lb of salt, $A(t) = 5(0.1)t = 0.5t$.

(b) $c(t) = \dfrac{A(t)}{V(t)} = \dfrac{0.5t}{5t + 50} = \dfrac{t}{10t + 100}$ lb/gal.

(c) Since $\lim\limits_{t \to \infty} \dfrac{t}{10t + 100} = 0.1$ lb/gal, $c(t)$ approaches 0.1.

$\boxed{42}$ Since $\lim\limits_{S \to \infty} R(S) = a$, we conclude that the number R of recruits approaches a.

$\boxed{\text{Exercises 2.5}}$

$\boxed{1}$ Jump $\boxed{2}$ Removable $\boxed{3}$ Removable $\boxed{4}$ Jump $\boxed{5}$ Jump

$\boxed{6}$ Jump $\boxed{7}$ Infinite $\boxed{8}$ Infinite $\boxed{9}$ Removable $\boxed{10}$ Removable

$\boxed{11}$ Since $\lim\limits_{x \to 1^-} f(x) = 0$ and $\lim\limits_{x \to 1^+} f(x) = 3$, there is a jump discontinuity at 1.

$\boxed{12}$ Since $\lim\limits_{x \to 1^-} f(x) = 1$ and $\lim\limits_{x \to 1^+} f(x) = 2$, there is a jump discontinuity at 1.

$\boxed{13}$ Since $\lim\limits_{x \to -2} f(x) = 1 \neq 2 = f(-2)$, the discontinuity is removable.

$\boxed{14}$ Since $\lim\limits_{x \to 1} f(x) = 0 \neq 1 = f(1)$, the discontinuity is removable.

$\boxed{15}$ Since $\lim\limits_{x \to 1} f(x) = 2 \neq 1 = f(1)$, the discontinuity is removable.

$\boxed{16}$ Since $\lim\limits_{x \to 1} f(x) = -1 \neq 2 = f(1)$, the discontinuity is removable.

$\boxed{17}$ Since $\lim\limits_{x \to 0} f(x) = \lim\limits_{x \to 0} \dfrac{\sin\left[\sin\left(x^2\right)\right]}{\sqrt[3]{x}} = 0$ and $f(0)$ does not exist,

the discontinuity is removable.

$\boxed{18}$ Since $\lim\limits_{x \to 1^-} f(x) = -\infty$ and $\lim\limits_{x \to 1^+} f(x) = \infty$, the discontinuity is infinite.

Note: In 19–22, we use the standard limit theorems to show that (2.20(iii)) is satisfied.

$\boxed{19}$ $\lim\limits_{x \to 4} f(x) = 12 + \sqrt{3} = f(4)$ $\boxed{20}$ $\lim\limits_{x \to -5} f(x) = 3 = f(-5)$

$\boxed{21}$ $\lim\limits_{x \to -2} f(x) = 19 - \dfrac{1}{\sqrt{2}} = f(-2)$ $\boxed{22}$ $\lim\limits_{x \to 8} f(x) = \dfrac{2}{17} = f(8)$

$\boxed{23}$ Since f is not defined at -2, (2.20)(i) is not satisfied.

$\boxed{24}$ Since f is not defined at 1, (2.20)(i) is not satisfied.

$\boxed{25}$ Since $\lim\limits_{x \to 3} f(x) = 6 \neq 4 = f(3)$, (2.20)(iii) is not satisfied.

$\boxed{26}$ Since $\lim\limits_{x \to -3} f(x) = -6 \neq 2 = f(-3)$, (2.20)(iii) is not satisfied.

$\boxed{27}$ Since $\lim\limits_{x \to 3} f(x) = 1 \neq 0 = f(3)$, (2.20)(iii) is not satisfied.

$\boxed{28}$ Since $\lim\limits_{x \to 3^-} f(x) = -1$ and $\lim\limits_{x \to 3^+} f(x) = 1$, $\lim\limits_{x \to 3} f(x)$ does not exist,

and (2.20)(ii) is not satisfied.

$\boxed{29}$ Since $\lim\limits_{x \to 0} f(x) = 1 \neq 0 = f(0)$, (2.20)(iii) is not satisfied.

$\boxed{30}$ Since $\lim\limits_{x \to 0} f(x) = 0 \neq 1 = f(0)$, (2.20)(iii) is not satisfied.

31 $f(x) = \dfrac{3}{x^2 + x - 6} = \dfrac{3}{(x+3)(x-2)}$; f is discontinuous at -3 and 2 by (2.21)(ii).

32 $f(x) = \dfrac{5}{x^2 - 4x - 12} = \dfrac{5}{(x+2)(x-6)}$; f is discontinuous at -2 and 6 by (2.21)(ii).

33 $f(x) = \dfrac{x-1}{x^2 + x - 2} = \dfrac{x-1}{(x+2)(x-1)}$; f is discontinuous at -2 and 1 by (2.21)(ii).

34 $f(x) = \dfrac{x-4}{x^2 - x - 12} = \dfrac{x-4}{(x-4)(x+3)}$; f is discontinuous at -3 and 4 by (2.21)(ii).

35 If $4 < c < 8$, $\displaystyle\lim_{x \to c} f(x) = \lim_{x \to c} \sqrt{x-4} = \sqrt{c-4} = f(c)$.

Similarly, $\displaystyle\lim_{x \to 4^+} f(x) = 0 = f(4)$ and $\displaystyle\lim_{x \to 8^-} f(x) = 2 = f(8)$.

Hence, f is continuous on $[4, 8]$ by (2.22).

36 If $c < 16$, then $\displaystyle\lim_{x \to c} f(x) = \lim_{x \to c} \sqrt{16 - x} = \sqrt{16 - c} = f(c)$.

Similarly, $\displaystyle\lim_{x \to 16^-} f(x) = 0 = f(16)$. Hence, f is continuous on $(-\infty, 16]$.

37 If $c > 0$, $\displaystyle\lim_{x \to c} f(x) = \lim_{x \to c} (1/x^2) = 1/c^2 = f(c)$. Hence, f is continuous on $(0, \infty)$.

38 If $1 < c < 3$, $\displaystyle\lim_{x \to c} f(x) = \lim_{x \to c} \dfrac{1}{x - 1} = \dfrac{1}{c - 1} = f(c)$.

Hence, f is continuous on $(1, 3)$.

Note: For 39–54, each function f is continuous on its domain.

39 $f(x) = \dfrac{3x - 5}{2x^2 - x - 3} = \dfrac{3x - 5}{(2x - 3)(x + 1)}$.　　　★ $\{x : x \neq -1, \frac{3}{2}\}$

40 $f(x) = \dfrac{x^2 - 9}{x - 3} = x + 3$ if $x \neq 3$.　　　★ $\{x : x \neq 3\}$

41 $f(x) = \sqrt{2x - 3} + x^2$ • $2x - 3 \geq 0 \Rightarrow x \geq \frac{3}{2}$　　　★ $[\frac{3}{2}, \infty)$

42 $f(x) = \dfrac{x}{\sqrt[3]{x - 4}}$ • $x - 4 \neq 0 \Rightarrow x \neq 4$　　　★ $\{x : x \neq 4\}$

43 $f(x) = \dfrac{x - 1}{\sqrt{x^2 - 1}}$ • $x^2 - 1 > 0 \Rightarrow x^2 > 1 \Rightarrow |x| > 1$　　　★ $(-\infty, -1) \cup (1, \infty)$

44 $f(x) = \dfrac{x}{\sqrt{1 - x^2}}$ • $1 - x^2 > 0 \Rightarrow 1 > x^2 \Rightarrow |x| < 1$　　　★ $(-1, 1)$

45 $f(x) = \dfrac{|x + 9|}{x + 9} = \begin{cases} 1 & \text{if } x > -9 \\ -1 & \text{if } x < -9 \end{cases}$　　　★ $\{x : x \neq -9\}$

46 $f(x) = \dfrac{x}{x^2 + 1}$ • $x^2 + 1 \neq 0$ for all real numbers x.　　　★ $\mathbb{R}$

47 $f(x) = \dfrac{5}{x^3 - x^2} = \dfrac{5}{x^2(x - 1)}$.　　　★ $\{x : x \neq 0, 1\}$

48 $f(x) = \dfrac{4x - 7}{(x + 3)(x^2 + 2x - 8)} = \dfrac{4x - 7}{(x + 3)(x + 4)(x - 2)}$.　　　★ $\{x : x \neq -4, -3, 2\}$

49 $f(x) = \dfrac{\sqrt{x^2 - 9}\,\sqrt{25 - x^2}}{x - 4}$ • $x^2 - 9 \geq 0 \Rightarrow |x| \geq 3$;

$25 - x^2 \geq 0 \Rightarrow |x| \leq 5$; $x \neq 4$　　　★ $[-5, -3] \cup [3, 4) \cup (4, 5]$

$\boxed{50}$ $f(x) = \dfrac{\sqrt{9-x}}{\sqrt{x-6}}$ • $9 - x \geq 0 \Rightarrow x \leq 9$; $x - 6 > 0 \Rightarrow x > 6$ ★ $(6, 9]$

$\boxed{51}$ $f(x) = \tan 2x$ • $2x \neq \frac{\pi}{2} + \pi n \Rightarrow x \neq \frac{\pi}{4} + \frac{\pi}{2}n$ ★ $\{x : x \neq \frac{\pi}{4} + \frac{\pi}{2}n\}$

$\boxed{52}$ $f(x) = \cot \frac{1}{3}x$ • $\frac{1}{3}x \neq \pi n \Rightarrow x \neq 3\pi n$ ★ $\{x : x \neq 3\pi n\}$

$\boxed{53}$ $f(x) = \csc \frac{1}{2}x$ • $\frac{1}{2}x \neq \pi n \Rightarrow x \neq 2\pi n$ ★ $\{x : x \neq 2\pi n\}$

$\boxed{54}$ $f(x) = \sec 3x$ • $3x \neq \frac{\pi}{2} + \pi n \Rightarrow x \neq \frac{\pi}{6} + \frac{\pi}{3}n$ ★ $\{x : x \neq \frac{\pi}{6} + \frac{\pi}{3}n\}$

$\boxed{55}$ $f(-1) \leq w \leq f(2) \Leftrightarrow 0 \leq w \leq 9$; $f(c) = w \Rightarrow c^3 + 1 = w \Rightarrow c = \sqrt[3]{w - 1}$

$\boxed{56}$ $f(0) \geq w \geq f(2) \Leftrightarrow 0 \geq w \geq -8$; $f(c) = w \Rightarrow -c^3 = w \Rightarrow c = \sqrt[3]{-w}$

$\boxed{57}$ $f(1) \leq w \leq f(3) \Leftrightarrow 0 \leq w \leq 6$; $f(c) = w \Rightarrow c^2 - c = w \Rightarrow c^2 - c - w = 0$

$$\Rightarrow c = \frac{1 \pm \sqrt{1 + 4w}}{2}. \text{ Choose } c = \frac{1 + \sqrt{1 + 4w}}{2} = \frac{1}{2} + \frac{1}{2}\sqrt{4w + 1} \text{ for } 1 \leq c \leq 3.$$

$\boxed{58}$ $f(-2) \leq w \leq f(-1) \Leftrightarrow -8 \leq w \leq -3$;

$$f(c) = w \Rightarrow 2c - c^2 = w \Rightarrow c^2 - 2c + w = 0 \Rightarrow c = \frac{2 \pm \sqrt{4 - 4w}}{2}.$$

$$\text{Choose } c = \frac{2 - \sqrt{4 - 4w}}{2} = 1 - \sqrt{1 - w} \text{ for } -2 \leq c \leq -1.$$

$\boxed{59}$ $f(0) = -9 < 100$ and $f(10) = 561 > 100$. Since f is continuous on $[0, 10]$,

there is at least one number a in $[0, 10]$ such that $f(a) = 100$.

$\boxed{60}$ Let $f(x) = x^5 - 3x^4 - 2x^3 - x + 1$. $f(0) = 1 > 0$ and $f(1) = -4 < 0$. Since f is

continuous on $[0, 1]$, there is at least one number a in $[0, 1]$ such that $f(a) = 0$.

$\boxed{61}$ $g(35°) \approx 9.79745 < 9.8$ and $g(40°) \approx 9.80180 > 9.8$. Since g is continuous on

$[35°, 40°]$, there is at least one latitude θ between $35°$ and $40°$ such that $g(\theta) = 9.8$.

$\boxed{62}$ $T(4000) \approx 98.0995 > 98$ and $T(4500) \approx 97.9478 < 98$.

Since T is continuous on $[4000, 4500]$, there is at least one elevation h between

4000 meters and 4500 meters such that $T(h) = 98$.

2.6 Review Exercises

$\boxed{1}$ $\displaystyle\lim_{x \to 3} \frac{5x + 11}{\sqrt{x + 1}} = \frac{26}{2} = 13$ $\boxed{2}$ $\displaystyle\lim_{x \to -2} \frac{6 - 7x}{(3 + 2x)^4} = \frac{20}{1} = 20$

$\boxed{3}$ $\displaystyle\lim_{x \to -2} (2x - \sqrt{4x^2 + x}) = -4 - \sqrt{14}$ $\boxed{4}$ $\displaystyle\lim_{x \to 4^-} (x - \sqrt{16 - x^2}) = 4 - 0 = 4$

$\boxed{5}$ $\displaystyle\lim_{x \to 3/2} \frac{2x^2 + x - 6}{4x^2 - 4x - 3} = \lim_{x \to 3/2} \frac{(2x - 3)(x + 2)}{(2x - 3)(2x + 1)} = \lim_{x \to 3/2} \frac{x + 2}{2x + 1} = \frac{7}{8}$

$\boxed{6}$ $\displaystyle\lim_{x \to 2} \frac{3x^2 - x - 10}{x^2 - x - 2} = \lim_{x \to 2} \frac{(3x + 5)(x - 2)}{(x + 1)(x - 2)} = \lim_{x \to 2} \frac{3x + 5}{x + 1} = \frac{11}{3}$

$\boxed{7}$ $\displaystyle\lim_{x \to 2} \frac{x^4 - 16}{x^2 - x - 2} = \lim_{x \to 2} \frac{(x^2 + 4)(x + 2)(x - 2)}{(x + 1)(x - 2)} = \lim_{x \to 2} \frac{(x^2 + 4)(x + 2)}{x + 1} = \frac{32}{3}$

$\boxed{8}$ The limit DNE since the ratio becomes unbounded $(+\infty)$ as $x \to 3^+$.

$\boxed{9}$ The limit DNE since the ratio becomes unbounded $(+\infty)$ as $x \to 0^+$.

$\boxed{10}\ \lim\limits_{x \to 5} \dfrac{(1/x) - (1/5)}{x - 5} = \lim\limits_{x \to 5} \dfrac{(5 - x)/(5x)}{x - 5} = \lim\limits_{x \to 5} \dfrac{-1}{5x} = -\dfrac{1}{25}$

$\boxed{11}\ \lim\limits_{x \to 1/2} \dfrac{8x^3 - 1}{2x - 1} = \lim\limits_{x \to 1/2} \dfrac{(2x - 1)(4x^2 + 2x + 1)}{2x - 1} = \lim\limits_{x \to 1/2} (4x^2 + 2x + 1) = 3$

$\boxed{12}\ \lim\limits_{x \to 2} 5 = 5$ $\boxed{13}\ \lim\limits_{x \to 3^+} \dfrac{3 - x}{|3 - x|} = \lim\limits_{x \to 3^+} \dfrac{3 - x}{-(3 - x)} = -1$

$\boxed{14}\ \lim\limits_{x \to 2} \dfrac{\sqrt{x} - \sqrt{2}}{x - 2} = \lim\limits_{x \to 2} \dfrac{\sqrt{x} - \sqrt{2}}{(\sqrt{x} + \sqrt{2})(\sqrt{x} - \sqrt{2})} = \lim\limits_{x \to 2} \dfrac{1}{\sqrt{x} + \sqrt{2}} = 1/(2\sqrt{2})$

$\boxed{15}\ \lim\limits_{h \to 0} \dfrac{(a + h)^4 - a^4}{h} = \lim\limits_{h \to 0} \dfrac{h(4a^3 + 6a^2h + 4ah^2 + h^3)}{h} = 4a^3$

$\boxed{16}\ \lim\limits_{h \to 0} \dfrac{(2 + h)^{-3} - 2^{-3}}{h} = \lim\limits_{h \to 0} \dfrac{8 - (2 + h)^3}{8h(2 + h)^3} = \lim\limits_{h \to 0} \dfrac{-12 - 6h - h^2}{8(2 + h)^3} = \dfrac{-12}{64} = -\dfrac{3}{16}$

$\boxed{17}\ \lim\limits_{x \to -3} \sqrt[3]{\dfrac{x + 3}{x^3 + 27}} = \lim\limits_{x \to -3} \sqrt[3]{\dfrac{x + 3}{(x + 3)(x^2 - 3x + 9)}} = \lim\limits_{x \to -3} \dfrac{1}{\sqrt[3]{x^2 - 3x + 9}} = \dfrac{1}{3}$

$\boxed{18}\ \lim\limits_{x \to 5/2^-} (\sqrt{5 - 2x} - x^2) = 0 - \dfrac{25}{4} = -\dfrac{25}{4}$, since $5 - 2x > 0$ for $x < \dfrac{5}{2}$

$\boxed{19}\ \lim\limits_{x \to -\infty} \dfrac{(2x - 5)(3x + 1)}{(x + 7)(4x - 9)} = \lim\limits_{x \to -\infty} \dfrac{(2 - 5/x)(3 + 1/x)}{(1 + 7/x)(4 - 9/x)} = \dfrac{2 \cdot 3}{1 \cdot 4} = \dfrac{3}{2}$

$\boxed{20}\ \lim\limits_{x \to \infty} \dfrac{2x + 11}{\sqrt{x + 1}} = \lim\limits_{x \to \infty} \dfrac{2\sqrt{x} + 11/\sqrt{x}}{\sqrt{1 + 1/x}} = \dfrac{\infty}{1} = \infty$

$\boxed{21}\ \lim\limits_{x \to -\infty} \dfrac{6 - 7x}{(3 + 2x)^4} = \lim\limits_{x \to -\infty} \dfrac{6/x^4 - 7/x^3}{(3/x + 2)^4} = \dfrac{0}{2^4} = 0$

$\boxed{22}\ \lim\limits_{x \to \infty} \dfrac{x - 100}{\sqrt{x^2 + 100}} = \lim\limits_{x \to \infty} \dfrac{1 - 100/x}{\sqrt{1 + 100/x^2}} = \dfrac{1}{1} = 1$

$\boxed{23}\ \lim\limits_{x \to 2/3^+} \dfrac{x^2}{4 - 9x^2} = -\infty$ $\boxed{24}\ \lim\limits_{x \to 3/5^-} \dfrac{1}{5x - 3} = -\infty$

$\boxed{25}\ \lim\limits_{x \to 0^+} \left(\sqrt{x} - \dfrac{1}{\sqrt{x}}\right) = -\infty$ $\boxed{26}\ \lim\limits_{x \to 1} \dfrac{x - 1}{\sqrt{(x - 1)^2}} = \lim\limits_{x \to 1} \dfrac{x - 1}{|x - 1|}$, DNE

$\boxed{27}$ (a) $\lim\limits_{x \to 2^-} f(x) = \lim\limits_{x \to 2^-} 3x = 6$ $\boxed{28}$ (a) $\lim\limits_{x \to 2^-} f(x) = \lim\limits_{x \to 2^-} x^3 = 8$

      (b) $\lim\limits_{x \to 2^+} f(x) = \lim\limits_{x \to 2^+} x^2 = 4$ (b) $\lim\limits_{x \to 2^+} f(x) = \lim\limits_{x \to 2^+} (4 - 2x) = 0$

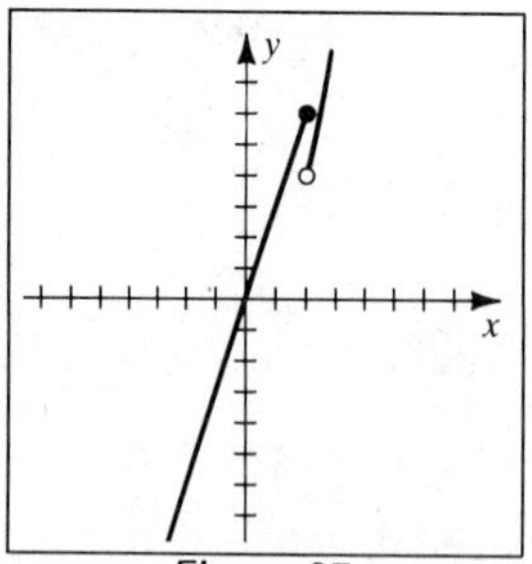

      (c) $\lim\limits_{x \to 2} f(x)$ DNE   (c) $\lim\limits_{x \to 2} f(x)$ DNE

Figure 27

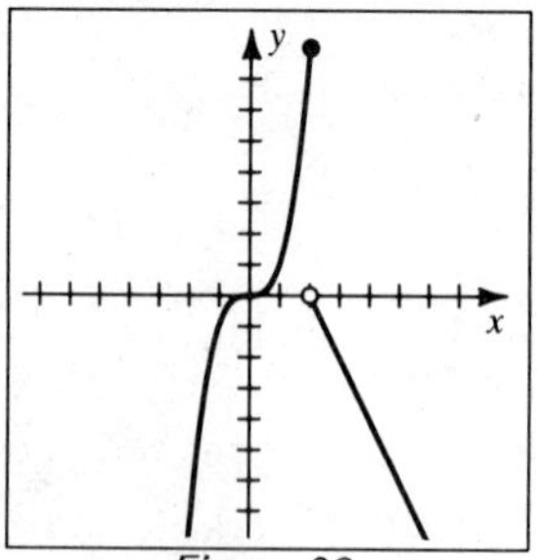

Figure 28

$\boxed{29}$ (a) $\lim\limits_{x \to -3^-} f(x) = \lim\limits_{x \to -3^-} \dfrac{1}{2 - 3x} = \dfrac{1}{11}$ $\boxed{30}$ (a) $\lim\limits_{x \to -3^-} f(x) = \lim\limits_{x \to -3^-} 9/x^2 = 1$

(b) $\lim\limits_{x \to -3^+} f(x) = \lim\limits_{x \to -3^+} \sqrt[3]{x + 2} = -1$ (b) $\lim\limits_{x \to -3^+} f(x) = \lim\limits_{x \to -3^+} (4 + x) = 1$

(c) $\lim\limits_{x \to -3} f(x)$ DNE   (c) $\lim\limits_{x \to -3} f(x) = 1$

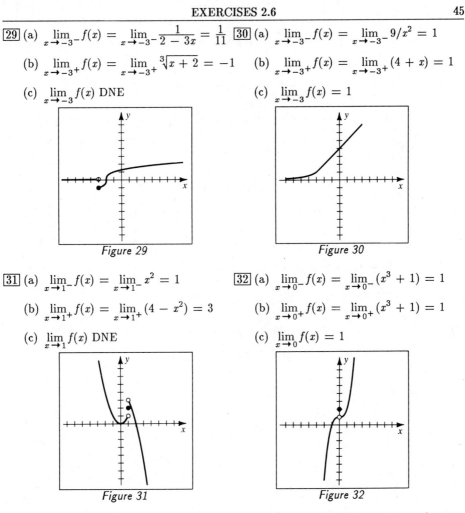

Figure 29   Figure 30

$\boxed{31}$ (a) $\lim\limits_{x \to 1^-} f(x) = \lim\limits_{x \to 1^-} x^2 = 1$ $\boxed{32}$ (a) $\lim\limits_{x \to 0^-} f(x) = \lim\limits_{x \to 0^-} (x^3 + 1) = 1$

(b) $\lim\limits_{x \to 1^+} f(x) = \lim\limits_{x \to 1^+} (4 - x^2) = 3$ (b) $\lim\limits_{x \to 0^+} f(x) = \lim\limits_{x \to 0^+} (x^3 + 1) = 1$

(c) $\lim\limits_{x \to 1} f(x)$ DNE   (c) $\lim\limits_{x \to 0} f(x) = 1$

Figure 31   Figure 32

$\boxed{33}$ Here, $f(x) = 5x - 21$, $L = 9$, and $a = 6$. Then $\left| f(x) - L \right| = \left| (5x - 21) - 9 \right|$
$= |5x - 30| = 5|x - 6|$. Thus, $\left| f(x) - L \right| < \epsilon \Leftrightarrow 5|x - 6| < \epsilon \Leftrightarrow |x - 6| < \frac{\epsilon}{5}$.
Hence, we may choose $\delta = \frac{\epsilon}{5}$. Now if $0 < |x - 6| < \delta$,
$$\text{then } \left| f(x) - L \right| = 5|x - 6| < 5\delta = 5(\tfrac{\epsilon}{5}) = \epsilon, \text{ as desired.}$$

$\boxed{34}$ Assume the limit L exists. If $\epsilon = \frac{1}{2}$ then there is a δ that satisfies (2.4). There exists rational and irrational numbers in the interval $(a - \delta, a + \delta)$. Let x_1 be a rational number and x_2 be an irrational number in this interval. Now,
$$2 = \left| f(x_1) - f(x_2) \right| = \left| \left[f(x_1) - L \right] - \left[f(x_2) - L \right] \right| \le \left| f(x_1) - L \right| + \left| f(x_2) - L \right|$$
$< \epsilon + \epsilon = \frac{1}{2} + \frac{1}{2} = 1$. But this is a contradiction and so the limit L does not exist.

$\boxed{35}$ $f(x) = \dfrac{\left| x^2 - 16 \right|}{x^2 - 16} = \dfrac{\left| x^2 - 16 \right|}{(x + 4)(x - 4)}$; f is discontinuous at -4 and 4 by (2.20)(i).

$\boxed{36}$ $f(x) = \dfrac{1}{x^2 - 16} = \dfrac{1}{(x + 4)(x - 4)}$; f is discontinuous at -4 and 4 by (2.21)(ii).

$\boxed{37}$ $f(x) = \dfrac{x^2 - x - 2}{x^2 - 2x} = \dfrac{(x-2)(x+1)}{x(x-2)}$; f is discontinuous at 0 and 2 by (2.21)(ii).

$\boxed{38}$ $f(x) = \dfrac{x+2}{x^3 - 8} = \dfrac{x+2}{(x-2)(x^2 + 2x + 4)}$; f is discontinuous at 2 by (2.21)(ii).

Note: For 39–42, since each f is a sum, difference, product, etc. of continuous functions,

each f is continuous on its domain.

$\boxed{39}$ $f(x) = 2x^4 - \sqrt[3]{x} + 1$ • $\star$ $\mathbb{R}$

$\boxed{40}$ $f(x) = \sqrt{(2+x)(3-x)}$ • $(2+x)(3-x) \geq 0 \Rightarrow -2 \leq x \leq 3$ $\star$ $[-2, 3]$

$\boxed{41}$ $f(x) = \dfrac{\sqrt{9 - x^2}}{x^4 - 16}$ • $9 - x^2 \geq 0 \Rightarrow 9 \geq x^2 \Rightarrow |x| \leq 3$; $x^4 - 16 \neq 0 \Rightarrow x \neq \pm 2$

$\star$ $[-3, -2) \cup (-2, 2) \cup (2, 3]$

$\boxed{42}$ $f(x) = \dfrac{\sqrt{x}}{x^2 - 1}$ • $x \geq 0$; $x^2 - 1 \neq 0 \Rightarrow x \neq \pm 1$ $\star$ $[0, 1) \cup (1, \infty)$

$\boxed{43}$ $f(x) = \sqrt{5x + 9}$; $a = 8$ • $\lim\limits_{x \to 8} f(x) = 7 = f(8)$

$\boxed{44}$ $f(x) = \sqrt[3]{x^2} - 4$; $a = 27$ • $\lim\limits_{x \to 27} f(x) = 5 = f(27)$

Chapter 3: The Derivative

Note: For solutions, the step $m_a = \lim\limits_{h \to 0} \dfrac{f(a+h) - f(a)}{h}$, or its equivalent, is omitted.

$\boxed{1}$ (a) $m_a = \lim\limits_{h \to 0} \dfrac{\left[5(a+h)^2 - 4(a+h)\right] - (5a^2 - 4a)}{h} = \lim\limits_{h \to 0} \dfrac{10ah + 5h^2 - 4h}{h} =$

$$\lim\limits_{h \to 0} (10a + 5h - 4) = 10a - 4$$

(b) $m_2 = 16$ and $f(2) = 12$; $y - 12 = 16(x - 2)$ or $y = 16x - 20$.

$\boxed{2}$ (a) $m_a = \lim\limits_{h \to 0} \dfrac{\left[3 - 2(a+h)^2\right] - (3 - 2a^2)}{h} = \lim\limits_{h \to 0} \dfrac{-4ah - 2h^2}{h} =$

$$\lim\limits_{h \to 0} (-4a - 2h) = -4a$$

(b) $m_2 = -8$ and $f(2) = -5$; $y + 5 = -8(x - 2)$ or $y = -8x + 11$.

$\boxed{3}$ (a) $m_a = \lim\limits_{h \to 0} \dfrac{(a+h)^3 - a^3}{h} = \lim\limits_{h \to 0} \dfrac{3a^2h + 3ah^2 + h^3}{h} =$

$$\lim\limits_{h \to 0} (3a^2 + 3ah + h^2) = 3a^2$$

(b) $m_2 = 12$ and $f(2) = 8$; $y - 8 = 12(x - 2)$ or $y = 12x - 16$.

$\boxed{4}$ (a) $m_a = \lim\limits_{h \to 0} \dfrac{(a+h)^4 - a^4}{h} = \lim\limits_{h \to 0} \dfrac{4a^3h + 6a^2h^2 + 4ah^3 + h^4}{h} =$

$$\lim\limits_{h \to 0} (4a^3 + 6a^2h + 4ah^2 + h^3) = 4a^3$$

(b) $m_2 = 32$ and $f(2) = 16$; $y - 16 = 32(x - 2)$ or $y = 32x - 48$.

$\boxed{5}$ (a) $m_a = \lim\limits_{h \to 0} \dfrac{\left[3(a+h) + 2\right] - (3a + 2)}{h} = \lim\limits_{h \to 0} \dfrac{3h}{h} = \lim\limits_{h \to 0} 3 = 3$

(b) $m_2 = 3$ and $f(2) = 8$; $y - 8 = 3(x - 2)$ or $y = 3x + 2$.

Note: The tangent line to a linear function is just the line itself.

$\boxed{6}$ (a) $m_a = \lim\limits_{h \to 0} \dfrac{\left[4 - 2(a+h)\right] - (4 - 2a)}{h} = \lim\limits_{h \to 0} \dfrac{-2h}{h} = \lim\limits_{h \to 0} (-2) = -2$

(b) $m_2 = -2$ and $f(2) = 0$; $y - 0 = -2(x - 2)$ or $y = -2x + 4$.

$\boxed{7}$ (a) $m_a = \lim\limits_{h \to 0} \dfrac{\sqrt{a+h} - \sqrt{a}}{h} \cdot \dfrac{\sqrt{a+h} + \sqrt{a}}{\sqrt{a+h} + \sqrt{a}} = \lim\limits_{h \to 0} \dfrac{h}{h(\sqrt{a+h} + \sqrt{a})} =$

$$\lim\limits_{h \to 0} \dfrac{1}{\sqrt{a+h} + \sqrt{a}} = \dfrac{1}{2\sqrt{a}}$$

(b) $m_4 = \frac{1}{4}$; $y - 2 = \frac{1}{4}(x - 4)$ or $y = \frac{1}{4}x + 1$.   (c) See *Figure 7*.

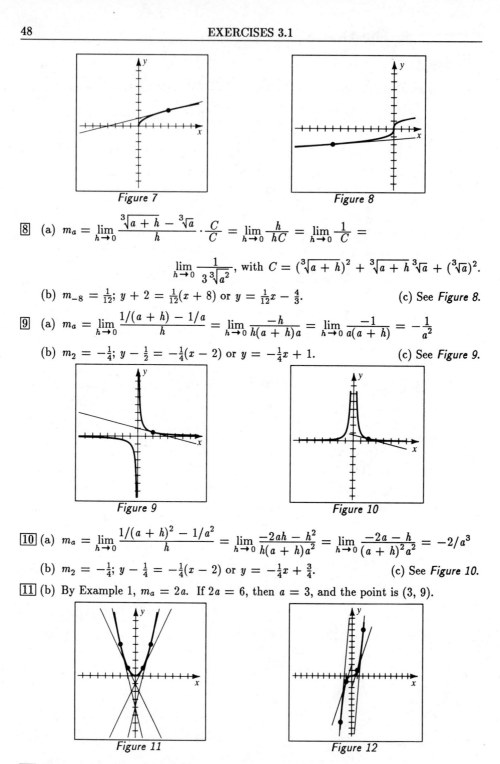

Figure 7　　　　　　　　　　*Figure 8*

$\boxed{8}$　(a) $m_a = \lim\limits_{h \to 0} \dfrac{\sqrt[3]{a+h} - \sqrt[3]{a}}{h} \cdot \dfrac{C}{C} = \lim\limits_{h \to 0} \dfrac{h}{hC} = \lim\limits_{h \to 0} \dfrac{1}{C} =$

$$\lim\limits_{h \to 0} \dfrac{1}{3\sqrt[3]{a^2}}, \text{ with } C = \left(\sqrt[3]{a+h}\right)^2 + \sqrt[3]{a+h}\,\sqrt[3]{a} + \left(\sqrt[3]{a}\right)^2.$$

(b) $m_{-8} = \frac{1}{12}$; $y + 2 = \frac{1}{12}(x + 8)$ or $y = \frac{1}{12}x - \frac{4}{3}$.　　　　(c) See *Figure 8*.

$\boxed{9}$　(a) $m_a = \lim\limits_{h \to 0} \dfrac{1/(a+h) - 1/a}{h} = \lim\limits_{h \to 0} \dfrac{-h}{h(a+h)a} = \lim\limits_{h \to 0} \dfrac{-1}{a(a+h)} = -\dfrac{1}{a^2}$

(b) $m_2 = -\frac{1}{4}$; $y - \frac{1}{2} = -\frac{1}{4}(x - 2)$ or $y = -\frac{1}{4}x + 1$.　　　(c) See *Figure 9*.

Figure 9　　　　　　　　　　*Figure 10*

$\boxed{10}$ (a) $m_a = \lim\limits_{h \to 0} \dfrac{1/(a+h)^2 - 1/a^2}{h} = \lim\limits_{h \to 0} \dfrac{-2ah - h^2}{h(a+h)a^2} = \lim\limits_{h \to 0} \dfrac{-2a - h}{(a+h)^2 a^2} = -2/a^3$

(b) $m_2 = -\frac{1}{4}$; $y - \frac{1}{4} = -\frac{1}{4}(x - 2)$ or $y = -\frac{1}{4}x + \frac{3}{4}$.　　(c) See *Figure 10*.

$\boxed{11}$ (b) By Example 1, $m_a = 2a$. If $2a = 6$, then $a = 3$, and the point is $(3, 9)$.

Figure 11　　　　　　　　　　*Figure 12*

$\boxed{12}$ (b) By Exercise 3, $m_a = 3a^2$.

$\quad$ If $3a^2 = 9$, then $a = \pm\sqrt{3}$, and the points are $(\pm\sqrt{3}, \pm 3\sqrt{3})$.

$\boxed{13}$ (a) Using (3.2), $v_{av} = \dfrac{d}{t} = \dfrac{s(a+h) - s(a)}{h}$. With $s(t) = 4t^2 + 3t$,

the average velocities (in cm/sec) for each interval are as follows.

$[1, 1.2]$: $\dfrac{s(1.2) - s(1)}{0.2} = \dfrac{9.36 - 7}{0.2} = 11.8$

$[1, 1.1]$: $\dfrac{s(1.1) - s(1)}{0.1} = \dfrac{8.14 - 7}{0.1} = 11.4$

$[1, 1.01]$: $\dfrac{s(1.01) - s(1)}{0.01} = \dfrac{7.1104 - 7}{0.01} = 11.04$

(b) Using (3.3), $v_a = \lim\limits_{h \to 0} \dfrac{\left[4(a+h)^2 + 3(a+h)\right] - (4a^2 + 3a)}{h} =$

$\lim\limits_{h \to 0} \dfrac{8ah + 4h^2 + 3h}{h} = \lim\limits_{h \to 0} (8a + 4h + 3) = 8a + 3.$ $v_1 = 11$ cm/sec.

$\boxed{14}$ (a) As in the previous exercise,

$[1, 1.2]$: $\dfrac{s(1.2) - s(1)}{0.2} = \dfrac{-1.92 - (-1)}{0.2} = -4.6$

$[1, 1.1]$: $\dfrac{s(1.1) - s(1)}{0.1} = \dfrac{-1.43 - (-1)}{0.1} = -4.3$

$[1, 1.01]$: $\dfrac{s(1.01) - s(1)}{0.01} = \dfrac{-1.0403 - (-1)}{0.01} = -4.03$

(b) Using (3.3), $v_a = \lim\limits_{h \to 0} \dfrac{\left[2(a+h) - 3(a+h)^2\right] - (2a - 3a^2)}{h} =$

$\lim\limits_{h \to 0} \dfrac{2h - 6ah - 3h^2}{h} = \lim\limits_{h \to 0} (2 - 6a - 3h) = 2 - 6a.$ $v_1 = -4$ cm/sec.

$\boxed{15}$ (a) $v_a = \lim\limits_{h \to 0} \dfrac{\left[160 - 16(a+h)^2\right] - (160 - 16a^2)}{h} = \lim\limits_{h \to 0} \dfrac{-32ah - 16h^2}{h} =$

$\lim\limits_{h \to 0} (-32a - 16h) = -32a.$

$v_1 = -32$ ft/sec.   (The negative sign indicates a downward direction.)

(b) Since $s(t) = 160 - 16t^2 = 0$ when $t = \sqrt{10}$, $v_a = -32\sqrt{10}$ ft/sec.

$\boxed{16}$ (a) $v_a = \lim\limits_{h \to 0} \dfrac{\left[112(a+h) - 16(a+h)^2\right] - (112a - 16a^2)}{h} =$

$\lim\limits_{h \to 0} \dfrac{112h - 32ah - 16h^2}{h} = \lim\limits_{h \to 0} (112 - 32a - 16h) = 112 - 32a.$

In ft/sec: $v_2 = 48$, $v_3 = 16$, and $v_4 = -16$.

(b) The projectile strikes the ground when $s(t) = 112t - 16t^2 = 0$,

or, equivalently, $t = 7$ for $t > 0$.

(c) The projectile's velocity at impact is $v_7 = -112$ ft/sec.

$\boxed{17}$ $m_a = \lim\limits_{h \to 0} \dfrac{\left[1 + 1/(a+h)\right] - (1 + 1/a)}{h} = \lim\limits_{h \to 0} \dfrac{-h}{h(a+h)a} = \lim\limits_{h \to 0} \dfrac{-1}{a(a+h)} = -\dfrac{1}{a^2}$

(a) At $P(1, 2)$, the equation of the tangent line is $(y - 2) = -1(x - 1)$ or

$y = -x + 3$. This line has x-intercept 3. The creature at $x = 3$ will be hit.

(b) At $Q(\frac{3}{2}, \frac{5}{3})$, the equation of the tangent line is $(y - \frac{5}{3}) = -\frac{4}{9}(x - \frac{3}{2})$ or

$y = -\frac{4}{9}x + \frac{7}{3}$. This line has x-intercept $\frac{21}{4}$. No creature is hit.

$\boxed{18}\ v_a = \lim\limits_{h\to 0} \dfrac{\left[\frac{1}{5}(a+h)^2 + 8(a+h)\right] - (\frac{1}{5}a^2 + 8a)}{h} = \lim\limits_{h\to 0}\dfrac{\frac{2}{5}ah + \frac{1}{5}h^2 + 8h}{h} = \frac{2}{5}a + 8$

(a) $v_0 = 8$ m/sec   (b) $v_5 = 10$ m/sec   (c) The athlete crosses the finish line when

$$s(t) = \tfrac{1}{5}t^2 + 8t = 100 \text{ or } t = 10 \text{ for } t > 0. \text{ Thus, } v_{10} = 12 \text{ m/sec.}$$

$\boxed{19}$ (a) Using (3.4)(i) with $f(x) = x^2 + 2$, $a = 3$, and $h = 3.5 - 3 = 0.5$,

$$\text{we have } y_{av} = \dfrac{f(3.5) - f(3)}{0.5} = \dfrac{14.25 - 11}{0.5} = 6.5.$$

(b) Using (3.4)(ii), $y_a = \lim\limits_{h\to 0}\dfrac{\left[(a+h)^2 + 2\right] - (a^2 + 2)}{h} = \lim\limits_{h\to 0}\dfrac{2ah + h^2}{h} =$

$$\lim\limits_{h\to 0}(2a + h) = 2a. \text{ Thus, } y_3 = 6.$$

$\boxed{20}$ (a) $y_{av} = \dfrac{f(2.4) - f(2)}{2.4 - 2} = \dfrac{-8.52 - (-5)}{0.4} = -8.8$

(b) $y_a = \lim\limits_{h\to 0}\dfrac{\left[3 - 2(a+h)^2\right] - (3 - 2a^2)}{h} = \lim\limits_{h\to 0}\dfrac{-4ah - 2h^2}{h} =$

$$\lim\limits_{h\to 0}(-4a - 2h) = -4a. \text{ Thus, } y_2 = -8.$$

$\boxed{21}$ (a) $p_v = \lim\limits_{h\to 0}\dfrac{200/(v+h) - 200/v}{h} = \lim\limits_{h\to 0}\dfrac{-200h}{h(v+h)v} = \lim\limits_{h\to 0}\dfrac{-200}{v(v+h)} = -\dfrac{200}{v^2}$

The negative sign indicates that the pressure decreases as the volume increases.

(b) $p_{10} = -200/10^2 = -2$

$\boxed{22}$ (a) Use $S = 4\pi r^2$.

$$S_r = \lim\limits_{h\to 0}\dfrac{4\pi(r+h)^2 - 4\pi r^2}{h} = \lim\limits_{h\to 0}\dfrac{8\pi rh + 4\pi h^2}{h} = \lim\limits_{h\to 0}(8\pi r + 4\pi h) = 8\pi r$$

(b) $S_3 = 24\pi$ ft^2/ft

$\boxed{23}$ (a) $m_{1.4} \approx -1$

(b) $\dfrac{f(1.4001) - f(1.4)}{0.0001} \approx -0.9703$ and $\dfrac{f(1.3999) - f(1.4)}{-0.0001} \approx -0.9713$.

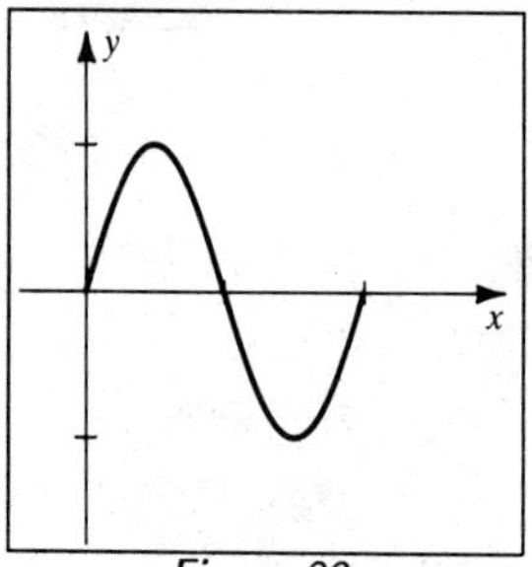

Figure 23

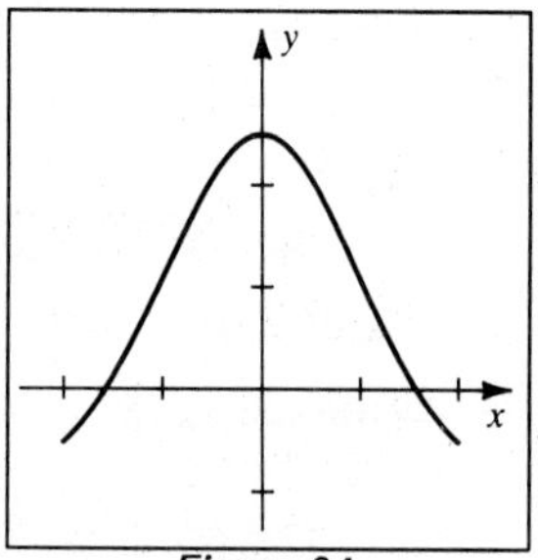

Figure 24

$\boxed{24}$ (a) $m_{-0.5} \approx 1.5$

(b) $\dfrac{f(-0.4999) - f(-0.5)}{0.0001} \approx 1.6138$; $\dfrac{f(-0.5001) - f(-0.5)}{-0.0001} \approx 1.6140$

(c) $y - 2.065 = 1.614(x + 0.5)$ or $y = 1.614x + 2.872$

$\boxed{25}$ $h = 0.01$: $v = \dfrac{s(2.01) - s(2)}{0.01} \approx \dfrac{0.761387164 - 0.762073579}{0.01} \approx -0.06864$ ft/sec

$h = 0.001$: $v = \dfrac{s(2.001) - s(2)}{0.001} \approx \dfrac{0.762009315 - 0.762073579}{0.001} \approx -0.06426$ ft/sec

$h = 0.0001$: $v = \dfrac{s(2.0001) - s(2)}{0.0001} \approx \dfrac{0.762067197 - 0.762073579}{0.0001} \approx -0.6382$ ft/sec

$\boxed{26}$ (b) From the figure, the object is moving in a positive direction when the slope is positive. Hence, the velocity is positive on the following intervals: $[0, 0.5)$, $(1.9, 4.7)$, $(7.9, 10]$.

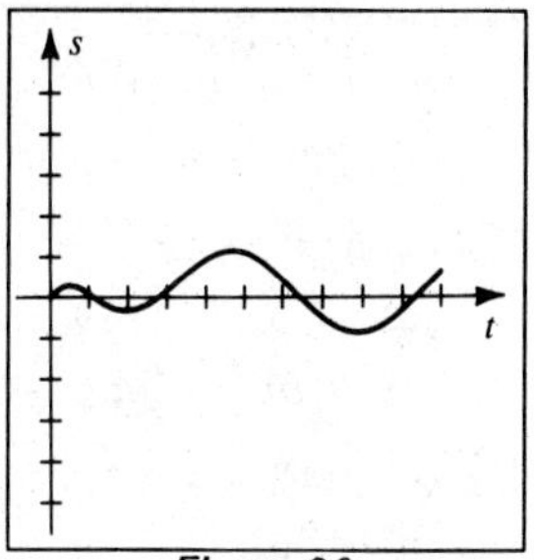

Figure 26

Exercises 3.2

Note: Use $f'(x) = \lim\limits_{h \to 0} \dfrac{f(x + h) - f(x)}{h}$ in Exercises 1–4.

$\boxed{1}$ (a) $f'(x) = \lim\limits_{h \to 0} \dfrac{\left[-5(x + h)^2 + 8(x + h) + 2\right] - (-5x^2 + 8x + 2)}{h} =$

$\lim\limits_{h \to 0} \dfrac{-10xh - 5h^2 + 8h}{h} = \lim\limits_{h \to 0} (-10x - 5h + 8) = -10x + 8$

(b) $\mathbb{R}$ (c) $f'(-1) = 18$; $y + 11 = 18(x + 1)$ or $y = 18x + 7$.

(d) $f'(x) = 0 \Rightarrow x = \frac{4}{5}$; $\left(\frac{4}{5}, \frac{26}{5}\right)$

$\boxed{2}$ (a) $f'(x) = \lim\limits_{h \to 0} \dfrac{\left[3(x + h)^2 - 2(x + h) - 4\right] - (3x^2 - 2x - 4)}{h} =$

$\lim\limits_{h \to 0} \dfrac{6xh + 3h^2 - 2h}{h} = \lim\limits_{h \to 0} (6x + 3h - 2) = 6x - 2$

(b) $\mathbb{R}$ (c) $f'(2) = 10$; $y - 4 = 10(x - 2)$ or $y = 10x - 16$.

(d) $f'(x) = 0 \Rightarrow x = \frac{1}{3}$; $\left(\frac{1}{3}, -\frac{13}{3}\right)$

$\boxed{3}$ (a) $f'(x) = \lim\limits_{h \to 0} \dfrac{\left[(x + h)^3 + (x + h)\right] - (x^3 + x)}{h} = \lim\limits_{h \to 0} \dfrac{3x^2 h + 3xh^2 + h^3 + h}{h} =$

$\lim\limits_{h \to 0} (3x^2 + 3xh + h^2 + 1) = 3x^2 + 1$

(b) $\mathbb{R}$ (c) $f'(1) = 4$; $y - 2 = 4(x - 1)$ or $y = 4x - 2$.

(d) $f'(x) \neq 0$ for any real value of x.

$\boxed{4}$ (a) $f'(x) = \lim\limits_{h \to 0} \dfrac{\left[(x + h)^3 - 4(x + h)\right] - (x^3 - 4x)}{h} =$

$\lim\limits_{h \to 0} \dfrac{3x^2 h + 3xh^2 + h^3 - 4h}{h} = \lim\limits_{h \to 0} (3x^2 + 3xh + h^2 - 4) = 3x^2 - 4$

(b) $\mathbb{R}$ (c) $f'(2) = 8$; $y - 0 = 8(x - 2)$ or $y = 8x - 16$.

(d) $f'(x) = 0 \Rightarrow x = \pm\frac{2}{\sqrt{3}}$; $\left(\pm\frac{2}{\sqrt{3}}, \mp\frac{16}{3\sqrt{3}}\right)$

$\boxed{5}$ (a) $f'(x) = 9$ (b) $\mathbb{R}$ (c) $y = 9x - 2$ (d) None

$\boxed{6}$ (a) $f'(x) = -4$ (b) $\mathbb{R}$ (c) $y = -4x + 3$ (d) None

$\boxed{7}$ (a) $f'(x) = 0$ (b) $\mathbb{R}$ (c) $y = 37$ (d) None

⑧ (a) $f'(x) = 0$ (b) $\mathbb{R}$ (c) $y = \pi^2$ (d) None

⑨ (a) $f(x) = 1/x^3 = x^{-3} \Rightarrow f'(x) = -3x^{-4} = -3/x^4$

   (b) $(-\infty, 0) \cup (0, \infty)$

   (c) $f'(2) = -\frac{3}{16}$; $y - \frac{1}{8} = -\frac{3}{16}(x - 2)$ or $y = -\frac{3}{16}x + \frac{1}{2}$.   (d) None

⑩ (a) $f(x) = 1/x^4 = x^{-4} \Rightarrow f'(x) = -4x^{-5} = -4/x^5$

   (b) $(-\infty, 0) \cup (0, \infty)$

   (c) $f'(1) = -4$; $y - 1 = -4(x - 1)$ or $y = -4x + 5$.   (d) None

⑪ (a) $f(x) = 4x^{1/4} \Rightarrow f'(x) = x^{-3/4} = 1/x^{3/4}$

   (b) $(-\infty, 0) \cup (0, \infty)$

   (c) $f'(81) = \frac{1}{27}$; $y - 12 = \frac{1}{27}(x - 81)$ or $y = \frac{1}{27}x + 9$.   (d) None

⑫ (a) $f(x) = 12x^{1/3} \Rightarrow f'(x) = 4x^{-2/3} = 4/x^{2/3}$

   (b) $(-\infty, 0) \cup (0, \infty)$

   (c) $f'(-27) = \frac{4}{9}$; $y + 36 = \frac{4}{9}(x + 27)$ or $y = \frac{4}{9}x - 24$.   (d) None

⑬ $f(x) = 3x^6 \Rightarrow f'(x) = 18x^5$, $f''(x) = 90x^4$, $f'''(x) = 360x^3$

⑭ $f(x) = 6x^4 \Rightarrow f'(x) = 24x^3$, $f''(x) = 72x^2$, $f'''(x) = 144x$

⑮ $f(x) = 9\sqrt[3]{x^2} = 9x^{2/3} \Rightarrow f'(x) = 6x^{-1/3}$, $f''(x) = -2x^{-4/3}$, $f'''(x) = \frac{8}{3}x^{-7/3}$

⑯ $f(x) = 3x^{7/3} \Rightarrow f'(x) = 7x^{4/3}$, $f''(x) = \frac{28}{3}x^{1/3}$, $f'''(x) = \frac{28}{9}x^{-2/3}$

⑰ $z = 25t^{9/5} \Rightarrow D_t z = 45t^{4/5}$ and $D_t^2 z = 36t^{-1/5}$

⑱ $y = 3x + 5 \Rightarrow D_x y = 3$, $D_x^2 y = 0$, and $D_x^3 y = 0$

⑲ $y = -4x + 7 \Rightarrow \dfrac{dy}{dx} = -4$, $\dfrac{d^2 y}{dx^2} = 0$, and $\dfrac{d^3 y}{dx^3} = 0$

⑳ $z = 64\sqrt[4]{t^3} = 64t^{3/4} \Rightarrow \dfrac{dz}{dt} = 48t^{-1/4}$ and $\dfrac{d^2 z}{dt^2} = -12t^{-5/4}$

㉑ (a) No, because f is not differentiable at $x = 0$.

   (b) Yes, because f' exists for every number in $[1, 3)$.

㉒ (a) No, because f is not differentiable at $x = 0$.

   (b) Yes, because f' exists for every number in $[-2, -1)$.

㉓ (a) From the graph we see that f is not differentiable at $x = 4$.

   (b) f' exists for every number in $[-5, 0]$.

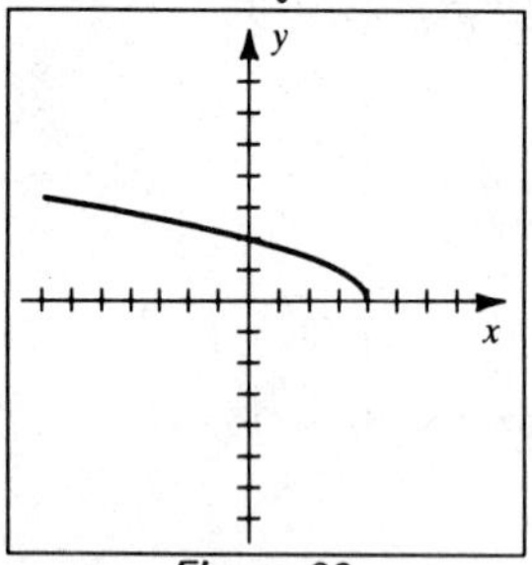

Figure 23

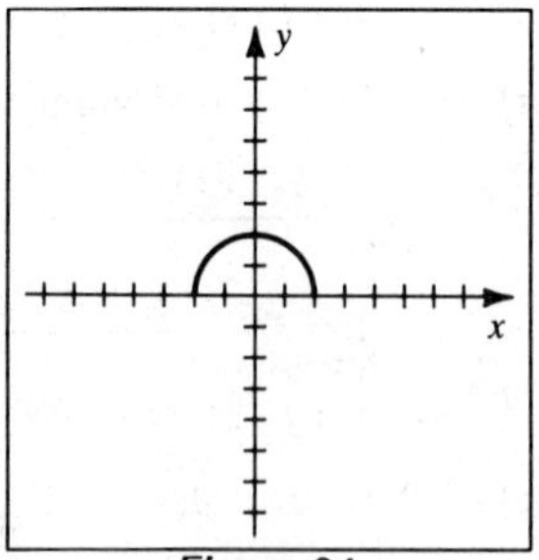

Figure 24

㉔ (a) From the graph we see that f is not differentiable at $x = \pm 2$.

   (b) f' exists for every number in $[-1, 1]$.

Note: It may be helpful to have the students graph each function in 25–30.

[25] $\lim_{x \to 0} |f'(x)| = \lim_{x \to 0} \left| \frac{1}{3} x^{-2/3} \right| = \infty \Rightarrow$ there is a vertical tangent line at $(0, 0)$.

Since f' is always positive, no cusp is formed.

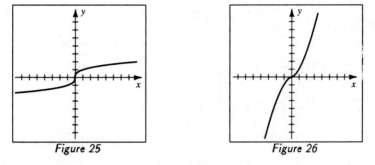

Figure 25   Figure 26

[26] $\lim_{x \to 0} |f'(x)| = \lim_{x \to 0} \left| \frac{5}{3} x^{2/3} \right| = 0 \Rightarrow$ no vertical tangent line at $(0, 0)$.

Since f' is always nonnegative, no cusp is formed.

[27] $\lim_{x \to 0} |f'(x)| = \lim_{x \to 0} \left| \frac{2}{5} x^{-3/5} \right| = \infty \Rightarrow$ there is a vertical tangent line at $(0, 0)$.

As $x \to 0^-$, $f'(x) \to -\infty$. As $x \to 0^+$, $f'(x) \to \infty$. By (3.10), there is a cusp.

Figure 27   Figure 28

[28] *Note:* We use a one-sided analogy to Definition (3.9) since $x = 0$ is an endpoint.

$\lim_{x \to 0^+} |f'(x)| = \lim_{x \to 0^+} \left| \frac{1}{4} x^{-3/4} \right| = \infty \Rightarrow$ there is a vertical tangent line at $(0, 0)$.

Since f' does not exist for negative values of x, no cusp is formed.

[29] $\lim_{x \to 0^+} |f'(x)| = \lim_{x \to 0^+} \left| \frac{15}{2} x^{1/2} \right| = 0 \Rightarrow$ no vertical tangent line at $(0, 0)$.

Since f' does not exist for negative values of x, no cusp is formed.

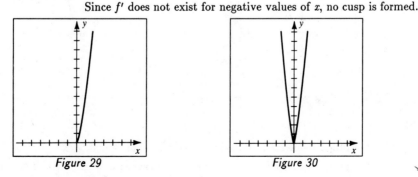

Figure 29   Figure 30

30 $\lim\limits_{x \to 0} |f'(x)| = \lim\limits_{x \to 0} \left| \frac{28}{3} x^{1/3} \right| = 0 \Rightarrow$ no vertical tangent line at $(0,\ 0)$.

Since $\lim\limits_{x \to 0} f'(x) = 0$, no cusp is formed. See *Figure 30*.

31 From the figure,

it appears that $f'(-1) = 1$, $f'(1) = 0$, $f'(2)$ is undefined, and $f'(3) = -1$.

32 From the figure,

it appears that $f'(-1) = -1$, $f'(1)$ is undefined, $f'(2)$ is undefined, and $f'(3) = 0$.

33 $\lim\limits_{h \to 0^+} \dfrac{|5 + h - 5| - |5 - 5|}{h} = \lim\limits_{h \to 0^+} \dfrac{|h|}{h} = \lim\limits_{h \to 0^+} \dfrac{h}{h} = 1$

$\lim\limits_{h \to 0^-} \dfrac{|5 + h - 5| - |5 - 5|}{h} = \lim\limits_{h \to 0^-} \dfrac{|h|}{h} = \lim\limits_{h \to 0^-} \dfrac{-h}{h} = -1$

Since the one-sided limits are not equal, the derivative fails to exist at $a = 5$.

34 $\lim\limits_{h \to 0^+} \dfrac{|-2 + h + 2| - |-2 + 2|}{h} = \lim\limits_{h \to 0^+} \dfrac{|h|}{h} = \lim\limits_{h \to 0^+} \dfrac{h}{h} = 1$

$\lim\limits_{h \to 0^-} \dfrac{|-2 + h + 2| - |-2 + 2|}{h} = \lim\limits_{h \to 0^-} \dfrac{|h|}{h} = \lim\limits_{h \to 0^-} \dfrac{-h}{h} = -1$

Since the one-sided limits are not equal, the derivative fails to exist at $a = -2$.

35 $\lim\limits_{h \to 0^+} \dfrac{[\![2 + h - 2]\!] - [\![2 - 2]\!]}{h} = \lim\limits_{h \to 0^+} \dfrac{[\![h]\!]}{h} = \lim\limits_{h \to 0^+} \dfrac{0}{h} = \lim\limits_{h \to 0^+} 0 = 0$

$\lim\limits_{h \to 0^-} \dfrac{[\![2 + h - 2]\!] - [\![2 - 2]\!]}{h} = \lim\limits_{h \to 0^-} \dfrac{[\![h]\!]}{h} = \lim\limits_{h \to 0^-} \dfrac{-1}{h}$, which DNE

Since the left-hand derivative fails to exist, the derivative fails to exist at $a = 2$.

36 $\lim\limits_{h \to 0^+} \dfrac{([\![2 + h]\!] - 2) - ([\![2]\!] - 2)}{h} = \lim\limits_{h \to 0^+} \dfrac{[\![2 + h]\!] - 2}{h} = \lim\limits_{h \to 0^+} \dfrac{0}{h} = \lim\limits_{h \to 0^+} 0 = 0$

$\lim\limits_{h \to 0^-} \dfrac{([\![2 + h]\!] - 2) - ([\![2]\!] - 2)}{h} = \lim\limits_{h \to 0^-} \dfrac{[\![2 + h]\!] - 2}{h} = \lim\limits_{h \to 0^-} \dfrac{-1}{h}$, which DNE

Since the left-hand derivative fails to exist, the derivative fails to exist at $a = 2$.

37 If $x < 0$, $f'(x) = 2$ and if $x > 0$, $f'(x) = 2x$.

At $x = 0$, the left-hand derivative is 2 and the right-hand derivative is 0.

Thus, the graph of f has a corner at $x = 0$. The domain of f' is $\{x : x \neq 0\}$.

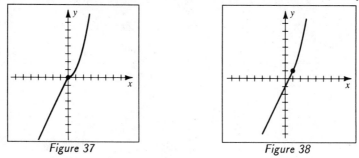

Figure 37　　　　　　　　　　　　Figure 38

38 If $x < 1$, $f'(x) = 2$ and if $x > 1$, $f'(x) = 2x$.

At $x = 1$, the left-hand and right-hand derivatives are equal to 2.

There is no corner at $x = 1$. The domain of f' is $\mathbb{R}$.

[39] If $x < -1$, $f'(x) = -2x$ and if $x > -1$, $f'(x) = 2$. The right-hand derivative, 2, is equal to the left-hand derivative at $x = -1$. However, the function is not continuous at $x = -1$ and hence, by the contrapositive of Theorem (3.11), cannot be differentiable at that point. The domain of f' is $\{x: x \neq 1\}$.

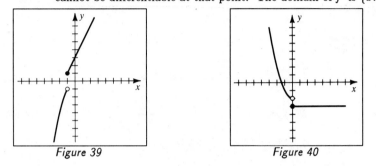

Figure 39   Figure 40

[40] If $x < 0$, $f'(x) = 2x$ and if $x > 0$, $f'(x) = 0$. The right-hand derivative, 0, is equal to the left-hand derivative at $x = 0$. However, the function is not continuous at $x = 0$ and hence, by the contrapositive of Theorem (3.11), cannot be differentiable at that point. The domain of f' is $\{x: x \neq 0\}$.

[41] f is not differentiable at $x = \pm 1$, ± 2, since f has a corner at these points.

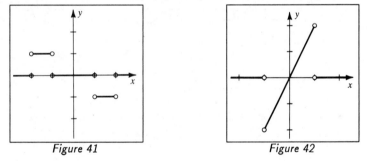

Figure 41   Figure 42

[42] f is not differentiable at $x = \pm 1$, since f has a corner at these points.

[43] $v(t) = s'(t) = 2t^{-1/3}$; $2t^{-1/3} = 4 \Rightarrow t^{-1/3} = 2 \Rightarrow t = 2^{-3} = \frac{1}{8}$.

[44] $v(t) = s'(t) = 12t^2$; $12t^2 = 300 \Rightarrow t^2 = 25 \Rightarrow t = \pm 5$.

[45] $C = \frac{5}{9}(F - 32) \Rightarrow F = \frac{9}{5}C + 32$; $F_C = \frac{9}{5}$

[46] $V = V_0(1 + \frac{1}{273}T) \Rightarrow T = 273\left(\frac{V}{V_0} - 1\right)$; $T_V = 273/V_0$

[47] $V = \frac{4}{3}\pi r^3 \Rightarrow V_r = 4\pi r^2$, the value of the surface area of a sphere with radius r.

[48] $C = 2\pi r \Rightarrow r = \frac{C}{2\pi}$; $r_C = \frac{1}{2\pi}$, a constant.

[49] (a) $A = \pi r^2 \Rightarrow A_r = 2\pi r$

(b) $r = 500$ ft $\Rightarrow A = 2\pi(500) = 1000\pi$ ft^2/ft

[50] (a) $V = \frac{4}{3}\pi r^3 \Rightarrow V_r = 4\pi r^2$

(b) $r = 10$ ft $\Rightarrow V = 4\pi(10)^2 = 400\pi$ ft^3/ft

[51] (a) The formula gives an approximation of the slope of the tangent line at $(a, f(a))$

by using the slope of the secant line through $P(a - h, f(a - h))$ and

$$Q(a + h, f(a + h)).$$

(b) $\displaystyle \lim_{h \to 0} \frac{f(a + h) - f(a - h)}{2h} = \lim_{h \to 0} \frac{f(a + h) - f(a) - f(a - h) + f(a)}{2h}$

$$= \frac{1}{2} \lim_{h \to 0} \frac{f(a + h) - f(a)}{h} - \frac{1}{2} \lim_{h \to 0} \frac{f(a - h) - f(a)}{h}$$

$$= \frac{1}{2} f'(a) + \frac{1}{2} \lim_{k \to 0} \frac{f(a + k) - f(a)}{k} \ \{\text{where } k = -h\} = \frac{1}{2} f'(a) + \frac{1}{2} f'(a) = f'(a)$$

(c) $h = 0.1$: $f'(1) \approx \dfrac{f(1.1) - f(0.9)}{0.2} = \dfrac{1/(1.1)^2 - 1/(0.9)^2}{0.2} \approx -2.0406$

$\quad\ h = 0.01$: $f'(1) \approx \dfrac{f(1.01) - f(0.99)}{0.02} = \dfrac{1/(1.01)^2 - 1/(0.99)^2}{0.02} \approx -2.0004$

$\quad\ h = 0.001$: $f'(1) \approx \dfrac{f(1.001) - f(0.999)}{0.002} = \dfrac{1/(1.001)^2 - 1/(0.999)^2}{0.002} \approx -2.0000$

(d) $f(x) = 1/x^2 \Rightarrow f'(x) = -2/x^3$; $f'(1) = -2$

[52] (a) $f''(a) = \left[f'(a)\right]' \approx \dfrac{f'(a + H) - f'(a - H)}{2H}$

$$\approx \dfrac{\dfrac{f(a + H + H) - f(a + H - H)}{2H} - \dfrac{f(a - H + H) - f(a - H - H)}{2H}}{2H}$$

$$= \dfrac{f(a + 2H) - 2f(a) + f(a - 2H)}{4H^2}$$

$$= \dfrac{f(a + h) - 2f(a) + f(a - h)}{h^2}, \text{ where } h = 2H.$$

(b) Using $h = 0.1, 0.01,$ and 0.001, respectively, $f''(1)$ is approximately equal to

$$\dfrac{f(1.1) - 2f(1) + f(0.9)}{(0.1)^2} = \dfrac{1/(1.1)^2 - 2 + 1/(0.9)^2}{0.01} \approx 6.1014$$

$$\dfrac{f(1.01) - 2f(1) + f(0.99)}{(0.01)^2} = \dfrac{1/(1.01)^2 - 2 + 1/(0.99)^2}{0.0001} \approx 6.0010$$

$$\dfrac{f(1.001) - 2f(1) + f(0.999)}{(0.001)^2} = \dfrac{1/(1.001)^2 - 2 + 1/(0.999)^2}{0.000001} \approx 6.0000$$

(c) $f(x) = 1/x^2 \Rightarrow f'(x) = -2/x^3 \Rightarrow f''(x) = 6/x^4$; $f''(1) = 6$

[53] (a) $a = 3, h = 1$:

$$v(3) = s'(3) \approx \dfrac{s(3 + 1) - s(3 - 1)}{2(1)} = \dfrac{149.0 - 42.6}{2} = 53.2 \text{ ft/sec}$$

(b) $a = 6, h = 1$:

$$v(6) = s'(6) \approx \dfrac{s(6 + 1) - s(6 - 1)}{2(1)} = \dfrac{396.7 - 220.1}{2} = 88.3 \text{ ft/sec}$$

[54] (a) $v'(3) = s''(3) \approx \dfrac{s(4) - 2\,s(3) + s(2)}{(1)^2} = \dfrac{149.0 - 2(89.1) + 42.6}{1} = 13.4 \text{ ft/sec}^2$

(b) $v'(6) = s''(6) \approx \dfrac{s(7) - 2\,s(6) + s(5)}{(1)^2} = \dfrac{396.7 - 2(303.7) + 220.1}{1} = 9.4 \text{ ft/sec}^2$

$\boxed{55}$ f is not differentiable at $x \approx -0.7$ since the graph of f has a corner there.

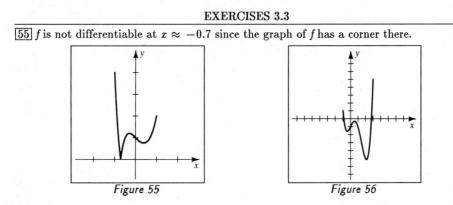

Figure 55   Figure 56

$\boxed{56}$ f has horizontal tangent lines at $x \approx -0.43, 0.54, 2.14$.

Exercises 3.3

$\boxed{1}$ $g'(t) = 6 \cdot \frac{5}{3} \cdot t^{2/3} = 10t^{2/3}$

$\boxed{2}$ $h'(z) = 8 \cdot \frac{3}{2} \cdot z^{1/2} = 12z^{1/2}$

$\boxed{3}$ $f'(s) = -1 + 8s - 20s^3$

$\boxed{4}$ $f'(t) = -12t^3 + 24t^5$

$\boxed{5}$ $f'(x) = 6x + \frac{4}{3}x^{1/3}$

$\boxed{6}$ $g'(x) = 4x^3 - \frac{3}{4}x^{-1/4}$

$\boxed{7}$ $g'(x) = (x^3 - 7)(4x) + (2x^2 + 3)(3x^2) = 10x^4 + 9x^2 - 28x$

$\boxed{8}$ $k'(x) = (2x^2 - 4x + 1)(6) + (6x - 5)(4x - 4) = 36x^2 - 68x + 26$

$\boxed{9}$ $f(x) = x^{5/2} + x^{3/2} - 4x^{1/2} \Rightarrow f'(x) = \frac{5}{2}x^{3/2} + \frac{3}{2}x^{1/2} - 2x^{-1/2}$

$\boxed{10}$ $h(x) = 3x^{8/3} - 2x^{5/3} + 5x^{2/3} \Rightarrow h'(x) = 8x^{5/3} - \frac{10}{3}x^{2/3} + \frac{10}{3}x^{-1/3}$

$\boxed{11}$ $h(r) = 3r^6 - 7r^3 + 2r^2 \Rightarrow h'(r) = 18r^5 - 21r^2 + 4r$

$\boxed{12}$ $k(v) = -2v^6 + v^4 - 3v^3 \Rightarrow k'(v) = -12v^5 + 4v^3 - 9v^2$

$\boxed{13}$ $g'(x) = (8x^2 - 5x)(26x) + (13x^2 + 4)(16x - 5) = 416x^3 - 195x^2 + 64x - 20$

$\boxed{14}$ $H'(z) = (z^5 - 2z^3)(14z + 1) + (7z^2 + z - 8)(5z^4 - 6z^2)$
$$= 49z^6 + 6z^5 - 110z^4 - 8z^3 - 48z^2$$

$\boxed{15}$ $f'(x) = \dfrac{(3x + 2)(4) - (4x - 5)(3)}{(3x + 2)^2} = \dfrac{23}{(3x + 2)^2}$

$\boxed{16}$ $h'(x) = \dfrac{(x - 1)(16x - 6) - (8x^2 - 6x + 11)(1)}{(x - 1)^2} = \dfrac{8x^2 - 16x - 5}{(x - 1)^2}$

$\boxed{17}$ $h'(z) = \dfrac{(2 - 9z)(-1 + 6z) - (8 - z + 3z^2)(-9)}{(2 - 9z)^2} = \dfrac{70 + 12z - 27z^2}{(2 - 9z)^2}$

$\boxed{18}$ $f'(w) = \dfrac{(w^3 - 7)(2) - (2w)(3w^2)}{(w^3 - 7)^2} = \dfrac{-4w^3 - 14}{(w^3 - 7)^2} = -\dfrac{4w^3 + 14}{(w^3 - 7)^2}$

$\boxed{19}$ $G'(v) = \dfrac{(v^3 + 1)(3v^2) - (v^3 - 1)(3v^2)}{(v^3 + 1)^2} = \dfrac{6v^2}{(v^3 + 1)^2}$

$\boxed{20}$ $f'(t) = \dfrac{(t^2 - 2t + 3)(8) - (8t + 15)(2t - 2)}{(t^2 - 2t + 3)^2} = \dfrac{-8t^2 - 30t + 54}{(t^2 - 2t + 3)^2}$

$\boxed{21}$ $g'(t) = \dfrac{(3t - 5)(\frac{2}{3}t^{-1/3}) - (t^{2/3})(3)}{(3t - 5)^2} = \dfrac{t^{-1/3}[2(3t - 5) - 9t]}{3(3t - 5)^2} = -\dfrac{3t + 10}{3\sqrt[3]{t}\,(3t - 5)^2}$

$\boxed{22}\ f'(x) = \dfrac{(2x^2 - 4x + 8)(\frac{1}{2}x^{-1/2}) - (x^{1/2})(4x - 4)}{(2x^2 - 4x + 8)^2}$

$\qquad\qquad = \dfrac{x^{-1/2}\left[(x^2 - 2x + 4) - x(4x - 4)\right]}{(2x^2 - 4x + 8)^2} = \dfrac{-3x^2 + 2x + 4}{\sqrt{x}\,(2x^2 - 4x + 8)^2}$

$\boxed{23}$ By the reciprocal rule, $f'(x) = -\dfrac{1 + 2x + 3x^2}{(1 + x + x^2 + x^3)^2}.$

$\boxed{24}\ p(x) = 1 + x^{-1} + x^{-2} + x^{-3} \Rightarrow p'(x) = -x^{-2} + (-2)x^{-3} + (-3)x^{-4} =$

$\qquad\qquad\qquad\qquad\qquad\qquad\qquad\qquad\qquad\qquad -\dfrac{1}{x^2} - \dfrac{2}{x^3} - \dfrac{3}{x^4}$

$\boxed{25}\ h'(x) = 7\left[-\dfrac{2x}{(x^2 + 5)^2}\right] = \dfrac{-14x}{(x^2 + 5)^2}\qquad \boxed{26}\ k'(z) = 6\left[-\dfrac{2z + 1}{(z^2 + z - 1)^2}\right]$

$\boxed{27}\ F'(t) = 2t - \dfrac{2t}{(t^2)^2} = 2t - \dfrac{2}{t^3}\qquad\qquad \boxed{28}\ s'(x) = 2 - \dfrac{2}{(2x)^2} = 2 - \dfrac{1}{2x^2}$

$\boxed{29}\ K'(s) = D_s\,(3^{-4}s^{-4}) = 3^{-4}(-4s^{-5}) = -\frac{4}{81}s^{-5}$

$\boxed{30}\ W'(s) = D_s\,(3^4 s^4) = 3^4(4s^3) = 324s^3$

$\boxed{31}\ h'(x) = D_x\,(25x^2 - 40x + 16) = 50x - 40 = 10(5x - 4)$

$\boxed{32}\ S'(w) = D_w\,(8w^3 + 12w^2 + 6w + 1) = 24w^2 + 24w + 6 = 6(4w^2 + 4w + 1)$

$\boxed{33}\ g'(r) = D_r\left[\dfrac{1}{(5r - 4)^2}\right] = -\dfrac{10(5r - 4)}{(5r - 4)^4} = \dfrac{-10}{(5r - 4)^3},$

$\qquad\qquad\qquad\qquad$ where we used Exercise 31 for $D_r\left[(5r - 4)^2\right].$

$\boxed{34}\ S'(x) = S_x\left[\dfrac{1}{(3x + 1)^2}\right] = S_x\left[\dfrac{1}{9x^2 + 6x + 1}\right] =$

$\qquad\qquad\qquad\qquad -\dfrac{18x + 6}{(9x^2 + 6x + 1)^2} = \dfrac{-6(3x + 1)}{(3x + 1)^4} = \dfrac{-6}{(3x + 1)^3}$

$\boxed{35}\ f'(t) = D_t\left(\dfrac{\frac{3}{5}t - t^2}{2 + 7t^2}\right) = \dfrac{(2 + 7t^2)(\frac{3}{5} - 2t) - (\frac{3}{5}t - t^2)(14t)}{(2 + 7t^2)^2} =$

$\qquad\qquad\qquad\qquad \dfrac{-\frac{21}{5}t^2 - 4t + \frac{6}{5}}{(2 + 7t^2)^2} = \dfrac{6 - 20t - 21t^2}{5(2 + 7t^2)^2}$

$\boxed{36}\ N'(z) = D_z\left(\dfrac{4}{3z + 2z^2}\right) = 4\left[-\dfrac{3 + 4z}{(3z + 2z^2)^2}\right] = \dfrac{-4(3 + 4z)}{(3z + 2z^2)^2}$

$\boxed{37}\ M'(x) = D_x\,(2x - 7 + 4x^{-1} + 3x^{-2}) = 2 - 4x^{-2} - 6x^{-3} = 2 - \dfrac{4}{x^2} - \dfrac{6}{x^3}$

$\boxed{38}\ T'(z) = D_z\,(5z + 1 - 2z^{-2}) = 5 + 4z^{-3}$

$\boxed{39}\ f'(x) = \frac{1}{7}D_x\,(3x^2 - 5x + 8) = \frac{1}{7}(6x - 5)$

$\boxed{40}\ h'(t) = \frac{1}{5}D_t\,(3t^5 + 2t) = \frac{1}{5}(15t^4 + 2)$

$\boxed{41}\ D_x\,y = 6x^2 - 6x - 36 = 6(x - 3)(x + 2);\ D_x\,y = 0 \Rightarrow x = -2, 3.$

$\boxed{42}\ D_x\,y = 12x^2 + 42x - 24 = 6(2x - 1)(x + 4);\ D_x\,y = 0 \Rightarrow x = -4, \frac{1}{2}.$

$\boxed{43}\ D_x\,y = \dfrac{(x - 2)(4x + 3) - (2x^2 + 3x - 6)(1)}{(x - 2)^2} = \dfrac{2x^2 - 8x}{(x - 2)^2} = \dfrac{2x(x - 4)}{(x - 2)^2};$

$\qquad\qquad\qquad\qquad\qquad\qquad\qquad\qquad\qquad D_x\,y = 0 \Rightarrow x = 0, 4.$

$\boxed{44}$ $D_x\,y = \dfrac{(x+1)(2x+2) - (x^2 + 2x + 5)(1)}{(x+1)^2} = \dfrac{x^2 + 2x - 3}{(x+1)^2} = \dfrac{(x+3)(x-1)}{(x+1)^2};$

$$D_x\,y = 0 \Rightarrow x = -3,\,1.$$

$\boxed{45}$ $D_x\,y = 24x^3 + 72x^2 - 1080x \Rightarrow D_x^2\,y = 72x^2 + 144x - 1080 = 72(x+5)(x-3);$

$$D_x^2\,y = 0 \Rightarrow x = -5,\,3.$$

$\boxed{46}$ $D_x\,y = 30x^4 - 20x^3 - 90x^2 + 11 \Rightarrow$

$$D_x^2\,y = 120x^3 - 60x^2 - 180x = 60x(2x-3)(x+1);\ D_x^2\,y = 0 \Rightarrow x = -1,\,0,\,\tfrac{3}{2}.$$

$\boxed{47}$ (a) $\dfrac{dy}{dx} = \dfrac{x^2(3) - (3x-1)(2x)}{(x^2)^2} = \dfrac{2x - 3x^2}{x^4} = \dfrac{2 - 3x}{x^3}$

(b) $\dfrac{dy}{dx} = D_x\left[(3x-1)(x^{-2})\right] = (3x-1)(-2x^{-3}) + (x^{-2})(3) =$

$$\dfrac{-6x+2}{x^3} + \dfrac{3}{x^2}\cdot\dfrac{x}{x} = \dfrac{2 - 3x}{x^3}$$

(c) $\dfrac{dy}{dx} = D_x\left(3x^{-1} - x^{-2}\right) = -3x^{-2} + 2x^{-3} = \dfrac{-3}{x^2}\cdot\dfrac{x}{x} + \dfrac{2}{x^3} = \dfrac{2 - 3x}{x^3}$

$\boxed{48}$ (a) $\dfrac{dy}{dx} = \dfrac{x^4(2x) - (x^2+1)(4x^3)}{(x^4)^2} = \dfrac{-2x^5 - 4x^3}{x^8} = \dfrac{-2(x^2+2)}{x^5}$

(b) $\dfrac{dy}{dx} = D_x\left[(x^2+1)(x^{-4})\right] = (x^2+1)(-4x^{-5}) + (x^{-4})(2x) =$

$$\dfrac{-4x^2 - 4}{x^5} + \dfrac{2x}{x^4}\cdot\dfrac{x}{x} = \dfrac{-2(x^2+2)}{x^5}$$

(c) $\dfrac{dy}{dx} = D_x\left(x^{-2} + x^{-4}\right) = -2x^{-3} - 4x^{-5} = \dfrac{-2}{x^3}\cdot\dfrac{x^2}{x^2} - \dfrac{4}{x^5} = \dfrac{-2(x^2+2)}{x^5}$

$\boxed{49}$ (a) $\dfrac{dy}{dx} = \dfrac{x^{2/3}(2x-3) - (x^2 - 3x)(\frac{2}{3}x^{-1/3})}{(x^{2/3})^2} = \dfrac{x^{-1/3}\left[3x(2x-3) - 2(x^2 - 3x)\right]}{3x^{4/3}} =$

$$\dfrac{4x^2 - 3x}{3x^{5/3}} = \dfrac{4x - 3}{3\sqrt[3]{x^2}}$$

(b) $\dfrac{dy}{dx} = D_x\left[(x^2 - 3x)(x^{-2/3})\right] = (x^2 - 3x)(-\tfrac{2}{3}x^{-5/3}) + (x^{-2/3})(2x-3) =$

$$\dfrac{-2(x^2 - 3x)}{3x^{5/3}} + \dfrac{2x-3}{x^{2/3}}\cdot\dfrac{3x}{3x} = \dfrac{4x^2 - 3x}{3x^{5/3}} = \dfrac{4x - 3}{3\sqrt[3]{x^2}}$$

(c) $\dfrac{dy}{dx} = D_x\left(x^{4/3} - 3x^{1/3}\right) = \tfrac{4}{3}x^{1/3} - x^{-2/3} = \dfrac{4x^{1/3}}{3}\cdot\dfrac{x^{2/3}}{x^{2/3}} - \dfrac{1}{x^{2/3}}\cdot\dfrac{3}{3} = \dfrac{4x - 3}{3\sqrt[3]{x^2}}$

$\boxed{50}$ (a) $\dfrac{dy}{dx} = \dfrac{x^{3/2}(2) - (2x+3)(\frac{3}{2}x^{1/2})}{(x^{3/2})^2} = \dfrac{x^{1/2}\left[4x - 3(2x+3)\right]}{2x^3} = -\dfrac{2x+9}{2\sqrt{x^5}}$

(b) $\dfrac{dy}{dx} = D_x\left[(2x+3)(x^{-3/2})\right] = (2x+3)(-\tfrac{3}{2}x^{-5/2}) + (x^{-3/2})(2) =$

$$-\dfrac{3(2x+3)}{2x^{5/2}} + \dfrac{2}{x^{3/2}}\cdot\dfrac{2x}{2x} = -\dfrac{2x+9}{2\sqrt{x^5}}$$

(c) $\dfrac{dy}{dx} = D_x\left(2x^{-1/2} + 3x^{-3/2}\right) = -x^{-3/2} - \tfrac{9}{2}x^{-5/2} =$

$$\dfrac{-1}{x^{3/2}}\cdot\dfrac{2x}{2x} - \dfrac{9}{2x^{5/2}} = -\dfrac{2x+9}{2\sqrt{x^5}}$$

$\boxed{51}$ $\dfrac{dy}{dx} = \dfrac{(x+1)(3) - (3x+4)(1)}{(x+1)^2} = -\dfrac{1}{(x+1)^2} = -\dfrac{1}{x^2 + 2x + 1}$;

$$\dfrac{d^2y}{dx^2} = -\left[-\dfrac{2x+2}{(x+1)^4}\right] = \dfrac{2}{(x+1)^3}$$

$\boxed{52}$ $\dfrac{dy}{dx} = \dfrac{(2x+3)(1) - (x+3)(2)}{(2x+3)^2} = \dfrac{-3}{(2x+3)^2} = \dfrac{-3}{4x^2 + 12x + 9}$;

$$\dfrac{d^2y}{dx^2} = -3\left[-\dfrac{8x+12}{(2x+3)^4}\right] = \dfrac{12}{(2x+3)^3}$$

$\boxed{53}$ $f'(x) = 5\left[-\dfrac{2x}{(1+x^2)^2}\right] = \dfrac{-10x}{(1+x^2)^2}$, $f'(-2) = \frac{20}{25}$;

$$y - 1 = \tfrac{4}{5}(x+2) \text{ or } y = \tfrac{4}{5}x + \tfrac{13}{5}$$

$\boxed{54}$ $f'(x) = 6x - x^{-1/2}$, $f'(4) = \frac{47}{2}$; $y - 44 = \frac{47}{2}(x-4)$ or $y = \frac{47}{2}x - 50$

$\boxed{55}$ (a) $f'(x) = 3x^2 + 4x - 4 = (3x - 2)(x + 2)$; $f'(x) = 0 \Rightarrow x = \frac{2}{3}, -2$

(b) The given line has slope -4. $f'(x) = -4 \Rightarrow$

$$3x^2 + 4x - 4 = -4 \Rightarrow 3x^2 + 4x = 0 \Rightarrow x(3x + 4) = 0 \Rightarrow x = 0, -\tfrac{4}{3}$$

$\boxed{56}$ Let $f(x) = x^3$. $f'(a) = 3a^2$ and the tangent line equation is $(y - a^3) = 3a^2(x - a)$.

If this line has x-intercept 4, then $(4, 0)$ must satisfy its equation.

Thus, $(0 - a^3) = 3a^2(4 - a) \Rightarrow 2a^2(a - 6) = 0 \Rightarrow a = 0, 6$.

If a were 0, then P would have x-intercept 0; so a must be 6 and P is $(6, 216)$.

$\boxed{57}$ The slope of the given line is 1. $y' = \frac{3}{2}x^{1/2} - \frac{1}{2}x^{-1/2} = \dfrac{3x - 1}{2\sqrt{x}}$.

Now, $\dfrac{3x - 1}{2\sqrt{x}} = 1 \Rightarrow 9x^2 - 6x + 1 = 4x \Rightarrow (9x - 1)(x - 1) = 0 \Rightarrow x = \frac{1}{9}, 1$.

The points are $(\frac{1}{9}, -\frac{8}{27})$ and $(1, 0)$.

$\boxed{58}$ The given line has slope $-\frac{1}{2}$, so the desired slope is 2.

$y' = \frac{5}{3}x^{2/3} + \frac{1}{3}x^{-2/3} = 2 \Rightarrow \frac{5}{3}x^{4/3} + \frac{1}{3} - 2x^{2/3} = 0 \Rightarrow$

$5(x^{2/3})^2 - 6(x^{2/3}) + 1 = 0 \Rightarrow (5x^{2/3} - 1)(x^{2/3} - 1) = 0 \Rightarrow x = \pm(\frac{1}{5})^{3/2}, \pm 1$.

The four points are $(\pm\frac{1}{5\sqrt{5}}, \pm\frac{26}{25\sqrt{5}})$ and $(\pm 1, \pm 2)$.

$\boxed{59}$ $y' = \frac{1}{2}x^{-1/2} = \dfrac{1}{2\sqrt{x}}$; $\lim\limits_{x \to 0^+}\left|\dfrac{1}{2\sqrt{x}}\right| = \infty \Rightarrow$ vertical tangent line at $x = 0$.

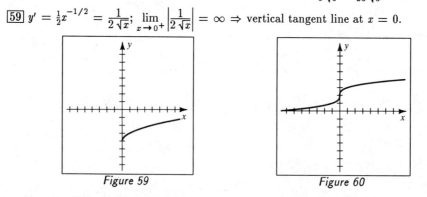

Figure 59   Figure 60

$\boxed{60}$ $y' = \frac{1}{3}x^{-2/3} = \dfrac{1}{3\sqrt[3]{x^2}}$; $\lim\limits_{x \to 0}\left|\dfrac{1}{3\sqrt[3]{x^2}}\right| = \infty \Rightarrow$ vertical tangent line at $x = 0$.

61 (a) $v(t) = s'(t) = 2 + 2t$; $v(1) = 4$, $v(4) = 10$, and $v(8) = 18$ (ft/sec)

(b) $s(t) = 50 \Rightarrow t^2 + 2t - 44 = 0 \Rightarrow t = -1 \pm 3\sqrt{5}$;

$$v(-1 + 3\sqrt{5}) = 6\sqrt{5} \text{ ft/sec} \approx 13.4 \text{ ft/sec}$$

62 (a) $v(t) = s'(t) = 6t^2 + 6t$; $v(2) = 36$ cm/sec

(b) $v(t) = 30 \Rightarrow 6t^2 + 6t - 30 = 0 \Rightarrow t = \frac{1}{2}(-1 + \sqrt{21}) \approx 1.79$ sec for $t \geq 0$.

63 $y' = a^3\left[-\dfrac{2x}{(a^2 + x^2)^2}\right] = \dfrac{-2a^3x}{(a^2 + x^2)^2}.$ $\quad$ At $x = a$, $y' = \dfrac{-2a^4}{4a^4} = -\dfrac{1}{2}.$

64 $y' = \dfrac{(a^2 + x^2)(ab) - (abx)(2x)}{(a^2 + x^2)^2} = \dfrac{a^3b - abx^2}{(a^2 + x^2)^2}.$ $\quad$ At $x = a$, $y' = \dfrac{a^3b - a^3b}{4a^4} = 0.$

65 Let (a, a^2) be the point of tangency. The slope of the tangent line is $2a$ and

$(a^2 - 9) = 2a(a - 5) \Rightarrow a^2 - 10a + 9 = 0 \Rightarrow a = 1, 9$. Thus, there are two such

lines: $(y - 9) = 2(x - 5)$ and $(y - 9) = 18(x - 5)$ or equivalently,

$$y = 2x - 1 \text{ and } y = 18x - 81.$$

66 Let $(a, 4/a)$ be the point of tangency. Since $y = 4/x$, the slope of the tangent line at

$x = a$ is $-4/a^2$. Thus, $(4/a - 1) = -4/a^2(a - 3) \Rightarrow (4a - a^2) = -4(a - 3) \Rightarrow$

$a^2 - 8a + 12 = 0 \Rightarrow a = 2, 6$. Thus, there are two such lines:

$(y - 1) = -1(x - 3)$ and $(y - 1) = -\frac{4}{36}(x - 3)$ or equivalently,

$$y = -x + 4 \text{ and } y = -\tfrac{1}{9}x + \tfrac{4}{3}.$$

67 (a) $(f + g)'(2) = f'(2) + g'(2) = -1 + 2 = 1$

(b) $(f - g)'(2) = f'(2) - g'(2) = -1 - 2 = -3$

(c) $(4f)'(2) = 4f'(2) = 4(-1) = -4$

(d) $(fg)'(2) = f(2)g'(2) + g(2)f'(2) = (3)(2) + (-5)(-1) = 11$

(e) $\left(\dfrac{f}{g}\right)'(2) = \dfrac{g(2)f'(2) - f(2)g'(2)}{[g(2)]^2} = \dfrac{(-5)(-1) - (3)(2)}{(-5)^2} = -\dfrac{1}{25}$

(f) $(1/f)'(2) = -\dfrac{f'(2)}{[f(2)]^2} = -\dfrac{-1}{3^2} = \dfrac{1}{9}$

68 (a) $(g - f)'(2) = g'(2) - f'(2) = 2 - (-1) = 3$

(b) $\left(\dfrac{g}{f}\right)'(2) = \dfrac{f(2)g'(2) - g(2)f'(2)}{[f(2)]^2} = \dfrac{(3)(2) - (-5)(-1)}{(3)^2} = \dfrac{1}{9}$

(c) $(4g)'(2) = 4g'(2) = 4(2) = 8$

(d) $(ff)'(2) = f(2)f'(2) + f(2)f'(2) = 2f(2)f'(2) = 2(3)(-1) = -6$

69 (a) $(2f - g)'(2) = 2f'(2) - g'(2) = 2(-1) - 2 = -4$

(b) $(5f + 3g)'(2) = 5f'(2) + 3g'(2) = (5)(-1) + (3)(2) = 1$

(c) $(gg)'(2) = g(2)g'(2) + g(2)g'(2) = 2g(2)g'(2) = 2(-5)(2) = -20$

(d) $\left(\dfrac{1}{f + g}\right)'(2) = -\dfrac{(f + g)'(2)}{[(f + g)(2)]^2} = -\dfrac{f'(2) + g'(2)}{[f(2) + g(2)]^2} = -\dfrac{-1 + 2}{(-2)^2} = -\dfrac{1}{4}$

$\boxed{70}$ (a) $(3f - 2g)'(2) = 3f'(2) - 2g'(2) = (3)(-1) - (2)(2) = -7$

(b) $\left(\dfrac{5}{g}\right)'(2) = 5\left[-\dfrac{g'(2)}{[g(2)]^2}\right] = -5 \cdot \dfrac{2}{(-5)^2} = -\dfrac{2}{5}$

(c) $(6f)'(2) = 6f'(2) = 6(-1) = -6$

(d) $\left(\dfrac{f}{f+g}\right)'(2) = \dfrac{(f+g)(2) \cdot f'(2) - f(2) \cdot (f+g)'(2)}{[(f+g)(2)]^2} = \dfrac{(-2)(-1) - (3)(1)}{(-2)^2} = -\dfrac{1}{4}$

$\boxed{71}$ For brevity, we suppress the argument of x for each function. $D_x(fgh) = D_x[(fg)h] =$
$(fg)h' + hD_x(fg) = fgh' + h(fg' + gf') = fgh' + fg'h + f'gh.$

$\qquad\qquad$ With $f = g = h$, we have $D_x(f^3) = f^2f' + f^2f' + f^2f' = 3f^2f'.$

$\boxed{72}$ $D_x[fghk] = D_x[f(ghk)] = f(ghk)' + f'(ghk) = fghk' + fgh'k + fg'hk + f'ghk.$

$\qquad\qquad$ With $f = g = h = k$, we have $D_x(f^4) = 4f^3f'.$

$\boxed{73}$ dy/dx $= (8x - 1)\ (x^2 + 4x + 7)\qquad (3x^2)\qquad$ { Writing the answer in the form
$\qquad\qquad\ + (8x - 1)\qquad (2x + 4)\qquad (x^3 - 5)\qquad$ shown is helpful for students. }
$\qquad\qquad\ +\qquad (8)\quad (x^2 + 4x + 7)\ (x^3 - 5)$

$\boxed{74}$ dy/dx $= (3x^4 - 10x^2 + 8)\ (2x^2 - 10)\qquad (6)$
$\qquad\qquad\ + (3x^4 - 10x^2 + 8)\qquad (4x)\qquad (6x + 7)$
$\qquad\qquad\ +\quad (12x^3 - 20x)\quad (2x^2 - 10)\ (6x + 7)$

$\boxed{75}$ dy/dx $= (x)\ (2x^3 - 5x - 1)\qquad (12x)$
$\qquad\qquad\ + (x)\qquad (6x^2 - 5)\qquad (6x^2 + 7)$
$\qquad\qquad\ + (1)\ (2x^3 - 5x - 1)\ (6x^2 + 7)$

$\boxed{76}$ dy/dx $= (4x)\quad (x - 1)\qquad (2)$
$\qquad\qquad\ + (4x)\qquad (1)\qquad (2x - 3)$
$\qquad\qquad\ + (4)\quad (x - 1)\quad (2x - 3)$

$\boxed{77}$ (a) $r(t) = 3t^{1/3}$; $r'(t) = 3(\frac{1}{3}t^{-2/3}) = t^{-2/3}$; $r'(8) = 8^{-2/3} = \frac{1}{4}$ cm/min

(b) $V = \frac{4}{3}\pi r^3$; $V(t) = \frac{4}{3}\pi(3\sqrt[3]{t})^3 = 36\pi t$; $V'(t) = 36\pi$; $V'(8) = 36\pi$ cm^3/min

(c) $S = 4\pi r^2$; $S(t) = 4\pi(3\sqrt[3]{t})^2 = 36\pi t^{2/3}$; $S'(t) = 36\pi \cdot \frac{2}{3}t^{-1/3} = \dfrac{24\pi}{\sqrt[3]{t}}$;

$\qquad\qquad\qquad\qquad\qquad\qquad\qquad\qquad\qquad\qquad\qquad\qquad S'(8) = 12\pi$ cm^2/min

$\boxed{78}$ $V(t) = 5000(t^2 + 2t + 1) \Rightarrow V'(t) = 5000(2t + 2) = 10{,}000(t + 1).$

$V'(0) = 10{,}000$ ft^3/month. $V'(2) = 30{,}000$ ft^3/month. When $V(t) = 5000(t + 1)^2$
$= 11{,}250$, we have $t^2 + 2t + 1 = \frac{9}{4}$ or $4t^2 + 8t - 5 = (2t - 1)(2t + 5) = 0.$

$\qquad\qquad$ Since $0 \le t \le 3$, $t = \frac{1}{2}$ and $V'(\frac{1}{2}) = 15{,}000$ ft^3/month.

$\boxed{79}$ $A = \pi r^2$ and $r(t) = 40t \Rightarrow A(t) = \pi(40t)^2 = 1600\pi t^2$; $A'(t) = 3200\pi t$;

(a) $A'(1) = 3200\pi$ $\qquad$ (b) $A'(2) = 6400\pi$ $\qquad$ (c) $A'(3) = 9600\pi$ (cm^2/sec)

$\boxed{80}$ $v = cp^{-1}$ and $p(t) = 20 + 2t \Rightarrow v(t) = c(20 + 2t)^{-1}$; $v(0) = 60 \Rightarrow c = 1200.$

Now $v(t) = 1200(20 + 2t)^{-1} = \dfrac{600}{t + 10}$ and $v'(t) = -\dfrac{600}{(t + 10)^2}$, so $v'(5) = -\dfrac{600}{225} =$

$-\frac{8}{3}$ cm^3/min. The volume of the gas is decreasing because the pressure is increasing.

$\boxed{81}$ (a) $f'(1) \approx \dfrac{f(1.1) - f(0.9)}{2(0.1)} = \dfrac{1.131 - 0.929}{0.2} = 1.01$

(c) $f'(x) = 3x^2 - 2 \Rightarrow f'(1) = 1.$

l_2 is nearly parallel to the tangent line, but l_1 is not.

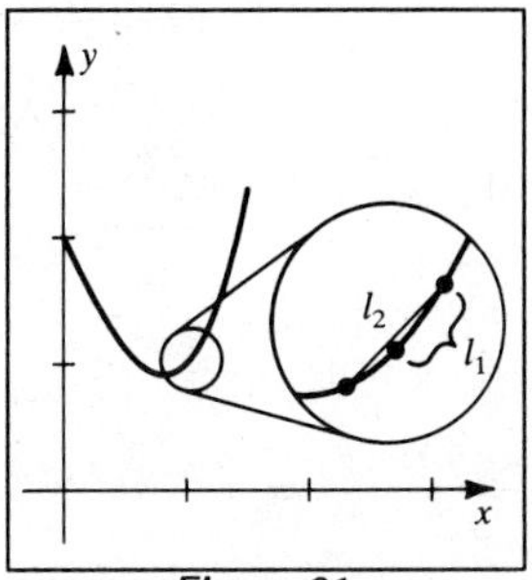

Figure 81

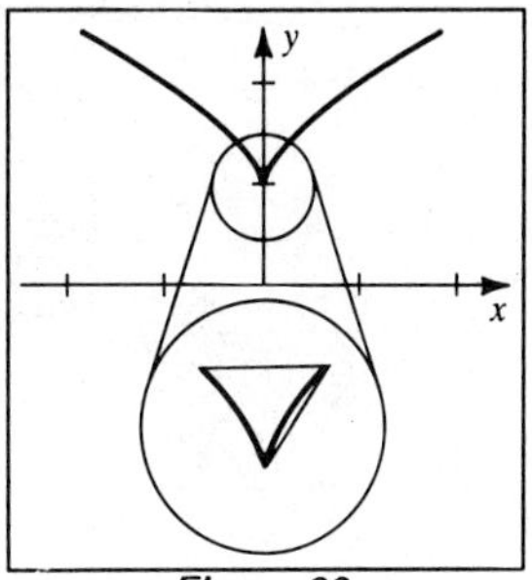

Figure 82

$\boxed{82}$ (a) $f'(0) \approx \dfrac{f(0.1) - f(-0.1)}{2(0.1)} \approx \dfrac{1.2154 - 1.2154}{0.2} = 0$

(c) $f'(0)$ does not exist.

Exercises 3.4

$\boxed{1}$ $f'(x) = -4\sin x$ $\boxed{2}$ $H'(z) = 7\sec^2 z$

$\boxed{3}$ $G'(v) = 5\big[v(-\csc v \cot v) + \csc v \cdot 1\big] = 5\csc v(1 - v\cot v)$

$\boxed{4}$ $f'(x) = 3(x\cos x + \sin x \cdot 1) = 3(\sin x + x\cos x)$

$\boxed{5}$ $k'(t) = 1 - \big[t^2(-\sin t) + 2t\cos t\big] = t^2\sin t - 2t\cos t + 1$

$\boxed{6}$ $p'(w) = 2w + w\cos w + \sin w$

$\boxed{7}$ $f'(\theta) = \dfrac{(\theta)(\cos\theta) - (\sin\theta)(1)}{(\theta)^2} = \dfrac{\theta\cos\theta - \sin\theta}{\theta^2}$

$\boxed{8}$ $g'(\alpha) = \dfrac{(\alpha)(\sin\alpha) - (1 - \cos\alpha)(1)}{(\alpha)^2} = \dfrac{\alpha\sin\alpha - 1 + \cos\alpha}{\alpha^2}$

$\boxed{9}$ $g'(t) = t^3\cos t + 3t^2\sin t = t^2(t\cos t + 3\sin t)$

$\boxed{10}$ $T'(r) = r^2\sec r \tan r + 2r\sec r = r\sec r(r\tan r + 2)$

$\boxed{11}$ $f'(x) = 2x(-\csc^2 x) + 2\cot x + x^2\sec^2 x + 2x\tan x$

$\boxed{12}$ $f'(x) = 3x^2\sec x \tan x + 6x\sec x - x^3\sec^2 x - 3x^2\tan x$

$\boxed{13}$ $h'(z) = \dfrac{(1 + \cos z)(\sin z) - (1 - \cos z)(-\sin z)}{(1 + \cos z)^2} = \dfrac{2\sin z}{(1 + \cos z)^2}$

$\boxed{14}$ $R'(w) = \dfrac{(1 - \sin w)(-\sin w) - (\cos w)(-\cos w)}{(1 - \sin w)^2} = \dfrac{1 - \sin w}{(1 - \sin w)^2} = \dfrac{1}{1 - \sin w}$

$\boxed{15}$ $g(x) = \csc x \cot x \Rightarrow g'(x) = \csc x(-\csc^2 x) + \cot x(-\csc x \cot x) =$

$-\csc x(\csc^2 x + \cot^2 x) = -\csc x(1 + 2\cot^2 x)$

$\boxed{16}$ $k(x) = \sec x \tan x \Rightarrow k'(x) = \sec x(\sec^2 x) + \tan x(\sec x \tan x) =$

$\sec x(\sec^2 x + \tan^2 x) = \sec x(1 + 2\tan^2 x)$

$\boxed{17}$ $g'(x) = (x + \csc x)(-\csc^2 x) + \cot x(1 - \csc x \cot x) =$

$$-x \csc^2 x - \csc^3 x + \cot x - \csc x \cot^2 x$$

$\boxed{18}$ $K'(\theta) = D_\theta\,(\sin^2\theta + 2\sin\theta\,\cos\theta + \cos^2\theta) = D_\theta\,(1 + 2\sin\theta\,\cos\theta) =$

$$2\Big[\sin\theta\,(-\sin\theta) + \cos\theta\,(\cos\theta)\Big] = 2\,(\cos^2\theta - \sin^2\theta)$$

$\boxed{19}$ $p(x) = \sin x \cdot \dfrac{\cos x}{\sin x} = \cos x$, so $p'(x) = -\sin x$

$\boxed{20}$ $g'(t) = D_t\big(\dfrac{1}{\sin t} \cdot \sin t\big) = D_t\,(1) = 0$

$\boxed{21}$ $f'(x) = \dfrac{(1 + x^2)(\sec^2 x) - (\tan x)(2x)}{(1 + x^2)^2} = \dfrac{\sec^2 x + x^2 \sec^2 x - 2x \tan x}{(1 + x^2)^2}$

$\boxed{22}$ $h'(\theta) = \dfrac{(1 - \sec\theta)(\sec\theta\,\tan\theta) - (1 + \sec\theta)(-\sec\theta\,\tan\theta)}{(1 - \sec\theta)^2} = \dfrac{2\sec\theta\,\tan\theta}{(1 - \sec\theta)^2}$

$\boxed{23}$ $K'(v) = D_v\Big(\dfrac{\cos v}{\sin v}\Big) = D_v\,(\cot v) = -\csc^2 v$

$\boxed{24}$ $q'(t) = D_t\Big[\sin t \cdot (1/\cos t)\Big] = D_t\,(\tan t) = \sec^2 t$

$\boxed{25}$ $g'(x) = D_x\,(-\sin x + \cos x) = -\cos x - \sin x$ {sine is odd, cosine is even}

$\boxed{26}$ $s'(z) = D_z\,(-\tan z + \sec z) = -\sec^2 z + \sec z \tan z$ {tangent is odd, secant is even}

$\boxed{27}$ $H'(\phi) = D_\phi\,(1 - \cos\phi + \sec\phi - 1) = \sin\phi + \sec\phi\,\tan\phi$

$\boxed{28}$ $f(x) = \dfrac{1 + \sec x}{\tan x + \sin x} = \dfrac{\cos x + 1}{\sin x + \sin x \cos x} = \dfrac{1 + \cos x}{\sin x(1 + \cos x)} = \dfrac{1}{\sin x} = \csc x;$

$$D_x\,[f(x)] = D_x\,(\csc x) = -\csc x \cot x$$

$\boxed{29}$ $f'(x) = \sec x \tan x \Rightarrow f'(\tfrac{\pi}{4}) = \sqrt{2}.$

tangent: $(y - \sqrt{2}) = \sqrt{2}(x - \tfrac{\pi}{4})$;   normal: $(y - \sqrt{2}) = -\tfrac{1}{\sqrt{2}}(x - \tfrac{\pi}{4})$

$\boxed{30}$ $f'(x) = -\csc x \cot x - \csc^2 x \Rightarrow f'(\tfrac{\pi}{4}) = -\sqrt{2} - 2.$ tangent:

$$y - (1 + \sqrt{2}) = -(\sqrt{2} + 2)(x - \tfrac{\pi}{4}); \ \text{normal: } y - (1 + \sqrt{2}) = \tfrac{1}{\sqrt{2} + 2}(x - \tfrac{\pi}{4})$$

$\boxed{31}$ On $[0, 2\pi]$, $f'(x) = -\sin x + \cos x = 0 \Rightarrow \cos x = \sin x \Rightarrow \tan x = 1 \Rightarrow x = \tfrac{\pi}{4}, \tfrac{5\pi}{4}.$

The points are $(\tfrac{\pi}{4}, \sqrt{2})$ and $(\tfrac{5\pi}{4}, -\sqrt{2}).$

$\boxed{32}$ On $[0, 2\pi]$, $f'(x) = -\sin x - \cos x = 0 \Rightarrow \sin x = -\cos x \Rightarrow \tan x = -1 \Rightarrow$

$$x = \tfrac{3\pi}{4}, \tfrac{7\pi}{4}. \text{ The points are } (\tfrac{3\pi}{4}, -\sqrt{2}) \text{ and } (\tfrac{7\pi}{4}, \sqrt{2}).$$

$\boxed{33}$ On $(0, \tfrac{\pi}{2})$, $f'(x) = -\csc x \cot x + \sec x \tan x = 0 \Rightarrow \dfrac{\sin x}{\cos^2 x} = \dfrac{\cos x}{\sin^2 x} \Rightarrow$

$$\sin^3 x = \cos^3 x \ \{\sin x \neq 0,\ \cos x \neq 0\} \Rightarrow x = \tfrac{\pi}{4}. \text{ The point is } (\tfrac{\pi}{4}, 2\sqrt{2}).$$

$\boxed{34}$ On $(-\tfrac{\pi}{2}, \tfrac{\pi}{2})$, $f'(x) = 2\sec x \tan x - \sec^2 x = 0 \Rightarrow 2\tan x - \sec x = 0 \ \{\sec x \neq 0 \ \forall x\}$

$$\Rightarrow \tfrac{2\sin x - 1}{\cos x} = 0 \Rightarrow \sin x = \tfrac{1}{2} \Rightarrow x = \tfrac{\pi}{6}. \text{ The point is } (\tfrac{\pi}{6}, \sqrt{3}).$$

$\boxed{35}$ (a) $f'(x) = 1 - 2\sin x = 0 \Rightarrow \sin x = \tfrac{1}{2} \Rightarrow x = \tfrac{\pi}{6} + 2\pi n, \tfrac{5\pi}{6} + 2\pi n$

(b) $f(0) = 2$ and $f'(0) = 1$; $(y - 2) = 1(x - 0)$ or $y = x + 2.$

$\boxed{36}$ (a) $f'(x) = 1 + \cos x = 0 \Rightarrow \cos x = -1 \Rightarrow x = \pi + 2\pi n$

(b) $f(\tfrac{\pi}{2}) = \tfrac{\pi}{2} + 1$ and $f'(\tfrac{\pi}{2}) = 1$; $y - (\tfrac{\pi}{2} + 1) = 1(x - \tfrac{\pi}{2})$ or $y = x + 1.$

$\boxed{37}$ (a) $y' = 2\cos x$ and the slope of the given line is $\sqrt{2}$; $y' = \sqrt{2} \Rightarrow \cos x = \sqrt{2}/2 \Rightarrow$

$$x = \tfrac{\pi}{4} + 2\pi n, \tfrac{7\pi}{4} + 2\pi n$$

(b) At $x = \tfrac{\pi}{6}$, $y = 4$ and $y' = \sqrt{3}$.

$$\text{The equation of the tangent line is } (y - 4) = \sqrt{3}(x - \tfrac{\pi}{6}).$$

$\boxed{38}$ (a) $y' = -2\sin x$ and the required slope is $-\sqrt{3}$; $y' = -\sqrt{3} \Rightarrow \sin x = \sqrt{3}/2 \Rightarrow$

$$x = \tfrac{\pi}{3} + 2\pi n, \tfrac{2\pi}{3} + 2\pi n$$

(b) The graph intersects the y-axis when $x = 0$. At $x = 0$, $y = 3$ and $y' = 0$.

$$\text{The equation of the tangent line is } (y - 3) = 0(x - 0) \text{ or } y = 3.$$

$\boxed{39}$ f is not differentiable at $x \approx 0.9, 2.4, 3.7$.

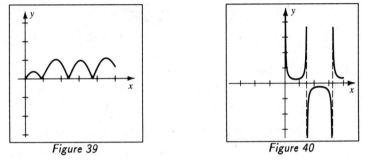

Figure 39   Figure 40

$\boxed{40}$ The x-coordinates of points at which the graph has a horizontal tangent line are

$$0.8, 2.4, \text{ and } 3.9.$$

$\boxed{41}$ $v(t) = s'(t) = 1 - 2\sin t = 0 \Rightarrow \sin t = \tfrac{1}{2} \Rightarrow t = \tfrac{\pi}{6} + 2\pi n, \tfrac{5\pi}{6} + 2\pi n$

$\boxed{42}$ $v(t) = s'(t) = 1 - \sqrt{2}\cos t = 0 \Rightarrow \cos t = \tfrac{1}{\sqrt{2}} \Rightarrow t = \tfrac{\pi}{4} + 2\pi n, \tfrac{7\pi}{4} + 2\pi n$

$\boxed{43}$ $y' = \tfrac{3}{2}x^{1/2} + 2 = 8 \Rightarrow x^{1/2} = 4 \Rightarrow x = 16$; $(16, 96)$

$\boxed{44}$ $y' = \tfrac{5}{3}x^{2/3} - 10 = 5 \Rightarrow x^{2/3} = 9 \Rightarrow x = 27$; $(27, -27)$

$\boxed{45}$ (a) $f'(x) = -\sin x$; $f''(x) = -\cos x$; $f'''(x) = \sin x$; $f^{(4)}(x) = \cos x$

(b) Due to the cyclic pattern, every fourth derivative is equal to $\cos x$.

$$\text{Since } 99 = 3 + 96 \text{ and } 96 \text{ is a multiple of } 4, \text{ the 99th derivative is } \sin x.$$

$\boxed{46}$ $f'(x) = -\csc^2 x = -(\csc x \cdot \csc x)$

$f''(x) = -\left[\csc x(-\csc x \cot x) + \csc x(-\csc x \cot x) \right] = 2\csc^2 x \cot x$

$f'''(x) = 2\left[\csc^2 x(-\csc^2 x) + \cot x(-2\csc^2 x \cot x) \right] =$

$$-2\csc^2 x(\csc^2 x + 2\cot^2 x) = -2\csc^2 x(3\cot^2 x + 1)$$

$\boxed{47}$ $D_x y = \sec^2 x = \sec x \cdot \sec x$

$D_x^2 y = \sec x(\sec x \tan x) + \sec x(\sec x \tan x) = 2\sec^2 x \tan x$

$D_x^3 y = 2\left[\sec^2 x(\sec^2 x) + \tan x(2\sec^2 x \tan x) \right] =$

$$2\sec^2 x(\sec^2 x + 2\tan^2 x) = 2\sec^2 x(3\tan^2 x + 1)$$

48 $\dfrac{dy}{dx} = \sec x \tan x$

$\dfrac{d^2y}{dx^2} = \sec x(\sec^2 x) + \tan x(\sec x \tan x) = \sec x(\sec^2 x + \tan^2 x) = \sec x(2\sec^2 x - 1)$

$\dfrac{d^3y}{dx^3} = \sec x(2 \cdot 2\sec^2 x \tan x)\ \{\text{from Exercise 47}\} + (2\sec^2 x - 1)(\sec x \tan x) =$

$$\sec x \tan x(4\sec^2 x + 2\sec^2 x - 1) = \sec x \tan x(6\sec^2 x - 1)$$

49 $D_x \cot x = D_x\left(\dfrac{\cos x}{\sin x}\right) = \dfrac{(\sin x)(-\sin x) - (\cos x)(\cos x)}{\sin^2 x} = \dfrac{-1(\sin^2 x + \cos^2 x)}{\sin^2 x} =$

$$-\dfrac{1}{\sin^2 x} = -\csc^2 x$$

50 $D_x(\csc x) = D_x\left(\dfrac{1}{\sin x}\right) = -\dfrac{\cos x}{(\sin x)^2} = -\dfrac{1}{\sin x} \cdot \dfrac{\cos x}{\sin x} = -\csc x \cot x$

51 $D_x \sin 2x = D_x(2\sin x \cos x) = 2\Big[\sin x(-\sin x) + \cos x \cos x\Big] = 2(\cos^2 x - \sin^2 x) =$

$$2\cos 2x$$

52 $D_x(\cos 2x) = D_x(1 - 2\sin^2 x) = D_x(1 - 2\sin x \sin x) =$

$$-2(\sin x \cos x + \sin x \cos x) = -2(2\sin x \cos x) = -2\sin 2x$$

Exercises 3.5

Note: In Exercises 1–10, the formulas for Δy and dy are obtained using

$$\Delta y = f(x + \Delta x) - f(x) \text{ and } dy = f'(x)\,dx.$$

1 (a) $\Delta y = \Big[2(x + \Delta x)^2 - 4(x + \Delta x) + 5\Big] - (2x^2 - 4x + 5)$

$\quad = 4x\,\Delta x + 2(\Delta x)^2 - 4\,\Delta x = (4x - 4)\,\Delta x + 2(\Delta x)^2;$

$dy = (4x - 4)\,dx$

(b) $x = 2$ and $\Delta x = -0.2 \Rightarrow$

$$\Delta y = 4(-0.2) + 2(-0.2)^2 = -0.72 \text{ and } dy = 4(-0.2) = -0.8$$

2 (a) $\Delta y = \Big[(x + \Delta x)^3 + 4\Big] - (x^3 + 4)$

$\quad = \Big[x^3 + 3x^2\,\Delta x + 3x(\Delta x)^2 + (\Delta x)^3 + 4\Big] - (x^3 + 4)$

$\quad = 3x^2\,\Delta x + 3x(\Delta x)^2 + (\Delta x)^3 = \Big[3x^2 + 3x\,\Delta x + (\Delta x)^2\Big]\Delta x;$

$dy = (3x^2)\,dx$

(b) $x = -1$ and $\Delta x = 0.1 \Rightarrow \Delta y = 2.71(0.1) = 0.271$ and $dy = 3(0.1) = 0.3$

3 (a) $\Delta y = \left[\dfrac{1}{(x + \Delta x)^2} - \dfrac{1}{x^2}\right] = \dfrac{x^2 - (x + \Delta x)^2}{x^2(x + \Delta x)^2} = \dfrac{-(2x + \Delta x)\,\Delta x}{x^2(x + \Delta x)^2};$

$dy = (-2/x^3)\,dx$

(b) $x = 3$ and $\Delta x = 0.3 \Rightarrow$

$$\Delta y = \dfrac{-1.89}{98.01} = -\dfrac{7}{363} \approx -0.01928 \text{ and } dy = -\dfrac{2}{27}(0.3) = -\dfrac{1}{45} = -0.0\bar{2}$$

4 (a) $\Delta y = \left[\dfrac{1}{2 + (x + \Delta x)} - \dfrac{1}{2 + x}\right] = \dfrac{(2 + x) - \Big[2 + (x + \Delta x)\Big]}{\Big[2 + (x + \Delta x)\Big](2 + x)}$

$$= \dfrac{-\Delta x}{\Big[2 + (x + \Delta x)\Big](2 + x)};$$

$dy = -\dfrac{1}{(2 + x)^2}\,dx$

(b) $x = 0$ and $\Delta x = -0.03 \Rightarrow$

$$\Delta y = \frac{0.03}{3.94} = \frac{3}{394} \approx 0.007614 \text{ and } dy = -\tfrac{1}{4}(-0.03) = \frac{3}{400} = 0.0075$$

$\boxed{5}$ (a) $\Delta y = \left[4 - 9(x + \Delta x)\right] - (4 - 9x) = -9\Delta x$

    (b) $dy = -9\,dx$ (c) $dy - \Delta y = 0$ (Recall that $\Delta x = dx$.)

$\boxed{6}$ (a) $\Delta y = \left[7(x + \Delta x) + 12\right] - (7x + 12) = 7\Delta x$

    (b) $dy = 7\,dx$ (c) $dy - \Delta y = 0$

$\boxed{7}$ (a) $\Delta y = \left[3(x + \Delta x)^2 + 5(x + \Delta x) - 2\right] - (3x^2 + 5x - 2)$

$$= (6x + 5)\Delta x + 3(\Delta x)^2$$

    (b) $dy = (6x + 5)\,dx$ (c) $dy - \Delta y = -3(\Delta x)^2$

$\boxed{8}$ (a) $\Delta y = \left[4 - 7(x + \Delta x) - 2(x + \Delta x)^2\right] - (4 - 7x - 2x^2)$

$$= (-7 - 4x)\Delta x - 2(\Delta x)^2$$

    (b) $dy = (-7 - 4x)\,dx$ (c) $dy - \Delta y = 2(\Delta x)^2$

$\boxed{9}$ (a) $\Delta y = \dfrac{1}{x + \Delta x} - \dfrac{1}{x} = \dfrac{-\Delta x}{x(x + \Delta x)}$ (b) $dy = -\dfrac{1}{x^2}\,dx$

    (c) $dy - \Delta y = \dfrac{-\Delta x}{x^2} \cdot \dfrac{x + \Delta x}{x + \Delta x} + \dfrac{\Delta x}{x(x + \Delta x)} \cdot \dfrac{x}{x} = \dfrac{-(\Delta x)^2}{x^2(x + \Delta x)}$

$\boxed{10}$ (a) $\Delta y = \dfrac{1}{(x + \Delta x)^2} - \dfrac{1}{x^2} = \dfrac{-2x\Delta x - (\Delta x)^2}{x^2(x + \Delta x)^2}$ (b) $dy = -\dfrac{2}{x^3}\,dx$

    (c) $dy - \Delta y = \dfrac{-2\Delta x}{x^3} \cdot \dfrac{(x + \Delta x)^2}{(x + \Delta x)^2} + \dfrac{2x\Delta x + (\Delta x)^2}{x^2(x + \Delta x)^2} \cdot \dfrac{x}{x} = \dfrac{-3x(\Delta x)^2 - 2(\Delta x)^3}{x^3(x + \Delta x)^2}$

$\boxed{11}$ $dy = (20x^4 - 24x^3 + 6x)\Delta x;$ $x = 1$ and $\Delta x = 0.03$ yield $dy = 2(0.03) = 0.06;$

$$f(1.03) \approx f(1) + dy = -4 + 0.06 = -3.94$$

$\boxed{12}$ $dy = (-9x^2 + 8)\Delta x;$ $x = 4$ and $\Delta x = -0.04$ yield $dy = -136(-0.04) = 5.44;$

$$f(3.96) \approx f(4) + dy = -167 + 5.44 = -161.56$$

$\boxed{13}$ $dy = (4x^3)\Delta x;$ $x = 1$ and $\Delta x = -0.02$ yield $dy = 4(-0.02) = -0.08;$

$$f(0.98) \approx f(1) + dy = 1 + (-0.08) = 0.92$$

$\boxed{14}$ $dy = (4x^3 - 9x^2 + 8x)\Delta x;$ $x = 2$ and $\Delta x = 0.01$ yield $dy = 12(0.01) = 0.12;$

$$f(2.01) \approx f(2) + dy = 3 + 0.12 = 3.12$$

$\boxed{15}$ $dy = f'(\theta)\,\Delta\theta = (2\cos\theta - \sin\theta)\,\Delta\theta;$

    $\theta = 30°$ and $\Delta\theta = -3°$ yield $dy = (\sqrt{3} - \tfrac{1}{2})(-3 \cdot \tfrac{\pi}{180})$ {radian measure must be

      used} $\approx -0.0645;$ $f(27°) \approx f(30°) + dy \approx (1 + \sqrt{3}/2) + (-0.0645) \approx 1.8015$

$\boxed{16}$ $dy = f'(\phi)\,\Delta\phi = (-\csc\phi\cot\phi - \csc^2\phi)\,\Delta\phi;$

    $\phi = 45°$ and $\Delta\phi = 1°$ yield $dy = (-\sqrt{2} \cdot 1 - 2)(1 \cdot \tfrac{\pi}{180}) \approx -0.0596;$

$$f(46°) \approx f(45°) + dy \approx (\sqrt{2} + 1) + (-0.0596) \approx 2.3546$$

$\boxed{17}$ $dy = f'(\alpha)\,\Delta\alpha = (\sec\alpha\tan\alpha)\,\Delta\alpha;$

    $\alpha = 60°$ and $\Delta\alpha = 2°$ yield $dy = (2 \cdot \sqrt{3})(2 \cdot \tfrac{\pi}{180}) = \tfrac{\pi\sqrt{3}}{45} \approx 0.1209;$

$$f(62°) \approx f(60°) + dy \approx 2 + 0.1209 = 2.1209$$

18. $dy = f'(\beta)\,\Delta\beta = \sec^2\beta\,\Delta\beta$;

$\beta = 30°$ and $\Delta\beta = -2°$ yield $dy = (\frac{4}{3})(-2 \cdot \frac{\pi}{180}) = -\frac{2\pi}{135} \approx -0.0465$;

$$f(28°) \approx f(30°) + dy \approx \sqrt{3}/3 + (-0.0465) \approx 0.5309$$

19. (a) With $h = 0.001$, $f'(2.5) \approx \dfrac{f(2.501) - f(2.499)}{2(0.001)} \approx -0.27315$.

$$y = f(2.5) + f'(2.5)(x - 2.5) \Rightarrow y \approx -0.98451 - 0.27315(x - 2.5)$$

(b) When $x = 2.6$, $y \approx -1.011825$.

(c) $f(2.6) \approx f(2.5) + dy =$

$$f(2.5) + f'(2.5)\Delta x \approx -0.98451 - 0.27315(0.1) = -1.011825$$

(d) They are equal because the tangent line approximation is equivalent to using

(3.31).

20. (a) $f'(x) = 3x^2 + 6x - 2$; $f'(0.4) = 0.88$;

$$y = f(0.4) + f'(0.4)(x - 0.4) \Rightarrow y = 4.744 + 0.88(x - 0.4)$$

(b) When $x = 0.43$, $y = 4.7704$.

(c) $f(0.43) \approx f(0.4) + dy = f(0.4) + f'(0.4)\Delta x = 4.744 + 0.88(0.03) = 4.7704$

(d) They are equal because the tangent line approximation is equivalent to using

(3.31).

21. The average error is $\dfrac{\Delta y}{y} \approx \dfrac{dy}{y} = \dfrac{12x^3\,dx}{3x^4} = \dfrac{4\,dx}{x} = \dfrac{4(\pm 0.01)}{2} = \pm 0.02$.

The percentage error is (average error) × 100%, i.e., $(\pm 0.02)(100\%)$ or $\pm 2\%$.

22. $\dfrac{\Delta y}{y} \approx \dfrac{dy}{y} = \dfrac{(3x^2 + 5)\,dx}{x^3 + 5x} = \dfrac{8(\pm 0.1)}{6} = \pm 0.1\overline{3}$; $\pm 13.\overline{3}\%$

23. $\dfrac{\Delta y}{y} \approx \dfrac{dy}{y} = \dfrac{(2/\sqrt{x} + 3)\,dx}{4\sqrt{x} + 3x} = \dfrac{4(\pm 0.2)}{20} = \pm 0.04$; $\pm 4\%$

24. $\dfrac{\Delta y}{y} \approx \dfrac{dy}{y} = \dfrac{2/\sqrt[3]{x^2}\,dx}{6\sqrt[3]{x}} = \dfrac{dx}{3x} = \dfrac{\pm 0.03}{3(8)} = \pm 0.00125$; $\pm 0.125\%$

25. $dA = (6x - 1)\,dx$; $x = 2$ and $dx = 0.1 \Rightarrow dA = 11(0.1) = 1.1$

26. $dP = (4t^{-1/3} + 2t)\,dt$; $t = 8$ and $dt = 0.2 \Rightarrow dP = 18(0.2) = 3.6$

27. $\dfrac{dy}{y} = \dfrac{12x^2\,dx}{4x^3} = 3\left(\dfrac{dx}{x}\right) = 3(\pm 15\%) = \pm 45\%$

28. $\dfrac{dz}{z} = \dfrac{16w^{-3/5}\,dw}{40w^{2/5}} = \dfrac{2}{5}\left(\dfrac{dw}{w}\right) = \dfrac{2}{5}(\pm 0.08) = \pm 0.032$

29. $\dfrac{dA}{A} = \dfrac{10s^{-1/3}\,ds}{15s^{2/3}} = \dfrac{2}{3}\left(\dfrac{ds}{s}\right) \Rightarrow \dfrac{ds}{s} = \dfrac{3}{2}\dfrac{dA}{A} = \dfrac{3}{2}(\pm 0.04) = \pm 0.06$

30. $\dfrac{dS}{S} = \dfrac{20\pi x\,dx}{10\pi x^2} = 2\left(\dfrac{dx}{x}\right) \Rightarrow \dfrac{dx}{x} = \dfrac{1}{2}\dfrac{dS}{S} = \dfrac{1}{2}(\pm 10\%) = \pm 5\%$

31. $A(r) = \pi r^2 \Rightarrow dA = 2\pi r\,dr$; $\Delta A \approx dA = 2\pi(16)(\pm 0.06) = \pm 1.92\pi$ in.^{2} $\approx$

$$\pm 6.03 \text{ in.}^2;\ A(16) = 256\pi \Rightarrow \dfrac{dA}{A} \approx \dfrac{\pm 1.92\pi}{256\pi} = \pm 0.0075;\ \pm 0.75\%$$

$\boxed{32}$ $A(x) = x^2 \Rightarrow dA = 2x\,dx$; $\Delta A \approx dA = 2(1)(\pm \frac{1}{16} \cdot \frac{1}{12}) = \pm \frac{1}{96} \approx \pm 0.0104 \text{ ft}^2$;

$$A(1) = 1 \Rightarrow \frac{dA}{A} = \pm \frac{1}{96} \approx \pm 0.0104; \pm 1.04\%$$

$\boxed{33}$ $V(x) = x^3 \Rightarrow dV = 3x^2\,dx$; $\Delta V \approx dV = 3(10)^2(0.1) = 30 \text{ in.}^3$.

The <u>exact</u> change is $\Delta V = V(10.1) - V(10) = (10.1)^3 - 10^3 = 30.301 \text{ in.}^3$.

$\boxed{34}$ $S(r) = 4\pi r^2 \Rightarrow dS = 8\pi r\,dr$; $\Delta S \approx dS = 8\pi(1)(0.01) = 0.08\pi \approx 0.251 \text{ ft}^2$.

$\boxed{35}$ If x is the length of the side of the square, then the base of the triangle is x and the

total area is $y = f(x) = x^2 + (\sqrt{3}/4)x^2$. $f'(x) = 2x + (\sqrt{3}/2)x$. $x = 48$ and

$\Delta x = \pm \frac{1}{12} \text{ ft} \Rightarrow dy = f'(x)\Delta x = (96 + 24\sqrt{3})(\pm \frac{1}{12}) = 8 + 2\sqrt{3} \approx \pm 11.4641 \text{ ft}$.

The actual area is $f(48) = 2304 + 576\sqrt{3} \approx 3301.66 \text{ ft}^2$.

$$\frac{dy}{y} = \frac{f'(48)(\pm \frac{1}{12})}{f(48)} \approx \pm 0.00347; \pm 0.347\%$$

$\boxed{36}$ Let r denote the radius of the cylinder and hemisphere. The volume of the silo is

$V(r) = \pi r^2(50) + \frac{2}{3}\pi r^3$. If C is the circumference of the cylinder, then

$r = \frac{C}{2\pi}$, and $C = 30 \pm 0.5 \text{ ft}$. $V(C) = 50\pi(\frac{C}{2\pi})^2 + \frac{2}{3}\pi(\frac{C}{2\pi})^3 =$

$(\frac{25}{2\pi})C^2 + (\frac{1}{12\pi^2})C^3$ and $V(30) = \frac{4500(5\pi + 1)}{2\pi^2} \approx 3808.96 \text{ ft}^3$.

$V'(C) = \frac{25C}{\pi} + \frac{C^2}{4\pi^2}$, so $\Delta V \approx V'(30)(\pm 0.5) = \pm \frac{150(10\pi + 3)}{4\pi^2} \approx \pm 130.8 \text{ ft}^3$.

$$\frac{dV}{V} \approx \frac{\pm 130.8}{3808.96} \approx \pm 0.0343; \pm 3.43\%$$

$\boxed{37}$ $V = \frac{1}{3}\pi r^2 h$ and $h = r \Rightarrow V = \frac{1}{3}\pi r^3$; $\Delta V \approx dV = \pi r^2\,dr$;

$$2 = \pi(10)^2\,dr \Rightarrow dr = \frac{1}{50\pi} \text{ cm} = 0.00637 \text{ cm}.$$

$\boxed{38}$ Using $A = \frac{1}{2}bc\sin\alpha$, we have $A = \frac{1}{2}(12)(12)\sin\theta = 72\sin\theta$ and $A' = 72\cos\theta$.

When $\theta = 30°$ and $\Delta\theta = 3°$, $dA = 72\cos 30°(3 \cdot \frac{\pi}{180}) = 3\sqrt{3}\pi/5 \approx 3.26 \text{ in.}^2$.

$\boxed{39}$ $F(s) = \frac{Gm_1 m_2}{s^2} \Rightarrow F'(s) = \frac{-2Gm_1 m_2}{s^3}$.

The average change is $\frac{\Delta F}{F} \approx \frac{dF}{F} = \frac{F'(s)\Delta s}{F} = \frac{(-2Gm_1 m_2/s^3)\Delta s}{Gm_1 m_2/s^2} = \frac{-2\Delta s}{s}$.

Now, $\frac{-2\Delta s}{s} = 0.1 \{10\%\}$ and $s = 20 \Rightarrow \Delta s = -\frac{1}{20}s = -1 \text{ cm}$.

$\boxed{40}$ $\frac{dT}{T} = \frac{(2\pi/\sqrt{g}) \cdot \frac{1}{2} \cdot l^{-1/2}\,dl}{(2\pi/\sqrt{g})\,l^{1/2}} = \frac{1}{2} \cdot \frac{dl}{l} = 30\% \Rightarrow \frac{dl}{l} = 2(30\%) = 60\%$ increase

$\boxed{41}$ Let r denote the radius of the arteriole, P the pressure difference, and c the

proportionality constant. Now, $P = \frac{c}{r^4}$ and $\frac{\Delta P}{P} \approx \frac{dP}{P} = \left(-\frac{4c}{r^5}dr\right)\left(\frac{r^4}{c}\right) = -4\left(\frac{dr}{r}\right)$.

$\frac{dr}{r} = -0.1 \{10\% \text{ decrease}\} \Rightarrow \frac{\Delta P}{P} = +0.4$, an increase of 40%.

$\boxed{42}$ Let L denote the wire's length, D the wire's diameter, and c the proportionality

constant. Now, $R = \frac{cL}{D^2}$ and $\frac{\Delta R}{R} \approx \frac{dR}{R} = \left(-\frac{2cL}{D^3}dD\right)\left(\frac{D^2}{cL}\right) = -2\left(\frac{dD}{D}\right)$.

Equivalently, $\frac{dD}{D} = -\frac{1}{2}\frac{dR}{R}$. Thus, $\frac{dR}{R} = \pm 3\% \Rightarrow \frac{dD}{D} = \pm 1.5\%$.

$\boxed{43}$ $F(\theta) = \dfrac{\mu W}{\mu \sin\theta + \cos\theta} = \dfrac{20}{0.2\sin\theta + \cos\theta}$ (since $\mu = 0.2$ and $W = 100$).

$\qquad F'(\theta) = -\dfrac{20(0.2\cos\theta - \sin\theta)}{(0.2\sin\theta + \cos\theta)^2} = \dfrac{20\sin\theta - 4\cos\theta}{(0.2\sin\theta + \cos\theta)^2}.$

$\qquad$ When $\theta = 45°$ and $\Delta\theta = 1°$, $dF = \dfrac{10\sqrt{2} - 2\sqrt{2}}{(\frac{1}{10}\sqrt{2} + \frac{1}{2}\sqrt{2})^2}(1 \cdot \frac{\pi}{180}) = \dfrac{5\sqrt{2}\pi}{81} \approx 0.274$ lb.

$\boxed{44}$ $dh = \dfrac{v_0^2 \sin\alpha \cos\alpha}{g}\, d\alpha$ and $dR = \dfrac{2v_0^2(\cos^2\alpha - \sin^2\alpha)}{g}\, d\alpha$. If $\Delta\alpha = 30' = \frac{\pi}{360}$, then

$\qquad \Delta h \approx dh = \dfrac{100^2 \sin 30° \cos 30°}{32} \cdot \dfrac{\pi}{360} = \dfrac{125\sqrt{3}\,\pi}{576} \approx 1.18$ ft

$\qquad\qquad$ and $\Delta R \approx dR = \dfrac{2(100)^2(\cos^2 30° - \sin^2 30°)}{32} \cdot \dfrac{\pi}{360} = \dfrac{125\pi}{144} \approx 2.73$ ft.

$\boxed{45}$ $h(\theta) = 20\tan\theta \Rightarrow dh = 20\sec^2\theta\, d\theta$. Let $\theta = \frac{\pi}{3}$ and $\Delta\theta = \pm\frac{15}{60} \cdot \frac{\pi}{180} = \pm\frac{\pi}{720}$.

$\qquad$ Thus $\Delta h \approx dh = 20\sec^2 60° \cdot (\pm\frac{\pi}{720}) = 20(4)(\pm\frac{\pi}{720}) = \pm\frac{\pi}{9} \approx \pm 0.35$ ft.

$\boxed{46}$ In the figure in the text, let A represent the spacelab's position, C the earth's center,

$\qquad$ and B the point of tangency on the earth. In right triangle ABC with hypotenuse

$\qquad$ AC, the equation relating r and θ is $\sin\theta = \dfrac{r}{380 + r} \Rightarrow r = \dfrac{380\sin\theta}{1 - \sin\theta}$ and

$\qquad$ $dr = \dfrac{380\cos\theta}{(1 - \sin\theta)^2}\, d\theta$. $\theta = 65.8°$ and $\Delta\theta = \pm\dfrac{0.5\,\pi}{180} \Rightarrow$

$\qquad\qquad\qquad\qquad dr = \dfrac{380\cos 65.8°}{(1 - \sin 65.8°)^2}\left(\pm\dfrac{\pi}{360}\right) \approx \pm 176$ miles.

$\boxed{47}$ From the text's figure, $\tan\phi = \dfrac{h}{\frac{1}{2} \cdot 230} \Rightarrow h = 115\tan\phi$ and $dh = 115\sec^2\phi\, d\phi \Rightarrow$

$\qquad$ $d\phi = \frac{1}{115}\cos^2\phi\, dh$. For $dh = \pm 1$ and $\phi = 52°$, we need $d\phi \approx \pm 0.0033 \approx \pm 0.19°$.

$\boxed{48}$ Let $E = \dfrac{k\cos\theta}{s^2}$, where k is a constant of proportionality.

$\qquad$ Then, $\dfrac{dE}{E} = \left(-\dfrac{k\sin\theta}{s^2}\, d\theta\right)\left(\dfrac{s^2}{k\cos\theta}\right) = -\tan\theta\, d\theta.$

$\qquad\qquad$ With $\theta = 21°$ and $d\theta = -1°$, $\dfrac{dE}{E} = \tan 21°(\frac{\pi}{180}) = 0.0067 \approx 0.67\%$.

$\boxed{49}$ $p = \dfrac{c}{v} \Rightarrow dp = -\dfrac{c}{v^2}\, dv \Rightarrow v\, dp = -\dfrac{c}{v}\, dv \Rightarrow v\, dp + \dfrac{c}{v}\, dv = 0 \Rightarrow v\, dp + p\, dv = 0.$

$\boxed{50}$ $I = \dfrac{V}{R} \Rightarrow dI = -\dfrac{V}{R^2}\, dR \Rightarrow R\, dI = -\dfrac{V}{R}\, dR \Rightarrow R\, dI + \dfrac{V}{R}\, dR = 0 \Rightarrow$

$\qquad\qquad\qquad\qquad\qquad\qquad\qquad\qquad\qquad\qquad R\, dI + I\, dR = 0.$

$\boxed{51}$ $dA = 2s\,\Delta s$ and $\Delta A = (s + \Delta s)^2 - s^2 = 2s\,\Delta s + (\Delta s)^2$;

$\qquad\qquad\qquad dA$ is the shaded area and $\Delta A - dA = (\Delta s)^2$ is as labeled.

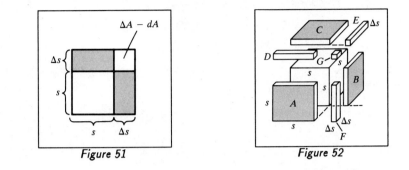

Figure 51   Figure 52

$\boxed{52}$ $dV = 3s^2\Delta s$, $\Delta V = (s + \Delta s)^3 - s^3 = 3s^2\Delta s + 3s(\Delta s)^2 + (\Delta s)^3$,

$$\text{and } \Delta V - dV = 3s(\Delta s)^2 + (\Delta s)^3.$$

Thus, dV is the sum of the volumes of shaded blocks A, B, and C,

while $\Delta V - dV$ is the sum of the volumes of the unshaded blocks D, E, F, and G.

$\boxed{\text{Exercises 3.6}}$

$\boxed{1}$ $\dfrac{dy}{dx} = \dfrac{dy}{du}\dfrac{du}{dx} = (2u)(3x^2) = 6x^2u = 6x^2(x^3 - 4)$

$\boxed{2}$ $\dfrac{dy}{dx} = \dfrac{dy}{du}\dfrac{du}{dx} = \dfrac{1}{3u^{2/3}} \cdot (2x + 5) = \dfrac{2x + 5}{3(x^2 + 5x)^{2/3}}$

$\boxed{3}$ $\dfrac{dy}{dx} = \dfrac{dy}{du}\dfrac{du}{dx} = -\dfrac{1}{u^2} \cdot \dfrac{3}{2(3x - 2)^{1/2}} = \dfrac{-3}{2(3x - 2)^{3/2}}$

$\boxed{4}$ $\dfrac{dy}{dx} = \dfrac{dy}{du}\dfrac{du}{dx} = (6u + 2)(4) = 8(3u + 1) = 8(12x + 1)$

$\boxed{5}$ $\dfrac{dy}{dx} = \dfrac{dy}{du}\dfrac{du}{dx} = (3\sec^2 3u)(2x) = 6x\sec^2 3u = 6x\sec^2(3x^2)$

$\boxed{6}$ $\dfrac{dy}{dx} = \dfrac{dy}{du}\dfrac{du}{dx} = (u\cos u - \sin u)(3x^2) = 3x^2(x^3\cos x^3 + \sin x^3)$

$\boxed{7}$ $f'(x) = 3(x^2 - 3x + 8)^2(2x - 3)$

$\boxed{8}$ $f'(x) = 2(4x^3 + 2x^2 - x - 3)(12x^2 + 4x - 1)$

$\boxed{9}$ $g'(x) = -5(8x - 7)^{-6}(8) = -40(8x - 7)^{-6}$

$\boxed{10}$ $k'(x) = -3(5x^2 - 2x + 1)^{-4}(10x - 2) = -6(5x^2 - 2x + 1)^{-4}(5x - 1)$

$\boxed{11}$ $f'(x) = \dfrac{(x^2 - 1)^4(1) - x(4)(x^2 - 1)^3(2x)}{(x^2 - 1)^8} = \dfrac{(x^2 - 1) - (4x)(2x)}{(x^2 - 1)^5} = -\dfrac{7x^2 + 1}{(x^2 - 1)^5}$

$\boxed{12}$ $g'(x) = \dfrac{(2x + 3)^4(4x^3 - 6x) - (x^4 - 3x^2 + 1)(4)(2x + 3)^3(2)}{(2x + 3)^8} =$

$$\dfrac{(2x + 3)(4x^3 - 6x) - (x^4 - 3x^2 + 1)(8)}{(2x + 3)^5} = \dfrac{12x^3 + 12x^2 - 18x - 8}{(2x + 3)^5}$$

$\boxed{13}$ $f'(x) = 5(8x^3 - 2x^2 + x - 7)^4(24x^2 - 4x + 1)$

$\boxed{14}$ $g'(w) = 4(w^4 - 8w^2 + 15)^3(4w^3 - 16w) = 16w(w^4 - 8w^2 + 15)^3(w^2 - 4)$

$\boxed{15}$ $F'(v) = 1000(17v - 5)^{999}(17) = 17{,}000(17v - 5)^{999}$

$\boxed{16}$ $s'(t) = -2(4t^5 - 3t^3 + 2t)^{-3}(20t^4 - 9t^2 + 2)$

$\boxed{17}$ $N'(x) = (6x - 7)^3(2)(8x^2 + 9)(16x) + 3(6x - 7)^2(6)(8x^2 + 9)^2$

$$= (6x - 7)^2(8x^2 + 9)\Big[32x(6x - 7) + 18(8x^2 + 9)\Big]$$

$$= (6x - 7)^2(8x^2 + 9)(336x^2 - 224x + 162) =$$

$$2(6x - 7)^2(8x^2 + 9)(168x^2 - 112x + 81)$$

$\boxed{18}$ $f'(w) = (2w^2 - 3w + 1)(4)(3w + 2)^3(3) + (4w - 3)(3w + 2)^4$

$$= (3w + 2)^3\Big[12(2w^2 - 3w + 1) + (4w - 3)(3w + 2)\Big] =$$

$$(3w + 2)^3(36w^2 - 37w + 6)$$

$\boxed{19}$ $f'(z) = 6\Big(z^2 - \dfrac{1}{z^2}\Big)^5\Big(2z + \dfrac{2}{z^3}\Big) = 12\Big(z^2 - \dfrac{1}{z^2}\Big)^5\Big(z + \dfrac{1}{z^3}\Big)$

$\boxed{20}$ $S'(t) = 3\Big(\dfrac{3t + 4}{6t - 7}\Big)^2\left[\dfrac{(6t - 7)(3) - (3t + 4)(6)}{(6t - 7)^2}\right] = \dfrac{-135(3t + 4)^2}{(6t - 7)^4}$

$\boxed{21}$ $k'(r) = \frac{1}{3}(8r^3 + 27)^{-2/3}(24r^2) = 8r^2(8r^3 + 27)^{-2/3}$

$\boxed{22}$ $h'(z) = -\frac{2}{3}(2z^2 - 9z + 8)^{-5/3}(4z - 9)$

$\boxed{23}$ $F'(v) = -5\dfrac{\frac{1}{5}(v^5 - 32)^{-4/5}(5v^4)}{(v^5 - 32)^{2/5}} = -\dfrac{5v^4}{(v^5 - 32)^{6/5}}$

$\boxed{24}$ $k'(s) = -\dfrac{\frac{1}{2}(3s - 4)^{-1/2}(3)}{3s - 4} = -\dfrac{3}{2(3s - 4)^{3/2}}$

$\boxed{25}$ $g'(w) = D_w\Big[w^{1/2} - 4w^{-1/2} + 3w^{-3/2}\Big]$

$$= \tfrac{1}{2}w^{-1/2} + 2w^{-3/2} - \tfrac{9}{2}w^{-5/2} = \dfrac{w^2 + 4w - 9}{2w^{5/2}}$$

$\boxed{26}$ $K'(x) = \frac{1}{2}(4x^2 + 2x + 3)^{-1/2}(8x + 2) = \dfrac{4x + 1}{\sqrt{4x^2 + 2x + 3}}$

$\boxed{27}$ $H'(x) = \dfrac{(4x^2 + 9)^{1/2}(2) - (2x + 3)(\frac{1}{2})(4x^2 + 9)^{-1/2}(8x)}{4x^2 + 9}$

$$= \dfrac{2(4x^2 + 9)^{-1/2}\Big[(4x^2 + 9) - 2x(2x + 3)\Big]}{4x^2 + 9} = \dfrac{6(3 - 2x)}{(4x^2 + 9)^{3/2}}$$

$\boxed{28}$ $f'(x) = 6(7x + \sqrt{x^2 + 3})^5\Big[7 + \frac{1}{2}(x^2 + 3)^{-1/2}(2x)\Big] =$

$$6(7x + \sqrt{x^2 + 3})^5\left[7 + \dfrac{x}{\sqrt{x^2 + 3}}\right]$$

$\boxed{29}$ $k'(x) = \cos(x^2 + 2) \cdot (2x) = 2x\cos(x^2 + 2)$

$\boxed{30}$ $f'(t) = -\sin(4 - 3t) \cdot (-3) = 3\sin(4 - 3t)$

$\boxed{31}$ $H'(\theta) = D_\theta(\cos 3\theta)^5 = 5(\cos 3\theta)^4(-\sin 3\theta)3 = -15\cos^4 3\theta \sin 3\theta$

$\boxed{32}$ $g'(x) = D_x(\sin x^3)^4 = 4(\sin x^3)^3(\cos x^3)(3x^2) = 12x^2 \sin^3(x^3)\cos(x^3)$

$\boxed{33}$ $g'(z) = \sec(2z + 1)^2 \tan(2z + 1)^2 (2)(2z + 1)(2) =$

$$4(2z + 1)\sec(2z + 1)^2 \tan(2z + 1)^2$$

$\boxed{34}$ $k'(z) = -\csc(z^2 + 4)\cot(z^2 + 4) \cdot (2z) = -2z\csc(z^2 + 4)\cot(z^2 + 4)$

$\boxed{35}$ $H'(s) = -\csc^2(s^3 - 2s) \cdot (3s^2 - 2) = (2 - 3s^2)\csc^2(s^3 - 2s)$

$\boxed{36}$ $f'(x) = \sec^2(2x^2 + 3) \cdot (4x) = 4x\sec^2(2x^2 + 3)$

$\boxed{37}$ $f'(x) = -\sin(3x^2) \cdot (6x) + 2(\cos 3x)(-\sin 3x)(3) = -6x\sin(3x^2) - 6\cos 3x \sin 3x$

$\boxed{38}$ $g'(w) = 3\,(\tan 6w)^2 \sec^2 6w\,(6) = 18\tan^2 6w \sec^2 6w$

$\boxed{39}$ $F'(\phi) = 2\,(\csc 2\phi)(-\csc 2\phi\,\cot 2\phi)(2) = -4\csc^2 2\phi\,\cot 2\phi$

$\boxed{40}$ $M'(x) = \sec(1/x^2)\,\tan(1/x^2)\,(-2/x^3) = -(2/x^3)\sec(1/x^2)\,\tan(1/x^2)$

$\boxed{41}$ $K'(z) = z^2\,(-\csc^2 5z)\,5 + \cot 5z\cdot(2z) = 2z\cot 5z - 5z^2\csc^2 5z$

$\boxed{42}$ $G'(s) = s\left[-\csc(s^2)\cot(s^2)\right]2s + (1)\csc(s^2) = \csc(s^2) - 2s^2\csc(s^2)\cot(s^2)$

$\boxed{43}$ $h'(\theta) = \tan^2\theta\,(3\sec^2\theta\,\sec\theta\,\tan\theta) + 2(\tan\theta)(\sec^2\theta)(\sec^3\theta) =$
$$2\tan\theta\,\sec^5\theta + 3\tan^3\theta\,\sec^3\theta$$

$\boxed{44}$ $H'(u) = u^2\left[3(\sec^2 4u)(\sec 4u\,\tan 4u)\,4\right] + 2u\sec^3 4u =$
$$2u\sec^3 4u + 12u^2\sec^3 4u\,\tan 4u$$

$\boxed{45}$ $N'(x) = 5(\sin 5x - \cos 5x)^4\,(5\cos 5x + 5\sin 5x) = 25(\sin 5x - \cos 5x)^4(\cos 5x + \sin 5x)$

$\boxed{46}$ $p'(v) = D_v\left[(\sin 4v)(1/\sin 4v)\right] = D_v(1) = 0$

$\boxed{47}$ $T'(w) = 3\cot^2(3w+1)\left[-\csc^2(3w+1)(3)\right] = -9\cot^2(3w+1)\csc^2(3w+1)$

$\boxed{48}$ $g'(r) = \left[\cos(2r+3)^4\right](4)(2r+3)^3(2) = 8(2r+3)^3\cos(2r+3)^4$

$\boxed{49}$ $h'(w) = \dfrac{(1-\sin 4w)(-4\sin 4w) - (\cos 4w)(-4\cos 4w)}{(1-\sin 4w)^2} =$
$$\frac{-4\sin 4w + 4\sin^2 4w + 4\cos^2 4w}{(1-\sin 4w)^2} = \frac{4(1-\sin 4w)}{(1-\sin 4w)^2} = \frac{4}{1-\sin 4w}$$

$\boxed{50}$ $f'(x) = \dfrac{(1+\tan 2x)(2\sec 2x\,\tan 2x) - (\sec 2x)(2\sec^2 2x)}{(1+\tan 2x)^2} =$
$$\frac{2\sec 2x\left[\tan 2x + \tan^2 2x - (1+\tan^2 2x)\right]}{(1+\tan 2x)^2} = \frac{2\sec 2x\,(\tan 2x - 1)}{(1+\tan 2x)^2}$$

$\boxed{51}$ $f'(x) = 3\tan^2 2x\,\sec^2 2x\,(2) - 3\sec^2 2x\,\sec 2x\,\tan 2x\,(2) =$
$$6\tan 2x\,\sec^2 2x\,(\tan 2x - \sec 2x)$$

$\boxed{52}$ $h'(\phi) = 3(\tan 2\phi - \sec 2\phi)^2\,(2\sec^2 2\phi - 2\sec 2\phi\,\tan 2\phi)$
$$= 6\sec 2\phi\,(\tan 2\phi - \sec 2\phi)^2\,(\sec 2\phi - \tan 2\phi) = 6\sec 2\phi\,(\sec 2\phi - \tan 2\phi)^3$$

$\boxed{53}$ $f'(x) = (\cos\sqrt{x})(\tfrac{1}{2}x^{-1/2}) + \tfrac{1}{2}(\sin x)^{-1/2}\cos x = \dfrac{\cos\sqrt{x}}{2\sqrt{x}} + \dfrac{\cos x}{2\sqrt{\sin x}}$

$\boxed{54}$ $f'(x) = \sec^2\sqrt[3]{5-6x}\left[\tfrac{1}{3}(5-6x)^{-2/3}(-6)\right] = -\dfrac{2\sec^2\sqrt[3]{5-6x}}{\sqrt[3]{(5-6x)^2}}$

$\boxed{55}$ $k'(\theta) = 2(\cos\sqrt{3-8\theta})(-\sin\sqrt{3-8\theta})\left[\tfrac{1}{2}(3-8\theta)^{-1/2}(-8)\right] =$
$$\frac{8\cos\sqrt{3-8\theta}\,\sin\sqrt{3-8\theta}}{\sqrt{3-8\theta}}$$

$\boxed{56}$ $r'(t) = \tfrac{1}{2}(\sin 2t - \cos 2t)^{-1/2}(2\cos 2t + 2\sin 2t) = \dfrac{\cos 2t + \sin 2t}{\sqrt{\sin 2t - \cos 2t}}$

$\boxed{57}$ $g'(x) = \sqrt{x^2+1}\,(\sec^2\sqrt{x^2+1})\left[\tfrac{1}{2}(x^2+1)^{-1/2}(2x)\right] +$
$$\left[\tfrac{1}{2}(x^2+1)^{-1/2}(2x)\right](\tan\sqrt{x^2+1}) = x\sec^2\sqrt{x^2+1} + \frac{x\tan\sqrt{x^2+1}}{\sqrt{x^2+1}}$$

$$\boxed{58}\ h'(\phi) = \frac{(\sqrt{\phi^2 + 4})(-4\csc^2 4\phi) - (\cot 4\phi)[\frac{1}{2}(\phi^2 + 4)^{-1/2}(2\phi)]}{(\sqrt{\phi^2 + 4})^2} =$$

$$\frac{-4(\phi^2 + 4)\csc^2 4\phi - \phi\cot 4\phi}{(\phi^2 + 4)^{3/2}}$$

$$\boxed{59}\ M'(x) = \sec\sqrt{4x + 1}\,\tan\sqrt{4x + 1}\,(\tfrac{1}{2})(4x + 1)^{-1/2}(4) = \frac{2\sec\sqrt{4x + 1}\,\tan\sqrt{4x + 1}}{\sqrt{4x + 1}}$$

$$\boxed{60}\ F'(s) = \tfrac{1}{2}(\csc 2s)^{-1/2}(-2\csc 2s \cot 2s) = -\frac{\csc 2s \cot 2s}{\sqrt{\csc 2s}}$$

$$\boxed{61}\ h'(x) = \tfrac{1}{2}(4 + \csc^2 3x)^{-1/2}(2)(\csc 3x)(-3\csc 3x \cot 3x) = -\frac{3\csc^2 3x \cot 3x}{\sqrt{4 + \csc^2 3x}}$$

$$\boxed{62}\ f'(t) = (\sin^2 2t)\Big[\tfrac{1}{2}(\cos 2t)^{-1/2}(-\sin 2t)(2)\Big] + 2(\sin 2t)(\cos 2t)(2)\sqrt{\cos 2t} =$$

$$\frac{\sin 2t(4\cos^2 2t - \sin^2 2t)}{\sqrt{\cos 2t}}$$

Note: Let $y = f(x)$ in Exercises 63–68. The answers are listed in the following order:

(a) $f'(x)$; the slope at P; the equation of the tangent line at P;

the equation of the normal line at P

(b) the roots of $f'(x) = 0$

$\boxed{63}$ (a) $f'(x) = 4(4x^2 - 8x + 3)^3(8x - 8) = 32(x - 1)(2x - 1)^3(2x - 3)^3$;

$$f'(2) = 864;\ y - 81 = 864(x - 2);\ y - 81 = -\tfrac{1}{864}(x - 2)$$

(b) $f'(x) = 0 \Rightarrow x = 1, \tfrac{1}{2}, \tfrac{3}{2}$

$\boxed{64}$ (a) $f'(x) = 10(2x - 1)^9(2) = 20(2x - 1)^9;\ f'(1) = 20;$

$$y - 1 = 20(x - 1);\ y - 1 = -\tfrac{1}{20}(x - 1)$$

(b) $f'(x) = 0 \Rightarrow x = \tfrac{1}{2}$

$\boxed{65}$ (a) $f'(x) = 5\Big(x + \tfrac{1}{x}\Big)^4\Big(1 - \tfrac{1}{x^2}\Big) = \dfrac{5(x^2 + 1)^4(x + 1)(x - 1)}{x^6}$;

$f'(1) = 0;\ y - 32 = 0(x - 1)$ or $y = 32$; the negative reciprocal of 0 is

undefined indicating that the normal line is vertical, namely, $x = 1$.

(b) $f'(x) = 0 \Rightarrow x = \pm 1$

$\boxed{66}$ (a) $f'(x) = \tfrac{1}{2}(2x^2 + 1)^{-1/2}(4x) = 2x(2x^2 + 1)^{-1/2};\ f'(-1) = -\tfrac{2}{\sqrt{3}}$;

$$y - \sqrt{3} = -\tfrac{2}{\sqrt{3}}(x + 1);\ y - \sqrt{3} = \tfrac{\sqrt{3}}{2}(x + 1)$$

(b) $f'(x) = 0 \Rightarrow x = 0$

$\boxed{67}$ (a) $f'(x) = 3 + 3\cos 3x;\ f'(0) = 6;\ y - 0 = 6(x - 0)$ or $y = 6x$;

$$y - 0 = -\tfrac{1}{6}(x - 0)\ \text{or}\ y = -\tfrac{1}{6}x$$

(b) $f'(x) = 0 \Rightarrow \cos 3x = -1 \Rightarrow 3x = \pi + 2\pi n \Rightarrow x = \tfrac{\pi}{3} + \tfrac{2\pi}{3}n$

$\boxed{68}$ (a) $f'(x) = 1 - 2\sin 2x;\ f'(0) = 1;\ y - 1 = 1(x - 0)$ or $y = x + 1$;

$$y - 1 = -1(x - 0)\ \text{or}\ y = -x + 1$$

(b) $f'(x) = 0 \Rightarrow \sin 2x = \tfrac{1}{2} \Rightarrow 2x = \tfrac{\pi}{6} + 2\pi n, \tfrac{5\pi}{6} + 2\pi n \Rightarrow x = \tfrac{\pi}{12} + \pi n, \tfrac{5\pi}{12} + \pi n$

69 $g'(z) = \frac{1}{2}(3z + 1)^{-1/2}(3) = \dfrac{3}{2(3z + 1)^{1/2}}$;

$$g''(z) = -\frac{3}{2}\frac{\frac{1}{2}(3z + 1)^{-1/2}(3)}{3z + 1} = -\frac{9}{4(3z + 1)^{3/2}}$$

70 $k'(s) = \frac{2}{3}(s^2 + 4)^{-1/3}(2s) = \dfrac{4s}{3(s^2 + 4)^{1/3}}$;

$$k''(s) = \frac{3(s^2 + 4)^{1/3}(4) - (4s)\cdot 3\cdot\frac{1}{3}(s^2 + 4)^{-2/3}(2s)}{9(s^2 + 4)^{2/3}}$$

$$= \frac{2(s^2 + 4)^{-2/3}\big[6(s^2 + 4) - (4s)(s)\big]}{9(s^2 + 4)^{2/3}} = \frac{4(s^2 + 12)}{9(s^2 + 4)^{4/3}}$$

71 $k'(r) = 5(4r + 7)^4(4) = 20(4r + 7)^4$;

$$k''(r) = 20\cdot 4(4r + 7)^3(4) = 320(4r + 7)^3$$

72 $f'(x) = \frac{1}{5}(10x + 7)^{-4/5}(10) = \dfrac{2}{(10x + 7)^{4/5}}$;

$$f''(x) = -2\frac{\frac{4}{5}(10x + 7)^{-1/5}(10)}{(10x + 7)^{8/5}} = -\frac{16}{(10x + 7)^{9/5}}$$

73 $f'(x) = 3\sin^2 x \cos x$;

$$f''(x) = 3\Big[\sin^2 x\cdot(-\sin x) + (\cos x)\,2\sin x \cos x\Big] = 6\sin x \cos^2 x - 3\sin^3 x$$

74 $G'(t) = 2\sec 4t(\sec 4t \tan 4t)\,4 = 8\tan 4t \sec^2 4t$;

$$G''(t) = 8\Big[\tan 4t \cdot 2\sec 4t \sec 4t \tan 4t \cdot 4 + \sec^2 4t \cdot \sec^2 4t \cdot 4\Big] =$$
$$32\sec^4 4t + 64\tan^2 4t \sec^2 4t$$

75 $y = f(x) = \sqrt[3]{x} \Rightarrow dy = \dfrac{1}{3(\sqrt[3]{x})^2}\,dx$. When $x = 64$ and $dx = 1$,

$$dy = \frac{1}{3(\sqrt[3]{64})^2}(1) = \frac{1}{48}.\ \ f(65) \approx f(64) + dy = 4 + \frac{1}{48} = 4\frac{1}{48}.$$

76 $y = f(x) = \sqrt[5]{x} \Rightarrow dy = \dfrac{1}{5(\sqrt[5]{x})^4}\,dx$. When $x = 32$ and $dx = 3$,

$$dy = \frac{1}{5(\sqrt[5]{32})^4}(3) = \frac{3}{80}.\ \ f(35) \approx f(32) + dy = 2 + \frac{3}{80} = 2\frac{3}{80}.$$

77 $K = \frac{1}{2}mv^2 \Rightarrow \dfrac{dK}{dt} = \dfrac{dK}{dv}\dfrac{dv}{dt} = mv\dfrac{dv}{dt}$ 　　78 $V = \frac{4}{3}\pi r^3 \Rightarrow \dfrac{dV}{dt} = \dfrac{dV}{dr}\dfrac{dr}{dt} = 4\pi r^2\dfrac{dr}{dt}$

79 $\dfrac{dW}{dt} = \dfrac{dW}{dx}\dfrac{dx}{dt} = 150(2)\left(\dfrac{6400}{6400 + x}\right)\left[\dfrac{-6400}{(6400 + x)^2}\right]\dfrac{dx}{dt} = -\dfrac{300\,(6400)^2}{(6400 + x)^3}\dfrac{dx}{dt}.$

At $x = 1000$ with $\dfrac{dx}{dt} = 6$, $\dfrac{dW}{dt} = -\dfrac{300\,(6400)^2}{(7400)^3}\cdot 6 \approx -0.1819$ lbs/sec.

80 (a) $W' = \dfrac{dW}{dt} = \dfrac{dW}{dL}\dfrac{dL}{dt} = (3\cdot 10.375\,L^2)\big[0.18(2 - L)\big] = 5.6025\,L^2\,(2 - L)$

(b) $W = 10.375\,L^3 \Rightarrow L = \sqrt[3]{W/10.375} \approx 1.245$ for $W = 20 \Rightarrow W' \approx 6.56$ kg/yr.

81 $k(2) = f(g(2)) = f(2) = -4$; $k'(2) = f'(g(2))\,g'(2) = f'(2)\,g'(2) = 3\cdot 5 = 15$

82 $p(3) = q(r(3)) = q(3) = -2$; $p'(3) = q'(r(3))\,r'(3) = q'(3)\,r'(3) = 6\cdot 4 = 24$

83 $f'(4) = g'(h(4))\,h'(4) \Rightarrow h'(4) = \dfrac{f'(4)}{g'(h(4))} = \dfrac{2}{g'(4)} = -\dfrac{2}{5}$

84 $u'(0) = v'(w(0))\,w'(0) \Rightarrow w'(0) = \dfrac{u'(0)}{v'(w(0))} = \dfrac{2}{v'(0)} = -\dfrac{2}{3}$

$\boxed{85}$ $h'(1.12) = f'(g(1.12)) \cdot g'(1.12) = f'(2.232) \cdot g'(1.12)$

$$\approx \left[\frac{f(2.243) - f(2.221)}{2(0.011)}\right]\left[\frac{g(1.13) - g(1.11)}{2(0.01)}\right]$$

$$= \left(\frac{5.0310 - 4.9328}{0.022}\right)\left(\frac{2.243 - 2.221}{0.02}\right) = 4.91$$

$\boxed{86}$ $h'(-2) = f'(g(-2)) \cdot g'(-2) = f'(-8.46) \cdot g'(-2)$

$$\approx \left[\frac{f(-8.43908) - f(-8.48092)}{2(0.02092)}\right]\left[\frac{g(-1.996) - g(-2.004)}{2(0.004)}\right]$$

$$= \left[\frac{-2.03594 - (-2.03930)}{0.04184}\right]\left[\frac{-8.43908 - (-8.48092)}{0.008}\right] = 0.42$$

$\boxed{87}$ (a) Since f is even, $f(-x) = f(x)$. Differentiating both sides yields:

$\quad\quad f'(-x)(-1) = f'(x) \Rightarrow f'(-x) = -f'(x) \Rightarrow f'$ is odd.

$\quad\quad\quad\quad$ Example : If $f(x) = x^4$ (an even function), then $f'(x) = 4x^3$ (an odd function).

$\quad$ (b) Since f is odd, $f(-x) = -f(x)$. Differentiating both sides yields:

$\quad\quad f'(-x)(-1) = -f'(x) \Rightarrow f'(-x) = f'(x) \Rightarrow f'$ is even.

$\quad\quad\quad\quad$ Example: If $f(x) = x^3$ (an odd function), then $f'(x) = 3x^2$ (an even function).

$\boxed{88}$ $D_x \cos x = D_x\left[\sin\left(\frac{\pi}{2} - x\right)\right] = \cos\left(\frac{\pi}{2} - x\right) \cdot (-1) = -\cos\left(\frac{\pi}{2} - x\right) = -\sin x$

$\boxed{89}$ (a) $\frac{dW}{dt} = \frac{dW}{dL}\frac{dL}{dt} = (1.644 \times 10^{-4})\, L^{1.74}\, \frac{dL}{dt}$.

$\quad$ (b) $W = (6 \times 10^{-5})\, L^{2.74} = 0.5 \Rightarrow L \approx 26.975$.

$$\text{Thus, } \frac{dL}{dt} = \frac{dW/dt}{dW/dL} \approx \frac{0.4}{(0.0001644)(26.975)^{1.74}} \approx 7.876 \text{ cm/month.}$$

$\boxed{90}$ $p = cv^{-1.4} \Rightarrow \frac{dp}{dv} = -1.4\, cv^{-2.4} = -\frac{1.4c}{v^{2.4}}$

$\boxed{91}$ (a) $S(8) = 60\pi$. $\Delta S \approx dS = S'(h)\, dh = \frac{6\pi h}{\sqrt{36 + h^2}}\, dh$.

$$\text{Thus, } \Delta S \approx \frac{6\pi(8)}{\sqrt{36 + 64}}(\pm 0.1) = \pm 0.48\pi \approx \pm 1.508 \,\text{cm}^2.$$

$\quad$ (b) % error $\approx \frac{\pm 1.508}{60\pi} \times 100\% \approx \pm 0.8\%$

$\boxed{92}$ $\frac{\Delta T}{T} \approx \frac{dT}{T} = \frac{\frac{1}{2}(2\pi/\sqrt{g})\, l^{-1/2}\, dl}{(2\pi/\sqrt{g})\, l^{1/2}} = \frac{dl}{2l} = 0.01 \Rightarrow$

$$dl = 0.02l \text{ or } l \text{ must increase by } 2\%.$$

Exercises 3.7

Note: For all exercises, we assume is that the denominators are nonzero.

Note: In Exercises 1–18, the first equation shown is the result of differentiating the original equation implicitly.

$\boxed{1}$ $16x + 2yy' = 0 \Rightarrow y' = -\frac{8x}{y}$ $\boxed{2}$ $12x^2 - 6y^2 y' = 1 \Rightarrow y' = \frac{12x^2 - 1}{6y^2}$

$\boxed{3}$ $6x^2 + (x^2 y' + 2xy) + 3y^2 y' = 0 \Rightarrow y' = -\frac{6x^2 + 2xy}{x^2 + 3y^2}$

4 $10x + (2x^2 y' + 4xy) + 2yy' = 0 \Rightarrow y' = -\dfrac{5x + 2xy}{x^2 + y}$

5 $10x - (xy' + y) - 8yy' = 0 \Rightarrow y' = \dfrac{10x - y}{x + 8y}$

6 $4x^3 + (8x^2 yy' + 8xy^2) - (9xy^2 y' + 3y^3) + 2 = 0 \Rightarrow y' = \dfrac{3y^3 - 4x^3 - 8xy^2 - 2}{8x^2 y - 9xy^2}$

7 $\frac{1}{2}x^{-1/2} + \frac{1}{2}y^{-1/2}y' = 0 \Rightarrow y'/\sqrt{y} = -1/\sqrt{x} \Rightarrow y' = -\sqrt{y/x}$

8 $\frac{2}{3}x^{-1/3} + \frac{2}{3}y^{-1/3}y' = 0 \Rightarrow y'/\sqrt[3]{y} = -1/\sqrt[3]{x} \Rightarrow y' = -\sqrt[3]{y/x}$

9 $2x + \frac{1}{2}(xy)^{-1/2}(xy' + y) = 0 \Rightarrow \dfrac{xy' + y}{2\sqrt{xy}} = -2x \Rightarrow y' = \dfrac{-4x\sqrt{xy} - y}{x}$

10 $2 - \frac{1}{2}(xy)^{-1/2}(xy' + y) + 3y^2 y' = 0 \Rightarrow$

$$\left(3y^2 - \dfrac{x}{2\sqrt{xy}}\right)y' = \dfrac{y}{2\sqrt{xy}} - 2 \Rightarrow y' = \dfrac{y - 4\sqrt{xy}}{6y^2\sqrt{xy} - x}$$

11 $2(\sin 3y)(\cos 3y)(3y') = 1 + y' \Rightarrow y' = \dfrac{1}{6\sin 3y \cos 3y - 1} = \dfrac{1}{3\sin 6y - 1}$

12 $1 = \big[\cos(xy)\big](xy' + y) \Rightarrow y' = \dfrac{1 - y\cos(xy)}{x\cos(xy)}$

13 $y' = \big[-\cot(xy)\csc(xy)\big](xy' + y) \Rightarrow$

$$y' + xy'\cot(xy)\csc(xy) = -y\cot(xy)\csc(xy) \Rightarrow y' = \dfrac{-y\cot(xy)\csc(xy)}{1 + x\cot(xy)\csc(xy)}$$

14 $2yy' = x^2(\sec y \tan y)y' + 2x \sec y \Rightarrow y' = \dfrac{2x \sec y}{2y - x^2 \sec y \tan y}$

15 $2yy' = x(-\sin y)y' + \cos y \Rightarrow (x\sin y + 2y)y' = \cos y \Rightarrow y' = \dfrac{\cos y}{x\sin y + 2y}$

16 $(xy' + y) = \sec^2 y\, y' \Rightarrow y'(x - \sec^2 y) = -y \Rightarrow y' = \dfrac{y}{\sec^2 y - x}$

17 $2x + \frac{1}{2}(\sin y)^{-1/2}(\cos y)y' - 2yy' = 0 \Rightarrow$

$$2x = \left(2y - \dfrac{\cos y}{2\sqrt{\sin y}}\right)y' \Rightarrow y' = \dfrac{4x\sqrt{\sin y}}{4y\sqrt{\sin y} - \cos y}$$

18 $\cos\sqrt{y} \cdot \frac{1}{2}y^{-1/2}\, y' - 3 = 0 \Rightarrow \dfrac{\cos\sqrt{y}}{2\sqrt{y}}\, y' = 3 \Rightarrow y' = \dfrac{6\sqrt{y}}{\cos\sqrt{y}}$

19 $2(x^2 + y^2 + a^2)(2x + 2yy') - 8a^2 x = 0 \Rightarrow y' = \dfrac{2a^2 x - x(x^2 + y^2 + a^2)}{y(x^2 + y^2 + a^2)}.$

At $P(2, \sqrt{2})$ with $a = 2$, $b = \sqrt{6}$, $y' = -\frac{1}{5}\sqrt{2}$.

20 $3x^2 + 3y^2 y' - 3a(xy' + y) = 0 \Rightarrow y' = \dfrac{3ay - 3x^2}{3y^2 - 3ax}.$

At $P(6, 6)$ with $a = 4$, $y' = -1$.

21 $2(x^2 + y^2)(2x + 2yy') = 2a^2(xy' + y) \Rightarrow y' = \dfrac{2a^2 y - 4x(x^2 + y^2)}{4y(x^2 + y^2) - 2a^2 x}.$

At $P(1, 1)$ with $a = \sqrt{2}$, $y' = -1$.

22 $(y - a)^2(2x + 2yy') + 2(y - a)y'(x^2 + y^2) = 2b^2 yy' \Rightarrow$

$$y' = \dfrac{-2x(y - a)^2}{2y(y - a)^2 + 2(y - a)(x^2 + y^2) - 2b^2 y}.$$

At $P(\sqrt{15}, 1)$ with $a = 2$, $b = 4$, $y' = \frac{1}{31}\sqrt{15}$.

Note: In Exercises 23–28, you do not need to explicitly solve for y' (see Exercise 26).

$\boxed{23}$ $xy' + y = 0 \Rightarrow y' = -\frac{y}{x}$. At $P(-2, 8)$, $y' = 4$.

$\boxed{24}$ $2yy' - 8x = 0 \Rightarrow y' = \frac{4x}{y}$. At $P(-1, 3)$, $y' = -\frac{4}{3}$.

$\boxed{25}$ $6x^2 - (x^2y' + 2xy) + 3y^2y' = 0 \Rightarrow y' = \dfrac{2xy - 6x^2}{3y^2 - x^2}$. At $P(2, -3)$, $y' = -\frac{36}{23}$.

$\boxed{26}$ $12y^3y' + 4 - (x^2y' \cos y + 2x \sin y) = 0$; $x = 1$, $y = 0 \Rightarrow 4 - y' = 0 \Rightarrow y' = 4$.

$\boxed{27}$ $x^2y' + y \cdot 2x + \cos y\, y' = 0 \Rightarrow y' = \dfrac{-2xy}{x^2 + \cos y}$. At $P(1, 2\pi)$, $y' = -2\pi$.

$\boxed{28}$ $x \cdot 2y\, y' + y^2 + 3y' = 0 \Rightarrow y' = \dfrac{-y^2}{2xy + 3}$. At $P(2, 3)$, $y' = -\frac{3}{5}$.

$\boxed{29}$ $6x + 8yy' = 0 \Rightarrow y' = -\frac{3x}{4y}$; $y'' = -\dfrac{(4y)(3) - (3x)(4y')}{16y^2} = -\dfrac{12y - 12x\left(-\frac{3x}{4y}\right)}{16y^2} =$

$$-\frac{48y^2 + 36x^2}{64y^3} = -\frac{12(3x^2 + 4y^2)}{64y^3} = -\frac{3}{4y^3} \text{ (since } 3x^2 + 4y^2 = 4)$$

$\boxed{30}$ $10x - 4yy' = 0 \Rightarrow y' = \frac{5x}{2y}$; $y'' = \dfrac{(2y)(5) - (5x)(2y')}{4y^2} = \dfrac{10y - 10x\left(\frac{5x}{2y}\right)}{4y^2} =$

$$\frac{20y^2 - 50x^2}{8y^3} = \frac{-10(5x^2 - 2y^2)}{8y^3} = -\frac{5}{y^3} \text{ (since } 5x^2 - 2y^2 = 4)$$

$\boxed{31}$ $3x^2 - 3y^2y' = 0 \Rightarrow y' = \frac{x^2}{y^2}$; $y'' = \dfrac{y^2(2x) - x^2(2yy')}{y^4} = \dfrac{2xy - 2x^2(x^2/y^2)}{y^3} =$

$$\frac{2x(y^3 - x^3)}{y^5} = -\frac{2x}{y^5} \text{ (since } y^3 - x^3 = -1)$$

$\boxed{32}$ $x^2(3y^2y') + y^3(2x) = 0 \Rightarrow y' = -\frac{2y}{3x}$;

$$y'' = -\frac{3x(2y') - 2y(3)}{9x^2} = \frac{-6xy' + 6y}{9x^2} = \frac{-6x\left(-\frac{2y}{3x}\right) + 6y}{9x^2} = \frac{30xy}{27x^3} = \frac{10y}{9x^2}$$

$\boxed{33}$ $\cos y\, y' + y' = 1 \Rightarrow y' = \dfrac{1}{1 + \cos y}$; $y'' = -\dfrac{-\sin y\, y'}{(1 + \cos y)^2} = \dfrac{\sin y}{(1 + \cos y)^3}$

$\boxed{34}$ $-\sin y\, y' = 1 \Rightarrow y' = -\csc y$;

$$y'' = -(-\csc y \cot y)\, y' = (\csc y \cot y)(-\csc y) = -\cot y \csc^2 y$$

$\boxed{35}$ $x^4 + y^4 - 1 = 0 \Leftrightarrow y^4 = 1 - x^4 \Leftrightarrow y = \pm\sqrt[4]{1 - x^4}$.

Let $f_c(x) = \begin{cases} (1 - x^4)^{1/4} & \text{if } -1 \le x \le c \\ -(1 - x^4)^{1/4} & \text{if } c < x \le 1 \end{cases}$ for any c in $[-1, 1]$.

There are an infinite number of solutions.

$\boxed{36}$ One, $f(x) = 0$ with domain $x = 0$.

$\boxed{37}$ None, since $(x^2 + y^2) \ge 0$ and hence $(x^2 + y^2) + 1 \ge 1 > 0$.

$\boxed{38}$ None, since $(\cos x + \sin y) \le 1 + 1 < 3$.

[39] Let $f_c(x) = \begin{cases} \sqrt{x} & \text{if } 0 \leq x \leq c \\ -\sqrt{x} & \text{if } x > c \end{cases}$

for any $c > 0$.

Then, $f_c(x)$ is a solution of $y^2 = x$.

A typical example with $c = 2$ is shown in *Figure 39*.

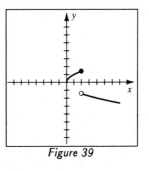

Figure 39

[40] $x^2 + y^2 = a^2 \Rightarrow y' = -\frac{x}{y}$. The slope of the tangent line at $P(x_0, y_0)$ is

$m = -\frac{x_0}{y_0}$, and $m_{OP} = \frac{y_0}{x_0}$. Thus, $m \cdot m_{OP} = -1$, provided $x_0 \neq 0$, $y_0 \neq 0$.

If $x_0 = 0$, the tangent line is horizontal and OP is vertical. If $y_0 = 0$, the tangent

line is vertical and OP is horizontal. In all cases, they are perpendicular.

[41] $3x^2 - x^2y^3 + 4y = 12 \Rightarrow 6x - (x^2 \cdot 3y^2y' + 2xy^3) + 4y' = 0 \Rightarrow y' = \dfrac{2xy^3 - 6x}{4 - 3x^2y^2}$.

At $(2, 0)$, $y' = -3$. Then, $\Delta y \approx dy = f'(2)\Delta x = (-3)(-0.03) = 0.09$.

[42] $x^3 + xy + y^4 = 19 \Rightarrow 3x^2 + (xy' + y) + 4y^3y' = 0 \Rightarrow y' = -\dfrac{3x^2 + y}{x + 4y^3}$.

At $(1, 2)$, $y' = -\frac{5}{33}$. Then, $\Delta y \approx dy = f'(1)\Delta x = -\frac{5}{33}(0.1) = -0.0\overline{15} \Rightarrow$

$$b \approx f(1) + dy = 2 - 0.0\overline{15} \approx 1.9848.$$

[43] (a) $y' = -\dfrac{2x + y^3}{3xy^2}$; at $(1.2, 1.3)$, $y' \approx -0.7556$.

$$f(1.23) \approx f(1.2) + f'(1.2)\Delta x \approx (1.3) + (-0.7556)(0.03) \approx 1.2773$$

(b) At $(1.23, 1.2773)$, $y' \approx -0.7548$.

$$f(1.26) \approx f(1.23) + f'(1.23)\Delta x \approx (1.2773) + (-0.7548)(0.03) \approx 1.2547$$

[44] (a) $y' = \dfrac{\cos x}{y \sin y - \cos y}$; at $(2.1, 3.3)$, $y' \approx -1.08123$.

$$f(2.12) \approx f(2.1) + f'(2.1)\Delta x \approx (3.3) + (-1.08123)(0.02) \approx 3.2784$$

(b) At $(2.12, 3.2784)$, $y' \approx -0.9604$.

$$f(2.14) \approx f(2.12) + f'(2.12)\Delta x \approx (3.2784) + (-0.9604)(0.02) \approx 3.2592$$

Exercises 3.8

[1] $A = x^2 \Rightarrow \frac{dA}{dt} = 2x\frac{dx}{dt} = 2(10)(3) = 60$.

[2] $S = z^3 \Rightarrow \frac{dS}{dt} = 3z^2\frac{dz}{dt} = 3(3^2)(-2) = -54$.

[3] $p = 4$ when $V = -40$.

$$V = -5p^{3/2} \Rightarrow \frac{dV}{dt} = -\frac{15}{2}p^{1/2}\frac{dp}{dt} \Rightarrow -4 = -\frac{15}{2}(4)^{1/2}\frac{dp}{dt} \Rightarrow \frac{dp}{dt} = \frac{4}{15}.$$

[4] $w = \frac{1}{3}$ when $P = 9$. $P = \frac{3}{w} \Rightarrow \frac{dP}{dt} = -\frac{3}{w^2}\frac{dw}{dt} \Rightarrow 5 = -\frac{3}{(1/3)^2}\frac{dw}{dt} \Rightarrow \frac{dw}{dt} = -\frac{5}{27}$.

[5] $x^2 + 3y^2 + 2y = 10 \Rightarrow$

$$2x\frac{dx}{dt} + 6y\frac{dy}{dt} + 2\frac{dy}{dt} = 0 \Rightarrow (3y + 1)\frac{dy}{dt} = -x\frac{dx}{dt} \Rightarrow -2\frac{dy}{dt} = -3(2) \Rightarrow \frac{dy}{dt} = 3.$$

$\boxed{6}$　$2y^3 - x^2 + 4x = -10 \Rightarrow$

$$6y^2 \frac{dy}{dt} - 2x\frac{dx}{dt} + 4\frac{dx}{dt} = 0 \Rightarrow 3y^2\frac{dy}{dt} = (x - 2)\frac{dx}{dt} \Rightarrow 3(-3) = -4\frac{dx}{dt} \Rightarrow \frac{dx}{dt} = \frac{9}{4}.$$

$\boxed{7}$　$3x^2y + 2x = -32 \Rightarrow 3x^2\frac{dy}{dt} + 6xy\frac{dx}{dt} + 2\frac{dx}{dt} = 0 \Rightarrow$

$$(6xy + 2)\frac{dx}{dt} = -3x^2\frac{dy}{dt} \Rightarrow -34\frac{dx}{dt} = -12(-4) \Rightarrow \frac{dx}{dt} = -\frac{24}{17}.$$

$\boxed{8}$　$-x^2y^2 - 4y = -44 \Rightarrow -2x^2y\frac{dy}{dt} - 2xy^2\frac{dx}{dt} - 4\frac{dy}{dt} = 0 \Rightarrow$

$$(x^2y + 2)\frac{dy}{dt} = -xy^2\frac{dx}{dt} \Rightarrow 20\frac{dy}{dt} = 12(5) \Rightarrow \frac{dy}{dt} = 3.$$

$\boxed{9}$　Let x denote the diameter.

$$A = \tfrac{1}{4}\pi x^2 \Rightarrow \frac{dA}{dt} = \tfrac{1}{2}\pi x\frac{dx}{dt} = \tfrac{1}{2}\pi(30)(0.01) = 0.15\pi \approx 0.471 \text{ cm}^2/\text{min}.$$

$\boxed{10}$　$A = \pi r^2 \Rightarrow \frac{dA}{dt} = 2\pi r\frac{dr}{dt} = 2\pi(150)(6) = 1800\pi \approx 5655 \text{ ft}^2/\text{min}.$

$\boxed{11}$　$\{ \text{diameter} = 18 \text{ in.} \Leftrightarrow \text{radius} = 9 \text{ in.} = \tfrac{3}{4} \text{ ft.} \}$

$$V = \tfrac{4}{3}\pi r^3 \Rightarrow \frac{dV}{dt} = 4\pi r^2\frac{dr}{dt} \Rightarrow \frac{dr}{dt} = \frac{1}{4\pi r^2}\frac{dV}{dt} = \frac{1}{4\pi(\frac{3}{4})^2}(5) = \frac{20}{9\pi} \approx 0.707 \text{ ft/min}.$$

$\boxed{12}$　$V = \tfrac{4}{3}\pi r^3 \Rightarrow \frac{dV}{dt} = 4\pi r^2\frac{dr}{dt} = 4\pi(10)^2(-\tfrac{4}{45}) = -\frac{320\pi}{9} \approx -111.7 \text{ in.}^3/\text{min}.$

$\boxed{13}$　Let x denote the distance between the base of the building and the bottom of the ladder and y denote the distance between the base of the building and the top of the ladder.　$x^2 + y^2 = 400 \Rightarrow x = \sqrt{336}$ when $y = 8$ and

$$2x\frac{dx}{dt} + 2y\frac{dy}{dt} = 0 \Rightarrow \frac{dy}{dt} = -\frac{x}{y}\frac{dx}{dt} = -\frac{\sqrt{336}}{8}(3) = -\tfrac{3}{8}\sqrt{336} \approx -6.9 \text{ ft/sec}.$$

$\boxed{14}$　Let x denote the distance of the first girl east of A, y the distance of the second girl north of A, and z the distance between the girls.

$$z^2 = x^2 + y^2 \Rightarrow 2z\frac{dz}{dt} = 2x\frac{dx}{dt} + 2y\frac{dy}{dt} \Rightarrow \frac{dz}{dt} = \frac{1}{z}\left(x\frac{dx}{dt} + y\frac{dy}{dt}\right).$$

$x = 10\frac{\text{ft}}{\text{sec}}(120 \text{ sec}) = 1200 \text{ ft}$, $y = 8\frac{\text{ft}}{\text{sec}}(60 \text{ sec}) = 480 \text{ ft} \Rightarrow z = 120\sqrt{116}$ ft.

$$\frac{dx}{dt} = 10 \text{ and } \frac{dy}{dt} = 8 \Rightarrow \frac{dz}{dt} = \frac{1}{120\sqrt{116}}\left[1200(10) + 480(8)\right] = \frac{132}{\sqrt{116}} \approx 12.3 \text{ ft/sec}.$$

$\boxed{15}$　Let x denote the distance of the tip of the shadow from the base of the pole, y the distance of the boy from the base, and z the length of the shadow.

$$z = x - y \Rightarrow \frac{dz}{dt} = \frac{dx}{dt} - \frac{dy}{dt}. \text{ By similar triangles, } \frac{x}{16} = \frac{x - y}{5} \Rightarrow x = \tfrac{16}{11}y \Rightarrow$$

$$\frac{dx}{dt} = \frac{16}{11}\frac{dy}{dt} = \tfrac{16}{11}(4) \approx 5.82 \text{ ft/sec. Thus, } \frac{dz}{dt} = \frac{64}{11} - 4 = \frac{20}{11} \approx 1.82 \text{ ft/sec}.$$

$\boxed{16}$　Let x denote the horizontal distance between the bow of the boat and the dock and L the length of rope between the boat and the pulley.

$$L^2 = x^2 + 7^2 \Rightarrow 2L\frac{dL}{dt} = 2x\frac{dx}{dt} \Rightarrow \frac{dx}{dt} = \frac{L}{x}\frac{dL}{dt} = \frac{\sqrt{674}}{25}(-2) = -\tfrac{2}{25}\sqrt{674} \approx$$

$$-2.08 \text{ ft/sec (negative since } x \text{ is decreasing).}$$

$\boxed{17}$ Let T denote the thickness of the ice and note that the radius is 120 in. The volume

of the ice (outer hemisphere − inner hemi.) is $V = \frac{2}{3}\pi(120 + T)^3 - \frac{2}{3}\pi(120)^3 \Rightarrow$

$$\frac{dV}{dt} = 2\pi(120 + T)^2 \frac{dT}{dt} = 2\pi(120 + 2)^2(-\frac{1}{4}) = -7442\pi \approx -23,380 \text{ in.}^3/\text{hr.}$$

$\boxed{18}$ Since $r = h$, $V = \frac{1}{3}\pi r^2 h = \frac{1}{3}\pi h^3$.

$$\frac{dV}{dt} = \pi h^2 \frac{dh}{dt} = \pi(10)^2(6) = 600\pi \approx 1885 \text{ in.}^3/\text{min.}$$

$\boxed{19}$ Let L denote the length of string and x the horizontal distance of the kite from the

boy. $L^2 = x^2 + 100^2 \Rightarrow$

$$2L\frac{dL}{dt} = 2x\frac{dx}{dt} \Rightarrow \frac{dx}{dt} = \frac{L}{x}\frac{dL}{dt} = \frac{125}{75}(2) = \frac{10}{3} \approx 3.33 \text{ ft/sec.}$$

$\boxed{20}$ Let h denote the height of the balloon and L the length of the rope. $L^2 = h^2 + 20^2$

$$\Rightarrow 2L\frac{dL}{dt} = 2h\frac{dh}{dt} \Rightarrow \frac{dh}{dt} = \frac{L}{h}\frac{dL}{dt} = \frac{500}{\sqrt{249,600}}(5) = \frac{2500}{\sqrt{249,600}} \approx 5.00 \text{ ft/sec.}$$

$\boxed{21}$ $pv = c \Rightarrow p\frac{dv}{dt} + v\frac{dp}{dt} = 0 \Rightarrow \frac{dv}{dt} = -\frac{v}{p}\frac{dp}{dt} = -\frac{75}{30}(-2) = 5 \text{ in.}^3/\text{min (increasing).}$

$\boxed{22}$ Let x denote the diameter of the cable in inches.

Hence, $A = \pi x(1200)$ is the curved surface area.

$$\frac{dA}{dt} = 1200\pi\frac{dx}{dt} \Rightarrow \frac{dx}{dt} = \frac{1}{1200\pi}\frac{dA}{dt} = \frac{1}{1200\pi}(750) = \frac{5}{8\pi} \approx 0.1989 \text{ in./yr.}$$

$\boxed{23}$ Let h denote the depth of the water. The area of the submerged triangular portion is

$A = \frac{1}{2}\left(\frac{2h}{\sqrt{3}}\right)h = \frac{h^2}{\sqrt{3}}$. $V = 8A = \frac{8h^2}{\sqrt{3}} \Rightarrow \frac{dV}{dt} = \frac{16h}{\sqrt{3}}\frac{dh}{dt} \Rightarrow$

$$\frac{dh}{dt} = \frac{1}{16h}\sqrt{3}\frac{dV}{dt} = \frac{1}{16(\frac{2}{3})}\sqrt{3}(5) = \frac{15}{32}\sqrt{3} \approx 0.81 \text{ ft/min.}$$

$\boxed{24}$ Using the same notation as in Exercise 23, $A = \frac{1}{2}h^2$ and $V = 4h^2 \Rightarrow$

$$\frac{dV}{dt} = 8h\frac{dh}{dt} \Rightarrow \frac{dh}{dt} = \frac{1}{8h}\frac{dV}{dt} = \frac{1}{8(\frac{2}{3})}(5) = \frac{15}{16} = 0.9375 \text{ ft/min.}$$

$\boxed{25}$ Let x denote the length of a side.

$A = \frac{\sqrt{3}}{4}x^2 \Rightarrow \frac{dA}{dt} = \frac{\sqrt{3}}{2}x\frac{dx}{dt} \Rightarrow \frac{dx}{dt} = \frac{2}{\sqrt{3}x}\frac{dA}{dt}$. $A = 200$, $x = \left(\frac{800}{\sqrt{3}}\right)^{1/2}$, and

$$\frac{dA}{dt} = -4 \Rightarrow \frac{dx}{dt} = \frac{2}{\sqrt{3}\left(\frac{800}{\sqrt{3}}\right)^{1/2}}(-4) = -\frac{\sqrt{2}}{5\sqrt[4]{3}} \approx -0.2149 \text{ cm/min.}$$

$\boxed{26}$ $V = \frac{4}{3}\pi r^3 \Rightarrow \frac{dV}{dt} = 4\pi r^2\frac{dr}{dt} \Rightarrow \frac{dr}{dt} = \frac{1}{4\pi r^2}\frac{dV}{dt}$. $V = 400$, $r = \sqrt[3]{\frac{300}{\pi}}$, and

$$\frac{dV}{dt} = -10 \Rightarrow \frac{dr}{dt} = \frac{1}{4\pi\left(\frac{300}{\pi}\right)^{2/3}}(-10) = -\frac{5}{2(\pi)^{1/3}(300)^{2/3}} \approx -0.038 \text{ ft/min.}$$

$\boxed{27}$ $C = 2\pi r \Rightarrow \frac{dC}{dt} = 2\pi\frac{dr}{dt} = 2\pi(0.5) = \pi \approx 3.14 \text{ m/sec.}$

Note: C is linear in r so its rate of change is constant.

$\boxed{28}$ Let x denote the runner's distance from third base and h her distance from home

plate. $h^2 = x^2 + 60^2 \Rightarrow$

$$2h\frac{dh}{dt} = 2x\frac{dx}{dt} \Rightarrow \frac{dh}{dt} = \frac{x}{h}\frac{dx}{dt} = \frac{20}{\sqrt{4000}}(-24) = -\frac{24}{\sqrt{10}} \approx -7.59 \text{ ft/sec.}$$

29 $\dfrac{1}{R} = \dfrac{1}{R_1} + \dfrac{1}{R_2} \Rightarrow -\dfrac{1}{R^2}\dfrac{dR}{dt} = -\dfrac{1}{R_1^2}\dfrac{dR_1}{dt} - \dfrac{1}{R_2^2}\dfrac{dR_2}{dt}.$

$R_1 = 30$ and $R_2 = 90 \Rightarrow R = \frac{45}{2}.$ $\dfrac{dR_1}{dt} = 0.01$ and $\dfrac{dR_2}{dt} = 0.02 \Rightarrow$

$$\dfrac{dR}{dt} = -\left(\tfrac{45}{2}\right)^2\left[-\dfrac{1}{(30)^2}\left(\tfrac{1}{100}\right) - \dfrac{1}{(90)^2}\left(\tfrac{2}{100}\right)\right] = \dfrac{11}{1600} = 0.006875 \text{ ohm/sec.}$$

30 $pv^{1.4} = c \Rightarrow v^{1.4}\dfrac{dp}{dt} + 1.4\,pv^{0.4}\dfrac{dv}{dt} = 0 \Rightarrow$

$$\dfrac{dv}{dt} = -\dfrac{v}{1.4p}\dfrac{dp}{dt} = -\dfrac{60}{1.4(40)}(3) = -\dfrac{45}{14} \approx -3.21 \text{ cm}^3/\text{sec.}$$

31 Since $a = 16$, $V = \frac{1}{3}\pi h^2[3(16) - h] \Rightarrow \dfrac{dV}{dt} = \pi h(32 - h)\dfrac{dh}{dt} \Rightarrow$

$$\dfrac{dh}{dt} = \dfrac{1}{\pi h(32 - h)}\dfrac{dV}{dt} \approx \dfrac{1}{\pi(4)(28)}(100)(0.1337) = \dfrac{13.37}{112\pi} \approx 0.038 \text{ ft/min.}$$

32 Let s denote the outside diameter of the sphere and V_0 the volume of the tank.

The volume of the ice is $V = \frac{4}{3}\pi(\frac{1}{2}s)^3 - V_0 \Rightarrow \dfrac{dV}{dt} = \dfrac{\pi}{2}s^2\dfrac{ds}{dt}.$

We also have $\dfrac{dV}{dt} = k\left[4\pi(\frac{1}{2}s)^2\right]$ for some constant $k > 0$.

$\dfrac{\pi}{2}s^2\dfrac{ds}{dt} = k\left[4\pi(\frac{1}{2}s)^2\right] \Rightarrow \dfrac{ds}{dt} = 2k$, two times the constant of proportionality.

33 Let L denote the distance between the two stones.

$$L = \left[16t^2\right] - \left[16(t - 2)^2\right] = 64t - 64. \text{ Thus, } \dfrac{dL}{dt} = 64 \text{ ft/sec, a constant rate.}$$

34 Let h denote the length of the rod and s the diameter. $V = \pi(\frac{1}{2}s)^2 h \Rightarrow$

$$\dfrac{dV}{dt} = \dfrac{\pi}{4}\left(2sh\dfrac{ds}{dt} + s^2\dfrac{dh}{dt}\right) = \dfrac{\pi}{4}\left[2(3)(40)(0.002) + 3^2(0.005)\right] =$$

$$\dfrac{21\pi}{160} \approx 0.41 \text{ cm}^3/\text{min.}$$

35 Orient the plane as in *Figure 35*. L is the distance between the plane and the control tower. Using the distance formula, $\{10{,}560 \text{ ft} = 2 \text{ miles}\}$

$$L = \sqrt{\left(\dfrac{z}{\sqrt{2}}\right)^2 + \left(\dfrac{z}{\sqrt{2}} + 2\right)^2} = \sqrt{z^2 + 2\sqrt{2}\,z + 4} \Rightarrow$$

$\dfrac{dL}{dt} = \frac{1}{2}(z^2 + 2\sqrt{2}\,z + 4)^{-1/2}(2z + 2\sqrt{2})\dfrac{dz}{dt}.$

$z = 360(\frac{1}{60}) = 6$ and $\dfrac{dz}{dt} = 360 \Rightarrow$

$$\dfrac{dL}{dt} = \dfrac{180(6 + \sqrt{2})}{\sqrt{10 + 3\sqrt{2}}} \approx 353.6 \text{ mi/hr.}$$

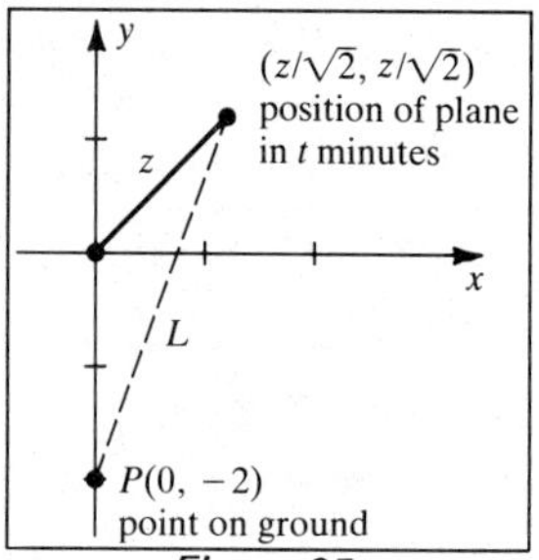

Figure 35

36 Let y denote the number of miles the car is north of P, x the number of miles the plane is *west* of P, and L the distance between the plane and the car.

$\{26{,}400 \text{ ft} = 5 \text{ miles}\}$ $L^2 = x^2 + y^2 + 5^2 \Rightarrow 2L\dfrac{dL}{dt} = 2x\dfrac{dx}{dt} + 2y\dfrac{dy}{dt}.$

$x = 100 - \frac{1}{4}(200) = 50$ and $y = 50(\frac{1}{4}) = 12.5 \Rightarrow L = \sqrt{2681.25}.$

$\dfrac{dy}{dt} = 50$ and $\dfrac{dx}{dt} = -200 \Rightarrow$

$$\dfrac{dL}{dt} = \dfrac{1}{\sqrt{2681.25}}\left[50(-200) + 12.5(50)\right] = -\dfrac{9375}{\sqrt{2681.25}} \approx -181.1 \text{ mi/hr.}$$

37 Consider the cup as shown in *Figure 37*. Let $b = 1$ and a vary with the depth of the water. The equation of line l is $y = 6(x - 1)$ and thus, $h = 6(a - 1) \Rightarrow$
$a = \frac{1}{6}(h + 6)$. $V = \frac{1}{3}\pi h(a^2 + b^2 + ab) =$

$$\frac{1}{3}\pi h\left[\frac{1}{36}(h^2 + 12h + 36) + 1 + \frac{1}{6}(h + 6)\right] = \frac{\pi}{108}h(h^2 + 18h + 108).$$

$\frac{dV}{dt} = (\frac{\pi}{36}h^2 + \frac{\pi}{3}h + \pi)\frac{dh}{dt}$. $\frac{dV}{dt} = -3$, $h = 4 \Rightarrow \frac{dh}{dt} = -\frac{27}{25\pi} \approx -0.3438$ in./hr.

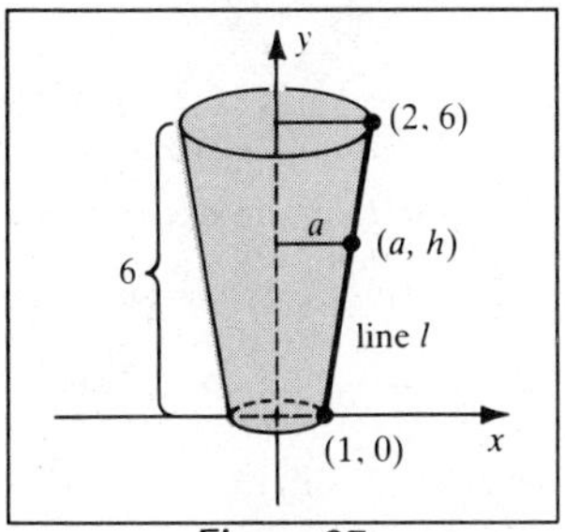

Figure 37

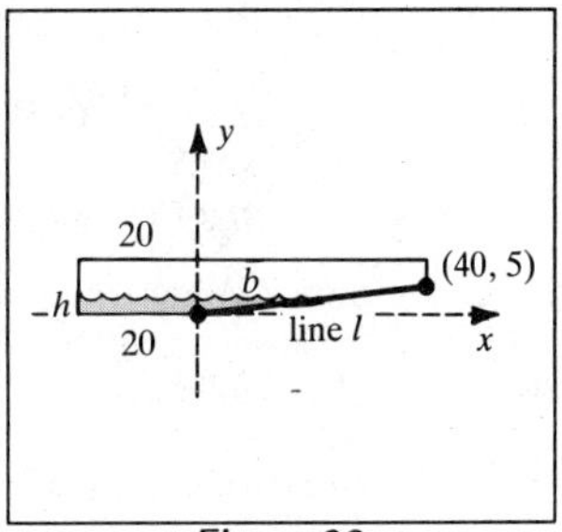

Figure 38

38 A cross section of water at depth h has the shape of a trapezoid with lower base 20, upper base $(20 + b)$, and height h as shown in *Figure 38*. Line l has equation $y = \frac{1}{8}x$ and so $y = h \Rightarrow b = 8h$. The area of the trapezoid is $\frac{1}{2}h\left[20 + (20 + 8h)\right]$ and the volume of the water is $V = 30(\frac{1}{2}h)(40 + 8h) = 600h + 120h^2 \Rightarrow$

$\frac{dV}{dt} = (600 + 240h)\frac{dh}{dt}$. $\frac{dV}{dt} = 500$ gal/min ≈ 66.85 ft^3/min and $h = 4 \Rightarrow$

$$\frac{dh}{dt} \approx \frac{66.85}{1560} \approx 0.043 \text{ ft/min.}$$

39 Let x denote the horizontal distance between the airplane and the observer and θ the angle of elevation. $x = 10,000 \cot\theta \Rightarrow \frac{dx}{dt} = -10,000 \csc^2\theta \frac{d\theta}{dt} =$

$$-10,000\left(\frac{2}{\sqrt{3}}\right)^2(1 \cdot \frac{\pi}{180}) = -\frac{10,000\pi}{135} \approx -232.7 \text{ ft/sec (toward the observer).}$$

40 Let L denote the rope's length. $L = 7\csc\theta \Rightarrow \frac{dL}{dt} = -7\csc\theta \cot\theta \frac{d\theta}{dt} \Rightarrow$

$\frac{d\theta}{dt} = -\frac{1}{7}\sin\theta \tan\theta \frac{dL}{dt} = -\frac{1}{7}(\frac{1}{2})(\frac{\sqrt{3}}{3})(-2) = \frac{1}{21}\sqrt{3} \approx 0.082$ rad/sec ≈ 4.7 deg/sec.

41 Using $A = \frac{1}{2}bc \sin\alpha$ for any triangle, we have $A = \frac{1}{2}(6)(6)\sin\theta = 18\sin\theta$.

$$\frac{dA}{dt} = 18\cos\theta \frac{d\theta}{dt} = 18(\frac{\sqrt{3}}{2})(2 \cdot \frac{\pi}{180}) = \frac{\pi}{10}\sqrt{3} \approx 0.54 \text{ in.}^2/\text{min.}$$

42 Let x denote the horizontal distance from the bottom of the ladder to the base of the building and y the distance from the top of the ladder to the base of the building.

$x = 20\cos\theta$, $y = 20\sin\theta$, and $\frac{dx}{dt} = -(20\sin\theta)\frac{d\theta}{dt} = -(y)\frac{d\theta}{dt} \Rightarrow \frac{d\theta}{dt} = -\frac{1}{y}\frac{dx}{dt}$.

$y = 12$ and $\frac{dx}{dt} = 2 \Rightarrow \frac{d\theta}{dt} = -\frac{1}{6} \approx -0.167$ rad/sec ≈ -9.55 deg/sec (decreasing).

$\boxed{43}$ Let s denote the distance between the top of the control tower and the airplane and x the distance the airplane is down the runway.

$$s^2 = x^2 + 300^2 + 20^2 \Rightarrow 2s\frac{ds}{dt} = 2x\frac{dx}{dt} \Rightarrow$$

$$\frac{ds}{dt} = \frac{x}{s}\frac{dx}{dt} = \frac{300}{\sqrt{180,400}}(8800 \text{ ft/min}) = \frac{2,640,000}{\sqrt{180,400}} \approx 6215.6 \text{ ft/min} \approx 70.63 \text{ mi/hr.}$$

$\boxed{44}$ $v = 1087\sqrt{T/273} \Rightarrow$

$$\frac{dv}{dt} = \frac{1087}{546\sqrt{T/273}}\frac{dT}{dt} = \frac{1087}{546\sqrt{303/273}}(3) = \frac{3261}{546\sqrt{303/273}} \approx 5.67 \text{ (ft/sec)/hr.}$$

$\boxed{45}$ Let x denote the horizontal distance between the plane and the observer, and θ the angle of elevation. When the plane is 60,000 ft from the observer $\{\theta = 30°\}$, the constant height is 30,000 ft. $x = 30,000\cot\theta \Rightarrow \frac{dx}{dt} = -30,000\csc^2\theta\frac{d\theta}{dt} =$

$$-30,000(2)^2(0.5 \cdot \tfrac{\pi}{180}) = -\tfrac{1000\pi}{3} \text{ ft/sec} \approx -714.0 \text{ mi/hr (toward the observer).}$$

$\boxed{46}$ Let h denote the missile's height and θ its angle of elevation. $h = 5\tan\theta \Rightarrow$

$$\frac{dh}{dt} = 5\sec^2\theta\frac{d\theta}{dt} = 5(\tfrac{2}{\sqrt{3}})^2(2 \cdot \tfrac{\pi}{180}) = \tfrac{2\pi}{27} \approx 0.233 \text{ mi/sec} \approx 837.8 \text{ mi/hr.}$$

$\boxed{47}$ Let ϕ represent the angle the wheel turns through when the pedals are rotated through an angle θ. Assuming no slippage in the chain, the length of chain moving around each sprocket must be equal. Using the arc length formula, $s_1 = 5\theta$, $s_2 = 2\phi$, and $s_1 = s_2 \Rightarrow \phi = \tfrac{5}{2}\theta$. The length x that the wheel travels is 14ϕ.

$$x = 14\phi = 35\theta \Rightarrow \frac{dx}{dt} = 35\frac{d\theta}{dt} \text{ in./sec} = \frac{175}{88}\frac{d\theta}{dt} \text{ mi/hr.}$$

$\boxed{48}$ Since $\theta = (\tfrac{\pi}{2} - \phi)$, $s = 20\csc\phi$ and $I = 100$,

$$E = \frac{100\cos(\tfrac{\pi}{2} - \phi)}{400\csc^2\phi} = \frac{100\sin^3\phi}{400} \Rightarrow \frac{dE}{dt} = \frac{300\sin^2\phi\,\cos\phi}{400}\frac{d\phi}{dt}.$$

$\boxed{49}$ (a) $r = l\sin\theta$ and $v^2 = rg\tan\theta \Rightarrow v^2 = gl\sin\theta\tan\theta$. $2v\frac{dv}{dt} =$

$$gl(\sin\theta\sec^2\theta + \tan\theta\,\cos\theta)\frac{d\theta}{dt} = g(l\sin\theta)(1 + \sec^2\theta)\frac{d\theta}{dt} = gr(1 + \sec^2\theta)\frac{d\theta}{dt}.$$

(b) $r = l\sin\theta \Rightarrow \frac{dr}{dt} = l\cos\theta\frac{d\theta}{dt} \Rightarrow \frac{d\theta}{dt} = \frac{1}{l\cos\theta}\frac{dr}{dt}$. Using the result from part (a)

yields $2v\frac{dv}{dt} = gr(1 + \sec^2\theta)\frac{1}{l\cos\theta}\frac{dr}{dt} = g(l\sin\theta)(1 + \sec^2\theta)\frac{1}{l\cos\theta}\frac{dr}{dt} =$

$$g\tan\theta\,(1 + \sec^2\theta)\frac{dr}{dt}.$$

$\boxed{50}$ By similar triangles, for the filter, $\frac{x}{4} = \frac{r}{2} \Rightarrow r = \tfrac{1}{2}x$.

$$V_{filter} + V_{cup} = 10 \Rightarrow \tfrac{1}{3}\pi(\tfrac{1}{2}x)^2x + \pi(2)^2y = 10 \Rightarrow \tfrac{\pi}{12}x^3 + 4\pi y = 10 \Rightarrow$$

$$\tfrac{1}{4}\pi x^2\frac{dx}{dt} + 4\pi\frac{dy}{dt} = 0 \Rightarrow \frac{dy}{dt} = -\tfrac{1}{16}x^2\frac{dx}{dt}.$$

$\boxed{51}$ $\dfrac{dy_A}{dt} = \dfrac{\Delta y}{\Delta t} = \dfrac{3.67 - 3.35}{5.00 - 3.75} = 0.256$ mi/min $= 15.36$ mi/hr

$\dfrac{dx_B}{dt} = \dfrac{\Delta x}{\Delta t} = \dfrac{6.08 - 5.80}{5.00 - 3.75} = 0.224$ mi/min $= 13.44$ mi/hr

Let z denote the distance between the two ships.

At $t = 5$, $z = \sqrt{(1.77 - 6.08)^2 + (3.67 - 1.24)^2} = \sqrt{24.481}$ mi.

$z^2 = (x_B - 1.77)^2 + (y_A - 1.24)^2 \Rightarrow \dfrac{dz}{dt} = \dfrac{(x_B - 1.77)\dfrac{dx_B}{dt} + (y_A - 1.24)\dfrac{dy_A}{dt}}{z} =$

$$\dfrac{(6.08 - 1.77)(13.44) + (3.67 - 1.24)(15.36)}{\sqrt{24.481}} \approx 19.25 \text{ mi/hr}$$

$\boxed{52}$ $3.3536 \cos(2.56x)\dfrac{dx}{dt} - \dfrac{1}{2\sqrt{y}}\dfrac{dy}{dt} = 2(x-1)\dfrac{dx}{dt} \Rightarrow$

$$\dfrac{dx}{dt} = \dfrac{\dfrac{1}{2\sqrt{y}}\dfrac{dy}{dt}}{3.3536\cos(2.56x) - 2(x-1)} \approx \dfrac{\dfrac{1}{2\sqrt{3.03}}(3.68)}{3.3536\cos(2.56\cdot1.71) - 2(1.71-1)} \approx$$

$$\dfrac{1.05705}{-2.52189} \approx -0.419$$

3.9 Review Exercises

$\boxed{1}$ $f'(x) = \lim\limits_{h \to 0} \dfrac{1}{h}\left[\dfrac{4}{3(x+h)^2 + 2} - \dfrac{4}{3x^2 + 2}\right] = \lim\limits_{h \to 0}\dfrac{4}{h}\left[\dfrac{3x^2 + 2 - 3(x+h)^2 - 2}{\left[3(x+h)^2 + 2\right](3x^2 + 2)}\right]$

$= \lim\limits_{h \to 0}\dfrac{4}{h}\left[\dfrac{-6xh - 3h^2}{\left[3(x+h)^2 + 2\right](3x^2 + 2)}\right] = \dfrac{-24x}{(3x^2 + 2)^2}$

$\boxed{2}$ $f'(x) = \lim\limits_{h \to 0}\dfrac{\sqrt{5 - 7(x+h)} - \sqrt{5 - 7x}}{h} \cdot \dfrac{\sqrt{5 - 7(x+h)} + \sqrt{5 - 7x}}{\sqrt{5 - 7(x+h)} + \sqrt{5 - 7x}} =$

$\lim\limits_{h \to 0}\dfrac{-7}{\sqrt{5 - 7(x+h)} + \sqrt{5 - 7x}} = \dfrac{-7}{2\sqrt{5 - 7x}}$

$\boxed{3}$ $f'(x) = 6x^2 - 7$

$\boxed{4}$ $k'(x) = -\dfrac{4x^3 - 2x}{(x^4 - x^2 + 1)^2} = -\dfrac{2x(2x^2 - 1)}{(x^4 - x^2 + 1)^2}$

$\boxed{5}$ $g'(t) = \tfrac{1}{2}(6t + 5)^{-1/2}(6) = \dfrac{3}{\sqrt{6t + 5}}$

$\boxed{6}$ $h'(t) = -\dfrac{\tfrac{1}{2}(6t + 5)^{-1/2}(6)}{6t + 5} = -\dfrac{3}{(6t + 5)^{3/2}}$

$\boxed{7}$ $F'(z) = \tfrac{1}{3}(7z^2 - 4z + 3)^{-2/3}(14z - 4) = \dfrac{2(7z - 2)}{3(7z^2 - 4z + 3)^{2/3}}$

$\boxed{8}$ $f'(w) = \tfrac{1}{5}(3w^2)^{-4/5}(6w) = \dfrac{6w}{5(3w^2)^{4/5}}$

$\boxed{9}$ $G'(x) = (-6)\dfrac{4(3x^2 - 1)^3(6x)}{(3x^2 - 1)^8} = -\dfrac{144x}{(3x^2 - 1)^5}$

$\boxed{10}$ $H'(x) = \tfrac{1}{6}\cdot 4(3x^2 - 1)^3(6x) = 4x(3x^2 - 1)^3$

$\boxed{11}$ $F'(r) = -2(r^2 - r^{-2})^{-3}(2r + 2r^{-3}) = -\dfrac{4(r + r^{-3})}{(r^2 - r^{-2})^3}$

12   $h'(z) = 5\big[(z^2 - 1)^5 - 1\big]^4\big[5(z^2 - 1)^4(2z)\big] = 50z(z^2 - 1)^4\big[(z^2 - 1)^5 - 1\big]^4$

13   $g'(x) = \frac{4}{5}(3x + 2)^{-1/5}(3) = \dfrac{12}{5(3x + 2)^{1/5}}$

14   $P'(x) = 2(x + x^{-1})(1 - x^{-2}) = 2(x + 1/x)(1 - 1/x^2)$

15   $r'(s) = 4\Big(\dfrac{8s^2 - 4}{1 - 9s^3}\Big)^3 \dfrac{(1 - 9s^3)(16s) - (8s^2 - 4)(-27s^2)}{(1 - 9s^3)^2} =$

$$\dfrac{4(8s^2 - 4)^3(72s^4 - 108s^2 + 16s)}{(1 - 9s^3)^5} = \dfrac{1024s(2s^2 - 1)^3(18s^3 - 27s + 4)}{(1 - 9s^3)^5}$$

16   $g'(w) = D_w\Big(\dfrac{w^2 - 4w + 3}{w^2 + 4w + 3}\Big) = \dfrac{(w^2 + 4w + 3)(2w - 4) - (w^2 - 4w + 3)(2w + 4)}{(w^2 + 4w + 3)^2}$

$$= \dfrac{8w^2 - 24}{(w + 1)^2(w + 3)^2} = \dfrac{8(w^2 - 3)}{(w + 1)^2(w + 3)^2}$$

17   $F'(x) = (x^6 + 1)^5(3)(3x + 2)^2(3) + (3x + 2)^3(5)(x^6 + 1)^4(6x^5)$

$\qquad = (x^6 + 1)^4(3x + 2)^2\big[9(x^6 + 1) + 30x^5(3x + 2)\big] =$

$$3(x^6 + 1)^4(3x + 2)^2(33x^6 + 20x^5 + 3)$$

18   $k'(z) = \frac{1}{2}\big[z^2 + (z^2 + 9)^{1/2}\big]^{-1/2}\big[2z + \frac{1}{2}(z^2 + 9)^{-1/2}(2z)\big] =$

$$\dfrac{2z(z^2 + 9)^{1/2} + z}{2\big[z^2 + (z^2 + 9)^{1/2}\big]^{1/2}(z^2 + 9)^{1/2}}$$

19   $k'(s) = (2s^2 - 3s + 1)(4)(9s - 1)^3(9) + (9s - 1)^4(4s - 3) =$

$\qquad (9s - 1)^3\big[36(2s^2 - 3s + 1) + (9s - 1)(4s - 3)\big] = (9s - 1)^3(108s^2 - 139s + 39)$

20   $p'(x) = D_x(2x^2 + 3 - x^{-2}) = 4x + (2/x^3)$

21   $f'(x) = 12x + \dfrac{5}{x^2} - \dfrac{4}{3x^{5/3}}$

22   $F'(t) = \dfrac{(t^2 + 2)(10t) - (5t^2 - 7)(2t)}{(t^2 + 2)^2} = \dfrac{34t}{(t^2 + 2)^2}$

23   $f'(w) = \frac{1}{2}\Big(\dfrac{2w + 5}{7w - 9}\Big)^{-1/2}\dfrac{(7w - 9)(2) - (2w + 5)(7)}{(7w - 9)^2} = \dfrac{-53}{2\sqrt{(2w + 5)(7w - 9)^3}}$

24   $S'(t) =$

$\qquad (t^2 + t + 1)^{1/2}(\frac{1}{3})(4t - 9)^{-2/3}(4) + (4t - 9)^{1/3}(\frac{1}{2})(t^2 + t + 1)^{-1/2}(2t + 1) =$

$$\dfrac{8(t^2 + t + 1) + 3(2t + 1)(4t - 9)}{6\big(\sqrt[3]{(4t - 9)^2}\big)\sqrt{t^2 + t + 1}} = \dfrac{32t^2 - 34t - 19}{6\sqrt[3]{(4t - 9)^2}\sqrt{t^2 + t + 1}}$$

25   $g'(r) = \frac{1}{2}(1 + \cos 2r)^{-1/2}(-2\sin 2r) = -\dfrac{\sin 2r}{\sqrt{1 + \cos 2r}}$

26   $g'(z) = -\csc(1/z)\cot(1/z)\,(-1/z^2) + D_z(\cos z) = (1/z^2)\csc(1/z)\cot(1/z) - \sin z$

27   $f'(x) = 2(\sin 4x^3)(\cos 4x^3)(12x^2) = 12x^2\sin 8x^3$

28   $H'(t) = 3(1 + \sin 3t)^2(3\cos 3t) = (9\cos 3t)(1 + \sin 3t)^2$

29   $h'(x) = 5(\sec x + \tan x)^4(\sec x \tan x + \sec^2 x) = 5\sec x(\sec x + \tan x)^5$

$\boxed{30}$ $K'(r) = \frac{1}{3}(r^3 + \csc 6r)^{-2/3}\Big[3r^2 - \csc(6r)\cot(6r)\cdot 6\Big] = \dfrac{r^2 - 2\csc(6r)\cot(6r)}{(r^3 + \csc 6r)^{2/3}}$

$\boxed{31}$ $f'(x) = x^2(-2\csc^2 2x) + 2x\cot 2x = 2x(\cot 2x - x\csc^2 2x)$

$\boxed{32}$ $P'(\theta) = \theta^2(2)\tan(\theta^2)\sec^2(\theta^2)(2\theta) + 2\theta\tan^2(\theta^2) =$

$$2\theta\tan^2(\theta^2) + 4\theta^3\tan(\theta^2)\sec^2(\theta^2)$$

$\boxed{33}$ $K'(\theta) = \dfrac{(1 + \cos 2\theta)(2\cos 2\theta) - (\sin 2\theta)(-2\sin 2\theta)}{(1 + \cos 2\theta)^2}$

$$= \dfrac{2\cos 2\theta + 2\cos^2 2\theta + 2\sin^2 2\theta}{(1 + \cos 2\theta)^2} = \dfrac{2(1 + \cos 2\theta)}{(1 + \cos 2\theta)^2} = \dfrac{2}{1 + \cos 2\theta}$$

$\boxed{34}$ $g'(v) = -\dfrac{2\cos 2v(-2\sin 2v)}{(1 + \cos^2 2v)^2} = \dfrac{2\sin 4v}{(1 + \cos^2 2v)^2}$

$\boxed{35}$ $g'(x) = 3(\cos\sqrt[3]{x} - \sin\sqrt[3]{x})^2\Big[-\sin\sqrt[3]{x}\,(\frac{1}{3})(x^{-2/3}) - \cos\sqrt[3]{x}(\frac{1}{3})(x^{-2/3})\Big] =$

$$-\dfrac{(\cos\sqrt[3]{x} - \sin\sqrt[3]{x})^2(\cos\sqrt[3]{x} + \sin\sqrt[3]{x})}{\sqrt[3]{x^2}}$$

$\boxed{36}$ $f'(x) = \dfrac{(2x + \sec^2 x)(1) - (x)(2 + 2\sec x\sec x\tan x)}{(2x + \sec^2 x)^2} = \dfrac{\sec^2 x(1 - 2x\tan x)}{(2x + \sec^2 x)^2}$

$\boxed{37}$ $G'(u) = \dfrac{(\cot u + 1)(-\csc u\cot u) - (\csc u + 1)(-\csc^2 u)}{(\cot u + 1)^2} =$

$$\dfrac{\csc u(-\cot^2 u - \cot u + \csc^2 u + \csc u)}{(\cot u + 1)^2} = \dfrac{\csc u(1 - \cot u + \csc u)}{(\cot u + 1)^2}$$

$\boxed{38}$ $k'(\phi) = \dfrac{(\cos\phi - \sin\phi)(\cos\phi) - (\sin\phi)(-\sin\phi - \cos\phi)}{(\cos\phi - \sin\phi)^2} = \dfrac{1}{(\cos\phi - \sin\phi)^2}$

$\boxed{39}$ $F'(x) = D_x(\tan^2 5x) = 2\tan 5x\sec^2 5x\,(5) = 10\tan 5x\sec^2 5x$

$\boxed{40}$ $H'(z) = \frac{1}{2}(\sin\sqrt{z})^{-1/2}(\cos\sqrt{z})(\frac{1}{2\sqrt{z}}) = \dfrac{\cos\sqrt{z}}{4\sqrt{z}\sqrt{\sin\sqrt{z}}}$

$\boxed{41}$ $g'(\theta) = 4(\tan^3\sqrt[4]{\theta})(\sec^2\sqrt[4]{\theta})(\frac{1}{4}\theta^{-3/4}) = \dfrac{\tan^3(\sqrt[4]{\theta})\sec^2(\sqrt[4]{\theta})}{\sqrt[4]{\theta^3}}$

$\boxed{42}$ $f'(x) = (\csc^3 3x)(2)(\cot 3x)(-3\csc^2 3x) + 3\csc^2 3x(-3\csc 3x\cot 3x)\cot^2 3x =$

$$-3\csc^3 3x\cot 3x\,(3\cot^2 3x + 2\csc^2 3x)$$

Note: In Exercises 43–44 and 46–48, the first equation shown is the result of differentiating the original equation implicitly. The assumption that the denominators are nonzero is made throughout.

$\boxed{43}$ $15x^2 - 2x^2\cdot 2yy' - 4xy^2 + 12y^2y' = 0 \Rightarrow y' = \dfrac{4xy^2 - 15x^2}{12y^2 - 4x^2 y}$

$\boxed{44}$ $6x - 2xyy' - y^2 - y^{-2}y' = 0 \Rightarrow y' = \dfrac{6x - y^2}{2xy + y^{-2}}\cdot\dfrac{y^2}{y^2} = \dfrac{6xy^2 - y^4}{2xy^3 + 1}$

$\boxed{45}$ $y^{3/2} + y = x^{1/2} + 1 \Rightarrow (\frac{3}{2}y^{1/2} + 1)y' = \frac{1}{2}x^{-1/2} \Rightarrow y' = \dfrac{1}{\sqrt{x}\,(3\sqrt{y} + 2)}$

$\boxed{46}$ $2yy' - \frac{1}{2}x^{1/2}y^{-1/2}y' - \frac{1}{2}y^{1/2}x^{-1/2} + 3 = 0 \Rightarrow$

$$y' = \frac{\frac{1}{2}\sqrt{y/x} - 3}{2y - \frac{1}{2}\sqrt{x/y}} \cdot \frac{-2\sqrt{xy}}{-2\sqrt{xy}} = \frac{6\sqrt{xy} - y}{x - 4y\sqrt{xy}}$$

$\boxed{47}$ $x(2yy') + y^2 = \cos(x + 2y)[1 + 2y'] \Rightarrow y' = \dfrac{\cos(x + 2y) - y^2}{2xy - 2\cos(x + 2y)}$

$\boxed{48}$ $y' = -\csc^2(xy)[xy' + y] \Rightarrow y' = -\dfrac{y\csc^2(xy)}{1 + x\csc^2(xy)}$

$\boxed{49}$ $y' = 2 + 2/\sqrt{x^3}$. At $P(4, 6)$, $y' = \frac{9}{4}$. Tangent line: $y - 6 = \frac{9}{4}(x - 4)$ or

$y = \frac{9}{4}x - 3$;   normal line: $y - 6 = -\frac{4}{9}(x - 4)$ or $y = -\frac{4}{9}x + \frac{70}{9}$.

$\boxed{50}$ $x^2y' + 2xy - 3y^2y' = 0 \Rightarrow y' = \dfrac{2xy}{3y^2 - x^2}$. At $P(-3, 1)$, $y' = 1$.

Tangent line: $y - 1 = 1(x + 3)$ or $y = x + 4$;

normal line: $y - 1 = -1(x + 3)$ or $y = -x - 2$.

$\boxed{51}$ The slope of the given line is $-\frac{1}{2}$. Thus, $y' = 3 + 2\sin 2x = 2 \Rightarrow \sin 2x = -\frac{1}{2} \Rightarrow$

$$2x = \frac{7\pi}{6} + 2\pi n \text{ or } \frac{11\pi}{6} + 2\pi n \Rightarrow x = \frac{7\pi}{12} + \pi n \text{ or } \frac{11\pi}{12} + \pi n.$$

$\boxed{52}$ $y' = 2\cos 2x + 2\sin 2x = 0 \Rightarrow \sin 2x = -\cos 2x \Rightarrow \tan 2x = -1 \Rightarrow$

$2x = \frac{3\pi}{4} + \pi n \Rightarrow x = \frac{3\pi}{8} + \frac{\pi}{2}n$. In $[0, 2\pi]$, the solutions are $\frac{3\pi}{8}$, $\frac{7\pi}{8}$, $\frac{11\pi}{8}$, and $\frac{15\pi}{8}$.

$\boxed{53}$ $y' = 15x^2 + \dfrac{2}{\sqrt{x}} \Rightarrow y'' = 30x - \dfrac{1}{\sqrt{x^3}} \Rightarrow y''' = 30 + \dfrac{3}{2\sqrt{x^5}}$

$\boxed{54}$ $y' = 4x - 3 + 5\sin 5x \Rightarrow y'' = 4 + 25\cos 5x \Rightarrow y''' = -125\sin 5x$

$\boxed{55}$ $2x + 4xy' + 4y - 2yy' = 0 \Rightarrow y' = \dfrac{x + 2y}{y - 2x}$. $y'' =$

$\dfrac{(y - 2x)(1 + 2y') - (x + 2y)(y' - 2)}{(y - 2x)^2}$. Substituting for y', the <u>numerator</u> becomes:

$$(y - 2x) + 2(x + 2y) - \left[\frac{(x + 2y)^2}{y - 2x}\right] + 2(x + 2y) = (2x + 9y) - \frac{(x + 2y)^2}{y - 2x}.$$

It now follows that $y'' = \dfrac{(2x + 9y)(y - 2x) - (x + 2y)^2}{(y - 2x)^3} = \dfrac{5(y^2 - 4xy - x^2)}{(y - 2x)^3} =$

$$\frac{5(-8)}{(y - 2x)^3} = -\frac{40}{(y - 2x)^3}.$$

$\boxed{56}$ (a) $m_{AB} = 3$; $f'(x) = 3x^2 - 2x - 5 = 3 \Rightarrow (3x + 4)(x - 2) \Leftrightarrow x = -\frac{4}{3}$ or 2.

(b) $f'(x) = 0 \Rightarrow 3x^2 - 2x - 5 = 0 \Rightarrow (3x - 5)(x + 1) = 0 \Rightarrow x = -1, \frac{5}{3}$.

$$f''(x) = 6x - 2 \Rightarrow f''(-1) = -8 \text{ and } f''(\tfrac{5}{3}) = 8.$$

$\boxed{57}$ (a) $\Delta y = f(x + \Delta x) - f(x) = \left[3(x + \Delta x)^2 - 7\right] - (3x^2 - 7) = 6x\Delta x + 3(\Delta x)^2$

(b) $dy = f'(x)\,dx = 6x\,dx$

(c) $dy - \Delta y = 6x\,dx - \left[6x\Delta x + 3(\Delta x)^2\right] = -3(\Delta x)^2$

$\boxed{58}$ $dy = \dfrac{5(1 - x^2)}{(x^2 + 1)^2}\,dx$; at $x = 2$ and $\Delta x = -0.02$, $dy = \dfrac{-15}{25}(-0.02) = 0.012$;

If $y = f(x)$, then $\Delta y = f(1.98) - f(2) = \frac{99,000}{49,204} - 2 = \frac{148}{12,301} \approx 0.01203154$.

$\boxed{59}$ $A = \frac{1}{4}\sqrt{3}\,x^2$, where x is the length of a side.

$$dA = \frac{1}{2}\sqrt{3}\,x\,dx = \frac{1}{2}\sqrt{3}(4)(\pm 0.03) = \pm 0.06\sqrt{3} \approx \pm 0.104 \text{ in.}^2.$$

$$\frac{\Delta A}{A} \approx \frac{dA}{A} = \frac{\pm 0.06\sqrt{3}}{4\sqrt{3}} = (\pm 0.015) = \pm 1.5\%$$

$\boxed{60}$ $\frac{ds}{dt} = \frac{ds}{dr}\frac{dr}{dt} = (6r - \frac{1}{\sqrt{r+1}})(3t^2 + 2t)$. At $t = 1$, $r = 3$ and $\frac{ds}{dt} = \frac{35}{2} \cdot 5 = \frac{175}{2}$.

$\boxed{61}$ Let $y = g(f(x))$. $dy = g'(f(x))f'(x)\,dx$. With $x = -1$ and $dx = -0.01$,

$$dy = g'(f(-1))f'(-1)(-0.01) = g'(1)f'(-1)(-0.01) = (19)(3)(-0.01) = -0.57.$$

$\boxed{62}$ Let $f(x) = \sqrt[3]{x}$. Using $f(x + \Delta x) \approx f(x) + f'(x)(\Delta x)$ with $x = 64$ and $\Delta x = 0.2$,

$$\sqrt[3]{64.2} \approx 4 + (\tfrac{1}{48})(0.2) \approx 4.004.$$

$\boxed{63}$ (a) $(2f - 3g)'(2) = 2f'(2) - 3g'(2) = 2(4) - 3(2) = 2$.

(b) $(2f - 3g)''(2) = 2f''(2) - 3g''(2) = 2(-2) - 3(1) = -7$.

(c) $(fg)'(2) = f(2)\,g'(2) + g(2)f'(2) = (-1)(2) + (-3)(4) = -14$.

(d) $(fg)'' = (fg' + gf')' = fg'' + 2f'g' + gf''$;

at $x = 2$, the value is $(-1)(1) + 2(4)(2) + (-3)(-2) = 21$.

(e) $\left(\dfrac{f}{g}\right)'(2) = \dfrac{g(2)f'(2) - f(2)\,g'(2)}{\left[g(2)\right]^2} = \dfrac{(-3)(4) - (-1)(2)}{(-3)^2} = -\dfrac{10}{9}$.

(f) $\left(\dfrac{f}{g}\right)'' = \left(\dfrac{gf' - fg'}{g^2}\right)' = \dfrac{g^2\left[(gf'' + g'f') - (fg'' + f'g')\right] - 2gg'(gf' - fg')}{g^4}$;

at $x = 2$, the value is $-\frac{57}{81} = -\frac{19}{27}$.

$\boxed{64}$ $(f \circ g)'(3) = f'(g(3))\,g'(3) = f'(-3) \cdot (-5) =$

$$f'(3) \cdot (-5) \ \{\text{since } f' \text{ is } even\} = 7(-5) = -35$$

$(g \circ f)'(3) = g'(f(3))f'(3) = g'(-3) \cdot 7 =$

$$-g'(3) \cdot 7 \ \{\text{since } g' \text{ is } odd\} = -(-5) \cdot 7 = 35$$

$\boxed{65}$ (a) $f'(x) = \dfrac{1}{(x + 1)^{2/3}}$, undefined at $x = -1$. $\lim\limits_{x \to -1^+} f'(x) = \infty$ and

$$\lim\limits_{x \to -1^-} f'(x) = \infty \Rightarrow f \text{ has a vertical tangent line at } (-1, -4).$$

(b) $f'(x) = \dfrac{4}{3(x - 8)^{1/3}}$, undefined at $x = 8$. $\lim\limits_{x \to 8^+} f'(x) = \infty$ and

$$\lim\limits_{x \to 8^-} f'(x) = -\infty \Rightarrow f \text{ has a cusp at } (8, -1).$$

66 $\lim\limits_{h \to 0^+} \dfrac{f(2+h) - f(2)}{h} = \lim\limits_{h \to 0^+} \dfrac{\left[2(2+h) - 1\right]^3 - 3^3}{h} =$

$$\lim\limits_{h \to 0^+} \dfrac{54h + 36h^2 + 8h^3}{h} = 54$$

$\lim\limits_{h \to 0^-} \dfrac{f(2+h) - f(2)}{h} = \lim\limits_{h \to 0^-} \dfrac{\left[5(2+h)^2 + 34(2+h) - 61\right] - 3^3}{h} =$

$$\lim\limits_{h \to 0^-} \dfrac{5h^2 + 54h}{h} = 54$$

Note: It is not sufficient to show that the derivative of each piece of the function

evaluated at 2 is equal to 54 since the second piece could be replaced by

$5x^2 + 34x + c$, $c \neq -61$, yielding similar results but not being continuous.

67 $dR = 4kT^3\, dT \Rightarrow \dfrac{dR}{R} = \dfrac{4kT^3}{kT^4}\, dT = 4\dfrac{dT}{T}$.

Since $\dfrac{dT}{T} \approx \dfrac{\Delta T}{T} = 0.5\%$, we have $\dfrac{\Delta R}{R} \approx \dfrac{dR}{R} = 4(0.5\%) = 2\%$.

68 $V = \frac{4}{3}\pi r^3 \Rightarrow dV = 4\pi r^2\, dr \Rightarrow dr = \dfrac{dV}{4\pi r^2}$ and $S = 4\pi r^2 \Rightarrow dS = 8\pi r\, dr$.

Thus, $dS = 8\pi r \cdot \dfrac{dV}{4\pi r^2} = \dfrac{2\, dV}{r} = \dfrac{2(12)}{4} = 6 \text{ cm}^2$.

69 $S = \pi r\sqrt{r^2 + 8^2} \Rightarrow \dfrac{dS}{dr} = \pi\left[r \cdot \frac{1}{2}(r^2 + 64)^{-1/2}(2r) + (r^2 + 64)^{1/2}\right] =$

$\pi(r^2 + 64)^{-1/2}\left[r^2 + (r^2 + 64)\right] = \dfrac{2\pi(r^2 + 32)}{(r^2 + 64)^{1/2}}$. When $r = 6$, $\dfrac{dS}{dr} = \dfrac{2\pi(68)}{10} =$

$\frac{68\pi}{5} \text{ ft}^2/\text{ft}$.

70 Let I denote the intensity and r the distance from the source.

$I = \frac{c}{r^2} \Rightarrow dI = -\frac{2c}{r^3}\, dr \Rightarrow \dfrac{dI}{I} = \dfrac{-2c/r^3}{c/r^2}\, dr = -2\dfrac{dr}{r}$ and $\dfrac{\Delta I}{I} \approx -2\dfrac{\Delta r}{r}$.

$\dfrac{\Delta I}{I} = 10\% \Rightarrow -2\dfrac{\Delta r}{r} = 10\% \Rightarrow \dfrac{\Delta r}{r} \approx -5\%$, or 5% closer.

71 Let h denote the depth of the water and w the width of

the surface of the water. Using similar triangles and

Figure 71, $\frac{x}{h} = \frac{1}{2} \Rightarrow h = 2x$ and hence, $w = 3 + h$.

The cross-sectional area of the water at one end of the

trough is $A = \frac{1}{2}\left[3 + (3 + h)\right]h = 3h + \frac{1}{2}h^2$. Hence,

the volume V of water is $V = 10A = 30h + 5h^2$.

$\dfrac{dV}{dt} = (30 + 10h)\dfrac{dh}{dt} = \left[30 + 10(1)\right] \cdot \left[\frac{1}{4}(\frac{1}{12})\right] = \frac{5}{6}\text{ft}^3/\text{min}$.

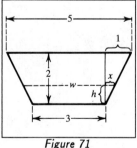

Figure 71

72 Let x and y denote the distances from the intersection of A and B, respectively, and L

the distance between A and B. $L^2 = x^2 + y^2 \Rightarrow 2L\dfrac{dL}{dt} = 2x\dfrac{dx}{dt} + 2y\dfrac{dy}{dt}$.

$x = \frac{1}{4}$, $y = \frac{1}{2}$, $\dfrac{dx}{dt} = -20$, $\dfrac{dy}{dt} = -40$, and $L = \frac{1}{4}\sqrt{5} \Rightarrow$

$$\dfrac{dL}{dt} = -20\sqrt{5} \approx -44.7\,\text{mi/hr}. \quad (\text{Distance is decreasing.})$$

73 Assuming p is a function of v, $pv = c \Rightarrow p + v\frac{dp}{dv} = 0 \Rightarrow \frac{dp}{dv} = -\frac{p}{v}$.

74 Let x denote the distance of the man in the train from the center of the bridge, y the distance of the man in the boat from a point (on the water) directly below the center of the bridge, and L the distance between the two men.

$L^2 = x^2 + y^2 + 20^2 \Rightarrow 2L\frac{dL}{dt} = 2x\frac{dx}{dt} + 2y\frac{dy}{dt}$. Ten seconds later, we have

(in ft and ft/sec) $x = 880$, $y = \frac{880}{3}$, $L = \sqrt{880^2 + (\frac{880}{3})^2 + 20^2} \approx 927.8$,

$\frac{dx}{dt} = 88$, and $\frac{dy}{dt} = \frac{88}{3}$. Thus, $\frac{dL}{dt} = \dfrac{880^2}{9\sqrt{880^2 + (\frac{880}{3})^2 + 20^2}} \approx 92.7\,\text{ft/sec}$.

75 (a) Consider the ferris wheel to be in the xy-plane with the origin centered at the rotating axis of the ferris wheel. The (x, y) coordinates of any passenger can be given by $(50\cos\theta, 50\sin\theta)$, where θ is the angle in standard position with terminal side passing through the point (x, y). Since ground level is at $y = -60$, $h = 50\sin\theta + 60$. The wheel rotates 2π radians every 30 seconds, so $\theta = \frac{2\pi}{30}t - \frac{\pi}{2}$. Note that at $t = 0$, $\theta = -\frac{\pi}{2}$. Thus,

$$h(t) = 50\sin\left(\tfrac{2\pi}{30}t - \tfrac{\pi}{2}\right) + 60 = 60 - 50\cos\tfrac{\pi}{15}t.$$

(b) $h = 55 \Rightarrow \cos\frac{\pi}{15}t = 0.1 \Rightarrow t_0 = \frac{15}{\pi}\cos^{-1}0.1 \approx 7.02$.

$$h'(t) = \tfrac{10\pi}{3}\sin\tfrac{\pi}{15}t \text{ and } h'(t_0) = \sqrt{11}\,\pi \approx 10.4\text{ ft/sec}.$$

76 (a) If θ is the angle in standard position with terminal side passing through A, then the coordinates of A are $(2\cos\theta, 2\sin\theta)$. The wheel rotates at 4π rad/sec and

$$t = 0 \Rightarrow \theta = 0, \text{ so } \theta = 4\pi t. \text{ Thus, } A \text{ is located at } (2\cos 4\pi t, 2\sin 4\pi t).$$

(b) The y-coordinate of B is always 0. The x-coordinate of B is the sum of the x-coordinate of A and $6\cos\phi$, where ϕ is the acute angle that the connecting rod makes with the x-axis. So $B(x, y) = (2\cos 4\pi t + 6\cos\phi, 0)$. Since $\overline{AB} = 6$,

$$\sin\phi = \frac{|2\sin(4\pi t)|}{6} = \frac{|\sin(4\pi t)|}{3} \text{ and } \cos\phi = \tfrac{1}{3}\sqrt{9 - \sin^2(4\pi t)}.$$

It follows that the x-coordinate of B is $2\cos(4\pi t) + 2\sqrt{9 - \sin^2(4\pi t)}$.

(c) Let $f(t) = 2\cos(4\pi t) + 2\sqrt{9 - \sin^2(4\pi t)}$.

$$f'(t) = -8\pi\sin(4\pi t) + \left[9 - \sin^2(4\pi t)\right]^{-1/2}\left[-8\pi\sin(4\pi t)\cos(4\pi t)\right].$$

At $A(0, 2)$, $\theta = \frac{\pi}{2}$ and $t = \frac{1}{8}$. $f'(\frac{1}{8}) = -8\pi$ in./sec. B is moving to the left.

Chapter 4: Applications of the Derivative

Note: In this chapter and subsequent chapters, we will use the following notation:

MAX for absolute maximum (maxima), *MIN* for absolute minimum (minima),

LMAX for local maximum (maxima), *LMIN* for local minimum (minima),

and *CN* for critical number(s).

1. *MAX* of 4 at 2; *MIN* of 0 at 4; *LMAX* at $x = 2$, $6 \leq x \leq 8$; *LMIN* at $x = 4$,
$6 < x < 8$, $x = 10$. *Note:* There is *not* a local minimum at $x = 6$ since there is no *open* interval containing 6 such that $f(x) \geq f(6)$ for every x in the interval.

   The same holds for $x = 8$. However, there are local maxima at $x = 6$ and $x = 8$.

2. *MAX* of 5 at 6; *MIN* of -1 at 11;

   LMAX at $3 \leq x < 4$, $x = 6$, $x = 9$; *LMIN* at $3 < x \leq 4$, $x = 8$

3. (a) *MIN:* $f(-3) = -6$; *MAX:* none   (b) *MIN:* none; *MAX:* $f(-1) = \frac{2}{3}$

   (c) *MIN:* none; *MAX:* $f(-1) = \frac{2}{3}$ (d) *MIN:* $f(1) = -\frac{2}{3}$; *MAX:* $f(3) = 6$

4. (a) *MIN:* $f(-1) = f(1) = -\frac{1}{4}$; *MAX:* $f(-2) = f(0) = f(2) = 0$

   (b) *MIN:* $f(1) = -\frac{1}{4}$; *MAX:* none

   (c) *MIN:* $f(1) = -\frac{1}{4}$; *MAX:* $f(0) = 0$ (d) *MIN:* none; *MAX:* $f(-2) = 0$

5. $f'(x) = x - 2$; $f'(x) = 0 \Rightarrow x = 2$.

   (a) *MIN:* $f(2) = -2$; *MAX:* none   (b) *MIN:* none; *MAX:* none

   (c) *MIN:* $f(2) = -2$; *MAX:* none   (d) *MIN:* $f(2) = -2$; *MAX:* $f(5) = \frac{5}{2}$

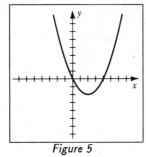

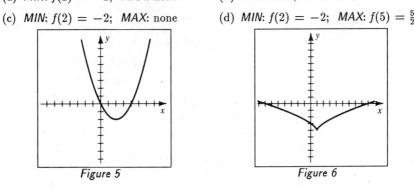

Figure 5   Figure 6

6. $f'(x) = \frac{2}{3}(x - 1)^{-1/3} = \frac{2}{3\sqrt[3]{x - 1}}$; $f'(x) \neq 0$; $f'(x)$ DNE if $x = 1$.

   (a) *MIN:* $f(1) = -4$; *MAX:* $f(9) = 0$ (b) *MIN:* none; *MAX:* $f(2) = -3$

   (c) *MIN:* $f(1) = -4$; *MAX:* none   (d) *MIN:* none; *MAX:* $f(0) = -3$

Note: In Exercises 7–10, the derivative and its *CN* are given first, then all candidates for the *MAX* and *MIN* are listed, and finally the *MAX* and *MIN* are given.

7. $f'(x) = -12x - 6x^2 = -6x(x + 2) = 0 \Rightarrow x = 0, -2$.

   $f(0) = 5, f(-2) = -3, f(-3) = 5,$ and $f(1) = -3$; *MAX:* 5, *MIN:* -3

[8] $f'(x) = 6x - 10 = 0 \Rightarrow x = \frac{5}{3}$.

$$f(\tfrac{5}{3}) = -\tfrac{4}{3}, \ f(-1) = 20, \text{ and } f(3) = 4; \quad \textit{MAX: } 20, \textit{ MIN: } -\tfrac{4}{3}$$

[9] $f'(x) = -\frac{2}{3}x^{-1/3} \neq 0$, however, $f'(x)$ is undefined at $x = 0$.

$$f(0) = 1, \ f(-1) = 0, \text{ and } f(8) = -3; \quad \textit{MAX: } 1, \textit{ MIN: } -3$$

[10] $f'(x) = 4x^3 - 10x = 2x(2x^2 - 5) = 0 \Rightarrow x = 0, \ \pm\sqrt{5/2}$, however, $-\sqrt{5/2} \notin [0, 2]$.

$$f(\sqrt{5/2}) = -\tfrac{9}{4}, \ f(0) = 4, \text{ and } f(2) = 0; \quad \textit{MAX: } 4, \textit{ MIN: } -\tfrac{9}{4}$$

[11] $f'(x) = 8x - 3 = 0 \Leftrightarrow x = \frac{3}{8}$ [12] $g'(x) = 2 \Rightarrow g$ has no *CN*

[13] $s'(t) = 6t^2 + 2t - 20 = 2(3t - 5)(t + 2) = 0 \Leftrightarrow t = \frac{5}{3}, -2$

[14] $K'(z) = 12z^2 + 10z - 42 = 2(2z - 3)(3z + 7) = 0 \Leftrightarrow z = \frac{3}{2}, -\frac{7}{3}$

[15] $F'(w) = 4w^3 - 32 = 4(w - 2)(w^2 + 2w + 4) = 0 \Rightarrow w = 2, \ w \in \mathbb{R}$

[16] $k'(r) = 5r^4 - 6r^2 + 1 = (5r^2 - 1)(r^2 - 1) = 0 \Leftrightarrow r = \pm\sqrt{1/5}, \ \pm 1$

[17] $f'(z) = \dfrac{z}{\sqrt{z^2 - 16}} = 0$ if $z = 0$, but 0 is not in the domain of f.

$f'(z)$ is undefined when $z = \pm 4$ — these are endpoint extrema.

$f'(z)$ is undefined for $|z| < 4$, but these values are not in the domain of f.

[18] $M'(x) = \dfrac{2x - 1}{3(x^2 - x - 2)^{2/3}} = 0$ at $x = \frac{1}{2}$ and does not exist at $x = -1, 2$.

[19] $h'(x) = \dfrac{4x^2 - 5x - 8}{\sqrt{x^2 - 4}} = 0 \Rightarrow x = \dfrac{5 \pm \sqrt{153}}{8} \approx 2.17, -0.92.$ Only $\dfrac{5 + \sqrt{153}}{8}$ is in

the domain of h. $h'(x)$ is undefined at $x = \pm 2$.

[20] $T'(v) = \dfrac{(4v + 1)v}{(v^2 - 16)^{1/2}} + 4(v^2 - 16)^{1/2} = \dfrac{8v^2 + v - 64}{(v^2 - 16)^{1/2}} = 0$ if $v = \dfrac{-1 \pm \sqrt{2049}}{16}$

$\approx 2.8, -2.9$, which are not in the domain of T. T' is undefined when $v = \pm 4$,

which are also endpoints. The *CN* are $v = \pm 4$.

[21] $g'(t) = \dfrac{2t^2}{3(2t - 5)^{2/3}} + 2t(2t - 5)^{1/3} = \dfrac{2t(7t - 15)}{3(2t - 5)^{2/3}} = 0$ at $t = 0, \frac{15}{7}$,

and fails to exist if $t = \frac{5}{2}$.

[22] $g'(x) = \dfrac{-2x^2 + 3x + 9}{\sqrt{9 - x^2}} = 0 \Rightarrow x = -\frac{3}{2}, 3.$ g' is undefined at ± 3.

[23] $G'(x) = \dfrac{-2x^2 + 6x - 18}{(x^2 - 9)^2} \neq 0$ and fails to exist at $x = \pm 3$.

Since ± 3 are not in the domain of G, there are no *CN*.

[24] $f'(s) = \dfrac{s(5s + 8)}{(5s + 4)^2} = 0 \Leftrightarrow s = 0, -\frac{8}{5}.$ f' is undefined at $s = -\frac{4}{5}$, but this value of s

is not in the domain of f. Thus, the *CN* are $s = 0, -\frac{8}{5}$.

[25] $f'(t) = 2\sin t \cos t + \sin t = \sin t(2\cos t + 1) = 0 \Leftrightarrow \sin t = 0$ or $\cos t = -\frac{1}{2} \Leftrightarrow$

$$t = \pi n, \ t = \tfrac{2\pi}{3} + 2\pi n, \ t = \tfrac{4\pi}{3} + 2\pi n$$

[26] $g'(t) = 12\sin^2 t \cos t - 6\sqrt{2}\cos t \sin t = 6\sin t \cos t(2\sin t - \sqrt{2}) = 0 \Leftrightarrow$

$\sin t = 0, \cos t = 0,$ or $\sin t = \sqrt{2}/2 \Leftrightarrow t = \pi n, \ \frac{\pi}{2} + \pi n, \ \frac{\pi}{4} + 2\pi n, \ \frac{3\pi}{4} + 2\pi n$

$\boxed{27}$ $K'(\theta) = 2\cos 2\theta - 2\sin\theta = 2(1 - 2\sin^2\theta) - 2\sin\theta = -4\sin^2\theta - 2\sin\theta + 2 = 0$

$\Leftrightarrow (2\sin\theta - 1)(\sin\theta + 1) = 0 \Leftrightarrow \sin\theta = \frac{1}{2}, -1 \Leftrightarrow$

$$\theta = \frac{\pi}{6} + 2\pi n, \frac{5\pi}{6} + 2\pi n, \text{ or } \frac{3\pi}{2} + 2\pi n$$

$\boxed{28}$ $f'(x) = -24\cos^2 x \sin x - 6\cos 2x - 6 = -24\cos^2 x \sin x - 6(2\cos^2 x - 1) - 6 = 0$

$\Leftrightarrow -12\cos^2 x(2\sin x + 1) = 0 \Leftrightarrow \cos x = 0 \text{ or } \sin x = -\frac{1}{2} \Leftrightarrow$

$$x = \frac{\pi}{2} + \pi n, \frac{7\pi}{6} + 2\pi n, \frac{11\pi}{6} + 2\pi n$$

$\boxed{29}$ $f'(x) = \dfrac{(1 - \sin x)\cos x - (1 + \sin x)(-\cos x)}{(1 - \sin x)^2} = \dfrac{2\cos x}{(1 - \sin x)^2} = 0 \Leftrightarrow \cos x = 0$

$\Leftrightarrow x = \frac{\pi}{2} + 2\pi n$ or $\frac{3\pi}{2} + 2\pi n$. Note that $x = \frac{\pi}{2} + 2\pi n$ are not in the domain of f.

Thus, the CN are $x = \frac{3\pi}{2} + 2\pi n$.

$\boxed{30}$ $g'(\theta) = 2\sqrt{3} + 4\cos 4\theta = 0 \Leftrightarrow \cos 4\theta = -\frac{1}{2}\sqrt{3} \Leftrightarrow 4\theta = \frac{5\pi}{6} + 2\pi n, \frac{7\pi}{6} + 2\pi n$

$\Leftrightarrow \theta = \frac{5\pi}{24} + \frac{\pi}{2}n, \frac{7\pi}{24} + \frac{\pi}{2}n$

$\boxed{31}$ $k'(u) = 1 - \sec^2 u = 0 \Rightarrow \sec u = \pm 1 \Rightarrow u = \pi n$. *Note:* $\tan u$ is undefined where

$\sec u$ is, so we do not need to look for CN where $k'(u)$ is undefined.

$\boxed{32}$ $p'(z) = 3\sec^2 z - 4 = 0 \Leftrightarrow \sec z = \pm\frac{2}{3}\sqrt{3} \Leftrightarrow z = \frac{\pi}{6} + \pi n, \frac{5\pi}{6} + \pi n$

$\boxed{33}$ $H'(\phi) = -\csc^2\phi - \csc\phi\cot\phi = 0 \Leftrightarrow \csc\phi(\csc\phi + \cot\phi) = 0 \Leftrightarrow$

$\csc\phi = 0$ or $\csc\phi = -\cot\phi$. Now, $\csc\phi \neq 0$ for all ϕ and $\csc\phi = -\cot\phi \Leftrightarrow$

$\dfrac{1}{\sin\phi} = -\dfrac{\cos\phi}{\sin\phi} \Leftrightarrow \cos\phi = -1$ and $\sin\phi \neq 0$, which is not possible.

Thus, there are no CN.

$\boxed{34}$ $g'(x) = 2 - \csc^2 x = 0 \Leftrightarrow \csc x = \pm\sqrt{2} \Leftrightarrow x = \frac{\pi}{4} + \pi n$ or $\frac{3\pi}{4} + \pi n \Leftrightarrow$

$$x = (2n + 1)\frac{\pi}{4}$$

$\boxed{35}$ $f'(x) = 2x\sec(x^2 + 1)\tan(x^2 + 1) = 0$ when $x = 0$ or $\tan(x^2 + 1) = 0$ since

$\sec(x^2 + 1) \neq 0$ for any x. Thus, $x = 0$ or $x^2 + 1 = k\pi \Leftrightarrow x = 0$ or

$x = \pm\sqrt{k\pi - 1}$, where k is any *positive* integer.

$\boxed{36}$ An equivalent form for $s(t)$ is $\dfrac{1 + \cos t}{1 - \cos t}$, $\cos t \neq 0$; $s'(t) = \dfrac{-2\sin t}{(1 - \cos t)^2} = 0 \Leftrightarrow$

$\sin t = 0 \Leftrightarrow t = \pi n$. $s'(t)$ is undefined when $\cos t = 1$, but these values are not in

the domain of s. Also, $\cos t = 1 \Rightarrow \sin t = 2\pi n$. Thus, the CN are $(2n + 1)\pi$.

$\boxed{37}$ (a) Since $f'(x) = \frac{1}{3}x^{-2/3}$, $f'(0)$ does not exist. If $a \neq 0$, then $f'(a) \neq 0$. Hence 0 is

the only critical number of f. The number $f(0) = 0$ is not a local extremum,

since $f(x) < 0$ if $x < 0$ and $f(x) > 0$ if $x > 0$.

(b) The only critical number is 0 for the same reasons given in part (a).

The number $f(0) = 0$ is a local minimum, since $f(x) > 0$ if $x \neq 0$.

$\boxed{38}$ $f'(0)$ does not exist by Example 4, Section 3.2. $f'(x) = 1$ if $x > 0$ and

$f'(x) = -1$ if $x < 0$. f has no tangent line at $x = 0$ and $x = 0$ is the only CN of f.

Since $f(x) > 0$ for $x \neq 0$, $f(0) = 0$ is a *LMIN* (and *MIN*).

[39] (a) There is a critical number, 0, but $f(0)$ is not a local extremum,

since $f(x) < f(0)$ if $x < 0$ and $f(x) > f(0)$ if $x > 0$.

(c) The function is continuous at every number a, since $\lim_{x \to a} f(x) = f(a)$.

If $0 < x_1 < x_2 < 1$, then $f(x_1) < f(x_2)$ and

hence there is neither a maximum nor a minimum on $(0, 1)$.

(d) This does not contradict Theorem (4.3) because the interval $(0, 1)$ is open.

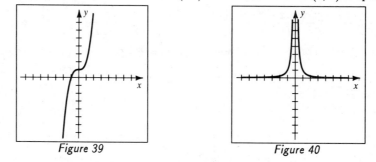

Figure 39　　　　　　　　　　　　Figure 40

[40] (a) There are no critical numbers, and hence, no local extrema.

(c) The function is continuous at every number a in $(0, 1)$, since $\lim_{x \to a} f(x) = f(a)$.

If $0 < x_1 < x_2 < 1$, then $f(x_1) > f(x_2)$ and

hence there is neither a maximum nor a minimum on $(0, 1)$.

(d) This does not contradict Theorem (4.3) because the interval $(0, 1)$ is open.

[41] (a) If $f(x) = cx + d$ and $c \neq 0$, then $f'(x) = c \neq 0$.

Hence there are no critical numbers.

(b) On $[a, b]$ the function has absolute extrema at a and b.

[42] Since $f(x) = f(c)$ for all x in (a, b), the conditions of (4.2) and (4.4) are satisfied.

[43] If $x = n$ is an integer, then $f'(n)$ does not exist.

Otherwise, $f'(x) = 0$ for every $x \neq n$.

[44] By Exercise 41 of §2.2,

$\lim_{x \to a} f(x)$ does not exist for any a, and thus f is not continuous at every x.

Hence, by (3.5), f is not differentiable at any x and every x must be a *CN*.

[45] If $f(x) = ax^2 + bx + c$ and $a \neq 0$, then $f'(x) = 2ax + b$.

Hence $-b/(2a)$ is the only critical number of f.

[46] The derivative is a quadratic. It exists everywhere and can have 0, 1, or 2 zeros.

The functions used to plot the figures are $f(x) = x^3 - x$, $f(x) = x^3$,

and $f(x) = x^3 + x$, respectively. See *Figures 46a, b, c*.

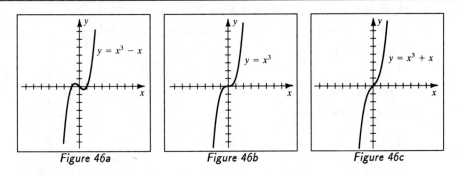

Figure 46a   Figure 46b   Figure 46c

47 Since $f'(x) = nx^{n-1}$, the only possible critical number is $x = 0$, and $f(0) = 0$.

If n is even, then $f(x) > 0$ if $x \neq 0$ and hence 0 is a local minimum.

If n is odd, then 0 is not an extremum, since $f(x) < 0$ if $x < 0$ and $f(x) > 0$ if $x > 0$.

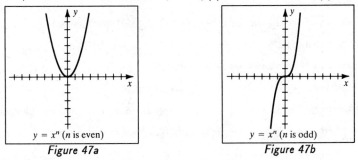

Figure 47a   Figure 47b

48 The derivative of a polynomial f of degree n is a polynomial of degree $n - 1$.

The derivative exists everywhere and has at most $n - 1$ distinct, real zeros.

By (4.5) and (4.6), these are the only points at which f can have local extrema.

49 When reading graphs it is generally difficult to estimate coordinates beyond $\pm\frac{1}{2}$ of the smallest grid marking. For example, if a graph is marked in units of 0.2, then we will usually have difficulty estimating coordinates beyond the accuracy of ± 0.1. The answers given carry more accuracy than most students will be able to achieve without some additional aid. *MIN:* $f(0.48) \approx 0.36$; *MAX:* $f(-1) = f(1) = 2$

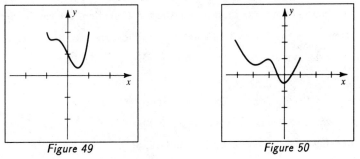

Figure 49   Figure 50

50 *MIN:* $f(-0.05) \approx -0.51$; *MAX:* $f(-\pi) \approx 2.11$

$\boxed{51}$ f is not differentiable at $x \approx -0.92$, 1.41. $f'(x) = 0$ at $x \approx -2.41$, 0.41.

The critical numbers are approximately -2.41, -0.92, 0.41, and 1.41.

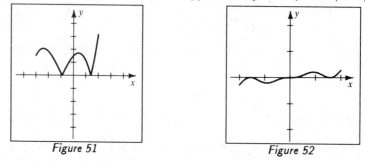

Figure 51   Figure 52

$\boxed{52}$ The critical numbers occur where $f'(x) = 0$ at approximately ± 1.57, 0, and ± 0.92.

<u>Exercises 4.2</u>

$\boxed{1}$ The idea is to find the values at which the slope of the tangent line is equal to the slope of the secant line. After drawing a line between the two endpoints of the graph, it appears that these values are approximately 3 and 7.

$\boxed{2}$ As in Exercise 1, we have the values 2, 4.5, and 9.

Note: In Exercises 3–8, since the given functions are continuous and differentiable everywhere, we only need to verify that $f(a) = f(b)$ and solve $f'(c) = 0$.

$\boxed{3}$ $f(0) = f(4) = 11$. $f'(c) = 6c - 12 = 0 \Rightarrow c = 2$.

$\boxed{4}$ $f(-7) = f(1) = -9$. $f'(c) = -12 - 4c = 0 \Rightarrow c = -3$.

$\boxed{5}$ $f(-3) = f(3) = 118$. $f'(c) = 4c(c^2 + 2) = 0 \Rightarrow c = 0$.

$\boxed{6}$ $f(-1) = f(1) = 0$. $f'(c) = 3c^2 - 1 = 0 \Rightarrow c = \pm 1/\sqrt{3}$.

$\boxed{7}$ $f(0) = f(\pi) = 0$. $f'(c) = 2\cos 2c = 0 \Rightarrow c = \frac{\pi}{4} + \frac{\pi}{2}n$.

In the open interval $(0, \pi)$, $c = \frac{\pi}{4}$ and $\frac{3\pi}{4}$.

$\boxed{8}$ $f(0) = f(2\pi) = 3$. $f'(c) = -2\sin 2c - 2\sin c = 0 \Rightarrow 2\sin c \cos c + \sin c = 0 \Rightarrow$ $\sin c(2\cos c + 1) = 0 \Rightarrow c = \pi n, \frac{2\pi}{3} + 2\pi n, \frac{4\pi}{3} + 2\pi n$.

In the open interval $(0, 2\pi)$, $c = \frac{2\pi}{3}$, π, and $\frac{4\pi}{3}$.

Note: In Exercises 9–24, unless otherwise specified, the functions are continuous on the indicated closed interval and differentiable on the associated open interval, thereby satisfying the hypotheses of the mean value theorem (MVT).

$\boxed{9}$ $f(3) - f(1) = f'(c)(3 - 1) \Rightarrow 37 - 3 = (10c - 3)(2) \Rightarrow c = 2$.

$\boxed{10}$ $f(5) - f(1) = f'(c)(5 - 1) \Rightarrow 76 - 0 = (6c + 1)(4) \Rightarrow c = 3$.

$\boxed{11}$ $f(1)$ is undefined $\Rightarrow f$ is not continuous on $[0, 2]$.

$\boxed{12}$ $f(2)$ is undefined $\Rightarrow f$ is not continuous on $[-2, 3]$.

$\boxed{13}$ $f'(0)$ does not exist $\Rightarrow f$ is not differentiable on $(-8, 8)$.

$\boxed{14}$ $f'(3)$ does not exist $\Rightarrow f$ is not differentiable on $(-1, 4)$.

15 $f(4) - f(1) = f'(c)(4 - 1) \Rightarrow 5 - 5 = (1 - 4/c^2)(3) \Rightarrow c = 2 \in (1, 4)$.

16 $f(1) - f(-1) = f'(c)\left[1 - (-1)\right] \Rightarrow 23 - (-23) = (15c^4 + 15c^2 + 15)(2) \Rightarrow$

$15c^4 + 15c^2 - 8 = 0 \Rightarrow c^2 = \frac{1}{30}(-15 + \sqrt{705})$ since $c^2 > 0$.

$$c = \pm\sqrt{\tfrac{1}{30}(-15 + \sqrt{705})} \approx \pm 0.62 \in (-1, 1).$$

17 $f(1) - f(-1) = f'(c)\left[1 - (-1)\right] \Rightarrow 3 - (-1) = (3c^2 - 4c + 1)(2) \Rightarrow$

$$3c^2 - 4c - 1 = 0 \Rightarrow c = \tfrac{1}{3}(2 - \sqrt{7}) \approx -0.22 \in (-1, 1).$$

18 $f(-1) - f(-8) = f'(c)\left[-1 - (-8)\right] \Rightarrow 4 - 7 = (-c^{-2/3})(7) \Rightarrow$

$c = \pm\left(\tfrac{7}{3}\right)^{3/2} \approx \pm 3.56$. Choose the negative value for the interval $(-8, -1)$.

19 $f(5) - f(1) = f'(c)(5 - 1) \Rightarrow 6 - 4 = \tfrac{1}{2}(c - 1)^{-1/2}(4) \Rightarrow c = 2$.

20 $f(6) - f(-1) = f'(c)\left[6 - (-1)\right] \Rightarrow 4 - 1 = \tfrac{2}{3}(c + 2)^{-1/3}(7) \Rightarrow$

$$c = \left(\tfrac{14}{9}\right)^3 - 2 = \tfrac{1286}{729} \approx 1.76.$$

21 $f(4) - f(-2) = f'(c)\left[4 - (-2)\right] \Rightarrow 65 - (-7) = 3c^2(6) \Rightarrow c = \pm 2$.

Choose 2 since the number c must be in the *open* interval $(-2, 4)$.

22 $f(6) - f(-3) = f'(c)\left[6 - (-3)\right] \Rightarrow 240 - (-39) = (3c^2 + 4)(9) \Rightarrow c = \pm 3$.

Choose 3 since the number c must be in the *open* interval $(-3, 6)$.

23 $f(\tfrac{\pi}{2}) - f(0) = f'(c)(\tfrac{\pi}{2} - 0) \Rightarrow 1 - 0 = (\cos c)(\tfrac{\pi}{2}) \Rightarrow$

$$\cos c = \tfrac{2}{\pi} \Rightarrow c \approx 0.88 \in (0, \tfrac{\pi}{2}).$$

24 $f(\tfrac{\pi}{4}) - f(0) = f'(c)(\tfrac{\pi}{4} - 0) \Rightarrow 1 - 0 = (\sec^2 c)(\tfrac{\pi}{4}) \Rightarrow$

$$\sec c = \tfrac{2}{\sqrt{\pi}} \Rightarrow c \approx 0.48 \in (0, \tfrac{\pi}{4}).$$

25 $f(-1) = f(1) = 1$. $f'(x) = 1$ if $x > 0$, $f'(x) = -1$ if $x < 0$, and $f'(0)$ does not exist.

This does not contradict Rolle's theorem,

because f is not differentiable throughout the open interval $(-1, 1)$.

26 $f(0) = 8 = f(2)$. $f'(x) = 2(x - 1)^{-1/3} \neq 0$.

Since $f'(x)$ does not exist at $x = 1$, f is not differentiable at each $x \in (0, 2)$.

27 $f(4) - f(-1) = f'(c)\left[4 - (-1)\right] \Rightarrow 1 - (-4) = (-4/c^2)(5) \Rightarrow c^2 = -4$.

The last equation has no real solutions.

This is not a contradiction, because f is not continuous on the interval $[-1, 4]$.

28 If $[\![a]\!] = n$ and $b - a \geq 1$, then $b \geq a + 1$ and $[\![b]\!] \geq n + 1$.

Thus, $f(b) - f(a) = [\![b]\!] - [\![a]\!] \geq 1$. Trying to solve $f(b) - f(a) = f'(c)(b - a)$,

we obtain $f'(c) = \dfrac{f(b) - f(a)}{b - a} \geq \dfrac{1}{b - a} > 0$. This equation has no solution since

$f'(x) = 0$ if x is not an integer, and $f'(x)$ does not exist if x is an integer.

There is no contradiction, since $b - a \geq 1 \Rightarrow [a, b]$ contains at least one integer at

which f is neither continuous nor differentiable.

29 Let $f(x) = px + q$. Since f is a polynomial, it is continuous on every closed interval $[a, b]$. Since $f'(x) = p$, f is differentiable on every open interval (a, b).

If c is in (a, b), then $f(b) - f(a) = (pb + q) - (pa + q) =$

$$p(b - a) = f'(c)(b - a) \text{ for every } c.$$

30 If $f(x) = rx^2 + sx + t \{ r \neq 0 \}$, then $f'(c) = 2rc + s$.

Hence, the equation $f(b) - f(a) = f'(c)(b - a)$ is linear in c for each a and b.

Therefore, there can be only one solution for c, that is,

$$c = \frac{1}{2r} \left[\frac{f(b) - f(a)}{b - a} - s \right] = \frac{1}{2r} \left[\frac{r(b^2 - a^2) - s(b - a)}{b - a} - s \right] = \tfrac{1}{2}(a + b),$$

the midpoint of the interval.

31 If f has degree 3, then $f'(x)$ is a polynomial of degree 2. Consequently the equation $f(b) - f(a) = f'(x)(b - a)$ has at most two solutions. If f has degree n,

then $f'(x)$ is a polynomial of degree $n - 1$ and there are at most $n - 1$ solutions.

32 Assume f has four distinct real zeros. Then by Rolle's theorem, f' must have 3 distinct real zeros located between consecutive zeros of f. However, f' is quadratic and can have at most 2 distinct real zeros. The proof can be extended to polynomials of degree n. Assume f is a polynomial of degree n with $(n + 1)$ zeros. Then, by repeated use of Rolle's theorem, f' is of degree $(n - 1)$ with n zeros, f'' is of degree $(n - 2)$ with $(n - 1)$ zeros and finally $f^{(n-2)}$ is of degree 2 (quadratic) with 3 zeros. This is a contradiction as above.

33 Let x be any number in $(a, b]$. Applying the mean value theorem to the interval $[a, x]$ yields $f(x) - f(a) = f'(c)(x - a) = 0(x - a) = 0$.

Thus, $f(x) = f(a)$, and hence f is a constant function.

34 Let $x \in (a, b]$. Applying the mean value theorem on the interval $[a, x]$,

$$f(x) - f(a) = (c)(x - a) \Rightarrow f(x) = c(x - a) + f(a) \Rightarrow f(x) = cx + d,$$

where $d = f(a) - ca$.

35 Let $s(t)$ be the distance traveled, $s'(t)$ the instantaneous velocity, t_A the time of departure, and t_B the time of arrival. By the mean value theorem,

$$s'(c) = \frac{s(t_B) - s(t_A)}{t_B - t_A} = \frac{50}{1} = 50 \text{ mi/hr for some time } c \text{ in } (0, 1).$$

36 Let t_1 be the time when the temperature was $44\,°\text{F}$ and t_2 the time it was $-56\,°\text{F}$. By the MVT, for some time t between t_1 and t_2,

$$\frac{dT}{dt} = \frac{T(t_2) - T(t_1)}{t_2 - t_1} = -\frac{100}{12} = (-8\tfrac{1}{3})\,°\text{F/hr} < -8\,°\text{F/hr}.$$

37 Let t_1 be the time when the person weighed 487 pounds and t_2 the time when the person weighed 130 pounds. By the MVT, for some time t between t_1 and t_2,

$$\frac{dW}{dt} = \frac{W(t_2) - W(t_1)}{t_2 - t_1} = -\frac{357}{8} = -44.625 \text{ lb/mo} < -44 \text{ lb/mo}.$$

38 Let t_1 be the time when the capacitor stored 2 millicoulombs and t_2 the time it stored 10. By the MVT, for some time t between t_1 and t_2,

$$I = \frac{dQ}{dt} = \frac{Q(t_2) - Q(t_1)}{t_2 - t_1} = \frac{8}{15} \frac{\text{millicoulombs}}{\text{milliseconds}} \approx 0.533 > \tfrac{1}{2} \text{ coulomb/sec (ampere)}.$$

39 Let $f(x) = \sin x$ on $[u, v]$. By the MVT,

$$|f(v) - f(u)| = |f'(c)||u - v| = |\cos c||u - v| \le |u - v| \text{ since } |\cos c| \le 1.$$

40 Let $f(h) = \sqrt{1 + h}$. For $h \ge 0$, f satisfies the MVT. Thus,

$$f(h) - f(0) = f'(c)\,(h - 0) \text{ for some } c > 0 \Rightarrow \sqrt{1 + h} = 1 + \frac{1}{2\sqrt{1 + c}}h < 1 + \tfrac{1}{2}h.$$

41 The slope of the line is equal to the slope of the tangent line at $c \approx 0.64$.

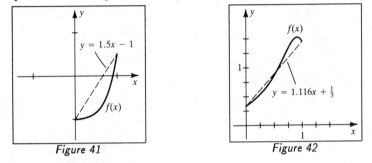

Figure 41   Figure 42

42 The slope of the line is equal to the slope of the tangent line at $c \approx 0.31, 0.84$.

Exercises 4.3

Note: We will use the notation ↑ for increasing and ↓ for decreasing in this chapter and subsequent chapters. Determining the sign of the derivative can be accomplished by using a table method as shown in the solution of Exercise 13.

1   $f'(x) = -7 - 8x = 0 \Leftrightarrow x = -\tfrac{7}{8}$. On $(-\infty, -\tfrac{7}{8})$, $f'(x) > 0$ and f is ↑ on $(-\infty, -\tfrac{7}{8}]$. On $(-\tfrac{7}{8}, \infty)$, $f'(x) < 0$ and f is ↓ on $[-\tfrac{7}{8}, \infty)$. $f(-\tfrac{7}{8}) = \frac{129}{16}$ is a *LMAX*.

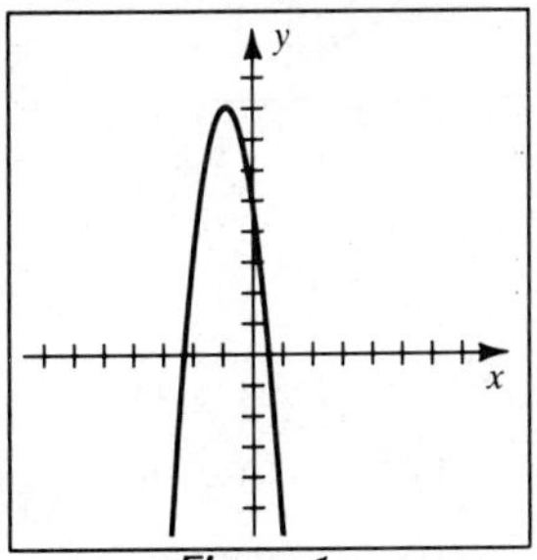

Figure 1 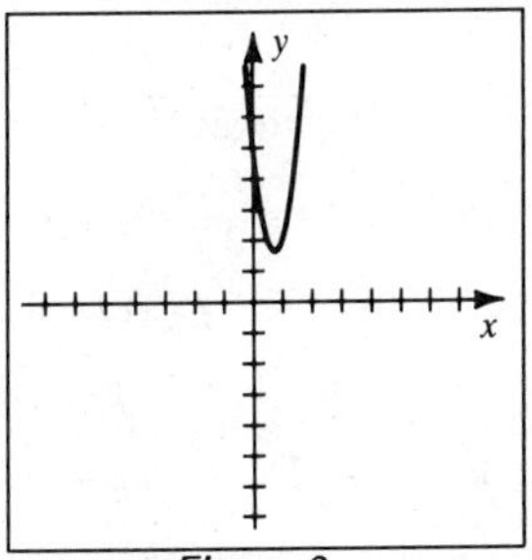   Figure 2

2   $f'(x) = 12x - 9 = 0 \Leftrightarrow x = \tfrac{3}{4}$. On $(-\infty, \tfrac{3}{4})$, $f'(x) < 0$ and f is ↓ on $(-\infty, \tfrac{3}{4}]$. On $(\tfrac{3}{4}, \infty)$, $f'(x) > 0$ and f is ↑ on $[\tfrac{3}{4}, \infty)$. Thus, $f(\tfrac{3}{4}) = \frac{13}{8}$ is a *LMIN*.

$\boxed{3}$ $f'(x) = 6x^2 + 2x - 20 = 2(3x - 5)(x + 2) = 0 \Leftrightarrow x = \frac{5}{3}, -2$. On $(-\infty, -2) \cup$

$(\frac{5}{3}, \infty)$, $f'(x) > 0$ and f is $\uparrow$ on $(-\infty, -2] \cup [\frac{5}{3}, \infty)$. On $(-2, \frac{5}{3})$, $f'(x) < 0$ and

f is $\downarrow$ on $[-2, \frac{5}{3}]$. Thus, $f(-2) = 29$ is a *LMAX* and $f(\frac{5}{3}) = -\frac{548}{27}$ is a *LMIN*.

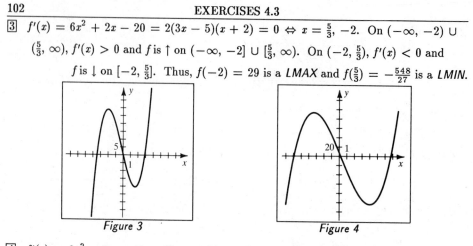

Figure 3   Figure 4

$\boxed{4}$ $f'(x) = 3x^2 - 2x - 40 = (3x + 10)(x - 4) = 0 \Leftrightarrow x = -\frac{10}{3}, 4$.

On $(-\infty, -\frac{10}{3}) \cup (4, \infty)$, $f'(x) > 0$ and f is $\uparrow$ on $(-\infty, -\frac{10}{3}] \cup [4, \infty)$.

On $(-\frac{10}{3}, 4)$, $f'(x) < 0$ and f is $\downarrow$ on $[-\frac{10}{3}, 4]$.

Thus, $f(-\frac{10}{3}) = \frac{2516}{27} \approx 93.2$ is a *LMAX* and $f(4) = -104$ is a *LMIN*.

$\boxed{5}$ $f'(x) = 4x^3 - 16x = 4x(x^2 - 4) = 0 \Leftrightarrow x = -2, 0, 2$.

On $(-\infty, -2) \cup (0, 2)$ $f'(x) < 0$ and f is $\downarrow$ on $(-\infty, -2] \cup [0, 2]$.

On $(-2, 0) \cup (2, \infty)$, $f'(x) > 0$ and f is $\uparrow$ on $[-2, 0] \cup [2, \infty)$.

Thus, $f(0) = 1$ is a *LMAX* and $f(-2) = f(2) = -15$ are *LMIN*.

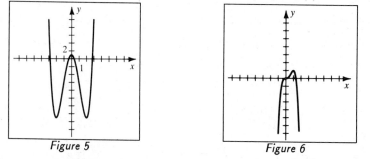

Figure 5   Figure 6

$\boxed{6}$ $f'(x) = 12x^2 - 12x^3 = 12x^2(1 - x) = 0 \Leftrightarrow x = 0, 1$.

On $(-\infty, 0) \cup (0, 1)$, $f'(x) > 0$ and f is $\uparrow$ on $(-\infty, 1]$.

On $(1, \infty)$, $f'(x) < 0$ and f is $\downarrow$ on $[1, \infty)$. Thus, $f(1) = 1$ is a *LMAX*.

$\boxed{7}$ $f'(x) = 30x^2(x - 1)^2 + 2(x - 1)(10x^3) = 10x^2(x - 1)(5x - 3) = 0 \Leftrightarrow x = 0, \frac{3}{5}, 1$.

The sign of f' is determined by the sign of the quadratic $(x - 1)(5x - 3)$.

f is $\uparrow$ on $(-\infty, \frac{3}{5}] \cup [1, \infty)$ and $\downarrow$ on $[\frac{3}{5}, 1]$.

Thus, $f(\frac{3}{5}) = \frac{216}{625} \approx 0.35$ is a *LMAX* and $f(1) = 0$ is a *LMIN*. See *Figure 7*.

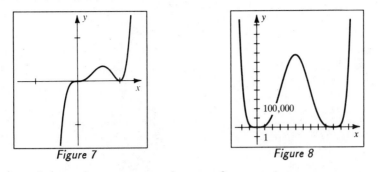

Figure 7   Figure 8

$\boxed{8}$ $f'(x) = 4(x^2 - 10x)^3(2x - 10) = 8x^3(x - 10)^3(x - 5) = 0 \Leftrightarrow x = 0, 5, 10.$

Since each factor is raised to an odd power, f' will change sign at each *CN*.

Hence, $f'(x) < 0$ on $(-\infty, 0) \cup (5, 10)$, and $f'(x) > 0$ on $(0, 5) \cup (10, \infty)$.

f is $\downarrow$ $(-\infty, 0] \cup [5, 10]$ and $\uparrow$ on $[0, 5] \cup [10, \infty)$.

$\qquad\qquad\qquad f(0) = f(10) = 0$ are *LMIN* and $f(5) = 390{,}625$ is a *LMAX*.

$\boxed{9}$ $f'(x) = \frac{4}{3}(x^{1/3} + x^{-2/3}) = \frac{4(x + 1)}{3x^{2/3}} = 0 \Leftrightarrow x = -1.$ f' fails to exist at $x = 0$.

The sign of f' is determined by the factor $(x + 1)$. On $(-\infty, -1)$, $f'(x) < 0$ and

f is $\downarrow$ on $(-\infty, -1]$. On $(-1, 0) \cup (0, \infty)$, $f'(x) > 0$ and f is $\uparrow$ on $[-1, \infty)$.

$\qquad\qquad$ Thus, $f(-1) = -3$ is a *LMIN*. There is a vertical tangent line at $x = 0$.

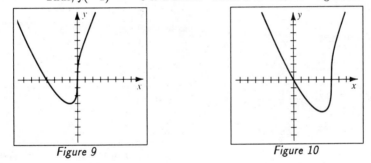

Figure 9   Figure 10

$\boxed{10}$ $f'(x) = x \cdot \frac{1}{3}(x - 5)^{-2/3} + (x - 5)^{1/3} = \frac{4x - 15}{3(x - 5)^{2/3}} = 0 \Leftrightarrow x = \frac{15}{4}.$

f' fails to exist at $x = 5$. On $(-\infty, \frac{15}{4})$, $f'(x) < 0$ and f is $\downarrow$ on $(-\infty, \frac{15}{4}]$.

On $(\frac{15}{4}, 5) \cup (5, \infty)$, $f'(x) > 0$ and f is $\uparrow$ on $[\frac{15}{4}, \infty)$.

Thus, $f(\frac{15}{4}) = -\frac{15}{4}\sqrt[3]{\frac{5}{4}} \approx -4.04$ is a *LMIN*. There is a vertical tangent line at $x = 5$.

$\boxed{11}$ $f'(x) = x^{2/3}(2)(x - 7) + (x - 7)^2(\frac{2}{3})x^{-1/3} = \frac{2(x - 7)(4x - 7)}{3x^{1/3}} = 0 \Leftrightarrow x = 7, \frac{7}{4}.$

f' fails to exist at $x = 0$. f' changes sign at each of its *CN*.

On $(-\infty, 0) \cup (\frac{7}{4}, 7)$, $f'(x) < 0$ and f is $\downarrow$ on $(-\infty, 0] \cup [\frac{7}{4}, 7]$.

On $(0, \frac{7}{4}) \cup (7, \infty)$ $f'(x) > 0$ and f is $\uparrow$ on $[0, \frac{7}{4}] \cup [7, \infty)$. Thus, $f(0) = f(7) = 2$

$\qquad\qquad$ are *LMIN* and $f(\frac{7}{4}) = \frac{441}{16}\sqrt[3]{\frac{49}{16}} + 2 \approx 42.03$ is a *LMAX*. See *Figure 11*.

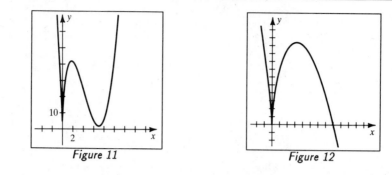

Figure 11   Figure 12

[12] $f'(x) = -x^{2/3} + \frac{2}{3}x^{-1/3}(8-x) = \dfrac{16-5x}{3x^{1/3}} = 0 \Leftrightarrow x = \frac{16}{5}$. f' fails to exist at

$x = 0$. The sign of f' changes at each critical number. On $(-\infty, 0) \cup (\frac{16}{5}, \infty)$,

$f'(x) < 0$ and f is $\downarrow$ on $(-\infty, 0] \cup [\frac{16}{5}, \infty)$. On $(0, \frac{16}{5})$, $f'(x) > 0$ and f is $\uparrow$ on

$[0, \frac{16}{5}]$. Thus, $f(0) = 0$ is a *LMIN* and $f(\frac{16}{5}) = \frac{24}{5}(\frac{16}{5})^{2/3} \approx 10.42$ is a *LMAX*.

[13] $f'(x) = \frac{2}{3}x^3(x^2-4)^{-2/3} + 2x(x^2-4)^{1/3} = \dfrac{8x(x^2-3)}{3(x^2-4)^{2/3}} = 0 \Leftrightarrow x = 0, \pm\sqrt{3}$.

f' fails to exist at $x = \pm 2$. Using a table, we find the following.

Interval	$8x$	$(x^2-4)^{2/3}$	(x^2-3)	f'	f
$(-\infty, -2)$	$-$	$+$	$+$	$-$	$\downarrow$
$(-2, -\sqrt{3})$	$-$	$+$	$+$	$-$	$\downarrow$
$(-\sqrt{3}, 0)$	$-$	$+$	$-$	$+$	$\uparrow$
$(0, \sqrt{3})$	$+$	$+$	$-$	$-$	$\downarrow$
$(\sqrt{3}, 2)$	$+$	$+$	$+$	$+$	$\uparrow$
$(2, \infty)$	$+$	$+$	$+$	$+$	$\uparrow$

Thus, f is $\uparrow$ on $[-\sqrt{3}, 0] \cup [\sqrt{3}, \infty)$ and f is $\downarrow$ on $(-\infty, -\sqrt{3}] \cup [0, \sqrt{3}]$.

$f(0) = 0$ is a *LMAX* and $f(\pm\sqrt{3}) = -3$ are *LMIN*.

There are no extrema at $x = \pm 2$, but there are vertical tangent lines at these values.

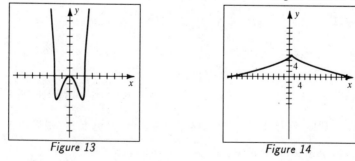

Figure 13   Figure 14

[14] $f'(x) = -\frac{1}{3}(x^2 - 2x + 1)^{-2/3}(2x - 2) = \dfrac{-2}{3(x-1)^{1/3}} \neq 0$.

f' fails to exist at 1. f is $\uparrow$ on $(-\infty, 1]$ and $\downarrow$ on $[1, \infty)$.

Thus, $f(1) = 8$ is a *LMAX*. There is a cusp at $x = 1$.

$\boxed{15}$ $f'(x) = x \cdot \frac{1}{2}(x^2 - 9)^{-1/2}(2x) + (x^2 - 9)^{1/2} = \dfrac{2x^2 - 9}{\sqrt{x^2 - 9}} = 0 \Leftrightarrow x = \pm\sqrt{\frac{9}{2}},$

which are not in the domain of f. f' fails to exist at ± 3.

f' is positive throughout its domain, and hence f is ↑ on $(-\infty, -3] \cup [3, \infty)$.

There are no extrema. There are vertical tangent lines at $x = \pm 3$.

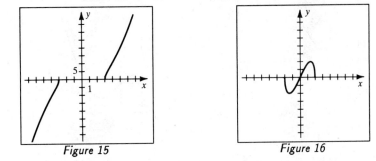

Figure 15   Figure 16

$\boxed{16}$ $f'(x) = -x^2(4 - x^2)^{-1/2} + (4 - x^2)^{1/2} = \dfrac{2(2 - x^2)}{(4 - x^2)^{1/2}} = 0$ at $x = \pm\sqrt{2}.$

f' fails to exist at $x = \pm 2$. Since the denominator is positive on $(-2, 2)$, $f'(x) < 0$

on $(-2, -\sqrt{2}) \cup (\sqrt{2}, 2)$ and $f'(x) > 0$ on $(-\sqrt{2}, \sqrt{2})$. Thus, f is ↓ on $[-2, -\sqrt{2}] \cup$

$[-\sqrt{2}, 2]$ and f is ↑ on $[-\sqrt{2}, \sqrt{2}]$. $f(-\sqrt{2}) = -2$ is a *LMIN* and $f(\sqrt{2}) = 2$ is

a *LMAX*. *Note:* $x = \pm 2$ are endpoints of the domain of f.

$\boxed{17}$ $f'(x) = \cos x - \sin x = 0$ if $x = \frac{\pi}{4}, \frac{5\pi}{4}$. Since $\cos x > \sin x$ on $[0, \frac{\pi}{4}) \cup (\frac{5\pi}{4}, 2\pi]$,

it follows that $f'(x) > 0$ on these intervals.   Hence, f is ↑ on $[0, \frac{\pi}{4}] \cup [\frac{5\pi}{4}, 2\pi]$.

Similarly, $\cos x < \sin x$ on $(\frac{\pi}{4}, \frac{5\pi}{4})$ and f is ↓ on $[\frac{\pi}{4}, \frac{5\pi}{4}]$.

Thus, $f(\frac{\pi}{4}) = \sqrt{2}$ is a *LMAX* and $f(\frac{5\pi}{4}) = -\sqrt{2}$ is a *LMIN*.

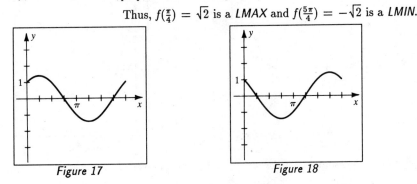

Figure 17   Figure 18

$\boxed{18}$ $f'(x) = -\sin x - \cos x = 0 \Leftrightarrow \sin x = -\cos x$ if $x = \frac{3\pi}{4}, \frac{7\pi}{4}$.

Since $-\sin x < \cos x$ on $[0, \frac{3\pi}{4}) \cup (\frac{7\pi}{4}, 2\pi]$, $f'(x) < 0$ on these intervals.

(To see this, consider the graphs of $y = -\sin x$ and $y = \cos x$.) Hence, f is ↓

on $[0, \frac{3\pi}{4}] \cup [\frac{7\pi}{4}, 2\pi]$. Similarly, $-\sin x > \cos x$ on $(\frac{3\pi}{4}, \frac{7\pi}{4})$ and f is ↑ on $[\frac{3\pi}{4}, \frac{7\pi}{4}]$.

Thus, $f(\frac{3\pi}{4}) = -\sqrt{2}$ is a *LMIN* and $f(\frac{7\pi}{4}) = \sqrt{2}$ is a *LMAX*.

$\boxed{19}$ $f'(x) = \frac{1}{2} - \cos x = 0$ if $x = \frac{\pi}{3}, \frac{5\pi}{3}$. Since $\cos x > \frac{1}{2}$ on $[0, \frac{\pi}{3}) \cup (\frac{5\pi}{3}, 2\pi]$,

$f'(x) < 0$ on these intervals and f is $\downarrow$ on $[0, \frac{\pi}{3}] \cup [\frac{5\pi}{3}, 2\pi]$.

Similarly, $\cos x < \frac{1}{2}$ on $(\frac{\pi}{3}, \frac{5\pi}{3})$ and f is $\uparrow$ on $[\frac{\pi}{3}, \frac{5\pi}{3}]$. Thus,

$\qquad f(\frac{\pi}{3}) = \frac{\pi}{6} - \frac{1}{2}\sqrt{3} \approx -0.34$ is a *LMIN* and $f(\frac{5\pi}{3}) = \frac{5\pi}{6} + \frac{1}{2}\sqrt{3} \approx 3.48$ is a *LMAX*.

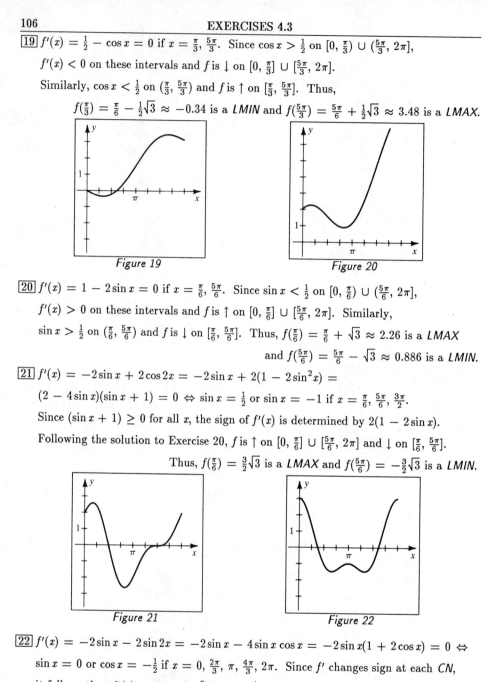

Figure 19   Figure 20

$\boxed{20}$ $f'(x) = 1 - 2\sin x = 0$ if $x = \frac{\pi}{6}, \frac{5\pi}{6}$. Since $\sin x < \frac{1}{2}$ on $[0, \frac{\pi}{6}) \cup (\frac{5\pi}{6}, 2\pi]$,

$f'(x) > 0$ on these intervals and f is $\uparrow$ on $[0, \frac{\pi}{6}] \cup [\frac{5\pi}{6}, 2\pi]$. Similarly,

$\sin x > \frac{1}{2}$ on $(\frac{\pi}{6}, \frac{5\pi}{6})$ and f is $\downarrow$ on $[\frac{\pi}{6}, \frac{5\pi}{6}]$. Thus, $f(\frac{\pi}{6}) = \frac{\pi}{6} + \sqrt{3} \approx 2.26$ is a *LMAX*

$\qquad\qquad\qquad\qquad\qquad\qquad$ and $f(\frac{5\pi}{6}) = \frac{5\pi}{6} - \sqrt{3} \approx 0.886$ is a *LMIN*.

$\boxed{21}$ $f'(x) = -2\sin x + 2\cos 2x = -2\sin x + 2(1 - 2\sin^2 x) =$

$(2 - 4\sin x)(\sin x + 1) = 0 \Leftrightarrow \sin x = \frac{1}{2}$ or $\sin x = -1$ if $x = \frac{\pi}{6}, \frac{5\pi}{6}, \frac{3\pi}{2}$.

Since $(\sin x + 1) \geq 0$ for all x, the sign of $f'(x)$ is determined by $2(1 - 2\sin x)$.

Following the solution to Exercise 20, f is $\uparrow$ on $[0, \frac{\pi}{6}] \cup [\frac{5\pi}{6}, 2\pi]$ and $\downarrow$ on $[\frac{\pi}{6}, \frac{5\pi}{6}]$.

$\qquad\qquad\qquad$ Thus, $f(\frac{\pi}{6}) = \frac{3}{2}\sqrt{3}$ is a *LMAX* and $f(\frac{5\pi}{6}) = -\frac{3}{2}\sqrt{3}$ is a *LMIN*.

Figure 21   Figure 22

$\boxed{22}$ $f'(x) = -2\sin x - 2\sin 2x = -2\sin x - 4\sin x \cos x = -2\sin x(1 + 2\cos x) = 0 \Leftrightarrow$

$\sin x = 0$ or $\cos x = -\frac{1}{2}$ if $x = 0, \frac{2\pi}{3}, \pi, \frac{4\pi}{3}, 2\pi$. Since f' changes sign at each *CN*,

it follows that $f'(x) < 0$ on $(0, \frac{2\pi}{3}) \cup (\pi, \frac{4\pi}{3})$ and $f'(x) > 0$ on $(\frac{2\pi}{3}, \pi) \cup (\frac{4\pi}{3}, 2\pi)$.

Hence f is $\downarrow$ on $[0, \frac{2\pi}{3}] \cup [\pi, \frac{4\pi}{3}]$ and $\uparrow$ on $[\frac{2\pi}{3}, \pi] \cup [\frac{4\pi}{3}, 2\pi]$.

$f(0) = f(2\pi) = 3$ are endpoint maxima. *Note:* These are not local extrema since

there is no *open* interval in $[0, 2\pi]$ that contains 0 or 2π.

$\qquad\qquad f(\pi) = -1$ is a *LMAX*. $f(\frac{2\pi}{3}) = f(\frac{4\pi}{3}) = -\frac{3}{2}$ are *LMIN*.

[23] $f'(x) = (x^3 - 9x)^{-2/3}(x^2 - 3)$. The first factor is positive wherever it is defined

$(x \neq 0, \pm 3)$ and so the sign of f' is determined by $(x^2 - 3)$. Hence,

$f'(x) > 0$ for $|x| > \sqrt{3}$ and $f'(x) < 0$ for $|x| < \sqrt{3}$.

     Thus, $f(-\sqrt{3}) = (6\sqrt{3})^{1/3} \approx 2.18$ is a *LMAX* and $f(\sqrt{3}) = -(6\sqrt{3})^{1/3}$ is a *LMIN*.

[24] $f'(x) = \dfrac{x}{\sqrt{x^2 + 4}} = 0 \Leftrightarrow x = 0$. $f'(x) < 0$ for $x < 0$ and $f'(x) > 0$ for $x > 0$.

     Thus, $f(0) = 2$ is a *LMIN*.

[25] $f'(x) = (x - 2)^2(x + 1)^3(7x - 5) = 0 \Leftrightarrow x = -1, \frac{5}{7}$, or 2. Since the first factor is

nonnegative and the second and third factors change sign at -1 and $\frac{5}{7}$, respectively,

it follows that $f'(x) > 0$ on $(-\infty, -1) \cup (\frac{5}{7}, 2) \cup (2, \infty)$ and $f'(x) < 0$ on $(-1, \frac{5}{7})$.

     Thus, $f(-1) = 0$ is a *LMAX* and $f(\frac{5}{7}) = -9^3(12)^4/7^7 \approx -18.36$ is a *LMIN*.

[26] $f'(x) = 2x(3x - 5)(x - 5)^3 = 0 \Leftrightarrow x = 0, \frac{5}{3}$, or 5. Since f' changes sign at each

CN, $f'(x) < 0$ on $(-\infty, 0) \cup (\frac{5}{3}, 5)$ and $f'(x) > 0$ on $(0, \frac{5}{3}) \cup (5, \infty)$.

     Thus, $f(0) = f(5) = 0$ are *LMIN* and $f(\frac{5}{3}) = (\frac{5}{3})^2(-\frac{10}{3})^4 \approx 342.94$ is a *LMAX*.

[27] $f'(x) = \dfrac{-3x + 12}{2x^3\sqrt{x - 3}} = 0 \Leftrightarrow x = 4$.

f' fails to exist at $x = 0$ and 3, but 0 is not in the domain of f.

     If $3 < x < 4$, $f'(x) > 0$ and if $x > 4$, $f'(x) < 0$. Thus, $f(4) = \frac{1}{16}$ is a *LMAX*.

[28] $f'(x) = \dfrac{x(3x + 28)}{2(x + 7)^{3/2}} = 0 \Leftrightarrow x = 0, -\frac{28}{3}$. f' fails to exist at $x = -7$.

However, -7 and $-\frac{28}{3}$ are not in the domain of f.

     If $-7 < x < 0$, $f'(x) < 0$ and if $x > 0$, $f'(x) > 0$. Thus, $f(0) = 0$ is a *LMIN*.

[29] $f'(x) = \frac{1}{2}\sec\frac{1}{2}x \tan\frac{1}{2}x = 0 \Leftrightarrow \tan\frac{1}{2}x = 0$ $(\sec\frac{1}{2}x \neq 0) \Leftrightarrow \frac{1}{2}x = \pi n \Leftrightarrow x = 2\pi n$.

On $[-\frac{\pi}{2}, \frac{\pi}{2}]$, the only *CN* is 0. Since $f'(x) < 0$ on $[-\frac{\pi}{2}, 0)$ and

                                    $f'(x) > 0$ on $(0, \frac{\pi}{2}]$, $f(0) = 1$ is a *LMIN*.

[30] $f'(x) = -2\cot x \csc^2 x - 2\csc^2 x = -2\csc^2 x(\cot x + 1) = 0$ on $[\frac{\pi}{6}, \frac{5\pi}{6}] \Rightarrow x = \frac{3\pi}{4}$

since $\csc^2 x \neq 0$. f' fails to exist at $x = \frac{\pi}{2}$ but $\frac{\pi}{2}$ is not in the domain of f. Since the

     sign of f' changes from negative to positive at $x = \frac{3\pi}{4}$, $f(\frac{3\pi}{4}) = -1$ is a *LMIN*.

[31] $f'(x) = 2\sec^2 x - 2\tan x \sec^2 x = 2\sec^2 x(1 - \tan x) = 0$ on $[-\frac{\pi}{3}, \frac{\pi}{3}] \Rightarrow x = \frac{\pi}{4}$ since

$\sec^2 x \neq 0$. Since f' changes from positive to negative at $x = \frac{\pi}{4}$, $f(\frac{\pi}{4}) = 1$ is a *LMAX*.

[32] $f'(x) = \sec^2 x - 2\sec x \tan x = \sec x(\sec x - 2\tan x) = 0 \Leftrightarrow$

$\sec x = 2\tan x$ {since $\sec x \neq 0$} $\Leftrightarrow 1 = 2\sin x$ on $[-\frac{\pi}{4}, \frac{\pi}{4}] \Rightarrow x = \frac{\pi}{6}$.

     Since f' changes from positive to negative at $x = \frac{\pi}{6}$, $f(\frac{\pi}{6}) = -\sqrt{3}$ is a *LMAX*.

[33] $y' = \frac{1}{2} - \sin x = 0$ on $[-2\pi, 2\pi] \Rightarrow x = -\frac{11\pi}{6}, -\frac{7\pi}{6}, \frac{\pi}{6}, \frac{5\pi}{6}$.

$\sin x > \frac{1}{2}$ on $(\frac{\pi}{6}, \frac{5\pi}{6}) \cup (-\frac{11\pi}{6}, -\frac{7\pi}{6})$ and $f'(x) < 0$ on these intervals.

$\sin x < \frac{1}{2}$ on $[-2\pi, -\frac{11\pi}{6}) \cup (-\frac{7\pi}{6}, \frac{\pi}{6}) \cup (\frac{5\pi}{6}, 2\pi]$ and $f'(x) > 0$ on these intervals.

     Thus, there are *LMIN* at $x = -\frac{7\pi}{6}, \frac{5\pi}{6}$ and *LMAX* at $x = -\frac{11\pi}{6}, \frac{\pi}{6}$.

$\boxed{34}$ $y' = \frac{1}{2}\sqrt{3} - \cos x = 0$ on $[-2\pi, 2\pi] \Rightarrow x = \pm\frac{11\pi}{6}, \pm\frac{\pi}{6}$.

$\cos x > \frac{1}{2}\sqrt{3}$ on $(-2\pi, -\frac{11\pi}{6}) \cup (-\frac{\pi}{6}, \frac{\pi}{6}) \cup (\frac{11\pi}{6}, 2\pi)$ and $f'(x) < 0$ on these intervals.

$\cos x < \frac{1}{2}\sqrt{3}$ on $(-\frac{11\pi}{6}, -\frac{\pi}{6}) \cup (\frac{\pi}{6}, \frac{11\pi}{6})$ and $f'(x) > 0$ on these intervals.

Thus, *LMIN* at $x = -\frac{11\pi}{6}, \frac{\pi}{6}$ and *LMAX* at $x = -\frac{\pi}{6}, \frac{11\pi}{6}$.

Note: In 35–39, the functions listed are the ones that were used to obtain the graphs.

The graph for Exercise 40 was drawn freehand.

$\boxed{35}$ $f(x) = \frac{7}{12\sqrt[3]{4}}x^{2/3}(x^2 - 16) + 3$

$\boxed{36}$ $f(x) = \frac{5}{3\sqrt[3]{4}}x(x - 5)^{2/3}$

$\boxed{37}$ $f(x) = \frac{5}{4}(x - 5)^2(x - 2)$

$\boxed{38}$ $f(x) = \frac{7}{16}x^4 - \frac{7}{2}x^2 + 3$

$\boxed{39}$ $f(x) = \frac{6}{3125}x^5 - \frac{2}{25}x^3$

$\boxed{40}$

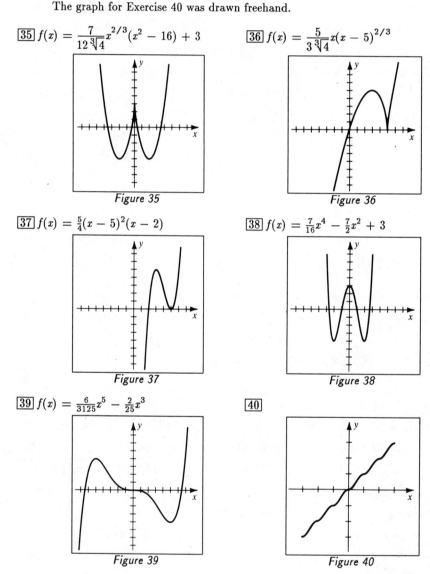

Figure 35   Figure 36

Figure 37   Figure 38

Figure 39   Figure 40

$\boxed{41}$ (a) Max: $f(-1.31) \approx 10.13$

    (b) increasing on $[-2, -1.31]$; decreasing on $[-1.31, 2]$

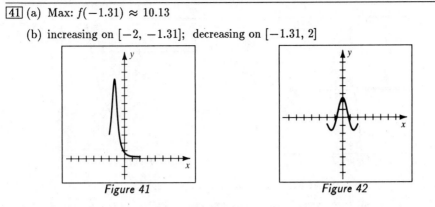

Figure 41   Figure 42

$\boxed{42}$ (a) Max: $f(0) = 2.5$; min: $f(\pm 1.45) \approx -1.59$

    (b) increasing on $[-1.45, 0]$ and $[1.45, 2]$; decreasing on $[-2, -1.45]$ and $[0, 1.45]$

$\boxed{43}$ At $x \approx -0.51$, $f'(x) = 0$ and changes sign from positive to negative.

    At $x \approx 0.49$, $f'(x) = 0$ and changes sign from negative to positive.

                 There is a *LMAX* at $x \approx -0.51$ and a *LMIN* at $x \approx 0.49$.

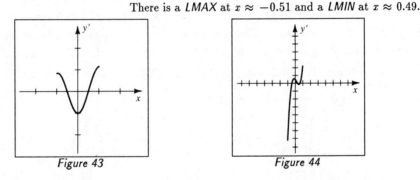

Figure 43   Figure 44

$\boxed{44}$ At $x \approx -0.44$ and $x \approx 0.63$, $f'(x) = 0$ and changes sign from negative to positive.

    At $x \approx 0.30$, $f'(x) = 0$ and changes sign from positive to negative.

                There is a *LMAX* at $x \approx 0.30$ and *LMIN* at $x \approx -0.44$ and 0.63.

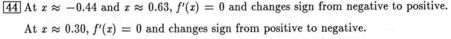

Exercises 4.4

Note: Throughout this section and all subsequent sections, *CU* denotes concave up, *CD*, concave down, and *PI*, point(s) of inflection.

$\boxed{1}$ $f'(x) = 3x^2 - 4x + 1 = (3x - 1)(x - 1) = 0 \Leftrightarrow x = \frac{1}{3}, 1$. $f''(x) = 6x - 4$.

    $f''(\frac{1}{3}) = -2 < 0 \Rightarrow f(\frac{1}{3}) = \frac{31}{27}$ is a *LMAX*; $f''(1) = 2 > 0 \Rightarrow f(1) = 1$ is a *LMIN*.

    Since $f''(x) < 0$ if $x < \frac{2}{3}$ and $f''(x) > 0$ if $x > \frac{2}{3}$, *PI* at $x = \frac{2}{3}$,

                  CD on $(-\infty, \frac{2}{3})$ and *CU* on $(\frac{2}{3}, \infty)$. See *Figure 1*.

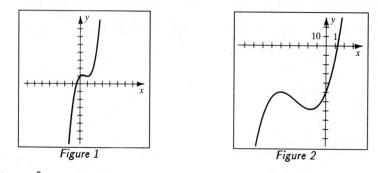

Figure 1   Figure 2

$\boxed{2}$ $f'(x) = 3x^2 + 20x + 25 = (3x + 5)(x + 5) = 0 \Leftrightarrow x = -5, -\frac{5}{3}$.

$f''(x) = 6x + 20$. $f''(-5) = -10 < 0 \Rightarrow f(-5) = -50$ is a *LMAX*.

$f''(-\frac{5}{3}) = 10 > 0 \Rightarrow f(-\frac{5}{3}) = -\frac{1850}{27} \approx -68.5$ is a *LMIN*.

Since $f''(x) < 0$ if $x < -\frac{10}{3}$ and $f''(x) > 0$ if $x > -\frac{10}{3}$,

$\qquad\qquad\qquad$ *PI* at $x = -\frac{10}{3}$, *CD* on $(-\infty, -\frac{10}{3})$ and *CU* on $(-\frac{10}{3}, \infty)$.

$\boxed{3}$ $f'(x) = 12x^3 - 12x^2 = 12x^2(x - 1) = 0 \Leftrightarrow x = 0, 1$.

$f''(x) = 36x^2 - 24x = 12x(3x - 2)$. $f''(1) = 12 > 0 \Rightarrow f(1) = 5$ is a *LMIN*.

$f''(0) = 0$ gives no information. By the first derivative test, $x = 0$ is not an

extremum. $f''(x) = 0$ at $x = 0, \frac{2}{3}$. f'' changes sign at each of these points.

$f''(x) > 0$ and f is *CU* on $(-\infty, 0) \cup (\frac{2}{3}, \infty)$. $f''(x) < 0$ and f is *CD* on $(0, \frac{2}{3})$.

$\qquad\qquad\qquad\qquad\qquad\qquad\qquad$ Thus, there are *PI* at $x = 0, \frac{2}{3}$.

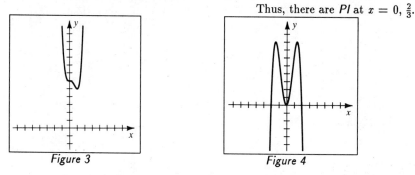

Figure 3   Figure 4

$\boxed{4}$ $f'(x) = 16x - 8x^3 = 8x(2 - x^2) = 0 \Leftrightarrow x = 0, \pm\sqrt{2}$. $f''(x) = 16 - 24x^2$.

$f''(0) = 16 > 0 \Rightarrow f(0) = 0$ is a *LMIN*. $f''(\pm\sqrt{2}) = -32 < 0 \Rightarrow$

$f(\pm\sqrt{2}) = 8$ are *LMAX*. $f''(x) > 0$ and f is *CU* on $(-\sqrt{2/3}, \sqrt{2/3})$.

$\qquad\qquad$ $f''(x) < 0$ and f is *CD* on $(-\infty, -\sqrt{2/3}) \cup (\sqrt{2/3}, \infty)$. *PI* at $x = \pm\sqrt{2/3}$.

$\boxed{5}$ $f'(x) = 12x^5 - 24x^3 = 12x^3(x^2 - 2) = 0 \Leftrightarrow x = 0, \pm\sqrt{2}$.

$f''(x) = 60x^4 - 72x^2 = 60x^2(x^2 - \frac{6}{5})$. $f''(\pm\sqrt{2}) = 96 > 0 \Rightarrow f(\pm\sqrt{2}) = -8$ are

LMIN. $f''(0) = 0$ gives no information. By the first derivative test, $f(0) = 0$ is a

LMAX. Since $60x^2 \geq 0$, the sign of f'' is determined by $(x^2 - \frac{6}{5})$, it follows that

$f''(x) > 0$ if $|x| > \sqrt{6/5}$ and $f''(x) < 0$ if $|x| < \sqrt{6/5}$ $(x \neq 0)$. Thus, f is

$\qquad$ *CU* on $(-\infty, -\sqrt{6/5}) \cup (\sqrt{6/5}, \infty)$ and *CD* on $(-\sqrt{6/5}, \sqrt{6/5})$. *PI* at $x = \pm\sqrt{6/5}$.

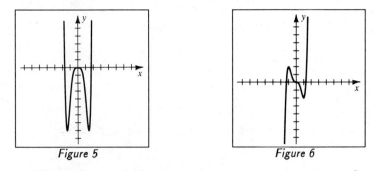

Figure 5   Figure 6

6 $f'(x) = 15x^4 - 15x^2 = 15x^2(x^2 - 1) = 0 \Leftrightarrow x = 0, \pm 1.$ $f''(x) = 60x^3 - 30x =$
$30x(2x^2 - 1).$ $f''(\pm 1) = \pm 30 \Rightarrow f(1) = -2$ is a *LMIN* and $f(-1) = 2$ is a *LMAX*.
$f''(0) = 0$ gives no information. By the first derivative test,

$f(0)$ not an extremum. The table indicates *PI* at $x = 0, \pm\sqrt{1/2}$.

Interval	$30x$	$2x^2 - 1$	f''	Concavity
$(-\infty, -\sqrt{1/2})$	−	+	−	CD
$(-\sqrt{1/2}, 0)$	−	−	+	CU
$(0, \sqrt{1/2})$	+	−	−	CD
$(\sqrt{1/2}, \infty)$	+	+	+	CU

7 $f'(x) = 4x(x^2 - 1) = 0 \Leftrightarrow x = 0, \pm 1.$ $f''(x) = 4(3x^2 - 1).$
$f''(0) = -4 < 0 \Rightarrow f(0) = 1$ is a *LMAX*. $f''(\pm 1) = 8 > 0 \Rightarrow f(\pm 1) = 0$ are *LMIN*.
$f''(x) > 0$ and f is *CU* on $(-\infty, -\sqrt{1/3}) \cup (\sqrt{1/3}, \infty).$

$f''(x) < 0$ and f is *CD* on $(-\sqrt{1/3}, \sqrt{1/3}).$ *PI* at $x = \pm\sqrt{1/3}.$

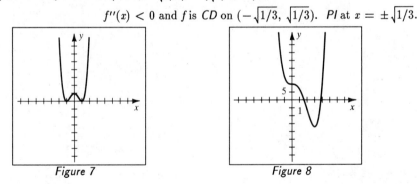

Figure 7   Figure 8

8 $f'(x) = 4x^2(x - 3) = 0 \Leftrightarrow x = 0, 3.$ $f''(x) = 12x(x - 2).$
$f''(3) = 36 > 0 \Rightarrow f(3) = -17$ is a *LMIN*. $f''(0) = 0$ gives no information.
By the first derivative test, $f(0) = 10$ is not a local extremum.
The sign of f'' changes at $x = 0, 2.$ $f''(x) > 0$ and f is *CU* on $(-\infty, 0) \cup (2, \infty).$

$f''(x) < 0$ and f is *CD* on $(0, 2).$ *PI* at $x = 0, 2.$

$\boxed{9}$ $f'(x) = \frac{1}{5}x^{-4/5}$ is undefined when $x = 0$, otherwise $f'(x) > 0$. No local extrema.

$f''(x) = -\frac{4}{25}x^{-9/5}$. $f''(x) > 0$ and f is *CU* on $(-\infty, 0)$.

$f''(x) < 0$ and f is *CD* on $(0, \infty)$. *PI* at $x = 0$.

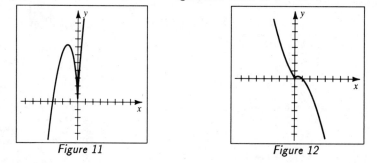

Figure 9   Figure 10

$\boxed{10}$ $f'(x) = -\frac{2}{3}x^{-1/3}$ is undefined when $x = 0$. $f''(x) = \frac{2}{9}x^{-4/3}$. Since $f''(0)$ is

undefined, use the first derivative test to show that $f(0) = 2$ is a *LMAX*.

Since $f''(x) > 0$, f is *CU* on $(-\infty, 0)$ and $(0, \infty)$. There are no *PI*.

$\boxed{11}$ $f'(x) = \dfrac{5(3x + 4)}{3x^{1/3}} = 0 \Leftrightarrow x = -\frac{4}{3}$. f' fails to exist at $x = 0$. $f''(x) = \dfrac{10(3x - 2)}{9x^{4/3}}$.

$f''(-\frac{4}{3}) < 0$ and $f(-\frac{4}{3}) = 4\sqrt[3]{6} \approx 7.27$ is a *LMAX*. Since $f''(0)$ is undefined, use the

first derivative test to show that $f(0) = 0$ is a *LMIN*. Since $9x^{4/3} \geq 0$, the sign of f''

is determined by $(3x - 2)$. Thus, $f''(x) < 0$ and f is *CD* on $(-\infty, 0) \cup (0, \frac{2}{3})$ and

$f''(x) > 0$ and f is *CU* on $(\frac{2}{3}, \infty)$. *PI* at $x = \frac{2}{3}$.

Note: f is not *CD* at $x = 0$ since no tangent line exists at $x = 0$.

Figure 11   Figure 12

$\boxed{12}$ $f'(x) = \dfrac{2 - 5x}{3x^{1/3}} = 0 \Leftrightarrow x = \frac{2}{5}$. f' fails to exist at $x = 0$. $f''(x) = \dfrac{-2(5x + 1)}{9x^{4/5}}$.

$f''(\frac{2}{5}) < 0 \Rightarrow f(\frac{2}{5}) = (0.4)^{2/3}(0.6) \approx 0.33$ is a *LMAX*. Since $f''(0)$ is undefined, use

the first derivative test to show that $f(0) = 0$ is a *LMIN*. Since $9x^{4/5} > 0$ for $x \neq 0$,

there is no *PI* at $x = 0$. $f''(x) > 0$ and f is *CU* on $(-\infty, -\frac{1}{5})$.

$f''(x) < 0$ and f is *CD* on $(-\frac{1}{5}, 0) \cup (0, \infty)$. *PI* at $x = -\frac{1}{5}$.

Note: f is not *CD* at $x = 0$ since f' does not exist at $x = 0$. Also, the *PI* is not

noticeable in the sketch of the graph since the concavity change is slight.

$\boxed{13}$ $f'(x) = \dfrac{x(7x - 10)}{(3x - 5)^{2/3}} = 0 \Leftrightarrow x = 0, \frac{10}{7}$. f' fails to exist at $x = \frac{5}{3}$.

$f''(x) = \dfrac{2(14x^2 - 40x + 25)}{(3x - 5)^{5/3}}$. $f''(0) = -2\sqrt[3]{5} < 0 \Rightarrow f(0) = 0$ is a *LMAX*.

$f''(\frac{10}{7}) = 2\sqrt[3]{245} > 0 \Rightarrow f(\frac{10}{7}) = -\frac{100}{343}\sqrt[3]{245} \approx -1.82$ is a *LMIN*.

By the first derivative test, $f(\frac{5}{3}) = 0$ is not an extremum.

$f''(x) = 0 \Rightarrow x = \dfrac{20 \pm 5\sqrt{2}}{14}$. Let $a = \dfrac{20 - 5\sqrt{2}}{14} \approx 0.92$ and $b = \dfrac{20 + 5\sqrt{2}}{14} \approx 1.93$.

f'' changes sign at a, $\frac{5}{3}$, and b. Hence, there are *PI* at $x = a$, $\frac{5}{3}$, and b. $f''(x) > 0$ and f is *CU* on $(a, \frac{5}{3})$ and (b, ∞). $f''(x) < 0$ and f is *CD* on $(-\infty, a)$ and $(\frac{5}{3}, b)$.

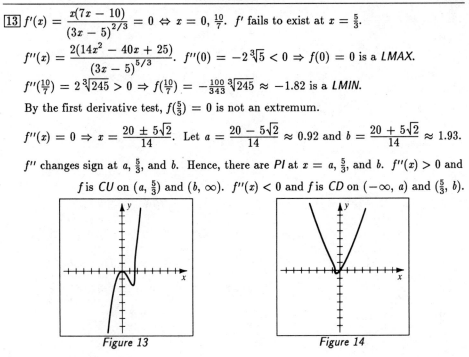

Figure 13   Figure 14

$\boxed{14}$ $f'(x) = \dfrac{2(2x + 1)}{(3x + 2)^{2/3}} = 0 \Leftrightarrow x = -\frac{1}{2}$. f' fails to exist at $x = -\frac{2}{3}$.

$f''(x) = \dfrac{4(x + 1)}{(3x + 2)^{5/3}}$. $f''(-\frac{1}{2}) = 4\sqrt[3]{4} > 0 \Rightarrow f(-\frac{1}{2}) = -\frac{1}{4}\sqrt[3]{4} \approx -0.4$ is a *LMIN*.

By the first derivative test, $f(-\frac{2}{3}) = 0$ is not an extremum.

$f''(x) > 0$ and f is *CU* on $(-\infty, -1)$ and $(-\frac{2}{3}, \infty)$.

$f''(x) < 0$ and f is *CD* on $(-1, -\frac{2}{3})$. x-coordinates of *PI* are -1 and $-\frac{2}{3}$.

$\boxed{15}$ $f'(x) = \dfrac{8 + 4x}{3x^{2/3}} = 0 \Leftrightarrow x = -2$. f' fails to exist at $x = 0$. $f''(x) = \dfrac{4(x - 4)}{9x^{5/3}} \Rightarrow$

$f''(-2) = \frac{2}{3}\sqrt[3]{2} > 0$ and $f(-2) = -6\sqrt[3]{2} \approx -7.55$ is a *LMIN*. $f''(0)$ is undefined.

By the first derivative test, $f(0) = 0$ is not a local extremum.

The sign of f'' changes at $x = 0, 4$. $f''(x) > 0$ and f is *CU* on $(-\infty, 0) \cup (4, \infty)$.

$f''(x) < 0$ and f is *CD* on $(0, 4)$. *PI* at $x = 0, 4$.

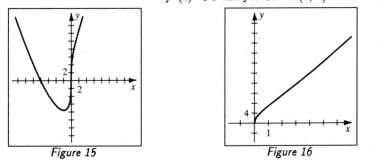

Figure 15   Figure 16

$\boxed{16}$ $f'(x) = \dfrac{3x + 6}{2\sqrt{x}} = 0 \Leftrightarrow x = -2$, which is not in the domain of f. f' fails to exist at

$x = 0$. $f(0) = 0$ is an endpoint extremum since $f > 0$ for $x > 0$. There are no local

extrema. $f''(x) = \dfrac{3x - 6}{4x^{3/2}}$. $f''(x) < 0$ for $0 < x < 2$ and f is CD on $(0, 2)$.

$\quad$ $f''(x) > 0$ for $x > 2$ and f is CU on $(2, \infty)$. x-coordinate of PI is 2. See *Figure 16*.

$\boxed{17}$ $f'(x) = \dfrac{3x(6 - x^2)}{\sqrt{9 - x^2}} = 0 \Leftrightarrow x = 0, \pm\sqrt{6}$. f' fails to exist at $x = \pm 3$, which are

endpoints of the domain. $f''(x) = \dfrac{3(54 - 27x^2 + 2x^4)}{(9 - x^2)^{3/2}}$. $f''(\pm\sqrt{6}) = -12\sqrt{3} < 0 \Rightarrow$

$f(\pm\sqrt{6}) = 6\sqrt{3} \approx 10.4$ are *LMAX*. $f''(0) = 6 > 0 \Rightarrow f(0) = 0$ is a *LMIN*.

$f''(x) = 0 \Rightarrow x = \pm\frac{1}{2}\sqrt{27 \pm 3\sqrt{33}} \Rightarrow x = \pm\frac{1}{2}\sqrt{27 - 3\sqrt{33}}$ for $|x| < 3$.

Let $a = -\frac{1}{2}\sqrt{27 - 3\sqrt{33}} \approx -1.56$ and $b = -a$. $f''(x) > 0$ and f is CU on (a, b).

$\quad$ $f''(x) < 0$ and f is CD on $(-3, a)$ and $(b, 3)$. x-coordinates of PI are a and b.

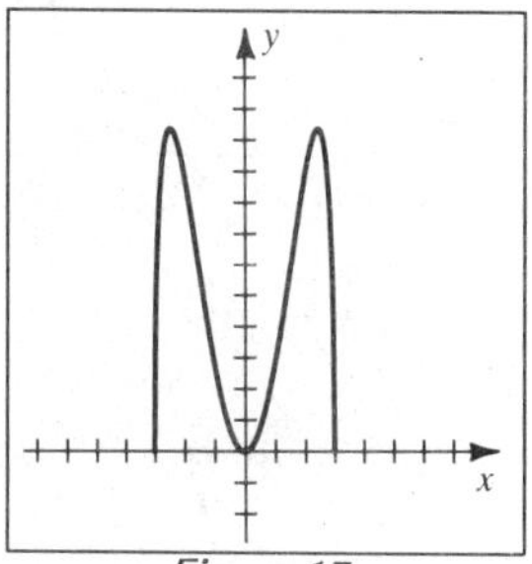

Figure 17

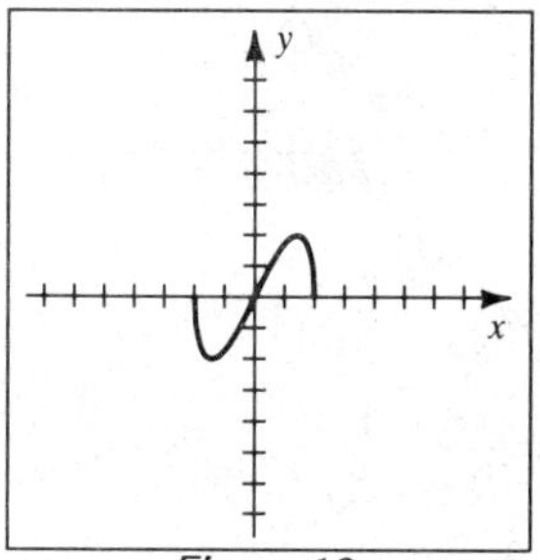

Figure 18

$\boxed{18}$ $f'(x) = \dfrac{4 - 2x^2}{(4 - x^2)^{1/2}} = 0 \Leftrightarrow x = \pm\sqrt{2}$. $f''(x) = \dfrac{2x(x^2 - 6)}{(4 - x^2)^{3/2}}$.

$f''(-\sqrt{2}) = 4 > 0 \Rightarrow f(-\sqrt{2}) = -2$ is a *LMIN*. $f''(\sqrt{2}) = -4 < 0 \Rightarrow$

$f(\sqrt{2}) = 2$ is a *LMAX*. $x = \pm 2$ are endpoints and cannot be local extrema.

$\quad$ The only value where f'' changes sign *in the domain* of f is $x = 0$.

$\quad$ $f''(x) > 0$ and f is CU on $(-2, 0)$. $f''(x) < 0$ and f is CD on $(0, 2)$. PI at $x = 0$.

Note: The solutions for Exercises 19–24 first appeared in the solutions of Exercises

$\quad$ 17–22 in §4.3, where they were solved using the first derivative test.

$\boxed{19}$ The CN are $x = \frac{\pi}{4}, \frac{5\pi}{4}$. $f''(x) = -\cos x - \sin x$. $f''(\frac{\pi}{4}) = -\sqrt{2} < 0 \Rightarrow$

$\qquad$ $f(\frac{\pi}{4}) = \sqrt{2}$ is a *LMAX*. $f''(\frac{5\pi}{4}) = \sqrt{2} > 0 \Rightarrow f(\frac{5\pi}{4}) = -\sqrt{2}$ is a *LMIN*.

$\boxed{20}$ The CN are $x = \frac{3\pi}{4}, \frac{7\pi}{4}$. $f''(x) = -\cos x + \sin x$. $f''(\frac{7\pi}{4}) = -\sqrt{2} < 0 \Rightarrow$

$\qquad$ $f(\frac{7\pi}{4}) = \sqrt{2}$ is a *LMAX*. $f''(\frac{3\pi}{4}) = \sqrt{2} > 0 \Rightarrow f(\frac{3\pi}{4}) = -\sqrt{2}$ is a *LMIN*.

$\boxed{21}$ The CN are $x = \frac{\pi}{3}, \frac{5\pi}{3}$. $f''(x) = \sin x$. $f''(\frac{5\pi}{3}) = -\frac{\sqrt{3}}{2} < 0 \Rightarrow$

$\qquad$ $f(\frac{5\pi}{3}) = \frac{5\pi}{6} + \frac{\sqrt{3}}{2}$ is a *LMAX*. $f''(\frac{\pi}{3}) = \frac{\sqrt{3}}{2} > 0 \Rightarrow f(\frac{\pi}{3}) = \frac{\pi}{6} - \frac{\sqrt{3}}{2}$ is a *LMIN*.

$\boxed{22}$ The CN are $x = \frac{\pi}{6}, \frac{5\pi}{6}$. $f''(x) = -2\cos x$. $f''(\frac{\pi}{6}) = -\sqrt{3} < 0 \Rightarrow$

$\quad\quad f(\frac{\pi}{6}) = \frac{\pi}{6} + \sqrt{3}$ is a *LMAX*. $f''(\frac{5\pi}{6}) = \sqrt{3} > 0 \Rightarrow f(\frac{5\pi}{6}) = \frac{5\pi}{6} - \sqrt{3}$ is a *LMIN*.

$\boxed{23}$ The CN are $x = \frac{\pi}{6}, \frac{5\pi}{6}, \frac{3\pi}{2}$. $f''(x) = -2\cos x - 4\sin 2x$. $f''(\frac{\pi}{6}) = -3\sqrt{3} < 0 \Rightarrow$

$\quad f(\frac{\pi}{6}) = \frac{3\sqrt{3}}{2}$ is a *LMAX*. $f''(\frac{5\pi}{6}) = 3\sqrt{3} > 0 \Rightarrow f(\frac{5\pi}{6}) = -\frac{3\sqrt{3}}{2}$ is a *LMIN*.

$\quad\quad\quad\quad\quad\quad\quad \frac{3\pi}{2}$ is also a CN, but $f''(\frac{3\pi}{2}) = 0$ gives no information.

$\boxed{24}$ The CN in $(0, 2\pi)$ are $x = \frac{2\pi}{3}, \pi, \frac{4\pi}{3}$. $f''(x) = -2\cos x - 4\cos 2x$.

$\quad f''(\pi) = -2 < 0 \Rightarrow f(\pi) = -1$ is a *LMAX*.

$\quad\quad\quad\quad f''(\frac{2\pi}{3}) = f''(\frac{4\pi}{3}) = 3 > 0 \Rightarrow f(\frac{2\pi}{3}) = -\frac{3}{2}$ and $f(\frac{4\pi}{3}) = -\frac{3}{2}$ are *LMIN*.

Note: For Exercises 25–30, see Exercises 29–34 in §4.3.

$\boxed{25}$ The only CN in $(-\frac{\pi}{2}, \frac{\pi}{2})$ is $x = 0$.

$\quad\quad f''(x) = \frac{1}{2}(\frac{1}{2}\sec\frac{1}{2}x\tan^2\frac{1}{2}x + \frac{1}{2}\sec^3\frac{1}{2}x) \Rightarrow f''(0) = \frac{1}{4} > 0 \Rightarrow f(0) = 1$ is a *LMIN*.

$\boxed{26}$ The only CN in $(\frac{\pi}{6}, \frac{5\pi}{6})$ is $x = \frac{3\pi}{4}$. $f''(x) = 4\csc^2 x\cot x(\cot x + 1) + 2\csc^4 x \Rightarrow$

$\quad\quad\quad\quad\quad\quad\quad f''(\frac{3\pi}{4}) = 8 > 0 \Rightarrow f(\frac{3\pi}{4}) = -1$ is a *LMIN*.

$\boxed{27}$ The only CN in $(-\frac{\pi}{3}, \frac{\pi}{3})$ is $x = \frac{\pi}{4}$. $f''(x) = 4\sec^2 x\tan x(1 - \tan x) - 2\sec^4 x \Rightarrow$

$\quad\quad\quad\quad\quad\quad\quad f''(\frac{\pi}{4}) = -8 < 0 \Rightarrow f(\frac{\pi}{4}) = 1$ is a *LMAX*.

$\boxed{28}$ The only CN in $(-\frac{\pi}{4}, \frac{\pi}{4})$ is $x = \frac{\pi}{6}$.

$\quad f''(x) = \sec x\tan x(\sec x - 2\tan x) + \sec x(\sec x\tan x - 2\sec^2 x) \Rightarrow$

$\quad\quad\quad\quad\quad\quad\quad f''(\frac{\pi}{6}) = -\frac{4}{\sqrt{3}} < 0, f(\frac{\pi}{6}) = -\sqrt{3}$ is a *LMAX*.

$\boxed{29}$ The CN on $(-2\pi, 2\pi)$ are $x = -\frac{11\pi}{6}, -\frac{7\pi}{6}, \frac{\pi}{6}, \frac{5\pi}{6}$. $f''(x) = -\cos x$.

$\quad$ Since $f''(-\frac{11\pi}{6}) = f''(\frac{\pi}{6}) = -\frac{\sqrt{3}}{2} < 0, f(-\frac{11\pi}{6}) = \frac{\sqrt{3}}{2} - \frac{11\pi}{12} \approx -2.01$ and

$\quad f(\frac{\pi}{6}) = \frac{\sqrt{3}}{2} + \frac{\pi}{12} \approx 1.13$ are *LMAX*. Since $f''(-\frac{7\pi}{6}) = f''(\frac{5\pi}{6}) = \frac{\sqrt{3}}{2} > 0$,

$\quad\quad\quad f(-\frac{7\pi}{6}) = -\frac{\sqrt{3}}{2} - \frac{7\pi}{12} \approx -2.70$ and $f(\frac{5\pi}{6}) = \frac{5\pi}{12} - \frac{\sqrt{3}}{2} \approx 0.44$ are *LMIN*.

$\boxed{30}$ The CN on $(-2\pi, 2\pi)$ are $x = -\frac{11\pi}{6}, -\frac{\pi}{6}, \frac{\pi}{6}, \frac{11\pi}{6}$. $f''(x) = \sin x$.

$\quad$ Since $f''(-\frac{11\pi}{6}) = f''(\frac{\pi}{6}) = \frac{1}{2} > 0, f(-\frac{11\pi}{6}) = -\frac{11\sqrt{3}\,\pi}{12} - \frac{1}{2} \approx -5.49$ and

$\quad f(\frac{\pi}{6}) = \frac{\sqrt{3}\,\pi}{12} - \frac{1}{2} \approx -0.05$ are *LMIN*. Since $f''(-\frac{\pi}{6}) = f''(\frac{11\pi}{6}) = -\frac{1}{2} < 0$,

$\quad\quad\quad f(-\frac{\pi}{6}) = \frac{1}{2} - \frac{\sqrt{3}\,\pi}{12} \approx 0.05$ and $f(\frac{11\pi}{6}) = \frac{11\sqrt{3}\,\pi}{12} + \frac{1}{2} \approx 5.49$ are *LMAX*.

$\boxed{31}$ $\boxed{32}$

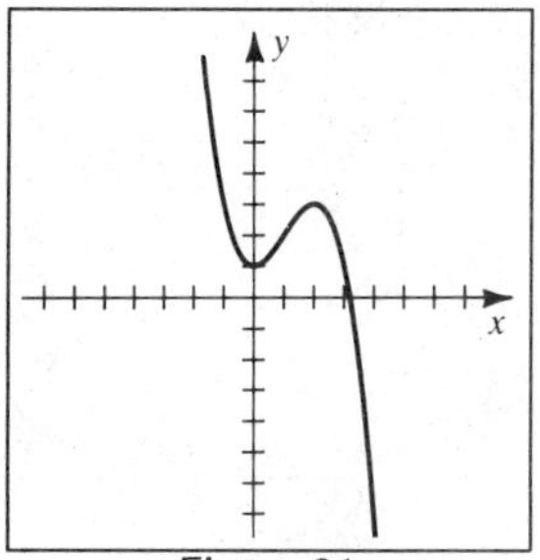

Figure 31

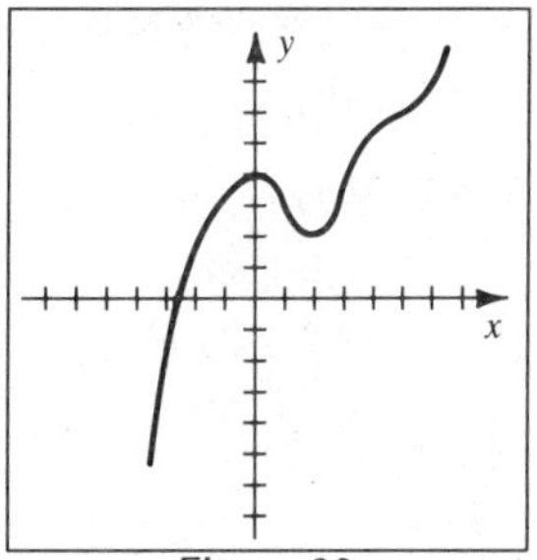

Figure 32

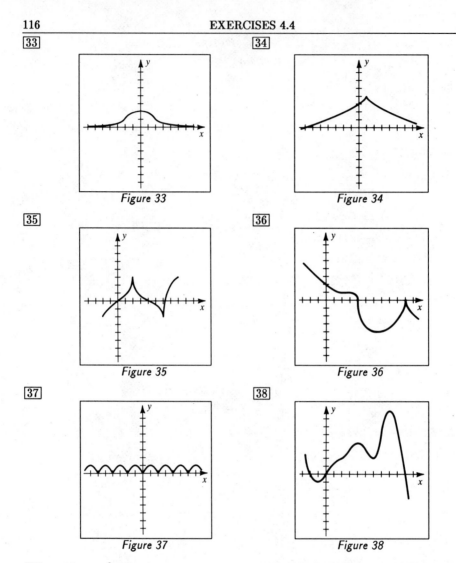

33

Figure 33

34

Figure 34

35

Figure 35

36

Figure 36

37

Figure 37

38

Figure 38

39 If $f(x) = ax^2 + bx + c$, then $f''(x) = 2a$, which does not change sign.

Thus, there is no point of inflection. (a) CU if $a > 0$. (b) CD if $a < 0$.

40 If $f(x) = ax^3 + bx^2 + cx + d$, then $f''(x) = 6ax + 2b$. Since $a \neq 0$, f'' changes

sign at $x = -b/(3a)$ and hence there is a point of inflection at this value of x.

41 Estimate from the screen.

(a) CU on $(-0.48, 1)$; CD on $(-1, -0.48)$ (b) -0.48

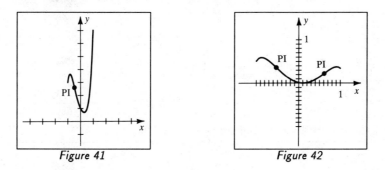

Figure 41   Figure 42

[42] Estimate from the screen.

   (a) CU on $(-0.53, 0.61)$; CD on $(-1, -0.53)$ and $(0.61, 1)$ (b) $-0.53, 0.61$

[43] $f''(x) = 0$ at $x = \frac{3}{10}, \frac{11}{5}$. However, f'' does not change sign at these values.

Since $f''(x) \geq 0$ on $[0, 3]$, f is *CU* on $(0, 3)$ with no *PI*.

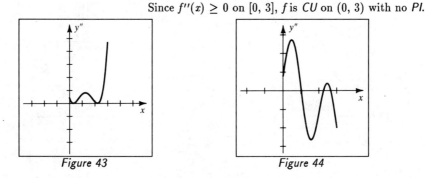

Figure 43   Figure 44

[44] $f''(x) = 0$ at $x \approx 1.02, 2.25, 2.66$. Since f'' changes sign at each of these points there

are *PI* at these x-coordinates. $f''(x) > 0$ on $(0, 1.02) \cup (2.25, 2.66)$ and f is *CU*.

$f''(x) < 0$ on $(1.02, 2.25) \cup (2.66, 3)$ and f is *CD*.

| Exercises 4.5 |

Note: It is helpful to know where the function intersects the horizontal or oblique
asymptote to determine how the function is approaching the asymptote. None of
the functions in the exercises have more than one point of intersection and it will
be denoted by $I(x, y)$. See the solutions to Exercises 6 and 12 for detailed work on
finding I.

[1] $f(x) = \dfrac{2x - 5}{x + 3}$; $f'(x) = \dfrac{11}{(x + 3)^2} \neq 0$; $f''(x) = -\dfrac{22}{(x + 3)^3}$. No extrema

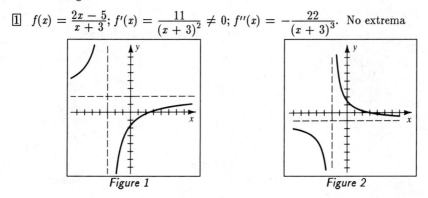

Figure 1   Figure 2

2. $f(x) = \dfrac{3-x}{x+2}$; $f'(x) = -\dfrac{5}{(x+2)^2} \neq 0$; $f''(x) = \dfrac{10}{(x+2)^3}$. No extrema.

See *Figure 2*.

3. $f(x) = \dfrac{x^2 + x - 6}{x^2 - 1} = \dfrac{(x+3)(x-2)}{(x+1)(x-1)}$; $I(5,\,1)$;

$f'(x) = -\dfrac{x^2 - 10x + 1}{(x^2 - 1)^2} = 0 \Leftrightarrow x = 5 \pm 2\sqrt{6}$; $f''(x) = \dfrac{2(x^3 - 15x^2 + 3x - 5)}{(x^2 - 1)^3}$.

Max: $f(5 + 2\sqrt{6}) \approx 1.05$; min: $f(5 - 2\sqrt{6}) \approx 5.95$

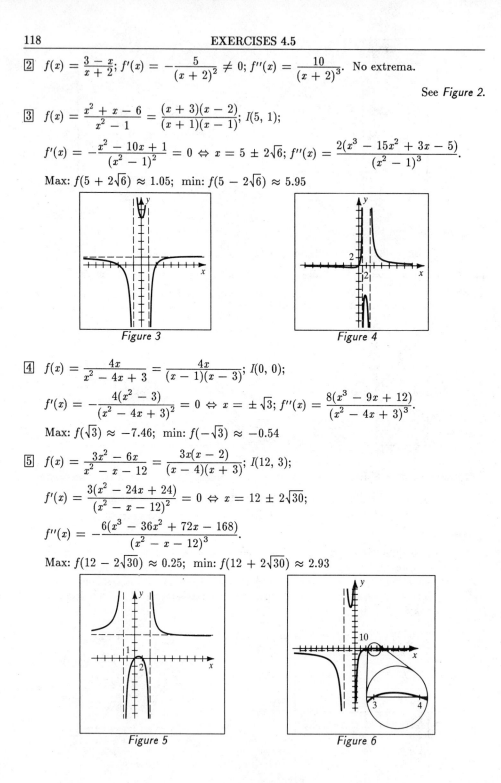

Figure 3   *Figure 4*

4. $f(x) = \dfrac{4x}{x^2 - 4x + 3} = \dfrac{4x}{(x-1)(x-3)}$; $I(0,\,0)$;

$f'(x) = -\dfrac{4(x^2 - 3)}{(x^2 - 4x + 3)^2} = 0 \Leftrightarrow x = \pm\sqrt{3}$; $f''(x) = \dfrac{8(x^3 - 9x + 12)}{(x^2 - 4x + 3)^3}$.

Max: $f(\sqrt{3}) \approx -7.46$; min: $f(-\sqrt{3}) \approx -0.54$

5. $f(x) = \dfrac{3x^2 - 6x}{x^2 - x - 12} = \dfrac{3x(x-2)}{(x-4)(x+3)}$; $I(12,\,3)$;

$f'(x) = \dfrac{3(x^2 - 24x + 24)}{(x^2 - x - 12)^2} = 0 \Leftrightarrow x = 12 \pm 2\sqrt{30}$;

$f''(x) = -\dfrac{6(x^3 - 36x^2 + 72x - 168)}{(x^2 - x - 12)^3}$.

Max: $f(12 - 2\sqrt{30}) \approx 0.25$; min: $f(12 + 2\sqrt{30}) \approx 2.93$

Figure 5   *Figure 6*

$\boxed{6}$ $f(x) = \dfrac{-2x^2 + 14x - 24}{x^2 + 2x} = \dfrac{-2(x-3)(x-4)}{x(x+2)}; f(x) = -2 \Rightarrow$

$\dfrac{-2x^2 + 14x - 24}{x^2 + 2x} = -2 \Rightarrow -2x^2 + 14x - 24 = -2x^2 - 4x \Rightarrow x = \frac{4}{3}; I(\frac{4}{3}, -2);$

$f'(x) = -\dfrac{6(3x^2 - 8x - 8)}{x^2(x+2)^2} = 0 \Leftrightarrow x = \frac{4}{3} \pm \frac{2}{3}\sqrt{10};$

$f''(x) = \dfrac{12(3x^3 - 12x^2 - 24x - 16)}{x^3(x+2)^3}.$

Max: $f(\frac{4}{3} + \frac{2}{3}\sqrt{10}) \approx 0.03$; min: $f(\frac{4}{3} - \frac{2}{3}\sqrt{10}) \approx 37.97$

$\boxed{7}$ $f(x) = \dfrac{2x^2}{x^2 + 1}; f'(x) = \dfrac{4x}{(x^2+1)^2} = 0 \Leftrightarrow x = 0;$

$f''(x) = -\dfrac{4(3x^2 - 1)}{(x^2+1)^3}.$ Min: $f(0) = 0$

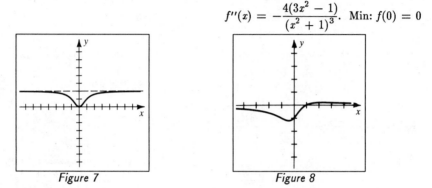

Figure 7   Figure 8

$\boxed{8}$ $f(x) = \dfrac{x-1}{x^2+1}; I(1, 0); f'(x) = -\dfrac{x^2 - 2x - 1}{(x^2+1)^2} = 0 \Leftrightarrow x = 1 \pm \sqrt{2};$

$f''(x) = \dfrac{2(x^3 - 3x^2 - 3x + 1)}{(x^2+1)^3}.$ Max: $f(1 + \sqrt{2}) \approx 0.21$; min: $f(1 - \sqrt{2}) \approx -1.21$

$\boxed{9}$ $f(x) = \dfrac{x+4}{\sqrt{x}}; f'(x) = \dfrac{x-4}{2x^{3/2}} = 0 \Leftrightarrow x = 4; f''(x) = -\dfrac{x-12}{4x^{5/2}}.$ Min: $f(4) = 4$

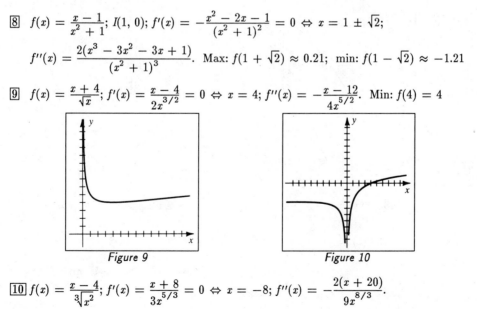

Figure 9   Figure 10

$\boxed{10}$ $f(x) = \dfrac{x-4}{\sqrt[3]{x^2}}; f'(x) = \dfrac{x+8}{3x^{5/3}} = 0 \Leftrightarrow x = -8; f''(x) = -\dfrac{2(x+20)}{9x^{8/3}}.$

Max: $f(-8) = -3$

11 $f(x) = \dfrac{-3x}{\sqrt{x^2 + 4}}$; $f'(x) = -\dfrac{12}{(x^2 + 4)^{3/2}} \neq 0$; $f''(x) = \dfrac{36x}{(x^2 + 4)^{5/2}}$. No extrema

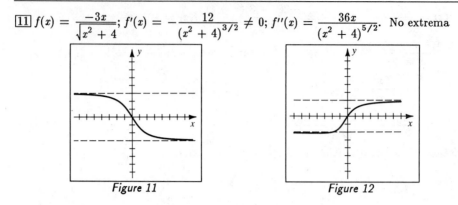

Figure 11   Figure 12

12 $f(x) = \dfrac{2x}{\sqrt{x^2 + x + 2}}$; $f'(x) = \dfrac{x + 4}{(x^2 + x + 2)^{3/2}} = 0 \Leftrightarrow x = -4$;

$f(x) = 2 \Rightarrow \dfrac{2x}{\sqrt{x^2 + x + 2}} = 2 \Rightarrow x = \sqrt{x^2 + x + 2} \Rightarrow x = -2$; $I(-2, 2)$;

$f''(x) = -\dfrac{4x^2 + 25x + 8}{2(x^2 + x + 2)^{5/2}}$. Min: $f(-4) \approx -2.14$

13 $f(x) = \dfrac{x^2 - x - 6}{x + 1} = \dfrac{(x - 3)(x + 2)}{x + 1}$; $f'(x) = \dfrac{x^2 + 2x + 5}{(x + 1)^2} \neq 0$;

$f''(x) = -\dfrac{8}{(x + 1)^3}$. No extrema

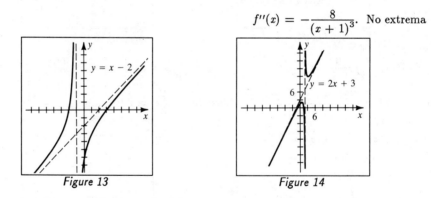

Figure 13   Figure 14

14 $f(x) = \dfrac{2x^2 - x - 3}{x - 2} = \dfrac{(2x - 3)(x + 1)}{x - 2}$; $f'(x) = \dfrac{2x^2 - 8x + 5}{(x - 2)^2} = 0 \Leftrightarrow$

$x = 2 \pm \tfrac{1}{2}\sqrt{6}$; $f''(x) = \dfrac{6}{(x - 2)^3}$. Max: $f(2 - \tfrac{1}{2}\sqrt{6}) \approx 2.10$; min: $f(2 + \tfrac{1}{2}\sqrt{6}) \approx 11.90$

15 $f(x) = \dfrac{x^2}{x + 1}$; $f'(x) = \dfrac{x(x + 2)}{(x + 1)^2} = 0 \Leftrightarrow x = 0, -2$; $f''(x) = \dfrac{2}{(x + 1)^3}$.

Max: $f(-2) = -4$; min: $f(0) = 0$

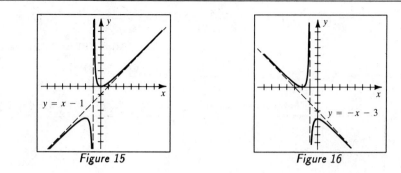

Figure 15   Figure 16

16 $f(x) = \dfrac{-x^2 - 4x - 4}{x + 1} = \dfrac{-1(x + 2)^2}{x + 1}$; $f'(x) = -\dfrac{x(x + 2)}{(x + 1)^2} = 0 \Leftrightarrow x = 0, -2$;

$$f''(x) = -\frac{2}{(x + 1)^3}.\ \ \text{Max: } f(0) = -4;\ \ \text{min: } f(-2) = 0$$

17 $f(x) = \dfrac{4 - x^2}{x + 3} = \dfrac{(2 + x)(2 - x)}{x + 3}$; $f'(x) = -\dfrac{x^2 + 6x + 4}{(x + 3)^2} = 0 \Leftrightarrow x = -3 \pm \sqrt{5}$;

$$f''(x) = -\frac{10}{(x + 3)^3}.\ \ \text{Max: } f(-3 + \sqrt{5}) \approx 1.53;\ \ \text{min: } f(-3 - \sqrt{5}) \approx 10.47$$

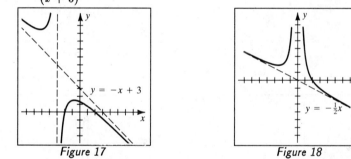

Figure 17   Figure 18

18 $f(x) = \dfrac{8 - x^3}{2x^2} = \dfrac{(2 - x)(4 + 2x + x^2)}{2x^2}$; $f'(x) = -\dfrac{x^3 + 16}{2x^3} = 0 \Leftrightarrow x = -2\sqrt[3]{2}$;

$$f''(x) = \frac{24}{x^4}.\ \ \text{Min: } f(-2\sqrt[3]{2}) \approx 1.89$$

19 $f(x) = \dfrac{3x}{(x + 8)^2}$; $I(0, 0)$; $f'(x) = -\dfrac{3(x - 8)}{(x + 8)^3}$; $f''(x) = \dfrac{6(x - 16)}{(x + 8)^4}$.

$$\text{Max: } f(8) = \tfrac{3}{32};\ \ \text{PI: } (16, \tfrac{1}{12})$$

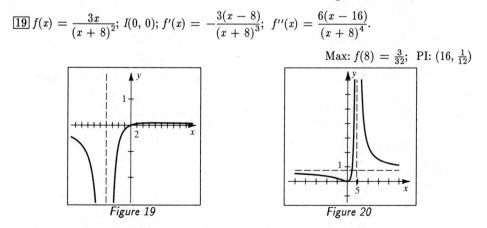

Figure 19   Figure 20

20 $f(x) = \dfrac{3x^2}{(2x-9)^2}$; $I(\frac{9}{4}, \frac{3}{4})$; $f'(x) = \dfrac{-54x}{(2x-9)^3}$; $f''(x) = \dfrac{54(4x+9)}{(2x-9)^4}$.

Min: $f(0) = 0$; PI: $(-\frac{9}{4}, \frac{1}{12})$

21 $f(x) = \dfrac{3x}{x^2+1}$; $I(0, 0)$; $f'(x) = \dfrac{-3(x^2-1)}{(x^2+1)^2}$; $f''(x) = \dfrac{6x(x^2-3)}{(x^2+1)^3}$.

Max: $f(1) = \frac{3}{2}$; min: $f(-1) = -\frac{3}{2}$; PI: $(0, 0)$, $(\pm\sqrt{3}, \pm\frac{3}{4}\sqrt{3})$

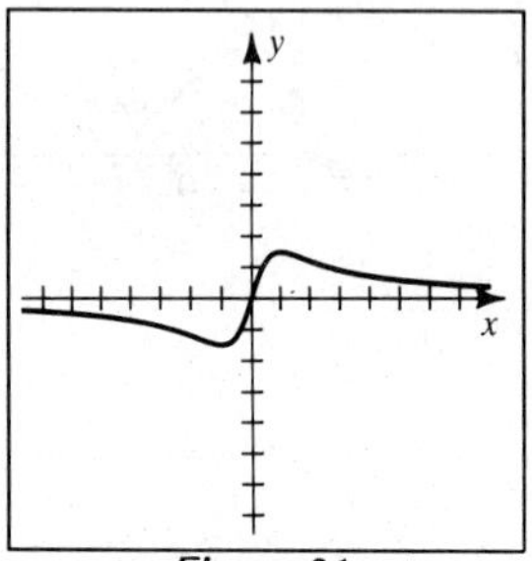

Figure 21

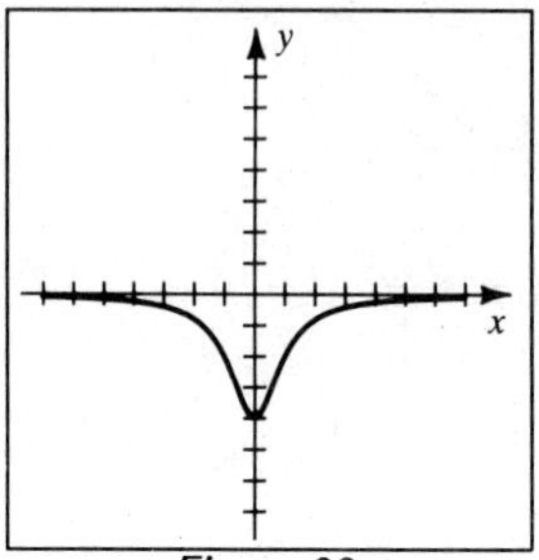

Figure 22

22 $f(x) = \dfrac{-4}{x^2+1}$; $f'(x) = \dfrac{8x}{(x^2+1)^2}$; $f''(x) = \dfrac{-8(3x^2-1)}{(x^2+1)^3}$.

Min: $f(0) = -4$; PI: $(\pm\frac{1}{3}\sqrt{3}, -3)$

23 $f(x) = x^2 - \dfrac{27}{x^2} = \dfrac{x^4-27}{x^2}$; $f'(x) = 2x + \dfrac{54}{x^3} = \dfrac{2(x^4+27)}{x^3}$;

$$f''(x) = 2 - \dfrac{162}{x^4} = \dfrac{2(x-3)(x+3)(x^2+9)}{x^4}.$$ PI: $(\pm 3, 6)$

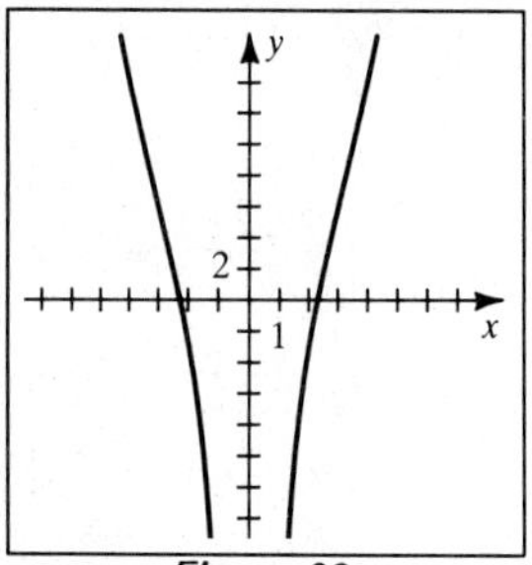

Figure 23

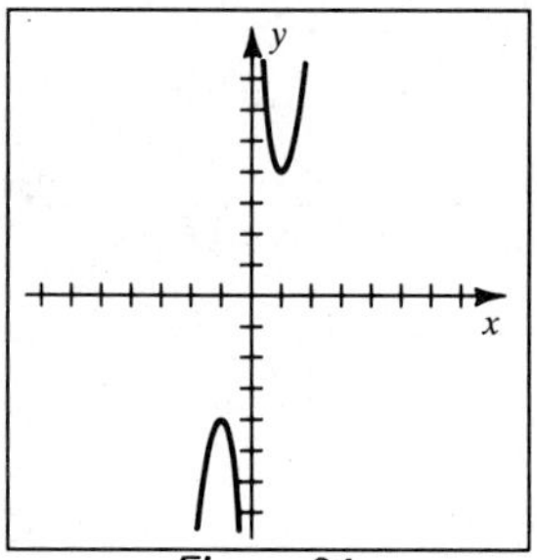

Figure 24

24 $f(x) = x^3 + \dfrac{3}{x} = \dfrac{x^4+3}{x}$; $f'(x) = 3x^2 - \dfrac{3}{x^2} = \dfrac{3(x-1)(x+1)(x^2+1)}{x^2}$;

$$f''(x) = 6x + \dfrac{6}{x^3} = \dfrac{6(x^4+1)}{x^3}.$$ Max: $f(-1) = -4$; min: $f(1) = 4$; No PI

25 $f(x) = \dfrac{2x^2+x-6}{x^2+3x+2} = \dfrac{(x+2)(2x-3)}{(x+2)(x+1)} = \dfrac{2x-3}{x+1}$ for $x \neq -2$.

To determine the value of y when $x = -2$, substitute -2 into $\dfrac{2x-3}{x+1}$ to get 7.

There is a hole in the graph at $(-2, 7)$.

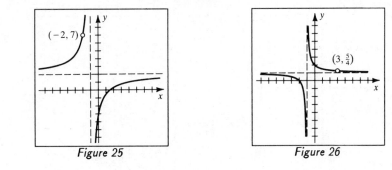

Figure 25   Figure 26

26 $f(x) = \dfrac{x^2 - x - 6}{x^2 - 2x - 3} = \dfrac{(x + 2)(x - 3)}{(x + 1)(x - 3)} = \dfrac{x + 2}{x + 1}$ for $x \neq 3$; hole at $(3, \frac{5}{4})$

27 $f(x) = \dfrac{x - 1}{1 - x^2} = \dfrac{x - 1}{(1 + x)(1 - x)} = \dfrac{-1}{x + 1}$ for $x \neq 1$; hole at $(1, -\frac{1}{2})$

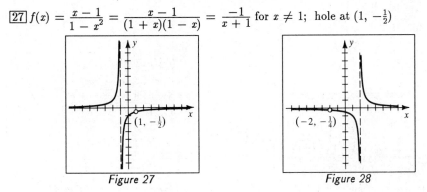

Figure 27   Figure 28

28 $f(x) = \dfrac{x + 2}{x^2 - 4} = \dfrac{x + 2}{(x + 2)(x - 2)} = \dfrac{1}{x - 2}$ for $x \neq -2$; hole at $(-2, -\frac{1}{4})$

29 $f(x) = \left| x^2 - 6x + 5 \right| = \left| (x - 1)(x - 5) \right|$

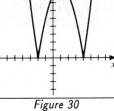

Figure 29   Figure 30

30 $f(x) = \left| 8 + 2x - x^2 \right| = \left| (4 - x)(2 + x) \right|$

31 $f(x) = |x^3 + 1|$

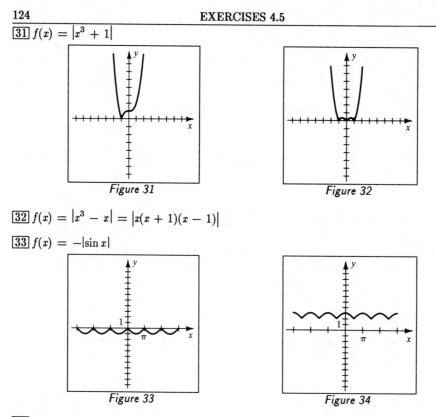

Figure 31   Figure 32

32 $f(x) = |x^3 - x| = |x(x + 1)(x - 1)|$

33 $f(x) = -|\sin x|$

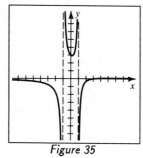

Figure 33

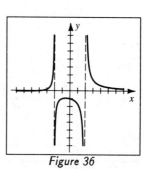

Figure 34

34 $f(x) = |\cos x| + 2$

Note: In 35–38, all pertinent information is listed in the problem.

35   36

Figure 35   Figure 36

[37] f intersects the horizontal asymptote, $y = 2$, at $I(5, 2)$.

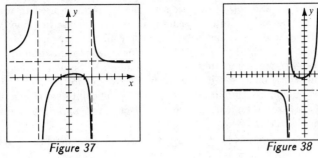

Figure 37   Figure 38

[38] f intersects the horizontal asymptote, $y = -3$, at $I(-7, -3)$.

[39] (a) Let $k > 0$ be a constant of proportionality.   (b)

The attraction to the particle at 0 is

$$F_1 = \frac{k(1)(-1)}{x^2} = -\frac{k}{x^2}. \text{ In this case,}$$

the negative sign indicates a force to the left.

The attraction to the particle at 2 is

$$F_2 = -\frac{k(1)(-1)}{(2 - x)^2} = \frac{k}{(x - 2)^2}.$$

The additional negative sign is used to indicate that

F_2 is in the opposite direction as F_1. Since $F = F_1 + F_2$ the result follows.

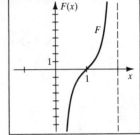

Figure 39

[40] (a) Not appropriate, since $\lim\limits_{I \to \infty} \dfrac{aI}{b + I} = a \neq 0$

(b) May be appropriate, since $\lim\limits_{I \to \infty} \dfrac{aI}{b + I^2} = 0$

[41].(a) CU on $(-0.43, 2)$; CD on $(-2, -0.43)$ (b) -0.43

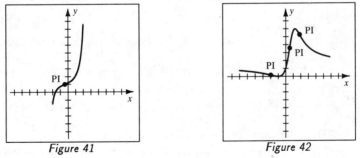

Figure 41   Figure 42

[42] (a) CU on $(-2, 0.54)$ and $(1.84, 6)$; CD on $(-6, -2)$ and $(0.54, 1.84)$

(b) $-2.00, 0.54, 1.84$

Note: In this exercise set and future exercise sets, the following is used to justify that a local extremum is an absolute extremum for a continuous function f. First, if $x_0 \in I$ for some interval I, and if $f'(x) > 0$ for all $x < x_0$ and $f'(x) < 0$ for all $x > x_0$ (where $x \in I$), then $f(x_0)$ must be an absolute maximum. (A similar statement can be made for an absolute minimum.) Second, if $(x_0, f(x_0))$ is a critical number of f on I, and if $f''(x) < 0$ $(f''(x) > 0)$ for all $x \in I$, then $f(x_0)$ is an absolute maximum (minimum) of f on I. The interval I can be open or unbounded. These statements assure that f does not approach a maximum or minimum *asymptotically.*

[1] Let x denote the length of a side of the square base and y the height of the box.

$V = x^2y = 4 \Rightarrow y = 4/x^2$. The surface area is given by

$S = 4xy + x^2 = 16/x + x^2$, where $x > 0$. $S' = -16/x^2 + 2x = 0$ if $x = 2$.

Since $S'' > 0$ for $x > 0$, this will be a minimum value. Thus, $x = 2$ and $y = 1$.

[2] As in Exercise 1, $V = x^2y = 4 \Rightarrow y = 4/x^2$. $S = 4xy + 2x^2 = 16/x + 2x^2$.

$S' = -16/x^2 + 4x = 0$ if $x = \sqrt[3]{4}$. Since $S'' > 0$ for $x > 0$,

this will give a minimum. $x = y = \sqrt[3]{4}$. (The optimal shape is a cube.)

[3] $V = \pi r^2 h = 1 \Rightarrow h = 1/(\pi r^2)$. The surface area S is to be minimized.

$S = 2\pi rh + \pi r^2 = 2/r + \pi r^2$, where $r > 0$. $S' = -2/r^2 + 2\pi r = 0$ if $r = 1/\sqrt[3]{\pi}$.

Since $S'' > 0$ for $r > 0$, this will be a minimum value. $r = h = 1/\sqrt[3]{\pi}$.

[4] The area M of the material used is to be minimized. The smallest square that the base can be cut from will be of length $2r$ on a side. As in Exercise 3,

$M = 2\pi rh + (2r)^2 = 2/r + 4r^2$. $M' = -2/r^2 + 8r = 0 \Rightarrow r = 1/\sqrt[3]{4}$.

Since $M'' > 0$ for $r > 0$, this will be a minimum value. $h = \sqrt[3]{16}/\pi$.

[5] The length of the fence used is $4y + 3x = 1000 \Rightarrow y = 250 - \frac{3}{4}x$.

$A = xy = x(250 - \frac{3}{4}x) = 250x - \frac{3}{4}x^2$, where $x \in [0, \frac{1000}{3}]$.

$A'(x) = 250 - \frac{3}{2}x = 0 \Rightarrow x = 166\frac{2}{3}$. $A(0) = A(\frac{1000}{3}) = 0$, and $A(166\frac{2}{3}) = 20{,}833\frac{1}{3}$.

Thus, $x = 166\frac{2}{3}$ ft and $y = 125$ ft give the maximum area.

[6] From Example 6, the time in the motorboat is $\dfrac{\sqrt{x^2 + 4}}{15}$. Thus, for $0 \le x \le 6$,

$T = \dfrac{\sqrt{x^2 + 4}}{15} + \dfrac{6 - x}{5}$. $T' = \dfrac{x}{15\sqrt{x^2 + 4}} - \dfrac{1}{5} < 0$ for $x \ge 0$ and T is

decreasing. The minimum time must occur at $x = 6$, that is,

the person should stay in the motorboat the entire trip.

[7] At a time t hours after 1:00 P.M., B is $10t$ miles west of its location at 1:00 P.M. and A is $30 - 15t$ miles south of B's 1:00 P.M. location. If $f(t)$ is the square of the distance between A and B, then $\sqrt{f(t)}$ or $f(t)$ is to be minimized.

$f(t) = (10t)^2 + (30 - 15t)^2 = 325t^2 - 900t + 900$. $f'(t) = 650t - 900 = 0 \Rightarrow$

$t = \frac{18}{13}$ hours. $f''(t) = 650 > 0 \Rightarrow$ this is a minimum distance.

Time $\approx$ 2:23:05 P.M. See *Figure 7.*

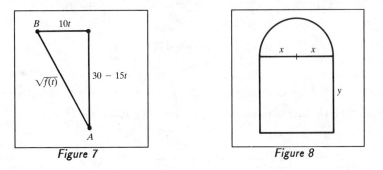

Figure 7   Figure 8

$\boxed{8}$ If y denotes the height of the rectangle and x the radius of the semicircle, then the curve has length πx and the perimeter is $\pi x + 2y + 2x = 15 \Rightarrow$ $2y = 15 - (2 + \pi)x$. The area A is to be maximized.

$A = 2xy + \frac{1}{2}\pi x^2 = 15x - (2 + \frac{\pi}{2})x^2$. $A' = 15 - (4 + \pi)x = 0 \Rightarrow x = \dfrac{15}{4 + \pi}$.

Since $A'' < 0$, this is a maximum value. $x = y = \dfrac{15}{4 + \pi}$.

$\boxed{9}$ Let x and y denote the distances shown in *Figure 9*, and L the length of the ladder.

Using similar triangles, $\dfrac{y}{x + 1} = \dfrac{8}{x}$, or $y = \dfrac{8(x + 1)}{x}$. Hence, $L^2 = (x + 1)^2 + y^2 =$ $x^2 + 2x + 65 + (128/x) + (64/x^2) = f(x)$. We can minimize L by minimizing $f(x)$.

$f'(x) = 2x + 2 - (128/x^2) - (128/x^3) = \dfrac{2(x^3 - 64)(x + 1)}{x^3} = 0$ if $x = -1, 4$.

$x = 4 \Rightarrow y = 10$ and $L = 5\sqrt{5} \approx 11.18$ ft.

This is a minimum, since $f'' = (2 + 256/x^3 + 384/x^4) > 0$ for $x > 0$.

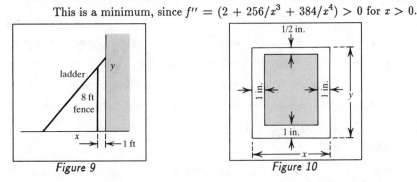

Figure 9   Figure 10

$\boxed{10}$ With x and y denoting the page dimensions as shown in *Figure 10*, $xy = 90$, or $y = 90/x$. If the printed area is A, then $A = (x - 2)(y - \frac{3}{2}) = 93 - (180/x) - \frac{3}{2}x$.

$A' = (180/x^2) - \frac{3}{2} = 0 \Rightarrow x = \sqrt{120} \approx 10.95$ in. Thus, $y = \dfrac{90}{\sqrt{120}} \approx 8.22$ in.

Since $A'' = -360/x^3 < 0$ for $x > 0$, this is a maximum.

$\boxed{11}$ Let w denote the width, l the length, and h the height. Then, $w = \frac{3}{4}l$.

Also, $V = lwh = \frac{3}{4}l^2h = 900 \Rightarrow h = 1200/l^2$. The cost is given by

$C = 4(wl) + 6(2lh) + 6(2wh) + 3(wl)$. Substituting for w and h yields

$C = 3l^2 + (14{,}400/l) + (10{,}800/l) + \frac{9}{4}l^2 = \frac{21}{4}l^2 + (25{,}200/l).$

$C' = \frac{21}{2}l - (25{,}200/l^2) = 0 \Rightarrow 21l^3 - 50{,}400 = 0 \Rightarrow$

$l = \sqrt[3]{2400} = 2(\sqrt[3]{300}) \approx 13.38$ ft, $w = \frac{3}{2}(\sqrt[3]{300}) \approx 10.04$ ft, $h = \sqrt[3]{300} \approx 6.69$ ft.

Since $C'' > 0$ for $l > 0$, this gives a minimum.

12 Let r denote the cup's radius, h its height, and a its slant height. Examining a cross section through the cup's vertical axis, we see the relationship $r^2 + h^2 = a^2$ holds. The volume of the cup is $V = \frac{1}{3}\pi r^2 h = \frac{1}{3}\pi(a^2 - h^2)h = \frac{1}{3}\pi(a^2 h - h^3)$.

$V' = \frac{1}{3}\pi(a^2 - 3h^2) = 0 \Rightarrow a^2 = 3h^2 \Rightarrow h^2 = \frac{1}{3}a^2 \; (h = \frac{1}{3}\sqrt{3}\, a).$

Thus, $V = \frac{1}{3}\pi(\frac{2}{3}a^2)(\frac{1}{3}\sqrt{3}\, a) = \frac{2}{27}\pi\sqrt{3}\, a^3 \approx 0.4a^3.$

$V'' = -2\pi h < 0$ for $h > 0 \Rightarrow$ this is a maximum.

13 Let x denote the width of the field, y the length, and k, a constant, the length of the barn, where $0 < k < y$. The area of the field is given by $A = xy$ and the amount of fence used is given by $2x + y + (y - k) = 500 \Rightarrow y = \dfrac{500 + k}{2} - x.$

Thus, $A = \left(\dfrac{500 + k}{2}\right)x - x^2.$ $A' = \dfrac{500 + k}{2} - 2x = 0 \Rightarrow x = \dfrac{500 + k}{4} = y.$

These values give a maximum since $A'' < 0$. $x = y \Rightarrow$ the rectangle is a square.

14 Let the variables be as in Exercise 13. We wish to minimize the amount of fence used, given by $F = 2x + y + (y - k)$. Since $y = \frac{A}{x}$, $F = 2x + \frac{2A}{x} - k.$

$F' = 2 - 2A/x^2 = 0 \Rightarrow x = y = \sqrt{A}.$ Since $F'' > 0$ for $x > 0$, this is a minimum.

15 Let x denote the number of rooms reserved, where $x \in [30, 60]$. The price for each room is given by $p(x) = \left[80 - (x - 30)\right] = 110 - x.$ The revenue received is $R(x) = x(110 - x) = 110x - x^2.$ Now, $R'(x) = 110 - 2x = 0 \Rightarrow x = 55.$

$R(30) = 2400$, $R(60) = 3000$, and $R(55) = 3025$. Thus, maximum revenue occurs when 55 rooms are rented. Note that the maximum will not occur on $[0, 30]$.

16 In this case, the cost is given by $C(x) = 6x$. The profit function is

$P(x) = R(x) - C(x) = 104x - x^2.$ $P'(x) = 104 - 2x = 0 \Rightarrow x = 52.$

$P(30) = 2220$, $P(60) = 2640$, and $P(52) = 2704.$

For $x \in [0, 30]$, $P(x) = 80x - 6x = 74x$, which has maximum when $x = 30$.

Thus, maximum profit occurs when 52 rooms are rented.

17 The volume of the cylindrical part is $\pi r^2 h$, and the volume of each hemisphere is $\frac{1}{2}(\frac{4}{3})\pi r^3$. The total volume is $V = \pi r^2 h + \frac{4}{3}\pi r^3 = 10\pi \Rightarrow h = \dfrac{30 - 4r^3}{3r^2}.$

The total surface area is $S = 2\pi rh + 4\pi r^2 = 2\pi r\left(\dfrac{30 - 4r^3}{3r^2}\right) + 4\pi r^2.$

Since the construction of the end piece is twice as expensive as the cylinder, the cost function is $C(r) = 2\pi r\left(\dfrac{30 - 4r^3}{3r^2}\right) + 2(4\pi r^2) = (20\pi/r) + \frac{16}{3}\pi r^2.$

$C'(r) = (-20\pi/r^2) + \frac{32}{3}\pi r$ and $C''(r) = (40\pi/r^3) + \frac{32}{3}\pi.$

$C'(r) = 0$ if $r^3 = \frac{60}{32} \Rightarrow r = \frac{1}{2}\sqrt[3]{15}.$ Since $C'' > 0$ for $r > 0,$

this value for r will give a minimum. $h = 2\sqrt[3]{15}$ for this value of $r.$

18 Let x denote the distance between the point C and the point on the shore opposite A,
where $0 \leq x \leq \sqrt{8}$ { $x = 0$ if $\angle ACB = 90°$ }. Let k denote the cost of pipe per mile
above the ground and $4k$ the cost per mile under the water. The length above ground
is $\sqrt{8} - x$, its cost is $k(\sqrt{8} - x)$. The length under water is $\sqrt{1 + x^2}$, its cost is
$4k\sqrt{1 + x^2}$. If $P(x)$ is total cost, then $P(x) = k(\sqrt{8} - x) + 4k\sqrt{1 + x^2}.$

$$P'(x) = -k + \frac{4kx}{\sqrt{1 + x^2}} = 0 \Rightarrow x = \sqrt{\frac{1}{15}} \approx 0.26 \text{ mi.}$$

This is a minimum since $P''(x) = \dfrac{4k}{(1 + x^2)^{3/2}} > 0.$

The distance from C to B would be $\sqrt{8} - \sqrt{\frac{1}{15}} \approx 2.57$ mi.

19 Consider *Figure 19*. The area $A = 2xy = 2x\sqrt{a^2 - x^2}.$ $A' = \dfrac{2(a^2 - 2x^2)}{\sqrt{a^2 - x^2}} = 0 \Rightarrow$

$x = \frac{1}{2}\sqrt{2}\, a.$ Thus, $y = \sqrt{a^2 - (\frac{1}{2}\sqrt{2}\, a)^2} = \frac{1}{2}\sqrt{2}\, a$ and the length of the base is $\sqrt{2}\, a.$

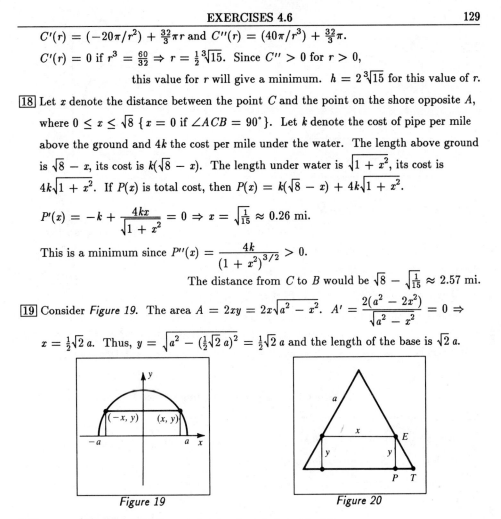

Figure 19   Figure 20

20 From *Figure 20*, $\triangle PET$ is a $30°\text{-}60°\text{-}90°$ triangle, with $ET = a - x,$
so $y = \frac{1}{2}\sqrt{3}(a - x).$ $A = xy = \frac{1}{2}\sqrt{3}(ax - x^2),$ where $0 \leq x \leq a.$
$A' = \frac{1}{2}\sqrt{3}(a - 2x) = 0 \Rightarrow x = \frac{1}{2}a.$

Since $A(0) = A(a) = 0,$ $x = \frac{1}{2}a,$ $y = \frac{1}{4}\sqrt{3}\, a$ give a maximum area.

21 $V = \frac{1}{3}\pi r^2 h.$ To relate r and h, consider the small right triangle in *Figure 21*.
The vertical leg is $h - a$ if $h > a$ (shown) or $a - h$ if $h < a.$
$r^2 + (h - a)^2 = a^2 \Rightarrow r^2 = 2ah - h^2$ (in either case).
$V = \frac{1}{3}\pi(2ah^2 - h^3) \Rightarrow V' = \frac{\pi}{3}(4a - 3h)h = 0$ if $h = \frac{4}{3}a$ and the volume is $\frac{32}{81}\pi a^3.$

This is a maximum since the endpoints of $h = 0, 2a$ yield $V = 0.$

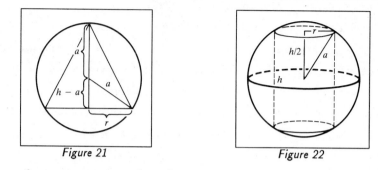

Figure 21   Figure 22

$\boxed{22}$ $V = \pi r^2 h$. From *Figure 22*, $r^2 = a^2 - \frac{1}{4}h^2$. $V = \pi(a^2 h - \frac{1}{4}h^3)$, where

$0 \le h \le 2a$. $V' = \pi(a^2 - \frac{3}{4}h^2) = 0$ if $h = \frac{2}{3}\sqrt{3}\,a$. The corresponding r is $\frac{1}{3}\sqrt{6}\,a$.

These values produce a maximum since the endpoints of $h = 0$, $2a$ yield $V = 0$.

$\boxed{23}$ If $f(x)$ is the square of the distance of a point $(x, x^2 + 1)$ on the parabola from $(3, 1)$,

then $f(x) = (x - 3)^2 + (x^2)^2$. $f'(x) = 2(x - 3) + 4x^3 = 0$ if $x = 1$.

{ Since the sum of the coefficients of f' is zero, 1 is a root. }

The point $(1, 2)$ gives a minimum, since $f''(x) = 2 + 12x^2 > 0$.

$\boxed{24}$ If $f(x)$ is the square of the distance of a point (x, x^3) on the graph from $(4, 0)$,

then $f(x) = (x - 4)^2 + (x^3)^2$. $f'(x) = 2(x - 4) + 6x^5 = 0$ if $x = 1$.

The point $(1, 1)$ gives a minimum, since $f''(x) = 2 + 30x^4 > 0$.

$\boxed{25}$ If S denotes the strength, w the width, and d the depth,

then $S = kwd^2$, where $k > 0$ is a proportionality constant.

With the circular cross section placed as shown in

Figure 25, we have $w = 2x$, $d = 2y$, and $y^2 = a^2 - x^2$.

$S = k(2x)4y^2 = 8k(a^2 x - x^3)$.

$S' = 8k(a^2 - 3x^2) = 0$ if $x = a/\sqrt{3}$.

Thus, $w = 2a/\sqrt{3}$ and $d = 2\sqrt{2}a/\sqrt{3}$.

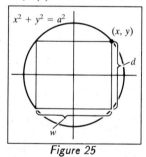

Figure 25

This is a maximum, since the endpoints of $x = 0$, a yield $S = 0$.

$\boxed{26}$ Let P be a point on the line segment x units from S_1. Let the illumination at P be

$I(x)$, which is the sum of the illumination from the two sources. Thus,

$I(x) = \dfrac{kS_1}{x^2} + \dfrac{kS_2}{(d - x)^2}$, where $k > 0$ is a constant of proportionality.

$I'(x) = \dfrac{-2kS_1}{x^3} + \dfrac{2kS_2}{(d - x)^3} = 0 \Leftrightarrow \dfrac{S_2}{S_1} = \left(\dfrac{d - x}{x}\right)^3 \Leftrightarrow x = \dfrac{d\,\sqrt[3]{S_1}}{\sqrt[3]{S_2} + \sqrt[3]{S_1}}$.

Since $I'' > 0$ for $x \in (0, d)$, this value of x will give minimal illumination.

$\boxed{27}$ If x is the number of pairs ordered and $p(x)$ the price (in dollars) per pair, then

$p(x) = 20$ on $[1, 49]$ and $20 - 0.02x$ on $[50, 600]$. Hence, if $R(x)$ is the revenue

function, $R(x) = xp(x) = 20x$ on $[1, 49]$ and $20x - 0.02x^2$ on $[50, 600]$. The maximum of R on $[1, 49]$ is $R(49) = 980$. On $(50, 600)$, $R'(x) = 20 - 0.04x = 0$

$\Leftrightarrow x = 500$. $R(50) = 950$, $R(500) = 5000$ and $R(600) = 4800$. Thus, $x = 500$.

[28] $V = \frac{1}{3}\pi r^2 h = 36\pi \Rightarrow h = 108/r^2$.

The surface area is given by $S = \pi r\sqrt{r^2 + h^2} = \pi r^{-1}(r^6 + 108^2)^{1/2}$.

$S'(r) = \dfrac{\pi(2r^6 - 108^2)}{r^2(r^6 + 108^2)^{1/2}} = 0$ if $r = 3\sqrt{2}$. Since $S' < 0$ if $0 \le r < 3\sqrt{2}$ and

$S' > 0$ if $r > 3\sqrt{2}$, $r = 3\sqrt{2}$ and $h = 6$ give minimal surface area.

[29] (a) Let $3y$ denote the length of the piece of wire bent into the equilateral triangle and

$6x$ { width x and length $2x$ } the amount bent into the rectangle. The triangle's

area is $\frac{1}{4}\sqrt{3}\,y^2$ { inside cover of text }. Now, $3y + 6x = 36 \Rightarrow y = 12 - 2x$.

The total area is $A(x) = \frac{1}{4}\sqrt{3}(12 - 2x)^2 + 2x^2 = \sqrt{3}(6 - x)^2 + 2x^2$.

$A' = (4 + 2\sqrt{3})x - 12\sqrt{3} = 0 \Leftrightarrow x = \dfrac{12\sqrt{3}}{4 + 2\sqrt{3}} \approx 2.785$.

Use $6x \approx 16.71$ cm for the rectangle. This is a minimum, since $A'' > 0$.

(b) The maximum must occur at an endpoint. $A(0) = 36\sqrt{3} < A(6) = 72$.

Use all the wire for the rectangle to obtain a maximum area.

[30] From *Figure 30*, $\triangle PQS$ is similar to $\triangle TRS$. Therefore, we have

$\dfrac{y}{\frac{1}{2}(b - x)} = \dfrac{\sqrt{a^2 - b^2/4}}{\frac{1}{2}b} \Rightarrow y = \dfrac{(b - x)\sqrt{4a^2 - b^2}}{2b}$. The area of the rectangle

is $A(x) = \dfrac{x(b - x)\sqrt{4a^2 - b^2}}{2b}$ and $A'(x) = \dfrac{(b - 2x)\sqrt{4a^2 - b^2}}{2b} = 0$ if $x = \frac{1}{2}b$. At

the endpoints $x = 0$ and b, $A = 0$. $x = \frac{1}{2}b$ and $y = \frac{1}{4}\sqrt{4a^2 - b^2}$ give a maximum.

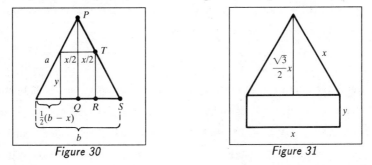

Figure 30   Figure 31

[31] From *Figure 31*, $3x + 2y = 12 \Rightarrow y = \frac{1}{2}(12 - 3x)$. The total area is given by

$A(x) = \frac{1}{4}\sqrt{3}\,x^2 + xy = \frac{1}{4}(\sqrt{3} - 6)x^2 + 6x$. $A'(x) = \frac{1}{2}(\sqrt{3} - 6)x + 6 = 0 \Rightarrow$

$x = \dfrac{12}{6 - \sqrt{3}} \approx 2.81$ ft and $y = \dfrac{18 - 6\sqrt{3}}{6 - \sqrt{3}} \approx 1.78$ ft.

Since $A(0) = 0$, $A(2.81) \approx 8.43$, and $A(4) = 4\sqrt{3} \approx 6.93$,

these values of x and y give a maximum area.

32 Let x denote the distance from the base of the shorter pole to the point S where the cable touches the ground. Let R denote the point at the top of the 6 ft pole and T the point at the top of the 8 ft pole. $\overline{RS} = \sqrt{x^2 + 36}$ and $\overline{TS} = \sqrt{(10 - x)^2 + 64}$. The total length of the cable is $f(x) = \sqrt{x^2 + 36} + \sqrt{(10 - x)^2 + 64}$ and

$$f'(x) = \frac{x}{\sqrt{x^2 + 36}} + \frac{x - 10}{\sqrt{(10 - x)^2 + 64}} = 0 \Leftrightarrow \frac{x^2}{x^2 + 36} = \frac{(x - 10)^2}{(10 - x)^2 + 64} \Leftrightarrow$$

$x^2(10 - x)^2 + 64x^2 = x^2(10 - x)^2 + 36(10 - x)^2 \Leftrightarrow 28x^2 + 720x - 3600 = 0 \Leftrightarrow$

$4(7x - 30)(x + 30) = 0 \Rightarrow x = \frac{30}{7}$. The endpoints are $x = 0, 10$.

$f(0) = 2\sqrt{41} + 6 \approx 18.8$, $f(\frac{30}{7}) = 2\sqrt{74} \approx 17.2$,

and $f(10) \approx 19.66$. Thus, 17.2 ft. is the minimum cable length.

33 If the dimensions are l by w, then $2l + 2w = p \Rightarrow w = \frac{1}{2}p - l$.

$A = lw = \frac{1}{2}pl - l^2 \Rightarrow A' = \frac{1}{2}p - 2l = 0 \Leftrightarrow l = \frac{1}{4}p$.

Thus, $l = w = \frac{1}{4}p$, a square. The area is maximum since $A'' < 0$.

34 Let x and y denote the dimensions of the rectangle with the rotation about an edge of length y.

$2x + 2y = p \Rightarrow y = \frac{1}{2}p - x$ and the volume is

$V = \pi x^2 y = \pi x^2(\frac{1}{2}p - x) = \pi(\frac{1}{2}px^2 - x^3)$.

$V' = \pi(px - 3x^2) = 0$ when $x = 0, \frac{1}{3}p$.

$x = \frac{1}{3}p$ and $y = \frac{1}{6}p$ will give a maximum volume,

since the endpoints of $x = 0, \frac{1}{2}p$ yield $V = 0$.

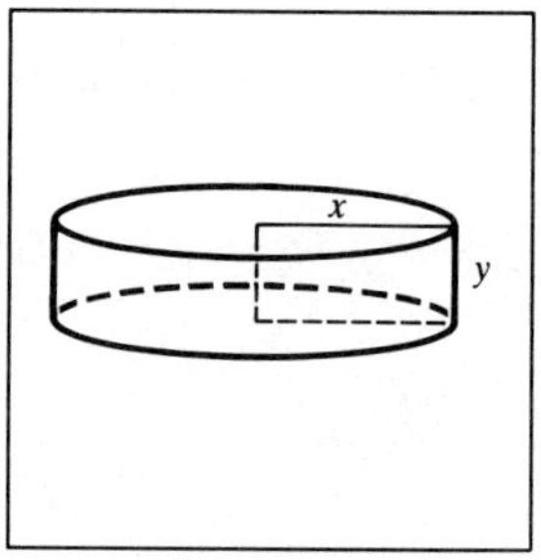

Figure 34

35 Let x denote the number of trees planted in *excess* of 24 per acre.

Thus, $(24 + x)$ is the number of trees per acre and $(600 - 12x)$ is the yield per tree.

The total yield per acre is $f(x) = (24 + x)(600 - 12x) = -12x^2 + 312x + 14,400$.

$f'(x) = -24x + 312 = 0 \Leftrightarrow x = 13$. $f''(x) < 0 \Rightarrow$ this is a maximum.

Plant 37 trees per acre.

36 Let x denote the number of \$10 increases. The rent per apartment is $300 + 10x$.

The number of occupied apartments is $180 - 5x$. The gross income is $G(x) =$

$(300 + 10x)(180 - 5x) = -50x^2 + 300x + 54,000$. $G'(x) = -100x + 300 = 0$

when $x = 3$. Since $G'' < 0$, this is a maximum. Charge \$330 per unit.

37 Let x denote the side of the square base, g the girth $(g = 4x)$, and l the length.

$l + g = 108 \Rightarrow l = 108 - 4x$. $V = x^2 l = 108x^2 - 4x^3$, where $0 \le x \le 27$.

$V'(x) = 216x - 12x^2 = 0$ when $x = 0, 18$.

$V(0) = V(27) = 0 \Rightarrow x = 18$ and $l = 36$ give a maximum volume.

38 Let $t = 0$ correspond to 10:00 A.M. and let y denote the distance north of P that the car is at time t. Hence, $y = 50t$. Let x denote the horizontal distance of the airplane from P at time t. Thus, $x = 100 - 200t$. Let d denote the distance between the airplane and the car. Since 26,400 ft = 5 mi, $f(t) = d^2 = x^2 + y^2 + 5^2 = (100 - 200t)^2 + (50t)^2 + 5^2$. We now have $f'(t) = 85,000t - 40,000 = 0 \Rightarrow$

$$t = \tfrac{8}{17} \text{ hr. This is minimum since } f'' > 0. \text{ Time} \approx 10{:}28 \text{ A.M.}$$

$\boxed{39}$ Let S_1 denote the amount of smoke from factory A and S_2 the amount of smoke from factory B. The pollution at a distance x from factory A on a straight line path to

factory B is $P = \dfrac{kS_1}{x^3} + \dfrac{kS_2}{(4 - x)^3}$, where $k > 0$ is a constant of proportionality.

Since $S_1 = 2S_2$, we have $P = \dfrac{2kS_2}{x^3} + \dfrac{kS_2}{(4 - x)^3} \Rightarrow P' = \dfrac{-6kS_2}{x^4} + \dfrac{3kS_2}{(4 - x)^4} = 0 \Rightarrow$

$\dfrac{4 - x}{x} = \sqrt[4]{1/2} \Rightarrow x = \dfrac{4}{1 + \sqrt[4]{1/2}} \approx 2.17$ mi from A.

Since $P'' > 0$ for $x \in (0, 4)$, this gives a minimum.

$\boxed{40}$ Let x denote the number of additional wells to be drilled. The average production per well is given by $200 - 10x$. The amount of oil produced is given by

$A = (8 + x)(200 - 10x) = 1600 + 120x - 10x^2$.

Now, $A' = 120 - 20x = 0 \Rightarrow x = 6$. Since $A'' < 0$, this is a maximum.

$\boxed{41}$ (a) The volume of the pyramid is $V = \tfrac{1}{3}x^2 h$. Let y denote its slant height. Then,

$y^2 = h^2 + (\tfrac{1}{2}x)^2$. The area of one of the triangular surfaces is

$\tfrac{1}{2}xy = \tfrac{1}{2}x\sqrt{h^2 + \tfrac{1}{4}x^2}$. Since there are 4 such surfaces, $S = 2x\sqrt{h^2 + \tfrac{1}{4}x^2}$.

Solving for h yields $h = \dfrac{\sqrt{S^2 - x^4}}{2x}$. Thus, $V = \tfrac{1}{6}x\sqrt{S^2 - x^4}$.

(b) $V'(x) = \dfrac{(S^2 - x^4) - 2x^4}{6(S^2 - x^4)^{1/2}} = \dfrac{4x^2 h^2 - 2x^4}{12xh}$ (since $4x^2 h^2 = S^2 - x^4$) $=$

$\dfrac{x^2(2h^2 - x^2)}{6xh} = 0 \Rightarrow x = \sqrt{2}\,h.$ (V' is undefined at $x = 0$.)

$V' > 0$ for $0 < x < \sqrt{2}\,h$ and $V' < 0$ for $x > \sqrt{2}\,h \Rightarrow$ maximum.

$\boxed{42}$ (a) If $v \leq 10$, the boat makes no progress. The number of gallons of gas used *each* hour is kv^2, where $k > 0$ is a constant. The total time for the trip is

$\dfrac{\text{distance}}{\text{rate}} = \dfrac{100}{v - 10}$. Thus, the total gas consumption is $y = \dfrac{100kv^2}{v - 10}$.

(b) $\dfrac{dy}{dv} = \dfrac{100kv(v - 20)}{(v - 10)^2} = 0 \Rightarrow v = 20$.

Since $\dfrac{dy}{dv} < 0$ on $(10, 20)$ and $\dfrac{dy}{dv} > 0$ on $(20, \infty)$, $v = 20$ mi/hr is a minimum.

$\boxed{43}$ (a) Since 1 mi = 5,280 ft and each car requires $(12 + d)$ ft,

it follows directly that the bridge can hold $[\![5280/(12 + d)]\!]$ cars.

The greatest integer function is necessary since a fraction of a car is not allowed.

(b) Since the bridge is 1 mile long, the car "density" is $\dfrac{5280}{12 + d}$ cars/mi. If each car

is moving at v mi/hr, then the flow rate is $F = [\![5280v/(12 + d)]\!]$ cars/hr.

(c) Since $d = 0.025v^2$, $F = \dfrac{5280v}{12 + 0.025v^2}$. $F' = \dfrac{63,360 - 132v^2}{(12 + 0.025v^2)^2} = 0 \Rightarrow$

$v = 4\sqrt{30} \approx 21.9$ mi/hr. $F' > 0$ for $0 < v < 4\sqrt{30}$ and $F' < 0$ for $v > 4\sqrt{30} \Rightarrow$

21.9 mi/hr is a maximum value.

$\boxed{44}$ Let $(x, f(x))$ be an arbitrary point on the graph of f. Then, the square of the

distance from (x_1, y_1) is given by $d^2 = \left[f(x) - y_1\right]^2 + \left[x - x_1\right]^2$. Differentiating to

find the critical numbers yields $\left[f(x) - y_1\right]f'(x) + (x - x_1) = 0$. Let x_0 be a

solution of this equation. Then, $\dfrac{f(x_0) - y_1}{x_0 - x_1} = -\dfrac{1}{f'(x_0)}$, that is, the slope of the line

is perpendicular to the slope of the tangent line at $(x_0, f(x_0))$. (If $f'(x_0) = 0$, then

the line is vertical but still perpendicular to the tangent line.) Since this is true for

all critical numbers, the shortest distance will be measured along a normal line.

$\boxed{45}$ Let x denote the distance from A to B. Then, the distance from B to C is

$\sqrt{(40 - x)^2 + 20^2}$ and the cost (times 10,000) is $C(x) = 5x + 10\sqrt{(40 - x)^2 + 400}$

$\Rightarrow C'(x) = 5 - \dfrac{10(40 - x)}{\left[(40 - x)^2 + 400\right]^{1/2}} = 0$ when $(40 - x) = \dfrac{20}{\sqrt{3}}$.

Now, $\tan\theta = \dfrac{20}{40 - x} = \sqrt{3} \Rightarrow \theta = 60°$. Since $C(20) \approx 383$,

$C(40) = 400$, and $C(20/\sqrt{3}) \approx 289$, the minimum occurs at $\theta = 60°$.

$\boxed{46}$ The capacity of the gutter is maximized when the cross-sectional area is maximized.

Let each of the turned up sides have length y and the bottom of the gutter have

width x. Then, $x + 2y = 12 \Rightarrow x = 12 - 2y$. If h is the height of the trough, then

the area A is the sum of a rectangle (x by h) and two triangles (height h and base b).

Since the triangles are 30°-60°-90°, $h = \frac{1}{2}\sqrt{3}\,y$ and $b = \frac{1}{2}y$.

$A = xh + 2(\frac{1}{2}hb) = \frac{1}{2}\sqrt{3}\,yx + \frac{1}{4}\sqrt{3}\,y^2 = \sqrt{3}(6y - \frac{3}{4}y^2)$, where $0 \le y \le 6$.

$A'(y) = \sqrt{3}(6 - \frac{3}{2}y) = 0 \Rightarrow y = 4$ in.

This is a maximum since $A(0) = 0$, $A(4) = 12\sqrt{3}$, and $A(6) = 9\sqrt{3}$.

$\boxed{47}$ From Exercise 12, we know $h^2 = \frac{1}{3}a^2$ and hence $r^2 = \frac{2}{3}a^2$ (or $r = \frac{1}{3}\sqrt{6}\,a$).

The following relationship holds:

(the circumference of the circular sheet of paper) $-$ (the arc of the circular sector) $=$

(the circumference of the cup's rim), i.e., $2\pi a - a\theta = 2\pi r \Rightarrow a\theta = 2\pi(a - r) \Rightarrow$

$$\theta = \dfrac{2\pi(a - \frac{1}{3}\sqrt{6}\,a)}{a} = 2\pi(1 - \frac{1}{3}\sqrt{6}) \approx 1.153 \text{ radians or } 66.06°.$$

[48] Using *Figure 48* and the law of cosines, we have

$$2^2 = (x^2 + 9) + (x^2 + 1) - 2\sqrt{x^2 + 1}\sqrt{x^2 + 9}\cos 2\theta \Rightarrow$$

$$\cos 2\theta = \frac{x^2 + 3}{\sqrt{(x^2 + 1)(x^2 + 9)}}. \text{ Since } 0 < 2\theta < \tfrac{\pi}{2},$$

2θ will be maximum when $\cos 2\theta$ is minimum.

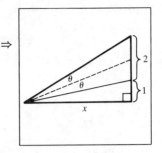

Let $f(x) = \dfrac{x^2 + 3}{(x^4 + 10x^2 + 9)^{1/2}}$.

So, $f'(x) = \dfrac{4x(x^2 - 3)}{(x^4 + 10x^2 + 9)^{3/2}}$ and $f'(x) = 0$ when $x = 0, \pm\sqrt{3}$.

Figure 48

Discard $x = 0, -\sqrt{3}$. Now, $0 < x < \sqrt{3} \Rightarrow f'(x) < 0$ and $x > \sqrt{3} \Rightarrow f'(x) > 0$.

Thus, $x = \sqrt{3}$ ft is a minimum value for f and hence, this value of x will maximize θ.

[49] Let $x = \overline{DC}$ and $h = \overline{BC}$. The volume of a cylinder is $V = \pi r^2 h$. Now, $h = L\sin\theta$

and $x = L\cos\theta$. Since x is the circumference of the cylinder, $x = 2\pi r \Rightarrow r = \dfrac{x}{2\pi}$.

Thus, $r = \dfrac{L\cos\theta}{2\pi}$. We can now write V in terms of θ. $V = \dfrac{L^3}{4\pi}(\cos^2\theta\,\sin\theta)$.

$$V'(\theta) = \frac{L^3}{4\pi}(-2\cos\theta\,\sin^2\theta + \cos^3\theta) = 0 \Leftrightarrow \cos\theta\,(\cos^2\theta - 2\sin^2\theta) = 0 \Leftrightarrow$$

$\cos\theta = 0$ or $\tan\theta = \pm\tfrac{1}{2}\sqrt{2}$. Since θ must be acute, we have

$\theta_0 = \tan^{-1}(\tfrac{1}{2}\sqrt{2}) \approx 35.3°$. Since $V' > 0$ for $0° < \theta < \theta_0$ and

$$V' < 0 \text{ for } \theta_0 < \theta < 90°, \theta_0 \text{ gives a maximum value.}$$

[50] (a) $F(\tfrac{\pi}{2b}) = A\left[\cos\left(b\cdot\tfrac{\pi}{2b}\right) - a\cos\left(3b\cdot\tfrac{\pi}{2b}\right)\right] = A\left(\cos\tfrac{\pi}{2} - a\cos\tfrac{3\pi}{2}\right) = 0.$

$\qquad\qquad\qquad\qquad\qquad F(-\tfrac{\pi}{2b}) = 0$, since F is an even function.

(b) $F'(t) = A(-b\sin bt + 3ab\sin 3bt) = 0 \Leftrightarrow$

$\qquad -b\sin bt + 3ab(3\sin bt - 4\sin^3 bt) = 0$ { since

$\qquad\qquad \sin 3bt = \sin(2bt + bt) = \sin 2bt\cos bt + \sin bt\cos 2bt$

$\qquad\qquad\quad = (2\sin bt\cos bt)\cos bt + \sin bt(1 - 2\sin^2 bt)$

$\qquad\qquad\quad = 2\sin bt\cos^2 bt + \sin bt - 2\sin^3 bt$

$\qquad\qquad\quad = 2\sin bt(1 - \sin^2 bt) + \sin bt - 2\sin^3 bt = 3\sin bt - 4\sin^3 bt$ }

$\qquad \Leftrightarrow b\sin bt\left[(9a - 1) - 12a\sin^2 bt\right] = 0 \Leftrightarrow$

$\qquad\qquad\qquad\qquad \sin bt = 0 \ (t = 0) \text{ or } \sin^2 bt = \dfrac{9a - 1}{12a}.$

(c) If $a = \tfrac{1}{3}$, then $\sin^2 bt = \tfrac{1}{2}$ and $\cos bt = \sqrt{1 - \sin^2 bt} = \tfrac{1}{2}\sqrt{2}$.

$\qquad$ In a manner similar to that of part (b), $\cos 3bt = 4\cos^3 bt - 3\cos bt$.

$$F_{max} = A\left[\cos bt - \tfrac{1}{3}(4\cos^3 bt - 3\cos bt)\right] = A\left[\tfrac{1}{\sqrt{2}} - \tfrac{1}{3}\left(\tfrac{4}{2\sqrt{2}} - \tfrac{3}{\sqrt{2}}\right)\right] = \tfrac{2}{3}\sqrt{2}\,A.$$

(d) If $0 < a \le \tfrac{1}{9}$, then $\sin^2 bt = \dfrac{9a - 1}{12a} < 0$, which is impossible.

$\qquad$ Thus, the only critical number is $t = 0 \Rightarrow F_{max} = A[1 - a(1)] = A(1 - a)$.

[51] $P(R) = I^2 R = \dfrac{V^2 R}{(R + r)^2}$. $P'(R) = \dfrac{V^2(r - R)}{(R + r)^3} = 0$ if $R = r$.

For $R < r$, $P' > 0$ and for $R > r$, $P' < 0$. Thus, $R = r$ yields maximum power.

[52] $P(I) = VI - I^2 r$. $P'(I) = V - 2Ir = 0 \Rightarrow I = \dfrac{V}{2r}$.

$$P''(I) = -2r < 0. \text{ Thus, } I = \dfrac{V}{2r} \text{ yields maximum power.}$$

[53] For each $0 < \theta < \frac{\pi}{2}$, there is exactly one rod of length L that touches the corner *and* both walls. We would like to find the *minimum* of all such rods. Divide the rod in the figure in the text at the corner into two parts. Then, $L = \dfrac{4}{\sin \theta} + \dfrac{3}{\cos \theta} \Rightarrow$

$L' = \dfrac{3 \sin^3 \theta - 4 \cos^3 \theta}{\cos^2 \theta \, \sin^2 \theta} = 0 \Rightarrow \tan^3 \theta = \frac{4}{3} \Rightarrow \tan \theta = \sqrt[3]{4/3} \Rightarrow \theta_0 \approx 47.74° \text{ and}$

$L \approx 9.87$ ft. Since for $0° < \theta < \theta_0$, $L' < 0$ and for $\theta_0 < \theta < 90°$, $L' > 0$,

this will be a minimum value for L.

[54] Let P have coordinates $(0, a)$, Q have coordinates $(k, -b)$, and the point A where the light enters the water have coordinates $(x, 0)$. The time $\{t = d/r\}$ for

light to travel from P to A is $\dfrac{\sqrt{a^2 + x^2}}{v_1}$ and from A to Q is $\dfrac{\sqrt{(k - x)^2 + b^2}}{v_2}$.

Let $T(x)$ be the sum of these terms which represents the total time from P to Q.

Then, $T'(x) = \dfrac{x}{v_1 \sqrt{a^2 + x^2}} - \dfrac{k - x}{v_2 \sqrt{(k - x)^2 + b^2}} = 0$ when these two terms are

equal. The first term is equal to $\dfrac{\sin \theta_1}{v_1}$ and the second is equal to $\dfrac{\sin \theta_2}{v_2}$. Since a path

of minimum time exists, it must satisfy this condition for a critical number.

Note: Since all points are distinct, neither denominator can be zero.

[55] (a) The volume of the cone and the cylinder is given by $V = \frac{1}{3}\pi R^2 h_1 + \pi R^2 h_2$,

where h_1 is the height of the cone and h_2 is the height of the cylinder. Thus,

$h_2 = \dfrac{V}{\pi R^2} - \frac{1}{3} h_1 = \dfrac{V}{\pi R^2} - \dfrac{R \cot \theta}{3}$ since $h_1 = R \cot \theta$. The total surface area is

$S = 2\pi R h_2 + \pi R \sqrt{R^2 + h_1^2} = 2\pi R \left(\dfrac{V}{\pi R^2} - \dfrac{R \cot \theta}{3} \right) + \pi R \sqrt{R^2 + R^2 \cot^2 \theta} =$

$\dfrac{2V}{R} - \frac{2}{3}\pi R^2 \cot \theta + \pi R^2 \sqrt{1 + \cot^2 \theta} = \dfrac{2V}{R} + \pi R^2 \left(\csc \theta - \frac{2}{3} \cot \theta \right) \{\theta \text{ acute}\}$.

(b) $S'(\theta) = 0 + \pi R^2 (-\csc \theta \cot \theta + \frac{2}{3} \csc^2 \theta) = 0 \Rightarrow \cot \theta - \frac{2}{3} \csc \theta = 0$

$\{\csc \theta \neq 0\} \Rightarrow \cos \theta = \frac{2}{3}$. Let $\theta_0 = \cos^{-1} \frac{2}{3} \approx 48.2°$. Since $S' < 0$ for

$0 < \theta < \theta_0$ and $S' > 0$ for $\theta_0 < \theta < \frac{\pi}{2}$, this value of θ_0 gives a minimum.

[56] $S'(\theta) = 0 + \frac{3}{2} R^2 \csc^2 \theta - \frac{3}{2}\sqrt{3} R^2 \csc \theta \cot \theta = 0 \Rightarrow$

$\csc \theta - \sqrt{3} \cot \theta = 0 \{\csc \theta \neq 0\} \Rightarrow \sqrt{3} \cos \theta = 1 \Rightarrow \theta = \cos^{-1}(\frac{1}{3}\sqrt{3}) \approx 54.7°$.

For the same reason as in Exercise 55(b), this value of θ will give a minimum.

Exercises 4.7

Note: In Exercises 1–8, $v(t) = s'(t)$ and $a(t) = v'(t) = s''(t)$.

The motion is to the *right* when $v(t) > 0$ and to the *left* when $v(t) < 0$.

⨌1 $v(t) = 6(t - 2)$; $a(t) = 6$; left in $[0, 2)$; right in $(2, 5]$

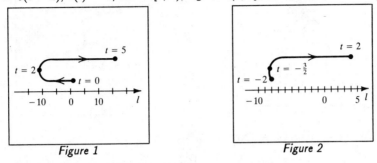

Figure 1   Figure 2

⨌2 $v(t) = 2t + 3$; $a(t) = 2$; left in $[-2, -\frac{3}{2})$; right in $(-\frac{3}{2}, 2]$

⨌3 $v(t) = 3(t^2 - 3)$; $a(t) = 6t$; right in $[-3, -\sqrt{3})$; left in $(-\sqrt{3}, \sqrt{3})$; right in $(\sqrt{3}, 3]$

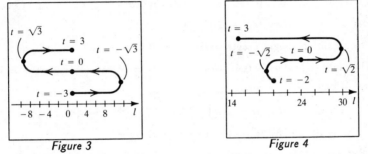

Figure 3   Figure 4

⨌4 $v(t) = 3(2 - t^2)$; $a(t) = -6t$; left in $[-2, -\sqrt{2})$; right in $(-\sqrt{2}, \sqrt{2})$; left in $(\sqrt{2}, 3]$

⨌5 $v(t) = -6(t - 1)(t - 4)$; $a(t) = -6(2t - 5)$;

left in $[0, 1)$; right in $(1, 4)$; left in $(4, 5]$

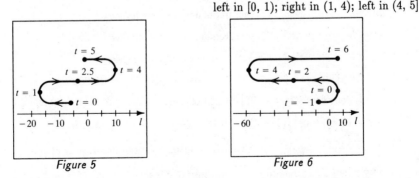

Figure 5   Figure 6

⨌6 $v(t) = 6t(t - 4)$; $a(t) = 12(t - 2)$; right in $[-1, 0)$; left in $(0, 4)$; right in $(4, 6]$

$\boxed{7}$ $v(t) = 4t(2t^2 - 3)$; $a(t) = 12(2t^2 - 1)$;

left in $[-2, -\sqrt{\frac{3}{2}})$; right in $(-\sqrt{\frac{3}{2}}, 0)$; left in $(0, \sqrt{\frac{3}{2}})$; right in $(\sqrt{\frac{3}{2}}, 2]$

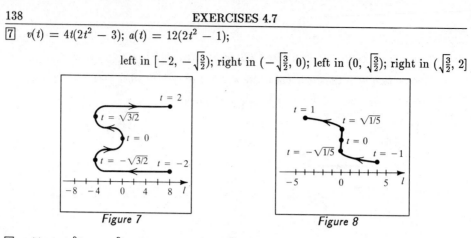

Figure 7   Figure 8

$\boxed{8}$ $v(t) = 6t^2(1 - 5t^2)$; $a(t) = 12t(1 - 10t^2)$;

left in $[-1, -\sqrt{\frac{1}{5}})$; right in $(-\sqrt{\frac{1}{5}}, 0) \cup (0, \sqrt{\frac{1}{5}})$; left in $(\sqrt{\frac{1}{5}}, 1]$

$\boxed{9}$ (a) $v(t) = 10t$; $v(3) = 30$ ft/sec   (b) $v(t) = 28 \Rightarrow t = \frac{28}{10}$ or 2.8 sec

$\boxed{10}$ (a) $v(t) = 6t$; $v(3) = 18$ ft/sec   (b) $v(t) = 88 \Rightarrow t = \frac{44}{3}$ or $14\frac{2}{3}$ sec

$\boxed{11}$ (a) $v(t) = 144 - 32t = 16(9 - 2t)$; $a(t) = -32$

(b) The maximum height occurs when $v(t) = 0$ $(t = \frac{9}{2})$; this height is $s(\frac{9}{2}) = 324$ ft.

(c) The flight ends when $s(t) = 0$ $\{t > 0\}$; $s(t) = 16t(9 - t) = 0 \Rightarrow t = 9$ sec.

$\boxed{12}$ (a) $v(t) = 192 - 32t = 32(6 - t)$; $a(t) = -32$

(b) $v(t) = 0 \Rightarrow t = 6$; $s(6) = 676$ ft.

(c) $s(t) = -4(2t - 25)(2t + 1) = 0 \Rightarrow t = 12.5$ sec.

Note: In Exercises 13–16, consider the general position function $s(t) = a\sin\omega t$ {or cos}.

The amplitude is $|a|$, the period is $\frac{2\pi}{\omega}$, and the frequency is $\frac{\omega}{2\pi}$, where $\omega > 0$.

$\boxed{13}$ amplitude = 5; period = 8 sec; frequency = $\frac{1}{8}$ cycle/sec

$\boxed{14}$ amplitude = 4; period = 2 sec; frequency = $\frac{1}{2}$ cycle/sec

$\boxed{15}$ amplitude = 6; period = 3 sec; frequency = $\frac{1}{3}$ cycle/sec

$\boxed{16}$ amplitude = 3; period = π sec; frequency = $\frac{1}{\pi}$ cycle/sec

$\boxed{17}$ $V' = 220(360\pi \cos 360\pi t) = 79{,}200\pi \cos 360\pi t$; $V'(1) = 79{,}200\pi$.

$I' = 20\left[360\pi \cos\left(360\pi t - \frac{\pi}{4}\right)\right] = 7200\pi \cos\left(360\pi t - \frac{\pi}{4}\right)$; $I'(1) = 3600\sqrt{2}\pi$.

$\boxed{18}$ $T'(t) = 14.8\left(\frac{\pi}{6}\right)\cos\left[\frac{\pi}{6}(t - 3)\right]$; $T'(3) = \frac{14.8\pi}{6} \approx 7.75\,°\text{C/month}$.

$T'(10) = \frac{14.8\pi}{6} \cdot \left(-\frac{\sqrt{3}}{2}\right) \approx -6.71\,°\text{C/month}$. The temperature is changing most

rapidly when T' is maximum or minimum. Since $-1 \le \cos\left[\frac{\pi}{6}(t - 3)\right] \le 1$,

$T' = \frac{14.8\pi}{6}$ is maximum and $T' = -\frac{14.8\pi}{6}$ is minimum.

These values occur at $t = 3$ and $t = 9$, respectively.

$\boxed{19}$ (a) Using the graph, the wave's amplitude is $\frac{1}{2}(12 - 3) = 4.5$, the period is 12, and

the phase shift is 10. Now $\frac{2\pi}{b} = 12 \Rightarrow b = \frac{\pi}{6}$ and $-\frac{c}{b} = 10 \Rightarrow c = -\frac{5\pi}{3}$. The

wave is shifted 7.5 units upward so $d = 7.5$ and $y = 4.5\sin\left[\frac{\pi}{6}(t - 10)\right] + 7.5$.

(b) $y' = \frac{3\pi}{4}\cos\left[\frac{\pi}{6}(t - 10)\right]$. At $t = 12$, $y' = \frac{3\pi}{8} \approx 1.178$ ft/hr.

$\boxed{20}$ (a) $y(t) = a\cos bt$; $y(0) = 25 \Rightarrow a = 25$. Since the period is 30 minutes,

$$\text{we have } \frac{2\pi}{b} = 30 \Rightarrow b = \frac{\pi}{15} \text{ and thus, } y = 25\cos\frac{\pi}{15}t.$$

(b) $y'(t) = -\frac{5\pi}{3}\sin\frac{\pi}{15}t$ indicates the rising (or falling) of the wave.

$$y = 10 \Rightarrow \cos\frac{\pi}{15}t = \frac{2}{5} \Rightarrow \sin\frac{\pi}{15}t = \pm\sqrt{1 - \left(\frac{2}{5}\right)^2} = \pm\frac{\sqrt{21}}{5}; \text{ Thus, when } y = 10,$$

$$y'(t) = \left(-\frac{5\pi}{3}\right)\left(\pm\frac{\sqrt{21}}{5}\right) = \pm\frac{5\pi}{3}\cdot\frac{\sqrt{21}}{5} = \pm\frac{\pi\sqrt{21}}{3} \approx \pm 4.8 \text{ ft/min.}$$

$\boxed{21}$ (a) $v(t) = -\pi\sin\pi t$; $v(0) = v(1) = v(2) = 0$, $v(\frac{1}{2}) = -\pi$, $v(\frac{3}{2}) = \pi$ (all in in./sec)

(b) It is rising when $v(t) = -\pi\sin\pi t > 0 \Rightarrow \sin\pi t < 0 \Rightarrow \pi < \pi t < 2\pi$,

$3\pi < \pi t < 4\pi$, etc. The motion is upward on the intervals

$$(1, 2), (3, 4), \ldots, (n, n + 1), \text{ where } n \text{ is an odd positive integer.}$$

$\boxed{22}$ (a) period $= \frac{2\pi}{100\pi} = \frac{1}{50}$ sec.   (b) $v(t) = 4\pi\cos 100\pi t$;

$$v(1.005) = v(1.015) = 0, v(1) = 4\pi, v(1.01) = -4\pi \text{ (all in cm/sec)}$$

$\boxed{23}$ $s(t) = k\cos(\omega t + b)$; $s'(t) = -k\omega\sin(\omega t + b)$;

$$s''(t) = -k\omega^2\cos(\omega t + b) = -\omega^2\left[k\cos(\omega t + b)\right] = -\omega^2 s(t)$$

$\boxed{24}$ $s(t) = k\sin(\omega t + b)$; $s'(t) = k\omega\cos(\omega t + b)$;

$$s''(t) = -k\omega^2\sin(\omega t + b) = -\omega^2\left[k\sin(\omega t + b)\right] = -\omega^2 s(t)$$

$\boxed{25}$ Let (x, y) be a point on the circle $x^2 + y^2 = a^2$ at some time t, and for simplicity,

assume that $(x, y) = (1, 0)$ at $t = 0$. Then, if the angle θ is drawn in standard

position with its terminal side passing through (x, y), we have $\frac{x}{a} = \cos\theta$,

or equivalently, $x = a\cos\theta$. This indicates that x is in simple harmonic motion.

$\boxed{26}$ (a) $s(t) = a\cos\omega t + b\sin\omega t \Rightarrow v(t) = -a\omega\sin\omega t + b\omega\cos\omega t \Rightarrow$

$a(t) = -a\omega^2\cos\omega t - b\omega^2\sin\omega t = -\omega^2(a\cos\omega t + b\sin\omega t) = -\omega^2 s(t)$,

$$\text{satisfying the simple harmonic motion condition in the remark.}$$

(b) Following the hint, let $s(t) = A\cos(\omega t - c) = A(\cos\omega t \cos c + \sin\omega t \sin c)$.

This must be equal to $s(t) = a\cos\omega t + b\sin\omega t$. Thus, $A\cos c = a$ and

$A\sin c = b$. Consequently, $a^2 + b^2 = A^2(\cos^2 c + \sin^2 c) = A^2$, so

$$A = \sqrt{a^2 + b^2}. \text{ Since } \frac{b}{a} = \frac{A\sin c}{A\cos c} = \tan c, \text{ we choose } c \text{ such that } \tan c = \frac{b}{a}.$$

27

t	0	1	2	3	4	5
s	0	4.21	1.82	0.14	−0.45	−0.37
v	10	−1.51	−2.29	−1.07	−0.18	0.25
a	0	−5.40	1.11	1.12	0.66	0.20

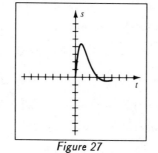

Figure 27

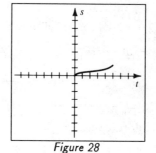

Figure 28

28

t	0	1	2	3	4	5
s	0	0.43	0.55	0.67	0.87	1.37
v	1.25	0.16	0.11	0.14	0.28	0.89
a	−5	−0.16	0	0.07	0.24	1.39

29 (a) $C(x) = 800 + 0.04x + 0.0002x^2$; $C(100) = 806$

(b) $c(x) = C(x)/x = (800/x) + 0.04 + 0.0002x$; $C'(x) = 0.04 + 0.0004x$;
$$c(100) = 8.06; \quad C'(100) = 0.08$$

30 (a) $C(x) = 6400 + 6.5x + 0.003x^2$; $C(100) = 7080$

(b) $c(x) = C(x)/x = (6400/x) + 6.5 + 0.003x$; $C'(x) = 6.5 + 0.006x$;
$$c(100) = 70.8; \quad C'(100) = 7.1$$

31 (a) $C(x) = 250 + 100x + 0.001x^3$; $C(100) = 11{,}250$

(b) $c(x) = C(x)/x = (250/x) + 100 + 0.001x^2$; $C'(x) = 100 + 0.003x^2$;
$$c(100) = 112.50; \quad C'(100) = 130$$

32 (a) $C(x) = 200 + 0.01x + \frac{100}{x}$; $C(100) = 202$

(b) $c(x) = C(x)/x = (200/x) + (100/x^2) + 0.01$; $C'(x) = 0.01 - (100/x^2)$;
$$c(100) = 2.02; \quad C'(100) = 0$$

33 $C'(x) = 50 - (100/x^2)$. The marginal cost at $x = 5$ is $C'(5) = \$46$, whereas the actual cost of the sixth motor is $C(6) - C(5) = 416\frac{2}{3} - 370 \approx \$46.67$.

34 $C'(x) = 1 - (10/x^2)$. The marginal cost at $x = 10$ is $C'(10) = \$0.90$, whereas the actual cost of the eleventh liter is $C(11) - C(10) = 14\frac{10}{11} - 14 \approx \$0.91$.

35 (a) $p'(x) = -0.1$ (b) $R(x) = xp(x) = 50x - 0.1x^2$

(c) $P(x) = R(x) - C(x) = -0.1x^2 + 48x - 10$ (d) $P'(x) = -0.2x + 48$

(e) $P'(x) = 0 \Leftrightarrow x = 240$. $P''(x) = -0.2 < 0 \Rightarrow P(240) = 5750$ is a *MAX*.

(f) $C'(x) = 2 \Rightarrow C'(10) = 2$, the marginal cost when the demand is 10 units.

$\boxed{36}$ (a) $p'(x) = \dfrac{-1}{2\sqrt{x-1}}$ (b) $R(x) = xp(x) = 80x - x\sqrt{x-1}$

(c) $P(x) = R(x) - C(x) = 5x - (x+2)\sqrt{x-1}$ (d) $P'(x) = \dfrac{10\sqrt{x-1} - 3x}{2\sqrt{x-1}}$

(e) $P'(x) = 0 \Leftrightarrow 10\sqrt{x-1} = 3x \Leftrightarrow 100(x-1) = 9x^2 \Leftrightarrow (9x-10)(x-10) = 0$

$\Leftrightarrow x = \frac{10}{9}, 10.$ $P(1) = 5$, $P(\frac{10}{9}) \approx 4.52$, and $P(10) = 14$.

Since $P \to -\infty$ as $x \to \infty$, $P(10) = 14$ will be a maximum profit.

(f) $C'(x) = 75 + \dfrac{1}{\sqrt{x-1}} \Rightarrow C'(10) = \frac{226}{3}$

$\boxed{37}$ $p(x) = 1800 - 2x$, $1 \le x \le 100$, $C(x) = 1000 + x + 0.01x^2$

(a) $R(x) = xp(x) = 1800x - 2x^2$

(b) $P(x) = R(x) - C(x) = -2.01x^2 + 1799x - 1000$

(c) $P'(x) = -4.02x + 1799 = 0 \Leftrightarrow x \approx 447.51$, which is not in the domain.

$P(1) = 796.99$ and $P(100) = 158,800$; the maximum profit occurs at $x = 100$.

(d) $P(100) = \$158,800$

$\boxed{38}$ $p(x) = 400 - 0.05x$, $C(x) = 500 + 10x$ (a) $R(x) = xp(x) = 400x - 0.05x^2$

(b) $P(x) = R(x) - C(x) = -0.05x^2 + 390x - 500$

(c) $P'(x) = -0.1x + 390 = 0 \Leftrightarrow x = 3900$, yielding a maximum since $P'' < 0$.

(d) $R'(x) = 400 - 0.1x = 300 \Leftrightarrow x = 1000$. Thus, $p(1000) = \$350$.

$\boxed{39}$ $p(x) = 8$ and $C(x) = 500 + 0.02x + 0.001x^2$.

(a) $R(x) = 8x$ and $P(x) = R(x) - C(x) = 7.98x - 500 - 0.001x^2$.

$P'(x) = 7.98 - 0.002x = 0$ when $x = 3990$ units,

yielding a maximum since $P'' < 0$.

(b) $P(3990) = \$15,420.10$.

$\boxed{40}$ The points $(1500, 7)$ and $(1000, 9)$ are on the linear demand function.

Its equation is $y - 7 = \frac{9-7}{1000-1500}(x - 1500)$, or $y = p(x) = -\frac{1}{250}x + 13$.

$R(x) = xp(x) = -\frac{1}{250}x^2 + 13x$ and $R'(x) = -\frac{1}{125}x + 13 = 0 \Leftrightarrow x = 1625$,

yielding a maximum since $R'' < 0$. $P(1625) = \$6.50$.

$\boxed{\text{Exercises 4.8}}$

Note: Determining the accuracy of x_n by requiring $|f(x_n)| < \epsilon$ is not a sound numerical technique. A better approach is to require $|x_{n+1} - x_n| < \epsilon$.

Note: Polynomials can be evaluated more easily (and accurately) using nested multiplication. Example: $3x^4 - 4x^3 + x - 6 = \{[(3x - 4)x]x + 1\}x - 6$.

Note: Numerical results may vary slightly. In the following, no rounding has been performed before the final result has been reached. This increases both accuracy and ease of calculation.

1 Let $f(x) = x^3 - 2$. $f(1) = -1$, $f(2) = 6 \Rightarrow$ there is a root in $[1, 2]$.

$$x_{n+1} = x_n - \frac{x_n^3 - 2}{3x_n^2} \text{ and } x_1 = 1 \text{ yield: } x_2 = 1.3333, \; x_3 = 1.2639, \; x_4 = 1.2599,$$

and $x_5 = 1.2599$. Root: $\approx \underline{1.2599}$

2 Let $f(x) = x^5 - 3$. $f(1) = -2$, $f(2) = 29 \Rightarrow$ there is a root in $[1, 2]$.

$$x_{n+1} = x_n - \frac{x_n^5 - 3}{5x_n^4} \text{ and } x_1 = 1 \text{ yield: } x_2 = 1.4000, \; x_3 = 1.2762, \; x_4 = 1.2472,$$

$x_5 = 1.2457$, and $x_6 = 1.2457$. Root: $\approx \underline{1.2457}$

3 $x_{n+1} = x_n - \dfrac{x_n^4 + 2x_n^3 - 5x_n^2 + 1}{4x_n^3 + 6x_n^2 - 10x_n}$. Since $f'(1) = 0$, we cannot use $x_1 = 1$.

Instead, $x_1 = 2$ yields: $x_2 = 1.6389$, $x_3 = 1.4319$, $x_4 = 1.3472$, $x_5 = 1.3320$,

$x_6 = 1.3315$, and $x_7 = 1.3315$. Root: $\approx \underline{1.3315}$

4 $x_{n+1} = x_n - \dfrac{x_n^4 - 5x_n^2 + 2x_n - 5}{4x_n^3 - 10x_n + 2}$ and $x_1 = 2$ yield: $x_2 = 2.3571$,

$x_3 = 2.2661$, $x_4 = 2.2573$, and $x_5 = 2.2573$. Root: $\approx \underline{2.2573}$

5 $x_{n+1} = x_n - \dfrac{x_n^5 + x_n^2 - 9x_n - 3}{5x_n^4 + 2x_n - 9}$ and $x_1 = -2$ yield: $x_2 = -1.8060$,

$x_3 = -1.7395$, $x_4 = -1.7321$, and $x_5 = -1.7321$. Root: $\approx \underline{-1.7321}$

Note: $x_1 = -1$ yields a root of -0.3222, which is outside the required interval.

6 Let $f(x) = \sin x + x \cos x - \cos x$.

$$x_{n+1} = x_n - \frac{\sin x_n + x_n \cos x_n - \cos x_n}{\sin x_n - x_n \sin x_n + 2\cos x_n} \text{ and } x_1 = 0 \text{ yield:}$$

$x_2 = 0.5$, $x_3 = 0.4796$, $x_4 = 0.4797$, and $x_5 = 0.4797$. Root: $\approx \underline{0.4797}$

7 Any zeros will occur where $x^4 = 11x^2 + 44x + 24$. From *Figure 7*, the largest zero

is in $[4, 5]$. $x_{n+1} = x_n - \dfrac{x_n^4 - 11x_n^2 - 44x_n - 24}{4x_n^3 - 22x_n - 44}$ and $x_1 = 4$ yield: $x_2 = 4.9677$,

$x_3 = 4.6860$, $x_4 = 4.6465$, $x_5 = 4.6458$, and $x_6 = 4.6458$. Root: $\approx \underline{4.6458}$

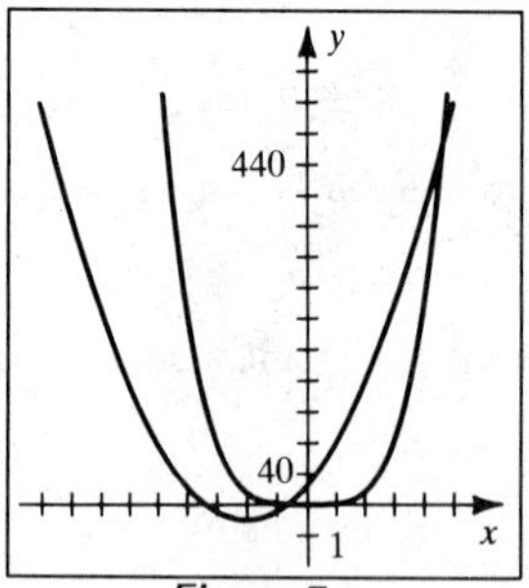

Figure 7

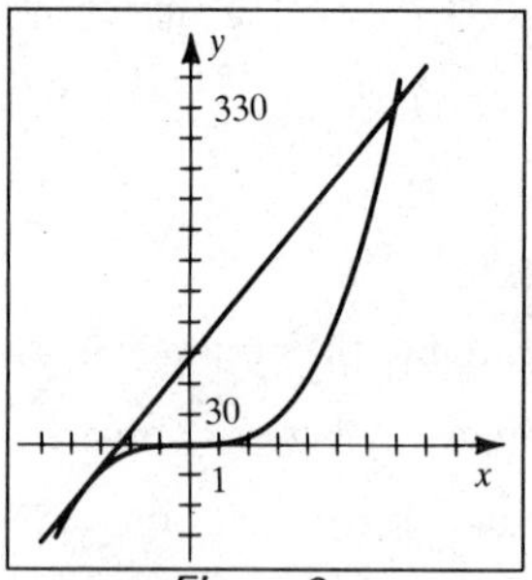

Figure 8

8 Any zeros will occur where $x^3 = 36x + 84$. From *Figure 8*, the largest zero is in

$[6, 8]$. $x_{n+1} = x_n - \dfrac{x_n^3 - 36x_n - 84}{3x_n^2 - 36}$ and $x_1 = 6$ yield: $x_2 = 7.1667$,

$x_3 = 6.9457$, $x_4 = 6.9362$, and $x_5 = 6.9362$. Root: $\approx \underline{6.9362}$

$\boxed{9}$ The roots of $x^3 + 5x - 3 = 0$ occur where the graphs of $y = x^3$ and $y = -5x + 3$

intersect. From *Figure 9*, the only root is in $[0, 1]$.

$$x_{n+1} = x_n - \frac{x_n^3 + 5x_n - 3}{3x_n^2 + 5} \text{ and } x_1 = 0 \text{ yield: } x_2 = 0.60, \ x_3 = 0.56,$$

and $x_4 = 0.56$. Root: ≈ 0.56

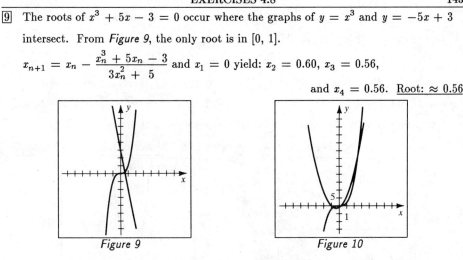

Figure 9   Figure 10

$\boxed{10}$ The roots of $2x^3 - 4x^2 - 3x + 1 = 0$ occur where the graphs of $y = 2x^3$ and

$y = 4x^2 + 3x - 1$ intersect. From *Figure 10*, the largest root is in $[2, 3]$.

$$x_{n+1} = x_n - \frac{2x_n^3 - 4x_n^2 - 3x_n + 1}{6x_n^2 - 8x_n - 3} \text{ and } x_1 = 2 \text{ yield: } x_2 = 3.00, \ x_3 = 2.63,$$

$x_4 = 2.53, \ x_5 = 2.52,$ and $x_6 = 2.52$. Root: ≈ 2.52

$\boxed{11}$ The root occurs where the graphs of $y = 2x$ and $y = 3\sin x$ intersect. From *Figure*

11, the positive root is in $[1, 2]$. $x_{n+1} = x_n - \dfrac{2x_n - 3\sin x_n}{2 - 3\cos x_n}$ and $x_1 = 1.5$ yield:

$x_2 = 1.50$. Root: ≈ 1.50

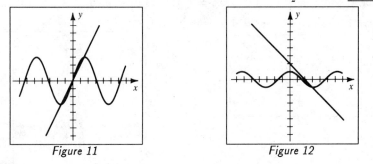

Figure 11   Figure 12

$\boxed{12}$ The root occurs where the graphs of $y = \cos x$ and $y = 2 - x$ intersect. From *Figure*

12, the root is in $[2, 4]$. $x_{n+1} = x_n - \dfrac{\cos x_n + x_n - 2}{1 - \sin x_n}$ and $x_1 = 3$ yield:

$x_2 = 2.99$ and $x_3 = 2.99$. Root: ≈ 2.99

Note: In Exercises 13–20, the formula for x_{n+1} is determined in a manner similar to that

in Exercises 1–12, and is therefore omitted.

$\boxed{13}$ Let $f(x) = x^4 - 125$. $f(3) = -44, f(4) = 131 \Rightarrow$ there is a root in $[3, 4]$.

Letting $x_1 = 3$ yields: $x_2 = 3.41, \ x_3 = 3.35, \ x_4 = 3.34,$ and $x_5 = 3.34$.

By symmetry, there is a root at -3.34. These are the only real roots since

$$f(x) = (x^2 - \sqrt{125})(x^2 + \sqrt{125}). \text{ Roots: } \approx \pm 3.34$$

$\boxed{14}$ Let $f(x) = 10x^2 - 1$. $f(0) = -1$, $f(1) = 9 \Rightarrow$ there is a root in $[0, 1]$.

Letting $x_1 = 1$ yields: $x_2 = 0.55$, $x_3 = 0.37$, $x_4 = 0.32$, and $x_5 = 0.32$.

By symmetry, there is a root at -0.32. Roots: $\approx \pm 0.32$

$\boxed{15}$ Any roots will occur where $x^4 = x + 2$. From *Figure 15*, there are roots near -1

and 1. With $x_1 = -1$ and $f(x) = x^4 - x - 2$, we find that $f(-1) = 0$, and hence,

Newton's method yields $x_n = -1$ for all n. Letting $x_1 = 1$ yields: $x_2 = 1.67$,

$x_3 = 1.44$, $x_4 = 1.36$, $x_5 = 1.35$, and $x_6 = 1.35$. Roots: ≈ 1.35 and -1 (exactly)

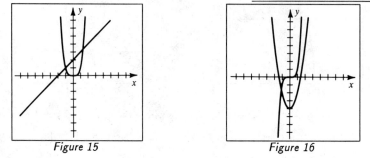

Figure 15   Figure 16

$\boxed{16}$ Any roots will occur where $x^5 = 2x^2 - 4$. From *Figure 16*, there is a root near -1.

Letting $x_1 = -1$ yields: $x_2 = -1.11$, $x_3 = -1.10$, and $x_4 = -1.10$.   Root: ≈ -1.10

$\boxed{17}$ Any roots will occur where $x^3 = 3x - 1$. From *Figure 17*, there are roots near -2, 0,

and 2. Letting $x_1 = -2$ yields: $x_2 = -1.89$, $x_3 = -1.88$, and $x_4 = -1.88$.

Letting $x_1 = 0$ yields: $x_2 = 0.33$, $x_3 = 0.35$, and $x_4 = 0.35$. Letting $x_1 = 2$ yields:

$x_2 = 1.67$, $x_3 = 1.55$, $x_4 = 1.53$, and $x_5 = 1.53$.   Roots: ≈ -1.88, 0.35, and 1.53

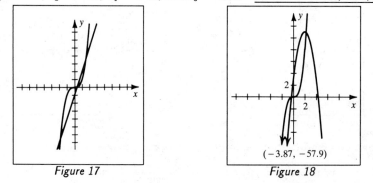

Figure 17   Figure 18

$\boxed{18}$ Any roots will occur where $x^3 = -2x^2 + 8x + 3$. From *Figure 18*, there are roots

near -4, 0, and 3. Letting $x_1 = -4$ yields: $x_2 = -3.88$, $x_3 = -3.87$, and

$x_4 = -3.87$. Letting $x_1 = 0$ yields: $x_2 = -0.38$, $x_3 = -0.35$, and $x_4 = -0.35$.

Letting $x_1 = 3$ yields: $x_2 = 2.42$, $x_3 = 2.24$, $x_4 = 2.22$, and $x_5 = 2.22$.

Roots: ≈ -3.87, -0.35, and 2.22

$\boxed{19}$ Any roots will occur where $\sin x = 2x - 5$. From *Figure 19*, there is a root near 3.

Letting $x_1 = 3$ yields: $x_2 = 2.71$ and $x_3 = 2.71$. <u>Root:</u> ≈ 2.71

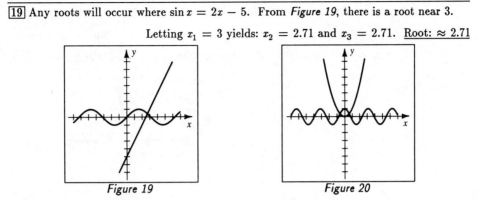

Figure 19   Figure 20

$\boxed{20}$ Any roots will occur where $x^2 = \cos 2x$. From *Figure 20*, there are roots near ± 1.

Letting $x_1 = 1$ yields: $x_2 = 0.62$, $x_3 = 0.60$, and $x_4 = 0.60$. By symmetry,

the other root is -0.60. <u>Roots:</u> $\approx \pm 0.60$

$\boxed{21}$ From *Figure 21*, the intersection points are in $[-2, -1]$ and $[1, 2]$.

Using (4.23) with $f(x) = x^2 - \sqrt{x + 3}$, $f'(x) = 2x - \frac{1}{2}(x + 3)^{-1/2}$,

and $x_1 = -1$ yields: $x_2 = -1.18$, $x_3 = -1.16$, and $x_4 = -1.16$.

Letting $x_1 = 1$ yields: $x_2 = 1.57$, $x_3 = 1.46$, $x_4 = 1.45$, and $x_5 = 1.45$.

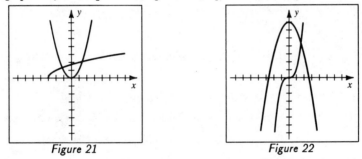

Figure 21   Figure 22

$\boxed{22}$ From *Figure 22*, the intersection point is in $[1, 2]$.

Using (4.23) with $f(x) = x^3 + x^2 - 7$, $f'(x) = 3x^2 + 2x$, and $x_1 = 2$ yields:

$x_2 = 1.69$, $x_3 = 1.63$, and $x_4 = 1.63$.

23 From *Figure 23*, an intersection point is near $x = 3$.

Using (4.23) with $f(x) = \cos\frac{1}{2}x + x^2 - 9$, $f'(x) = -\frac{1}{2}\sin\frac{1}{2}x + 2x$, and $x_1 = 3$ yields:

$x_2 = 2.99$, and $x_3 = 2.99$. By symmetry, the other point is near $x = -2.99$.

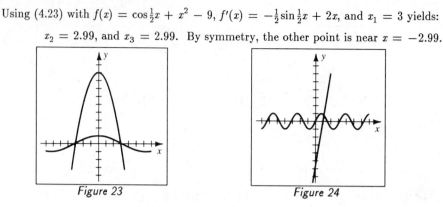

Figure 23   Figure 24

24 From *Figure 24*, the intersection point is in $[1, 2]$.

Using (4.23) with $f(x) = \sin 2x - 6x + 6$, $f'(x) = 2\cos 2x - 6$, and $x_1 = 1$ yields:

$x_2 = 1.13$, and $x_3 = 1.13$.

25 (a) $x_{n+1} = x_n - \frac{\sin x_n}{\cos x_n} = x_n - \tan x_n$ and $x_1 = 3$ yields:

$x_2 = 3.1425465$, $x_3 = 3.1415927$, $x_4 = 3.1415926$, and $x_5 = 3.1415926$.

(b) They approach the nearest root, which is 2π.

26 We must determine where $f'(x) = 0$ for $1 \leq x \leq 2$.

Let $g(x) = f'(x) = \cos 2x - 2x \sin 2x$. Then, $g'(x) = -4\sin 2x - 4x \cos 2x$ and

$x_{n+1} = x_n - \frac{g(x_n)}{g'(x_n)}$. Letting $x_1 = 1.5$ yields: $x_2 = 1.763$, $x_3 = 1.714$, $x_4 = 1.713$,

and $x_5 = 1.713$.   Root: $\approx$ 1.713

27 (a) $f'(\frac{1}{2}) = 0$ and hence the expression for x_2 would be undefined.

(b) Actually, Newton's method does not fail for 0.4. This value is just a poor choice

for x_1. It converges to the approximate root 0.1031497.

28 If x_n is any nonzero approximation, then, by (4.23), $x_{n+1} = -2x_n$

and hence each successive approximation will be farther from the zero of f.

29 (a) f: $x_1 = 1.1$, $x_2 = 1.066485$, $x_3 = 1.044237$, $x_4 = 1.029451$

g: $x_1 = 1.1$, $x_2 = 0.9983437$, $x_3 = 0.9999995$, $x_4 = 1.000000$

(b) $x = 1$ is a multiple root of the equation $f(x) = 0$.

As a result, $f'(1) = 0$ and Newton's method will converge more slowly.

The higher the multiplicity, the slower the convergence.

30 (a) f: $x_1 = 1.1$, $x_2 = 1.050154$, $x_3 = 1.025116$, $x_4 = 1.012568$

g: $x_1 = 1.1$, $x_2 = 1.000613$, $x_3 = 1.000000$, $x_4 = 1.000000$

(b) See the solution for Exercise 29(b).

31 $x_1 = 0.5$, $x_2 = 0.55$, $x_3 = 0.5266846$, $x_4 = 0.5250390$, $x_5 = 0.5251374$

32 $x_1 = 0.4$, $x_2 = 0.5$, $x_3 = 0.4848726$, $x_4 = 0.4913568$, $x_5 = 0.4918413$,

$x_6 = 0.4918152$

$\boxed{33}$ (a) $x_1 = 1.5$ (b) $x_2 = 1.363039$, $x_3 = 1.343602$, $x_4 = 1.343222$

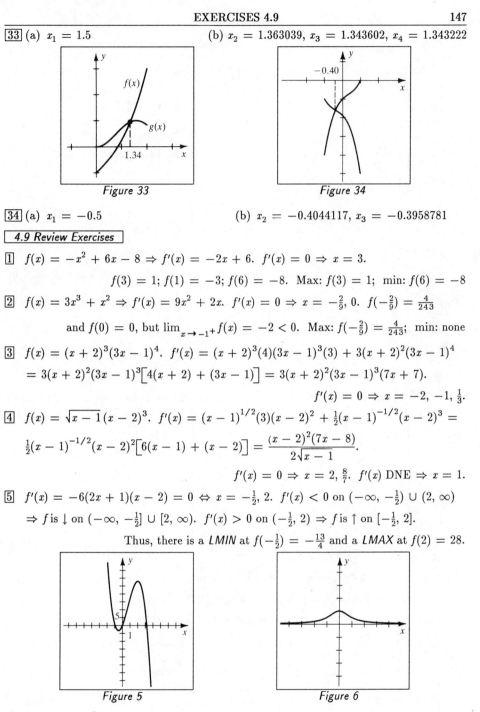

Figure 33   Figure 34

$\boxed{34}$ (a) $x_1 = -0.5$ (b) $x_2 = -0.4044117$, $x_3 = -0.3958781$

4.9 Review Exercises

$\boxed{1}$ $f(x) = -x^2 + 6x - 8 \Rightarrow f'(x) = -2x + 6.$ $f'(x) = 0 \Rightarrow x = 3.$

$f(3) = 1; f(1) = -3; f(6) = -8.$ Max: $f(3) = 1$;   min: $f(6) = -8$

$\boxed{2}$ $f(x) = 3x^3 + x^2 \Rightarrow f'(x) = 9x^2 + 2x.$ $f'(x) = 0 \Rightarrow x = -\frac{2}{9}, 0.$ $f(-\frac{2}{9}) = \frac{4}{243}$

and $f(0) = 0$, but $\lim_{x \to -1^+} f(x) = -2 < 0.$ Max: $f(-\frac{2}{9}) = \frac{4}{243}$;   min: none

$\boxed{3}$ $f(x) = (x + 2)^3(3x - 1)^4.$ $f'(x) = (x + 2)^3(4)(3x - 1)^3(3) + 3(x + 2)^2(3x - 1)^4$

$= 3(x + 2)^2(3x - 1)^3 \big[4(x + 2) + (3x - 1)\big] = 3(x + 2)^2(3x - 1)^3(7x + 7).$

$$f'(x) = 0 \Rightarrow x = -2, -1, \tfrac{1}{3}.$$

$\boxed{4}$ $f(x) = \sqrt{x - 1}\,(x - 2)^3.$ $f'(x) = (x - 1)^{1/2}(3)(x - 2)^2 + \frac{1}{2}(x - 1)^{-1/2}(x - 2)^3 =$

$\frac{1}{2}(x - 1)^{-1/2}(x - 2)^2 \big[6(x - 1) + (x - 2)\big] = \dfrac{(x - 2)^2(7x - 8)}{2\sqrt{x - 1}}.$

$$f'(x) = 0 \Rightarrow x = 2, \tfrac{8}{7}. \quad f'(x) \text{ DNE} \Rightarrow x = 1.$$

$\boxed{5}$ $f'(x) = -6(2x + 1)(x - 2) = 0 \Leftrightarrow x = -\frac{1}{2}, 2.$ $f'(x) < 0$ on $(-\infty, -\frac{1}{2}) \cup (2, \infty)$

$\Rightarrow f$ is $\downarrow$ on $(-\infty, -\frac{1}{2}] \cup [2, \infty).$ $f'(x) > 0$ on $(-\frac{1}{2}, 2) \Rightarrow f$ is $\uparrow$ on $[-\frac{1}{2}, 2].$

Thus, there is a *LMIN* at $f(-\frac{1}{2}) = -\frac{13}{4}$ and a *LMAX* at $f(2) = 28.$

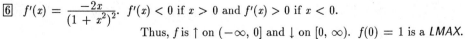

Figure 5   Figure 6

$\boxed{6}$ $f'(x) = \dfrac{-2x}{(1 + x^2)^2}.$ $f'(x) < 0$ if $x > 0$ and $f'(x) > 0$ if $x < 0.$

Thus, f is $\uparrow$ on $(-\infty, 0]$ and $\downarrow$ on $[0, \infty).$ $f(0) = 1$ is a *LMAX*.

$\boxed{7}$ $f'(x) = \dfrac{4(1-x)}{3x^{2/3}} = 0$ at $x = 1$. f' is undefined at $x = 0$.

     f is $\uparrow$ on $(-\infty, 1]$ and $\downarrow$ on $[1, \infty)$. *LMAX* at $f(1) = 3$. Vertical tangent at $(0, 0)$.

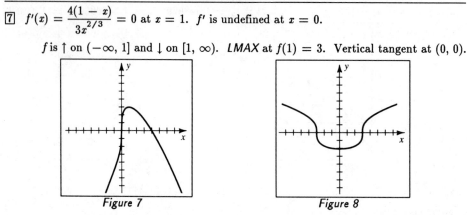

               Figure 7   *Figure 8*

$\boxed{8}$ $f'(x) = \dfrac{2x}{3(x^2-9)^{2/3}} = 0$ at $x = 0$. f' is undefined at $x = \pm 3$.

                       f is $\downarrow$ on $(-\infty, 0]$ and $\uparrow$ on $[0, \infty)$. *LMIN* at $f(0) = -\sqrt[3]{9}$.

$\boxed{9}$ $f'(x) = \dfrac{-x^2}{(8-x^3)^{2/3}}$. $f''(x) = -\dfrac{16x}{(8-x^3)^{5/3}}$.

     The *CN* of f are 0 and 2. Since $f''(0) = 0$ and $f''(2)$ is undefined, use the first derivative test to show that there are no extrema. $f'(x) < 0$ for all $x \ne 0, 2$. Hence, f is $\downarrow$ on $\mathbb{R}$. $f'' > 0$ when $x < 0$ or $x > 2$. $f'' < 0$ when $0 < x < 2$.

       Thus, *CU* on $(-\infty, 0)$ and $(2, \infty)$;   *CD* on $(0, 2)$; x-coordinates of *PI* are 0 and 2.

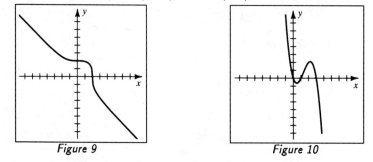

               Figure 9   *Figure 10*

$\boxed{10}$ $f'(x) = -3x^2 + 8x - 3 = 0$ at $x = a, b$; where $a = \tfrac{1}{3}(4 - \sqrt{7})$ and $b = \tfrac{1}{3}(4 + \sqrt{7})$.

     $f''(x) = -6x + 8 \Rightarrow f''(a) = 2\sqrt{7} > 0$ and $f''(b) = -2\sqrt{7} < 0$.

     Thus, $f(a) \approx -0.631$ is a *LMIN* and $f(b) \approx 2.11$ is a *LMAX*. $f''(x) > 0$ if $x < \tfrac{4}{3}$ and

               $f''(x) < 0$ if $x > \tfrac{4}{3} \Rightarrow$ is *CU* on $(-\infty, \tfrac{4}{3})$ and *CD* on $(\tfrac{4}{3}, \infty)$. *PI* at $x = \tfrac{4}{3}$.

$\boxed{11}$ Using Exercise 6, $f''(x) = \dfrac{6x^2 - 2}{(x^2 + 1)^3} \Rightarrow f''(0) = -2 \Rightarrow f(0)$ is a *LMAX*.

     f'' has the same sign as $6x^2 - 2$. Thus, f is *CU* on $(-\infty, -\tfrac{1}{3}\sqrt{3}) \cup (\tfrac{1}{3}\sqrt{3}, \infty)$ and

               CD on $(-\tfrac{1}{3}\sqrt{3}, \tfrac{1}{3}\sqrt{3})$. *PI* at $x = \pm\tfrac{1}{3}\sqrt{3}$. See *Figure 6* for the graph.

12 $f'(x) = 6x^2(20 - x^3) = 0$ at $x = 0, \sqrt[3]{20}$. $f''(x) = 30x(8 - x^3) \Rightarrow f''(0) = 0$ which

gives no information. Since f' does not change sign near 0, there is no extremum at

$x = 0$. $f''(\sqrt[3]{20}) < 0 \Rightarrow f(\sqrt[3]{20}) = 400$ is a *LMAX*. $f''(x) = 0$ at $x = 0, 2$.

$f''(x) < 0$ and f is *CD* on $(-\infty, 0) \cup (2, \infty)$. $f''(x) > 0$ and f is *CU* on $(0, 2)$.

PI at $x = 0, 2$.

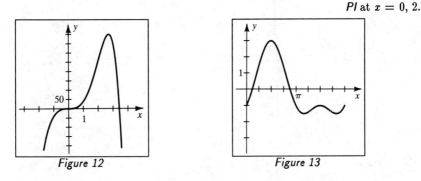

Figure 12   Figure 13

13 $f'(x) = 2\cos x + 2\sin 2x = 2\cos x + 4\sin x \cos x = 2\cos x(1 + 2\sin x) = 0 \Leftrightarrow$

$\cos x = 0$ or $\sin x = -\frac{1}{2}$. On $[0, 2\pi]$, the solutions are $\frac{\pi}{2}$, $\frac{3\pi}{2}$ and $\frac{7\pi}{6}$, $\frac{11\pi}{6}$.

$f''(x) = -2\sin x + 4\cos 2x$. $f''(\frac{\pi}{2}) = -6$ and $f''(\frac{3\pi}{2}) = -2 \Rightarrow$ *LMAX* at $f(\frac{\pi}{2}) = 3$

and $f(\frac{3\pi}{2}) = -1$. $f''(\frac{7\pi}{6}) = f''(\frac{11\pi}{6}) = 3$. There are *LMIN* of $-\frac{3}{2}$ at both points.

14 $f'(x) = 2\cos x + 2\sin 2x \Rightarrow f'(\frac{\pi}{6}) = 2\sqrt{3}$.   Tangent line: $y - \frac{1}{2} = 2\sqrt{3}(x - \frac{\pi}{6})$.

Normal line: $y - \frac{1}{2} = -\frac{1}{6}\sqrt{3}(x - \frac{\pi}{6})$.

15   16

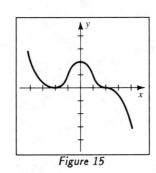

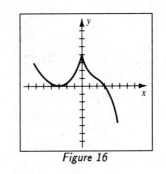

Figure 15   Figure 16

Note: HA, OA, and VA denote horizontal, oblique, and vertical asymptotes, respectively.

$\boxed{17}$ $f'(x) = -\dfrac{150x}{(9x^2 - 25)^2}$; $f''(x) = \dfrac{150(27x^2 + 25)}{(9x^2 - 25)^3}$. Since $f'(0) = 0$ and $f''(0) < 0$,

there is a *LMAX* at $f(0) = 0$. VA: $x = \pm\frac{5}{3}$; HA: $y = \frac{1}{3}$.

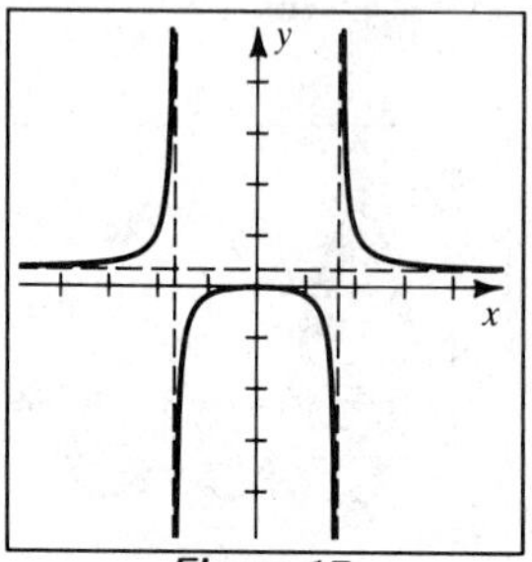

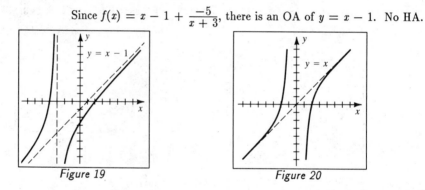

Figure 17 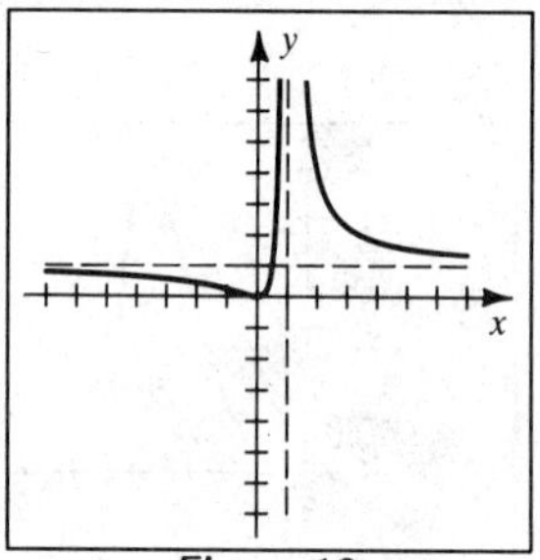   Figure 18

$\boxed{18}$ $f'(x) = -\dfrac{2x}{(x - 1)^3}$; $f''(x) = \dfrac{2(2x + 1)}{(x - 1)^4}$. Since $f'(0) = 0$ and $f''(0) > 0$,

there is a *LMIN* at $f(0) = 0$. VA: $x = 1$; HA: $y = 1$.

$\boxed{19}$ $f'(x) = \dfrac{x^2 + 6x + 14}{(x + 3)^2}$; $f''(x) = -\dfrac{10}{(x + 3)^3}$.

$x^2 + 6x + 14 \neq 0 \Rightarrow f'(x) \neq 0$; there are no extrema. VA: $x = -3$.

Since $f(x) = x - 1 + \dfrac{-5}{x + 3}$, there is an OA of $y = x - 1$. No HA.

$y = x - 1$

$y = x$

Figure 19   Figure 20

$\boxed{20}$ $f'(x) = \dfrac{x^4 + 48}{x^4}$; $f''(x) = -\dfrac{192}{x^5}$. $x^4 + 48 \neq 0 \Rightarrow f'(x) \neq 0$; there are no extrema.

VA: $x = 0$. Since $f(x) = x - 16/x^3$, there is an OA of $y = x$. No HA.

$\boxed{21}$ $f'(x) = -\dfrac{x^2 - 6x + 2}{(x^2 + 2x - 8)^2}$; $f''(x) = \dfrac{2(x^3 - 9x^2 + 6x - 20)}{(x^2 + 2x - 8)^3}$.

$f'(x) = 0 \Rightarrow x = 3 \pm \sqrt{7}$. The sign of f' is determined by $-(x^2 - 6x + 2)$.

$f' > 0$ on $(3 - \sqrt{7}, 3 + \sqrt{7})$ and $f' < 0$ on $(-\infty, 3 - \sqrt{7}) \cup (3 + \sqrt{7}, \infty)$.

Thus, $f(3 + \sqrt{7}) \approx 0.08$ is a *LMAX* and $f(3 - \sqrt{7}) \approx 0.37$ is a *LMIN*.

VA: $x = -4, 2$; HA: $y = 0$.

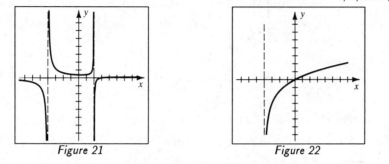

Figure 21   Figure 22

$\boxed{22}$ $f'(x) = \dfrac{x + 8}{2(x + 4)^{3/2}}$; $f''(x) = -\dfrac{x + 16}{4(x + 4)^{5/2}}$. The domain of f is $x > -4$.

$f'(x) > 0$ on $(-4, \infty)$ and so f is always $\uparrow$ and has no extrema.

$\boxed{23}$ $f(4) - f(0) = f'(c)(4 - 0) \Rightarrow 85 - 1 = (3c^2 + 2c + 1)(4 - 0) \Rightarrow$

$$3c^2 + 2c - 20 = 0 \Rightarrow c = \tfrac{1}{3}(-1 + \sqrt{61}) \approx 2.3 \in (0, 4).$$

$\boxed{24}$ Let $s(t)$ be the position of the car, t_1 the time of departure, and t_2 the time of

arrival. By the mean value theorem, $s'(c) = \dfrac{s(t_2) - s(t_1)}{t_2 - t_1}$ for some $c \in (t_1, t_2)$.

Since the distance is 125 mi, and if $t_2 - t_1 = \tfrac{5}{3}$ hr, then there exists a time c_0 such

that $s'(c_0) = \tfrac{125}{5/3} = 75$ mi/hr.

If $t_2 - t_1 < \tfrac{5}{3}$ hr, then there exists a time c_0 when $s'(c_0) > 75$ mi/hr.

boxed{25} With x and y as shown in *Figure 25*, $4x + 2y = 1000 \Rightarrow y = 500 - 2x$.

$A = xy = 500x - 2x^2 \Rightarrow A' = 500 - 4x = 0$ if $x = 125$ yd and $y = 250$ yd.

$A'' < 0$ for all $x \Rightarrow$ a maximum.

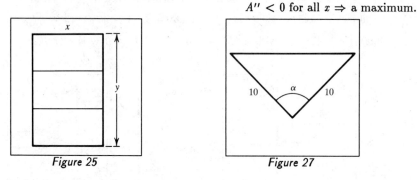

Figure 25   Figure 27

boxed{26} Let x denote the height and y the width of the shelter. The cost is given by

$C(x) = 2(4x) + 2(4x) + 5(4y) = 16x + 20y = 400 \Rightarrow y = 20 - \frac{4}{5}x$.

The volume is given by $V(x) = 4xy = 4x(20 - \frac{4}{5}x) \Rightarrow$

$V'(x) = 80 - \frac{32}{5}x = 0 \Leftrightarrow x = 12.5$ and $y = 10$.

Since V is quadratic and $V'' < 0$, these dimensions give a maximum volume.

boxed{27} See *Figure 27*. Let α be the angle between the two sheets as shown.

The volume will be maximized when the cross-sectional area is maximized.

$A = \frac{1}{2}bc\sin\alpha = \frac{1}{2}(10)(10)\sin\alpha = 50\sin\alpha$.

This is maximum when $\sin\alpha = 1$, or $\alpha = \frac{\pi}{2}$. (No differentiation is necessary.)

boxed{28} With h and r as shown in *Figure 28*, $r^2 + \frac{1}{4}h^2 = a^2$. The curved surface area of the

cylinder is $A = 2\pi rh = 2\pi h\sqrt{a^2 - h^2/4} \Rightarrow A' = \dfrac{2\pi(2a^2 - h^2)}{\sqrt{4a^2 - h^2}} = 0$ if $h = a\sqrt{2}$.

At the endpoints, $A(0) = A(2a) = 0 \Rightarrow$ this is a maximum.

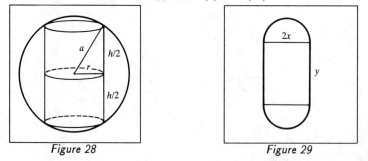

Figure 28   Figure 29

boxed{29} Let x denote the radius of the semicircles and y the length of the rectangle as shown

in *Figure 29*. The perimeter is $2y + 2\pi x = \frac{1}{2} \Rightarrow y = \frac{1}{4} - \pi x$. The area of the

rectangle is $A = (2x)y = \frac{1}{2}x - 2\pi x^2 \Rightarrow A' = \frac{1}{2} - 4\pi x = 0$ if $x = \frac{1}{8\pi}$ mi and

$y = \frac{1}{8}$ mi. This is a maximum area for the rectangle, since $A'' < 0$ for all x.

30 Let x be the number of \$1 decreases in the monthly cost of cable television. Then, the revenue is given by $R(x) = (20 - x)(5000 + 500x) = 100,000 + 5000x - 500x^2$. $R'(x) = 5000 - 1000x = 0 \Rightarrow x = 5$.

Since $R'' < 0$ for all x, \$20 - \$5 = \$15 will give a maximum revenue.

31 (a) Let x and $(5 - x)$ be the perimeters of the circle and square, respectively. The radius of the circle is $\frac{1}{2\pi}x$ and its area is $\pi r^2 = \frac{1}{4\pi}x^2$. The length of one side of the square is $\frac{1}{4}(5 - x)$ and the area of the square is $\frac{1}{16}(5 - x)^2$. The total area is

$A = \frac{1}{4\pi}x^2 + \frac{1}{16}(5 - x)^2$, where $0 \le x \le 5$. $A' = \frac{x}{2\pi} - \frac{5 - x}{8} = 0 \Rightarrow$

$\frac{x}{2\pi} = \frac{5 - x}{8} \Rightarrow 8x = 2\pi(5 - x) \Rightarrow 8x + 2\pi x = 10\pi \Rightarrow x = \frac{5\pi}{4 + \pi} \approx 2.2$.

Since $A(0) = \frac{25}{16} \approx 1.56$, $A(2.2) \approx 0.875$, and $A(5) = \frac{25}{4\pi} \approx 1.99$,

$A(5)$ is a maximum, that is, the entire wire should be bent into a circle.

(b) From above, the minimum occurs when $x \approx 2.2$ ft is bent into a circle.

32 $R = \frac{kS^n}{S^n + a^n} \Rightarrow R'(S) = \frac{nka^n S^{n-1}}{(S^n + a^n)^2} > 0$ since all variables and constants are

positive. Thus, R is an increasing function of S. $\lim\limits_{S \to \infty} R(S) = k \Rightarrow$ HA: $R = k$.

33 $v(t) = s'(t) = \frac{3(1 - t^2)}{(t^2 + 1)^2}$; $a(t) = v'(t) = \frac{6t(t^2 - 3)}{(t^2 + 1)^3}$. The direction of the motion is

determined by the sign of $(1 - t^2)$ in $v(t)$. The motion is to the left in $[-2, -1)$,

to the right in $(-1, 1)$, and to the left in $(1, 2]$.

34 $v(t) = s'(t) = ak\cos(kt + m) - bk\sin(kt + m) \Rightarrow$

$a(t) = v'(t) = -ak^2\sin(kt + m) - bk^2\cos(kt + m) = -k^2 s(t)$. The distance from

the origin is $|s(t)|$, so $|a(t)| = k^2|s(t)|$, where k^2 is the constant of proportionality.

35 $C'(x) = 100 + 0.1x + 0.0006x^2$. $C'(100) = 116$.

The actual cost is $C(101) - C(100) = 14,816.11 - 14,700 = 116.11$.

36 The cost is $C(2000) = 25,000$. The average cost is $\frac{C(2000)}{2000} = 12.5$.

The marginal cost is $C'(x) = 2 + 0.01x$ and $C'(2000) = 22$. The marginal average

cost is $c'(x) = \left(\frac{C(x)}{x}\right)' = \left(\frac{1000}{x} + 2 + 0.005x\right)' = -\frac{1000}{x^2} + 0.005$.

$c'(2000) = 0.00475$.

37 (a) $R(x) = px = 18x$ (b) $P(x) = R(x) - C(x) = -0.02x^2 + 12x - 500$

(c) $P'(x) = -0.04x + 12 = 0 \Rightarrow x = 300$, which yields a maximum since $P'' < 0$.

(d) $P(300) = \$1300$

38 (a) The total length of the walls is given by $x + 2(x - 3) + 2y$.

The area is given by $xy = 500 \Rightarrow y = 500/x$. Thus, the total length of the walls

is given by $x + 2(x - 3) + 1000/x = 3x - 6 + 1000/x$ and the cost is

$$C(x) = 100\left[3x - 6 + (1000/x)\right].$$

(b) VA: $x = 0$, OA: $y = 300x - 600$

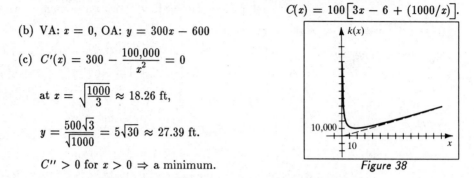

(c) $C'(x) = 300 - \dfrac{100,000}{x^2} = 0$

at $x = \sqrt{\dfrac{1000}{3}} \approx 18.26$ ft,

$y = \dfrac{500\sqrt{3}}{\sqrt{1000}} = 5\sqrt{30} \approx 27.39$ ft.

$C'' > 0$ for $x > 0 \Rightarrow$ a minimum.

Figure 38

39 Choose $x_1 = 4$, since $\pi < 4 < \frac{3\pi}{2}$. $x_{n+1} = x_n - \dfrac{\sin x_n - x_n \cos x_n}{x_n \sin x_n}$ and

$x_1 = 4$ yield: $x_2 = 4.614$, $x_3 = 4.496$, $x_4 = 4.493$, and $x_5 = 4.493$. Root ≈ 4.493

40 Let $f(x) = x^4 - 5$. $f(1) = -4 < 0$, $f(2) = 11 > 0 \Rightarrow$ there is a root in $[1, 2]$.

$x_{n+1} = x_n - \dfrac{x_n^4 - 5}{4x_n^3}$ and $x_1 = 1$ yield: $x_2 = 2$, $x_3 = 1.656$, $x_4 = 1.517$,

$x_5 = 1.496$, $x_6 = 1.495$, and $x_7 = 1.495$. Root ≈ 1.495

Chapter 5: Integrals

☐1 $\int (4x + 3)\, dx = 4 \cdot \frac{x^2}{2} + 3x + C = 2x^2 + 3x + C$

☐2 $\int (4x^2 - 8x + 1)\, dx = \frac{4}{3}x^3 - 4x^2 + x + C$

☐3 $\int (9t^2 - 4t + 3)\, dt = 3t^3 - 2t^2 + 3t + C$

☐4 $\int (2t^3 - t^2 + 3t - 7)\, dt = \frac{1}{2}t^4 - \frac{1}{3}t^3 + \frac{3}{2}t^2 - 7t + C$

☐5 $\int \left(\frac{1}{z^3} - \frac{3}{z^2} \right) dz = -\frac{1}{2z^2} + \frac{3}{z} + C$

☐6 $\int \left(\frac{4}{z^7} - \frac{7}{z^4} + z \right) dz = -\frac{2}{3z^6} + \frac{7}{3z^3} + \frac{1}{2}z^2 + C$

☐7 $\int \left(3\sqrt{u} + \frac{1}{\sqrt{u}} \right) du = 2u^{3/2} + 2u^{1/2} + C$

☐8 $\int (\sqrt{u^3} - \frac{1}{2}u^{-2} + 5)\, du = \frac{2}{5}u^{5/2} + \frac{1}{2}u^{-1} + 5u + C$

☐9 $\int (2v^{5/4} + 6v^{1/4} + 3v^{-4})\, dv = \frac{8}{9}v^{9/4} + \frac{24}{5}v^{5/4} - v^{-3} + C$

☐10 $\int (3v^5 - v^{5/3})\, dv = \frac{1}{2}v^6 - \frac{3}{8}v^{8/3} + C$

☐11 $\int (3x - 1)^2\, dx = \int (9x^2 - 6x + 1)\, dx = 3x^3 - 3x^2 + x + C$

☐12 $\int \left(x - \frac{1}{x} \right)^2 dx = \int (x^2 - 2 + x^{-2})\, dx = \frac{1}{3}x^3 - 2x - \frac{1}{x} + C$

☐13 $\int x(2x + 3)\, dx = \int (2x^2 + 3x)\, dx = \frac{2}{3}x^3 + \frac{3}{2}x^2 + C$

☐14 $\int (2x - 5)(3x + 1)\, dx = \int (6x^2 - 13x - 5)\, dx = 2x^3 - \frac{13}{2}x^2 - 5x + C$

☐15 $\int \frac{8x - 5}{\sqrt[3]{x}}\, dx = \int (8x^{2/3} - 5x^{-1/3})\, dx = \frac{24}{5}x^{5/3} - \frac{15}{2}x^{2/3} + C$

☐16 $\int \frac{2x^2 - x + 3}{\sqrt{x}}\, dx = \int (2x^{3/2} - x^{1/2} + 3x^{-1/2})\, dx = \frac{4}{5}x^{5/2} - \frac{2}{3}x^{3/2} + 6x^{1/2} + C$

☐17 $\int \frac{x^3 - 1}{x - 1}\, dx = \int (x^2 + x + 1)\, dx\ (x \neq 1) = \frac{1}{3}x^3 + \frac{1}{2}x^2 + x + C$

☐18 $\int \frac{x^3 + 3x^2 - 9x - 2}{x - 2}\, dx = \int (x^2 + 5x + 1)\, dx\ (x \neq 2) = \frac{1}{3}x^3 + \frac{5}{2}x^2 + x + C$

☐19 $\int \frac{(t^2 + 3)^2}{t^6}\, dt = \int \frac{t^4 + 6t^2 + 9}{t^6}\, dt =$

$$\int (t^{-2} + 6t^{-4} + 9t^{-6})\, dt = -t^{-1} - 2t^{-3} - \frac{9}{5}t^{-5} + C$$

☐20 $\int \frac{(\sqrt{t} + 2)^2}{t^3}\, dt = \int \frac{t + 4\sqrt{t} + 4}{t^3}\, dt =$

$$\int (t^{-2} + 4t^{-5/2} + 4t^{-3})\, dt = -t^{-1} - \frac{8}{3}t^{-3/2} - 2t^{-2} + C$$

☐21 $\int \frac{3}{4}\cos u\, du = \frac{3}{4}\int \cos u\, du = \frac{3}{4}\sin u + C$

☐22 $\int -\frac{1}{5}\sin u\, du = -\frac{1}{5}\int \sin u\, du = \frac{1}{5}\cos u + C$

☐23 $\int \frac{7}{\csc x}\, dx = 7\int \sin x\, dx = -7\cos x + C$

[24] $\int \frac{1}{4 \sec x} dx = \frac{1}{4} \int \cos x \, dx = \frac{1}{4} \sin x + C$

[25] $\int (\sqrt{t} + \cos t) \, dt = \frac{2}{3} t^{3/2} + \sin t + C$ [26] $\int (\sqrt[3]{t^2} - \sin t) \, dt = \frac{3}{5} t^{5/3} + \cos t + C$

[27] $\int \frac{\sec t}{\cos t} dt = \int \sec^2 t \, dt = \tan t + C$ [28] $\int \frac{1}{\sin^2 t} dt = \int \csc^2 t \, dt = -\cot t + C$

[29] $\int (\csc v \cot v \sec v) \, dv = \int \csc^2 v \, dv = -\cot v + C$

[30] $\int (4 + 4 \tan^2 v) \, dv = 4 \int (1 + \tan^2 v) \, dv = 4 \int \sec^2 v \, dv = 4 \tan v + C$

[31] $\int \frac{\sec w \sin w}{\cos w} dw = \int \sec w \tan w \, dw = \sec w + C$

[32] $\int \frac{\csc w \cos w}{\sin w} dw = \int \csc w \cot w \, dw = -\csc w + C$

[33] $\int \frac{(1 + \cot^2 z) \cot z}{\csc z} dz = \int \frac{\csc^2 z \cot z}{\csc z} dz = \int \csc z \cot z \, dz = -\csc z + C$

[34] $\int \frac{\tan z}{\cos z} dz = \int \tan z \sec z \, dz = \sec z + C$

[35] By Theorem (5.5)(i), $\int D_x \sqrt{x^2 + 4} \, dx = \sqrt{x^2 + 4} + C.$

[36] By Theorem (5.5)(i), $\int D_x \sqrt[3]{x^3 - 8} \, dx = \sqrt[3]{x^3 - 8} + C.$

[37] By Theorem (5.5)(i), $\int \frac{d}{dx} (\sin \sqrt[3]{x}) \, dx = \sin \sqrt[3]{x} + C.$

[38] By Theorem (5.5)(i), $\int \frac{d}{dx} (\sqrt{\tan x}) \, dx = \sqrt{\tan x} + C.$

[39] By Theorem (5.5)(ii), $D_x \int (x^3 \sqrt{x - 4}) \, dx = x^3 \sqrt{x - 4}.$

[40] By Theorem (5.5)(ii), $D_x \int (x^4 \sqrt[3]{x^2 + 9}) \, dx = x^4 \sqrt[3]{x^2 + 9}.$

[41] By Theorem (5.5)(ii), $\frac{d}{dx} \int \cot x^3 \, dx = \cot x^3.$

[42] By Theorem (5.5)(ii), $\frac{d}{dx} \int \cos \sqrt{x^2 + 1} \, dx = \cos \sqrt{x^2 + 1}.$

[43] $\int a^2 \, dx = a^2 \int dx = a^2 x + C$ [44] $\int ab \, dx = ab \int dx = abx + C$

[45] $\int (at + b) \, dt = a \cdot \frac{t^2}{2} + bt + C = \frac{1}{2} at^2 + bt + C$

[46] $\int \left(\frac{a}{b^2} t \right) dt = \frac{a}{b^2} \int t \, dt = \frac{a}{2b^2} t^2 + C$

[47] $\int (a + b) \, du = (a + b) \int du = (a + b) u + C$

[48] $\int (b - a^2) \, du = (b - a^2) \int du = (b - a^2) u + C$

[49] $f'(x) = 12x^2 - 6x + 1 \Rightarrow f(x) = 4x^3 - 3x^2 + x + C.$

$$f(1) = 5 \Rightarrow 2 + C = 5 \Rightarrow C = 3.$$

[50] $f'(x) = 9x^2 + x - 8 \Rightarrow f(x) = 3x^3 + \frac{1}{2}x^2 - 8x + C.$

$$f(-1) = 1 \Rightarrow \frac{11}{2} + C = 1 \Rightarrow C = -\frac{9}{2}.$$

[51] $\frac{dy}{dx} = 4x^{1/2} \Rightarrow y = \frac{8}{3} x^{3/2} + C.$ $x = 4 \Rightarrow y = \frac{64}{3} + C = 21 \Rightarrow C = -\frac{1}{3}.$

[52] $\frac{dy}{dx} = 5x^{-1/3} \Rightarrow y = \frac{15}{2} x^{2/3} + C.$ $x = 27 \Rightarrow y = \frac{135}{2} + C = 70 \Rightarrow C = \frac{5}{2}.$

[53] $f''(x) = 4x - 1 \Rightarrow f'(x) = 2x^2 - x + C.$ $f'(2) = -2 \Rightarrow C = -8.$

$$f(x) = \frac{2}{3}x^3 - \frac{1}{2}x^2 - 8x + D. \ f(1) = 3 \Rightarrow D = \frac{65}{6}.$$

$\boxed{54}$ $f''(x) = 6x - 4 \Rightarrow f'(x) = 3x^2 - 4x + C.$ $f'(2) = 5 \Rightarrow C = 1.$

$$f(x) = x^3 - 2x^2 + x + D.\ f(2) = 4 \Rightarrow D = 2.$$

$\boxed{55}$ $\dfrac{d^2y}{dx^2} = 3\sin x - 4\cos x \Rightarrow \dfrac{dy}{dx} = -3\cos x - 4\sin x + C.$ $x = 0 \Rightarrow -3 + C = 2 \Rightarrow$

$$C = 5.\ \ y = -3\sin x + 4\cos x + 5x + D.\ \ x = 0 \Rightarrow 4 + D = 7 \Rightarrow D = 3.$$

$\boxed{56}$ $\dfrac{d^2y}{dx^2} = 2\cos x - 5\sin x \Rightarrow \dfrac{dy}{dx} = 2\sin x + 5\cos x + C.$

$x = \pi \Rightarrow -5 + C = 3 \Rightarrow C = 8.\ \ y = -2\cos x + 5\sin x + 8x + D.$

$$x = \pi \Rightarrow 2 + 8\pi + D = 2 + 6\pi \Rightarrow D = -2\pi.$$

$\boxed{57}$ Since $a(t) = v'(t),$ $v(t) = 2t - 3t^2 + C.$ $v(0) = -5 \Rightarrow C = -5.$

$$\text{Since } v(t) = s'(t),\ s(t) = t^2 - t^3 - 5t + D.\ \ s(0) = 4 \Rightarrow D = 4.$$

$\boxed{58}$ Since $a(t) = v'(t),$ $v(t) = t^3 + C.$ $v(0) = 20 \Rightarrow C = 20.$

$$\text{Since } v(t) = s'(t),\ s(t) = \tfrac{1}{4}t^4 + 20t + D.\ \ s(0) = 5 \Rightarrow D = 5.$$

$\boxed{59}$ (a) $a(t) = -32 \Rightarrow v(t) = -32t + C.$ $v(0) = 1600 \Rightarrow C = 1600.$

$$s(t) = -16t^2 + 1600t + D.\ \ s(0) = 0 \Rightarrow D = 0.$$

(b) The maximum height occurs when $v(t) = -32t + 1600 = 0,$ or $t = 50.$

$$s(50) = 40{,}000 \text{ ft.}$$

$\boxed{60}$ (a) $a(t) = -32 \Rightarrow v(t) = -32t + C.$ $v(0) = 0 \Rightarrow C = 0.$ $s(t) = -16t^2 + D.$

$s(0) = 1000 \Rightarrow D = 1000$ and $s(t) = -16t^2 + 1000.$

$$\text{Hence, the object falls } 16t^2 \text{ feet in } t \text{ seconds.}$$

(b) $v(3) = -32(3) = -96$ ft/sec.

(c) When $s(t) = 0,$ $-16t^2 + 1000 = 0$ and $t = \tfrac{5}{2}\sqrt{10} \approx 7.9$ sec.

$\boxed{61}$ (a) $a(t) = -32 \Rightarrow v(t) = -32t + C.$ $v(0) = -16 \Rightarrow C = -16.$

$$s(t) = -16t^2 - 16t + D.\ \ s(0) = 96 \Rightarrow D = 96.$$

(b) $s(t) = -16t^2 - 16t + 96 = 0$ when $t = 2$ (-3 is rejected.).

(c) $v(2) = -32(2) - 16 = -80$ ft/sec.

$\boxed{62}$ (a) For the general situation, $a(t) = -g \Rightarrow v(t) = -gt + C.$ $v(0) = v_0 \Rightarrow$

$v(t) = -gt + v_0.$ $s(t) = -\tfrac{1}{2}gt^2 + v_0t + D.$ $s(0) = s_0 \Rightarrow s(t) =$

$-\tfrac{1}{2}gt^2 + v_0t + s_0.$ Maximum altitude occurs when $v(t) = 0.$ Since $g = 5.3$ and

$v_0 = 60,$ we have $v(t) = -5.3t + 60 = 0$ when $t = \tfrac{60}{5.3} \approx 11.32.$

$$s(t) = -\tfrac{1}{2}(5.3)t^2 + 60t \Rightarrow s\!\left(\tfrac{60}{5.3}\right) \approx 339.6 \text{ ft (since } s_0 = 0).$$

(b) On earth, $g = 32 \Rightarrow t = \tfrac{60}{32} \Rightarrow s\!\left(\tfrac{60}{32}\right) = 56.25$ ft.

$\boxed{63}$ See the solution of Exercise 62(a).

$\boxed{64}$ (a) $a(t) = 2 \Rightarrow v(t) = 2t + C.$ $v(0) = 0 \Rightarrow v(t) = 2t.$ Thus, $s(t) = t^2 + D.$

In t seconds, the ball will roll a distance of $s(t) - s(0) = t^2$ ft.

(b) If $v(0) = v_0,$ then $s(t) = t^2 + v_0t + D.$ The distance traveled in 5 sec is

$$s(5) - s(0) = 5^2 + v_05 = 100 \text{ if } v_0 = 15 \text{ ft/sec.}$$

$\boxed{65}$ $a(t) = a \Rightarrow v(t) = at + C.$ $v(0) = 0 \Rightarrow v(t) = at.$ $s(t) = \frac{1}{2}at^2 + D$ and

$$s(0) = 0 \Rightarrow s(t) = \frac{1}{2}at^2. \quad s(10) = 50a = 500 \Rightarrow a = 10 \text{ ft/sec}^2.$$

$\boxed{66}$ $a(t) = a \Rightarrow v(t) = at + C.$ $v(0) = 60 \text{ mi/hr} = 88 \text{ ft/sec} \Rightarrow v(t) = at + 88.$

$$v(9) = 9a + 88 = 0 \Rightarrow a = -\frac{88}{9} \text{ ft/sec}^2.$$

$\boxed{67}$ Since $A'(t) = 5 + 0.01t,$ $A(t) = 5t + 0.005t^2 + C.$ $A(0) = 0 \Rightarrow$

$$A(t) = 0.005t^2 + 5t. \quad A(t) = 100 \text{ (for } t > 0) \Rightarrow t = -500 + 300\sqrt{3} \approx 19.62 \text{ yr.}$$

$\boxed{68}$ Since $A'(t) = 2.74 - 0.11t - 0.01t^2,$ we have $A(t) = 2.74t - 0.055t^2 - \frac{0.01}{3}t^3 + C.$

$$A(0) = 0 \Rightarrow C = 0. \quad A(4) \approx 9.87 \text{ billion gal.}$$

$\boxed{69}$ $C'(x) = 20 - 0.015x \Rightarrow C(x) = 20x - 0.0075x^2 + D.$ $C(1) = 25 \Rightarrow D = 5.0075.$

$$\text{Thus, } C(x) = 20x - 0.0075x^2 + 5.0075 \text{ and } C(50) \approx \$986.26.$$

$\boxed{70}$ $C'(x) = 2x^{-1/3} \Rightarrow C(x) = 3x^{2/3} + D.$ $C(8) = 20 \Rightarrow D = 8.$

$$\text{Thus, } C(x) = 3x^{2/3} + 8 \text{ and } C(64) = \$56.00.$$

Exercises 5.2

Note: Let I denote the given integral.

Note: The final step of substituting for u in the evaluation of the integral has been eliminated when the substitution is straightforward.

$\boxed{1}$ $u = 2x^2 + 3,$ $\frac{1}{4}du = x\,dx \Rightarrow I = \frac{1}{4}\int u^{10}\,du = \frac{1}{44}u^{11} + C$

$\boxed{2}$ $u = x^2 + 5,$ $\frac{1}{2}du = x\,dx \Rightarrow I = \frac{1}{2}\int u^{-3}\,du = -\frac{1}{4}u^{-2} + C$

$\boxed{3}$ $u = 3x^3 + 7,$ $\frac{1}{9}du = x^2\,dx \Rightarrow I = \frac{1}{9}\int u^{1/3}\,du = \frac{1}{12}u^{4/3} + C$

$\boxed{4}$ $u = x^2 - 3,$ $\frac{1}{2}du = x\,dx \Rightarrow I = \frac{5}{2}\int u^{-1/2}\,du = 5u^{1/2} + C$

$\boxed{5}$ $u = 1 + \sqrt{x},$ $2\,du = \frac{dx}{\sqrt{x}} \Rightarrow I = 2\int u^3\,du = \frac{1}{2}u^4 + C$

$\boxed{6}$ $u = 5x - 4,$ $\frac{1}{5}du = dx \Rightarrow I = \frac{1}{5}\int u^{-10}\,du = -\frac{1}{45}u^{-9} + C$

$\boxed{7}$ $u = x^{3/2},$ $\frac{2}{3}du = \sqrt{x}\,dx \Rightarrow I = \frac{2}{3}\int \cos u\,du = \frac{2}{3}\sin u + C$

$\boxed{8}$ $u = \tan x,$ $du = \sec^2 x\,dx \Rightarrow I = \int u\,du = \frac{1}{2}u^2 + C$

$\boxed{9}$ $u = 3x - 2,$ $\frac{1}{3}du = dx \Rightarrow I = \frac{1}{3}\int u^{1/2}\,du = \frac{2}{9}u^{3/2} + C$

$\boxed{10}$ $u = 2x + 5,$ $\frac{1}{2}du = dx \Rightarrow I = \frac{1}{2}\int u^{1/4}\,du = \frac{2}{5}u^{5/4} + C$

$\boxed{11}$ $u = 8t + 5,$ $\frac{1}{8}du = dt \Rightarrow I = \frac{1}{8}\int u^{1/3}\,du = \frac{3}{32}u^{4/3} + C$

$\boxed{12}$ $u = 4 - 5t,$ $-\frac{1}{5}du = dt \Rightarrow I = -\frac{1}{5}\int u^{-1/2}\,du = -\frac{2}{5}u^{1/2} + C$

$\boxed{13}$ $u = 3z + 1,$ $\frac{1}{3}du = dz \Rightarrow I = \frac{1}{3}\int u^4\,du = \frac{1}{15}u^5 + C$

$\boxed{14}$ $u = 2z^2 - 3,$ $\frac{1}{4}du = z\,dz \Rightarrow I = \frac{1}{4}\int u^5\,du = \frac{1}{24}u^6 + C$

$\boxed{15}$ $u = v^3 - 1,$ $\frac{1}{3}du = v^2\,dv \Rightarrow I = \frac{1}{3}\int u^{1/2}\,du = \frac{2}{9}u^{3/2} + C$

$\boxed{16}$ $u = 9 - v^2,$ $-\frac{1}{2}du = v\,dv \Rightarrow I = -\frac{1}{2}\int u^{1/2}\,du = -\frac{1}{3}u^{3/2} + C$

$\boxed{17}$ $u = 1 - 2x^2,$ $-\frac{1}{4}du = x\,dx \Rightarrow I = -\frac{1}{4}\int u^{-1/3}\,du = -\frac{3}{8}u^{2/3} + C$

$\boxed{18}$ $u = 3 - x^4,$ $-\frac{1}{4}du = x^3\,dx \Rightarrow I = -\frac{1}{4}\int u^3\,du = -\frac{1}{16}u^4 + C$

$\boxed{19}$ $\int (s^2 + 1)^2\,ds = \int (s^4 + 2s^2 + 1)\,ds = \frac{1}{5}s^5 + \frac{2}{3}s^3 + s + C$

$\boxed{20}$ $\int (3 - s^3)^2 \, s \, ds = \int (9s - 6s^4 + s^7) \, ds = \frac{9}{2}s^2 - \frac{6}{5}s^5 + \frac{1}{8}s^8 + C$

$\boxed{21}$ $u = \sqrt{x} + 3,\ 2 \, du = \frac{dx}{\sqrt{x}} \Rightarrow I = 2\int u^4 \, du = \frac{2}{5}u^5 + C$

$\boxed{22}$ $u = 1 + (1/x),\ -du = (1/x^2) \, dx \Rightarrow I = -\int u^{-3} \, du = \frac{1}{2}u^{-2} + C$

$\boxed{23}$ $u = t^2 - 4t + 3,\ \frac{1}{2} \, du = (t - 2) \, dt \Rightarrow I = \frac{1}{2}\int u^{-3} \, du = -\frac{1}{4}u^{-2} + C$

$\boxed{24}$ $u = 4 - 3t^2 - 2t^3,\ -\frac{1}{6} \, du = (t^2 + t) \, dt \Rightarrow I = -\frac{1}{6}\int u^{-4} \, du = \frac{1}{18}u^{-3} + C$

$\boxed{25}$ $u = 4x,\ \frac{1}{4} \, du = dx \Rightarrow I = (3 \cdot \frac{1}{4}) \int \sin u \, du = -\frac{3}{4}\cos u + C$

$\boxed{26}$ $u = \frac{1}{2}x,\ 2 \, du = dx \Rightarrow I = (4 \cdot 2) \int \cos u \, du = 8 \sin u + C$

$\boxed{27}$ $u = 4x - 3,\ \frac{1}{4} \, du = dx \Rightarrow I = \frac{1}{4}\int \cos u \, du = \frac{1}{4}\sin u + C$

$\boxed{28}$ $u = 1 + 6x,\ \frac{1}{6} \, du = dx \Rightarrow I = \frac{1}{6}\int \sin u \, du = -\frac{1}{6}\cos u + C$

$\boxed{29}$ $u = v^2,\ \frac{1}{2} \, du = v \, dv \Rightarrow I = \frac{1}{2}\int \sin u \, du = -\frac{1}{2}\cos u + C$

$\boxed{30}$ $u = \sqrt[3]{v},\ 3 \, du = v^{-2/3} \, dv \Rightarrow I = 3 \int \cos u \, du = 3 \sin u + C$

$\boxed{31}$ $u = \sin 3x,\ \frac{1}{3} \, du = \cos 3x \, dx \Rightarrow I = \frac{1}{3}\int u^{1/3} \, du = \frac{1}{4}u^{4/3} + C$

$\boxed{32}$ $u = 1 - \cos 2x,\ \frac{1}{2} \, du = \sin 2x \, dx \Rightarrow I = \frac{1}{2}\int u^{-1/2} \, du = u^{1/2} + C$

$\boxed{33}$ $I = \int (\sin^2 x + 2 \sin x \cos x + \cos^2 x) \, dx = \int (1 + \sin 2x) \, dx = x - \frac{1}{2}\cos 2x + C$

$\boxed{34}$ $\int \frac{\sin 4x}{\cos 2x} \, dx = \int \frac{\sin (2 \cdot 2x)}{\cos 2x} \, dx = \int \frac{2 \sin 2x \cos 2x}{\cos 2x} \, dx = 2 \int \sin 2x \, dx = -\cos 2x + C$

$\boxed{35}$ $u = 1 + \cos x,\ -du = \sin x \, dx \Rightarrow I = -\int u^2 \, du = -\frac{1}{3}u^3 + C =$
$\qquad -\frac{1}{3}(1 + \cos x)^3 + C = -\frac{1}{3} - \cos x - \cos^2 x - \frac{1}{3}\cos^3 x + D,\ \text{with } D = C + \frac{1}{3}$

$\boxed{36}$ $u = \sin x,\ du = \cos x \, dx \Rightarrow I = \int u^3 \, du = \frac{1}{4}u^4 + C$

$\boxed{37}$ $u = \cos x,\ -du = \sin x \, dx \Rightarrow I = -\int u^{-4} \, du = \frac{1}{3}u^{-3} + C$

$\boxed{38}$ $I = \int \frac{\sin 2x}{\cos^5 2x} \, dx;\ u = \cos 2x,\ -\frac{1}{2} \, du = \sin 2x \, dx \Rightarrow I = -\frac{1}{2}\int u^{-5} \, du = \frac{1}{8}u^{-4} + C$

$\boxed{39}$ $u = 1 - \sin t,\ -du = \cos t \, dt \Rightarrow I = -\int u^{-2} \, du = u^{-1} + C$

$\boxed{40}$ $u = 2 + 5 \cos t,\ -\frac{1}{5} \, du = \sin t \, dt \Rightarrow I = -\frac{1}{5}\int u^3 \, du = -\frac{1}{20}u^4 + C$

$\boxed{41}$ $u = 3x - 4,\ \frac{1}{3} \, du = dx \Rightarrow I = \frac{1}{3}\int \sec^2 u \, du = \frac{1}{3}\tan u + C$

$\boxed{42}$ $I = \int \csc^2 2x \, dx;\ u = 2x,\ \frac{1}{2} \, du = dx \Rightarrow I = \frac{1}{2}\int \csc^2 u \, du = -\frac{1}{2}\cot u + C$

$\boxed{43}$ $u = \sec 3x,\ \frac{1}{3} \, du = \sec 3x \tan 3x \, dx \Rightarrow I = \frac{1}{3}\int u \, du = \frac{1}{6}u^2 + C$

Note: Letting $u = \tan 3x$ yields $\frac{1}{6}\tan^2 3x + C$. Since $1 + \tan^2 3x = \sec^2 3x$, these answers differ by a constant.

$\boxed{44}$ $I = \int \cot 4x \csc 4x \, dx;\ u = 4x,\ \frac{1}{4} \, du = dx \Rightarrow I = \frac{1}{4}\int \cot u \csc u \, du = -\frac{1}{4}\csc u + C$

$\boxed{45}$ $I = \int \csc^2 5x \, dx;\ u = 5x,\ \frac{1}{5} \, du = dx \Rightarrow I = \frac{1}{5}\int \csc^2 u \, du = -\frac{1}{5}\cot u + C$

$\boxed{46}$ $I = \int x \sec^2 (x^2) \, dx;\ u = x^2,\ \frac{1}{2} \, du = x \, dx \Rightarrow I = \frac{1}{2}\int \sec^2 u \, du = \frac{1}{2}\tan u + C$

$\boxed{47}$ $u = x^2,\ \frac{1}{2} \, du = x \, dx \Rightarrow I = \frac{1}{2}\int \cot u \csc u \, du = -\frac{1}{2}\csc u + C$

$\boxed{48}$ $u = \frac{1}{3}x,\ 3 \, du = dx \Rightarrow I = 3 \int \sec u \tan u \, du = 3 \sec u + C$

$\boxed{49}$ $f'(x) = \sqrt[3]{3x + 2} \Rightarrow f(x) = \frac{1}{4}(3x + 2)^{4/3} + C.\ f(2) = 4 + C = 9 \Rightarrow C = 5.$

$\boxed{50}$ $\frac{dy}{dx} = x\sqrt{x^2 + 5} \Rightarrow y = \frac{1}{3}(x^2 + 5)^{3/2} + C.$
$\qquad\qquad\qquad y = 12 \text{ if } x = 2 \Rightarrow 12 = 9 + C \Rightarrow C = 3.$

$\boxed{51}$ $f''(x) = 16\cos 2x - 3\sin x \Rightarrow f'(x) = 8\sin 2x + 3\cos x + C.$

$f'(0) = 4 \Rightarrow 3 + C = 4 \Rightarrow C = 1.$ $f(x) = -4\cos 2x + 3\sin x + x + D.$

$$f(0) = -2 \Rightarrow -4 + D = -2 \Rightarrow D = 2.$$

$\boxed{52}$ $f''(x) = 4\sin 2x + 16\cos 4x \Rightarrow f'(x) = -2\cos 2x + 4\sin 4x + C.$

$f'(0) = -2 + C = 1 \Rightarrow C = 3.$ $f(x) = -\sin 2x - \cos 4x + 3x + D.$

$$f(0) = -1 + D = 6 \Rightarrow D = 7.$$

$\boxed{53}$ (a) $u = x + 4,\ du = dx \Rightarrow I = \int u^2\, du = \frac{1}{3}u^3 + C_1 =$

$$\tfrac{1}{3}(x+4)^3 + C_1 = \tfrac{1}{3}x^3 + 4x^2 + 16x + \tfrac{64}{3} + C_1$$

(b) $I = \int(x^2 + 8x + 16)\, dx = \frac{1}{3}x^3 + 4x^2 + 16x + C_2;\ C_2 = C_1 + \frac{64}{3}$

$\boxed{54}$ (a) $u = x^2 + 4,\ \frac{1}{2}\,du = x\,dx \Rightarrow I = \frac{1}{2}\int u^2\, du = \frac{1}{6}u^3 + C_1 =$

$$\tfrac{1}{6}(x^2+4)^3 + C_1 = \tfrac{1}{6}x^6 + 2x^4 + 8x^2 + \tfrac{64}{6} + C_1$$

(b) $I = \int(x^5 + 8x^3 + 16x)\, dx = \frac{1}{6}x^6 + 2x^4 + 8x^2 + C_2;\ C_2 = C_1 + \frac{64}{6}$

$\boxed{55}$ (a) $u = \sqrt{x} + 3,\ 2\,du = \frac{1}{\sqrt{x}}\,dx \Rightarrow I = 2\int u^2\, du = \frac{2}{3}u^3 + C_1 =$

$$\tfrac{2}{3}(\sqrt{x}+3)^3 + C_1 = \tfrac{2}{3}x^{3/2} + 6x + 18x^{1/2} + 18 + C_1$$

(b) $I = \int \dfrac{x + 6\sqrt{x} + 9}{\sqrt{x}}\, dx = \int(x^{1/2} + 6 + 9x^{-1/2})\, dx =$

$$\tfrac{2}{3}x^{3/2} + 6x + 18x^{1/2} + C_2;\ C_2 = C_1 + 18$$

$\boxed{56}$ (a) $u = (1 + x^{-1}),\ -du = x^{-2}\, dx \Rightarrow I = -\int u^2\, du = -\frac{1}{3}u^3 + C_1 =$

$-\tfrac{1}{3}(1 + x^{-1})^3 + C_1 = -\tfrac{1}{3}(x^{-3} + 3x^{-2} + 3x^{-1} + 1) + C_1 =$

$$-\tfrac{1}{3}x^{-3} - x^{-2} - x^{-1} - \tfrac{1}{3} + C_1$$

(b) $I = \int(1 + x^{-1})^2\, x^{-2}\, dx = \int(1 + 2x^{-1} + x^{-2})x^{-2}\, dx =$

$$\int(x^{-2} + 2x^{-3} + x^{-4})\, dx = -x^{-1} - x^{-2} - \tfrac{1}{3}x^{-3} + C_2;\ C_2 = C_1 - \tfrac{1}{3}$$

$\boxed{57}$ Since $s'(t) = v(t) = \frac{1}{2}\sin(3t - \frac{\pi}{4}),\ s(t) = -\frac{1}{6}\cos(3t - \frac{\pi}{4}) + C.$

$$\text{Thus, the motion is simple harmonic if } C = 0.$$

$\boxed{58}$ Since $v'(t) = a(t) = k\cos(\omega t + \phi),\ v(t) = \frac{k}{\omega}\sin(\omega t + \phi) + C_1.$

Since $s'(t) = v(t),\ s(t) = -(k/\omega^2)\cos(\omega t + \phi) + C_1 t + C_2.$

$$\text{Thus, the motion is simple harmonic if } C_1 = C_2 = 0.$$

$\boxed{59}$ $dA/dt = 4000 + 2000\sin(\frac{\pi}{90}t) \Rightarrow A(t) = 4000t - \dfrac{180{,}000}{\pi}\cos(\frac{\pi}{90}t) + C.$

$A(90) - A(0) = (360{,}000 + \dfrac{180{,}000}{\pi} + C) - (-\dfrac{180{,}000}{\pi} + C) \approx 474{,}592\ \text{ft}^3.$

$\boxed{60}$ (a) $dV/dt = a\sin bt.$ Since the maximum flow rate is 8, we know that $a = 8$ (the amplitude of the sine wave.) Using the graph, we see that the period is

$$\tfrac{1}{2}\ \sec = \tfrac{1}{120}\ \min.\quad b = \tfrac{2\pi}{1/120} = 240\pi \text{ and } dV/dt = 8\sin(240\pi t).$$

(b) Since $dV/dt = 8\sin(240\pi t),\ V(t) = -\frac{8}{240\pi}\cos(240\pi t) + C.$ The volume pumped into the aorta during the systolic phase over the interval $[0, 0.25]$ is

given by $V(\frac{1}{4} \cdot \frac{1}{60}) - V(0) = (\frac{8}{240\pi} + C) - (-\frac{8}{240\pi} + C) = \frac{1}{15\pi} \approx 0.021\ \text{L}.$

$\boxed{61}$ (a) $dV/dt = a\sin bt$. If the maximum of dV/dt is 0.6, then $a = 0.6$.

Since the period is 5 seconds, $b = \frac{2\pi}{5}$. Thus, we have $dV/dt = 0.6\sin\left(\frac{2\pi}{5}t\right)$.

(b) $V(t) = -\frac{3}{2\pi}\cos\left(\frac{2\pi}{5}t\right) + C$. Since the inhaling process requires $\frac{5}{2}$ sec and

we assume that at $t = 0$ the volume starts to increase,

a person is inhaling while $dV/dt > 0$ from $t = 0$ to $t = \frac{5}{2}$.

Thus, the volume inhaled is given by $V(\frac{5}{2}) - V(0) = \frac{3}{\pi} \approx 0.95$ L.

$\boxed{62}$ $\frac{dN}{dt} = 1000\cos\left(\frac{\pi}{5}t\right) \Rightarrow N(t) = \frac{5000}{\pi}\sin\left(\frac{\pi}{5}t\right) \div C$. $N(5) = 3000 \Rightarrow C = 3000$.

The maximum of N {when $\sin\left(\frac{\pi}{5}t\right) = 1$, or $t = \frac{5}{2}$} is $\frac{5000}{\pi} + 3000 \approx 4592$ rabbits.

$\boxed{63}$ First way: $u = \sin x$, $du = \cos x\, dx \Rightarrow I = \int u\, du = \frac{1}{2}u^2 + C = \frac{1}{2}\sin^2 x + C$.

Second way:

$$u = \cos x, \ -du = \sin x\, dx \Rightarrow I = -\int u\, du = -\frac{1}{2}u^2 + D = -\frac{1}{2}\cos^2 x + D.$$

Third way: $\sin x \cos x = \frac{1}{2}\sin 2x \Rightarrow I = \frac{1}{2}\int \sin 2x\, dx = -\frac{1}{4}\cos 2x + E.$

They are all antiderivatives of $\sin x \cos x$. They simply differ by a constant.

(Note that $\frac{1}{2}\sin^2 x = \frac{1}{4} - \frac{1}{4}\cos 2x$ and $-\frac{1}{2}\cos^2 x = -\frac{1}{4} - \frac{1}{4}\cos 2x$.)

Exercises 5.3

$\boxed{1}$ $\displaystyle\sum_{j=1}^{4} (j^2 + 1) = 2 + 5 + 10 + 17 = 34$

$\boxed{2}$ $\displaystyle\sum_{j=1}^{4} (2^j + 1) = 3 + 5 + 9 + 17 = 34$

$\boxed{3}$ $\displaystyle\sum_{k=0}^{5} k(k - 1) = 0 + 0 + 2 + 6 + 12 + 20 = 40$

$\boxed{4}$ $\displaystyle\sum_{k=0}^{4} (k - 2)(k - 3) = 6 + 2 + 0 + 0 + 2 = 10$

$\boxed{5}$ $\displaystyle\sum_{n=1}^{10} \left[1 + (-1)^n\right] = 0 + 2 + 0 + 2 + 0 + 2 + 0 + 2 + 0 + 2 = 10$

$\boxed{6}$ $\displaystyle\sum_{n=1}^{4} (-1)^n \left(\frac{1}{n}\right) = -1 + \frac{1}{2} - \frac{1}{3} + \frac{1}{4} = \frac{-12 + 6 - 4 + 3}{12} = -\frac{7}{12}$

$\boxed{7}$ $\displaystyle\sum_{i=1}^{50} 10 = 50(10) = 500$, by (5.10). $\boxed{8}$ $\displaystyle\sum_{k=1}^{1000} 2 = 1000(2) = 2000$, by (5.10).

$\boxed{9}$ $\displaystyle\sum_{k=1}^{n} (k^2 + 3k + 5) = \sum_{k=1}^{n} k^2 + 3\sum_{k=1}^{n} k + \sum_{k=1}^{n} 5 =$

$\dfrac{n(n + 1)(2n + 1)}{6} + \dfrac{3n(n + 1)}{2} + 5n = (\frac{1}{3}n^3 + \frac{1}{2}n^2 + \frac{1}{6}n) + \frac{3}{2}(n^2 + n) + 5n =$

$\frac{1}{3}n(n^2 + 6n + 20)$

$\boxed{10}$ $\displaystyle\sum_{k=1}^{n} (3k^2 - 2k + 1) = 3\sum_{k=1}^{n} k^2 - 2\sum_{k=1}^{n} k + \sum_{k=1}^{n} 1 =$

$\dfrac{3n(n + 1)(2n + 1)}{6} - \dfrac{2n(n + 1)}{2} + n = 3(\frac{1}{3}n^3 + \frac{1}{2}n^2 + \frac{1}{6}n) - (n^2 + n) + n =$

$\frac{1}{2}n(2n^2 + n + 1)$

$\boxed{11}$ $\sum\limits_{k=1}^{n} (k^3 + 2k^2 - k + 4) = \sum\limits_{k=1}^{n} k^3 + 2\sum\limits_{k=1}^{n} k^2 - \sum\limits_{k=1}^{n} k + \sum\limits_{k=1}^{n} 4 =$

$$\left[\frac{n(n+1)}{2}\right]^2 + \frac{2n(n+1)(2n+1)}{6} - \frac{n(n+1)}{2} + 4n =$$

$$(\tfrac{1}{4}n^4 + \tfrac{1}{2}n^3 + \tfrac{1}{4}n^2) + 2(\tfrac{1}{3}n^3 + \tfrac{1}{2}n^2 + \tfrac{1}{6}n) - \tfrac{1}{2}(n^2 + n) + 4n =$$

$$\tfrac{1}{12}n(3n^3 + 14n^2 + 9n + 46)$$

$\boxed{12}$ $\sum\limits_{k=1}^{n} (3k^3 + k) = 3\sum\limits_{k=1}^{n} k^3 + \sum\limits_{k=1}^{n} k = 3\left[\frac{n(n+1)}{2}\right]^2 + \frac{n(n+1)}{2} =$

$$\tfrac{1}{4}n(n+1)\big[3n(n+1) + 2\big] = \tfrac{1}{4}n(n+1)(3n^2 + 3n + 2)$$

$\boxed{13}$ $1 + 5 + 9 + 13 + 17$ • Since the difference in terms is 4, the coefficient of the summation variable will be 4. Consider the term $4k + a$.

When $k = 1$, $4k + a$ should be 1, $\therefore a = -3$. $\quad\quad$ ★ $\sum\limits_{k=1}^{5} (4k - 3)$

$\boxed{14}$ $2 + 5 + 8 + 11 + 14$ • Since the difference in terms is 3, the coefficient of the summation variable will be 3. Consider the term $3k + a$.

When $k = 1$, $3k + a$ should be 2, $\therefore a = -1$. $\quad\quad$ ★ $\sum\limits_{k=1}^{5} (3k - 1)$

$\boxed{15}$ $\tfrac{1}{2} + \tfrac{2}{5} + \tfrac{3}{8} + \tfrac{4}{11}$ • Let the numerator be k and the denominator $3k + a$.

When $k = 1$, $3k + a$ should be 2, $\therefore a = -1$. $\quad\quad$ ★ $\sum\limits_{k=1}^{4} \dfrac{k}{3k - 1}$

$\boxed{16}$ $\tfrac{1}{4} + \tfrac{2}{9} + \tfrac{3}{14} + \tfrac{4}{19}$ • Let the numerator be k and the denominator $5k + a$.

When $k = 1$, $5k + a$ should be 4, $\therefore a = -1$. $\quad\quad$ ★ $\sum\limits_{k=1}^{4} \dfrac{k}{5k - 1}$

$\boxed{17}$ $1 - \dfrac{x^2}{2} + \dfrac{x^4}{4} - \dfrac{x^6}{6} + \cdots + (-1)^n \dfrac{x^{2n}}{2n}$ • The pattern begins with the second term

and the general term is listed. $\quad\quad$ ★ $1 + \sum\limits_{k=1}^{n} (-1)^k \dfrac{x^{2k}}{2k}$

$\boxed{18}$ $1 + x + \dfrac{x^2}{2} + \dfrac{x^3}{3} + \cdots + \dfrac{x^n}{n}$ • The pattern begins with the second term and the

general term is listed. $\quad\quad$ ★ $1 + \sum\limits_{k=1}^{n} \dfrac{x^k}{k}$

Note: If a function f is decreasing on an interval, use the right-hand endpoint for A_{IP} and the left-hand endpoint for A_{CP}. Reverse this choice if f is increasing.

$\boxed{19}$ (a) $f'(x) = -1 < 0$ on $[-2, 2] \Rightarrow f$ is ↓. $n = \dfrac{b - a}{\Delta x} = \dfrac{2 - (-2)}{1} = 4$.

$$A_{IP} = \sum\limits_{k=1}^{4} f(u_k)\,\Delta x = \sum\limits_{k=1}^{4} f(u_k) \,\{\text{since } \Delta x = 1\} =$$

$$f(-1) + f(0) + f(1) + f(2) = 4 + 3 + 2 + 1 = 10$$

(b) $A_{CP} = \sum\limits_{k=1}^{4} f(v_k)\,\Delta x = A_{IP} + f(-2)\,\Delta x - f(2)\,\Delta x = 10 + 5(1) - 1(1) = 14$

See *Figures 19a* and *19b*.

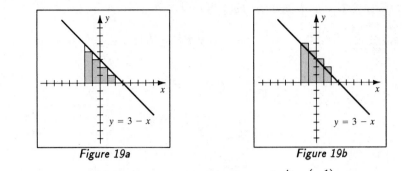

Figure 19a   Figure 19b

20 (a) $f'(x) = 1 > 0$ on $[-1\ 4] \Rightarrow f$ is $\uparrow$. $n = \dfrac{b - a}{\Delta x} = \dfrac{4 - (-1)}{1} = 5$.

$$A_{IP} = \sum_{k=1}^{5} f(u_k)\,\Delta x = \sum_{k=1}^{5} f(u_k) \ \{\text{since } \Delta x = 1\} =$$

$$f(-1) + f(0) + f(1) + f(2) + f(3) = 1 + 2 + 3 + 4 + 5 = 15$$

(b) $A_{CP} = \displaystyle\sum_{k=1}^{5} f(v_k)\,\Delta x = A_{IP} + f(4)\,\Delta x - f(-1)\,\Delta x = 15 + 6(1) - 1(1) = 20$

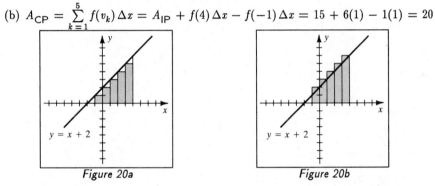

Figure 20a   Figure 20b

21 (a) $f'(x) = 2x > 0$ on $[1, 3] \Rightarrow f$ is $\uparrow$. $n = \dfrac{b - a}{\Delta x} = \dfrac{3 - 1}{1/2} = 4$.

$$A_{IP} = \sum_{k=1}^{4} f(u_k)\,\Delta x = \tfrac{1}{2}\sum_{k=1}^{4} f(u_k) = \tfrac{1}{2}\Big[f(1) + f(\tfrac{3}{2}) + f(2) + f(\tfrac{5}{2})\Big] =$$

$$\tfrac{1}{2}\Big[2 + \tfrac{13}{4} + 5 + \tfrac{29}{4}\Big] = \tfrac{35}{4}$$

(b) $A_{CP} = \displaystyle\sum_{k=1}^{4} f(v_k)\,\Delta x = A_{IP} + f(3)\,\Delta x - f(1)\,\Delta x = \tfrac{35}{4} + 10(\tfrac{1}{2}) - 2(\tfrac{1}{2}) = \tfrac{51}{4}$

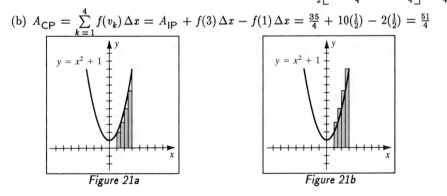

Figure 21a   Figure 21b

$\boxed{22}$ (a) $f'(x) = -2x < 0$ on $[0, 2] \Rightarrow f$ is $\downarrow$. $\quad n = \dfrac{b-a}{\Delta x} = \dfrac{2-0}{1/2} = 4$.

$$A_{\mathsf{IP}} = \sum_{k=1}^{4} f(u_k)\,\Delta x = \tfrac{1}{2} \sum_{k=1}^{4} f(u_k) = \tfrac{1}{2}\Big[f(\tfrac{1}{2}) + f(1) + f(\tfrac{3}{2}) + f(2) \Big] =$$

$$\tfrac{1}{2}\Big[\tfrac{15}{4} + 3 + \tfrac{7}{4} + 0 \Big] = \tfrac{17}{4}$$

(b) $A_{\mathsf{CP}} = \sum_{k=1}^{4} f(v_k)\,\Delta x = A_{\mathsf{IP}} + f(0)\,\Delta x - f(2)\,\Delta x = \tfrac{17}{4} + 4(\tfrac{1}{2}) - 0(\tfrac{1}{2}) = \tfrac{25}{4}$

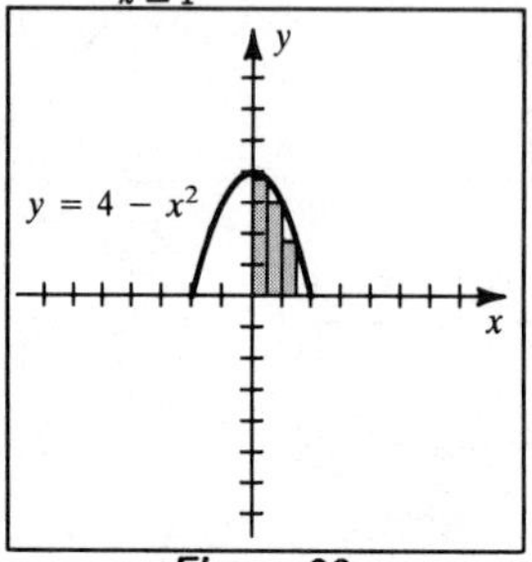

Figure 22a 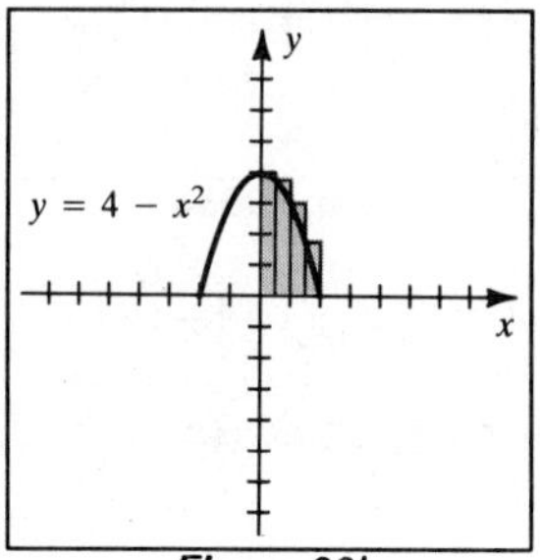   Figure 22b

$\boxed{23}$ (a) $f'(x) = \dfrac{\cos x}{2\sqrt{\sin x}} > 0$ on $[0, 1.5] \Rightarrow f$ is $\uparrow$. $\quad n = \dfrac{b-a}{\Delta x} = \dfrac{1.5-0}{0.15} = 10$.

$$A_{\mathsf{IP}} = \sum_{k=1}^{10} f(u_k)\,\Delta x = \Big[f(0) + f(0.15) + f(0.3) + \cdots + f(1.2) + f(1.35) \Big]\Delta x$$

$$\approx (6.9364)(0.15) \approx 1.0405$$

(b) $A_{\mathsf{CP}} = \sum_{k=1}^{10} f(v_k)\,\Delta x = A_{\mathsf{IP}} + f(1.5)\,\Delta x - f(0)\,\Delta x \approx 1.1903$

$\boxed{24}$ (a) $f'(x) = \dfrac{-3x^2}{2(x^3 + 1)^{3/2}} < 0$ on $[0, 3] \Rightarrow f$ is $\downarrow$. $\quad n = \dfrac{b-a}{\Delta x} = \dfrac{3-0}{0.3} = 10$.

$$A_{\mathsf{IP}} = \sum_{k=1}^{10} f(u_k)\Delta x = \Big[f(0.3) + f(0.6) + f(0.9) + \cdots + f(2.7) + f(3) \Big]\Delta x$$

$$\approx (5.1010)(0.3) \approx 1.5303$$

(b) $A_{\mathsf{CP}} = \sum_{k=1}^{10} f(v_k)\,\Delta x = A_{\mathsf{IP}} + f(0)\,\Delta x - f(3)\,\Delta x \approx 1.7736$

$\boxed{25}$ (a) $b = 4 \Rightarrow \Delta x = \dfrac{4}{n}$ and $x_k = \dfrac{4k}{n}$. Since f is $\uparrow$, $u_k = x_{k-1} = \dfrac{4(k-1)}{n}$ and

$$v_k = x_k = \dfrac{4k}{n}. \quad A_{\mathsf{IP}} = \sum_{k=1}^{n} f(u_k)\,\Delta x = \sum_{k=1}^{n} (2u_k + 3)\,\Delta x =$$

$$\sum_{k=1}^{n} \Big[\dfrac{2(4)(k-1)}{n} + 3 \Big]\dfrac{4}{n} = \dfrac{4}{n}\Big(\sum_{k=1}^{n} \dfrac{8k}{n} - \sum_{k=1}^{n} \dfrac{8}{n} + \sum_{k=1}^{n} 3 \Big) =$$

$$\dfrac{32}{n^2}\sum_{k=1}^{n} k - \dfrac{32}{n^2}\sum_{k=1}^{n} 1 + \dfrac{12}{n}\sum_{k=1}^{n} 1 = \dfrac{32}{n^2} \cdot \dfrac{(n)(n+1)}{2} - \dfrac{32}{n^2}\cdot n + \dfrac{12}{n}\cdot n =$$

$$\dfrac{16(n)(n+1)}{n^2} - \dfrac{32}{n} + 12. \quad \lim_{n \to \infty} A_{\mathsf{IP}} = 16 - 0 + 12 = 28.$$

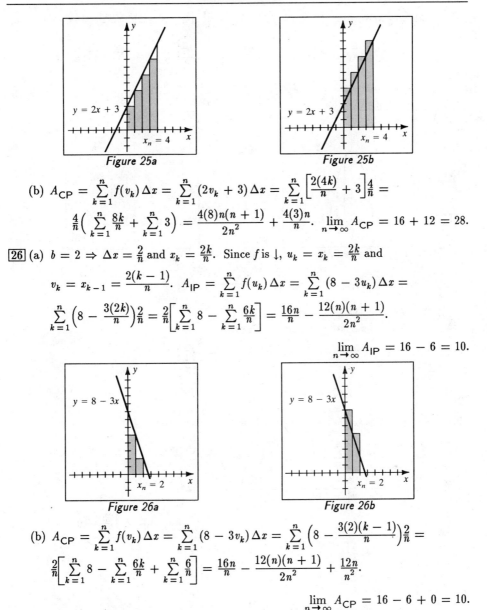

Figure 25a   Figure 25b

(b) $A_{\text{CP}} = \sum\limits_{k=1}^{n} f(v_k)\,\Delta x = \sum\limits_{k=1}^{n} (2v_k + 3)\,\Delta x = \sum\limits_{k=1}^{n} \left[\frac{2(4k)}{n} + 3\right]\frac{4}{n} =$

$\frac{4}{n}\left(\sum\limits_{k=1}^{n} \frac{8k}{n} + \sum\limits_{k=1}^{n} 3\right) = \frac{4(8)n(n+1)}{2n^2} + \frac{4(3)n}{n}. \quad \lim\limits_{n\to\infty} A_{\text{CP}} = 16 + 12 = 28.$

26 (a) $b = 2 \Rightarrow \Delta x = \frac{2}{n}$ and $x_k = \frac{2k}{n}$. Since f is $\downarrow$, $u_k = x_k = \frac{2k}{n}$ and

$v_k = x_{k-1} = \frac{2(k-1)}{n}. \quad A_{\text{IP}} = \sum\limits_{k=1}^{n} f(u_k)\,\Delta x = \sum\limits_{k=1}^{n} (8 - 3u_k)\,\Delta x =$

$\sum\limits_{k=1}^{n}\left(8 - \frac{3(2k)}{n}\right)\frac{2}{n} = \frac{2}{n}\left[\sum\limits_{k=1}^{n} 8 - \sum\limits_{k=1}^{n} \frac{6k}{n}\right] = \frac{16n}{n} - \frac{12(n)(n+1)}{2n^2}.$

$\lim\limits_{n\to\infty} A_{\text{IP}} = 16 - 6 = 10.$

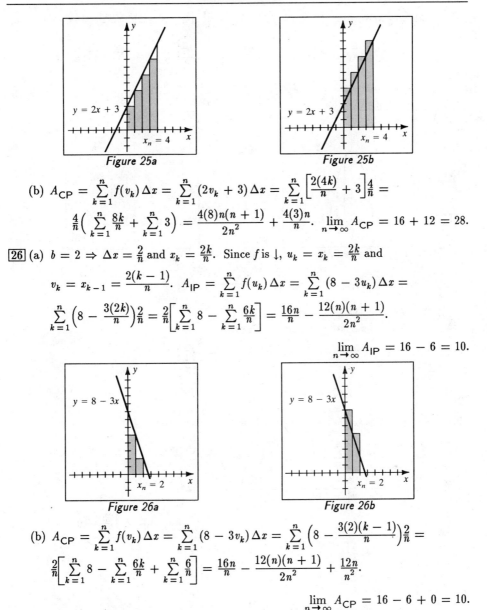

Figure 26a   Figure 26b

(b) $A_{\text{CP}} = \sum\limits_{k=1}^{n} f(v_k)\,\Delta x = \sum\limits_{k=1}^{n} (8 - 3v_k)\,\Delta x = \sum\limits_{k=1}^{n}\left(8 - \frac{3(2)(k-1)}{n}\right)\frac{2}{n} =$

$\frac{2}{n}\left[\sum\limits_{k=1}^{n} 8 - \sum\limits_{k=1}^{n} \frac{6k}{n} + \sum\limits_{k=1}^{n} \frac{6}{n}\right] = \frac{16n}{n} - \frac{12(n)(n+1)}{2n^2} + \frac{12n}{n^2}.$

$\lim\limits_{n\to\infty} A_{\text{CP}} = 16 - 6 + 0 = 10.$

27 (a) $\Delta x = \frac{3}{n}$ and $x_k = \frac{3k}{n}$. Since f is $\downarrow$, $u_k = \frac{3k}{n}$ and $v_k = \frac{3(k-1)}{n}$.

$$A_{IP} = \sum_{k=1}^{n} f(u_k)\,\Delta x = \sum_{k=1}^{n}\left(9 - \frac{9k^2}{n^2}\right)\left(\frac{3}{n}\right) = \frac{27}{n}\left[\sum_{k=1}^{n} 1 - \sum_{k=1}^{n}\frac{k^2}{n^2}\right] =$$

$$\frac{27n}{n} - \frac{27n(n+1)(2n+1)}{6n^3}. \quad \lim_{n\to\infty} A_{IP} = 27 - 9 = 18.$$

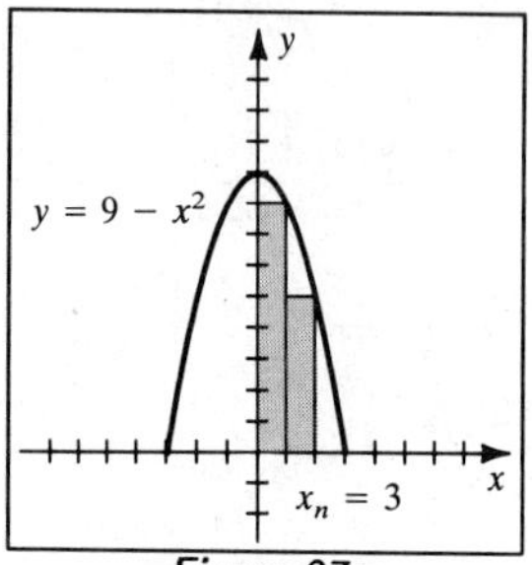

Figure 27a

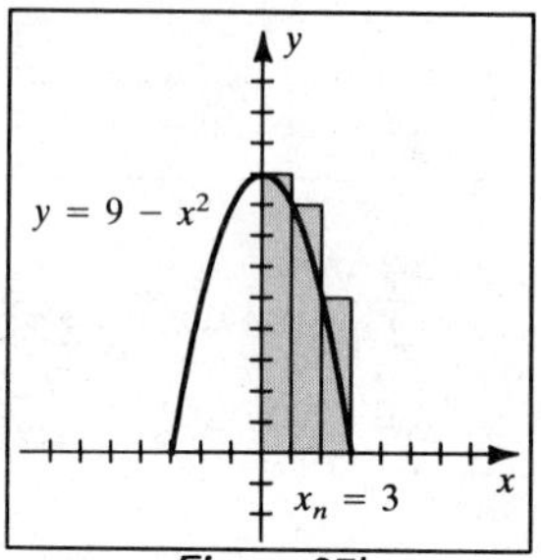

Figure 27b

(b) $A_{CP} = \sum_{k=1}^{n} f(v_k)\,\Delta x = \sum_{k=1}^{n}\left(9 - \frac{9(k-1)^2}{n^2}\right)\left(\frac{3}{n}\right) =$

$$\frac{27}{n}\left[\sum_{k=1}^{n} 1 - \sum_{k=1}^{n}\frac{k^2}{n^2} + \sum_{k=1}^{n}\frac{2k}{n^2} - \sum_{k=1}^{n}\frac{1}{n^2}\right] =$$

$$\frac{27n}{n} - \frac{27n(n+1)(2n+1)}{6n^3} + \frac{54n(n+1)}{2n^3} - \frac{27n}{n^3}.$$

$$\lim_{n\to\infty} A_{CP} = 27 - 9 + 0 - 0 = 18.$$

28 (a) $\Delta x = \frac{5}{n}$ and $x_k = \frac{5k}{n}$. Since f is $\uparrow$, $u_k = \frac{5(k-1)}{n}$ and $v_k = \frac{5k}{n}$. $A_{IP} =$

$$\sum_{k=1}^{n} f(u_k)\,\Delta x = \sum_{k=1}^{n}\left(\frac{5(k-1)}{n}\right)^2\left(\frac{5}{n}\right) = \frac{125}{n^3}\left[\sum_{k=1}^{n} k^2 - 2\sum_{k=1}^{n} k + \sum_{k=1}^{n} 1\right] =$$

$$\frac{125(n)(n+1)(2n+1)}{6n^3} - \frac{250(n)(n+1)}{2n^3} + \frac{125n}{n^3}.$$

$$\lim_{n\to\infty} A_{IP} = \frac{125}{3} - 0 + 0 = \frac{125}{3}.$$

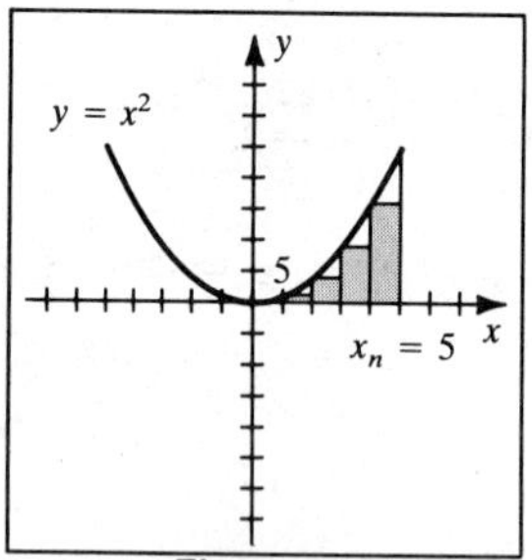

Figure 28a

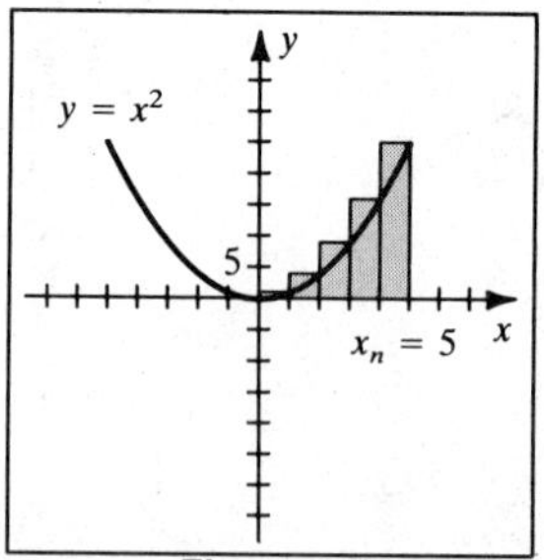

Figure 28b

(b) $A_{CP} = \sum_{k=1}^{n} f(v_k)\,\Delta x = \sum_{k=1}^{n}\left(\frac{5k}{n}\right)^2\left(\frac{5}{n}\right) = \frac{125}{n^3}\sum_{k=1}^{n} k^2 = \frac{125n(n+1)(2n+1)}{6n^3}.$

$$\lim_{n\to\infty} A_{CP} = \frac{125}{3}.$$

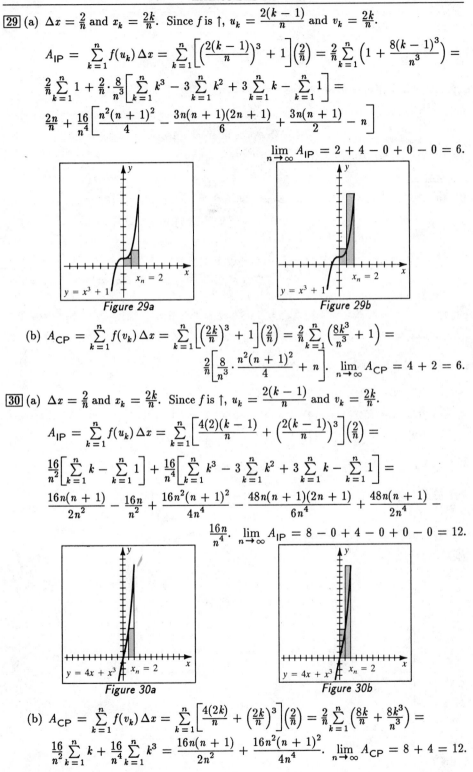

$\boxed{29}$ (a) $\Delta x = \frac{2}{n}$ and $x_k = \frac{2k}{n}$. Since f is $\uparrow$, $u_k = \frac{2(k-1)}{n}$ and $v_k = \frac{2k}{n}$.

$$A_{\text{IP}} = \sum_{k=1}^{n} f(u_k)\,\Delta x = \sum_{k=1}^{n}\left[\left(\frac{2(k-1)}{n}\right)^3 + 1\right]\left(\frac{2}{n}\right) = \frac{2}{n}\sum_{k=1}^{n}\left(1 + \frac{8(k-1)^3}{n^3}\right) =$$

$$\frac{2}{n}\sum_{k=1}^{n} 1 + \frac{2}{n}\cdot\frac{8}{n^3}\left[\sum_{k=1}^{n} k^3 - 3\sum_{k=1}^{n} k^2 + 3\sum_{k=1}^{n} k - \sum_{k=1}^{n} 1\right] =$$

$$\frac{2n}{n} + \frac{16}{n^4}\left[\frac{n^2(n+1)^2}{4} - \frac{3n(n+1)(2n+1)}{6} + \frac{3n(n+1)}{2} - n\right]$$

$$\lim_{n\to\infty} A_{\text{IP}} = 2 + 4 - 0 + 0 - 0 = 6.$$

Figure 29a   Figure 29b

(b) $A_{\text{CP}} = \sum_{k=1}^{n} f(v_k)\,\Delta x = \sum_{k=1}^{n}\left[\left(\frac{2k}{n}\right)^3 + 1\right]\left(\frac{2}{n}\right) = \frac{2}{n}\sum_{k=1}^{n}\left(\frac{8k^3}{n^3} + 1\right) =$

$$\frac{2}{n}\left[\frac{8}{n^3}\cdot\frac{n^2(n+1)^2}{4} + n\right]. \quad \lim_{n\to\infty} A_{\text{CP}} = 4 + 2 = 6.$$

$\boxed{30}$ (a) $\Delta x = \frac{2}{n}$ and $x_k = \frac{2k}{n}$. Since f is $\uparrow$, $u_k = \frac{2(k-1)}{n}$ and $v_k = \frac{2k}{n}$.

$$A_{\text{IP}} = \sum_{k=1}^{n} f(u_k)\,\Delta x = \sum_{k=1}^{n}\left[\frac{4(2)(k-1)}{n} + \left(\frac{2(k-1)}{n}\right)^3\right]\left(\frac{2}{n}\right) =$$

$$\frac{16}{n^2}\left[\sum_{k=1}^{n} k - \sum_{k=1}^{n} 1\right] + \frac{16}{n^4}\left[\sum_{k=1}^{n} k^3 - 3\sum_{k=1}^{n} k^2 + 3\sum_{k=1}^{n} k - \sum_{k=1}^{n} 1\right] =$$

$$\frac{16n(n+1)}{2n^2} - \frac{16n}{n^2} + \frac{16n^2(n+1)^2}{4n^4} - \frac{48n(n+1)(2n+1)}{6n^4} + \frac{48n(n+1)}{2n^4} -$$

$$\frac{16n}{n^4}. \quad \lim_{n\to\infty} A_{\text{IP}} = 8 - 0 + 4 - 0 + 0 - 0 = 12.$$

Figure 30a   Figure 30b

(b) $A_{\text{CP}} = \sum_{k=1}^{n} f(v_k)\,\Delta x = \sum_{k=1}^{n}\left[\frac{4(2k)}{n} + \left(\frac{2k}{n}\right)^3\right]\left(\frac{2}{n}\right) = \frac{2}{n}\sum_{k=1}^{n}\left(\frac{8k}{n} + \frac{8k^3}{n^3}\right) =$

$$\frac{16}{n^2}\sum_{k=1}^{n} k + \frac{16}{n^4}\sum_{k=1}^{n} k^3 = \frac{16n(n+1)}{2n^2} + \frac{16n^2(n+1)^2}{4n^4}. \quad \lim_{n\to\infty} A_{\text{CP}} = 8 + 4 = 12.$$

31 Let A_k denote the area under the graph of $f(x) = x^3$ from 0 to k, $k > 0$.

(a) $A = A_3 - A_1 = \frac{3^4}{4} - \frac{1^4}{4} = 20$

(b) $A = A_b - A_a = \frac{b^4}{4} - \frac{a^4}{4} = \frac{1}{4}(b^4 - a^4)$

32 (a) This is the graph of $f(x) = x^3$ { from Exercise 31 } shifted up 2 units.

The area of the rectangle being added to the answer in Exercise 31 is 2 times the length of the interval. Hence, $A = 20 + 2(3 - 1) = 24$.

(b) As in part (a), $A = \frac{1}{4}(b^4 - a^4) + 2(b - a)$.

Exercises 5.4

1 (a) $\Delta x_1 = (1.1 - 0) = 1.1$, $\Delta x_2 = (2.6 - 1.1) = 1.5$, $\Delta x_3 = (3.7 - 2.6) = 1.1$,
$$\Delta x_4 = (4.1 - 3.7) = 0.4, \; \Delta x_5 = (5 - 4.1) = 0.9.$$

(b) $\|P\| = \text{maximum } \Delta x_k = 1.5$.

2 (a) $\Delta x_1 = (3 - 2) = 1$, $\Delta x_2 = (3.7 - 3) = 0.7$, $\Delta x_3 = (4 - 3.7) = 0.3$,
$$\Delta x_4 = (5.2 - 4) = 1.2, \; \Delta x_5 = (6 - 5.2) = 0.8.$$

(b) $\|P\| = \text{maximum } \Delta x_k = 1.2$.

3 (a) $\Delta x_1 = 0.3$, $\Delta x_2 = 1.7$, $\Delta x_3 = 1.4$, $\Delta x_4 = 0.5$, $\Delta x_5 = 0.1$.   (b) $\|P\| = 1.7$.

4 (a) $\Delta x_1 = 0.6$, $\Delta x_2 = 0.4$, $\Delta x_3 = 1.5$, $\Delta x_4 = 0.5$.   (b) $\|P\| = 1.5$.

5 $R_P = \sum\limits_{k=1}^{3} f(w_k)\,\Delta x_k = \sum\limits_{k=1}^{3} (2w_k + 3)\,\Delta x_k =$

(a) $f(3) \cdot 2 + f(4) \cdot 1 + f(5) \cdot 1 = 18 + 11 + 13 = 42$

(b) $f(1) \cdot 2 + f(3) \cdot 1 + f(4) \cdot 1 = 10 + 9 + 11 = 30$

(c) $f(2) \cdot 2 + f(\frac{7}{2}) \cdot 1 + f(\frac{9}{2}) \cdot 1 = 14 + 10 + 12 = 36$

6 $R_P = \sum\limits_{k=1}^{j} f(w_k)\,\Delta x_k = \sum\limits_{k=1}^{3} (3 - 4w_k)\,\Delta x_k =$

(a) $f(3) \cdot 2 + f(4) \cdot 1 + f(5) \cdot 1 = -18 - 13 - 17 = -48$

(b) $f(1) \cdot 2 + f(3) \cdot 1 + f(4) \cdot 1 = -2 - 9 - 13 = -24$

(c) $f(2) \cdot 2 + f(\frac{7}{2}) \cdot 1 + f(\frac{9}{2}) \cdot 1 = -10 - 11 - 15 = -36$

7 $\Delta x_k = 1$, $\forall k$.

$$R_P = \sum\limits_{k=1}^{6} f(w_k)\,\Delta x_k = f(\tfrac{1}{2}) + f(\tfrac{3}{2}) + f(\tfrac{5}{2}) + f(\tfrac{7}{2}) + f(\tfrac{9}{2}) + f(\tfrac{11}{2}) = \tfrac{49}{4}.$$

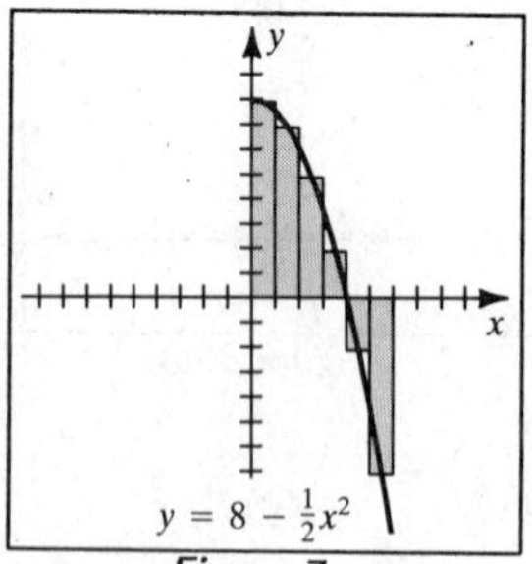

$y = 8 - \frac{1}{2}x^2$

Figure 7

$y = 8 - \frac{1}{2}x^2$

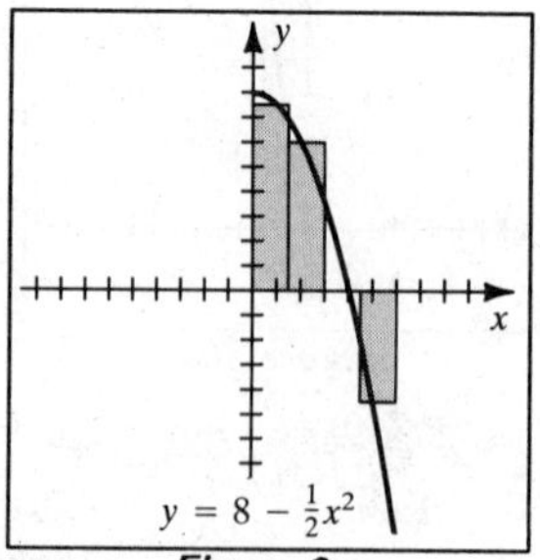

Figure 8

$\boxed{8}$ $\Delta x_k = \frac{3}{2}$, $\forall k$. $R_P = \sum\limits_{k=1}^{4} f(w_k)\,\Delta x_k = \left[f(1) + f(2) + f(4) + f(5)\right]\left(\frac{3}{2}\right) = \frac{27}{2}$.

$\boxed{9}$ $R_P = \sum\limits_{k=1}^{4} f(w_k)\,\Delta x_k = f(-1)\cdot 2 + f(1)\cdot 1 + f(2)\cdot 2 + f(4)\cdot 1 =$
$$-2 + 1 + 16 + 64 = 79.$$

$\boxed{10}$ $R_P = \sum\limits_{k=1}^{5} f(w_k)\,\Delta x_k = f(1)\cdot 2 + f(4)\cdot 2 + f(5)\cdot 2 + f(9)\cdot 2 + f(9)\cdot 7 =$
$$2 + 4 + 2\sqrt{5} + 6 + 21 = 33 + 2\sqrt{5} \approx 37.47.$$

$\boxed{11}$ $\Delta x_k = \frac{1}{10}$, $\forall k$. $R_P = \sum\limits_{k=1}^{10} f(w_k)\,\Delta x_k =$
$$\left[f(0.05) + f(0.15) + f(0.25) + \cdots + f(0.85) + f(0.95)\right]\Delta x \approx (2.810)(0.1) \approx 0.28$$

$\boxed{12}$ $\Delta x_1 = 0.35$, $\Delta x_2 = 0.42$, $\Delta x_3 = 0.74$, $\Delta x_4 = 0.34$, $\Delta x_5 = 0.15$
$$R_P = \sum\limits_{k=1}^{5} f(w_k)\,\Delta x_k = [f(-0.75)\,\Delta x_1 + f(-0.5)\,\Delta x_2 + f(0)\,\Delta x_3 +$$
$$f(0.6)\,\Delta x_4 + f(0.9)\,\Delta x_5] \approx 1.5217$$

$\boxed{13}$ $\lim\limits_{\|P\|\to 0} \sum\limits_{k=1}^{n} (3w_k^2 - 2w_k + 5)\,\Delta x_k;$ $\qquad [-1, 2]$ $\bullet$ $\qquad \star \displaystyle\int_{-1}^{2} (3x^2 - 2x + 5)\,dx$

$\boxed{14}$ $\lim\limits_{\|P\|\to 0} \sum\limits_{k=1}^{n} \pi(w_k^2 - 4)\,\Delta x_k;$ $\qquad [2, 3]$ $\bullet$ $\qquad \star \displaystyle\int_{2}^{3} \pi(x^2 - 4)\,dx$

$\boxed{15}$ $\lim\limits_{\|P\|\to 0} \sum\limits_{k=1}^{n} 2\pi w_k(1 + w_k^3)\,\Delta x_k;$ $\qquad [0, 4]$ $\bullet$ $\qquad \star \displaystyle\int_{0}^{4} 2\pi x(1 + x^3)\,dx$

$\boxed{16}$ $\lim\limits_{\|P\|\to 0} \sum\limits_{k=1}^{n} (\sqrt[3]{w_k} + 4w_k)\,\Delta x_k;$ $\qquad [-4, -3]$ $\bullet$ $\qquad \star \displaystyle\int_{-4}^{-3} (\sqrt[3]{x} + 4x)\,dx$

$\boxed{17}$ $\displaystyle\int_{4}^{1} \sqrt{x}\,dx = -\int_{1}^{4} \sqrt{x}\,dx = -\frac{14}{3}$, by (5.17).

$\boxed{18}$ $\displaystyle\int_{1}^{4} \sqrt{s}\,ds = \frac{14}{3}$, since s is a dummy variable.

$\boxed{19}$ $\displaystyle\int_{1}^{4} \sqrt{t}\,dt = \frac{14}{3}$, since t is a dummy variable.

$\boxed{20}$ $\displaystyle\int_{1}^{4} \sqrt{x}\,dx + \int_{4}^{1} \sqrt{x}\,dx = \frac{14}{3} + -\int_{1}^{4} \sqrt{x}\,dx = \frac{14}{3} + (-\frac{14}{3}) = 0$, by (5.17).

$\boxed{21}$ $\displaystyle\int_{4}^{4} \sqrt{x}\,dx + \int_{4}^{1} \sqrt{x}\,dx = 0 + -\int_{1}^{4} \sqrt{x}\,dx = -\frac{14}{3}$, by (5.18) and (5.17).

$\boxed{22}$ $\displaystyle\int_{4}^{4} \sqrt{x}\,dx = 0$, by (5.18).

$\boxed{23}$ $5x + 4y = 20 \Leftrightarrow y = -\frac{5}{4}x + 5$. The integral that represents the area under the
line from $x = 0$ to $x = 4$ is $\displaystyle\int_{0}^{4} (-\frac{5}{4}x + 5)\,dx$.

$\boxed{24}$ $3x - 4y = -11 \Leftrightarrow y = \frac{3}{4}x + \frac{11}{4}$. The integral that represents the area under the
line from $x = -1$ to $x = 3$ is $\displaystyle\int_{-1}^{3} (\frac{3}{4}x + \frac{11}{4})\,dx$.

$\boxed{25}$ $(x - 2)^2 + y^2 = 9$ $(y \geq 0) \Leftrightarrow y = \sqrt{9 - (x - 2)^2}$. The integral that represents the
area under the semicircle from $x = -1$ to $x = 5$ is $\displaystyle\int_{-1}^{5} \sqrt{9 - (x - 2)^2}\,dx$.

[26] $(x - 1)^2 + (y - 2)^2 = 16 \ (y \geq 2) \Leftrightarrow y = 2 + \sqrt{16 - (x - 1)^2}$.

The integral that represents the area under the semicircle from $x = -3$ to $x = 5$ is

$$\int_{-3}^{5} \left(2 + \sqrt{16 - (x - 1)^2}\right) dx.$$

[27] The area bounded by $x = -1$, $x = 5$, the x-axis, and $f(x) = 6$ is that of a rectangle with base $5 - (-1) = 6$ and height 6. Hence, the value is $(6)(6) = 36$.

[28] The area bounded by $x = -2$, $x = 3$, the x-axis, and $f(x) = 4$ is that of a rectangle with base $3 - (-2) = 5$ and height 4. Hence, the value is $(5)(4) = 20$.

[29] The area bounded by $x = -3$, $x = 2$, the x-axis, and $f(x) = 2x + 6$ is that of a triangle of base $2 - (-3) = 5$ and height $f(2) = 10$.

Hence, the value is $\frac{1}{2}(5)(10) = 25$.

[30] The area bounded by $x = -1$, $x = 2$, the x-axis, and $f(x) = 7 - 3x$ is that of a trapezoid of bases $f(-1) = 10$ and $f(2) = 1$ and height $2 - (-1) = 3$.

Hence, the value is $\frac{1}{2}(3)(10 + 1) = 16.5$.

[31] The area bounded by $x = 0$, $x = 3$, the x-axis, and $f(x) = |x - 1|$ is that of two triangles. Value $= \frac{1}{2}(1)(1) + \frac{1}{2}(2)(2) = 2.5$.

[32] The area bounded by $x = -1$, $x = 4$, the x-axis, and $f(x) = |x|$ is that of two triangles. Value $= \frac{1}{2}(1)(1) + \frac{1}{2}(4)(4) = 8.5$.

[33] The area bounded by $x = 0$, $x = 3$, the x-axis, and $f(x) = \sqrt{9 - x^2}$ is that of the first quadrant portion of a circle {quarter circle} centered at the origin with radius 3.

Value $= \frac{1}{4}\pi(3)^2 = \frac{9\pi}{4}$.

[34] The area bounded by $x = 0$, $x = a$, the x-axis, and $f(x) = \sqrt{a^2 - x^2}$ is that of the first quadrant portion of a circle {quarter circle} centered at the origin with radius a.

Value $= \frac{1}{4}\pi(a)^2 = \frac{\pi}{4}a^2$.

[35] $y = 3 + \sqrt{4 - x^2} \Rightarrow x^2 + (y - 3)^2 = 4 \ (y \geq 3)$. The area bounded by $x = -2$, $x = 2$, the x-axis, and $f(x) = 3 + \sqrt{4 - x^2}$ is that of the top half of a circle centered at $(0, 3)$ with radius 2 and a rectangle of height 3 and base 4.

Value $= \frac{1}{2}\pi(2)^2 + (3)(4) = 12 + 2\pi$.

[36] $y = 3 - \sqrt{4 - x^2} \Rightarrow x^2 + (y - 3)^2 = 4 \ (y \leq 3)$. The area bounded by $x = -2$, $x = 2$, the x-axis, and $f(x) = 3 - \sqrt{4 - x^2}$ is that of the bottom half of a circle centered at $(0, 3)$ with radius 2 subtracted from the area of the rectangle formed by $-2 \leq x \leq 2$ and $0 \leq y \leq 3$. Value $= (3)(4) - \frac{1}{2}\pi(2)^2 = 12 - 2\pi$.

Exercises 5.5

[1] By (5.21), $I = 5[4 - (-2)] = 30$.   [2] By (5.21), $I = \sqrt{2}(10 - 1) = 9\sqrt{2}$.

[3] By (5.21), $I = 3(2 - 6) = -12$.

[4] By (5.21), $I = \int_{4}^{-3} 1 \, dx = 1(-3 - 4) = -7$.

⑤ By (5.21), $I = \int_{-1}^{1} 1\, dx = 1\big[1 - (-1)\big] = 2.$

⑥ By (5.18) or (5.21), $I = 0.$

⑦ $I = 3\int_{1}^{4} x^2\, dx + \int_{1}^{4} 5\, dx = 3(21) + 5(4 - 1) = 78$

⑧ $I = 6\int_{1}^{4} x\, dx - \int_{1}^{4} 1\, dx = 6(\frac{15}{2}) - 1(4 - 1) = 42$

⑨ $I = \int_{1}^{4} 2\, dx - 9\int_{1}^{4} x\, dx - 4\int_{1}^{4} x^2\, dx = 2(4 - 1) - 9(\frac{15}{2}) - 4(21) = -\frac{291}{2}$

⑩ $I = \int_{1}^{4} (9x^2 + 12x + 4)\, dx = 9\int_{1}^{4} x^2\, dx + 12\int_{1}^{4} x\, dx + \int_{1}^{4} 4\, dx =$

$$9(21) + 12(\tfrac{15}{2}) + 4(4 - 1) = 291$$

⑪ $3x^2 + 4 \geq 2x^2 + 5 \Leftrightarrow x^2 \geq 1.$ Using (5.27) and the fact that $3x^2 + 4 \geq 2x^2 + 5$

on $[1, 2]$, we have $\int_{1}^{2} (3x^2 + 4)\, dx \geq \int_{1}^{2} (2x^2 + 5)\, dx.$

⑫ $3x + 1 \geq 2x + 2 \Leftrightarrow x \geq 1.$

Using (5.27) and the fact that $3x + 1 \geq 2x + 2$ on $[1, 4]$, we have

$$\int_{1}^{4} (3x + 1)\, dx \geq \int_{1}^{4} (2x + 2)\, dx, \text{ or equivalently, } \int_{1}^{4} (2x + 2)\, dx \leq \int_{1}^{4} (3x + 1)\, dx.$$

⑬ $x^2 - 6x + 8 = (x - 2)(x - 4) \leq 0$ on $[2, 4]$ so $-(x^2 - 6x + 8) \geq 0$ on $[2, 4]$.

By (5.26), $\int_{2}^{4} -(x^2 - 6x + 8)\, dx = -\int_{2}^{4} (x^2 - 6x + 8)\, dx \geq 0,$ or equivalently,

$$\int_{2}^{4} (x^2 - 6x + 8)\, dx \leq 0.$$

⑭ Let $f(x) = 5x^2 - x + 1$ and $f'(x) = 10x - 1.$ $f(2) = 19$ and f is ↑ on $[2, 4] \Rightarrow$

$$f(x) \geq 0 \text{ on } [2, 4]. \text{ By (5.26), } \int_{2}^{4} (5x^2 - x + 1)\, dx \geq 0.$$

⑮ $-1 \leq \sin x \leq 1 \Rightarrow 0 \leq (1 + \sin x) \leq 2.$ By (5.26), $\int_{0}^{2\pi} (1 + \sin x)\, dx \geq 0.$

⑯ On $[-\frac{\pi}{3}, \frac{\pi}{3}]$, $1 \leq \sec x \leq 2$ and hence $-1 \leq \sec x - 2 \leq 0$, or $1 \geq -(\sec x - 2) \geq 0.$

By (5.26), $\int_{-\pi/3}^{\pi/3} -(\sec x - 2)\, dx = -\int_{-\pi/3}^{\pi/3} (\sec x - 2)\, dx \geq 0,$ or equivalently,

$$\int_{-\pi/3}^{\pi/3} (\sec x - 2)\, dx \leq 0.$$

⑰ $\int_{5}^{1} f(x)\, dx + \int_{-3}^{5} f(x)\, dx = \int_{-3}^{5} f(x)\, dx + \int_{5}^{1} f(x)\, dx = \int_{-3}^{1} f(x)\, dx,$ by (5.25).

⑱ $\int_{4}^{1} f(x)\, dx + \int_{6}^{4} f(x)\, dx = \int_{6}^{4} f(x)\, dx + \int_{4}^{1} f(x)\, dx = \int_{6}^{1} f(x)\, dx,$ by (5.25).

⑲ $\int_{c}^{d} f(x)\, dx + \int_{e}^{c} f(x)\, dx = \int_{e}^{c} f(x)\, dx + \int_{c}^{d} f(x)\, dx = \int_{e}^{d} f(x)\, dx,$ by (5.25).

20 $\int_{-2}^{6} f(x)\,dx - \int_{-2}^{2} f(x)\,dx = \int_{-2}^{6} f(x)\,dx + \int_{2}^{-2} f(x)\,dx =$

$$\int_{2}^{-2} f(x)\,dx + \int_{-2}^{6} f(x)\,dx = \int_{2}^{6} f(x)\,dx, \text{ by (5.25).}$$

21 $\int_{c}^{c+h} f(x)\,dx - \int_{c}^{h} f(x)\,dx = \int_{c}^{c+h} f(x)\,dx + \int_{h}^{c} f(x)\,dx =$

$$\int_{h}^{c} f(x)\,dx + \int_{c}^{c+h} f(x)\,dx = \int_{h}^{c+h} f(x)\,dx, \text{ by (5.25).}$$

22 $\int_{c}^{m} f(x)\,dx - \int_{d}^{m} f(x)\,dx = \int_{c}^{m} f(x)\,dx + \int_{m}^{d} f(x)\,dx = \int_{c}^{d} f(x)\,dx, \text{ by (5.25).}$

23 (a) $27 = (3z^2)(3 - 0) \Rightarrow z^2 = 3 \Rightarrow z = \sqrt{3}$, since $-\sqrt{3} \notin (0, 3)$.

  (b) $f_{av} = \frac{1}{3-0}(27) = 9$.

24 (a) $\frac{9}{4} = 3z^{-2}\left[-1 - (-4)\right] \Rightarrow \frac{9}{4} = \frac{9}{z^2} \Rightarrow z^2 = 4 \Rightarrow z = -2$, since $2 \notin (-4, -1)$.

  (b) $f_{av} = \frac{1}{-1-(-4)}(\frac{9}{4}) = \frac{3}{4}$.

25 (a) $6 = (z^2 + 1)\left[1 - (-2)\right] \Rightarrow z^2 = 1 \Rightarrow z = -1$, since $1 \notin (-2, 1)$.

  (b) $f_{av} = \frac{1}{1-(-2)}(6) = 2$.

26 (a) $32 = (3z^2 - 2z + 3)\left[3 - (-1)\right] \Rightarrow 3z^2 - 2z - 5 = 0 \Rightarrow$

$$(3z - 5)(z + 1) = 0 \Rightarrow z = \frac{5}{3}, \text{ since } -1 \notin (-1, 3).$$

  (b) $f_{av} = \frac{1}{3-(-1)}(32) = 8$.

27 (a) $54 = 3\sqrt{z+1}\left[8 - (-1)\right] \Rightarrow \sqrt{z+1} = 2 \Rightarrow z + 1 = 4 \Rightarrow z = 3$.

  (b) $f_{av} = \frac{1}{8-(-1)}(54) = 6$.

28 (a) $-3 = 8z^{-3}\left[-1 - (-2)\right] \Rightarrow z^3 = -\frac{8}{3} \Rightarrow z = \frac{-2}{\sqrt[3]{3}}$.

  (b) $f_{av} = \frac{1}{-1-(-2)}(-3) = -3$.

29 (a) $14 = (4z^3 - 1)(2 - 1) \Rightarrow 4z^3 = 15 \Rightarrow z = \sqrt[3]{\frac{15}{4}}$.

  (b) $f_{av} = \frac{1}{2-1}(14) = 14$.

30 (a) $20 = (2 + 3\sqrt{z})(4 - 1) \Rightarrow 9\sqrt{z} = 14 \Rightarrow z = \frac{196}{81}$.

  (b) $f_{av} = \frac{1}{4-1}(20) = \frac{20}{3}$.

31 $(8z^3 + 3z - 1)\left[3 - (-2)\right] = 132.5 \Leftrightarrow 40z^3 + 15z - 137.5 = 0$.

  Let $f(x) = 40x^3 + 15x - 137.5$. $x_{n+1} = x_n - \dfrac{40x_n^3 + 15x_n - 137.5}{120x_n^2 + 15}$

$$\text{If } x_1 = 1.5, \ x_2 = 1.430, \ x_3 = 1.426, \text{ and } x_4 = 1.426.$$

32 $(1 - \cos 4z)(\frac{\pi}{4} - \frac{\pi}{6}) = \frac{\pi}{12} + \frac{\sqrt{3}}{8} \Leftrightarrow \frac{\pi}{12}\cos 4z + \frac{\sqrt{3}}{8} = 0$.

  Let $f(x) = \frac{\pi}{12}\cos 4x + \frac{\sqrt{3}}{8}$. $x_{n+1} = x_n - \dfrac{\frac{\pi}{12}\cos 4x_n + \frac{1}{8}\sqrt{3}}{-\frac{\pi}{3}\sin 4x_n}$

$$\text{If } x_1 = \frac{\pi}{6}, \ x_2 = 0.618, \ x_3 = 0.635, \ x_4 = 0.636, \text{ and } x_5 = 0.636.$$

33 $\int_{a}^{b}\left[cf(x) + dg(x)\right]dx = \int_{a}^{b} cf(x)\,dx + \int_{a}^{b} dg(x)\,dx = c\int_{a}^{b} f(x)\,dx + d\int_{a}^{b} g(x)\,dx$

$$\text{by (5.23)(i) and (5.22).}$$

34 Since $-|f(x)| \le f(x) \le |f(x)|$, it follows from (5.27) that

$$-\int_a^b |f(x)|\, dx \le \int_a^b f(x)\, dx \le \int_a^b |f(x)|\, dx \Rightarrow \left| \int_a^b f(x)\, dx \right| \le \int_a^b |f(x)|\, dx.$$

Note that the definite integral is a real number and so the property

$$-a \le b \le a \Rightarrow |b| \le a \text{ for all real numbers } b \text{ and nonnegative } a \text{ applies.}$$

Exercises 5.6

1   $I = \left[\frac{1}{3}x^3 - 2x^2 - 3x \right]_1^4 = (\frac{64}{3} - 32 - 12) - (\frac{1}{3} - 2 - 3) = -18$

2   $I = \left[5x + \frac{1}{2}x^2 - 2x^3 \right]_{-2}^3 = (15 + \frac{9}{2} - 54) - (-10 + 2 + 16) = -\frac{85}{2}$

3   $I = \left[2z^4 + \frac{3}{2}z^2 - z \right]_{-2}^3 = (162 + \frac{27}{2} - 3) - (32 + 6 + 2) = \frac{265}{2}$

4   $I = \left[\frac{1}{5}z^5 - \frac{1}{2}z^4 \right]_0^2 = (\frac{32}{5} - 8) - 0 = -\frac{8}{5}$

5   $I = 1(12 - 7) = 5$ 6 $I = 8\left[-1 - (-6) \right] = 40$

7   $I = 5\int_1^2 x^{-6}\, dx = 5\left[-\frac{1}{5}x^{-5} \right]_1^2 = -(\frac{1}{32} - 1) = \frac{31}{32}$

8   $I = 4\int_1^4 x^{5/2}\, dx = 4\left[\frac{2}{7}x^{7/2} \right]_1^4 = \frac{8}{7}(2^7 - 1) = \frac{1016}{7}$

9   $I = \int_4^9 (t^{1/2} - 3t^{-1/2})\, dt = \left[\frac{2}{3}t^{3/2} - 6t^{1/2} \right]_4^9 = 0 - (\frac{16}{3} - 12) = \frac{20}{3}$

10   $I = \int_{-1}^{-2} (2t^{-2} - 7t^{-3})\, dt = \left[-2t^{-1} + \frac{7}{2}t^{-2} \right]_{-1}^{-2} = \frac{15}{8} - \frac{11}{2} = -\frac{29}{8}$

11   By (5.34)(i), $I = 2\int_0^8 (s^{2/3} + 2)\, ds = 2\left[\frac{3}{5}s^{5/3} + 2s \right]_0^8 = 2\left[\frac{3}{5}(2^5) + 16 \right] = \frac{352}{5}.$

12   $I = \int_1^0 (s^{7/3} - s^{5/2})\, ds = \left[\frac{3}{10}s^{10/3} - \frac{2}{7}s^{7/2} \right]_1^0 = 0 - (\frac{3}{10} - \frac{2}{7}) = -\frac{1}{70}$

13   $I = \int_{-1}^0 (4x^2 + 12x + 9)\, dx = \left[\frac{4}{3}x^3 + 6x^2 + 9x \right]_{-1}^0 = 0 - (-\frac{13}{3}) = \frac{13}{3}$

14   $I = \left[-x^{-4} - x^5 \right]_1^2 = (-\frac{1}{16} - 32) - (-1 - 1) = -\frac{481}{16}$

15   Since $x \ne 1$, $I = \int_3^2 (x + 1)\, dx = \left[\frac{1}{2}x^2 + x \right]_3^2 = 4 - \frac{15}{2} = -\frac{7}{2}.$

16   Since $x \ne -2$, $I = \int_0^{-1} (x^2 - 2x + 4)\, dx = \left[\frac{1}{3}x^3 - x^2 + 4x \right]_0^{-1} = -\frac{16}{3}.$

17   $I = 0$ by (5.18).   18 $I = 0$ by (5.18).

19   $I = \int_1^3 (2x - 4 + 5x^{-2})\, dx = \left[x^2 - 4x - 5x^{-1} \right]_1^3 = -\frac{14}{3} - (-8) = \frac{10}{3}$

20   $I = \int_{-2}^{-1} (x^2 - 2 + x^{-2})\, dx = \left[\frac{1}{3}x^3 - 2x - x^{-1} \right]_{-2}^{-1} = \frac{8}{3} - \frac{11}{6} = \frac{5}{6}$

$\boxed{21}$ $I = \int_{-3}^{4} -(x-4)\,dx + \int_{4}^{6} (x-4)\,dx = \left[4x - \frac{1}{2}x^2\right]_{-3}^{4} + \left[\frac{1}{2}x^2 - 4x\right]_{4}^{6} =$

$$\left[8 - \left(-\frac{33}{2}\right)\right] + \left[-6 - (-8)\right] = \frac{53}{2}$$

$\boxed{22}$ $I = \int_{-1}^{3/2} -(2x-3)\,dx + \int_{3/2}^{5} (2x-3)\,dx = \left[3x - x^2\right]_{-1}^{3/2} + \left[x^2 - 3x\right]_{3/2}^{5} =$

$$\left[\frac{9}{4} - (-4)\right] + \left[10 - \left(-\frac{9}{4}\right)\right] = \frac{37}{2}$$

$\boxed{23}$ $u = 5 - x \Rightarrow -du = dx.$ $x = 1, 4 \Rightarrow u = 4, 1.$

$$\text{Thus, } I = -\int_{4}^{1} u^{1/2}\,du = -\left[\frac{2}{3}u^{3/2}\right]_{4}^{1} = -\frac{2}{3}(1 - 2^3) = \frac{14}{3}.$$

$\boxed{24}$ $u = 2x - 1 \Rightarrow \frac{1}{2}\,du = dx.$ $x = 1, 5 \Rightarrow u = 1, 9.$

$$\text{Thus, } I = \frac{1}{2}\int_{1}^{9} u^{1/3}\,du = \frac{1}{2}\left[\frac{3}{4}u^{4/3}\right]_{1}^{9} = \frac{3}{8}(9^{4/3} - 1) \approx 6.65.$$

$\boxed{25}$ Since $\left[(v^2 - 1)^3 v\right]$ is an odd function, $I = 0$ by (5.34)(ii).

$\boxed{26}$ $u = v^3 - 2 \Rightarrow \frac{1}{3}\,du = v^2\,dv.$ $v = -2, 0 \Rightarrow u = -10, -2.$

$$\text{Thus, } I = \frac{1}{3}\int_{-10}^{-2} u^{-2}\,du = \frac{1}{3}\left[-\frac{1}{u}\right]_{-10}^{-2} = -\frac{1}{3}\left[-\frac{1}{2} - \left(-\frac{1}{10}\right)\right] = \frac{2}{15}.$$

$\boxed{27}$ $u = 3 - 2x \Rightarrow -\frac{1}{2}\,du = dx.$ $x = 0, 1 \Rightarrow u = 3, 1.$

$$\text{Thus, } I = -\frac{1}{2}\int_{3}^{1} u^{-2}\,du = -\frac{1}{2}\left[-\frac{1}{u}\right]_{3}^{1} = \frac{1}{2}(1 - \frac{1}{3}) = \frac{1}{3}.$$

$\boxed{28}$ $u = x^2 + 9 \Rightarrow \frac{1}{2}\,du = x\,dx.$ $x = 0, 4 \Rightarrow u = 9, 25.$

$$\text{Thus, } I = \frac{1}{2}\int_{9}^{25} u^{-1/2}\,du = \frac{1}{2}\left[2u^{1/2}\right]_{9}^{25} = 5 - 3 = 2.$$

$\boxed{29}$ $u = \sqrt{x} + 1 \Rightarrow 2\,du = \frac{dx}{\sqrt{x}}.$ $x = 1, 4 \Rightarrow u = 2, 3.$

$$\text{Thus, } I = 2\int_{2}^{3} u^{-3}\,du = 2\left[-\frac{1}{2}u^{-2}\right]_{2}^{3} = -(\frac{1}{9} - \frac{1}{4}) = \frac{5}{36}.$$

$\boxed{30}$ $u = 3 - x^4 \Rightarrow -\frac{1}{4}\,du = x^3\,dx.$ $x = 0, 1 \Rightarrow u = 3, 2.$

$$\text{Thus, } I = -\frac{1}{4}\int_{3}^{2} u^3\,du = -\frac{1}{4}\left[\frac{1}{4}u^4\right]_{3}^{2} = -\frac{1}{16}(16 - 81) = \frac{65}{16}.$$

$\boxed{31}$ $\int_{\pi/2}^{\pi} \cos(\frac{1}{3}x)\,dx = \left[3\sin(\frac{1}{3}x)\right]_{\pi/2}^{\pi} = 3(\frac{1}{2}\sqrt{3} - \frac{1}{2}) = \frac{3}{2}(\sqrt{3} - 1) \approx 1.10$

$\boxed{32}$ $\int_{0}^{\pi/2} 3\sin(\frac{1}{2}x)\,dx = \left[-6\cos(\frac{1}{2}x)\right]_{0}^{\pi/2} = -6(\frac{1}{2}\sqrt{2} - 1) = 6 - 3\sqrt{2} \approx 1.76$

$\boxed{33}$ $\int_{\pi/4}^{\pi/3} (4\sin 2\theta + 6\cos 3\theta)\,d\theta = \left[-2\cos 2\theta + 2\sin 3\theta\right]_{\pi/4}^{\pi/3} =$

$$(1 + 0) - (0 + \sqrt{2}) = 1 - \sqrt{2} \approx -0.41$$

$\boxed{34}$ $\int_{\pi/6}^{\pi/4} (1 - \cos 4\theta)\,d\theta = \left[\theta - \frac{1}{4}\sin 4\theta\right]_{\pi/6}^{\pi/4} = \left[\frac{\pi}{4} - 0\right] - \left[\frac{\pi}{6} - \frac{1}{4}(\frac{1}{2}\sqrt{3})\right] =$

$$\frac{\pi}{12} + \frac{1}{8}\sqrt{3} \approx 0.48$$

$\boxed{35}$ Since $(x + \sin 5x)$ is an odd function, $I = 0$ by (5.34)(ii).

$\boxed{36}$ $u = \cos x, -du = \sin x\,dx.$ $x = 0, \frac{\pi}{3} \Rightarrow u = 1, \frac{1}{2}.$

$$\text{Thus, } I = -\int_{1}^{1/2} u^{-2}\,du = -\left[-\frac{1}{u}\right]_{1}^{1/2} = 2 - 1 = 1.$$

$\boxed{37}$ (a) From Exercise 28, $I = 2. \ 2 = \dfrac{z}{\sqrt{z^2 + 9}}(4 - 0) \Rightarrow 2z = \sqrt{z^2 + 9} \Rightarrow$

$$4z^2 = z^2 + 9 \Rightarrow 3z^2 = 9 \Rightarrow z = \sqrt{3}, \text{ since } -\sqrt{3} \notin (0, 4).$$

(b) $f_{av} = \frac{1}{4-0}(2) = \frac{1}{2}.$

$\boxed{38}$ (a) Let $u = x + 1$ and $du = dx.$ $x = -2, 0 \Rightarrow u = -1, 1.$

Thus, $I = \displaystyle\int_{-1}^{1} u^{1/3} \, du = 0$ by (5.34)(ii). $0 = \sqrt[3]{z + 1}\big[0 - (-2)\big] \Rightarrow z = -1.$

(b) $f_{av} = \frac{1}{0-(-2)}(0) = 0.$

$\boxed{39}$ (a) $\displaystyle\int_{0}^{5}(x + 4)^{1/2} \, dx = \frac{2}{3}\Big[(x + 4)^{3/2}\Big]_0^5 = \frac{2}{3}(27 - 8) = \frac{38}{3}.$

$$\tfrac{38}{3} = \sqrt{z + 4}\,(5 - 0) \Rightarrow z = \left(\tfrac{38}{15}\right)^2 - 4 = \tfrac{544}{225}.$$

(b) $f_{av} = \frac{1}{5-0}\left(\frac{38}{3}\right) = \frac{38}{15}.$

$\boxed{40}$ (a) $\displaystyle\int_{-3}^{2}\sqrt{6 - x} \, dx = \Big[-\tfrac{2}{3}(6 - x)^{3/2}\Big]_{-3}^{2} = -\tfrac{2}{3}(8 - 27) = \tfrac{38}{3}.$

$$\tfrac{38}{3} = \sqrt{6 - z}\,\big[2 - (-3)\big] \Rightarrow z = 6 - \left(\tfrac{38}{15}\right)^2 = -\tfrac{94}{225}.$$

(b) $f_{av} = \frac{1}{2-(-3)}\left(\frac{38}{3}\right) = \frac{38}{15}.$

$\boxed{41}$ $D_x \displaystyle\int_{0}^{3}\sqrt{x^2 + 16} \, dx = 0$, since the definite integral is equal to a constant.

$\boxed{42}$ $D_x \displaystyle\int_{0}^{1}x\sqrt{x^2 + 4} \, dx = 0$, since the definite integral is equal to a constant.

$\boxed{43}$ $D_x \displaystyle\int_{0}^{x}\frac{1}{t + 1} \, dt = \frac{1}{x + 1}$, by (5.35).

$\boxed{44}$ $D_x \displaystyle\int_{0}^{x}\frac{1}{\sqrt{1 - t^2}} \, dt, \ |x| < 1 = \frac{1}{\sqrt{1 - x^2}}$, by (5.35).

$\boxed{45}$ $a_{av} = \dfrac{1}{t_2 - t_1}\displaystyle\int_{t_1}^{t_2} a(t) \, dt = \dfrac{1}{t_2 - t_1}\Big[v(t)\Big]_{t_1}^{t_2} = \dfrac{v(t_2) - v(t_1)}{t_2 - t_1} = \text{average acceleration}$

$\boxed{46}$ The average rate of change of f on $[a, b]$ is $\dfrac{f(b) - f(a)}{b - a}$. By (5.29),

the average value of f' on $[a, b]$ is $\dfrac{1}{b - a}\displaystyle\int_{a}^{b} f'(x) \, dx = \dfrac{1}{b - a}\big[f(x)\big]_a^b = \dfrac{f(b) - f(a)}{b - a}.$

$\boxed{47}$ (a) $v_{av} = \dfrac{1}{d - 0}\displaystyle\int_{0}^{d} v \, dy = \dfrac{1}{d}\displaystyle\int_{0}^{d} c(d - y)^{1/6} \, dy = \dfrac{c}{d}\Big[-\tfrac{6}{7}(d - y)^{7/6}\Big]_0^d =$

$$-\tfrac{6c}{7d}(0 - d^{7/6}) = \tfrac{6}{7}cd^{1/6}$$

(b) At the surface, $y = 0$ and $v = cd^{1/6} = v_0.$ From part (a), $v_{av} = \tfrac{6}{7}cd^{1/6} = \tfrac{6}{7}v_0.$

$\boxed{48}$ $P_{av} = \dfrac{1}{t_2 - t_1}\displaystyle\int_{t_1}^{t_2} P(t) \, dt = \dfrac{1}{2\pi/\omega - 0}\displaystyle\int_{0}^{2\pi/\omega} (I_M^2 \sin^2 \omega t)\, R \, dt =$

$$\left(\dfrac{\omega R I_M^2}{2\pi}\right)\displaystyle\int_{0}^{2\pi/\omega} \tfrac{1}{2}(1 - \cos 2\omega t) \, dt = \left(\dfrac{\omega R I_M^2}{4\pi}\right)\Big[t - \dfrac{\sin 2\omega t}{2\omega}\Big]_0^{2\pi/\omega} = \left(\dfrac{\omega R I_M^2}{4\pi}\right)\left(\dfrac{2\pi}{\omega} - 0\right)$$

$$= \tfrac{1}{2}R I_M^2$$

$\boxed{49}$ If $s(t)$ denotes the height of the ball, then $s(t) = s_0 - 16t^2$.

The ball is in the air from $t_0 = 0$ $\{s(t) = s_0\}$ to $t_1 = \frac{1}{4}\sqrt{s_0}$ $\{s(t) = 0\}$.

Thus, $v_{av} = \dfrac{1}{t_1 - t_0}\displaystyle\int_{t_0}^{t_1} v(t)\,dt = \dfrac{4}{\sqrt{s_0}}\Big[s(t)\Big]_{t_0}^{t_1} = \dfrac{4}{\sqrt{s_0}}\Big[0 - s_0\Big] = -4\sqrt{s_0}.$

(The answer is negative since the ball is moving toward the ground.)

$\boxed{50}$ At 6 A.M., $t_0 = 6$ and at noon, $t_1 = 12$. Then, $T_{av} = \dfrac{1}{t_1 - t_0}\displaystyle\int_{t_0}^{t_1} T(t)\,dt =$

$\dfrac{1}{12 - 6}\displaystyle\int_6^{12} \frac{1}{20}(t^3 - 36t^2 + 288t)\,dt = \frac{1}{120}\Big[\frac{1}{4}t^4 - 12t^3 + 144t^2\Big]_6^{12} =$

$\frac{1}{120}\Big[(5184 - 20{,}736 + 20{,}736) - (324 - 2592 + 5184)\Big] = \frac{1}{120}(2268) = 18.9\,°\text{F}.$

$\boxed{51}$ By Part I of Theorem (5.30), the function $G(u) = \displaystyle\int_a^u f(t)\,dt$ is an antiderivative of f.

By the chain rule, we have $D_x\, G(u) = D_u\, G(u)\, D_x\, u = f(u)\, D_x\, u.$

Replacing u by $g(x)$ yields the desired result, namely, $f(g(x))\, g'(x).$

$\boxed{52}$ By (5.25), $D_x\displaystyle\int_{k(x)}^{g(x)} f(t)\,dt = D_x\displaystyle\int_{k(x)}^0 f(t)\,dt + D_x\displaystyle\int_0^{g(x)} f(t)\,dt =$

$D_x\displaystyle\int_0^{g(x)} f(t)\,dt - D_x\displaystyle\int_0^{k(x)} f(t)\,dt = f(g(x))\, g'(x) - f(k(x))\, k'(x)$ using Exercise 51.

$\boxed{53}$ By Exercise 51 with $g(x) = x^4$ and $f(t) = \dfrac{t}{\sqrt{t^3 + 2}}$, we have $D_x\displaystyle\int_2^{x^4} \dfrac{t}{\sqrt{t^3 + 2}}\,dt =$

$f(g(x))\, g'(x) = \dfrac{x^4}{\sqrt{(x^4)^3 + 2}}(4x^3) = \dfrac{4x^7}{\sqrt{x^{12} + 2}}.$

$\boxed{54}$ Using Exercise 51, $D_x\displaystyle\int_0^{x^2} \sqrt[3]{t^4 + 1}\,dt = \sqrt[3]{(x^2)^4 + 1}\,(2x) = (2x)\sqrt[3]{x^8 + 1}.$

$\boxed{55}$ By Exercise 52 with $g(x) = x^3$, $k(x) = 3x$ and $f(t) = (t^3 + 1)^{10}$,

we have $D_x\displaystyle\int_{3x}^{x^3} (t^3 + 1)^{10}\,dt = f(g(x))\, g'(x) - f(k(x))\, k'(x) =$

$\Big[(x^3)^3 + 1\Big]^{10}(3x^2) - \Big[(3x)^3 + 1\Big]^{10}(3) = 3x^2(x^9 + 1)^{10} - 3(27x^3 + 1)^{10}.$

$\boxed{56}$ Using Exercise 52, $D_x\displaystyle\int_{1/x}^{\sqrt{x}} \sqrt{t^4 + t^2 + 4}\,dt$

$= \sqrt{(\sqrt{x})^4 + (\sqrt{x})^2 + 4}\left(\dfrac{1}{2\sqrt{x}}\right) - \sqrt{(\tfrac{1}{x})^4 + (\tfrac{1}{x})^2 + 4}\left(-\dfrac{1}{x^2}\right)$

$= \left(\dfrac{1}{2\sqrt{x}}\right)\sqrt{x^2 + x + 4} + \left(\dfrac{1}{x^2}\right)\sqrt{\dfrac{1}{x^4} + \dfrac{1}{x^2} + 4}$

$= \left(\dfrac{1}{2\sqrt{x}}\right)\sqrt{x^2 + x + 4} + \left(\dfrac{1}{x^4}\right)\sqrt{4x^4 + x^2 + 1}$

Note: Let T denote the trapezoidal rule and S, Simpson's rule, in this section and all subsequent sections using numerical integration. The first step listed is

$$T = \frac{b-a}{2n}\left\{ f(x_0) + 2\sum_{k=1}^{n-1} f(x_k) + f(x_n) \right\} \text{ or}$$

$$S = \frac{b-a}{3n}\left[f(x_0) + 4f(x_1) + 2f(x_2) + \cdots + f(x_n) \right].$$

1.   (a) $f(x) = x^2 + 1$; $T = \frac{3-1}{2(4)}\left\{ f(1) + 2\left[f(1.5) + f(2) + f(2.5) \right] + f(3) \right\} =$

$$\frac{1}{4}\left[2 + 2(3.25 + 5 + 7.25) + 10 \right] = \frac{1}{4}(43) = 10.75$$

   (b) $S = \frac{3-1}{3(4)}\left[f(1) + 4f(1.5) + 2f(2) + 4f(2.5) + 2f(3) \right] =$

$$\frac{1}{6}\left[2 + 4(3.25) + 2(5) + 4(7.25) + 10 \right] = \frac{1}{6}(64) = 10\frac{2}{3} \approx 10.67$$

2.   (a) $f(x) = x^3$; $T = \frac{5-1}{2(4)}\left\{ f(1) + 2\left[f(2) + f(3) + f(4) \right] + f(5) \right\} =$

$$\frac{1}{2}\left[1 + 2(8 + 27 + 64) + 125 \right] = \frac{1}{2}(324) = 162$$

   (b) $S = \frac{5-1}{3(4)}\left[f(1) + 4f(2) + 2f(3) + 4f(4) + f(5) \right] =$

$$\frac{1}{3}\left[1 + 4(8) + 2(27) + 4(64) + 125 \right] = \frac{1}{3}(468) = 156$$

3. $f(x) = 2x - 1$

   (a) $T = \frac{1.6-1}{2(6)}\left\{ f(1) + 2\left[f(1.1) + f(1.2) + f(1.3) + f(1.4) + f(1.5) \right] + f(1.6) \right\} =$

$$\frac{1}{20}\left[1 + 2(1.2 + 1.4 + 1.6 + 1.8 + 2) + 2.2 \right] = \frac{1}{20}(19.2) = 0.96$$

   (b) $S = \frac{1.6-1}{3(6)}\left[f(1) + 4f(1.1) + 2f(1.2) + 4f(1.3) + 2f(1.4) + 4f(1.5) + f(1.6) \right]$

$$= \frac{1}{30}\left[1 + 4(1.2) + 2(1.4) + 4(1.6) + 2(1.8) + 4(2) + 2.2 \right] = \frac{1}{30}(28.8) = 0.96$$

   Note: Since f is linear, both methods give the correct result.

4. $f(x) = \frac{1}{2}x + 1$

   (a) $T = \frac{3.2-2}{2(6)}\left\{ f(2) + 2\left[f(2.2) + f(2.4) + f(2.6) + f(2.8) + f(3) \right] + f(3.2) \right\} =$

$$\frac{1}{10}\left[2 + 2(2.1 + 2.2 + 2.3 + 2.4 + 2.5) + 2.6 \right] = \frac{1}{10}(27.6) = 2.76$$

   (b) $S = \frac{3.2-2}{3(6)}\left[f(2) + 4f(2.2) + 2f(2.4) + 4f(2.6) + 2f(2.8) + 4f(3) + f(3.2) \right]$

$$= \frac{1}{15}\left[2 + 4(2.1) + 2(2.2) + 4(2.3) + 2(2.4) + 4(2.5) + 2.6 \right] = \frac{1}{15}(41.4) = 2.76$$

   Note: Since f is linear, both methods give the correct result.

5. $f(x) = 1/x$

   (a) $T = \frac{4-1}{2(6)}\left\{ f(1) + 2\left[f(1.5) + f(2) + f(2.5) + f(3) + f(3.5) \right] + f(4) \right\} \approx$

$$\frac{1}{4}\left[1 + 2(0.6667 + 0.5 + 0.4 + 0.3333 + 0.2857) + 0.25 \right] = \frac{1}{4}(5.6214) =$$

$$1.40535 \approx 1.41$$

   (b) $S = \frac{4-1}{3(6)}\left[f(1) + 4f(1.5) + 2f(2) + 4f(2.5) + 2f(3) + 4f(3.5) + f(4) \right] \approx$

$$\frac{1}{6}\left[1 + 4(0.6667) + 2(0.5) + 4(0.4) + 2(0.3333) + 4(0.2857) + 0.25 \right] =$$

$$\frac{1}{6}(8.3262) = 1.3877 \approx 1.39$$

6 (a) $f(x) = 1/(1 + x)$; $T = \frac{3-0}{2(8)} \{ f(0) + 2 [f(\frac{3}{8}) + f(\frac{6}{8}) + f(\frac{9}{8}) + f(\frac{12}{8}) +$

$$f(\tfrac{15}{8}) + f(\tfrac{18}{8}) + f(\tfrac{21}{8})] + f(3) \} \approx$$

$$\tfrac{3}{16} [1 + 2(0.7273 + 0.5714 + 0.4706 + 0.4 + 0.3478 + 0.3077 + 0.2759) +$$

$$0.25] = \tfrac{3}{16}(7.4514) \approx 1.3971 \approx 1.40$$

(b) $S = \frac{3-0}{3(8)} [f(0) + 4f(\frac{3}{8}) + 2f(\frac{6}{8}) + 4f(\frac{9}{8}) + 2f(\frac{12}{8}) + 4f(\frac{15}{8}) +$

$$2f(\tfrac{18}{8}) + 4f(\tfrac{21}{8}) + f(3)] \approx$$

$$\tfrac{1}{8} [1 + 4(0.7273) + 2(0.5714) + 4(0.4706) + 2(0.4) + 4(0.3478) +$$

$$2(0.3077) + 4(0.2759) + 0.25] = \tfrac{1}{8}(11.0946) \approx 1.3868 \approx 1.39$$

7 (a) $f(x) = 1/\sqrt{1 + x^2}$; $T = \frac{1-0}{2(4)} \{ f(0) + 2 \left[f(\frac{1}{4}) + f(\frac{1}{2}) + f(\frac{3}{4}) \right] + f(1) \} \approx$

$$\tfrac{1}{8} \left[1 + 2(0.9701 + 0.8944 + 0.8) + 0.7071 \right] = \tfrac{1}{8}(7.0361) \approx 0.8795 \approx 0.88$$

(b) $S = \frac{1-0}{3(4)} \left[f(0) + 4f(\frac{1}{4}) + 2f(\frac{1}{2}) + 4f(\frac{3}{4}) + f(1) \right] \approx$

$$\tfrac{1}{12} \left[1 + 4(0.9701) + 2(0.8944) + 4(0.8) + 0.7071 \right] = \tfrac{1}{12}(10.5763) \approx$$

$$0.8814 \approx 0.88$$

8 (a) $f(x) = \sqrt{1 + x^3}$; $T = \frac{3-2}{2(4)} \{ f(2) + 2 \left[f(2.25) + f(2.5) + f(2.75) \right] + f(3) \} \approx$

$$\tfrac{1}{8} \left[3 + 2(3.5200 + 4.0774 + 4.6687) + 5.2915 \right] = \tfrac{1}{8}(32.8237) \approx 4.1030 \approx 4.10$$

(b) $S = \frac{3-2}{3(4)} \left[f(2) + 4f(2.25) + 2f(2.5) + 4f(2.75) + f(3) \right]$

$$\approx \tfrac{1}{12} \left[3 + 4(3.5200) + 2(4.0774) + 4(4.6687) + 5.2915 \right] = \tfrac{1}{12}(49.2011) \approx$$

$$4.1001 \approx 4.10$$

9 $f(x) = 1/(4 + x^2)$

(a) $T = \frac{2-0}{2(6)} \{ f(0) + 2 \left[f(\frac{1}{3}) + f(\frac{2}{3}) + f(1) + f(\frac{4}{3}) + f(\frac{5}{3}) \right] + f(2) \} \approx$

$$\tfrac{1}{6} \left[0.25 + 2(0.2432 + 0.225 + 0.2 + 0.1731 + 0.1475) + 0.125 \right] =$$

$$\tfrac{1}{6}(2.3526) = 0.3921 \approx 0.39$$

(b) $S = \frac{2-0}{3(6)} \left[f(0) + 4f(\frac{1}{3}) + 2f(\frac{2}{3}) + 4f(1) + 2f(\frac{4}{3}) + 4f(\frac{5}{3}) + f(2) \right] \approx$

$$\tfrac{1}{9} \left[0.25 + 4(0.2432) + 2(0.225) + 4(0.2) + 2(0.1731) + 4(0.1475) + 0.125 \right] =$$

$$\tfrac{1}{9}(3.534) \approx 0.3927 \approx 0.39$$

10 $f(x) = 1/\sqrt{4 - x^2}$

(a) $T = \frac{0.6-0}{2(6)} \{ f(0) + 2 \left[f(0.1) + f(0.2) + f(0.3) + f(0.4) + f(0.5) \right] + f(0.6) \} \approx$

$$\tfrac{1}{20} \left[0.5 + 2(0.5006 + 0.5025 + 0.5057 + 0.5103 + 0.5164) + 0.5241 \right] =$$

$$\tfrac{1}{20}(6.0951) \approx 0.3048 \approx 0.30$$

(b) $S = \frac{0.6-0}{3(6)} \left[f(0) + 4f(0.1) + 2f(0.2) + 4f(0.3) + 2f(0.4) + 4f(0.5) + f(0.6) \right]$

$$\approx \tfrac{1}{30} [0.5 + 4(0.5006) + 2(0.5025) + 4(0.5057) + 2(0.5103) + 4(0.5164) +$$

$$0.5241] = \tfrac{1}{30}(9.1405) \approx 0.3047 \approx 0.30$$

$\boxed{11}$ $f(x) = \sqrt{\sin x}$

(a) $T = \frac{\pi - 0}{2(6)}\left\{f(0) + 2\left[f(\frac{\pi}{6}) + f(\frac{\pi}{3}) + f(\frac{\pi}{2}) + f(\frac{2\pi}{3}) + f(\frac{5\pi}{6})\right] + f(\pi)\right\} \approx$

$\frac{\pi}{12}\left[0 + 2(0.7071 + 0.9306 + 1 + 0.9306 + 0.7071) + 0\right] = \frac{\pi}{12}(8.5508) \approx$

$$2.2386 \approx 2.24$$

(b) $S = \frac{\pi - 0}{3(6)}\left[f(0) + 4f(\frac{\pi}{6}) + 2f(\frac{\pi}{3}) + 4f(\frac{\pi}{2}) + 2f(\frac{2\pi}{3}) + 4f(\frac{5\pi}{6}) + f(\pi)\right] \approx$

$\frac{\pi}{18}\left[0 + 4(0.7071) + 2(0.9306) + 4(1) + 2(0.9306) + 4(0.7071) + 0\right] =$

$$\frac{\pi}{18}(13.3792) \approx 2.3351 \approx 2.34$$

$\boxed{12}$ (a) $f(x) = \sin\sqrt{x}$; $T = \frac{\pi - 0}{2(4)}\left\{f(0) + 2\left[f(\frac{\pi}{4}) + f(\frac{\pi}{2}) + f(\frac{3\pi}{4})\right] + f(\pi)\right\} \approx$

$\frac{\pi}{8}\left[0 + 2(0.7747 + 0.9500 + 0.9994) + 0.9797\right] = \frac{\pi}{8}(6.4279) \approx 2.5242 \approx 2.52$

(b) $S = \frac{\pi - 0}{3(4)}\left[f(0) + 4f(\frac{\pi}{4}) + 2f(\frac{\pi}{2}) + 4f(\frac{3\pi}{4}) + f(\pi)\right] \approx$

$\frac{\pi}{12}\left[0 + 4(0.7747) + 2(0.9500) + 4(0.9994) + 0.9797\right] = \frac{\pi}{12}(9.9761) \approx$

$$2.6117 \approx 2.61$$

$\boxed{13}$ (a) We must find the maximum value M of $|f''(x)|$ on $[-2, 3]$.

If $f(x) = \frac{1}{360}x^6 + \frac{1}{60}x^5$, then $f''(x) = \frac{1}{12}x^4 + \frac{1}{3}x^3$ and $f'''(x) = \frac{1}{3}x^3 + x^2$.

$f'''(x) = 0 \Rightarrow x = -3, 0$; $-3 \notin [-2, 3]$. $|f''(-2)| = \frac{4}{3}, |f''(0)| = 0$, and

$|f''(3)| = \frac{63}{4} \Rightarrow M = \frac{63}{4}$. $|\text{error}| \le \dfrac{M(b-a)^3}{12n^2} = \dfrac{63(5)^3}{4 \cdot 12 \cdot 4^2} = \dfrac{2625}{256} \approx 10.25$.

(b) $f^{(4)}(x) = x^2 + 2x$ and $f^{(5)}(x) = 2x + 2$. $f^{(5)}(x) = 0 \Rightarrow x = -1$.

$\left|f^{(4)}(-2)\right| = 0, \left|f^{(4)}(-1)\right| = 1$, and $\left|f^{(4)}(3)\right| = 15 \Rightarrow M = 15$.

$$|\text{error}| \le \dfrac{M(b-a)^5}{180n^4} = \dfrac{15(5)^5}{180(4)^4} = \dfrac{3125}{3072} \approx 1.02.$$

$\boxed{14}$ (a) If $f(x) = -\frac{1}{12}x^4 + \frac{2}{3}x^3$, then $f''(x) = -x^2 + 4x$ and $f'''(x) = -2x + 4$.

$f'''(x) = 0 \Rightarrow x = 2$. $|f''(0)| = 0, |f''(2)| = 4$, and $|f''(3)| = 3 \Rightarrow M = 4$.

$$|\text{error}| \le \dfrac{M(b-a)^3}{12n^2} = \dfrac{4(3)^3}{12(4)^2} = \dfrac{9}{16} = 0.5625.$$

(b) $f^{(4)}(x) = -2$ and $M = \left|f^{(4)}(x)\right| = 2$.

$$|\text{error}| \le \dfrac{M(b-a)^5}{180n^4} = \dfrac{2(3)^5}{180(4)^4} = \dfrac{27}{2560} \approx 0.01.$$

$\boxed{15}$ (a) $f''(x) = 6/x^4$ and $f'''(x) = -24/x^5$. Since there are no critical numbers for f''

in $[1, 5]$, we need only examine the endpoints. $|f''(1)| = 6$ and $|f''(5)| = \frac{6}{625} \Rightarrow$

$$M = 6. \quad |\text{error}| \le \dfrac{M(b-a)^3}{12n^2} = \dfrac{6(4)^3}{12(8)^2} = \dfrac{1}{2} = 0.5.$$

(b) $f^{(4)}(x) = 120/x^6$ and $f^{(5)}(x) = -720/x^7$. As in part (a), $\left|f^{(4)}(1)\right| = 120$ and

$\left|f^{(4)}(5)\right| = \frac{120}{15,625} \Rightarrow M = 120$. $|\text{error}| \le \dfrac{M(b-a)^5}{180n^4} = \dfrac{120(4)^5}{180(8)^4} = \dfrac{1}{6} \approx 0.17$.

16 (a) $f''(x) = \frac{1}{4}x^{3/2}$ and $f'''(x) = \frac{3}{8}x^{1/2}$. Since there are no critical numbers for f''

in $[1, 4]$, we need only examine the endpoints. $\left|f''(1)\right| = \frac{1}{4}$ and $\left|f''(4)\right| = 2 \Rightarrow$

$$M = 2. \quad |\text{error}| \leq \frac{M(b-a)^3}{12n^2} = \frac{2(3)^3}{12(6)^2} = \frac{1}{8} = 0.125.$$

(b) $f^{(4)}(x) = \frac{3}{16}x^{-1/2}$ and $f^{(5)}(x) = -\frac{3}{32}x^{-3/2}$. As in part (a), $\left|f^{(4)}(1)\right| = \frac{3}{16}$ and

$\left|f^{(4)}(4)\right| = \frac{3}{32} \Rightarrow M = \frac{3}{16}$. $|\text{error}| \leq \dfrac{M(b-a)^5}{180n^4} = \dfrac{3(3)^5}{16 \cdot 180(6)^4} = \dfrac{1}{5120} \approx 0.0002.$

17 (a) See Exercises 13–16 for help in finding M. $f''(x) = 360x^{2/3}$. $\left|f''(1)\right| = 360$ and

$\left|f''(8)\right| = 1440 \Rightarrow M = 1440.$ $|\text{error}| \leq \dfrac{1440(7)^3}{12n^2} \leq 0.001 \Rightarrow$

$$n^2 \geq \frac{1440(7)^3(1000)}{12} = 41,160,000 \Rightarrow n \geq 6415.6..., \text{ or } n \geq 6416.$$

(b) $f^{(4)}(x) = -80/x^{4/3}$. $\left|f^{(4)}(1)\right| = 80$ and $\left|f^{(4)}(8)\right| = 5 \Rightarrow M = 80.$

$|\text{error}| \leq \dfrac{80(7)^5}{180n^4} \leq 0.001 \Rightarrow n^4 \geq \dfrac{80(7)^5(1000)}{180} \Rightarrow n \geq 52.2..., \text{ or } n \geq 54,$

since n must be even.

18 (a) $f''(x) = \frac{1}{20}x^{-4}$. $\left|f''(1)\right| = \frac{1}{20}$ and $\left|f''(2)\right| = \frac{1}{320} \Rightarrow M = \frac{1}{20}.$

$|\text{error}| \leq \dfrac{1(1)^3}{20 \cdot 12n^2} \leq 0.001 \Rightarrow n^2 \geq \dfrac{1000}{20 \cdot 12} \Rightarrow n \geq 2.04..., \text{ or } n \geq 3.$

(b) $f^{(4)}(x) = 1/x^6$. $\left|f^{(4)}(1)\right| = 1$ and $\left|f^{(4)}(2)\right| = \frac{1}{64} \Rightarrow M = 1.$

$|\text{error}| \leq \dfrac{1(1)^5}{180n^4} \leq 0.001 \Rightarrow n^4 \geq \dfrac{1000}{180} \Rightarrow n \geq 1.53..., \text{ or } n \geq 2.$

19 (a) Since $f''(x) = 2/x^3, \left|f''(x)\right| \leq 2(2)^3 = 16 = M$ on $[\frac{1}{2}, 1]$.

$|\text{error}| \leq \dfrac{M(b-a)^3}{12n^2} = \dfrac{16(\frac{1}{2})^3}{12n^2} \leq 0.0001 \Rightarrow n \geq \dfrac{100}{\sqrt{6}} \approx 40.82 \Rightarrow n = 41.$

(b) Since $f^{(4)}(x) = 24/x^5, \left|f^{(4)}(x)\right| \leq 24(2^5) = 768 = M$ on $[\frac{1}{2}, 1]$.

$|\text{error}| \leq \dfrac{M(b-a)^5}{180n^4} \leq \dfrac{768(\frac{1}{2})^5}{180n^4} \leq 0.0001 \Rightarrow n \geq \sqrt[4]{\dfrac{4000}{3}} \approx 6.04 \Rightarrow n = 8,$

since n must be even.

20 (a) Since $f''(x) = 2/(1 + x)^3, \left|f''(x)\right| \leq 2 = M$ on $[0, 3]$.

$|\text{error}| \leq \dfrac{M(b-a)^3}{12n^2} = \dfrac{2(3)^3}{12n^2} \leq 0.001 \Rightarrow n \geq \sqrt{4500} \approx 67.08 \Rightarrow n = 68.$

(b) Since $f^{(4)}(x) = 24/(1 + x)^5, \left|f^{(4)}(x)\right| \leq 24 = M$ on $[0, 3]$.

$|\text{error}| \leq \dfrac{M(b-a)^5}{180n^4} \leq \dfrac{24(3)^5}{180n^4} \leq 0.001 \Rightarrow n \geq \sqrt[4]{32,400} \approx 13.4 \Rightarrow n = 14.$

21 (a) $T = \frac{4-2}{2(4)}\left[3 + 2(2 + 4 + 3) + 5\right] = \frac{1}{4}(26) = 6.5$

(b) $S = \frac{4-2}{3(4)}\left[3 + 4(2) + 2(4) + 4(3) + 5\right] = \frac{1}{6}(36) = 6$

22 (a) $T = \frac{4-2}{2(2)}\left[5 + 2(4) + 3\right] = \frac{1}{2}(16) = 8$

   (b) $S = \frac{4-2}{3(2)}\left[5 + 4(4) + 3\right] = \frac{1}{3}(24) = 8$

23 (a) $T = \frac{4-2}{2(8)}\{4.12 + 2\left[3.76 + 3.21 + 3.58 + 3.94 + 4.15 + 4.69 + 5.44\right] +$

$$7.52\} = \frac{1}{8}(69.18) \approx 8.65$$

   (b) $S = \frac{4-2}{3(8)}[4.12 + 4(3.76) + 2(3.21) + 4(3.58) + 2(3.94) + 4(4.15) +$

$$2(4.69) + 4(5.44) + 7.52] = \frac{1}{12}(103.04) \approx 8.59$$

24 (a) $T = \frac{4-2}{2(10)}\{12.1 + 2\left[11.4 + 9.7 + 8.4 + 6.3 + 6.2 + 5.8 + 5.4 + 5.1 + 5.9\right]$

$$+ 5.6\} = \frac{1}{10}(146.1) = 14.61$$

   (b) $S = \frac{4-2}{3(10)}[12.1 + 4(11.4) + 2(9.7) + 4(8.4) + 2(6.3) + 4(6.2) + 2(5.8) +$

$$4(5.4) + 2(5.1) + 4(5.9) + 5.6] = \frac{1}{15}(220.7) \approx 14.71$$

25 Let $A = \int_{1}^{2.7} \frac{dx}{x}$ and $B = \int_{1}^{2.8} \frac{dx}{x}$. With $\frac{b-a}{n} = 0.1$, the trapezoidal rule gives

0.9940 and 1.0304 for approximations of A and B, respectively (details omitted).

Since $f''(x) = 2/x^3$, it follows that $\left|f''(x)\right| \le 2 = M$ on $[1, \infty)$. Thus, the error in

both of these approximations is bounded by $\dfrac{M(b-a)^3}{12n^2} \le \dfrac{2(2.8-1)(0.1)^2}{12} = 0.003$.

Moreover, $0.9910 \le A \le 0.9970$ and $1.0274 \le B \le 1.0334$. Hence, $A < 1 < B$.

26 $f(x) = 1/(x^2 + 1);$ $S = \frac{1-0}{3(8)}[f(0) + 4f(\frac{1}{8}) + 2f(\frac{1}{4}) + 4f(\frac{3}{8}) + 2f(\frac{1}{2}) +$

$$4f(\tfrac{5}{8}) + 2f(\tfrac{3}{4}) + 4f(\tfrac{7}{8}) + f(1)] \approx$$

$\frac{1}{24}\left[1 + 4(\frac{64}{65}) + 2(\frac{16}{17}) + 4(\frac{64}{73}) + 2(\frac{4}{5}) + 4(\frac{64}{89}) + 2(\frac{16}{25}) + 4(\frac{64}{113}) + \frac{1}{2}\right] \approx$

$$\frac{1}{24}(18.8496) = 0.7854; \ 4 \times 0.7854 = 3.1416.$$

27 (5.39) is valid for any $M \ge \left|f^{(4)}(x)\right|$. Since $f^{(4)}(x) = 0$ for a polynomial of degree 3

or less, it follows that we can let $M = 0$ and the error bound can be set at zero.

(It is interesting to note that Simpson's rule, with equal subintervals, is exact for a

cubic polynomial even though it is using only a quadratic polynomial to interpolate

the function.)

28 Since $f''(x) > 0$ on $[a, b]$, f is CU throughout $[a, b]$. Let

L_k denote the line segment connecting $(x_k, f(x_k))$ and

$(x_{k+1}, f(x_{k+1}))$. Since $f(x) > 0$ on $[a, b]$, $f(x)$ lies below

L_k on (x_k, x_{k+1}) and the area of the trapezoid T_k is

greater than the area under the graph of f on $[a, b]$.

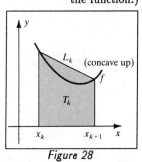

Figure 28

[29] (a) $T = \frac{7-1}{2(6)}\{f(1) + 2[f(2) + f(3) + f(4) + f(5) + f(6)] + f(7)\} =$

$$\frac{1}{2}[5 + 2(10 + 30 + 35 + 15 + 25) + 20] = \frac{1}{2}(255) \approx 127.5$$

(b) $S = \frac{7-1}{3(6)}[f(1) + 4f(2) + 2f(3) + 4f(4) + 2f(5) + 4f(6) + f(7)] =$

$$\frac{1}{3}[5 + 4(10) + 2(30) + 4(35) + 2(15) + 4(25) + 20] = \frac{1}{3}(395) \approx 131.7$$

Note: Answers may vary due to different interpretations of the graph.

[30] From the figure, we see that $n = 7$ and $\frac{b-a}{n} = 20$. In this exercise,

we approximate $\int_0^{140} f(x)\, dx = \int_0^{140} [u(x) - l(x)]\, dx$, where $[u(x) - l(x)]$ represents

the distance between the upper and lower boundaries at each grid point. Thus,

$$T = \frac{20}{2}[0 + 2(30 + 50 + 70 + 60 + 60 + 40) + 0] = 10(620) = 6200 \text{ ft}^2.$$

[31] $\bar{v}_x = \frac{1}{k}\int_0^k v(y)\, dy \approx$

$$\frac{1}{k} \cdot \frac{k-0}{2(5)}\{v(0) + 2[v(0.2k) + v(0.4k) + v(0.6k) + v(0.8k)] + v(k)\} =$$

$$\frac{1}{10}[0.28 + 2(0.23 + 0.19 + 0.17 + 0.13) + 0.02] = 0.174 \text{ m/sec}$$

[32] Let $g(x) = \bar{v}_x\, h(x)$. Then, $F = \int_0^L g(x)\, dx \approx$

$\frac{24-0}{3(8)}[g(0) + 4g(3) + 2g(6) + 4g(9) + 2g(12) + 4g(15) + 2g(18) + 4g(21) + g(24)]$

$= [0 + 4(0.0459) + 2(0.1314) + 4(0.3381) + 2(0.7596) + 4(0.6464) +$

$$2(0.2907) + 4(0.0704) + 0] \approx 6.77 \text{ m}^3/\text{sec}$$

[33] $f(x) = 1/(x^4 + 1)$. $S = \frac{4-0}{3(8)}[f(0) + 4f(0.5) + 2f(1) + 4f(1.5) + 2f(2) +$

$4f(2.5) + 2f(3) + 4f(3.5) + f(4)] = \frac{1}{6}[1 + 4(0.9412) + 2(0.5) + 4(0.1649) +$

$2(5.8824) + 4(2.4961) + 2(1.2195) + 4(6.6198) + 4]$

$$\approx \frac{1}{6}(6.6968) \approx 1.1161. \quad f_{av} \approx \frac{1}{4-0}(1.1161) \approx 0.2790.$$

[34] $f(x) = \sqrt{\cos x}$; $S = \frac{1-(-1)}{3(8)}[f(-1) + 4f(-0.75) + 2f(-0.5) + 4f(-0.25) +$

$2f(0) + 4f(0.25) + 2f(0.5) + 4f(0.75) + f(1)] = \frac{1}{12}[0.7351 + 4(0.8554) +$

$2(0.9368) + 4(0.9843) + 2(1) + 4(0.9843) + 2(0.9368) + 4(0.8554) + 1]$

$$\approx \frac{1}{12}(21.9351) \approx 1.8279. \quad f_{av} \approx \frac{1}{1-(-1)}(1.8279) \approx 0.9140.$$

[35] By the fundamental theorem of calculus, $f(1) = f(0) + \int_0^1 \frac{\sqrt{x}}{x^2 + 1}\, dx.$

$T = \frac{1-0}{2(10)}\{f'(0) + 2[f'(0.1) + f'(0.2) + \cdots + f'(0.9)] + f'(1)\}$

$= \frac{1}{20}[0 + 2(0.3131 + 0.4300 + 0.5025 + 0.5452 + 0.5657 +$

$$0.5696 + 0.5615 + 0.5454 + 0.5241) + 0.5]$$

$\approx \frac{1}{20}(9.6142) \approx 0.4807.$ $f(1) \approx f(0) + 0.4807 = 1.4807.$

36 By the fundamental theorem of calculus, $f(1) = f(0) + \int_0^1 \sqrt{\tan x}\, dx$.

$$T = \tfrac{1-0}{2(10)}\{f'(0) + 2\left[f'(0.1) + f'(0.2) + \cdots + f'(0.9)\right] + f'(1)\}$$

$$= \tfrac{1}{20}[\, 0 + 2(0.3168 + 0.4502 + 0.5562 + 0.6502 + 0.7391 +$$

$$0.8271 + 0.9178 + 1.0147 + 1.1226) + 1.2480]$$

$$\approx \tfrac{1}{20}(14.4373) \approx 0.7219. \qquad\qquad f(1) \approx f(0) + 0.7219 = 2.7219.$$

5.8 Review Exercises

1 $\displaystyle\int \frac{8x^2 - 4x + 5}{x^4}\, dx = \int(8x^{-2} - 4x^{-3} + 5x^{-4})\, dx = -\frac{8}{x} + \frac{2}{x^2} - \frac{5}{3x^3} + C$

2 $\int(3x^5 + 2x^3 - x)\, dx = \frac{3}{6}x^6 + \frac{2}{4}x^4 - \frac{1}{2}x^2 + C = \frac{1}{2}(x^6 + x^4 - x^2) + C$

3 $\int 100\, dx = 100x + C$

4 $\int x^{3/5}(2x - \sqrt{x})\, dx = \int(2x^{8/5} - x^{11/10})\, dx = \frac{10}{13}x^{13/5} - \frac{10}{21}x^{21/10} + C$

5 $u = 2x + 1,\ \frac{1}{2}du = dx \Rightarrow I = \frac{1}{2}\int u^7\, du = \frac{1}{16}u^8 + C$

6 $u = 5x + 1,\ \frac{1}{5}du = dx \Rightarrow I = \frac{1}{5}\int u^{1/3}\, du = \frac{3}{20}u^{4/3} + C$

7 $u = 1 - 2x^2,\ -\frac{1}{4}du = x\, dx \Rightarrow I = -\frac{1}{4}\int u^3\, du = -\frac{1}{16}u^4 + C$

8 $\displaystyle\int \frac{(1 + \sqrt{x})^2}{\sqrt[3]{x}}\, dx = \int(x^{-1/3} + 2x^{1/6} + x^{2/3})\, dx = \frac{3}{2}x^{2/3} + \frac{12}{7}x^{7/6} + \frac{3}{5}x^{5/3} + C$

9 $u = 1 + \sqrt{x},\ 2\,du = \frac{1}{\sqrt{x}}\, dx \Rightarrow I = 2\int u^{-2}\, du = -\frac{2}{u} + C$

10 $\int(x^2 + 4)^2\, dx = \int(x^4 + 8x^2 + 16)\, dx = \frac{1}{5}x^5 + \frac{8}{3}x^3 + 16x + C$

11 $\int(3 - 2x - 5x^3)\, dx = 3x - x^2 - \frac{5}{4}x^4 + C$

12 $\int(x + x^{-1})^2\, dx = \int(x^2 + 2 + x^{-2})\, dx = \frac{1}{3}x^3 + 2x - (1/x) + C$

13 $u = 4x^2 + 2x - 7,\ \frac{1}{2}du = (4x + 1)\, dx \Rightarrow I = \frac{1}{2}\int u^2\, du = \frac{1}{6}u^3 + C$

14 $u = 1 - x^{-1},\ du = x^{-2}\, dx \Rightarrow I = \int u^{1/4}\, du = \frac{4}{5}u^{5/4} + C$

15 $\int(2x^{-3} - 3x^2)\, dx = 2\cdot\frac{x^{-2}}{-2} - 3\cdot\frac{x^3}{3} + C = (-1/x^2) - x^3 + C$

16 $\int(x^{3/2} + x^{-3/2})\, dx = \frac{2}{5}x^{5/2} - 2x^{-1/2} + C$

17 $\displaystyle\int_0^1 \sqrt[3]{8x^7}\, dx = 2\int_0^1 x^{7/3}\, dx = 2\left[\frac{3}{10}x^{10/3}\right]_0^1 = \frac{3}{5}(1 - 0) = \frac{3}{5}$

18 Since $x \neq -2$, $I = \displaystyle\int_1^2 (x - 3)\, dx = \left[\frac{1}{2}x^2 - 3x\right]_1^2 = \left[-4 - (-\frac{5}{2})\right] = -\frac{3}{2}$.

19 $u = 1 + x^3 \Rightarrow \frac{1}{3}du = x^2\, dx.\ x = 0, 1 \Rightarrow u = 1, 2.$

$$I = \frac{1}{3}\int_1^2 u^{-2}\, du = \frac{1}{3}\left[-\frac{1}{u}\right]_1^2 = -\frac{1}{3}(\frac{1}{2} - 1) = \frac{1}{6}.$$

20 $u = 2x + 7 \Rightarrow \frac{1}{2}du = dx.\ x = 1, 9 \Rightarrow u = 9, 25.$

$$I = \frac{1}{2}\int_9^{25} u^{1/2}\, du = \frac{1}{2}\left[\frac{2}{3}u^{3/2}\right]_9^{25} = \frac{1}{3}(125 - 27) = \frac{98}{3}.$$

21 $u = x^2 + 2x \Rightarrow \frac{1}{2}du = (x + 1)\, dx.\ x = 1, 2 \Rightarrow u = 3, 8.$

$$I = \frac{1}{2}\int_3^8 u^{-1/2}\, du = \frac{1}{2}\left[2u^{1/2}\right]_3^8 = \sqrt{8} - \sqrt{3} \approx 1.10.$$

22   $\displaystyle\int_1^2 \frac{x^2+2}{x^2}\,dx = \int_1^2 (1+2x^{-2})\,dx = \left[x - \frac{2}{x}\right]_1^2 = \left[1-(-1)\right] = 2$

23   $u = x^3+1 \Rightarrow \frac{1}{3}\,du = x^2\,dx.\ \ x = 0,\,2 \Rightarrow u = 1,\,9.$

$$I = \frac{1}{3}\int_1^9 u^{1/2}\,du = \frac{1}{3}\left[\frac{2}{3}u^{3/2}\right]_1^9 = \frac{2}{9}(27-1) = \frac{52}{9}.$$

24   $I = 0$ by (5.18).

25   $\displaystyle\int_0^1 (2x-3)(5x+1)\,dx = \int_0^1 (10x^2 - 13x - 3)\,dx = \left[\frac{10}{3}x^3 - \frac{13}{2}x^2 - 3x\right]_0^1 =$

$$\left(\frac{10}{3} - \frac{13}{2} - 3\right) = -\frac{37}{6}$$

26   $\displaystyle\int_{-1}^1 (x^2+1)^2\,dx = 2\int_0^1 (x^4 + 2x^2 + 1)\,dx \ \{\text{even integrand}\} =$

$$2\left[\frac{1}{5}x^5 + \frac{2}{3}x^3 + x\right]_0^1 = 2\left(\frac{28}{15}\right) = \frac{56}{15}$$

27   $\displaystyle\int_0^4 \sqrt{3x}\,(\sqrt{x} + \sqrt{3})\,dx = \int_0^4 (\sqrt{3}\,x + 3x^{1/2})\,dx = \left[\frac{1}{2}\sqrt{3}\,x^2 + 2x^{3/2}\right]_0^4 =$

$$8\sqrt{3} + 16 \approx 29.86$$

28   $\displaystyle\int_{-1}^1 (x+1)(x+2)(x+3)\,dx = \int_{-1}^1 (x^3 + 6x^2 + 11x + 6)\,dx = \int_{-1}^1 (6x^2 + 6)\,dx$

$\{\text{since } x^3 \text{ and } 11x \text{ are odd}\} = 2\int_0^1 6(x^2+1)\,dx \ \{\text{even integrand}\} = 12\left[\frac{1}{3}x^3 + x\right]_0^1$

$$= 12\left(\frac{4}{3}\right) = 16$$

29   $u = 3 - 5x,\ -\frac{1}{5}\,du = dx \Rightarrow I = -\frac{1}{5}\int \sin u\,du = \frac{1}{5}\cos u + C$

30   $u = 2x^3,\ \frac{1}{6}\,du = x^2\,dx \Rightarrow I = \frac{1}{6}\int \cos u\,du = \frac{1}{6}\sin u + C$

31   $u = \sin 3x,\ \frac{1}{3}\,du = \cos 3x\,dx \Rightarrow I = \frac{1}{3}\int u^4\,du = \frac{1}{15}u^5 + C$

32   $u = 1/x,\ -du = (1/x^2)\,dx \Rightarrow I = -\int \sin u\,du = \cos u + C$

33   $u = \sin 3x,\ \frac{1}{3}\,du = \cos 3x\,dx \Rightarrow I = \frac{1}{3}\int u^{-3}\,du = -\frac{1}{6}u^{-2} + C$

34   $\int (3\cos 2\pi t - 5\sin 4\pi t)\,dt = \frac{3}{2\pi}\sin 2\pi t + \frac{5}{4\pi}\cos 4\pi t + C$

35   $u = 3 + 5\sin x \Rightarrow \frac{1}{5}\,du = \cos x\,dx.\ \ x = 0,\,\frac{\pi}{2} \Rightarrow u = 3,\,8.$

$$I = \frac{1}{5}\int_3^8 u^{1/2}\,du = \frac{1}{5}\left[\frac{2}{3}u^{3/2}\right]_3^8 = \frac{2}{15}(16\sqrt{2} - 3\sqrt{3}) \approx 2.32.$$

36   $\displaystyle\int_{-\pi/4}^0 (\sin x + \cos x)^2\,dx = \int_{-\pi/4}^0 (\sin^2 x + 2\sin x \cos x + \cos^2 x)\,dx =$

$\displaystyle\int_{-\pi/4}^0 (1 + \sin 2x)\,dx = \left[x - \frac{1}{2}\cos 2x\right]_{-\pi/4}^0 = (-\frac{1}{2}) - (-\frac{\pi}{4}) = \frac{\pi}{4} - \frac{1}{2} \approx 0.29$

37   $u = \cos 2x \Rightarrow -\frac{1}{2}\,du = \sin 2x\,dx.\ \ x = 0,\,\frac{\pi}{4} \Rightarrow u = 1,\,0.$

$$I = -\frac{1}{2}\int_1^0 u^2\,du = -\frac{1}{2}\left[\frac{1}{3}u^3\right]_1^0 = -\frac{1}{6}(0-1) = \frac{1}{6}.$$

38   Note that $(\sec x + \tan x)(1 - \sin x) = \dfrac{1 + \sin x}{\cos x}(1 - \sin x) = \dfrac{\cos^2 x}{\cos x} = \cos x.$

$$\text{Thus, } I = \int_{\pi/6}^{\pi/4} \cos x\,dx = \left[\sin x\right]_{\pi/6}^{\pi/4} = \frac{\sqrt{2}}{2} - \frac{1}{2} = \frac{1}{2}(\sqrt{2} - 1) \approx 0.21.$$

39   By (5.5)(i), $\int D_x \sqrt[5]{x^4 + 2x^2 + 1}\,dx = \sqrt[5]{x^4 + 2x^2 + 1} + C.$

$\boxed{40}$ By (5.5)(i) and (5.32), $\int_0^{\pi/2} D_x \left(x \sin^3 x\right) dx = \left[x \sin^3 x\right]_0^{\pi/2} = \frac{\pi}{2}\sin^3(\frac{\pi}{2}) - 0 = \frac{\pi}{2}$.

$\boxed{41}$ Since the definite integral is a constant, the answer is 0.

$\boxed{42}$ By (5.35), $D_x \int_0^x (t^2 + 1)^{10}\, dt = (x^2 + 1)^{10}$.

$\boxed{43}$ $\dfrac{d^2 y}{dx^2} = 6x - 4 \Rightarrow \dfrac{dy}{dx} = 3x^2 - 4x + C$. $x = 2$ and $y' = 5 \Rightarrow 5 = 4 + C \Rightarrow$

$\qquad C = 1$. $y = x^3 - 2x^2 + x + D$. $x = 2$ and $y = 4 \Rightarrow 4 = 2 + D \Rightarrow D = 2$.

$\boxed{44}$ $f''(x) = x^{1/3} - 5 \Rightarrow f'(x) = \frac{3}{4}x^{4/3} - 5x + C$. $f'(1) = -\frac{17}{4} + C = 2 \Rightarrow C = \frac{25}{4}$.

$\qquad f(x) = \frac{9}{28}x^{7/3} - \frac{5}{2}x^2 + \frac{25}{4}x + D$. $f(1) = \frac{57}{14} + D = -8 \Rightarrow D = -\frac{169}{14}$.

$\boxed{45}$ $\forall\, k,\ \Delta x_k = 1 \Rightarrow$

$\qquad R_P = f(-\frac{3}{2}) + f(-\frac{1}{2}) + f(\frac{1}{2}) + f(\frac{3}{2}) + f(\frac{5}{2}) = \frac{27}{4} + \frac{35}{4} + \frac{35}{4} + \frac{27}{4} + \frac{11}{4} = \frac{135}{4}$.

$\boxed{46}$ (a) f increases on $[-2,\, 0]$ and decreases on $[0,\, 3]$. Hence, for A_{IP}, we use the left-

$\qquad$ hand endpoint of each subinterval in $[-2,\, 0]$ and the right-hand endpoint in

$\qquad$ $[0,\, 3]$. Since each $\Delta x_k = 1$,

$\qquad A_{\text{IP}} = f(-2) + f(-1) + f(1) + f(2) + f(3) = 5 + 8 + 8 + 5 + 0 = 26$.

$\quad$ (b) $A_{\text{CP}} = f(-1) + f(0) + f(0) + f(1) + f(2) = 8 + 9 + 9 + 8 + 5 = 39$

$\boxed{47}$ Using (5.27) and the fact that $x^2 \ge x^3$ on $[0,\, 1]$, we have $\int_0^1 x^2\, dx \ge \int_0^1 x^3\, dx$.

$\boxed{48}$ Using (5.27) and the fact that $x^3 \ge x^2$ on $[1,\, 2]$, we have $\int_1^2 x^3\, dx \ge \int_1^2 x^2\, dx$.

$\boxed{49}$ Omitting $f(x)\, dx$, $\int_c^e + \int_a^b - \int_c^b - \int_d^d = \int_c^e + \int_b^c + \int_a^b = \int_b^e + \int_a^b = \int_a^e$.

$\boxed{50}$ $\int_a^d - \int_t^b - \int_g^g + \int_m^b + \int_t^a = \int_a^d + \int_b^t + \int_m^b + \int_t^a = \int_t^d + \int_m^t = \int_m^d$.

$\boxed{51}$ (a) $a(t) = -32 \Rightarrow v(t) = -32t + C$. $v(0) = -30 \Rightarrow C = -30$.

$\qquad v(t) = -32t - 30 \Rightarrow s(t) = -16t^2 - 30t + D$. $s(0) = 900 \Rightarrow D = 900$.

$\quad$ (b) $v(5) = -32(5) - 30 = -190$ ft/sec.

$\quad$ (c) $s(t) = 0\ (t > 0)$ when $t = \frac{1}{16}(-15 + \sqrt{14{,}625}) = \frac{15}{16}(-1 + \sqrt{65}) \approx 6.6$ sec.

$\boxed{52}$ (a) $\int_1^4 (x^2 + 2x - 5)\, dx = 21$. $21 = (z^2 + 2z - 5)(4 - 1) \Rightarrow$

$\qquad z^2 + 2z - 12 = 0 \Rightarrow z = -1 + \sqrt{13} \approx 2.61 \in (1,\, 4)$.

$\quad$ (b) Average value $= \frac{1}{4-1}(21) = 7$.

[53] (a) $f(x) = \sqrt{1 + x^4}$; $T = \frac{10 - 0}{2(5)} \{ f(0) + 2[f(2) + f(4) + f(6) + f(8)] + f(10) \} =$

$(1)[1 + 2(4.1231 + 16.0312 + 36.0139 + 64.0078) + 100.0050] =$

$$341.3570 \approx 341.36$$

(b) $S = \frac{10 - 0}{3(8)} [f(0) + 4f(1.25) + 2f(2.5) + 4f(3.75) + 2f(5) + 4f(6.25) +$

$$2f(7.5) + 4f(8.75) + f(10)] =$$

$\frac{5}{12}[1 + 4(1.8551) + 2(6.3295) + 4(14.0980) + 2(25.0200) + 4(39.0753) +$

$$2(56.2589) + 4(76.5690) + 100.0050] = \frac{5}{12}(802.6114) \approx 334.42$$

[54] $T_{av} = \frac{1}{t_2 - t_1} \int_{t_1}^{t_2} T(t)\, dt = \frac{1}{8} \int_0^8 T(t)\, dt$, where $t = 0$ corresponds to 9 A.M. and

$t = 8$ corresponds to 5 P.M. Using Simpson's rule, with $n = 8$, yields

$S = \frac{8 - 0}{3(8)} [75.3 + 4(77.0) + 2(83.1) + 4(84.8) + 2(86.5) + 4(86.4) + 2(81.1) +$

$$4(78.6) + 75.1] = \frac{1}{3}(1959) = 653. \text{ Thus, } T_{av} \approx \frac{653}{8} = 81.625\,°\text{F}.$$

Chapter 6: Applications of the Definite Integral

$\boxed{1}$ The shaded region is an R_x region. $A = \int_{-2}^{2} \left[(x^2 + 1) - (x - 2) \right] dx.$

$\boxed{2}$ The shaded region is an R_x region. $A = \int_{1}^{4} \left[(-x + 6) - \sqrt{x} \right] dx.$

$\boxed{3}$ The shaded region is an R_y region. $A = \int_{-2}^{1} \left[(-3y^2 + 4) - y^3 \right] dy.$

$\boxed{4}$ The shaded region is an R_y region. $A = \int_{-1}^{8} \left[(y + 2) - y^{2/3} \right] dy.$

$\boxed{5}$ $x^2 = 4x \Rightarrow x = 0, 4.$ $4x \geq x^2$ on $[0, 4] \Rightarrow$

$$A = \int_{0}^{4} (4x - x^2) \, dx = \left[2x^2 - \tfrac{1}{3}x^3 \right]_{0}^{4} = 32 - \tfrac{64}{3} = \tfrac{32}{3}.$$

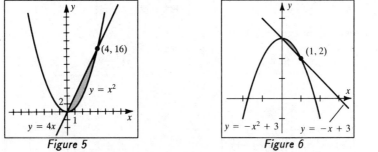

Figure 5 Figure 6

$\boxed{6}$ $3 - x = 3 - x^2 \Rightarrow x = 0, 1.$ $3 - x^2 \geq 3 - x$ on $[0, 1] \Rightarrow$

$$A = \int_{0}^{1} \left[(3 - x^2) - (3 - x) \right] dx = \left[-\tfrac{1}{3}x^3 + \tfrac{1}{2}x^2 \right]_{0}^{1} = -\tfrac{1}{3} + \tfrac{1}{2} = \tfrac{1}{6}.$$

Note: Symmetry is used without mention whenever possible in the solutions and answers.

$\boxed{7}$ $x^2 + 1 = 5 \Rightarrow x = \pm 2.$ $5 \geq (x^2 + 1)$ on $[-2, 2] \Rightarrow$

$$A = 2 \int_{0}^{2} \left[5 - (x^2 + 1) \right] dx = 2 \left[4x - \tfrac{1}{3}x^3 \right]_{0}^{2} = 2(\tfrac{16}{3}) = \tfrac{32}{3}.$$

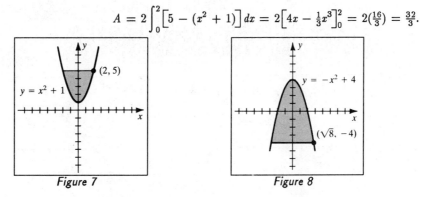

Figure 7 Figure 8

$\boxed{8}$ $4 - x^2 = -4 \Rightarrow x = \pm \sqrt{8}.$ $4 - x^2 \geq -4$ on $[-\sqrt{8}, \sqrt{8}] \Rightarrow$

$$A = 2 \int_{0}^{\sqrt{8}} \left[(4 - x^2) - (-4) \right] dx = 2 \left[8x - \tfrac{1}{3}x^3 \right]_{0}^{\sqrt{8}} = 2(\tfrac{16\sqrt{8}}{3}) = \tfrac{64\sqrt{2}}{3}.$$

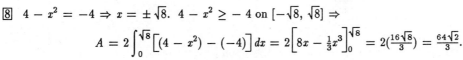

$\boxed{9}$ $1/x^2 > -x^2 \Rightarrow A = \int_1^2 \left[x^{-2} - (-x^2) \right] dx = \left[-\frac{1}{x} + \frac{1}{3}x^3 \right]_1^2 = \frac{13}{6} - (-\frac{2}{3}) = \frac{17}{6}.$

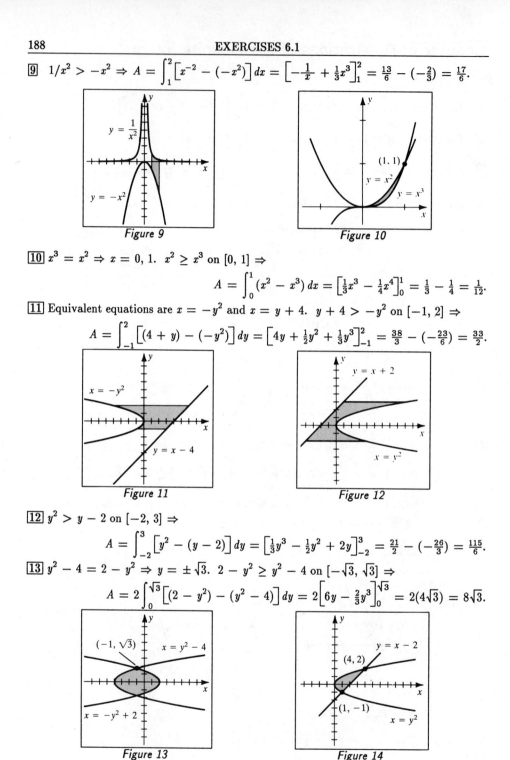

Figure 9

Figure 10

$\boxed{10}$ $x^3 = x^2 \Rightarrow x = 0, 1.$ $x^2 \geq x^3$ on $[0, 1] \Rightarrow$

$$A = \int_0^1 (x^2 - x^3)\, dx = \left[\frac{1}{3}x^3 - \frac{1}{4}x^4 \right]_0^1 = \frac{1}{3} - \frac{1}{4} = \frac{1}{12}.$$

$\boxed{11}$ Equivalent equations are $x = -y^2$ and $x = y + 4.$ $y + 4 > -y^2$ on $[-1, 2] \Rightarrow$

$$A = \int_{-1}^2 \left[(4 + y) - (-y^2) \right] dy = \left[4y + \frac{1}{2}y^2 + \frac{1}{3}y^3 \right]_{-1}^2 = \frac{38}{3} - (-\frac{23}{6}) = \frac{33}{2}.$$

Figure 11

Figure 12

$\boxed{12}$ $y^2 > y - 2$ on $[-2, 3] \Rightarrow$

$$A = \int_{-2}^3 \left[y^2 - (y - 2) \right] dy = \left[\frac{1}{3}y^3 - \frac{1}{2}y^2 + 2y \right]_{-2}^3 = \frac{21}{2} - (-\frac{26}{3}) = \frac{115}{6}.$$

$\boxed{13}$ $y^2 - 4 = 2 - y^2 \Rightarrow y = \pm\sqrt{3}.$ $2 - y^2 \geq y^2 - 4$ on $[-\sqrt{3}, \sqrt{3}] \Rightarrow$

$$A = 2\int_0^{\sqrt{3}} \left[(2 - y^2) - (y^2 - 4) \right] dy = 2\left[6y - \frac{2}{3}y^3 \right]_0^{\sqrt{3}} = 2(4\sqrt{3}) = 8\sqrt{3}.$$

Figure 13

Figure 14

$\boxed{14}$ $y^2 = y + 2 \Rightarrow y = -1, 2.$ $y + 2 \geq y^2$ on $[-1, 2] \Rightarrow$

$$A = \int_{-1}^2 \left[(y + 2) - y^2 \right] dy = \left[\frac{1}{2}y^2 + 2y - \frac{1}{3}y^3 \right]_{-1}^2 = \frac{10}{3} - (-\frac{7}{6}) = \frac{9}{2}.$$

15 $x = y(2 - y)(2 + y) \geq 0$ on $[0, 2]$ and $x \leq 0$ on $[-2, 0]$.

$$A = 2\int_0^2 \left[(4y - y^3) - 0\right] dy = 2\left[2y^2 - \tfrac{1}{4}y^4\right]_0^2 = 2(4) = 8.$$

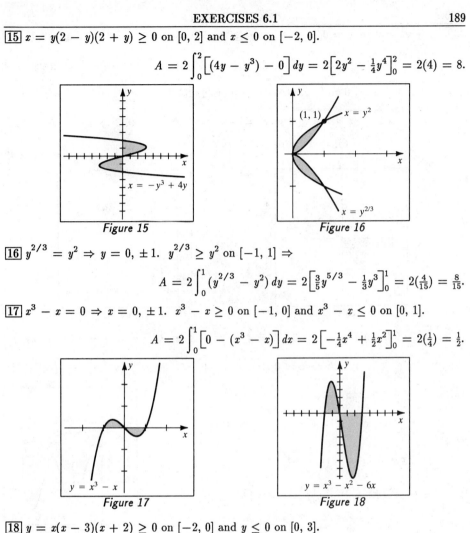

Figure 15   Figure 16

16 $y^{2/3} = y^2 \Rightarrow y = 0, \pm 1.$ $y^{2/3} \geq y^2$ on $[-1, 1] \Rightarrow$

$$A = 2\int_0^1 (y^{2/3} - y^2)\, dy = 2\left[\tfrac{3}{5}y^{5/3} - \tfrac{1}{3}y^3\right]_0^1 = 2(\tfrac{4}{15}) = \tfrac{8}{15}.$$

17 $x^3 - x = 0 \Rightarrow x = 0, \pm 1.$ $x^3 - x \geq 0$ on $[-1, 0]$ and $x^3 - x \leq 0$ on $[0, 1]$.

$$A = 2\int_0^1 \left[0 - (x^3 - x)\right] dx = 2\left[-\tfrac{1}{4}x^4 + \tfrac{1}{2}x^2\right]_0^1 = 2(\tfrac{1}{4}) = \tfrac{1}{2}.$$

Figure 17   Figure 18

18 $y = x(x - 3)(x + 2) \geq 0$ on $[-2, 0]$ and $y \leq 0$ on $[0, 3]$.

$$A = \int_{-2}^0 \left[(x^3 - x^2 - 6x) - 0\right] dx + \int_0^3 \left[0 - (x^3 - x^2 - 6x)\right] dx = \tfrac{16}{3} + \tfrac{63}{4} = \tfrac{253}{12}.$$

19 $x = y(y + 3)(y - 1) \geq 0$ on $[-3, 0]$ and $x \leq 0$ on $[0, 1]$. $A =$

$$\int_{-3}^0 \left[(y^3 + 2y^2 - 3y) - 0\right] dy + \int_0^1 \left[0 - (y^3 + 2y^2 - 3y)\right] dy = \tfrac{45}{4} + \tfrac{7}{12} = \tfrac{71}{6}.$$

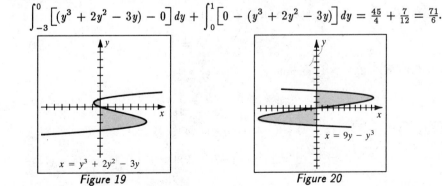

Figure 19   Figure 20

$\boxed{20}$ $9y - y^3 = 0 \Rightarrow y = 0, \pm 3.$ $9y - y^3 \geq 0$ on $[0, 3]$ and $9y - y^3 \leq 0$ on $[-3, 0]$.

$$A = 2\int_0^3 (9y - y^3)\, dy = 2\left[\tfrac{9}{2}y^2 - \tfrac{1}{4}y^4\right]_0^3 = 2(\tfrac{81}{4}) = \tfrac{81}{2}.$$

$\boxed{21}$ $y = x\sqrt{4 - x^2} \leq 0$ on $[-2, 0]$ and $y \geq 0$ on $[0, 2]$.

$$A = 2\int_0^2 x\sqrt{4 - x^2}\, dx.\quad u = 4 - x^2 \Rightarrow -du = 2x\, dx.\quad x = 0, 2 \Rightarrow u = 4, 0.$$

$$A = -\int_4^0 u^{1/2}\, du = -\left[\tfrac{2}{3}u^{3/2}\right]_4^0 = -\tfrac{2}{3}(0 - 8) = \tfrac{16}{3}.$$

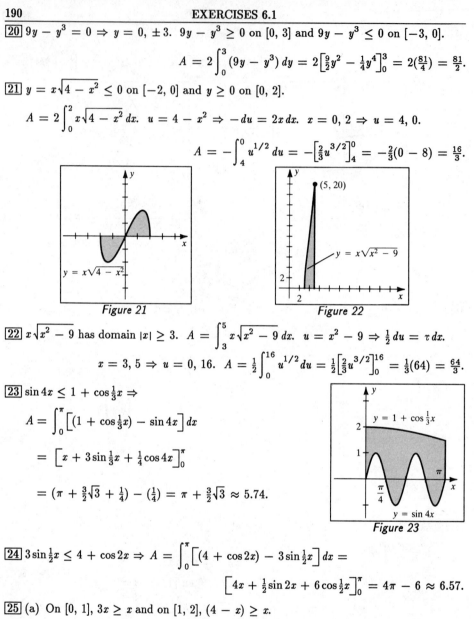

Figure 21　　　　　　　　　　Figure 22

$\boxed{22}$ $x\sqrt{x^2 - 9}$ has domain $|x| \geq 3.$ $A = \int_3^5 x\sqrt{x^2 - 9}\, dx.$ $u = x^2 - 9 \Rightarrow \tfrac{1}{2}du = x\, dx.$

$$x = 3, 5 \Rightarrow u = 0, 16.\quad A = \tfrac{1}{2}\int_0^{16} u^{1/2}\, du = \tfrac{1}{2}\left[\tfrac{2}{3}u^{3/2}\right]_0^{16} = \tfrac{1}{3}(64) = \tfrac{64}{3}.$$

$\boxed{23}$ $\sin 4x \leq 1 + \cos\tfrac{1}{3}x \Rightarrow$

$$A = \int_0^\pi \left[(1 + \cos\tfrac{1}{3}x) - \sin 4x\right] dx$$

$$= \left[x + 3\sin\tfrac{1}{3}x + \tfrac{1}{4}\cos 4x\right]_0^\pi$$

$$= (\pi + \tfrac{3}{2}\sqrt{3} + \tfrac{1}{4}) - (\tfrac{1}{4}) = \pi + \tfrac{3}{2}\sqrt{3} \approx 5.74.$$

Figure 23

$\boxed{24}$ $3\sin\tfrac{1}{2}x \leq 4 + \cos 2x \Rightarrow A = \int_0^\pi \left[(4 + \cos 2x) - 3\sin\tfrac{1}{2}x\right] dx =$

$$\left[4x + \tfrac{1}{2}\sin 2x + 6\cos\tfrac{1}{2}x\right]_0^\pi = 4\pi - 6 \approx 6.57.$$

$\boxed{25}$ (a) On $[0, 1]$, $3x \geq x$ and on $[1, 2]$, $(4 - x) \geq x.$

$$A = \int_0^1 (3x - x)\, dx + \int_1^2 \left[(4 - x) - x\right] dx.$$

(b) On $[0, 2]$, $y \geq \tfrac{1}{3}y$ and on $[2, 3]$, $(4 - y) \geq \tfrac{1}{3}y.$

$$A = \int_0^2 (y - \tfrac{1}{3}y)\, dy + \int_2^3 \left[(4 - y) - \tfrac{1}{3}y\right] dy.$$

$\boxed{26}$ (a) On $[-1, \tfrac{5}{3}]$, $(x + 1) \geq (-2x - 2)$ and on $[\tfrac{5}{3}, 3]$, $(x + 1) \geq (7x - 17).$

$$A = \int_{-1}^{5/3} \left[(x + 1) - (-2x - 2)\right] dx + \int_{5/3}^3 \left[(x + 1) - (7x - 17)\right] dx.$$

(b) On $[-\frac{16}{3}, 0]$, $(\frac{1}{7}y + \frac{17}{7}) \geq (-\frac{1}{2}y - 1)$ and on $[0, 4]$, $(\frac{1}{7}y + \frac{17}{7}) \geq (y - 1)$.

$$A = \int_{-16/3}^{0} \left[(\tfrac{1}{7}y + \tfrac{17}{7}) - (-\tfrac{1}{2}y - 1)\right] dy + \int_{0}^{4} \left[(\tfrac{1}{7}y + \tfrac{17}{7}) - (y - 1)\right] dy.$$

27 (a) On $[1, 4]$, $\sqrt{x} > -x$. $A = \int_{1}^{4} \left[\sqrt{x} - (-x)\right] dx.$

(b) On $[-4, -1]$, $4 \geq -y$; on $[-1, 1]$, $4 \geq 1$; and on $[1, 2]$, $4 \geq y^2$.

$$A = \int_{-4}^{-1} \left[4 - (-y)\right] dy + \int_{-1}^{1} (4 - 1) \, dy + \int_{1}^{2} (4 - y^2) \, dy.$$

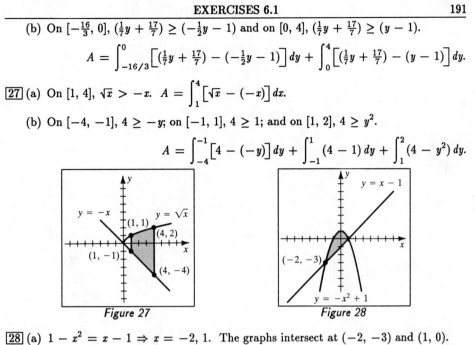

Figure 27   Figure 28

28 (a) $1 - x^2 = x - 1 \Rightarrow x = -2, 1$. The graphs intersect at $(-2, -3)$ and $(1, 0)$.

$$\text{On } [-2, 1],\ 1 - x^2 \geq x - 1.\quad A = \int_{-2}^{1} \left[(1 - x^2) - (x - 1)\right] dx.$$

(b) On $[-3, 0]$, $(y + 1) \geq -\sqrt{1 - y}$ and on $[0, 1]$, $\sqrt{1 - y} \geq -\sqrt{1 - y}$.

$$A = \int_{-3}^{0} \left[(y + 1) - (-\sqrt{1 - y})\right] dy + 2\int_{0}^{1} \sqrt{1 - y} \, dy.$$

29 (a) $y - 3 = -y^2 + 3 \Rightarrow y = -3, 2$. The graphs intersect at

$(-6, -3)$ and $(-1, 2)$. On $[-6, -1]$, $(x + 3) \geq -\sqrt{3 - x}$ and on $[-1, 3]$,

$$\sqrt{3 - x} \geq -\sqrt{3 - x}.\quad A = \int_{-6}^{-1} \left[(x + 3) - (-\sqrt{3 - x})\right] dx + 2\int_{-1}^{3} \sqrt{3 - x} \, dx.$$

(b) On $[-3, 2]$, $(3 - y^2) \geq (y - 3)$. $A = \int_{-3}^{2} \left[(3 - y^2) - (y - 3)\right] dy.$

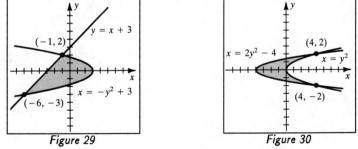

Figure 29   Figure 30

$\boxed{30}$ (a) $y^2 = 2y^2 - 4 \Rightarrow y = \pm 2$. The graphs intersect at $(4, 2)$ and $(4, -2)$.

On $[-4, 0]$, $\sqrt{\frac{1}{2}(x + 4)} \geq -\sqrt{\frac{1}{2}(x + 4)}$. On $[0, 4]$, $\sqrt{\frac{1}{2}(x + 4)} \geq \sqrt{x}$ for $y \geq 0$.

$$A = 2\int_{-4}^{0} \sqrt{\tfrac{1}{2}(x + 4)}\, dx + 2\int_{0}^{4} (\sqrt{\tfrac{1}{2}(x + 4)} - \sqrt{x})\, dx.$$

(b) On $[-2, 2]$, $y^2 \geq 2y^2 - 4$. $A = 2\int_{0}^{2} \left[y^2 - (2y^2 - 4) \right] dy$.

$\boxed{31}$ On $[0, 2]$, $f(x) = g(x)$ at $x = 1$. $f(x) \geq g(x)$ on $[0, 1]$ and $f(x) \leq g(x)$ on $[1, 2]$.

$$A = \int_{0}^{1} \left[(6 - 3x^2) - 3x \right] dx + \int_{1}^{2} \left[3x - (6 - 3x^2) \right] dx = \tfrac{7}{2} + \tfrac{11}{2} = 9.$$

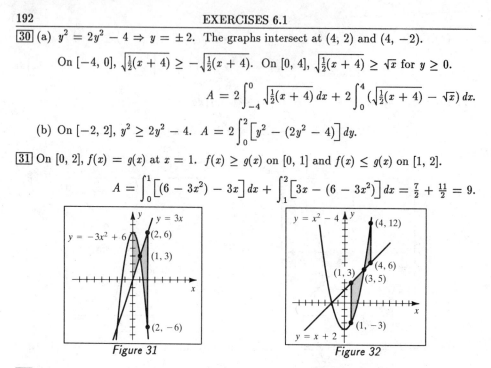

Figure 31   Figure 32

$\boxed{32}$ On $[1, 4]$, $f(x) = g(x)$ at $x = 3$. $f(x) \geq g(x)$ on $[3, 4]$ and $f(x) \leq g(x)$ on $[1, 3]$.

$$A = \int_{1}^{3} \left[(x + 2) - (x^2 - 4) \right] dx + \int_{3}^{4} \left[(x^2 - 4) - (x + 2) \right] dx = \tfrac{44}{6} + \tfrac{17}{6} = \tfrac{61}{6}.$$

$\boxed{33}$ On $[-1, 3]$, $f(x) = g(x)$ at $x = 0, 2$. $f(x) \geq g(x)$ on $[-1, 0]$ and $[2, 3]$.

$f(x) \leq g(x)$ on $[0, 2]$. $A = \int_{-1}^{0} \left[(x^3 - 4x + 2) - 2 \right] dx +$

$$\int_{0}^{2} \left[2 - (x^3 - 4x + 2) \right] dx + \int_{2}^{3} \left[(x^3 - 4x + 2) - 2 \right] dx = \tfrac{7}{4} + 4 + \tfrac{25}{4} = 12.$$

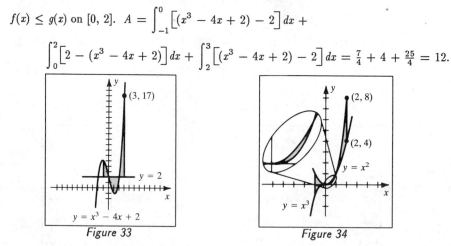

Figure 33   Figure 34

$\boxed{34}$ $f(x) = g(x)$ at $x = 0, 1$. $f(x) \geq g(x)$ on $[-1, 1]$ and $f(x) \leq g(x)$ on $[1, 2]$.

$$A = \int_{-1}^{1} (x^2 - x^3)\, dx + \int_{1}^{2} (x^3 - x^2)\, dx = \tfrac{2}{3} + \tfrac{17}{12} = \tfrac{25}{12}.$$

$\boxed{35}$ On $[0, 2\pi]$, $f(x) = g(x)$ at $x = \frac{\pi}{4}$, $\frac{5\pi}{4}$. $f(x) \ge g(x)$ on $[\frac{\pi}{4}, \frac{5\pi}{4}]$, $f(x) \le g(x)$ on

$[0, \frac{\pi}{4}] \cup [\frac{5\pi}{4}, 2\pi]$. $A = \int_0^{\pi/4} (\cos x - \sin x)\, dx + \int_{\pi/4}^{5\pi/4} (\sin x - \cos x)\, dx +$

$$\int_{5\pi/4}^{2\pi} (\cos x - \sin x)\, dx = (\sqrt{2} - 1) + 2\sqrt{2} + (1 + \sqrt{2}) = 4\sqrt{2}.$$

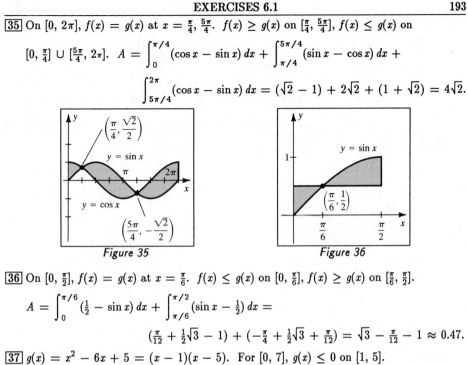

Figure 35   Figure 36

$\boxed{36}$ On $[0, \frac{\pi}{2}]$, $f(x) = g(x)$ at $x = \frac{\pi}{6}$. $f(x) \le g(x)$ on $[0, \frac{\pi}{6}]$, $f(x) \ge g(x)$ on $[\frac{\pi}{6}, \frac{\pi}{2}]$.

$A = \int_0^{\pi/6} (\frac{1}{2} - \sin x)\, dx + \int_{\pi/6}^{\pi/2} (\sin x - \frac{1}{2})\, dx =$

$$(\frac{\pi}{12} + \frac{1}{2}\sqrt{3} - 1) + (-\frac{\pi}{4} + \frac{1}{2}\sqrt{3} + \frac{\pi}{12}) = \sqrt{3} - \frac{\pi}{12} - 1 \approx 0.47.$$

$\boxed{37}$ $g(x) = x^2 - 6x + 5 = (x - 1)(x - 5)$. For $[0, 7]$, $g(x) \le 0$ on $[1, 5]$.

Hence, $A = \int_0^1 (x^2 - 6x + 5)\, dx + \int_1^5 -(x^2 - 6x + 5)\, dx + \int_5^7 (x^2 - 6x + 5)\, dx$.

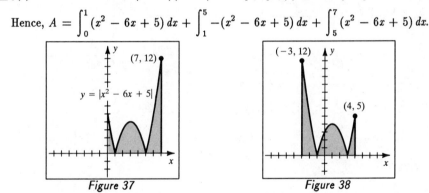

Figure 37   Figure 38

$\boxed{38}$ $g(x) = -x^2 + 2x + 3 = (3 - x)(x + 1)$.

For $[-3, 4]$, $g(x) \le 0$ on $[-3, -1]$ and $[3, 4]$. Hence,

$$A = \int_{-3}^{-1} -(-x^2 + 2x + 3)\, dx + \int_{-1}^3 (-x^2 + 2x + 3)\, dx + \int_3^4 -(-x^2 + 2x + 3)\, dx.$$

$\boxed{39}$ *Note*: Answers may vary depending upon the estimates of the function values.

Let $f(x)$ be the difference between the ordinates of the top and the bottom curves,

that is, $f(x_k) = y_k(\text{top}) - y_k(\text{bottom})$. Then, $\int_0^6 f(x)\, dx \approx$

(a) $T = \frac{6 - 0}{2(6)} \{ f(0) + 2[f(1) + f(2) + f(3) + f(4) + f(5)] + f(6) \} =$

$$\frac{1}{2}[0 + 2(0.5 + 0.75 + 1 + 1 + 1) + 0] = \frac{1}{2}(8.5) = 4.25$$

(b) $S = \frac{6-0}{3(6)}\left[f(0) + 4f(1) + 2f(2) + 4f(3) + 2f(4) + 4f(5) + f(6)\right] =$

$\frac{1}{3}\left[0 + 4(0.5) + 2(0.75) + 4(1) + 2(1) + 4(1) + 0\right] = \frac{1}{3}(13.5) = 4.50$

$\boxed{40}$ Let $h(x) = f(x) - g(x)$. Then, $\int_1^5 h(x)\,dx \approx$

(a) $T = \frac{5-1}{2(8)}\{h(1) + 2[h(1.5) + h(2) + h(2.5) + h(3) + h(3.5) + h(4) + h(4.5)]$

$+ h(5)\} = \frac{1}{4}\left[2 + 2(0.5 + 1 + 2.5 + 2.5 + 2 + 1 + 0.5) + 2\right] = 6$

(b) $S = \frac{5-1}{3(8)}[h(1) + 4h(1.5) + 2h(2) + 4h(2.5) + 2h(3) + 4h(3.5) + 2h(4)$

$+ 4h(4.5) + h(5)]$

$= \frac{1}{6}\left[2 + 4(0.5) + 2(1) + 4(2.5) + 2(2.5) + 4(2) + 2(1) + 4(0.5) + 2\right]$

$= \frac{35}{6} \approx 5.83$

$\boxed{41}$ f has a zero at $x \approx -1.10$. $f(x) \le 0$ on $[-1.5, -1.10]$ and $f(x) \ge 0$ on $[-1.10, 1.5]$.

$$\text{Area} \approx \int_{-1.5}^{-1.1} -(x^3 - 0.7x^2 - 0.8x + 1.3)\,dx + \int_{-1.1}^{1.5} (x^3 - 0.7x^2 - 0.8x + 1.3)\,dx$$

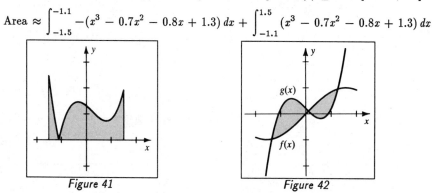

Figure 41   Figure 42

$\boxed{42}$ The graphs intersect at $x \approx -1.37, 0.1, 1.26$.

$f(x) \le g(x)$ on $[-1.37, 0.1]$ and $f(x) \ge g(x)$ on $[0.1, 1.26]$.

$$\text{Area} \approx \int_{-1.37}^{0.1} (x^3 - x + 0.2 - \sin x)\,dx + \int_{0.1}^{1.26}\left[\sin x - (x^3 - x + 0.2)\right]dx.$$

Exercises 6.2

$\boxed{1}$ The radius of each disk generated is $r = \frac{1}{2}x^2 + 2$. $V = \pi\int_{-1}^2 \left(\frac{1}{2}x^2 + 2\right)^2 dx$.

$\boxed{2}$ The radius of each disk generated is $r = y^2 - 4$. $V = \pi\int_0^2 (y^2 - 4)^2\,dy$.

$\boxed{3}$ For each washer generated, the outer radius is $R = \sqrt{25 - y^2}$ and the inner radius is

$$r = 3. \text{ Using symmetry on } [-4, 4], \ V = 2\cdot\pi\int_0^4\left[(\sqrt{25 - y^2})^2 - 3^2\right]dy.$$

$\boxed{4}$ For each washer generated, the outer radius is $R = -2x^2 + 2$ and the inner radius is

$r = -x^2 + 1$. Using symmetry on $[-1, 1]$,

$$V = 2\cdot\pi\int_0^1\left[(-2x^2 + 2)^2 - (-x^2 + 1)^2\right]dx.$$

$\boxed{5}$ By (6.5) with $f(x) = 1/x$, $V = \pi \int_1^3 (1/x)^2\, dx = \pi\left[-\frac{1}{x}\right]_1^3 = -\pi(\frac{1}{3} - 1) = \frac{2\pi}{3}$.

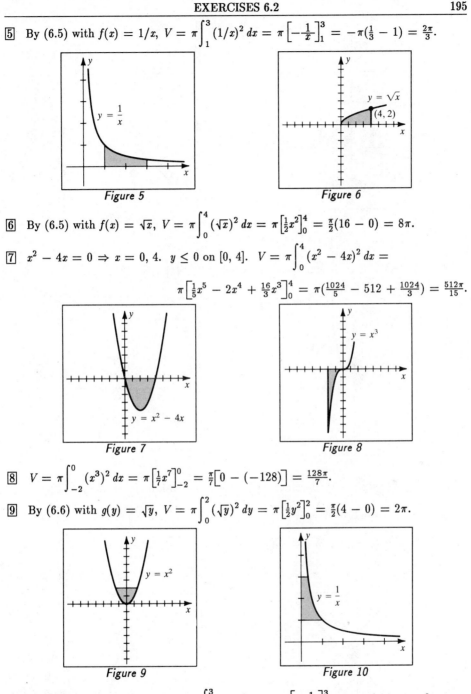

Figure 5   Figure 6

$\boxed{6}$ By (6.5) with $f(x) = \sqrt{x}$, $V = \pi \int_0^4 (\sqrt{x})^2\, dx = \pi\left[\frac{1}{2}x^2\right]_0^4 = \frac{\pi}{2}(16 - 0) = 8\pi$.

$\boxed{7}$ $x^2 - 4x = 0 \Rightarrow x = 0, 4$. $y \le 0$ on $[0, 4]$. $V = \pi \int_0^4 (x^2 - 4x)^2\, dx =$

$$\pi\left[\tfrac{1}{5}x^5 - 2x^4 + \tfrac{16}{3}x^3\right]_0^4 = \pi\left(\tfrac{1024}{5} - 512 + \tfrac{1024}{3}\right) = \tfrac{512\pi}{15}.$$

Figure 7   Figure 8

$\boxed{8}$ $V = \pi \int_{-2}^0 (x^3)^2\, dx = \pi\left[\tfrac{1}{7}x^7\right]_{-2}^0 = \tfrac{\pi}{7}\left[0 - (-128)\right] = \tfrac{128\pi}{7}$.

$\boxed{9}$ By (6.6) with $g(y) = \sqrt{y}$, $V = \pi \int_0^2 (\sqrt{y})^2\, dy = \pi\left[\tfrac{1}{2}y^2\right]_0^2 = \tfrac{\pi}{2}(4 - 0) = 2\pi$.

Figure 9   Figure 10

$\boxed{10}$ By (6.6) with $g(y) = 1/y$, $V = \pi \int_1^3 (1/y)^2\, dy = \pi\left[-\frac{1}{y}\right]_1^3 = -\pi(\frac{1}{3} - 1) = \frac{2\pi}{3}$.

$\boxed{11}$ $4y - y^2 = 0 \Rightarrow y = 0, 4.$ $4y - y^2 \geq 0$ on $[0, 4]$.

$$V = \pi \int_0^4 (4y - y^2)^2 \, dy = \pi \left[\tfrac{16}{3}y^3 - 2y^4 + \tfrac{1}{5}y^5 \right]_0^4 = \pi(\tfrac{1024}{3} - 512 + \tfrac{1024}{5}) = \tfrac{512\pi}{15}.$$

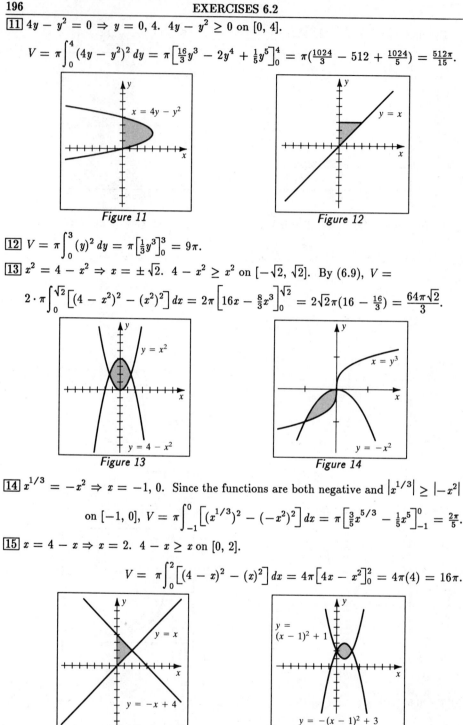

Figure 11   Figure 12

$\boxed{12}$ $V = \pi \int_0^3 (y)^2 \, dy = \pi \left[\tfrac{1}{3}y^3 \right]_0^3 = 9\pi.$

$\boxed{13}$ $x^2 = 4 - x^2 \Rightarrow x = \pm \sqrt{2}.$ $4 - x^2 \geq x^2$ on $[-\sqrt{2}, \sqrt{2}]$. By (6.9), $V =$

$$2 \cdot \pi \int_0^{\sqrt{2}} \left[(4 - x^2)^2 - (x^2)^2 \right] dx = 2\pi \left[16x - \tfrac{8}{3}x^3 \right]_0^{\sqrt{2}} = 2\sqrt{2}\pi(16 - \tfrac{16}{3}) = \tfrac{64\pi\sqrt{2}}{3}.$$

Figure 13   Figure 14

$\boxed{14}$ $x^{1/3} = -x^2 \Rightarrow x = -1, 0.$ Since the functions are both negative and $\left| x^{1/3} \right| \geq \left| -x^2 \right|$

on $[-1, 0]$, $V = \pi \int_{-1}^0 \left[(x^{1/3})^2 - (-x^2)^2 \right] dx = \pi \left[\tfrac{3}{5}x^{5/3} - \tfrac{1}{5}x^5 \right]_{-1}^0 = \tfrac{2\pi}{5}.$

$\boxed{15}$ $x = 4 - x \Rightarrow x = 2.$ $4 - x \geq x$ on $[0, 2]$.

$$V = \pi \int_0^2 \left[(4 - x)^2 - (x)^2 \right] dx = 4\pi \left[4x - x^2 \right]_0^2 = 4\pi(4) = 16\pi.$$

Figure 15   Figure 16

$\boxed{16}$ $(x-1)^2 + 1 = -(x-1)^2 + 3 \Rightarrow x = 0, 2.$ $-(x-1)^2 + 3 \geq (x-1)^2 + 1$ on

$[0, 2].$ $V = \pi \int_0^2 \left\{ \left[-(x-1)^2 + 3 \right]^2 - \left[(x-1)^2 + 1 \right]^2 \right\} dx$

$= \pi \int_0^2 \left[(-x^2 + 2x + 2)^2 - (x^2 - 2x + 2)^2 \right] dx$

$= \pi \int_0^2 \left[(-x^2 + 2x + 2) - (x^2 - 2x + 2) \right]\left[(-x^2 + 2x + 2) + (x^2 - 2x + 2) \right] dx$

$= \pi \int_0^2 (-2x^2 + 4x)(4)\, dx = -8\pi \int_0^2 (x^2 - 2x)\, dx = -8\pi \left[\tfrac{1}{3}x^3 - x^2 \right]_0^2$

$= -8\pi(-\tfrac{4}{3}) = \tfrac{32\pi}{3}.$

$\boxed{17}$ $y^2 = 2y \Rightarrow y = 0, 2.$ $2y \geq y^2$ on $[0, 2].$

$$V = \pi \int_0^2 \left[(2y)^2 - (y^2)^2 \right] dy = \pi \left[\tfrac{4}{3}y^3 - \tfrac{1}{5}y^5 \right]_0^2 = \pi(\tfrac{32}{3} - \tfrac{32}{5}) = \tfrac{64\pi}{15}.$$

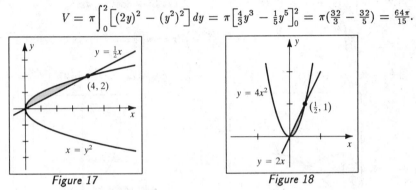

Figure 17   Figure 18

$\boxed{18}$ $x = \tfrac{1}{2}y$ and $x = \tfrac{1}{2}\sqrt{y}$ intersect when $y = 0, 1.$ $\tfrac{1}{2}\sqrt{y} \geq \tfrac{1}{2}y$ on $[0, 1].$

$$V = \pi \int_0^1 \left[(\tfrac{1}{2}\sqrt{y})^2 - (\tfrac{1}{2}y)^2 \right] dy = \tfrac{\pi}{4} \left[\tfrac{1}{2}y^2 - \tfrac{1}{3}y^3 \right]_0^1 = \tfrac{\pi}{4}(\tfrac{1}{2} - \tfrac{1}{3}) = \tfrac{\pi}{24}.$$

$\boxed{19}$ $y^2 = y + 2 \Rightarrow y = -1, 2.$ $y + 2 \geq y^2$ on $[-1, 2].$

$V = \pi \int_{-1}^2 \left[(y+2)^2 - (y^2)^2 \right] dy = \pi \left[\tfrac{1}{3}(y+2)^3 - \tfrac{1}{5}y^5 \right]_{-1}^2 = \pi(\tfrac{224}{15} - \tfrac{8}{15}) = \tfrac{72\pi}{5}.$

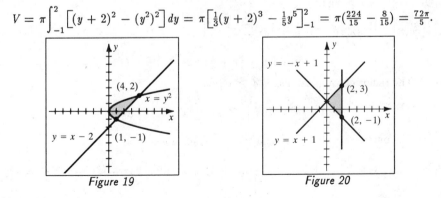

Figure 19   Figure 20

$\boxed{20}$ The lines intersect at $(0, 1), (2, -1), (2, 3).$ If $-1 \leq y \leq 1,$

the left boundary is $x = 1 - y$ and if $1 \leq y \leq 3,$ it is $x = y - 1.$ By symmetry,

$$V = 2 \cdot \pi \int_1^3 \left[2^2 - (y-1)^2 \right] dy = 2\pi \left[4y - \tfrac{1}{3}(y-1)^3 \right]_1^3 = \tfrac{32\pi}{3}.$$

$\boxed{21}$ $V = \pi \displaystyle\int_0^\pi (\sin 2x)^2\, dx = \frac{\pi}{2}\displaystyle\int_0^\pi (1 - \cos 4x)\, dx = \frac{\pi}{2}\Big[x - \frac{1}{4}\sin 4x\Big]_0^\pi = \frac{1}{2}\pi^2.$

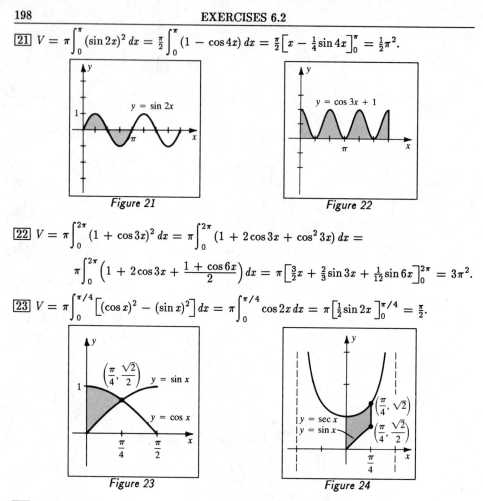

Figure 21   *Figure 22*

$\boxed{22}$ $V = \pi \displaystyle\int_0^{2\pi} (1 + \cos 3x)^2\, dx = \pi \displaystyle\int_0^{2\pi} (1 + 2\cos 3x + \cos^2 3x)\, dx =$

$\qquad \pi\displaystyle\int_0^{2\pi}\Big(1 + 2\cos 3x + \frac{1 + \cos 6x}{2}\Big)\, dx = \pi\Big[\frac{3}{2}x + \frac{2}{3}\sin 3x + \frac{1}{12}\sin 6x\Big]_0^{2\pi} = 3\pi^2.$

$\boxed{23}$ $V = \pi \displaystyle\int_0^{\pi/4} \Big[(\cos x)^2 - (\sin x)^2\Big]\, dx = \pi \displaystyle\int_0^{\pi/4} \cos 2x\, dx = \pi\Big[\frac{1}{2}\sin 2x\Big]_0^{\pi/4} = \frac{\pi}{2}.$

Figure 23   *Figure 24*

$\boxed{24}$ On $[0, \frac{\pi}{4}]$, $\sec x \geq \sin x$.

$\qquad V = \pi \displaystyle\int_0^{\pi/4} \Big[(\sec x)^2 - (\sin x)^2\Big]\, dx = \pi \displaystyle\int_0^{\pi/4} \Big[\sec^2 x - \Big(\frac{1 - \cos 2x}{2}\Big)\Big]\, dx =$

$\qquad\qquad \pi\Big[\tan x - \frac{1}{2}x + \frac{1}{4}\sin 2x\Big]_0^{\pi/4} = \pi(1 - \frac{\pi}{8} + \frac{1}{4}) = \frac{5\pi}{4} - \frac{1}{8}\pi^2.$

$\boxed{25}$ (a) The radius of a typical disk is $4 - x^2$.

$$V = 2\cdot\pi \int_0^2 (4 - x^2)^2\, dx = 2\pi\Big[16x - \frac{8}{3}x^3 + \frac{1}{5}x^5\Big]_0^2 = \frac{512\pi}{15}.$$

(b) The outer radius is $5 - x^2$ and the inner radius is $5 - 4$.

$$V = 2\cdot\pi \int_0^2 \Big[(5 - x^2)^2 - (5 - 4)^2\Big]\, dx = 2\pi\Big[24x - \frac{10}{3}x^3 + \frac{1}{5}x^5\Big]_0^2 = \frac{832\pi}{15}.$$

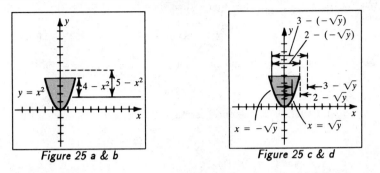

Figure 25 a & b   Figure 25 c & d

(c) For the revolution about the vertical line $x = 2$, the y-interval is $0 \le y \le 4$.

The outer radius is $2 - (-\sqrt{y})$ and the inner radius is $2 - \sqrt{y}$.

$$V = \pi \int_0^4 \{[2 - (-\sqrt{y})]^2 - [2 - \sqrt{y}]^2\}\, dy = \pi \int_0^4 8\sqrt{y}\, dy = 8\pi \left[\tfrac{2}{3} y^{3/2}\right]_0^4 = \tfrac{128\pi}{3}.$$

(d) The outer radius is $3 - (-\sqrt{y})$ and the inner radius is $3 - \sqrt{y}$. $V =$

$$\pi \int_0^4 \{[3 - (-\sqrt{y})]^2 - [3 - \sqrt{y}]^2\}\, dy = \pi \int_0^4 12\sqrt{y}\, dy = 12\pi \left[\tfrac{2}{3} y^{3/2}\right]_0^4 = 64\pi.$$

26 (a) On the y-interval $[0, 2]$, the radius is $4 - y^2$.

$$V = \pi \int_0^2 (4 - y^2)^2\, dy = \pi \left[16y - \tfrac{8}{3}y^3 + \tfrac{1}{5}y^5\right]_0^2 = \tfrac{256\pi}{15}.$$

(b) The outer radius is $6 - y^2$ and the inner radius is $6 - 4$.

$$V = \pi \int_0^2 \left[(6 - y^2)^2 - (6 - 4)^2\right] dy = \pi \left[32y - 4y^3 + \tfrac{1}{5}y^5\right]_0^2 = \tfrac{192\pi}{5}.$$

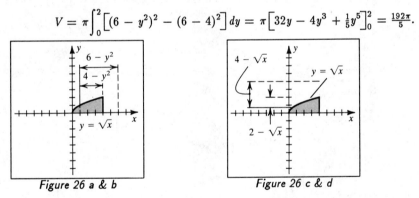

Figure 26 a & b   Figure 26 c & d

(c) On the x-interval $[0, 4]$, the outer radius is $2 - 0$ and the inner radius is $2 - \sqrt{x}$.

$$V = \pi \int_0^4 \left[(2 - 0)^2 - (2 - \sqrt{x})^2\right] dx = \pi \left[\tfrac{8}{3} x^{3/2} - \tfrac{1}{2}x^2\right]_0^4 = \tfrac{40\pi}{3}.$$

(d) The outer radius is $4 - 0$ and the inner radius is $4 - \sqrt{x}$.

$$V = \pi \int_0^4 \left[(4 - 0)^2 - (4 - \sqrt{x})^2\right] dx = \pi \left[\tfrac{16}{3} x^{3/2} - \tfrac{1}{2}x^2\right]_0^4 = \tfrac{104\pi}{3}.$$

$\boxed{27}$ (a) On the x-interval $[0, 4]$, the outer radius is $(-\frac{1}{2}x + 2) - (-2)$ and the inner

radius is $0 - (-2)$. $V = \pi \displaystyle\int_0^4 \{ [(-\frac{1}{2}x + 2) - (-2)]^2 - [0 - (-2)]^2 \} \, dx$.

(b) The outer radius is $5 - 0$ and the inner radius is $5 - (-\frac{1}{2}x + 2)$.

$$V = \pi \int_0^4 \{ (5 - 0)^2 - [5 - (-\frac{1}{2}x + 2)]^2 \} \, dx.$$

(c) On the y-interval $[0, 2]$, the outer radius is $7 - 0$ and the inner radius is

$7 - (-2y + 4)$. $V = \pi \displaystyle\int_0^2 \{ (7 - 0)^2 - [7 - (-2y + 4)]^2 \} \, dy$.

(d) The outer radius is $(-2y + 4) - (-4)$ and the inner radius is $0 - (-4)$.

$$V = \pi \int_0^2 \{ [(-2y + 4) - (-4)]^2 - [0 - (-4)]^2 \} \, dy.$$

$\boxed{28}$ (a) On the x-interval $[0, 2]$, the outer radius is $x^2 - (-2)$ and the inner radius is

$0 - (-2)$. $V = \pi \displaystyle\int_0^2 \{ [x^2 - (-2)]^2 - [0 - (-2)]^2 \} \, dx$.

(b) The outer radius is $5 - 0$ and the inner radius is $5 - x^2$.

$$V = \pi \int_0^2 \left[(5 - 0)^2 - (5 - x^2)^2 \right] \, dx.$$

(c) On the y-interval $[0, 4]$, the outer radius is $7 - \sqrt{y}$ and the inner radius is $7 - 2$.

$$V = \pi \int_0^4 \left[(7 - \sqrt{y})^2 - (7 - 2)^2 \right] \, dy.$$

(d) The outer radius is $2 - (-4)$ and the inner radius is $\sqrt{y} - (-4)$.

$$V = \pi \int_0^4 \{ [2 - (-4)]^2 - [\sqrt{y} - (-4)]^2 \} \, dy.$$

$\boxed{29}$ $x^3 = 4x \Rightarrow x = 0, \pm 2$. For $x \le 0$, the radius of the outer disk is $(8 - 4x)$ and the

radius of the inner disk is $(8 - x^3)$. For $x \ge 0$, the outer disk has radius $(8 - x^3)$

and the inner disk has radius $(8 - 4x)$.

$$V = \pi \int_{-2}^0 \left[(8 - 4x)^2 - (8 - x^3)^2 \right] \, dx + \pi \int_0^2 \left[(8 - x^3)^2 - (8 - 4x)^2 \right] \, dx.$$

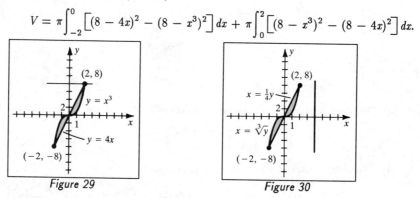

Figure 29   Figure 30

$\boxed{30}$ For $y \le 0$, the outer radius is $(4 - y^{1/3})$ and the inner radius is $(4 - \frac{1}{4}y)$.

For $y \ge 0$, the outer radius is $(4 - \frac{1}{4}y)$ and the inner radius is $(4 - y^{1/3})$.

$$V = \pi \int_{-8}^0 \left[(4 - y^{1/3})^2 - (4 - \frac{1}{4}y)^2 \right] \, dy + \pi \int_0^8 \left[(4 - \frac{1}{4}y)^2 - (4 - y^{1/3})^2 \right] \, dy.$$

$\boxed{31}$ The outer radius is $\left[2 - (3 - y)\right]$ and the inner radius is $(2 - \sqrt{3 - y})$.

$$V = \pi \int_2^3 \left\{ [2 - (3 - y)]^2 - [2 - \sqrt{3 - y}]^2 \right\} dy.$$

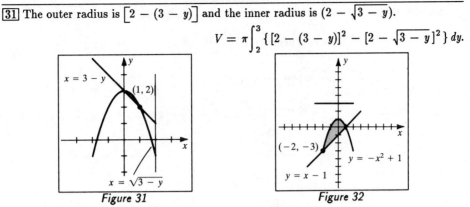

Figure 31   Figure 32

$\boxed{32}$ For $-2 \leq x \leq 1$, the outer radius is $\left[3 - (x - 1)\right]$ and the inner radius is

$$\left[3 - (1 - x^2)\right]. \quad V = \pi \int_{-2}^1 \left\{ [3 - (x - 1)]^2 - [3 - (1 - x^2)]^2 \right\} dx.$$

$\boxed{33}$ For $-1 \leq y \leq 1$, the outer radius is $\left[5 - (-\sqrt{1 - y^2})\right]$ and the inner radius is

$$(5 - \sqrt{1 - y^2}). \quad V = 2 \cdot \pi \int_0^1 \left\{ [5 - (-\sqrt{1 - y^2})]^2 - [5 - \sqrt{1 - y^2}]^2 \right\} dy.$$

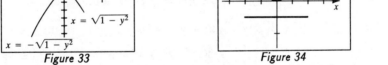

Figure 33   Figure 34

$\boxed{34}$ $x^{2/3} = x^2 \Rightarrow x = 0, \pm 1$. For $-1 \leq x \leq 1$, the outer radius is $\left[x^{2/3} - (-1)\right]$ and

the inner radius is $\left[x^2 - (-1)\right]$. $V = 2 \cdot \pi \int_0^1 \left\{ [x^{2/3} - (-1)]^2 - [x^2 - (-1)]^2 \right\} dx.$

$\boxed{35}$ Revolve the rectangle with vertices $(0, 0)$, $(0, h)$, (r, h), and $(r, 0)$ about the y-axis

using $g(y) = r$. $V = \pi \int_0^h r^2 \, dy = \pi r^2 \left[\, y \, \right]_0^h = \pi r^2 h.$

$\boxed{36}$ Revolve the rectangle with vertices $(r, 0)$, (r, h), (R, h), and $(R, 0)$ about the y-axis.

The outer radius is $R - 0$ and the inner radius is $r - 0$.

$$V = \pi \int_0^h (R^2 - r^2) \, dy = \pi (R^2 - r^2) \left[\, y \, \right]_0^h = \pi (R^2 - r^2) h.$$

$\boxed{37}$ Revolve the triangle with vertices $(0, 0)$, $(h, 0)$ and (h, r) about the x-axis using

$$f(x) = \tfrac{r}{h} x. \quad V = \pi \int_0^h (\tfrac{r}{h} x)^2 \, dx = \pi (\tfrac{r}{h})^2 \left[\tfrac{1}{3} x^3 \right]_0^h = \tfrac{1}{3} \pi r^2 h.$$

$\boxed{38}$ Revolve the semicircle $y = \sqrt{r^2 - x^2}$ on $[-r, r]$ about the x-axis.

$$V = 2 \cdot \pi \int_0^r (\sqrt{r^2 - x^2})^2 \, dx = 2\pi \int_0^r (r^2 - x^2) \, dx = 2\pi \left[r^2 x - \tfrac{1}{3} x^3 \right]_0^r = \tfrac{4}{3} \pi r^3.$$

39 Revolve the trapezoid with vertices $(0, 0)$, $(0, r)$, $(h, 0)$ and (h, R) about the x-axis

using $y = \left(\dfrac{R-r}{h}\right)x + r$. Then, $V = \pi\displaystyle\int_0^h \left(\dfrac{R-r}{h}\cdot x + r\right)^2 dx$

$$= \pi\int_0^h \left[\left(\dfrac{R-r}{h}\right)^2 x^2 + 2r\left(\dfrac{R-r}{h}\right)x + r^2\right] dx$$

$$= \pi\left[\left(\dfrac{R-r}{h}\right)^2 \dfrac{x^3}{3} + 2r\left(\dfrac{R-r}{h}\right)\dfrac{x^2}{2} + r^2 x\right]_0^h = \tfrac{1}{3}\pi h\left[(R-r)^2 + 3r(R-r) + 3r^2\right]$$

$$= \tfrac{1}{3}\pi h(R^2 + Rr + r^2).$$

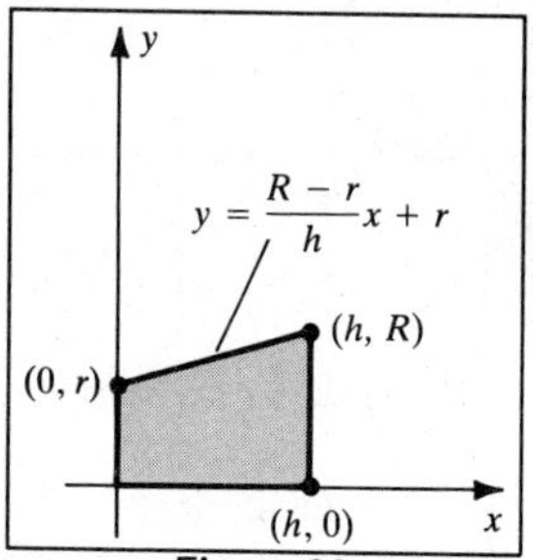

$y = \dfrac{R-r}{h}x + r$

(h, R)

$(0, r)$

$(h, 0)$

Figure 39

$x = \sqrt{r^2 - y^2}$

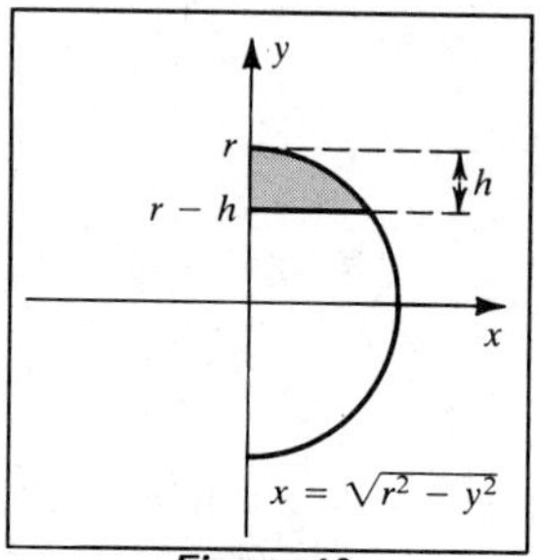

Figure 40

40 Revolve the region bounded by $x = \sqrt{r^2 - y^2}$, $y = r$ and, $y = r - h$ about the

y-axis. $V = \pi\displaystyle\int_{r-h}^r \left(\sqrt{r^2 - y^2}\right)^2 dy = \tfrac{1}{3}\pi\left[3r^2 y - y^3\right]_{r-h}^r =$

$$\tfrac{1}{3}\pi\left[(2r^3) - (2r^3 - 3rh^2 + h^3)\right] = \tfrac{1}{3}\pi h^2(3r - h).$$

41 The volume $V = \pi\displaystyle\int_0^6 [f(x)]^2 dx$. Let $g(x) = [f(x)]^2$ to estimate V.

$$\mathrm{T} = \pi\cdot\tfrac{6-0}{2(6)}\left\{g(0) + 2\left[g(1) + g(2) + g(3) + g(4) + g(5)\right] + g(6)\right\} =$$

$$\tfrac{\pi}{2}\left[2^2 + 2(1^2 + 2^2 + 4^2 + 2^2 + 2^2) + 1^2\right] = \tfrac{63\pi}{2} \approx 98.96.$$

42 The volume $V = \pi\displaystyle\int_0^8 [f(x)]^2 dx$. Let $g(x) = [f(x)]^2$ to estimate V. $\mathrm{S} =$

$$\pi\cdot\tfrac{8-0}{3(8)}\left\{g(0) + 4g(1) + 2g(2) + 4g(3) + 2g(4) + 4g(5) + 2g(6) + 4g(7) + g(8)\right\} =$$

$$\tfrac{\pi}{3}\left[0 + 4(1)^2 + 0 + 4(2)^2 + 0 + 4(3)^2 + 0 + 4(4)^2 + 0\right] =$$

$$\tfrac{\pi}{3}(120) = 40\pi \approx 125.66.$$

43 (a) The graphs intersect at $x \approx 0.45$, 2.01.

(b) $V \approx \pi\displaystyle\int_{0.45}^{2.01}\left[\left(\dfrac{\sin x}{1+x}\right)^2 - (0.3)^2\right] dx$. Let $f(x) = \left(\dfrac{\sin x}{1+x}\right)^2 - (0.3)^2$.

$$\mathrm{S} \approx (\pi)\tfrac{2.01 - 0.45}{3(4)}\left[f(0.45) + 4f(0.84) + 2f(1.23) + 4f(1.62) + f(2.01)\right] \approx$$

$$0.28.$$

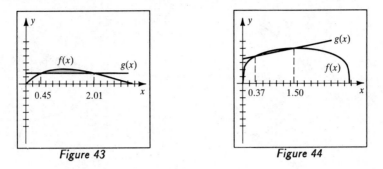

Figure 43   Figure 44

44 (a) The graphs intersect at $x \approx 0.37, 1.50$.

(b) $V \approx \pi \int_{0.37}^{1.50} \left[(\sqrt[4]{|\sin x|})^2 - (0.2x + 0.7)^2 \right] dx =$

$\pi \int_{0.37}^{1.50} \left[\sqrt{\sin x} - (0.2x + 0.7)^2 \right] dx.$ Let $f(x) = \sqrt{\sin x} - (0.2x + 0.7)^2$.

$S \approx (\pi)\frac{1.50-0.37}{3(4)} \left[f(0.37) + 4f(0.6525) + 2f(0.935) + 4f(1.2175) + f(1.50) \right]$
$\approx 0.26.$

Exercises 6.3

1 Radius $= x$; altitude $= \sqrt{x - 2}$; $V = 2\pi \int_{2}^{11} x\sqrt{x - 2}\, dx.$

2 Radius $= x$; altitude $= (x^2 + 1)$; $V = 2\pi \int_{0}^{3} x(x^2 + 1)\, dx.$

3 Radius $= y$; altitude $= (-\frac{1}{2}y + 3)$; $V = 2\pi \int_{0}^{6} y(-\frac{1}{2}y + 3)\, dy.$

4 Radius $= y$; altitude $= \sqrt[3]{y - 1}$; $V = 2\pi \int_{1}^{9} y\sqrt[3]{y - 1}\, dy.$

5 $V = 2\pi \int_{0}^{4} x\sqrt{x}\, dx = 2\pi \left[\frac{2}{5}x^{5/2} \right]_{0}^{4} = \frac{4\pi}{5}(32) = \frac{128\pi}{5}.$

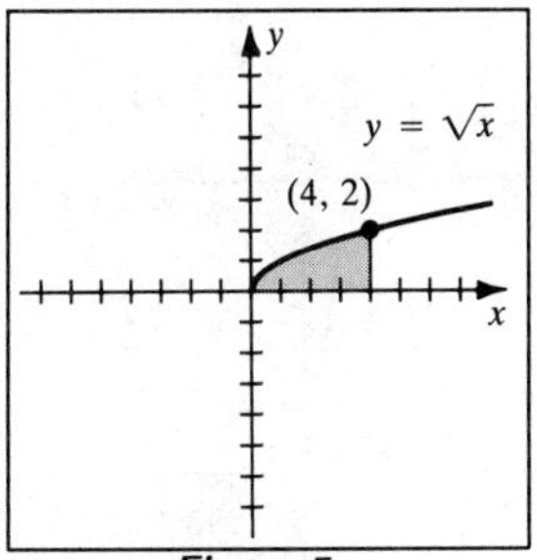

Figure 5 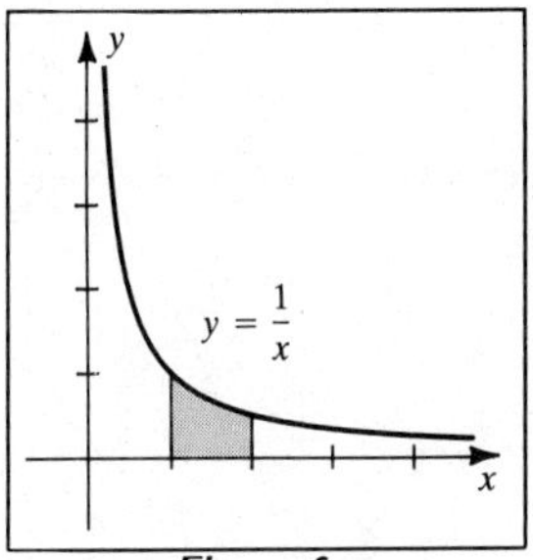   Figure 6

$y = \sqrt{x}$

$(4, 2)$

$y = \frac{1}{x}$

6 $V = 2\pi \int_{1}^{2} x(1/x)\, dx = 2\pi \left[x \right]_{1}^{2} = 2\pi.$

7 $x^2 = \sqrt{8x} \Rightarrow x = 0, 2.$ $\sqrt{8x} \geq x^2$ on $[0, 2]$.

$V = 2\pi \int_{0}^{2} x(\sqrt{8x} - x^2)\, dx = 2\pi \left[\sqrt{8}(\frac{2}{5}x^{5/2}) - \frac{1}{4}x^4 \right]_{0}^{2} = 2\pi(\frac{32}{5} - 4) = \frac{24\pi}{5}.$

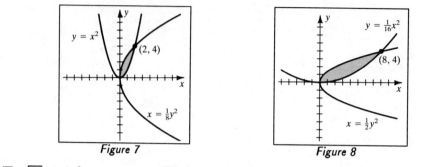

Figure 7   Figure 8

$\boxed{8}$ $\sqrt{2x} = \frac{1}{16}x^2 \Rightarrow x = 0, 8.$ $\sqrt{2x} \ge \frac{1}{16}x^2$ on $[0, 8]$.

$$V = 2\pi \int_0^8 x\left(\sqrt{2x} - \tfrac{1}{16}x^2\right) dx = 2\pi\left[\tfrac{2\sqrt{2}}{5}x^{5/2} - \tfrac{1}{64}x^4\right]_0^8 = 2\pi\left(\tfrac{512}{5} - 64\right) = \tfrac{384\pi}{5}.$$

$\boxed{9}$ $y = 2x - 12$ and $y = \frac{1}{2}x - \frac{3}{2}$ intersect at $(7, 2)$. $2x - 12 \le \frac{1}{2}x - \frac{3}{2}$ on $[4, 7]$.

$$V = 2\pi \int_4^7 x\left[\left(\tfrac{1}{2}x - \tfrac{3}{2}\right) - (2x - 12)\right] dx = \pi\left[\tfrac{21}{2}x^2 - x^3\right]_4^7 = \pi\left(\tfrac{343}{2} - 104\right) = \tfrac{135\pi}{2}.$$

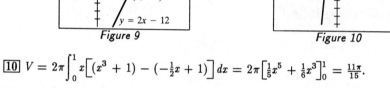

Figure 9   Figure 10

$\boxed{10}$ $V = 2\pi \int_0^1 x\left[(x^3 + 1) - (-\tfrac{1}{2}x + 1)\right] dx = 2\pi\left[\tfrac{1}{5}x^5 + \tfrac{1}{6}x^3\right]_0^1 = \tfrac{11\pi}{15}.$

$\boxed{11}$ $2x - 4 \le 0$ on $[0, 2]$.

$$V = 2\pi \int_0^2 x\left[0 - (2x - 4)\right] dx = 2\pi\left[2x^2 - \tfrac{2}{3}x^3\right]_0^2 = 2\pi\left(8 - \tfrac{16}{3}\right) = \tfrac{16\pi}{3}.$$

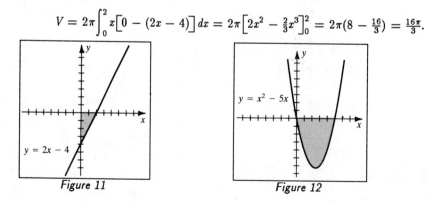

Figure 11   Figure 12

$\boxed{12}$ $x^2 - 5x \le 0$ on $[0, 5]$.

$$V = 2\pi \int_0^5 x\left[0 - (x^2 - 5x)\right] dx = 2\pi\left[-\tfrac{1}{4}x^4 + \tfrac{5}{3}x^3\right]_0^5 = 2\pi\left(\tfrac{625}{3} - \tfrac{625}{4}\right) = \tfrac{625\pi}{6}.$$

$\boxed{13}$ Using symmetry with $g(y) = \sqrt{4y}$, $V = 2 \cdot 2\pi \int_0^4 y(\sqrt{4y})\, dy = 8\pi \left[\frac{2}{5}y^{5/2}\right]_0^4 = \frac{512\pi}{5}$.

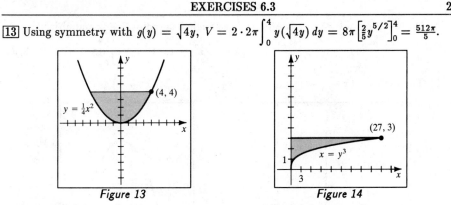

Figure 13   Figure 14

$\boxed{14}$ With $g(y) = y^3$, $V = 2\pi \int_0^3 y(y^3)\, dy = 2\pi \left[\frac{1}{5}y^5\right]_0^3 = \frac{486\pi}{5}$.

$\boxed{15}$ With $g(y) = \frac{1}{2}y$, $V = 2\pi \int_0^6 y(\frac{1}{2}y)\, dy = \pi \left[\frac{1}{3}y^3\right]_0^6 = 72\pi$.

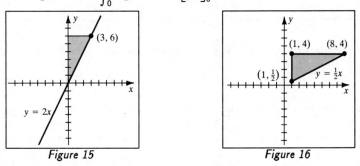

Figure 15   Figure 16

$\boxed{16}$ $x = 2y$ and $x = 1$ intersect at $y = \frac{1}{2}$. The altitude of a cylindrical shell is $2y - 1$.

$$V = 2\pi \int_{1/2}^4 y(2y - 1)\, dy = 2\pi \left[\frac{2}{3}y^3 - \frac{1}{2}y^2\right]_{1/2}^4 = 2\pi \left[\frac{104}{3} - (-\frac{1}{24})\right] = \frac{833\pi}{12}.$$

$\boxed{17}$ $y^2 - 4 \le 0$ on $0 \le y \le 2$.

$$V = 2\pi \int_0^2 y \left[0 - (y^2 - 4)\right] dy = 2\pi \left[2y^2 - \frac{1}{4}y^4\right]_0^2 = 2\pi(8 - 4) = 8\pi.$$

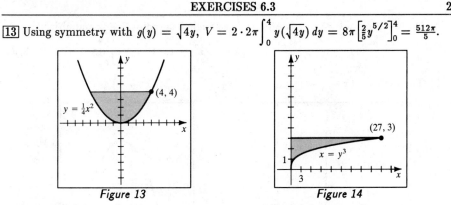

Figure 17   Figure 18

$\boxed{18}$ $-y \ge y - 4$ on $0 \le y \le 2$. The altitude of a cylindrical shell is $(-y) - (y - 4)$.

$$V = 2\pi \int_0^2 y \left[(-y) - (y - 4)\right] dy = 2\pi \left[2y^2 - \frac{2}{3}y^3\right]_0^2 = 2\pi(8 - \frac{16}{3}) = \frac{16\pi}{3}.$$

19 (a) On the interval $0 \le x \le 2$, a typical rectangle has radius $3 - x$ and altitude

$$x^2 + 1. \quad V = 2\pi \int_0^2 (3 - x)(x^2 + 1)\, dx.$$

(b) The radius is $\left[x - (-1)\right]$ and $V = 2\pi \int_0^2 [x - (-1)](x^2 + 1)\, dx.$

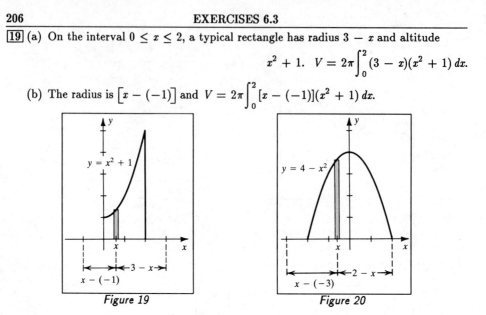

Figure 19   Figure 20

20 (a) On the interval $-2 \le x \le 2$, a typical rectangle has radius $2 - x$ and altitude

$$4 - x^2. \quad V = 2\pi \int_{-2}^2 (2 - x)(4 - x^2)\, dx.$$

(b) The radius is $\left[x - (-3)\right]$ and $V = 2\pi \int_{-2}^2 [x - (-3)](4 - x^2)\, dx.$

21 (a) On the interval $0 \le y \le 4$, the radius is $(4 - y)$ and the altitude is

$$\left[\sqrt{y} - (-\sqrt{y})\right] = 2\sqrt{y}. \quad V = 2 \cdot 2\pi \int_0^4 (4 - y)\sqrt{y}\, dy.$$

(b) The radius is $5 - y$ and $V = 2 \cdot 2\pi \int_0^4 (5 - y)\sqrt{y}\, dy.$

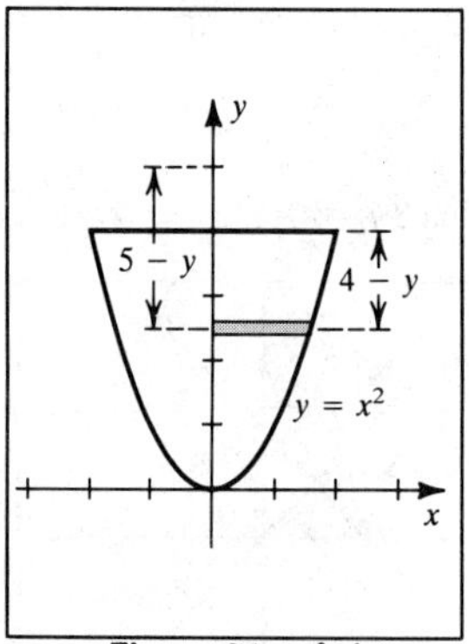

Figure 21 a & b 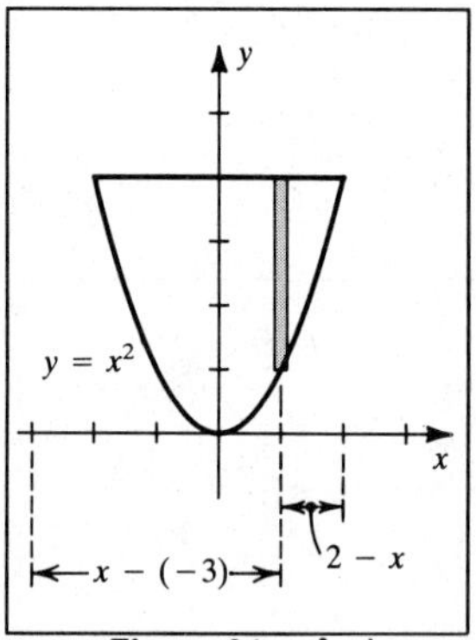   Figure 21 c & d

(c) On the interval $-2 \le x \le 2$, the radius is $(2 - x)$ and the altitude is $(4 - x^2)$.

$$V = 2\pi \int_{-2}^2 (2 - x)(4 - x^2)\, dx.$$

(d) The radius is $\left[x - (-3)\right]$ and $V = 2\pi \int_{-2}^2 [x - (-3)](4 - x^2)\, dx.$

22 (a) On the interval $0 \le x \le 4$, the radius is $(4 - x)$ and the altitude is $\sqrt{x}$.

$$V = 2\pi \int_0^4 (4 - x)\sqrt{x}\, dx.$$

(b) The radius is $6 - x$ and $V = 2\pi \int_0^4 (6 - x)\sqrt{x}\, dx.$

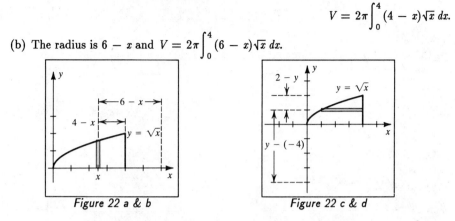

Figure 22 a & b   Figure 22 c & d

(c) On the interval $0 \le y \le 2$, the radius is $(2 - y)$ and the altitude is $(4 - y^2)$.

$$V = 2\pi \int_0^2 (2 - y)(4 - y^2)\, dy.$$

(d) The radius is $\left[y - (-4)\right]$ and $V = 2\pi \int_0^2 [y - (-4)](4 - y^2)\, dy.$

Note: In Exercises 23–26, refer to the figures of Exercises 31–34 in §6.2.

23 Let $y = 3 - x$ and $y = 3 - x^2$ be the two functions on $0 \le x \le 1$.

The radius is $(2 - x)$ and the altitude is $\left[(3 - x^2) - (3 - x)\right]$.

$$V = 2\pi \int_0^1 (2 - x)\left[(3 - x^2) - (3 - x)\right] dx.$$

24 Let $x = -\sqrt{1 - y}$ and $x = y + 1$ be the two functions on $-3 \le y \le 0$.

Let $x = -\sqrt{1 - y}$ and $x = \sqrt{1 - y}$ be the two functions on $0 \le y \le 1$.

For $y \le 0$, the radius is $(3 - y)$ and the altitude is $\left[(y + 1) - (-\sqrt{1 - y})\right]$.

For $y \ge 0$, the altitude is $\left[\sqrt{1 - y} - (-\sqrt{1 - y})\right] = 2\sqrt{1 - y}.$

$$V = 2\pi \int_{-3}^0 (3 - y)\left[(y + 1) - (-\sqrt{1 - y})\right] dy + 2\cdot 2\pi \int_0^1 (3 - y)\sqrt{1 - y}\, dy.$$

25 Let $y = \pm\sqrt{1 - x^2}$ be the two functions on $-1 \le x \le 1$.

The radius is $(5 - x)$ and the altitude is $\left[\sqrt{1 - x^2} - (-\sqrt{1 - x^2})\right] = 2\sqrt{1 - x^2}.$

$$V = 2\cdot 2\pi \int_{-1}^1 (5 - x)\sqrt{1 - x^2}\, dx.$$

26 Let $x = y^{3/2}$ and $x = y^{1/2}$ be the two functions in the first quadrant.

On $0 \le y \le 1$, the radius is $\left[y - (-1)\right]$ and the altitude is $(y^{1/2} - y^{3/2})$.

Using symmetry on $-1 \le x \le 1$, $V = 2\cdot 2\pi \int_0^1 [y - (-1)](y^{1/2} - y^{3/2})\, dy.$

27 (a) On $0 \le y \le \frac{1}{2}$, the altitude of a cylinder is $(4 - 1)$. On $\frac{1}{2} \le y \le 1$, the altitude

is $\left[(1/y^2) - 1\right]$. $V = 2\pi \int_0^{1/2} y(4 - 1) \, dy + 2\pi \int_{1/2}^1 y\left[(1/y^2) - 1\right] dy$.

(b) On $1 \le x \le 4$, the radius of a disk is $1/\sqrt{x}$. $V = \pi \int_1^4 \left(\frac{1}{\sqrt{x}}\right)^2 dx$.

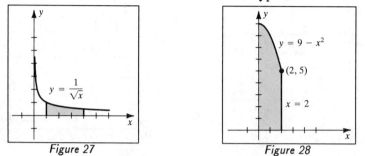

Figure 27   Figure 28

28 (a) On $0 \le y \le 5$, the altitude of a cylinder is $(2 - 0)$.

On $5 \le y \le 9$, the altitude is $\sqrt{9 - y}$. $V = 2\pi \int_0^5 y(2 - 0) \, dy + 2\pi \int_5^9 y\sqrt{9 - y} \, dy$.

(b) On $0 \le x \le 2$, the radius of a disk is $(9 - x^2)$. $V = \pi \int_0^2 (9 - x^2)^2 \, dx$.

29 (a) On $0 \le x \le 1$, the altitude of a cylinder is $\left[(x^2 + 2) - 0\right]$.

$$V = 2\pi \int_0^1 x(x^2 + 2) \, dx.$$

(b) On $0 \le y \le 2$, the radius of a disk is $(1 - 0)$. On $2 \le y \le 3$,

the outer radius of a disk is $(1 - 0)$ and the inner radius is $(\sqrt{y - 2} - 0)$.

$$V = \pi \int_0^2 (1)^2 \, dy + \pi \int_2^3 \left[(1)^2 - (\sqrt{y - 2})^2\right] dy.$$

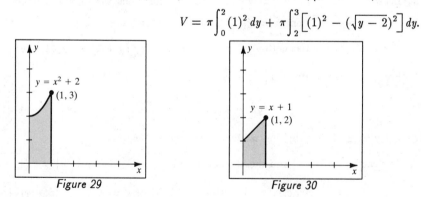

Figure 29   Figure 30

30 (a) On $0 \le x \le 1$, the altitude of a cylinder is $\left[(x + 1) - 0\right]$.

$$V = 2\pi \int_0^1 x(x + 1) \, dx.$$

(b) On $0 \le y \le 1$, the radius of a disk is $(1 - 0)$. On $1 \le y \le 2$,

the outer radius of a disk is $(1 - 0)$ and the inner radius is $\left[(y - 1) - 0\right]$.

$$V = \pi \int_0^1 (1)^2 \, dy + \pi \int_1^2 \left[(1)^2 - (y - 1)^2\right] dy.$$

$\boxed{31}$ The volume $V = 2\pi \int_0^6 x f(x)\, dx$. Let $g(x) = x f(x)$ to estimate V.

$T = 2\pi \cdot \frac{6-0}{2(6)} \{ g(0) + 2\left[g(1) + g(2) + g(3) + g(4) + g(5) \right] + g(6) \} =$

$\qquad \pi\left[0 \cdot 2 + 2(1 \cdot 1 + 2 \cdot 2 + 3 \cdot 4 + 4 \cdot 2 + 5 \cdot 2) + 6 \cdot 1 \right] = 76\pi \approx 238.76.$

$\boxed{32}$ The volume $V = 2\pi \int_0^8 x f(x)\, dx$. Let $g(x) = x f(x)$ to estimate V. $S =$

$2\pi \cdot \frac{8-0}{3(8)} \{ g(0) + 4g(1) + 2g(2) + 4g(3) + 2g(4) + 4g(5) + 2g(6) + 4g(7) + g(8) \}$

$= \frac{2\pi}{3} [0 \cdot 0 + 4(1 \cdot 1) + 2(2 \cdot 0) + 4(3 \cdot 2) + 2(4 \cdot 0) + 4(5 \cdot 3) + 2(6 \cdot 0) +$

$\qquad\qquad\qquad 4(7 \cdot 4) + (8 \cdot 0)] = \frac{2\pi}{3}(200) = \frac{400\pi}{3} \approx 418.88.$

$\boxed{33}$ (a) The x-intercepts occur at $x \approx 0.68,\ 1.44$.

(b) $V \approx 2\pi \int_{0.68}^{1.44} x(-x^4 + 2.21x^3 - 3.21x^2 + 4.42x - 2)\, dx$

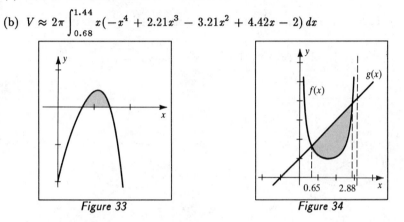

Figure 33   Figure 34

$\boxed{34}$ (a) $f(x) = \csc x - x - 1$; $f'(x) = -\csc x \cot x - 1$;

$\qquad x_{n+1} = x_n - \dfrac{\csc x_n - x_n - 1}{-\csc x_n \cot x_n - 1};$

$\qquad x_1 = 0.5,\ x_2 = 0.621590,\ x_3 = 0.649746,\ x_4 = 0.650751;$

$\qquad x_1 = 3.0,\ x_2 = 2.936644,\ x_3 = 2.893489,\ x_4 = 2.881633,\ x_5 = 2.880988;$

$\qquad\qquad\qquad\qquad\qquad\qquad\qquad\qquad\qquad\qquad x \approx 0.65,\ 2.88$

(b) $V \approx 2\pi \int_{0.65}^{2.88} x(x + 1 - \csc x)\, dx$. Let $f(x) = x(x + 1 - \csc x)$.

$\qquad T \approx (2\pi) \frac{2.88 - 0.65}{2(6)} \{ f(0.65) +$

$\qquad\qquad 2\left[f(1.022) + f(1.393) + f(1.765) + f(2.137) + f(2.508) \right] + f(2.88) \} \approx 34.1.$

$\boxed{\text{Exercises 6.4}}$

Note: Exercises 1–26: The first integral represents a general formula for the volume. In

Exercises 1–8, the vertical distance between the graphs of $y = \sqrt{x}$ and $y = -\sqrt{x}$ is

$\left[\sqrt{x} - (-\sqrt{x}) \right]$, denoted by $2\sqrt{x}$.

$\boxed{1}$ $V = \int_c^d s^2\, dx = \int_0^9 A(x)\, dx = \int_0^9 (2\sqrt{x})^2\, dx = 4\left[\frac{1}{2}x^2\right]_0^9 = 162.$

$\boxed{2}$ $V = \int_c^d lw\, dx = \int_0^9 A(x)\, dx = \int_0^9 2(2\sqrt{x})\, dx = 4\left[\frac{2}{3}x^{3/2}\right]_0^9 = 72.$

$\boxed{3}$ $V = \int_c^d \frac{1}{2}\pi r^2 \, dx = \int_0^9 A(x) \, dx = \int_0^9 \frac{1}{2}\pi(\sqrt{x})^2 \, dx = \frac{\pi}{2}\left[\frac{1}{2}x^2\right]_0^9 = \frac{81\pi}{4}.$

$\boxed{4}$ $V = \int_c^d \frac{1}{4}\pi r^2 \, dx = \int_0^9 A(x) \, dx = \int_0^9 \frac{1}{4}\pi(2\sqrt{x})^2 \, dx = \pi\left[\frac{1}{2}x^2\right]_0^9 = \frac{81\pi}{2}.$

$\boxed{5}$ $V = \int_c^d \frac{\sqrt{3}}{4}s^2 \, dx = \int_0^9 A(x) \, dx = \int_0^9 \frac{\sqrt{3}}{4}(2\sqrt{x})^2 \, dx = \sqrt{3}\left[\frac{1}{2}x^2\right]_0^9 = \frac{81\sqrt{3}}{2}.$

$\boxed{6}$ $V = \int_c^d \frac{1}{2}bh \, dx = \int_0^9 A(x) \, dx = \int_0^9 \frac{1}{2}(2\sqrt{x})\left[\frac{1}{4}(2\sqrt{x})\right] dx = \frac{1}{2}\left[\frac{1}{2}x^2\right]_0^9 = \frac{81}{4}.$

$\boxed{7}$ $V = \int_c^d \frac{1}{2}(B + b)h \, dx = \int_0^9 A(x) \, dx = \int_0^9 \frac{1}{2}\left[2\sqrt{x} + \frac{1}{2}(2\sqrt{x})\right]\left[\frac{1}{4}(2\sqrt{x})\right] dx =$

$$\frac{3}{4}\left[\frac{1}{2}x^2\right]_0^9 = \frac{243}{8}.$$

$\boxed{8}$ $V = \int_c^d bh \, dx = \int_0^9 A(x) \, dx = \int_0^9 (2\sqrt{x})\left[2(2\sqrt{x})\right] dx = 8\left[\frac{1}{2}x^2\right]_0^9 = 324.$

$\boxed{9}$ $V = \int_c^d s^2 \, dx = \int_{-a}^a A(x) \, dx = 2\int_0^a \left[\sqrt{a^2 - x^2} - (-\sqrt{a^2 - x^2})\right]^2 dx =$

$$8\left[a^2 x - \frac{1}{3}x^3\right]_0^a = \frac{16}{3}a^3.$$

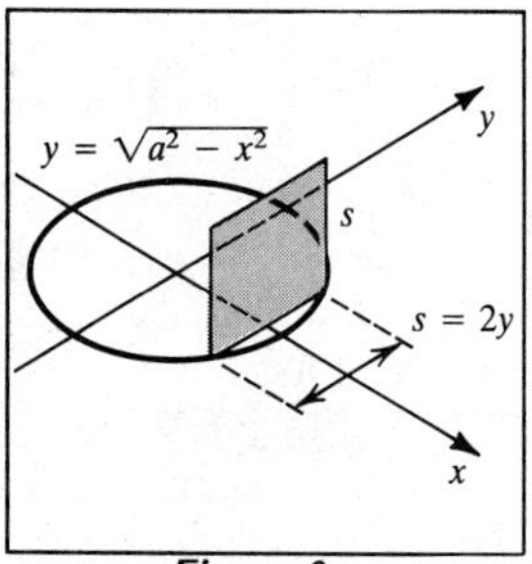

Figure 9

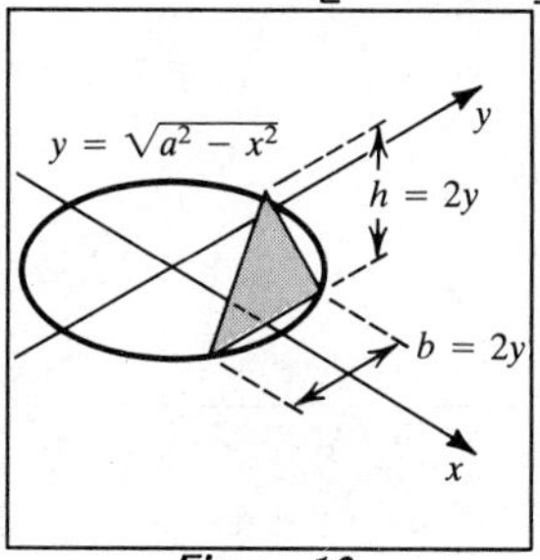

Figure 10

$\boxed{10}$ $V = \int_c^d \frac{1}{2}bh \, dx = \int_{-a}^a A(x) \, dx = 2\int_0^a \frac{1}{2}(2\sqrt{a^2 - x^2})(2\sqrt{a^2 - x^2}) \, dx =$

$$4\left[a^2 x - \frac{1}{3}x^3\right]_0^a = \frac{8}{3}a^3.$$

$\boxed{11}$ If $-2 \le x \le 2$, the hypotenuse of the cross-sectional triangle is $4 - x^2$;

its height and base are $\frac{1}{\sqrt{2}}(4 - x^2)$.

$$V = \int_c^d \frac{1}{2}bh \, dx = \int_{-2}^2 A(x) \, dx = 2\int_0^2 \frac{1}{2}\left[\frac{1}{\sqrt{2}}(4 - x^2)\right]\left[\frac{1}{\sqrt{2}}(4 - x^2)\right] dx =$$

$$\frac{1}{2}\int_0^2 (16 - 8x^2 + x^4) \, dx = \frac{1}{2}\left[16x - \frac{8}{3}x^3 + \frac{1}{5}x^5\right]_0^2 = \frac{128}{15}.$$

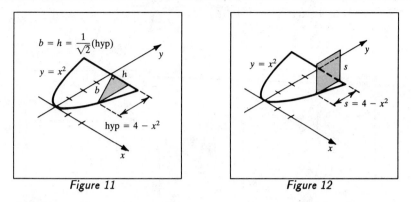

Figure 11   Figure 12

[12] $V = \int_c^d s^2\, dx = \int_{-2}^2 A(x)\, dx = 2\int_0^2 (4 - x^2)^2\, dx = 2\left[16x - \frac{8}{3}x^3 + \frac{1}{5}x^5\right]_0^2 = \frac{512}{15}.$

[13] The cross-sectional rectangle x units from O will have dimensions $2y$ by $4y$.

By Example 1, $y = \frac{ax}{2h}$. $\quad V = \int_c^d lw\, dx = \int_0^h A(x)\, dx = \int_0^h (4y)(2y)\, dx =$

$$\int_0^h \left(\frac{2ax}{h}\right)\left(\frac{ax}{h}\right) dx = \frac{2a^2}{h^2}\left[\frac{1}{3}x^3\right]_0^h = \frac{2}{3}a^2 h.$$

[14] If $0 \le x \le 1$, the semicircle's base diameter has length $\sqrt{x} - x$. Thus, the radius is

$\frac{1}{2}(\sqrt{x} - x)$. $\quad V = \int_c^d \frac{1}{2}\pi r^2\, dx = \int_0^1 A(x)\, dx = \int_0^1 \frac{1}{2}\pi\left[\frac{1}{2}(\sqrt{x} - x)\right]^2 dx =$

$$\frac{\pi}{8}\int_0^1 (x - 2x^{3/2} + x^2)\, dx = \frac{\pi}{8}\left[\frac{1}{2}x^2 - \frac{4}{5}x^{5/2} + \frac{1}{3}x^3\right]_0^1 = \frac{\pi}{240}.$$

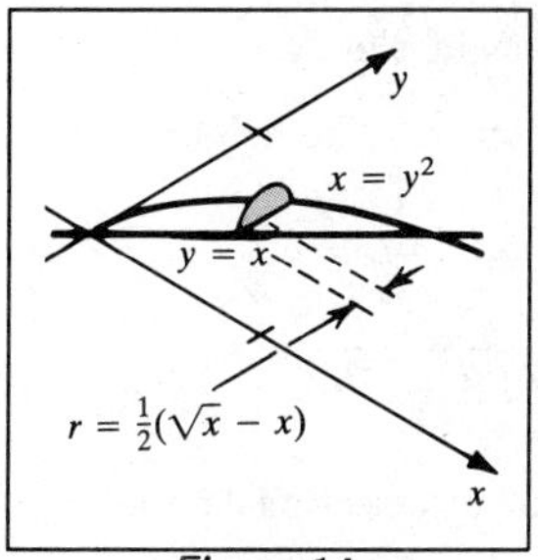

Figure 14 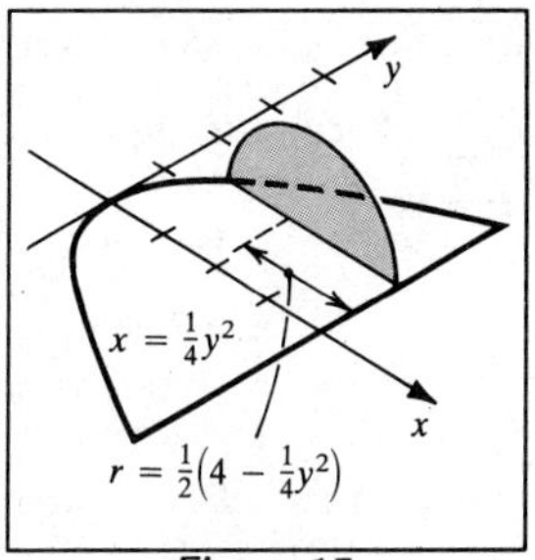   Figure 15

[15] If $-4 \le y \le 4$, the base diameter of the semicircle has length $4 - \frac{1}{4}y^2$.

$$V = \int_c^d \frac{1}{2}\pi r^2\, dy = \int_{-4}^4 A(y)\, dy = 2\int_0^4 \frac{1}{2}\pi\left[\frac{1}{2}(4 - \frac{1}{4}y^2)\right]^2 dy =$$

$$\frac{\pi}{4}\int_0^4 (16 - 2y^2 + \frac{1}{16}y^4)\, dy = \frac{\pi}{4}\left[16y - \frac{2}{3}y^3 + \frac{1}{80}y^5\right]_0^4 = \frac{128\pi}{15}.$$

$\boxed{16}$ $V = \int_c^d bh \, dy = \int_0^2 A(y) \, dy = \int_0^2 \left[\sqrt{16y} - (-\sqrt{16y})\right]\left[2(\sqrt{16y} - (-\sqrt{16y}))\right] dy =$

$$128 \int_0^2 y \, dy = 128 \left[\tfrac{1}{2}y^2\right]_0^2 = 256.$$

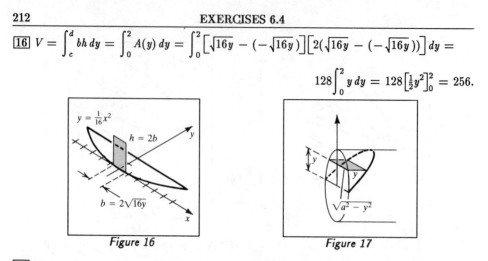

Figure 16   Figure 17

$\boxed{17}$ The wedge can be considered as a solid whose base is a semicircle of radius a and every cross section of the wedge, by a plane perpendicular to the vertical radius, is a rectangle. Using $x^2 + y^2 = a^2$ for the circle, then if $0 \le y \le a$, the length of this rectangle is $2\sqrt{a^2 - y^2}$. Because of the 45° cut, the width of this rectangle is y.

$V = \int_c^d lw \, dy = \int_0^a A(y) \, dy = \int_0^a \left[\sqrt{a^2 - y^2} - (-\sqrt{a^2 - y^2})\right] y \, dy =$

$2 \int_0^a \sqrt{a^2 - y^2} \, y \, dy = -\int_{a^2}^0 \sqrt{u} \, du \ \{u = a^2 - y^2\} = -\left[\tfrac{2}{3}u^{3/2}\right]_{a^2}^0 =$

$$-\tfrac{2}{3}(0 - a^3) = \tfrac{2}{3}a^3.$$

Alternate solution: If the x-axis is the intersection of the two cuts, we can sum the areas of the isosceles triangles from $x = -a$ to $x = a$. The height of each triangle is $y = \sqrt{a^2 - x^2}$, which is also the base. $V = \int_c^d \tfrac{1}{2}bh \, dx =$

$$\int_{-a}^a A(x) \, dx = 2 \int_0^a \tfrac{1}{2} \sqrt{a^2 - x^2} \sqrt{a^2 - x^2} \, dx = \left[a^2 x - \tfrac{1}{3}x^3\right]_0^a = \tfrac{2}{3}a^3.$$

$\boxed{18}$ Position the x-axis with the origin at the point of intersection of the cylindrical axes and perpendicular to the plane they lie in. The figure depicts only $\tfrac{1}{8}$ of the entire solid, the nearest $\tfrac{1}{4}$ of the top half. Restricting our attention to this portion, we see that for $x \in [0, a]$, the plane through x perpendicular to the x-axis cuts the solid in a square. If s is the length of a side, then $s = \sqrt{a^2 - x^2}$ (see the small triangle).

$$V = 8 \int_c^d s^2 \, dx = 8 \int_0^a A(x) \, dx = 8 \int_0^a (\sqrt{a^2 - x^2})^2 \, dx = 8\left[a^2 x - \tfrac{1}{3}x^3\right]_0^a = \tfrac{16}{3}a^3.$$

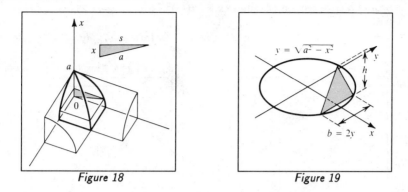

Figure 18　　　　　　　　Figure 19

19 $V = \int_c^d \tfrac{1}{2}bh\,dx = \int_{-a}^a A(x)\,dx = \int_{-a}^a \tfrac{1}{2}\left[\sqrt{a^2 - x^2} - \left(-\sqrt{a^2 - x^2}\right)\right]h\,dx$

$= h\int_{-a}^a \sqrt{a^2 - x^2}\,dx = h(\tfrac{1}{2}\pi a^2) = \tfrac{1}{2}\pi a^2 h,$

since the last integral represents the area of a semicircle of radius a.

20 The radius of each circle is $r = \tfrac{1}{2}(6 + \tfrac{1}{36}s^2)$. $V = \int_c^d \pi r^2\,dx = \int_0^{24} A(s)\,ds =$

$\int_0^{24} \pi\left[\tfrac{1}{2}(6 + \tfrac{1}{36}s^2)\right]^2 ds = \pi\int_0^{24}(9 + \tfrac{1}{12}s^2 + \tfrac{1}{5184}s^4)\,ds = \left[9s + \tfrac{1}{36}s^3 + \tfrac{1}{25{,}920}s^5\right]_0^{24}$

$= \pi(216 + 384 + 307.2) \approx (907.2)\pi \approx 2850.1 \text{ in.}^3.$

21 We place a coordinate line along the 4-cm side with the origin at the vertex as shown. Consider a point on this line x units from the vertex. A plane through this point, perpendicular to the coordinate line, intersects the solid in a triangular cross section. Let b be the base and h the height of this triangle. We can express b and h in terms of x using similar triangles. From *Figure 21b*, $b = \tfrac{2}{4}x$. From *Figure 21c*,

$h = \tfrac{3}{4}x$. $V = \int_c^d \tfrac{1}{2}bh\,dx = \int_0^4 A(x)\,dx = \int_0^4 \tfrac{1}{2}(\tfrac{2}{4}x)(\tfrac{3}{4}x)\,dx = \tfrac{3}{16}\left[\tfrac{1}{3}x^3\right]_0^4 = 4 \text{ cm}^3.$

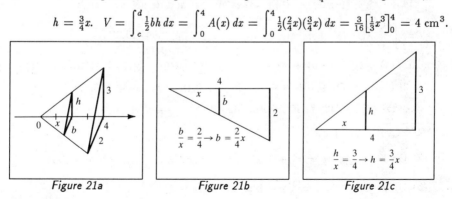

Figure 21a　　　　　　Figure 21b　　　　　　Figure 21c

22 Place each solid so that an altitude is on the x-axis, extending from 0 to h.

If $A(x)$ and $B(x)$ are the cross-sectional areas of the two solids,

then $A(x) = B(x)$ for every x in $[0, h]$, and hence $\int_0^h A(x)\,dx = \int_0^h B(x)\,dx.$

Thus, by (6.13), the two volumes are equal.

23 The area of a cross section of radius $\frac{1}{2}x$ is $\frac{1}{2}\pi(\frac{1}{2}x)^2$. From *Figure 23*, we see that

$$x = a - y. \quad V = \int_c^d \tfrac{1}{2}\pi r^2\, dy = \int_0^a A(y)\, dy = \int_0^a \tfrac{1}{2}\pi\left[\tfrac{1}{2}(a - y)\right]^2 dy =$$

$$\tfrac{\pi}{8}\left[a^2 y - ay^2 + \tfrac{1}{3}y^3\right]_0^a = \tfrac{\pi}{24}a^3.$$

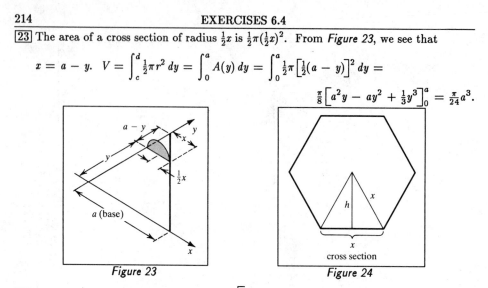

Figure 23   Figure 24

24 One-sixth the area of a cross section is $\frac{\sqrt{3}}{4}x^2$ (an equilateral triangle).

$$V = 6\int_c^d \tfrac{\sqrt{3}}{4}s^2\, dy = 6\int_0^a A(y)\, dy = 6\int_0^a \tfrac{\sqrt{3}}{4}(a - y)^2\, dy =$$

$$\tfrac{3\sqrt{3}}{2}\left[a^2 y - ay^2 + \tfrac{1}{3}y^3\right]_0^a = \tfrac{\sqrt{3}}{2}a^3.$$

25 The areas of cross sections of typical disks and washers are

$\pi\,[f(x)]^2$ and $\pi\,\{\,[f(x)]^2 - [g(x)]^2\,\}$, respectively.

   In each case, the integrand represents $A(x)$ in (6.13).

26 Center the top of the pool at $(0, 0)$ with $x = -14$ at A and $x = 14$ at B.

The equation of the perimeter of the pool is given by $x^2 + y^2 = 14^2$. Hence, the width of a rectangular, vertical cross section of the pool perpendicular to the x-axis is

$$\left[\sqrt{14^2 - x^2} - (-\sqrt{14^2 - x^2}\,)\right] = 2\sqrt{196 - x^2} \text{ and its height is } h(x).$$

$$V = \int_{-14}^{14} A(x)\, dx, \text{ where } A(x) = 2\sqrt{196 - x^2}\,h(x). \quad T = \tfrac{14 - (-14)}{2(7)}.$$

$$\{\,A(-14) + 2\big[A(-10) + A(-6) + A(-2) + A(2) + A(6) + A(10)\big] + A(14)\,\}$$

$$\approx 2\big[0 + 2(68.59 + 101.19 + 138.56 + 180.13 + 202.39 + 166.57) + 0\big]$$

$$= 4(857.43) = 3429.72 \text{ ft}^3. \text{ Also, } 3429.72 \text{ ft}^3 \times \tfrac{1}{0.134} \text{ (gal/ft}^3) \approx 25{,}595 \text{ gal.}$$

Exercises 6.5

1 (a) On $1 \le x \le 3$, $y = x^3 + 1 \Rightarrow y' = 3x^2$ and $L = \int_1^3 \sqrt{1 + (3x^2)^2}\, dx$.

   (b) On $2 \le y \le 28$, $x = \sqrt[3]{y - 1} \Rightarrow x' = \tfrac{1}{3}(y - 1)^{-2/3}$ and

$$L = \int_2^{28} \sqrt{1 + \left[\tfrac{1}{3}(y - 1)^{-2/3}\right]^2}\, dy.$$

2 (a) On $8 \le x \le 27$, $y = x^{2/3} \Rightarrow y' = \tfrac{2}{3}x^{-1/3}$ and $L = \int_8^{27} \sqrt{1 + (\tfrac{2}{3}x^{-1/3})^2}\, dx$.

(b) On $4 \le y \le 9$, $x = y^{3/2} \Rightarrow x' = \frac{3}{2}y^{1/2}$ and $L = \int_4^9 \sqrt{1 + (\frac{3}{2}y^{1/2})^2}\, dy$.

$\boxed{3}$ (a) On $-3 \le x \le -1$, $y = 4 - x^2 \Rightarrow y' = -2x$ and $L = \int_{-3}^{-1} \sqrt{1 + (-2x)^2}\, dx$.

(b) On $-5 \le y \le 3$, $x = -\sqrt{4 - y} \Rightarrow x' = -\frac{1}{2}(4 - y)^{-1/2}(-1)$ and
$$L = \int_{-5}^3 \sqrt{1 + \left[\frac{1}{2}(4 - y)^{-1/2}\right]^2}\, dy.$$

$\boxed{4}$ (a) On $-4 \le x \le -1$, $y = x^{-2} \Rightarrow y' = -2x^{-3}$ and $L = \int_{-4}^{-1} \sqrt{1 + (-2x^{-3})^2}\, dx$.

(b) On $\frac{1}{16} \le y \le 1$, $x = -y^{-1/2} \Rightarrow x' = \frac{1}{2}y^{-3/2}$ and $L = \int_{1/16}^1 \sqrt{1 + (\frac{1}{2}y^{-3/2})^2}\, dy$.

$\boxed{5}$ $y = f(x) = \frac{2}{3}x^{2/3} \Rightarrow f'(x) = \frac{4}{9}x^{-1/3}$. Thus, $\sqrt{1 + [f'(x)]^2} = \sqrt{1 + \frac{16}{81}x^{-2/3}} =$

$\sqrt{x^{-2/3}(x^{2/3} + \frac{16}{81})} = x^{-1/3}\sqrt{x^{2/3} + \frac{16}{81}}$ and $L = \int_1^8 x^{-1/3}\sqrt{x^{2/3} + \frac{16}{81}}\, dx$.

$u = x^{2/3} + \frac{16}{81} \Rightarrow \frac{3}{2}\, du = x^{-1/3}\, dx$.

$x = 1 \Rightarrow u = 1 + \frac{16}{81} = c$ and $x = 8 \Rightarrow u = 4 + \frac{16}{81} = d$.
$$L = \frac{3}{2}\int_c^d u^{1/2}\, du = d^{3/2} - c^{3/2} = (4 + \tfrac{16}{81})^{3/2} - (1 + \tfrac{16}{81})^{3/2} \approx 7.29.$$

$\boxed{6}$ $(y + 1)^2 = (x - 4)^3$ and $y + 1 \ge 0$ from A to $B \Rightarrow$

$y = f(x) = -1 + (x - 4)^{3/2} \Rightarrow 1 + [f'(x)]^2 = 1 + \left[\frac{3}{2}(x - 4)^{1/2}\right]^2 = \frac{9}{4}x - 8$.
$$L = \int_5^8 (\tfrac{9}{4}x - 8)^{1/2}\, dx = \frac{8}{27}\left[(\tfrac{9}{4}x - 8)^{3/2}\right]_5^8 = \frac{8}{27}\left[10^{3/2} - (\tfrac{13}{4})^{3/2}\right] \approx 7.63.$$

$\boxed{7}$ $f'(x) = -\frac{3}{2}x^{1/2} \Rightarrow 1 + [f'(x)]^2 = 1 + \frac{9}{4}x$.
$$L = \int_1^4 (1 + \tfrac{9}{4}x)^{1/2}\, dx = \frac{8}{27}\left[(1 + \tfrac{9}{4}x)^{3/2}\right]_1^4 = \frac{8}{27}\left[10^{3/2} - (\tfrac{13}{4})^{3/2}\right] \approx 7.63.$$

$\boxed{8}$ $1 + [f'(x)]^2 = 1 + 16x^{-2/3} = x^{-2/3}(x^{2/3} + 16)$. Note that $\sqrt{x^{-2/3}} = |x^{-1/3}| =$

$-x^{-1/3}$ since $x < 0$. $L = \int_{-8}^{-1} (-x^{-1/3})(x^{2/3} + 16)^{1/2}\, dx =$

$-\frac{3}{2}\int_{20}^{17} u^{1/2}\, du \; \{ u = x^{2/3} + 16 \text{ and } -\frac{3}{2}\, du = -x^{-1/3}\, dx \} = -\frac{3}{2}\left[\frac{2}{3}u^{3/2}\right]_{20}^{17} =$
$$20^{3/2} - 17^{3/2} \approx 19.35.$$

$\boxed{9}$ $y' = f'(x) = \frac{1}{4}x^2 - 1/x^2 \Rightarrow 1 + [f'(x)]^2 = 1 + (\frac{1}{16}x^4 - \frac{1}{2} + 1/x^4) =$

$(\frac{1}{4}x^2 + 1/x^2)^2$. Hence, $L = \int_1^2 (\frac{1}{4}x^2 + x^{-2})\, dx = \left[\frac{1}{12}x^3 - \frac{1}{x}\right]_1^2 = \frac{13}{12}$.

$\boxed{10}$ $y' = f'(x) = \dfrac{1}{4x^2} - x^2 \Rightarrow 1 + [f'(x)]^2 = 1 + \left(\dfrac{1}{16x^4} - \dfrac{1}{2} + x^4\right) = \left(\dfrac{1}{4x^2} + x^2\right)^2$.

Hence, $L = \int_2^3 (\frac{1}{4}x^{-2} + x^2)\, dx = \left[-\dfrac{1}{4x} + \dfrac{1}{3}x^3\right]_2^3 = \frac{153}{24}$.

$\boxed{11}$ $x = g(y) = \dfrac{15 + y^8}{30y^3} = \frac{1}{2}y^{-3} + \frac{1}{30}y^5 \Rightarrow g'(y) = -\frac{3}{2}y^{-4} + \frac{1}{6}y^4 \Rightarrow$

$1 + [g'(y)]^2 = 1 + (\frac{9}{4}y^{-8} - \frac{1}{2} + \frac{1}{36}y^8) = (\frac{3}{2}y^{-4} + \frac{1}{6}y^4)^2.$

$$\text{Hence, } L = \int_1^2 (\tfrac{3}{2}y^{-4} + \tfrac{1}{6}y^4)\, dy = \left[-\tfrac{1}{2}y^{-3} + \tfrac{1}{30}y^5 \right]_1^2 = \tfrac{353}{240}.$$

$\boxed{12}$ $x = g(y) = \frac{1}{16}y^4 + \frac{1}{2}y^{-2} \Rightarrow g'(y) = \frac{1}{4}y^3 - y^{-3} \Rightarrow$

$1 + [g'(y)]^2 = 1 + (\frac{1}{16}y^6 - \frac{1}{2} + y^{-6}) = (\frac{1}{4}y^3 + y^{-3})^2.$

Since $y < 0$ on $[-2, -1]$, $\sqrt{1 + [g'(y)]^2} = -(\frac{1}{4}y^3 + y^{-3})$ and

$$L = -\int_{-2}^{-1} (\tfrac{1}{4}y^3 + y^{-3})\, dy = -\left[\tfrac{1}{16}y^4 - \tfrac{1}{2y^2} \right]_{-2}^{-1} = \tfrac{21}{16}.$$

$\boxed{13}$ $x = g(y) = 4 + \frac{7}{2}y - y^3 \Rightarrow 1 + [g'(y)]^2 = 1 + (\frac{7}{2} - 3y^2)^2.$ Hence,

$$L = \int_0^2 \sqrt{1 + (\tfrac{7}{2} - 3y^2)^2}\, dy.$$

$\boxed{14}$ $y = f(x) = 1 - \frac{4}{7}x^3 + \frac{11}{7}x \Rightarrow 1 + [f'(x)]^2 = 1 + (-\frac{12}{7}x^2 + \frac{11}{7})^2.$ Hence,

$$L = \int_0^1 \sqrt{1 + (-\tfrac{12}{7}x^2 + \tfrac{11}{7})^2}\, dx.$$

$\boxed{15}$ Let $y = x$ intersect the graph at $x = a$, $a > 0$. The point of intersection occurs

when $a^{2/3} + a^{2/3} = 1$, or $a = (\frac{1}{2})^{3/2}$. Since $y > 0$, $y = +(1 - x^{2/3})^{3/2}$ and

$y' = -\dfrac{(1 - x^{2/3})^{1/2}}{x^{1/3}}.$ Thus, $\sqrt{1 + (y')^2} = \left(1 + \dfrac{1 - x^{2/3}}{x^{2/3}}\right)^{1/2} = x^{-1/3}.$

By symmetry, $L = 8\displaystyle\int_a^1 x^{-1/3}\, dx = 8\left[\tfrac{3}{2}x^{2/3}\right]_a^1 = 12\{1 - \left[(\tfrac{1}{2})^{3/2}\right]^{2/3}\} = 6.$

$\{$ Note that if $L = 4\displaystyle\int_0^1 x^{-1/3}\, dx = 6$ is used, the integral is improper. $\}$

$\boxed{16}$ $f(x) = \frac{1}{10}x^5 + \frac{1}{6}x^{-3} \Rightarrow f'(x) = \frac{1}{2}x^4 - \frac{1}{2}x^{-4} \Rightarrow$

$1 + [f'(x)]^2 = 1 + (\frac{1}{4}x^8 - \frac{1}{2} + \frac{1}{4}x^{-8}) = \left[\frac{1}{2}(x^4 + x^{-4})\right]^2 \Rightarrow$

$$L = \tfrac{1}{2}\int_1^2 (x^4 + x^{-4})\, dx = \tfrac{1}{2}\left[\tfrac{1}{5}x^5 - \tfrac{1}{3x^3}\right]_1^2 = \tfrac{779}{240}.$$

$\boxed{17}$ (a) $f'(x) = \frac{2}{3}x^{-1/3} \Rightarrow 1 + [f'(x)]^2 = 1 + \frac{4}{9}x^{-2/3} = (x^{2/3} + \frac{4}{9})x^{-2/3} \Rightarrow$

$s(x) = \displaystyle\int_1^x \sqrt{t^{2/3} + \tfrac{4}{9}}\, (t^{-1/3})\, dt = \left[(t^{2/3} + \tfrac{4}{9})^{3/2}\right]_1^x =$

$(x^{2/3} + \frac{4}{9})^{3/2} - (1 + \frac{4}{9})^{3/2} = \left(\dfrac{9x^{2/3} + 4}{9}\right)^{3/2} - \left(\dfrac{13}{9}\right)^{3/2} =$

$$\tfrac{1}{27}\left[(9x^{2/3} + 4)^{3/2} - 13^{3/2}\right] \{(\tfrac{1}{9})^{3/2} = \tfrac{1}{27}\}.$$

(b) $\Delta s = s(1.1) - s(1) = \frac{1}{27}\left[9(1.1)^{2/3} + 4\right]^{3/2} - 13^{3/2}] \approx 0.1196.$

By the fundamental theorem of calculus, $s'(x) = \sqrt{x^{2/3} + \tfrac{4}{9}}\,(x^{-1/3}).$

$ds = \sqrt{1 + [f'(x)]^2}\, dx = s'(x)\, dx = s'(1)(0.1) = \sqrt{(1)^{2/3} + \tfrac{4}{9}}\,(1)^{-1/3}(0.1) =$

$$\dfrac{\sqrt{13}}{30} \approx 0.1202.$$

$\boxed{18}$ (a) $f'(x) = \frac{3}{2}x^{1/2} \Rightarrow 1 + [f'(x)]^2 = 1 + \frac{9}{4}x \Rightarrow s(x) = \int_1^x \sqrt{1 + \frac{9}{4}t}\, dt =$

$$\frac{8}{27}\left[(1 + \frac{9}{4}t)^{3/2}\right]_1^x = \frac{8}{27}\left[(1 + \frac{9}{4}x)^{3/2} - (1 + \frac{9}{4})^{3/2}\right] =$$

$$\frac{8}{27}\left[\left(\frac{4 + 9x}{4}\right)^{3/2} - \left(\frac{13}{4}\right)^{3/2}\right] = \frac{1}{27}\left[(9x + 4)^{3/2} - 13^{3/2}\right]\{(\frac{1}{4})^{3/2} = \frac{1}{8}\}.$$

(b) $\Delta s = s(1.1) - s(1) = \frac{1}{27}(13.9^{3/2} - 13^{3/2}) \approx 0.1834.$

By the fundamental theorem of calculus, $s'(x) = \sqrt{1 + \frac{9}{4}x}.$

$$ds = \sqrt{1 + [f'(x)]^2}\, dx = s'(x)\, dx = s'(1)(0.1) = \sqrt{1 + \frac{9}{4}(1)}(0.1) = \frac{\sqrt{13}}{20} \approx 0.1803.$$

$\boxed{19}$ $\Delta s \approx ds = \sqrt{1 + [f'(x)]^2}\, dx = \sqrt{1 + (2x)^2}\, dx.$ With $x = 2$, $dx = 0.1$,

$$ds = \sqrt{17}(0.1) \approx 0.4123. \quad d(A, B) = \sqrt{0.1^2 + 0.41^2} = \sqrt{0.1781} \approx 0.4220.$$

$\boxed{20}$ $\Delta s \approx ds = \sqrt{1 + [f'(x)]^2}\, dx = \sqrt{1 + (-3x^2)^2}\, dx.$ With $x = 1$, $dx = 0.1$,

$$ds = \sqrt{10}(0.1) \approx 0.3162. \quad d(A, B) = \sqrt{0.1^2 + 0.331^2} = \sqrt{0.119561} \approx 0.3458.$$

$\boxed{21}$ $f(x) = \cos x$, $ds = \sqrt{1 + (-\sin x)^2}\, dx.$

With $x = \frac{\pi}{6}$ and $dx = \frac{31\pi}{180} - \frac{\pi}{6}$, $ds = \sqrt{1 + (-\frac{1}{2})^2}(\frac{\pi}{180}) = \frac{\pi\sqrt{5}}{360} \approx 0.0195.$

$\boxed{22}$ $f(x) = \sin x$, $ds = \sqrt{1 + (\cos x)^2}\, dx.$

With $x = 0$ and $dx = \frac{\pi}{90} - 0$, $ds = \sqrt{1 + (1)^2}(\frac{\pi}{90}) = \frac{\pi\sqrt{2}}{90} \approx 0.0494.$

$\boxed{23}$ $L = \int_{-2}^2 \sqrt{1 + [f'(x)]^2}\, dx = \int_{-2}^2 \sqrt{1 + (2x + 1)^2}\, dx = \int_{-2}^2 g(x)\, dx.$

$S = \frac{2 - (-2)}{3(4)}\left[g(-2) + 4g(-1) + 2g(0) + 4g(1) + g(2)\right] =$

$$\frac{1}{3}(\sqrt{10} + 4\sqrt{2} + 2\sqrt{2} + 4\sqrt{10} + \sqrt{26}) \approx 9.80.$$

$\boxed{24}$ $L = \int_0^2 \sqrt{1 + [f'(x)]^2}\, dx = \int_0^2 \sqrt{1 + (3x^2)^2}\, dx = \int_0^2 g(x)\, dx.$

$S = \frac{2 - 0}{3(4)}\left[g(0) + 4g(\frac{1}{2}) + 2g(1) + 4g(\frac{3}{2}) + g(2)\right] =$

$$\frac{1}{6}\left[1 + 4(1.25) + 2\sqrt{10} + 4\sqrt{46.5625} + \sqrt{145}\right] \approx 8.61.$$

$\boxed{25}$ $L = \int_0^{\pi/2} \sqrt{1 + [f'(x)]^2}\, dx = \int_0^{\pi/2} \sqrt{1 + (\cos x)^2}\, dx = \int_0^{\pi/2} g(x)\, dx.$

$S = \frac{\pi/2 - 0}{3(4)}\left[g(0) + 4g(\frac{\pi}{8}) + 2g(\frac{\pi}{4}) + 4g(\frac{3\pi}{8}) + g(\frac{\pi}{2})\right] \approx$

$$\frac{\pi}{24}\left[\sqrt{2} + 4(1.36) + 2(1.22) + 4(1.07) + 1\right] \approx \frac{\pi}{24}(14.57) \approx 1.91.$$

$\boxed{26}$ $L = \int_0^{\pi/4} \sqrt{1 + [f'(x)]^2}\, dx = \int_0^{\pi/4} \sqrt{1 + (\sec^2 x)^2}\, dx = \int_0^{\pi/4} g(x)\, dx.$

$S = \frac{\pi/4 - 0}{3(4)}\left[g(0) + 4g(\frac{\pi}{16}) + 2g(\frac{\pi}{8}) + 4g(\frac{3\pi}{16}) + g(\frac{\pi}{4})\right] \approx$

$$\frac{\pi}{48}\left[\sqrt{2} + 4(1.44) + 2(1.54) + 4(1.76) + \sqrt{5}\right] \approx \frac{\pi}{48}(19.53) \approx 1.28.$$

$\boxed{27}$ (a) $d_1 = d_4 = \sqrt{(\frac{\pi}{4})^2 + (\frac{1}{\sqrt{2}})^2} \approx 1.0568.$

$$d_2 = d_3 = \sqrt{(\frac{\pi}{4})^2 + (1 - \frac{1}{\sqrt{2}})^2} \approx 0.8382 \Rightarrow \text{sum} \approx 3.79.$$

(b) It is smaller because it is the sum of the straight line distances between the points, but will approach the exact arc length as n increases.

$\boxed{28}$ (a) $\displaystyle\int_0^{\pi} \sqrt{1 + \cos^2 x}\, dx$

(b) Let $f(x) = \sqrt{1 + \cos^2 x}$.

$$T = \tfrac{\pi - 0}{2(4)}\{f(0) + 2\left[f(\tfrac{\pi}{4}) + f(\tfrac{\pi}{2}) + f(\tfrac{3\pi}{4})\right] + f(\pi)\} \approx 3.82.$$

$\boxed{29}$ $y = f(x) = 2\sqrt{x},\ x > 0 \Rightarrow f'(x) = \frac{1}{\sqrt{x}}.$

$$S = \int_a^b 2\pi f(x)\sqrt{1 + [f'(x)]^2}\, dx = 2\pi\int_0^1 2\sqrt{x}\,\sqrt{1 + \tfrac{1}{x}}\, dx = 4\pi\int_0^1 \sqrt{x + 1}\, dx =$$

$$4\pi\left[\tfrac{2}{3}(x+1)^{3/2}\right]_0^1 = \tfrac{8\pi}{3}(2^{3/2} - 1) \approx 15.32.$$

$\boxed{30}$ $S = 2\pi\displaystyle\int_1^2 x^3\sqrt{1 + (3x^2)^2}\, dx = 2\pi\left[\tfrac{1}{36}\cdot\tfrac{2}{3}(1 + 9x^4)^{3/2}\right]_1^2$

$$\{u = 1 + 9x^4,\ \tfrac{1}{36}\, du = x^3\, dx\} = \tfrac{\pi}{27}(145^{3/2} - 10^{3/2}) \approx 199.48.$$

$\boxed{31}$ $f(x) = \tfrac{1}{4}x^4 + \tfrac{1}{8}x^{-2} \Rightarrow f'(x) = x^3 - \tfrac{1}{4}x^{-3} \Rightarrow 1 + [f'(x)]^2 = x^6 + \tfrac{1}{2} + x^{-6} =$

$(x^3 + \tfrac{1}{4}x^{-3})^2.$ $S = 2\pi\displaystyle\int_1^2 (\tfrac{1}{4}x^4 + \tfrac{1}{8}x^{-2})(x^3 + \tfrac{1}{4}x^{-3})\, dx =$

$2\pi\displaystyle\int_1^2 (\tfrac{1}{4}x^7 + \tfrac{3}{16}x + \tfrac{1}{32}x^{-5})\, dx = 2\pi\left[\tfrac{1}{32}x^8 + \tfrac{3}{32}x^2 - \tfrac{1}{128}x^{-4}\right]_1^2 =$

$$\tfrac{2\pi}{128}\left[4x^8 + 12x^2 - x^{-4}\right]_1^2 = \tfrac{\pi}{64}(\tfrac{17{,}151}{16} - 15) = \tfrac{\pi}{64}(\tfrac{16{,}911}{16}) \approx 51.88.$$

$\boxed{32}$ $f(x) = 2\sqrt{x + 1} \Rightarrow 1 + [f'(x)]^2 = 1 + 1/(x + 1).$

$$S = 2\pi\int_0^3 2\sqrt{x + 1}\,\sqrt{1 + \tfrac{1}{x + 1}}\, dx = 4\pi\int_0^3 \sqrt{x + 2}\, dx = 4\pi\left[\tfrac{2}{3}(x + 2)^{3/2}\right]_0^3 =$$

$$\tfrac{8\pi}{3}(5^{3/2} - 2^{3/2}) \approx 69.97.$$

$\boxed{33}$ $g(y) = \tfrac{1}{8}y^3 \Rightarrow 1 + [g'(y)]^2 = 1 + \tfrac{9}{64}y^4 = \tfrac{1}{64}(64 + 9y^4).$

$$S = 2\pi\int_2^4 \tfrac{1}{8}y^3\left(\tfrac{1}{8}\sqrt{64 + 9y^4}\right) dy = \tfrac{\pi}{32}\left[\tfrac{1}{36}\cdot\tfrac{2}{3}(64 + 9y^4)^{3/2}\right]_2^4 \ \{u = 64 + 9y^4,$$

$$\tfrac{1}{36}\, du = y^3\, dy\} = \tfrac{\pi}{1728}(2368^{3/2} - 208^{3/2}) = \tfrac{\pi}{1728}\left[(64\cdot 37)^{3/2} - (16\cdot 13)^{3/2}\right] =$$

$$\tfrac{\pi}{1728}\left[512(37)^{3/2} - 64(13)^{3/2}\right] = \tfrac{\pi}{27}\left[8(37)^{3/2} - 13^{3/2}\right] \approx 204.04.$$

$\boxed{34}$ $g(y) = 4\sqrt{y} \Rightarrow 1 + [g'(y)]^2 = 1 + \tfrac{4}{y}.$ $S = 2\pi\displaystyle\int_1^9 4\sqrt{y}\,\sqrt{1 + \tfrac{4}{y}}\, dy =$

$$8\pi\int_1^9 \sqrt{y + 4}\, dy = 8\pi\left[\tfrac{2}{3}(y + 4)^{3/2}\right]_1^9 = \tfrac{16\pi}{3}(13^{3/2} - 5^{3/2}) \approx 598.02.$$

$\boxed{35}$ The entire surface is generated when the arc between the points $(3, 4)$ and $(0, 5)$ is revolved about the y-axis.

$$x > 0 \Rightarrow g(y) = \sqrt{25 - y^2} \Rightarrow 1 + [g'(y)]^2 = 1 + \left(\frac{-y}{\sqrt{25 - y^2}}\right)^2 = \frac{25}{25 - y^2}.$$

$$S = 2\pi \int_4^5 \sqrt{25 - y^2} \sqrt{\frac{25}{25 - y^2}}\, dy = 2\pi \int_4^5 5\, dy = 10\pi(5 - 4) = 10\pi.$$

[36] $y > 0 \Rightarrow f(x) = \sqrt{25 - x^2} \Rightarrow 1 + [f'(x)]^2 = 1 + \left(\frac{-x}{\sqrt{25 - x^2}}\right)^2 = \frac{25}{25 - x^2}.$

$$S = 2 \cdot 2\pi \int_0^3 \sqrt{25 - x^2} \sqrt{\frac{25}{25 - x^2}}\, dx = 4\pi \int_0^3 5\, dy = 20\pi(3 - 0) = 60\pi.$$

[37] The cone can be obtained by revolving the line segment with endpoints (0, 0) and

(h, r) about the x-axis. Then, $y = \frac{r}{h}x$ and $1 + [y']^2 = 1 + \frac{r^2}{h^2} = \frac{h^2 + r^2}{h^2} \Rightarrow$

$$S = 2\pi \int_0^a \frac{r}{h}x \left(\frac{h^2 + r^2}{h^2}\right)^{1/2} dx = 2\pi \cdot \frac{r}{h} \cdot \frac{\sqrt{h^2 + r^2}}{h} \left[\frac{1}{2}x^2\right]_0^h = \pi r \sqrt{h^2 + r^2}.$$

[38] The spherical segment can be obtained by revolving the curve $y = \sqrt{r^2 - x^2}$ from

$x = 0$ to $x = h$ about the x-axis. $1 + [y']^2 = 1 + \left(\frac{-x}{\sqrt{r^2 - x^2}}\right)^2 = \frac{r^2}{r^2 - x^2} \Rightarrow$

$$S = 2\pi \int_0^h \sqrt{r^2 - x^2} \sqrt{\frac{r^2}{r^2 - x^2}}\, dx = 2\pi \int_0^h r\, dx = 2\pi r h.$$

[39] The sphere can be obtained by revolving the curve

$y = \sqrt{r^2 - x^2}$ from $x = -r$ to $x = r$ about the x-axis.

$$1 + [y']^2 = \frac{r^2}{r^2 - x^2} \Rightarrow S = 2\pi \int_{-r}^r \sqrt{r^2 - x^2} \sqrt{\frac{r^2}{r^2 - x^2}}\, dx = 2 \cdot 2\pi \int_0^r r\, dx = 4\pi r^2.$$

[40] Let h_1, $h_2 \in [-a,\, a]$ be the points on a diameter of the sphere where the parallel
planes intersect the diameter perpendicularly. If $0 \le h_1 < h_2 \le a$, then surface areas
of the spherical segments determined by h_1 and h_2 are $2\pi a h_1$ and $2\pi a h_2$, respectively.
Their difference is $2\pi a h_2 - 2\pi a h_1 = 2\pi a(h_2 - h_1)$. Thus the area of the surface
between the two planes depends only on the distance between them. Similarly, if
$-a \le h_1 < 0 < h_2 \le a$, the surface area is given by $2\pi a |h_1| + 2\pi a |h_2| =$
$2\pi a(|h_1| + |h_2|)$, and the area depends only on the distance between the two planes.

[41] Regard ds as the slant height of the frustum of a cone that has average radius x.

The surface area of this frustum is $2\pi x\, ds = 2\pi x \sqrt{1 + \big[f'(x)\big]^2}\, dx$.

Apply the limit of sums operator $\int_a^b$ to obtain the formula.

[42] $y = f(x) = 3x^{1/3} \Rightarrow 1 + [f'(x)]^2 = 1 + x^{-4/3} = x^{-4/3}(x^{4/3} + 1).$

$$S = 2\pi \int_1^8 x(x^{-2/3}) \sqrt{x^{4/3} + 1}\, dx = 2\pi \left[\frac{2}{3} \cdot \frac{3}{4}(x^{4/3} + 1)^{3/2}\right]_1^8 \{u = x^{4/3} + 1,$$

$$\tfrac{3}{4}\, du = x^{1/3}\, dx\} = \pi(17^{3/2} - 2^{3/2}) \approx 211.32.$$

43 For $k = 1$, the expression is $\pi\left[f(0) + f(0.25)\right] d\left[(0, 1), (0.25, 0.984375)\right] =$

$$\pi\left(1 + 0.984375\right)\sqrt{(0.25 - 0)^2 + (0.984375 - 1)^2} \approx 1.561566.$$

$$S = \sum_{k=1}^{4} 2\pi\frac{f(x_{k-1}) + f(x_k)}{2} d(Q_{k-1}, Q_k) \approx$$

$$1.561566 + 1.593994 + 1.771803 + 1.143980 \approx 6.07.$$

44 (a) $S = 2\pi\displaystyle\int_0^1 (1 - x^3)\sqrt{1 + 9x^4}\,dx$

(b) Let $g(x) = (1 - x^3)\sqrt{1 + 9x^4}$.

$$S = 2\pi \cdot \tfrac{1-0}{3(4)}\left[g(0) + 4g(0.25) + 2g(0.5) + 4g(0.75) + g(1)\right] \approx$$

$$\tfrac{\pi}{6}\left[1 + 4(1.0015) + 2(1.0938) + 4(1.1340) + 1\right] \approx 6.14.$$

| Exercises 6.6 |

1 (a) and (b) The elapsed time is not relevant to the amount of work done.

It is relevant to Power = Work/Time. Thus, $F = (400)(15) = 6000$ ft-lb.

2 $W = Fd = (80)(4) = 320$ ft-lb.

3 $f(x) = kx$; $f(1.5) = 1.5k = 8 \Rightarrow k = \tfrac{16}{3}$.

(a) $W = \displaystyle\int_0^{14-10} \tfrac{16}{3}x\,dx = \left[\tfrac{8}{3}x^2\right]_0^4 = \tfrac{128}{3}$ in.-lb.

(b) $W = \displaystyle\int_{11-10}^{13-10} \tfrac{16}{3}x\,dx = \left[\tfrac{8}{3}x^2\right]_1^3 = \tfrac{64}{3}$ in.-lb.

4 $f(0.75 - 0.80) = k(-0.05) = -25 \Rightarrow k = 500$.

(Compression $\Rightarrow x < 0$ and $F < 0$.) $W = \displaystyle\int_0^{-0.1} 500x\,dx = 250(-0.1)^2 = 2.5$ ft-lb.

5 $W_1 = \displaystyle\int_0^1 kx\,dx = \tfrac{1}{2}k$. $W_2 = \displaystyle\int_1^2 kx\,dx = \tfrac{3}{2}k$. Hence, $W_2 = 3W_1$.

6 Let c be the natural length of the spring.

$$W_1 = \int_{6-c}^{7-c} kx\,dx = 60 \Rightarrow k\left[\tfrac{1}{2}x^2\right]_{6-c}^{7-c} = \tfrac{1}{2}k\left[(7 - c)^2 - (6 - c)^2\right] = 60 \Rightarrow$$

$$k(13 - 2c) = 120, \text{ or } k = 120/(13 - 2c).$$

$$W_2 = \int_{7-c}^{8-c} kx = 120 \Rightarrow k\left[\tfrac{1}{2}x^2\right]_{7-c}^{8-c} = \tfrac{1}{2}k\left[(8 - c)^2 - (7 - c)^2\right] = 120 \Rightarrow$$

$$k(15 - 2c) = 240, \text{ or } k = 240/(15 - 2c).$$

Solving for c, $\dfrac{120}{13 - 2c} = \dfrac{240}{15 - 2c} \Rightarrow 15 - 2c = 26 - 4c \Rightarrow c = 5.5$ inches.

$$\text{Also, } k = \frac{120}{13 - 2(5.5)} = 60.$$

7 The work done in lifting only the elevator is $(3000)(9) = 27,000$ ft-lb. We must add the work of lifting the cable to this value. Let the cable be placed along the y-axis with $y = 0$ corresponding to the initial position of the bottom of the cable. On $0 \le y \le 9$, if the bottom of the cable is at y, there is $(12 - y)$ ft of cable still

suspended with a weight of $14(12 - y)$ and $W = \int_0^9 14(12 - y)\, dy =$

$$14\left[12y - \tfrac{1}{2}y^2\right]_0^9 = 945.$$ Total work $= 27{,}000 + 945 = 27{,}945$ ft-lb.

8 As in Exercise 7,

$$W = 50(60) + \int_0^{60} (60 - y)\tfrac{1}{4}\, dy = 3000 + \left[15y - \tfrac{1}{8}y^2\right]_0^{60} = 3450 \text{ ft-lb.}$$

9 Since the rates of vertical lift and water loss are constant with respect to time, the rate of water loss with respect to vertical lift is $\frac{-0.25}{1.5} = -\tfrac{1}{6}$ lb/ft. The bucket will still contain some water at 12 feet and the work required to lift just the water is

$$\int_0^{12} (20 - \tfrac{1}{6}x)\, dx = \left[20x - \tfrac{1}{12}x^2\right]_0^{12} = 228 \text{ ft-lb.}$$ The work required to lift the empty

bucket is $(4)(12) = 48$ ft-lb. Thus, the total work is $48 + 228 = 276$ ft-lb.

10 Half the water (10 lbs.) will have leaked out at a height of 60 ft.

Using Exercise 9, we see that $W = (4)(60) + \int_0^{60} (20 - \tfrac{1}{6}x)\, dx = \left[20x - \tfrac{1}{12}x^2\right]_0^{60} =$

$$240 + 900 = 1140 \text{ ft-lb.}$$

11 The volume of the kth slice is $(2)(4)\,dy$ and it is lifted a distance of $(3 - y)$.

$$W = 62.5\int_0^3 8(3 - y)\, dy = 500\left[3y - \tfrac{1}{2}y^2\right]_0^3 = 2250 \text{ ft-lb.}$$

12 Refer to Figure 6.58. The cone intersects the xy-plane along the line with equation $y = \tfrac{h}{a}x$. On $0 \le y \le h$, the volume of the kth slice is $\pi x^2\, dy = \pi\left(\tfrac{a}{h}y\right)^2 dy$ and it is

lifted a distance of $(h - y)$. $W = \dfrac{\pi \rho a^2}{h^2}\int_0^h y^2(h - y)\, dy = \tfrac{\pi}{12}\rho a^2 h^2$ ft-lb.

13 (a) Place the cylinder as shown in *Figure 13*. On $0 \le y \le 6$, a slice of water at height y has a weight of $62.5\pi(\tfrac{3}{2})^2\, dy$ and is lifted a distance of $(6 - y)$.

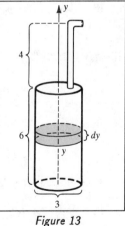

Figure 13

$$W = 62.5\pi(\tfrac{9}{4})\int_0^6 (6 - y)\, dy = 62.5\pi(\tfrac{9}{4})\left[6y - \tfrac{1}{2}y^2\right]_0^6$$

$$= \tfrac{81\pi}{2}(62.5) \approx 7952 \text{ ft-lb.}$$

    (b) $W = 62.5\pi(\tfrac{9}{4})\displaystyle\int_0^6 (10 - y)\, dy$

$$= 62.5\pi(\tfrac{9}{4})\left[10y - \tfrac{1}{2}y^2\right]_0^6 = \tfrac{189\pi}{2}(62.5)$$

$$\approx 18{,}555 \text{ ft-lb.}$$

14 (a) This is the same as Exercise 13, except that $0 \le y \le 3$ is partitioned, and the upper limit of integration is 3 instead of 6. $W = \tfrac{243\pi}{8}(62.5) \approx 5964$ ft-lb.

    (b) $W = \tfrac{459\pi}{8}(62.5) \approx 11{,}266$ ft-lb.

[15] Place the trough as shown in *Figure 15*. Partition $0 \le y \le \sqrt{3}$. At height y the width of the trough is $2x$, where $x = y/\sqrt{3}$. The kth slice is nearly a rectangle with a volume of $8(2x)\, dy = \dfrac{16y}{\sqrt{3}}\, dy$ and must be lifted a distance of $(\sqrt{3} - y)$.

$$W = \frac{16(62.5)}{\sqrt{3}} \int_0^{\sqrt{3}} y(\sqrt{3} - y)\, dy = \frac{1000}{\sqrt{3}} \left[\frac{\sqrt{3}}{2} y^2 - \tfrac{1}{3} y^3 \right]_0^{\sqrt{3}} = 500 \text{ ft-lb.}$$

Figure 15   Figure 16

[16] From *Figure 16*, $r = \sqrt{5^2 - (5 - y)^2} = \sqrt{10y - y^2}$.

The kth slice is a disk of volume $\pi(10y - y^2)\, dy$ and must be lifted $(9 - y)$ ft.

$$W = (62.5)\pi \int_0^5 (9 - y)(10y - y^2)\, dy = 62.5\pi \left[45y^2 - \tfrac{19}{3} y^3 + \tfrac{1}{4} y^4 \right]_0^5 =$$

$$62.5\pi \left(\tfrac{5875}{12} \right) \approx 96{,}129 \text{ ft-lb.}$$

[17] $W = \displaystyle\int_{32}^{40} p \, dv = 115 \int_{32}^{40} v^{-1.2}\, dv = -575 \left[\frac{1}{\sqrt[5]{v}} \right]_{32}^{40} = 575(\tfrac{1}{2} - 40^{-1/5}) \approx 12.55 \text{ in.-lb.}$

[18] From the initial data, $c = p_0 v_0^{1.14}$ and $p = cv^{-1.14} \;\Rightarrow\; p = p_0 v_0^{1.14} v^{-1.14}$.

$$W = \int_{v_0}^{2v_0} p\, dv = p_0 v_0^{1.14} \int_{v_0}^{2v_0} v^{-1.14}\, dv = p_0 v_0^{1.14} \left[\frac{v^{-0.14}}{-0.14} \right]_{v_0}^{2v_0} =$$

$$\frac{p_0 v_0}{0.14} (1 - 2^{-0.14}) \approx 0.66\, p_0 v_0.$$

[19] $F(s) = \dfrac{Gm_1 m_2}{s^2}.$

Hence, $W = Gm_1 m_2 \displaystyle\int_{4000}^{4000+h} s^{-2}\, ds = Gm_1 m_2 \left[-\frac{1}{s} \right]_{4000}^{4000+h} = \dfrac{Gm_1 m_2 h}{(4000)(4000 + h)}.$

[20] Since $F(r) = \dfrac{kq}{r^2}$, it follows that $W = \displaystyle\int_d^{d/2} \frac{kq}{r^2}\, dr = -kq \left[\frac{1}{r} \right]_d^{d/2} = -\dfrac{kq}{d} \text{ J.}$

(Note that it is usually assumed that $k < 0$ since like charges repel.)

[21] Since $W = \displaystyle\int_0^5 f(x)\, dx$, we can approximate this using the trapezoidal rule $(n = 10)$.

$$T = \tfrac{5-0}{2(10)} \{ 7.4 + 2[8.1 + 8.4 + 7.8 + 6.3 + 7.1 + 5.9 + 6.8 + 7.0 + 8.0] + 9.2 \}$$
$$= \tfrac{1}{4}(147.4) = 36.85 \text{ ft-lb.}$$

[22] Since $W = \displaystyle\int_1^9 f(x)\, dx$, we can approximate this using the trapezoidal rule $(n = 8)$.

$$T = \tfrac{9-1}{2(8)} \{ 125 + 2[120 + 130 + 146 + 165 + 157 + 150 + 143] + 140 \}$$
$$= \tfrac{1}{2}(2287) = 1143.5 \text{ J.}$$

[23] (a) $f(x) = k/d^2$, where k is a constant and d is the distance between the electrons.

The distance between the two electrons is given by $5 - x$, where x is the

x-coordinate of the moving electron. $W = \int_0^3 \dfrac{k}{(5-x)^2}\, dx = k\left[\dfrac{1}{5-x}\right]_0^3 = \frac{3}{10}k$ J.

(b) The distance between the moving electron and the electron at $(-5, 0)$ is

$\left[x - (-5)\right]$. Since the forces are in opposite directions they have opposite signs.

The net force is the sum of these two forces, i.e., $f(x) = \dfrac{k}{(5-x)^2} - \dfrac{k}{(5+x)^2}$.

$$W = \int_0^3 \left[\dfrac{k}{(5-x)^2} - \dfrac{k}{(5+x)^2}\right] dx = k\left[\dfrac{1}{5-x} + \dfrac{1}{5+x}\right]_0^3 = \frac{9}{40}k \text{ J.}$$

[24] In (6.21), if $f(x) = F$, with F a constant, then $W = \int_a^b F\, dx = F(b-a)$,

where $(b - a)$ is the distance the object travels. Thus, $W = Fd$, as in (6.20).

Exercises 6.7

[1] $m = \displaystyle\sum_{k=1}^{3} m_k = 100 + 80 + 70 = 250.$

$M_0 = \displaystyle\sum_{k=1}^{3} m_k x_k = 100(-3) + 80(2) + 70(4) = 140.$ $\bar{x} = M_0/m = \frac{140}{250} = 0.56.$

[2] $m = \displaystyle\sum_{k=1}^{3} m_k = 50 + 100 + 50 = 200.$ $M_0 = \displaystyle\sum_{k=1}^{3} m_k x_k =$

$50(-10) + 100(2) + 50(3) = -150.$ $\bar{x} = M_0/m = \frac{-150}{200} = -0.75.$

[3] $m = \displaystyle\sum_{k=1}^{3} m_k = 2 + 7 + 5 = 14.$

$M_x = \displaystyle\sum_{k=1}^{3} m_k y_k = 2(-1) + 7(0) + 5(-5) = -27.$

$M_y = \displaystyle\sum_{k=1}^{3} m_k x_k = 2(4) + 7(-2) + 5(-8) = -46.$

$\bar{x} = M_y/m = \frac{-46}{14} = -\frac{23}{7}$ and $\bar{y} = M_x/m = -\frac{27}{14}.$

[4] $m = \displaystyle\sum_{k=1}^{5} m_k = 10 + 3 + 4 + 1 + 8 = 26.$

$M_x = \displaystyle\sum_{k=1}^{5} m_k y_k = 10(-2) + 3(7) + 4(-3) + 1(-3) + 8(0) = -14.$

$M_y = \displaystyle\sum_{k=1}^{5} m_k x_k = 10(-5) + 3(3) + 4(0) + 1(-8) + 8(0) = -49.$

$\bar{x} = M_y/m = -\frac{49}{26}$ and $\bar{y} = M_x/m = -\frac{7}{13}.$

Note: Without loss of generality, assume $\rho = 1$ throughout this section.

$\boxed{5}$ Let $f(x) = x^3$ and $g(x) = 0$ in (6.25).

$$m = \int_0^1 (x^3 - 0)\, dx = \tfrac{1}{4}. \quad M_x = \tfrac{1}{2}\int_0^1 (x^3 + 0)(x^3 - 0)\, dx = \tfrac{1}{14}.$$

$$M_y = \int_0^1 x(x^3 - 0)\, dx = \tfrac{1}{5}. \quad \bar{x} = \frac{M_y}{m} = \tfrac{4}{5} \text{ and } \bar{y} = \frac{M_x}{m} = \tfrac{2}{7}.$$

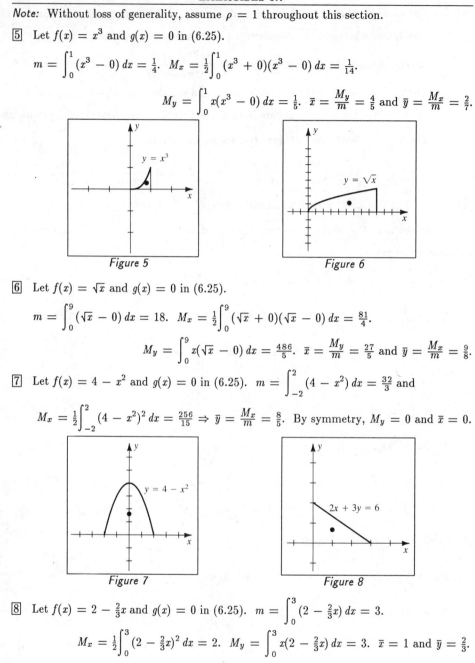

Figure 5   Figure 6

$\boxed{6}$ Let $f(x) = \sqrt{x}$ and $g(x) = 0$ in (6.25).

$$m = \int_0^9 (\sqrt{x} - 0)\, dx = 18. \quad M_x = \tfrac{1}{2}\int_0^9 (\sqrt{x} + 0)(\sqrt{x} - 0)\, dx = \tfrac{81}{4}.$$

$$M_y = \int_0^9 x(\sqrt{x} - 0)\, dx = \tfrac{486}{5}. \quad \bar{x} = \frac{M_y}{m} = \tfrac{27}{5} \text{ and } \bar{y} = \frac{M_x}{m} = \tfrac{9}{8}.$$

$\boxed{7}$ Let $f(x) = 4 - x^2$ and $g(x) = 0$ in (6.25). $m = \int_{-2}^2 (4 - x^2)\, dx = \tfrac{32}{3}$ and

$$M_x = \tfrac{1}{2}\int_{-2}^2 (4 - x^2)^2\, dx = \tfrac{256}{15} \Rightarrow \bar{y} = \frac{M_x}{m} = \tfrac{8}{5}. \text{ By symmetry, } M_y = 0 \text{ and } \bar{x} = 0.$$

Figure 7   Figure 8

$\boxed{8}$ Let $f(x) = 2 - \tfrac{2}{3}x$ and $g(x) = 0$ in (6.25). $m = \int_0^3 (2 - \tfrac{2}{3}x)\, dx = 3.$

$$M_x = \tfrac{1}{2}\int_0^3 (2 - \tfrac{2}{3}x)^2\, dx = 2. \quad M_y = \int_0^3 x(2 - \tfrac{2}{3}x)\, dx = 3. \quad \bar{x} = 1 \text{ and } \bar{y} = \tfrac{2}{3}.$$

9 Let $f(x) = \sqrt{x}$ and $g(x) = \frac{1}{2}x$ in (6.25). $\sqrt{x} = \frac{1}{2}x \Rightarrow x = 0, 4$.

$m = \int_0^4 (\sqrt{x} - \frac{1}{2}x)\,dx = \frac{4}{3}$. $M_x = \frac{1}{2}\int_0^4 \left[(\sqrt{x})^2 - (\frac{1}{2}x)^2\right] dx = \frac{4}{3}$.

$M_y = \int_0^4 x(\sqrt{x} - \frac{1}{2}x)\,dx = \frac{32}{15}$. $\bar{x} = \frac{8}{5}$ and $\bar{y} = 1$.

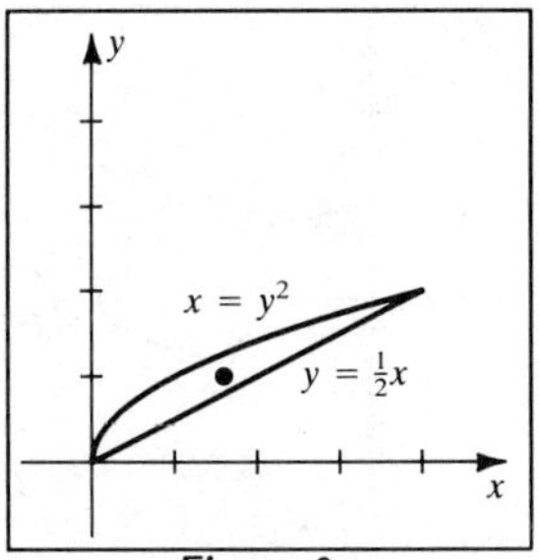

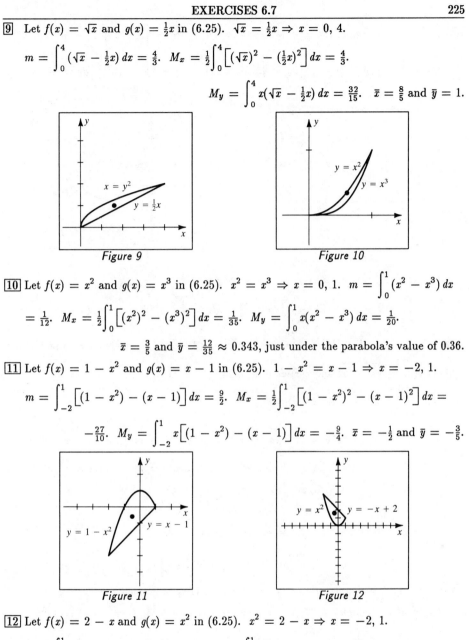

Figure 9

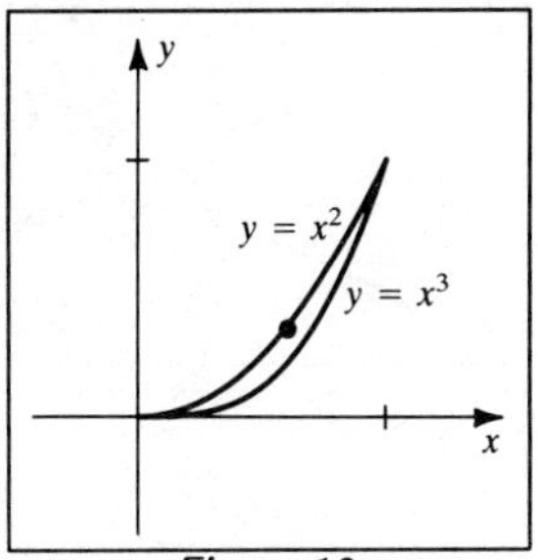

Figure 10

10 Let $f(x) = x^2$ and $g(x) = x^3$ in (6.25). $x^2 = x^3 \Rightarrow x = 0, 1$. $m = \int_0^1 (x^2 - x^3)\,dx$

$= \frac{1}{12}$. $M_x = \frac{1}{2}\int_0^1 \left[(x^2)^2 - (x^3)^2\right] dx = \frac{1}{35}$. $M_y = \int_0^1 x(x^2 - x^3)\,dx = \frac{1}{20}$.

$\bar{x} = \frac{3}{5}$ and $\bar{y} = \frac{12}{35} \approx 0.343$, just under the parabola's value of 0.36.

11 Let $f(x) = 1 - x^2$ and $g(x) = x - 1$ in (6.25). $1 - x^2 = x - 1 \Rightarrow x = -2, 1$.

$m = \int_{-2}^1 \left[(1 - x^2) - (x - 1)\right] dx = \frac{9}{2}$. $M_x = \frac{1}{2}\int_{-2}^1 \left[(1 - x^2)^2 - (x - 1)^2\right] dx =$

$-\frac{27}{10}$. $M_y = \int_{-2}^1 x\left[(1 - x^2) - (x - 1)\right] dx = -\frac{9}{4}$. $\bar{x} = -\frac{1}{2}$ and $\bar{y} = -\frac{3}{5}$.

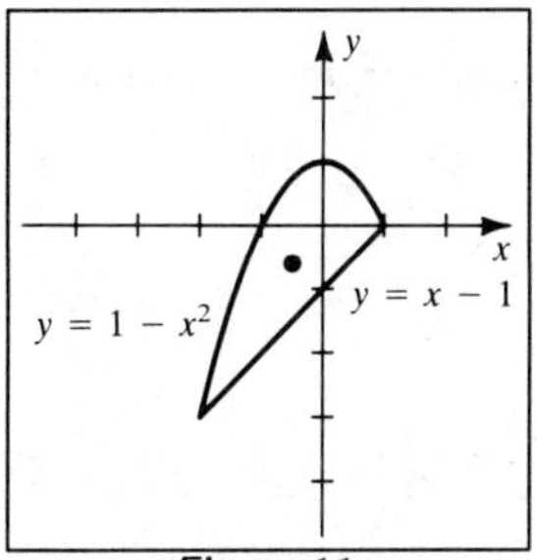

Figure 11

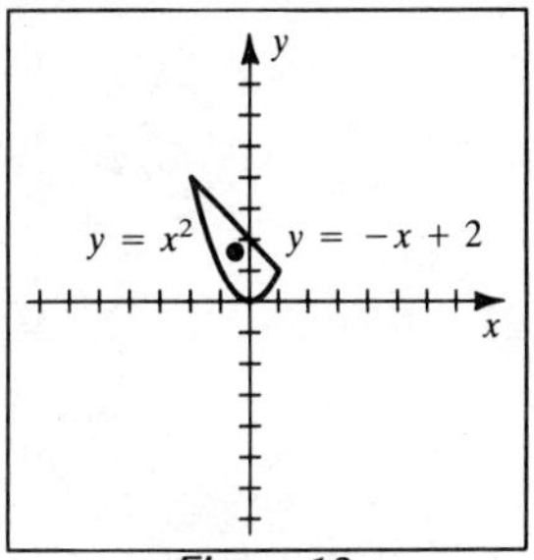

Figure 12

12 Let $f(x) = 2 - x$ and $g(x) = x^2$ in (6.25). $x^2 = 2 - x \Rightarrow x = -2, 1$.

$m = \int_{-2}^1 \left[(2 - x) - x^2\right] dx = \frac{9}{2}$. $M_x = \frac{1}{2}\int_{-2}^1 \left[(2 - x)^2 - (x^2)^2\right] dx = \frac{36}{5}$.

$M_y = \int_{-2}^1 x\left[(2 - x) - x^2\right] dx = -\frac{9}{4}$. $\bar{x} = -\frac{1}{2}$ and $\bar{y} = \frac{8}{5}$.

13 This is an R_y region. $y^2 = y + 2 \Rightarrow y = -1, 2.$ $m = \int_{-1}^{2} \left[(y + 2) - y^2\right] dy = \frac{9}{2}.$

$$M_x = \int_{-1}^{2} y\left[(y + 2) - y^2\right] dy = \frac{9}{4}. \quad M_y = \frac{1}{2}\int_{-1}^{2} \left[(y + 2)^2 - (y^2)^2\right] dy = \frac{36}{5}.$$

$$\bar{x} = \frac{8}{5} \text{ and } \bar{y} = \frac{1}{2}.$$

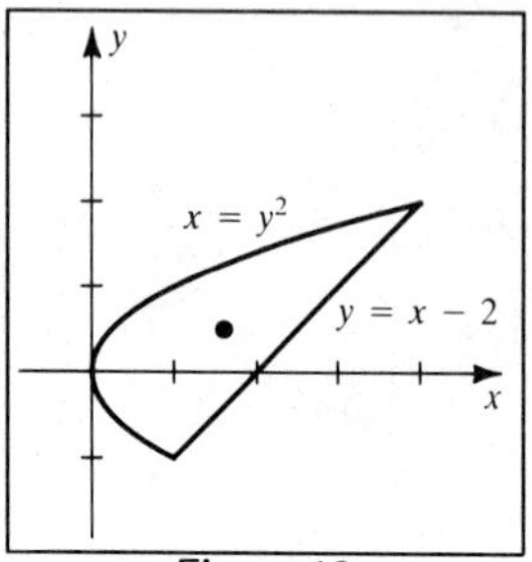

Figure 13

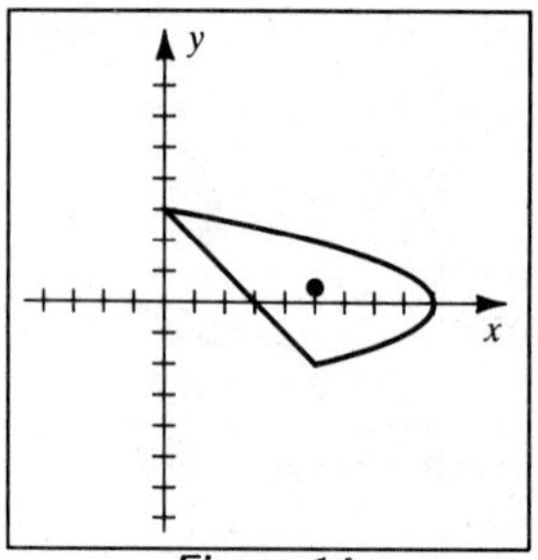

Figure 14

14 This is an R_y region. $9 - y^2 = 3 - y \Rightarrow y = -2, 3.$

$$m = \int_{-2}^{3} \left[(9 - y^2) - (3 - y)\right] dy = \frac{125}{6}. \quad M_x = \int_{-2}^{3} y\left[(9 - y^2) - (3 - y)\right] dy =$$

$$\frac{125}{12}. \quad M_y = \frac{1}{2}\int_{-2}^{3} \left[(9 - y^2)^2 - (3 - y)^2\right] dy = \frac{625}{6}. \quad \bar{x} = 5 \text{ and } \bar{y} = \frac{1}{2}.$$

15 Let $f(x) = \sqrt{a^2 - x^2}$ and $g(x) = 0$ in (6.25). $m = $ area $= \frac{1}{4}\pi a^2.$

$$M_y = \int_{0}^{a} x\sqrt{a^2 - x^2}\, dx = \left[(\tfrac{2}{3})(-\tfrac{1}{2})(a^2 - x^2)^{3/2}\right]_{0}^{a} = \frac{1}{3}a^3.$$

$$M_x = \frac{1}{2}\int_{0}^{a} (\sqrt{a^2 - x^2})^2\, dx = \frac{1}{2}\left[a^2 x - \frac{1}{3}x^3\right]_{0}^{a} = \frac{1}{3}a^3. \quad \bar{x} = \bar{y} = \frac{4a}{3\pi}.$$

16 From the figure, $y^2 = cx$, and hence, $b^2 = ca$. Thus, $c = b^2/a$ and $a = b^2/c$.

$$m = \int_{0}^{a} \sqrt{cx}\, dx = \sqrt{c}\left[\frac{2}{3}x^{3/2}\right]_{0}^{a} = \frac{2}{3}\sqrt{c}\, a^{3/2} = \frac{2}{3}\sqrt{c}\left(\frac{b^3}{c^{3/2}}\right) = \frac{2b^3}{3c}.$$

$$M_x = \frac{1}{2}\int_{0}^{a} (\sqrt{cx})^2\, dx = \frac{1}{4}ca^2. \quad M_y = \int_{0}^{a} x\sqrt{cx}\, dx = \frac{2}{5}\sqrt{c}\, a^{5/2} = \frac{2}{5}\sqrt{c}\left(\frac{b^2}{c}\right)^{5/2} = \frac{2b^5}{5c^2}.$$

$$\bar{x} = \frac{3b^2}{5c} = \frac{3}{5}a \text{ and } \bar{y} = \frac{3a^2c^2}{8b^3} = \frac{3b^4}{8b^3} = \frac{3}{8}b.$$

17 In *Figure 17*, $\bar{x} = 0$ by symmetry. By the additivity of moments,

$M_x = M_x(\text{semicircle}) + M_x(\text{square})$. From Example 5, $M_x(\text{semicircle}) = \frac{2}{3}a^3.$

$$M_x(\text{square}) = \frac{1}{2}\int_{-a}^{a} \left[0^2 - (2a)^2\right] dx = -4a^3. \quad \text{Thus, } M_x = \frac{2}{3}a^3 + (-4a^3) = -\frac{10}{3}a^3.$$

$$m = \text{area} = 4a^2 + \frac{1}{2}\pi a^2 = \frac{1}{2}a^2(8 + \pi) \text{ and so } \bar{y} = \frac{-20a}{3(8 + \pi)},$$

about 30% of the distance from the origin to the bottom of the square.

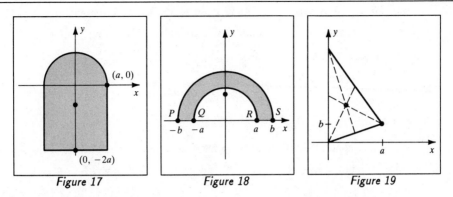

Figure 17   Figure 18   Figure 19

[18] From Example 5, M_x for a semicircle of radius r is $\frac{2}{3}r^3$. Since moments are additive and the region has the semicircle of radius a missing, we negate M_x for the semicircle of radius a. Hence, $M_x = \frac{2}{3}(b^3 - a^3)$. $m = \text{area} = \frac{1}{2}\pi(b^2 - a^2)$.

$$\text{Thus, } \bar{y} = \frac{4(b^3 - a^3)}{3\pi(b^2 - a^2)} = \frac{4(b^2 + ab + a^2)}{3\pi(b + a)} \text{ and } \bar{x} = 0 \text{ by symmetry.}$$

[19] The midpoints of the three sides are $(\frac{a}{2}, \frac{b}{2})$, $(\frac{a}{2}, \frac{b+c}{2})$, and $(0, \frac{c}{2})$. The three

medians have equations $y = (\frac{b+c}{a})x$, $y = (\frac{2b-c}{2a})x + \frac{1}{2}c$, and

$y = (\frac{b-2c}{a})x + c$. All three intersect at $(\frac{1}{3}a, \frac{1}{3}(b + c))$. The triangle has area $\frac{1}{2}ac$.

The upper boundary is $f(x) = (\frac{b-c}{a})x + c$ and the lower boundary is $g(x) = \frac{b}{a}x$.

$$M_y = \int_0^a x[f(x) - g(x)]\,dx = c\int_0^a (x - x^2/a)\,dx = c\left[\frac{1}{2}x^2 - \frac{x^3}{3a}\right]_0^a = \frac{1}{6}ca^2.$$

$$M_x = \frac{1}{2}\int_0^a \{[f(x)]^2 - [g(x)]^2\}\,dx = \frac{1}{2}\int_0^a \left\{\left[\left(\frac{b-c}{a}\right)x + c\right]^2 - \left[\frac{b}{a}x\right]^2\right\}dx$$

$$= \frac{1}{2}\int_0^a \left[\left(\frac{b-c}{a}\right)^2 x^2 + 2c\left(\frac{b-c}{a}\right)x + c^2 - \frac{b^2}{a^2}x^2\right]dx$$

$$= \frac{1}{2}\int_0^a \left[\left(\frac{b^2 - 2bc + c^2}{a^2}\right)x^2 + 2c\left(\frac{b-c}{a}\right)x + c^2 - \frac{b^2}{a^2}x^2\right]dx$$

$$= \frac{1}{2}\int_0^a \left[\left(\frac{c^2 - 2bc}{a^2}\right)x^2 + 2c\left(\frac{b-c}{a}\right)x + c^2\right]dx$$

$$= \frac{c}{2}\int_0^a \left[\frac{c - 2b}{a^2}x^2 + \frac{2(b-c)}{a}x + c\right]dx = \frac{c}{2}\left[\frac{c - 2b}{3a^2}x^3 + \frac{b-c}{a}x^2 + cx\right]_0^a$$

$$= \frac{1}{6}ac(b + c). \quad \bar{x} = \frac{M_y}{m} = \frac{\frac{1}{6}ca^2}{\frac{1}{2}ac} = \frac{1}{3}a \text{ and } \bar{y} = \frac{M_x}{m} = \frac{\frac{1}{6}ac(b + c)}{\frac{1}{2}ac} = \frac{1}{3}(b + c).$$

20 In *Figure 20*, $\bar{x} = 0$ by symmetry. As in Exercise 17, $M_x = M_x(\text{triangle}) +$

$M_x(\text{square})$. From Exer. 19, we know that $\bar{y}(\text{triangle}) = \frac{1}{3}(\text{height}) = \frac{1}{3}(\frac{\sqrt{3}}{2}a) = \frac{\sqrt{3}}{6}a$.

$\bar{y} = \frac{M_x}{m} \Rightarrow M_x(\text{triangle}) = \text{area} \times \bar{y}(\text{triangle}) = \frac{1}{2}a(\frac{\sqrt{3}}{2}a)(\frac{\sqrt{3}}{6}a) = \frac{1}{8}a^3$.

$M_x(\text{square}) = \frac{1}{2}\int_{-a/2}^{a/2}(-a^2)\,dx = -\frac{1}{2}a^3$. Hence, $M_x = \frac{1}{8}a^3 + (-\frac{1}{2}a^3) = -\frac{3}{8}a^3$.

Since $m = \text{area} = a^2 + \frac{\sqrt{3}}{4}a^2$, it follows that $\bar{y} = \frac{M_x}{m} = \frac{-3a}{2(4 + \sqrt{3})}$,

about 26% of the distance from the origin to the bottom of the square.

21 The sides of the rectangle have length $\sqrt{2}$ and $\sqrt{18}$. By symmetry, $\bar{x} = \bar{y} = 3$.

$$V = 2\pi\bar{x}A = (2\pi \cdot 3)(\sqrt{2}\sqrt{18}) = 36\pi.$$

22 By symmetry, $\bar{x} = 2$. $V = 2\pi\bar{x}A = (2\pi \cdot 2)(\frac{1}{2} \cdot 2 \cdot 1) = 4\pi$.

23 The area of the quarter circle is $\frac{\pi}{4}a^2$ and its volume of revolution (a hemisphere)

about the y-axis is $\frac{2}{3}\pi a^3$. Thus, $\bar{x} = \frac{V}{2\pi A} = \frac{\frac{2}{3}\pi a^3}{2\pi(\frac{\pi}{4}a^2)} = \frac{4a}{3\pi}$. By symmetry, $\bar{y} = \frac{4a}{3\pi}$.

24 The area of the triangle is $\frac{1}{2}ab$ and its volume of revolution (a cone)

about the y-axis is $\frac{1}{3}\pi ab^2$. Thus, $\bar{x} = \frac{\frac{1}{3}\pi ab^2}{2\pi(\frac{1}{2}ab)} = \frac{1}{3}b$. Similarly, $\bar{y} = \frac{\frac{1}{3}\pi ba^2}{2\pi(\frac{1}{2}ab)} = \frac{1}{3}a$.

25 (a) The graphs intersect at $x \approx \pm 0.89$. Thus, $m = \rho\int_{-0.89}^{0.89}(\sqrt{|\cos x|} - x^2)\,dx$.

(b) Let $f(x) = \sqrt{|\cos x|} - x^2$.

$$S \approx \rho\frac{0.89-(-0.89)}{3(4)}\Big[f(-0.89) + 4f(-0.445) + 2f(0) + 4f(0.445) + f(0.89)\Big]$$

$$\approx 1.19\rho.$$

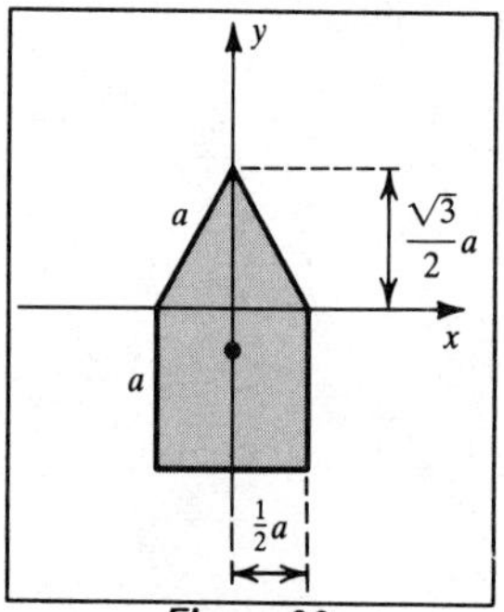

Figure 20

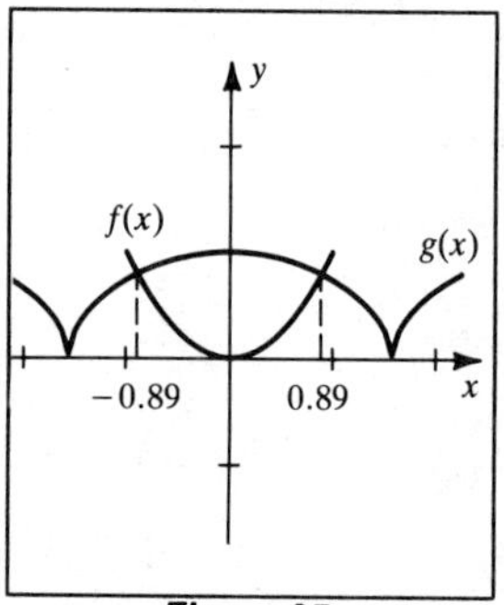

Figure 25

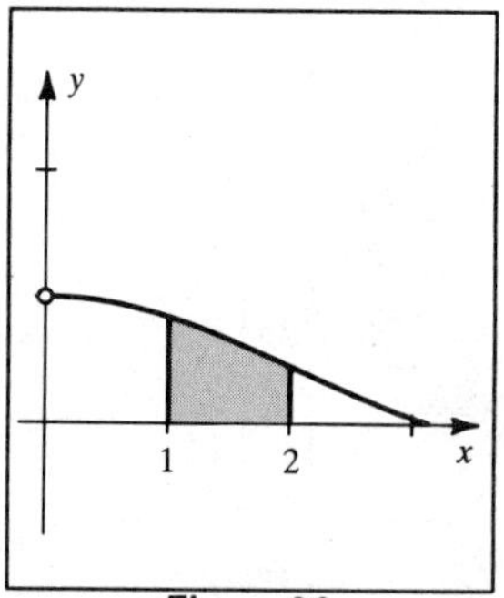

Figure 26

25 $m = \rho\int_1^2 \frac{\sin x}{x}\,dx \approx 0.659331\rho$ using Simpson's rule.

$M_y = \rho\int_1^2 x\frac{\sin x}{x}\,dx = \rho\int_1^2 \sin x\,dx = -\rho\Big[\cos x\Big]_1^2 \approx 0.956449\rho$.

$M_x = \frac{\rho}{2}\int_1^2 \frac{\sin^2 x}{x^2}\,dx \approx 0.223721\rho$ using Simpson's rule.

$$\bar{x} = \frac{M_y}{m} \approx \frac{0.956449\rho}{0.659331\rho} \approx 1.45; \quad \bar{y} = \frac{M_x}{m} \approx \frac{0.223721\rho}{0.659331\rho} \approx 0.34$$

$\boxed{1}$ (a) $F = \int_c^d \rho\, h(y)\, L(y)\, dy = \rho \int_0^1 (1 - y)(1)\, dy = \frac{1}{2}\rho = \frac{1}{2}(62.5) = 31.25$ lb.

  (b) $F = \int_c^d \rho\, h(y)\, L(y)\, dy = \rho \int_0^1 (1 - y)(3)\, dy = \frac{3}{2}\rho = \frac{3}{2}(62.5) = 93.75$ lb.

$\boxed{2}$ In *Figure 2*, the diagonal is $y = x$. On the upper half, $h(y) = 1 - y$ and $L(y) = y$.

  Thus, $F_1 = \rho \int_0^1 (1 - y)y\, dy = \frac{1}{6}\rho = \frac{1}{6}(62.5) \approx 10.42$ lb. On the lower half,

  $h(y) = 1 - y$ and $L(y) = 1 - y$. Hence, $F_2 = \rho \int_0^1 (1 - y)(1 - y)\, dy =$

  $\frac{1}{3}\rho = \frac{1}{3}(62.5) \approx 20.83$ lb. Note that $F_1 + F_2 = F$ in Exercise 1(a).

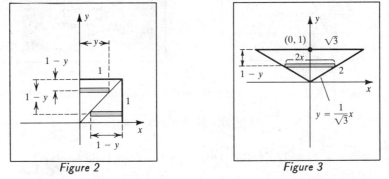

Figure 2   Figure 3

$\boxed{3}$ (a) The height of the trough is 1. The equations of the right and left edges of the

    trough are $x = \pm\sqrt{3}y$, respectively. Thus, $h(y) = 1 - y$ and $L(y) = 2\sqrt{3}y$ and

$$F = \rho \int_0^1 (1 - y)(2\sqrt{3}y)\, dy = 2\sqrt{3}\rho(\tfrac{1}{6}) = \frac{\sqrt{3}}{3}(62.5) \approx 36.08 \text{ lb.}$$

  (b) $F = \rho \int_0^{1/2} (\tfrac{1}{2} - y)(2\sqrt{3}y)\, dy = 2\sqrt{3}\rho(\tfrac{1}{48}) = \frac{\sqrt{3}}{24}(62.5) \approx 4.51$ lb.

$\boxed{4}$ The equations of the right and left edges of the end plates are $x = \pm\sqrt{y}$.

  $L(y) = 2\sqrt{y}$ and $h(y) = 4 - y \Rightarrow F = \rho \int_0^4 (4 - y)(2\sqrt{y})\, dy =$

$$2\rho\Big[4(\tfrac{2}{3})y^{3/2} - \tfrac{2}{5}y^{5/2}\Big]_0^4 = \tfrac{256}{15}\rho = \tfrac{256}{15}(62.5) = 1066\tfrac{2}{3} \text{ lb.}$$

$\boxed{5}$ Let the center of one of the circular ends of the tank be placed at the origin. This

  circle has equation $x^2 + y^2 = 4$. The right and left boundaries of the circle are

  $x = \pm\sqrt{4 - y^2}$. The surface of the oil coincides with $y = 0$. $F =$

  $\rho \int_{-2}^0 (0 - y)(2\sqrt{4 - y^2})\, dy = -2\rho\Big[(-\tfrac{1}{3})(4 - y^2)^{3/2}\Big]_{-2}^0 = \tfrac{16}{3}\rho = \tfrac{16}{3}(60) = 320$ lb.

$\boxed{6}$ Let the bottom edge of the gate be located along the line $y = 0$. $h(y) = 9 - y$ and

$$L(y) = 5.\quad F = \rho \int_0^3 (9 - y)(5)\, dy = \tfrac{225}{2}\rho = \tfrac{225}{2}(62.5) = 7031.25 \text{ lb.}$$

$\boxed{7}$ From *Figure 7*, an equation for the right edge is $y = -2(x - 4)$, or $x = 4 - \frac{1}{2}y$.

An equation for the left edge is $y = 2(x + 4)$, or $x = \frac{1}{2}y - 4$. $h(y) = 10 - y$.

$$F = \int_0^4 (10 - y)\Big[(4 - \tfrac{1}{2}y) - (\tfrac{1}{2}y - 4)\Big]\, dy = \Big[80y - 9y^2 + \tfrac{1}{3}y^3\Big]_0^4 =$$

$$\tfrac{592}{3}\rho = \tfrac{592}{3}(62.5) = 12{,}333\tfrac{1}{3} \text{ lb.}$$

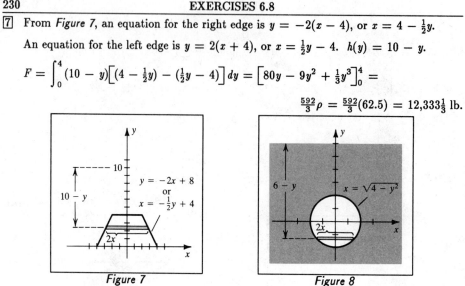

Figure 7   Figure 8

$\boxed{8}$ From *Figure 8*, $h(y) = 6 - y$. The right and left boundaries of the circular plate are

$x = \pm\sqrt{4 - y^2}$. $F = \rho\int_{-2}^{2}(6 - y)(2\sqrt{4 - y^2})\, dy = 2\rho\int_{-2}^{2} 6\sqrt{4 - y^2}\, dy -$

$2\rho\int_{-2}^{2} y\sqrt{4 - y^2}\, dy = 12\rho\Big[\tfrac{1}{2}\pi(2)^2\Big]\{\text{semicircle}\} - 2\rho(0)\{\text{odd function}\} =$

$$24\pi\rho = 24\pi(62.5) \approx 4712.39 \text{ lb.}$$

$\boxed{9}$ (a) Place the left edge of the plate along the y-axis and the bottom edge on the

x-axis. Then, the right edge has equation $x = 3$ and the left, $x = 0$. $L(y) = 3$

and $h(y) = 8 - y \Rightarrow F = \rho\int_0^6 (8 - y)(3)\, dy = 90\rho = 90(50) = 4500 \text{ lb.}$

(b) The diagonal is $y = 2x$, or $x = \frac{1}{2}y$. On the lower triangle, $h(y) = 8 - y$ and

$L(y) = 3 - \tfrac{1}{2}y \Rightarrow F = \rho\int_0^6 (8 - y)(3 - \tfrac{1}{2}y)\, dy = 54(50) = 2700 \text{ lb.}$ On the

other part, $L(y) = \tfrac{1}{2}y - 0 \Rightarrow F = \rho\int_0^6 (8 - y)(\tfrac{1}{2}y)\, dy = 36(50) = 1800 \text{ lb.}$

$\boxed{10}$ $F = \rho\int_1^4 h(y)\, L(y)\, dy$. Let $g(y) = h(y)\, L(y)$, where h and L are given in the table.

(a) $T = \frac{4-1}{2(6)}\rho\{ g(1) + 2[g(1.5) + g(2) + g(2.5) + g(3) + g(3.5)] + g(4) \}$

$= \tfrac{1}{4}\rho\Big[0 + 2(3 + 6 + 13.75 + 13.5 + 12.25) + 0\Big]$

$= \tfrac{97}{4}\rho = \tfrac{97}{4}(62.5) = 1515.625 \text{ lb.}$

(b) $S = \frac{4-1}{3(6)}\rho\Big[g(1) + 4g(1.5) + 2g(2) + 4g(2.5) + 2g(3) + 4g(3.5) + g(4)\Big]$

$= \tfrac{1}{6}\rho\Big[0 + 4(3) + 2(6) + 4(13.75) + 2(13.5) + 4(12.25) + 0\Big]$

$= \tfrac{155}{6}\rho = \tfrac{155}{6}(62.5) \approx 1614.58 \text{ lb.}$

11 Note that both $c(t)$ and Q_0 are given using milligrams. Estimating $\int_0^{12} c(t)\, dt$,

$$S = \tfrac{12-0}{3(12)}[0 + 4(0) + 2(0.15) + 4(0.48) + 2(0.86) + 4(0.72) + 2(0.48) +$$
$$4(0.26) + 2(0.15) + 4(0.09) + 2(0.05) + 4(0.01) + 0] = \tfrac{1}{3}(9.62).$$

Solving (6.28) for F, we have $F = \frac{5}{9.62/3} \approx 1.56$ liters/min.

12 Use the trapezoidal rule to estimate $\int_0^{360} c(t)\, dt$.

$$T = \tfrac{360-0}{2(12)}[0 + 2(2.14 + 3.89 + 5.81 + 8.95 + 7.31 + 6.15 + 4.89 + 2.98 +$$
$$1.42 + 0.89 + 0.29) + 0] = 15(89.44) = 1341.6.$$

Solving (6.28) for F and converting 1200 kilograms to grams yields

$$F = \tfrac{1,200,000}{1341.6} \approx 894.45 \text{ m}^3/\text{sec}.$$

13 (a) $f(1) = 20(1 + 1)^{-0.4} + 3 \approx 18.16$ min.

Using a definite integral from 0 to 1 yields 20.19.

(b) $\int_0^4 \left[20(x + 1)^{-0.4} + 3\right] dx = \left[\tfrac{20}{0.6}(x + 1)^{0.6} + 3x\right]_0^4 \approx$

$$99.55 - 33.33 \approx 66.2 \text{ min.}$$

(c) $\left[\tfrac{20}{0.6}(x + 1)^{0.6} + 3x\right]_0^8 \approx 115.2$ min.   (d) $\left[\tfrac{20}{0.6}(x + 1)^{0.6} + 3x\right]_0^{16} \approx 197.1$ min.

14 Since $f(x) = 5x^{-1/2}$ is discontinuous at $x = 0$, we use $f(1)$ rather than find

$$\int_0^1 f(x)\, dx. \quad \sum_{k=1}^{10} 5k^{-1/2} = 5 + \sum_{k=2}^{10} 5k^{-1/2} \approx 5 + \int_1^{10} 5x^{-1/2}\, dx =$$
$$10\sqrt{10} - 5 \approx 26.62 \text{ min.}$$

15 (a) The time required to keyboard 600 registrations can be estimated by

$$\int_0^{600} 6(1 + x)^{-1/3}\, dx = 6\left[\tfrac{3}{2}(1 + x)^{2/3}\right]_0^{600} = 9\left[(601)^{2/3} - 1\right] \approx 632 \text{ min.}$$

(b) $2\int_0^{300} 6(1 + x)^{-1/3}\, dx = 2 \cdot 9\left[(301)^{2/3} - 1\right] \approx 790$ min.

16 Over $[0, 5]$, the amount is $\int_0^5 2t(3t + 1)\, dt = \left[2t^3 + t^2\right]_0^5 = 275$, or \$275,000.

Over $[5, 10]$, the amount is $\int_5^{10} 2t(3t + 1)\, dt = 1825$, or \$1,825,000.

17 $\sum_{k=1}^{100} k(k^2 + 1)^{-1/4} \approx \int_0^{100} x(x^2 + 1)^{-1/4}\, dx = \left[\tfrac{2}{3}(x^2 + 1)^{3/4}\right]_0^{100} =$

$$\tfrac{2}{3}\left[(10,001)^{3/4} - 1\right] \approx 666.$$

18 $\sum_{k=1}^{200} 5k(k^2 + 10)^{-1/3} \approx \int_0^{200} 5x(x^2 + 10)^{-1/3}\, dx = 5\left[\tfrac{3}{4}(x^2 + 10)^{2/3}\right]_0^{200} =$

$$\tfrac{15}{4}\left[(40,010)^{2/3} - (10)^{2/3}\right] \approx 4369.$$

19 The distance traveled (in miles) is $\int_0^{12/60} v(t)\, dt$, where time is in <u>hours</u>, not minutes.

$$T = \tfrac{12/60 - 0}{2(12)}\left\{v(0) + 2\left[v(\tfrac{1}{60}) + v(\tfrac{2}{60}) + v(\tfrac{3}{60}) + \cdots + v(\tfrac{11}{60})\right] + v(\tfrac{12}{60})\right\}$$
$$= \tfrac{1}{120}[40 + 2(45 + 40 + 50 + 55 + 65 + 60 + 55 + 55 + 60 + 65 + 65) + 55]$$
$$= \tfrac{1}{120}(1325) \approx 11 \text{ mi. \{Answers may vary depending on graph interpretations.\}}$$

[20] The net change in velocity is $\int_0^8 a(t)\, dt$. {Answers may vary.}

$$T = \tfrac{8-0}{2(8)}\{a(0) + 2[a(1) + a(2) + a(3) + a(4) + a(5) + a(6) + a(7)] + a(8)\} =$$
$$\tfrac{1}{2}[0 + 2(2 + 7 + 18 + 22 + 22 + 20 + 12) + 10] = 108 \text{ ft/sec.}$$

[21] Since $W = \int_1^7 f(x)\, dx$, we have the following results.

(a) $T = \tfrac{7-1}{2(6)}[20 + 2(23 + 25 + 22 + 26 + 30) + 28] = \tfrac{1}{2}(300) = 150$ J.

(b) $S = \tfrac{7-1}{3(6)}[20 + 4(23) + 2(25) + 4(22) + 2(26) + 4(30) + 28] = \tfrac{1}{3}(450) =$
$$150 \text{ J.}$$

[22] Distance $= \int_0^{10} v(t)\, dt$. $\;T = \tfrac{10-0}{2(5)}[24 + 2(22 + 16 + 10 + 2) + 0] = 124$ ft.

[23] Gasoline used $= \int_0^2 t\sqrt{9 - t^2}\, dt = \left[-\tfrac{1}{3}(9 - t^2)^{3/2}\right]_0^2 = 9 - \tfrac{5\sqrt{5}}{3} \approx 5.27$ gal.

[24] The change in population (in thousands) from 1985 to 1994 is given by
$$\int_0^9 (1.5 + 0.3\sqrt{t} + 0.006t^2)\, dt = 20{,}358.$$

The 1994 population will be approximately 70,358.

[25] The total charge transferred is $\int_0^3 \dfrac{dQ}{dt}\, dt = \int_0^3 I(t)\, dt$.

$$T = \tfrac{3-0}{2(6)}[0 + 2(0.2 + 0.6 + 0.7 + 0.8 + 0.5) + 0.2] = \tfrac{1}{4}(5.8) = 1.45 \text{ coulombs.}$$

[26] (a) $T = \tfrac{42-6}{2(6)}[0.0052 + 2(0.0124 + 0.0132 + 0.0136 + 0.0084 + 0.0034) + 0.0017]$
$$= 3(0.1089) = 0.3267 \text{ cm in the spring.}$$

$$T = \tfrac{42-6}{2(6)}[0.0043 + 2(0.0076 + 0.0104 + 0.0109 + 0.0072 + 0.0034) + 0.0016]$$
$$= 3(0.0849) = 0.2547 \text{ cm in the autumn.}$$

(b) $S = \tfrac{42-6}{3(6)}[0.0052 + 4(0.0124) + 2(0.0132) + 4(0.0136) + 2(0.0084) +$
$$4(0.0034) + 0.0017] = 2(0.1677) = 0.3354 \text{ cm in the spring.}$$

$$S = \tfrac{42-6}{3(6)}[0.0043 + 4(0.0076) + 2(0.0104) + 4(0.0109) + 2(0.0072) +$$
$$4(0.0034) + 0.0016] = 2(0.1287) = 0.2574 \text{ cm in the autumn.}$$

[27] (a) $v'(t) > 0$ on $[0, \tfrac{1}{30}]$. Thus, $\int_0^{1/30} 12{,}450\pi \sin(30\pi t)\, dt =$

$$12{,}450\pi\left[-\tfrac{1}{30\pi}\cos(30\pi t)\right]_0^{1/30} = -415(-1 - 1) = 830 \text{ cm}^3.$$

(b) One cycle of inhaling and exhaling corresponds to a period of $V'(t)$.

Period $= \tfrac{2\pi}{30\pi} = \tfrac{1}{15}\,\dfrac{\min}{\text{breath}}$. $\;15\,\dfrac{\text{breaths}}{\min} = 15 \times 60 \times 24 \times 365 =$

$7.884 \times 10^6\,\dfrac{\text{breaths}}{\text{yr}}$. $\;(7.884 \times 10^6)\,\dfrac{\text{breaths}}{\text{yr}} \times (830 \times 4.1 \times 10^{-12})\dfrac{\text{joule}}{\text{breath}} \approx$

$$26.8 \times 10^{-3} \text{ joule} \approx 0.026 \text{ joule. No, it is not safe.}$$

$\boxed{28}$ $T = 16 \Rightarrow$ total number of calories $=$

$$\int_0^8 \left(5 + 3\cdot3 - 6\cdot\tfrac{3}{16}\left|t - \tfrac{1}{2}\cdot16\right|\right) dt + \int_8^{16}\left(5 + 3\cdot2 - 6\cdot\tfrac{2}{16}\left|t - \tfrac{1}{2}\cdot16\right|\right) dt =$$

$$\int_0^8 \left[14 - \tfrac{9}{8}(8 - t)\right] dt + \int_8^{16}\left[11 - \tfrac{3}{4}(t - 8)\right] dt =$$

$$\int_0^8 \left(5 + \tfrac{9}{8}t\right) dt + \int_8^{16}\left(17 - \tfrac{3}{4}t\right) dt = 76 + 64 = 140 \text{ calories.}$$

$\boxed{29}$ $T = \frac{15-10}{2(5)}\{R(10) + 2\left[R(11) + R(12) + R(12) + R(13) + R(14)\right] + R(15)\} =$

$$\tfrac{1}{2}\left[5.3 + 2(5.2 + 4.9 + 6.5 + 9.3) + 7.0\right] = 32.05 \approx 32 \text{ cm.}$$

$\boxed{30}$ $S = \frac{80-0}{3(8)}[\rho(0) + 4\rho(10) + 2\rho(20) + 4\rho(30) + 2\rho(40) + 4\rho(50) +$

$$2\rho(60) + 4\rho(70) + \rho(80)]$$

$$= \tfrac{10}{3}\left[0 + 4(10) + 2(25) + 4(30) + 2(20) + 4(15) + 2(10) + 4(5) +0\right] =$$

$$\tfrac{10}{3}(350) = 1166\tfrac{2}{3} \approx 1167 \text{ zooplankton.}$$

6.9 Review Exercises

$\boxed{1}$ (a) $-x^2 = x^2 - 8 \Rightarrow x = \pm2.$ $A = 2\int_0^2\left[(-x^2) - (x^2 - 8)\right] dx = \frac{64}{3}.$

(b) Using symmetry on the fourth quadrant region if $-4 \le y \le 0$,

$$A = 4\int_{-4}^0 \sqrt{-y}\,dy = \tfrac{64}{3}.$$

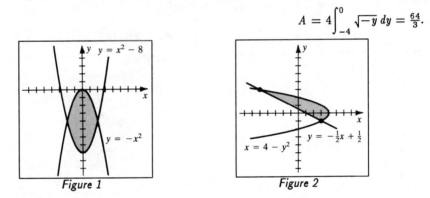

Figure 1   Figure 2

$\boxed{2}$ (a) $4 - y^2 = 1 - 2y \Rightarrow y = -1, 3;\ x = 3, -5.$

$$A = \int_{-5}^3\left[\sqrt{4 - x} - (-\tfrac{1}{2}x + \tfrac{1}{2})\right] dx + 2\int_3^4 \sqrt{4 - x}\,dx = \tfrac{28}{3} + \tfrac{4}{3} = \tfrac{32}{3}.$$

(b) $A = \int_{-1}^3\left[(4 - y^2) - (-2y + 1)\right] dy = \tfrac{32}{3}.$

$\boxed{3}$ $y^2 = 1 - y \Rightarrow y = a, b,$ where $a = \frac{1}{2}(-1 - \sqrt{5})$ and $b = \frac{1}{2}(-1 + \sqrt{5})$. $A =$

$$\int_a^b \left[(1 - y) - y^2\right] dy = \left[y - \frac{1}{2}y^2 - \frac{1}{3}y^3\right]_a^b = \left(\frac{5\sqrt{5}}{12} - \frac{7}{12}\right) - \left(-\frac{5\sqrt{5}}{12} - \frac{7}{12}\right) = \frac{5\sqrt{5}}{6}.$$

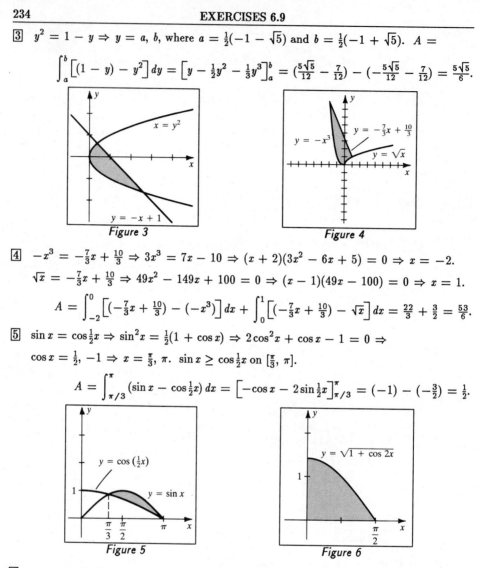

Figure 3   Figure 4

$\boxed{4}$ $-x^3 = -\frac{7}{3}x + \frac{10}{3} \Rightarrow 3x^3 = 7x - 10 \Rightarrow (x + 2)(3x^2 - 6x + 5) = 0 \Rightarrow x = -2.$

$\sqrt{x} = -\frac{7}{3}x + \frac{10}{3} \Rightarrow 49x^2 - 149x + 100 = 0 \Rightarrow (x - 1)(49x - 100) = 0 \Rightarrow x = 1.$

$$A = \int_{-2}^0 \left[\left(-\frac{7}{3}x + \frac{10}{3}\right) - (-x^3)\right] dx + \int_0^1 \left[\left(-\frac{7}{3}x + \frac{10}{3}\right) - \sqrt{x}\right] dx = \frac{22}{3} + \frac{3}{2} = \frac{53}{6}.$$

$\boxed{5}$ $\sin x = \cos \frac{1}{2}x \Rightarrow \sin^2 x = \frac{1}{2}(1 + \cos x) \Rightarrow 2\cos^2 x + \cos x - 1 = 0 \Rightarrow$

$\cos x = \frac{1}{2}, -1 \Rightarrow x = \frac{\pi}{3}, \pi.$ $\sin x \geq \cos \frac{1}{2}x$ on $[\frac{\pi}{3}, \pi].$

$$A = \int_{\pi/3}^{\pi} \left(\sin x - \cos \frac{1}{2}x\right) dx = \left[-\cos x - 2\sin \frac{1}{2}x\right]_{\pi/3}^{\pi} = (-1) - \left(-\frac{3}{2}\right) = \frac{1}{2}.$$

Figure 5   Figure 6

$\boxed{6}$ $y \geq 0$ on $[0, \frac{\pi}{2}].$

Using disks, $V = \pi \displaystyle\int_0^{\pi/2} \left(\sqrt{1 + \cos 2x}\right)^2 dx = \pi \left[x + \frac{1}{2}\sin 2x\right]_0^{\pi/2} = \frac{1}{2}\pi^2.$

$\boxed{7}$ Using disks, $V = \pi\int_0^2 (\sqrt{4x+1})^2\, dx = \pi\left[2x^2 + x\right]_0^2 = 10\pi.$

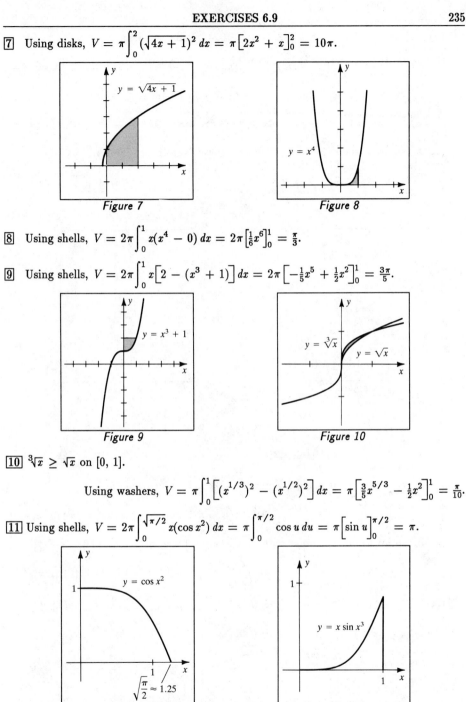

Figure 7   Figure 8

$\boxed{8}$ Using shells, $V = 2\pi\int_0^1 x(x^4 - 0)\, dx = 2\pi\left[\frac{1}{6}x^6\right]_0^1 = \frac{\pi}{3}.$

$\boxed{9}$ Using shells, $V = 2\pi\int_0^1 x\left[2 - (x^3 + 1)\right] dx = 2\pi\left[-\frac{1}{5}x^5 + \frac{1}{2}x^2\right]_0^1 = \frac{3\pi}{5}.$

Figure 9   Figure 10

$\boxed{10}$ $\sqrt[3]{x} \geq \sqrt{x}$ on $[0, 1]$.

Using washers, $V = \pi\int_0^1\left[(x^{1/3})^2 - (x^{1/2})^2\right] dx = \pi\left[\frac{3}{5}x^{5/3} - \frac{1}{2}x^2\right]_0^1 = \frac{\pi}{10}.$

$\boxed{11}$ Using shells, $V = 2\pi\int_0^{\sqrt{\pi/2}} x(\cos x^2)\, dx = \pi\int_0^{\pi/2}\cos u\, du = \pi\left[\sin u\right]_0^{\pi/2} = \pi.$

Figure 11   Figure 12

$\boxed{12}$ Using shells, $V = 2\pi\int_0^1 x(x \sin x^3)\, dx = \frac{2\pi}{3}\int_0^1 \sin u\, du = \frac{2\pi}{3}\left[-\cos u\right]_0^1 =$

$$-\frac{2\pi}{3}(\cos 1 - 1) = \frac{2\pi}{3}(1 - \cos 1) \approx 0.963.$$

$\boxed{13}$ (a) $4x^2 = -4x + 8 \Rightarrow x = -2, 1; \; y = 16, 4.$ Using washers, $V =$

$$\pi \int_{-2}^{1} \left[(-4x + 8)^2 - (4x^2)^2\right] dx = \pi \left[-\tfrac{16}{5}x^5 + \tfrac{16}{3}x^3 - 32x^2 + 64x\right]_{-2}^{1} = \tfrac{1152\pi}{5}.$$

(b) A typical shell has radius $(1 - x)$ and altitude $\left[(-4x + 8) - 4x^2\right].$

$$V = 2\pi \int_{-2}^{1} (1 - x)\left[(-4x + 8) - 4x^2\right] dx = 2\pi \left[x^4 - 6x^2 + 8x\right]_{-2}^{1} = 54\pi.$$

(c) A typical washer has outer radius $(16 - 4x^2)$ and inner radius

$$\left[16 - (-4x + 8)\right]. \quad V = \pi \int_{-2}^{1} \left\{(16 - 4x^2)^2 - \left[16 - (-4x + 8)\right]^2\right\} dx =$$

$$\pi \left[\tfrac{16}{5}x^5 - 48x^3 - 32x^2 + 192x\right]_{-2}^{1} = \tfrac{1728\pi}{5}.$$

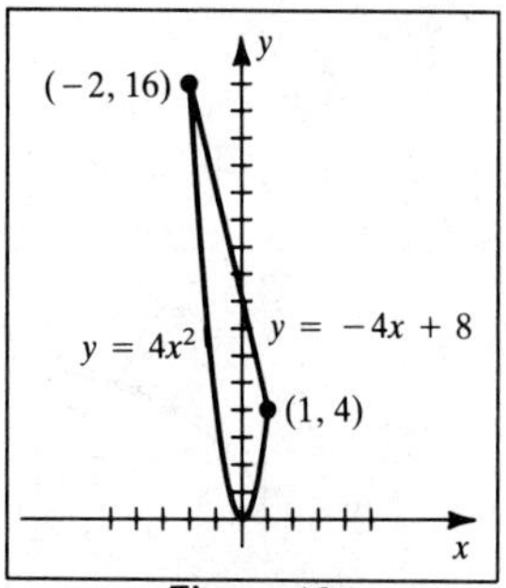

Figure 13

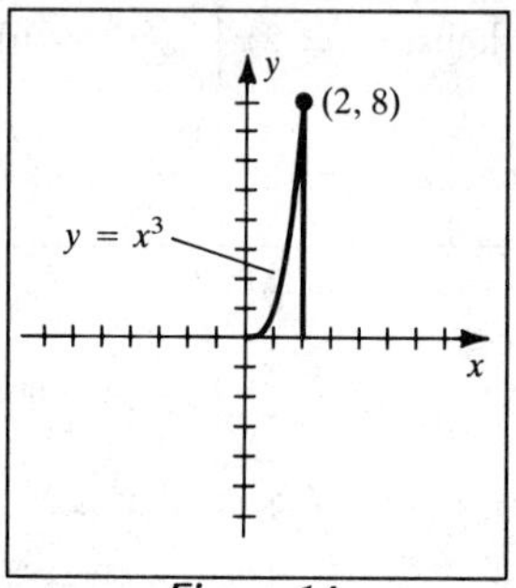

Figure 14

$\boxed{14}$ (a) $V = \pi \int_{0}^{2} (x^3)^2 \, dx = \tfrac{128\pi}{7}.$ (b) $V = 2\pi \int_{0}^{2} x(x^3) \, dx = \tfrac{64\pi}{5}.$

(c) $V = 2\pi \int_{0}^{2} (2 - x)x^3 \, dx = \tfrac{16\pi}{5}.$ (d) $V = 2\pi \int_{0}^{2} (3 - x)x^3 \, dx = \tfrac{56\pi}{5}.$

(e) A typical washer has outer radius $(8 - 0)$ and inner radius $(8 - x^3).$

$$V = \pi \int_{0}^{2} \left[(8 - 0)^2 - (8 - x^3)^2\right] dx = \pi \int_{0}^{2} (16x^3 - x^6) \, dx = \tfrac{320\pi}{7}.$$

(f) A typical washer has outer radius $\left[x^3 - (-1)\right]$ and inner radius $\left[0 - (-1)\right].$

$$V = \pi \int_{0}^{2} \left\{\left[x^3 - (-1)\right]^2 - \left[0 - (-1)\right]^2\right\} dx = \tfrac{184\pi}{7}.$$

$\boxed{15}$ $f(x) = 1 + \tfrac{1}{2}(x + 3)^{2/3} \Rightarrow f'(x) = \tfrac{1}{3}(x + 3)^{-1/3} \Rightarrow$

$$1 + [f'(x)]^2 = 1 + \tfrac{1}{9}(x + 3)^{-2/3} = \tfrac{1}{9}\left[9(x + 3)^{2/3} + 1\right](x + 3)^{-2/3} \Rightarrow$$

$$L = \tfrac{1}{3}\int_{-2}^{5} (x + 3)^{-1/3} \sqrt{9(x + 3)^{2/3} + 1} \, dx = \tfrac{1}{3}\int_{10}^{37} \tfrac{1}{6}\sqrt{u} \, du \; \{ u = 9(x + 3)^{2/3} + 1,$$

$$\tfrac{1}{6} \, du = (x + 3)^{-1/3} \, dx\} = \tfrac{1}{18}\left[\tfrac{2}{3}u^{3/2}\right]_{10}^{37} = \tfrac{1}{27}(37^{3/2} - 10^{3/2}) \approx 7.16.$$

$$\boxed{16}\int_c^d \tfrac{1}{2}bh\,dx = \int_0^4 A(x)\,dx = \int_0^4 \tfrac{1}{2}\left[\sqrt{4x} - (-\sqrt{4x})\right]\left[\sqrt{4x} - (-\sqrt{4x})\right]dx = \tfrac{1}{2}\int_0^4 16x\,dx =$$

$$8\left[\tfrac{1}{2}x^2\right]_0^4 = 64.$$

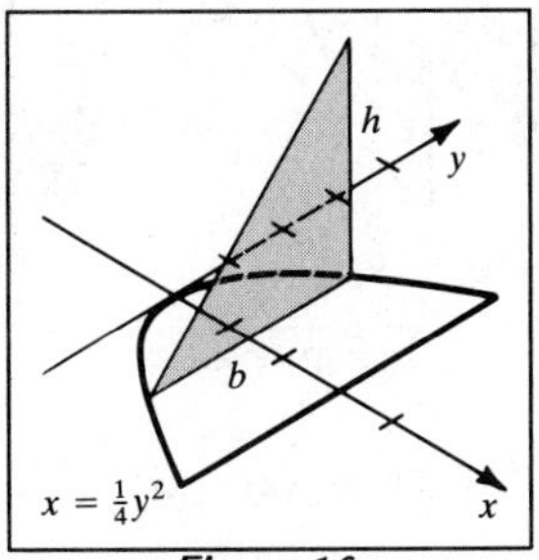

Figure 16

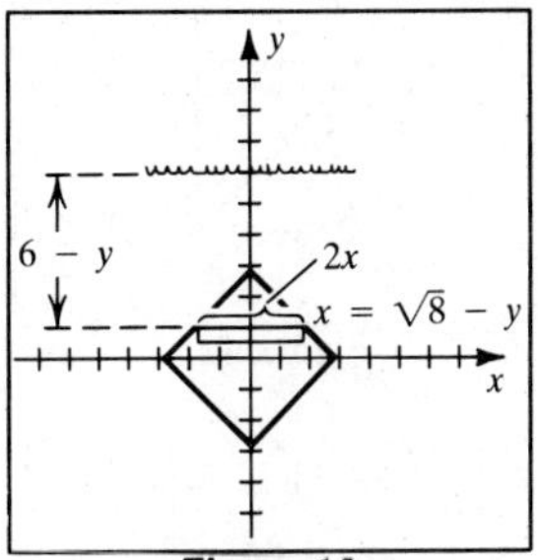

Figure 19

$\boxed{17}$ Center the y-axis vertically in the pool with $y = 0$ at the bottom of the pool.

On $0 \le y \le 4$, each slice of water at height y is lifted a distance of $(5 - y)$ and has

an area of $\pi(6)^2$. $W = \int_0^4 (5 - y)(62.5)\pi(6)^2\,dy = 432(62.5)\pi \approx 84,823$ ft-lb.

$\boxed{18}$ Position the y-axis vertically so that $y = 0$ is at the bottom of the well,

and $y = 30$ at is the top. The bucket loses $\frac{24/3}{30}$ lb/ft. The mass of the bucket is

$$\left[4 + (24 - \tfrac{8}{30}y)\right]. \quad W = \int_0^{30}\left[4 + (24 - \tfrac{8}{30}y)\right]dy = 720 \text{ ft-lb.}$$

$\boxed{19}$ See *Figure 19*. The corners of the plate are at $(\pm\sqrt{8}, 0)$ and $(0, \pm\sqrt{8})$,

and the surface is at $y = 6$. Consider the upper half of the plate $(y > 0)$.

The right edge is $x = f(y) = \sqrt{8} - y$. By symmetry, $L(y) = 2(\sqrt{8} - y)$ and

$$F_1 = \rho\int_0^{\sqrt{8}}(6 - y)\,2(\sqrt{8} - y)\,dy = \rho(48 - \tfrac{16}{3}\sqrt{2}). \text{ Consider the lower half } (y < 0).$$

$$L(y) = 2(y + \sqrt{8}) \text{ and } F_2 = \rho\int_{-\sqrt{8}}^0 (6 - y)\,2(y + \sqrt{8})\,dy = \rho(48 + \tfrac{16}{3}\sqrt{2}).$$

$$\text{Total force} = F_1 + F_2 = 96(62.5) = 6000 \text{ lb.}$$

$\boxed{20}$ Use (6.17(i)) with $f(x) = 2\sin\tfrac{1}{3}x$.

$$ds = \sqrt{1 + \tfrac{4}{9}(\cos\tfrac{1}{3}x)^2}\,dx = \sqrt{1 + \tfrac{4}{9}\cos^2\tfrac{\pi}{3}\left(\tfrac{\pi}{90}\right)} = \tfrac{\pi}{270}\sqrt{10} \approx 0.0368.$$

Note: For Exercises 21–22, without loss of generality, assume $\rho = 1$.

$\boxed{21}$ From *Figure 21*, we see that $m = \text{area} = \int_{-1}^1 \left[(x^3 + 1) - (-x - 1)\right]dx = 4.$

$$M_x = \tfrac{1}{2}\int_{-1}^1 \left[(x^3 + 1)^2 - (-x - 1)^2\right]dx = -\tfrac{4}{21}.$$

$$M_y = \int_{-1}^1 x\left[(x^3 + 1) - (-x - 1)\right]dx = \tfrac{16}{15}. \qquad \bar{x} = \frac{M_y}{m} = \tfrac{4}{15} \text{ and } \bar{y} = \frac{M_x}{m} = -\tfrac{1}{21}.$$

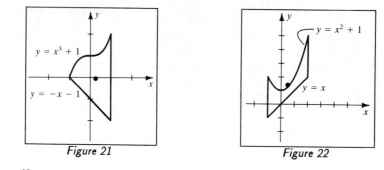

Figure 21   Figure 22

22 $m = \displaystyle\int_{-1}^{2} \left[(x^2 + 1) - x \right] dx = \frac{9}{2}.$ $M_x = \frac{1}{2}\displaystyle\int_{-1}^{2} \left[(x^2 + 1)^2 - (x)^2 \right] dx = \frac{63}{10}.$

$M_y = \displaystyle\int_{-1}^{2} x\left[(x^2 + 1) - x \right] dx = \frac{9}{4}.$ $\bar{x} = \frac{M_y}{m} = \frac{1}{2}$ and $\bar{y} = \frac{M_x}{m} = \frac{7}{5}.$

Note that the centroid is *not* in the bounded region.

23 $f(x) = \frac{1}{3}x^3 + \frac{1}{4}x^{-1} \Rightarrow 1 + [f'(x)]^2 = 1 + (x^4 - \frac{1}{2} + x^{-4}) = (x^2 + \frac{1}{4}x^{-2})^2.$

$S = 2\pi \displaystyle\int_{1}^{2} (\frac{1}{3}x^3 + \frac{1}{4}x^{-1})(x^2 + \frac{1}{4}x^{-2}) \, dx = 2\pi \int_{1}^{2} (\frac{1}{3}x^5 + \frac{1}{3}x + \frac{1}{16}x^{-3}) \, dx = \frac{515\pi}{64} \approx 25.3.$

24 An equation describing the shape is $x = ay^2$.

$x = 1$ and $y = \pm 2 \Rightarrow x = \frac{1}{4}y^2$ or $y = \pm \sqrt{4x}.$

The surface of the reflector may be generated by revolving $f(x) = \sqrt{4x}$ about the x-

axis. $S = 2\pi \displaystyle\int_{0}^{1} \sqrt{4x} \sqrt{1 + (x^{-1/2})^2} \, dx = 4\pi \int_{0}^{1} \sqrt{x + 1} \, dx = \frac{8\pi}{3}(2^{3/2} - 1) \approx 15.32.$

25 The distance the rocket travels is $\displaystyle\int_{0}^{5} v(t) \, dt.$

$T = \frac{5-0}{2(5)}\left[100 + 2(120 + 150 + 190 + 240) + 300 \right] = \frac{1}{2}(1800) = 900 \text{ ft.}$

26 (a) The total consumption is given by $\displaystyle\int_{0}^{60} R(t) \, dt.$

$S = \frac{60-0}{3(6)}\left[1.31 + 4(1.43) + 2(1.45) + 4(1.39) + 2(1.36) + 4(1.47) + 1.29 \right] =$

$\frac{10}{3}(25.38) = 84.6 \text{ kwh.}$

(b) Since the meter showed a consumption of $48{,}953 - 48{,}792 = 161$ kwh—a

percentage difference of 90%—it may be reasonable to assume that the meter is

not operating properly.

27 (a) The area under the graph of $y = 2\pi x^4$

(b) (i)   The volume obtained by revolving $y = \sqrt{2}\, x^2$ about the x-axis

(ii)   The volume obtained by revolving $y = x^3$ about the y-axis

(c) The work done by a force of magnitude $y = 2\pi x^4$ as it moves from

$x = 0$ to $x = 1$

28 The semicircle has radius 3. By symmetry, $\bar{x} = 7.$

$V = 2\pi\bar{x}A = (2\pi \cdot 7)(\frac{1}{2}\pi \cdot 3^2) = 63\pi^2.$

Chapter 7: Logarithmic and Exponential Functions

1. $y = 3x + 5 \Rightarrow y - 5 = 3x \Rightarrow x = \dfrac{y - 5}{3} \Rightarrow f^{-1}(x) = \dfrac{x - 5}{3}$

2. $y = 7 - 2x \Rightarrow 2x = 7 - y \Rightarrow x = \dfrac{7 - y}{2} \Rightarrow f^{-1}(x) = \dfrac{7 - x}{2}$

3. $y = \dfrac{1}{3x - 2} \Rightarrow 3xy - 2y = 1 \Rightarrow 3xy = 2y + 1 \Rightarrow x = \dfrac{2y + 1}{3y} \Rightarrow f^{-1}(x) = \dfrac{2x + 1}{3x}$

4. $y = \dfrac{1}{x + 3} \Rightarrow xy + 3y = 1 \Rightarrow xy = 1 - 3y \Rightarrow x = \dfrac{1 - 3y}{y} \Rightarrow f^{-1}(x) = \dfrac{1 - 3x}{x}$

5. $y = \dfrac{3x + 2}{2x - 5} \Rightarrow 2xy - 5y = 3x + 2 \Rightarrow 2xy - 3x = 5y + 2 \Rightarrow$

$$x = \dfrac{5y + 2}{2y - 3} \Rightarrow f^{-1}(x) = \dfrac{5x + 2}{2x - 3}$$

6. $y = \dfrac{4x}{x - 2} \Rightarrow xy - 2y = 4x \Rightarrow xy - 4x = 2y \Rightarrow x = \dfrac{2y}{y - 4} \Rightarrow f^{-1}(x) = \dfrac{2x}{x - 4}$

7. $y = 2 - 3x^2, \; x \le 0 \Rightarrow y + 3x^2 = 2 \Rightarrow x^2 = \dfrac{2 - y}{3} \Rightarrow$

$$x = \pm\tfrac{1}{3}\sqrt{6 - 3y} \; \{\text{Choose the ``$-$'' since } x \le 0.\} \Rightarrow f^{-1}(x) = -\tfrac{1}{3}\sqrt{6 - 3x}$$

8. $y = 5x^2 + 2, \; x \ge 0 \Rightarrow y - 2 = 5x^2 \Rightarrow x^2 = \dfrac{y - 2}{5} \Rightarrow$

$$x = \pm\tfrac{1}{5}\sqrt{5y - 10} \; \{\text{Choose the ``$+$'' since } x \ge 0.\} \Rightarrow f^{-1}(x) = \tfrac{1}{5}\sqrt{5x - 10}$$

9. $y = \sqrt{3 - x} \Rightarrow y^2 = 3 - x \Rightarrow$

$$x = 3 - y^2 \; \{\text{Since } y \ge 0 \text{ for } f, \; x \ge 0 \text{ for } f^{-1}.\} \Rightarrow f^{-1}(x) = 3 - x^2, \; x \ge 0$$

10. $y = \sqrt{4 - x^2}, \; 0 \le x \le 2 \Rightarrow y^2 = 4 - x^2 \Rightarrow x^2 = 4 - y^2 \Rightarrow x = \pm\sqrt{4 - y^2}$

$$\{\text{Choose the ``$+$'' since } 0 \le x \le 2.\} \Rightarrow f^{-1}(x) = \sqrt{4 - x^2}, \; 0 \le x \le 2$$

11. $y = \sqrt[3]{x} + 1 \Rightarrow y - 1 = \sqrt[3]{x} \Rightarrow x = (y - 1)^3 \Rightarrow f^{-1}(x) = (x - 1)^3$

12. $y = (x^3 + 1)^5 \Rightarrow \sqrt[5]{y} = x^3 + 1 \Rightarrow x^3 = \sqrt[5]{y} - 1 \Rightarrow$

$$x = \sqrt[3]{\sqrt[5]{y} - 1} \Rightarrow f^{-1}(x) = \sqrt[3]{\sqrt[5]{x} - 1}$$

13. (a) Since f is one-to-one, an inverse exists. If $f(x) = ax + b$, then $f^{-1}(x) = \dfrac{x - b}{a}$

for $a \ne 0$. (b) No, because a constant function is not one-to-one.

14. (i) If $P(a, b)$ is on the graph of f, then $f(a) = b$.

Also, $f^{-1}(b) = f^{-1}(f(a)) = a$. So $Q(b, a)$ is on the graph of f^{-1}.

(ii) $M(P, Q) = \left(\dfrac{a + b}{2}, \dfrac{b + a}{2}\right)$.

Since the x and y coordinates are equal, the point is on the line $y = x$.

(iii) $m_{PQ} = \dfrac{a - b}{b - a} = -1$ and the slope of the line $y = x$ is 1. Since the slopes of

the lines are negative reciprocals of each other, the lines are perpendicular.

15 (b) $f: D = [-1, 2]; R = [\frac{1}{2}, 4]$ (c) $f^{-1}: D = [\frac{1}{2}, 4]; R = [-1, 2]$

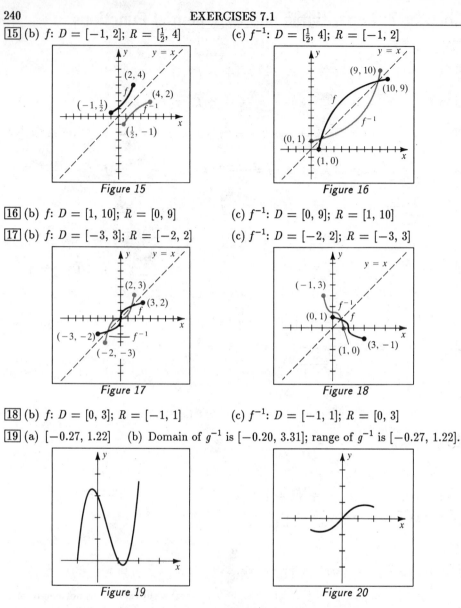

Figure 15   Figure 16

16 (b) $f: D = [1, 10]; R = [0, 9]$ (c) $f^{-1}: D = [0, 9]; R = [1, 10]$

17 (b) $f: D = [-3, 3]; R = [-2, 2]$ (c) $f^{-1}: D = [-2, 2]; R = [-3, 3]$

Figure 17   Figure 18

18 (b) $f: D = [0, 3]; R = [-1, 1]$ (c) $f^{-1}: D = [-1, 1]; R = [0, 3]$

19 (a) $[-0.27, 1.22]$ (b) Domain of g^{-1} is $[-0.20, 3.31]$; range of g^{-1} is $[-0.27, 1.22]$.

Figure 19   Figure 20

20 (a) $[-1.43, 1.43]$ (b) Domain of g^{-1} is $[-0.84, 0.84]$; range of g^{-1} is $[-1.43, 1.43]$.

21 (a) $f'(x) = \dfrac{1}{\sqrt{2x + 3}} > 0 \Rightarrow f$ is increasing on $[-\frac{3}{2}, \infty)$ and hence is one-to-one.

Thus, f has an inverse function and $f^{-1}(x) = \dfrac{x^2 - 3}{2}$.

(b) The range of f is $[0, \infty)$. This is also the domain of f^{-1}.

(c) Using (7.8) with $g = f^{-1}$, $D_x f^{-1}(x) =$

$$\frac{1}{f'(f^{-1}(x))} = \sqrt{2f^{-1}(x) + 3} = \sqrt{(x^2 - 3) + 3} = \sqrt{x^2} = |x| = x \, (x > 0).$$

$\boxed{22}$ (a) $f'(x) = \dfrac{5}{3(5x+2)^{2/3}} > 0 \Rightarrow f$ is increasing on $(-\infty, \infty)$ and hence is one-to-

one. Thus, f has an inverse function and $f^{-1}(x) = \dfrac{x^3 - 2}{5}$.

(b) The range of f is $\mathbb{R}$. This is also the domain of f^{-1}.

(c) Using (7.8) with $g = f^{-1}$,

$$D_x f^{-1}(x) = \frac{1}{f'(f^{-1}(x))} = \tfrac{3}{5}\big[5 f^{-1}(x) + 2\big]^{2/3} = \tfrac{3}{5}(x^3 - 2 + 2)^{2/3} = \tfrac{3}{5}x^2.$$

$\boxed{23}$ (a) $f'(x) = -2x < 0$ if $x \geq 0 \Rightarrow f$ is decreasing on $[0, \infty)$ and hence is one-to-one.

Thus, f has an inverse function. $y = 4 - x^2$ and $x \geq 0 \Rightarrow f^{-1}(x) = \sqrt{4 - x}$.

(b) The range of f is $(-\infty, 4]$. This is also the domain of f^{-1}.

(c) $D_x f^{-1}(x) = \dfrac{1}{f'(f^{-1}(x))} = \dfrac{1}{-2 f^{-1}(x)} = \dfrac{-1}{2\sqrt{4 - x}}$.

$\boxed{24}$ (a) $f'(x) = 2x - 4 > 0$ if $x \geq 2 \Rightarrow f$ is increasing on $[2, \infty)$ and hence is one-to-one.
Thus, f has an inverse function.

$$y = x^2 - 4x + 5 = (x - 2)^2 + 1 \text{ and } x \geq 2 \Rightarrow f^{-1}(x) = 2 + \sqrt{x - 1}.$$

(b) f has a *LMIN* at $(2, 1)$. Thus, the range of $f = [1, \infty) =$ the domain of f^{-1}.

(c) $D_x f^{-1}(x) = \dfrac{1}{f'(f^{-1}(x))} = \dfrac{1}{2 f^{-1}(x) - 4} = \dfrac{1}{(4 + 2\sqrt{x - 1}) - 4} = \dfrac{1}{2\sqrt{x - 1}}$.

$\boxed{25}$ (a) $f'(x) = -1/x^2 < 0$ if $x \neq 0 \Rightarrow f$ is decreasing on $(-\infty, 0)$ and $(0, \infty)$ and

hence is one-to-one. Thus, f has an inverse function and $f^{-1}(x) = 1/x = f(x)$.

(b) The range of f, and the domain of f^{-1}, is all real numbers except zero.

(c) $D_x f^{-1}(x) = \dfrac{1}{f'(f^{-1}(x))} = -[f^{-1}(x)]^2 = -(1/x)^2 = -1/x^2$.

$\boxed{26}$ (a) $f'(x) = \dfrac{-x}{\sqrt{9 - x^2}} < 0$ if $0 \leq x < 3 \Rightarrow f$ is decreasing on $[0, 3]$ and hence is one-

to-one. Thus, f has an inverse function and $f^{-1}(x) = \sqrt{9 - x^2} = f(x)$.

(b) The range of f is $[0, 3]$. This is also the domain of f^{-1}.

(c) $D_x f^{-1}(x) = \dfrac{1}{f'(f^{-1}(x))} = \dfrac{-\sqrt{9 - [f^{-1}(x)]^2}}{f^{-1}(x)} = \dfrac{-\sqrt{x^2}}{\sqrt{9 - x^2}} = \dfrac{-x}{\sqrt{9 - x^2}}$.

$\boxed{27}$ (a) $f'(x) = 5x^4 + 9x^2 + 2 > 0 \Rightarrow f$ is $\uparrow \Rightarrow f^{-1}$ exists.

(b) The point $(1, 5)$ is on the graph of $f \Rightarrow P(5, 1)$ is on the graph of f^{-1}.

$$\text{Using (7.7) with } g = f^{-1}, \; D_x f^{-1}(5) = \frac{1}{f'(f^{-1}(5))} = \frac{1}{f'(1)} = \frac{1}{16}.$$

$\boxed{28}$ (a) $f'(x) = -1 - 3x^2 = -(1 + 3x^2) < 0 \Rightarrow f$ is $\downarrow \Rightarrow f^{-1}$ exists.

(b) Using (7.7) with $g = f^{-1}$, $D_x f^{-1}(-8) = \dfrac{1}{f'(f^{-1}(-8))} = \dfrac{1}{f'(2)} = \dfrac{1}{-13} = -\dfrac{1}{13}$.

$\boxed{29}$ (a) $f'(x) = -2 - 24/x^4 = -2(1 + 12/x^4) < 0$ for $x > 0 \Rightarrow f$ is $\downarrow \Rightarrow f^{-1}$ exists.

(b) $D_x f^{-1}(-3) = \dfrac{1}{f'(f^{-1}(-3))} = \dfrac{1}{f'(2)} = \dfrac{1}{-7/2} = -\dfrac{2}{7}$.

$\boxed{30}$ (a) $f'(x) = 20x^4 + 3/x^4 > 0$ for $x > 0 \Rightarrow f$ is $\uparrow \Rightarrow f^{-1}$ exists.

(b) $D_x f^{-1}(3) = \dfrac{1}{f'(f^{-1}(3))} = \dfrac{1}{f'(1)} = \dfrac{1}{23}.$

$\boxed{31}$ (a) $f'(x) = 3x^2 + 4 > 0 \Rightarrow f$ is $\uparrow \Rightarrow f^{-1}$ exists.

(b) $D_x f^{-1}(15) = \dfrac{1}{f'(f^{-1}(15))} = \dfrac{1}{f'(2)} = \dfrac{1}{16}.$

$\boxed{32}$ (a) $f'(x) = 5x^4 + 1 > 0 \Rightarrow f$ is $\uparrow \Rightarrow f^{-1}$ exists.

(b) $D_x f^{-1}(2) = \dfrac{1}{f'(f^{-1}(2))} = \dfrac{1}{f'(1)} = \dfrac{1}{6}.$

$\boxed{\text{Exercises 7.2}}$

$\boxed{1}$ $f(x) = \ln(9x + 4) \Rightarrow f'(x) = \dfrac{1}{9x + 4} \cdot D_x(9x + 4) = \dfrac{1}{9x + 4} \cdot 9 = \dfrac{9}{9x + 4}$

$\boxed{2}$ $f(x) = \ln(x^4 + 1) \Rightarrow f'(x) = \dfrac{1}{x^4 + 1} \cdot D_x(x^4 + 1) = \dfrac{1}{x^4 + 1} \cdot 4x^3 = \dfrac{4x^3}{x^4 + 1}$

$\boxed{3}$ $f(x) = \ln(3x^2 - 2x + 1) \Rightarrow f'(x) = \dfrac{1}{3x^2 - 2x + 1} \cdot (6x - 2) = \dfrac{2(3x - 1)}{3x^2 - 2x + 1}$

$\boxed{4}$ $f(x) = \ln(4x^3 - x^2 + 2) \Rightarrow f'(x) = \dfrac{1}{4x^3 - x^2 + 2} \cdot (12x^2 - 2x) = \dfrac{2x(6x - 1)}{4x^3 - x^2 + 2}$

$\boxed{5}$ $f(x) = \ln|3 - 2x| \Rightarrow f'(x) = \dfrac{1}{3 - 2x} \cdot (-2) = \dfrac{2}{2x - 3}$

$\boxed{6}$ $f(x) = \ln|4 - 3x| \Rightarrow f'(x) = \dfrac{1}{4 - 3x} \cdot (-3) = \dfrac{3}{3x - 4}$

$\boxed{7}$ $f(x) = \ln|2 - 3x|^5 = 5\ln|2 - 3x| \Rightarrow f'(x) = 5 \cdot \dfrac{1}{2 - 3x} \cdot (-3) = \dfrac{15}{3x - 2}$

$\boxed{8}$ $f(x) = \ln|5x^2 - 1|^3 = 3\ln|5x^2 - 1| \Rightarrow f'(x) = 3 \cdot \dfrac{1}{5x^2 - 1} \cdot 10x = \dfrac{30x}{5x^2 - 1}$

$\boxed{9}$ $f(x) = \ln\sqrt{7 - 2x^3} = \frac{1}{2}\ln(7 - 2x^3) \Rightarrow f'(x) = \frac{1}{2} \cdot \dfrac{-6x^2}{7 - 2x^3} = \dfrac{3x^2}{2x^3 - 7}$

$\boxed{10}$ $f(x) = \ln\sqrt[3]{6x + 7} = \frac{1}{3}\ln(6x + 7) \Rightarrow f'(x) = \frac{1}{3} \cdot \dfrac{6}{6x + 7} = \dfrac{2}{6x + 7}$

$\boxed{11}$ $f(x) = x\ln x \Rightarrow f'(x) = x \cdot \dfrac{1}{x} + 1 \cdot \ln x = 1 + \ln x$

$\boxed{12}$ $f(x) = \ln(\ln x) \Rightarrow f'(x) = \dfrac{1}{\ln x} \cdot D_x(\ln x) = \dfrac{1}{\ln x} \cdot \dfrac{1}{x} = \dfrac{1}{x\ln x}$

$\boxed{13}$ $f(x) = \ln\sqrt{x} + \sqrt{\ln x} = \frac{1}{2}\ln x + (\ln x)^{1/2} \Rightarrow$

$$f'(x) = \frac{1}{2} \cdot \frac{1}{x} + \frac{1}{2}(\ln x)^{-1/2} \cdot \frac{1}{x} = \frac{1}{2x}\left(1 + \frac{1}{\sqrt{\ln x}}\right)$$

$\boxed{14}$ $f(x) = \ln x^3 + (\ln x)^3 = 3\ln x + (\ln x)^3 \Rightarrow$

$$f'(x) = \frac{3}{x} + 3(\ln x)^2 \cdot \frac{1}{x} = \frac{3}{x}\left[1 + (\ln x)^2\right]$$

$\boxed{15}$ $f(x) = \dfrac{1}{\ln x} + \ln\dfrac{1}{x} = (\ln x)^{-1} + \ln(x^{-1}) = (\ln x)^{-1} - \ln x \Rightarrow$

$$f'(x) = -(\ln x)^{-2} \cdot \frac{1}{x} - \frac{1}{x} = -\frac{1}{x}\left[\frac{1}{(\ln x)^2} + 1\right]$$

$\boxed{16}$ $f(x) = \dfrac{x^2}{\ln x} \Rightarrow f'(x) = \dfrac{(\ln x)(2x) - x^2(1/x)}{(\ln x)^2} = \dfrac{2x\ln x - x}{(\ln x)^2} = \dfrac{x(2\ln x - 1)}{(\ln x)^2}$

$\boxed{17}$ $f(x) = \ln\left[(5x-7)^4(2x+3)^3\right] = 4\ln(5x-7) + 3\ln(2x+3) \Rightarrow$

$$f'(x) = 4 \cdot \frac{1}{5x-7} \cdot 5 + 3 \cdot \frac{1}{2x+3} \cdot 2 = \frac{20}{5x-7} + \frac{6}{2x+3}$$

$\boxed{18}$ $f(x) = \ln\left[\sqrt[3]{4x-5}(3x+8)^2\right] = \frac{1}{3}\ln(4x-5) + 2\ln(3x+8) \Rightarrow$

$$f'(x) = \frac{1}{3} \cdot \frac{1}{4x-5} \cdot 4 + 2 \cdot \frac{1}{3x+8} \cdot 3 = \frac{4}{3(4x-5)} + \frac{6}{3x+8}$$

$\boxed{19}$ $f(x) = \ln\dfrac{\sqrt{x^2+1}}{(9x-4)^2} = \frac{1}{2}\ln(x^2+1) - 2\ln(9x-4) \Rightarrow f'(x) = \dfrac{x}{x^2+1} - \dfrac{18}{9x-4}$

$\boxed{20}$ $f(x) = \ln\dfrac{x^2(2x-1)^3}{(x+5)^2} = 2\ln x + 3\ln(2x-1) - 2\ln(x+5) \Rightarrow$

$$f'(x) = \frac{2}{x} + \frac{6}{2x-1} - \frac{2}{x+5}$$

$\boxed{21}$ $f(x) = \ln\sqrt{\dfrac{x^2-1}{x^2+1}} = \frac{1}{2}\left[\ln(x^2-1) - \ln(x^2+1)\right] \Rightarrow$

$$f'(x) = \frac{1}{2}\left(\frac{2x}{x^2-1} - \frac{2x}{x^2+1}\right) = \frac{x}{x^2-1} - \frac{x}{x^2+1}$$

$\boxed{22}$ $f(x) = \ln\sqrt{\dfrac{4+x^2}{4-x^2}} = \frac{1}{2}\left[\ln(4+x^2) - \ln(4-x^2)\right] \Rightarrow$

$$f'(x) = \frac{1}{2}\left(\frac{2x}{4+x^2} - \frac{-2x}{4-x^2}\right) = \frac{x}{4+x^2} + \frac{x}{4-x^2}$$

$\boxed{23}$ $f(x) = \ln(x + \sqrt{x^2-1}) \Rightarrow$

$$f'(x) = \frac{1 + x/\sqrt{x^2-1}}{x + \sqrt{x^2-1}} = \frac{\sqrt{x^2-1}+x}{\sqrt{x^2-1}\,(x+\sqrt{x^2-1})} = \frac{1}{\sqrt{x^2-1}}$$

$\boxed{24}$ $f(x) = \ln(x + \sqrt{x^2+1}) \Rightarrow$

$$f'(x) = \frac{1 + x/\sqrt{x^2+1}}{x + \sqrt{x^2+1}} = \frac{\sqrt{x^2+1}+x}{\sqrt{x^2+1}\,(x+\sqrt{x^2+1})} = \frac{1}{\sqrt{x^2+1}}$$

$\boxed{25}$ $f(x) = \ln\cos 2x \Rightarrow f'(x) = \dfrac{-2\sin 2x}{\cos 2x} = -2\tan 2x$

$\boxed{26}$ $f(x) = \cos(\ln 2x) \Rightarrow f'(x) = \left[-\sin(\ln 2x)\right]\left(\dfrac{2}{2x}\right) = (-1/x)\sin(\ln 2x)$

$\boxed{27}$ $f(x) = \ln\tan^3 3x = 3\ln(\tan 3x) \Rightarrow f'(x) = 3 \cdot \dfrac{3\sec^2 3x}{\tan 3x} = 9\csc 3x \sec 3x$

$\boxed{28}$ $f(x) = \ln\cot(x^2) \Rightarrow f'(x) = \dfrac{\left[-\csc^2(x^2)\right]\cdot 2x}{\cot(x^2)} = -2x\csc(x^2)\sec(x^2)$

$\boxed{29}$ $f(x) = \ln\ln\sec 2x \Rightarrow f'(x) = \dfrac{(1/\sec 2x)(2\sec 2x \tan 2x)}{\ln\sec 2x} = \dfrac{2\tan 2x}{\ln\sec 2x}$

$\boxed{30}$ $f(x) = \ln\csc^2 4x = 2\ln\csc 4x \Rightarrow f'(x) = 2 \cdot \dfrac{-4\csc 4x \cot 4x}{\csc 4x} = -8\cot 4x$

$\boxed{31}$ $f(x) = \ln|\sec x| \Rightarrow f'(x) = \dfrac{1}{\sec x} \cdot \sec x \tan x = \tan x$

$\boxed{32}$ $f(x) = \ln|\sin x| \Rightarrow f'(x) = \dfrac{1}{\sin x} \cdot \cos x = \cot x$

$\boxed{33}$ $f(x) = \ln|\sec x + \tan x| \Rightarrow$

$$f'(x) = \frac{1}{\sec x + \tan x} \cdot (\sec x \tan x + \sec^2 x) = \frac{\sec x(\tan x + \sec x)}{\sec x + \tan x} = \sec x$$

$\boxed{34}$ $f(x) = \ln|\csc x - \cot x| \Rightarrow$

$$f'(x) = \frac{1}{\csc x - \cot x} \cdot (-\csc x \cot x + \csc^2 x) = \frac{\csc x(\csc x - \cot x)}{\csc x - \cot x} = \csc x$$

$\boxed{35}$ $3y - x^2 + \ln xy = 2 \Leftrightarrow 3y - x^2 + \ln x + \ln y = 2 \Rightarrow$

$$3y' - 2x + \tfrac{1}{x} + \tfrac{y'}{y} = 0 \Rightarrow y'(3 + \tfrac{1}{y}) = 2x - \tfrac{1}{x} \Rightarrow y' = \frac{y(2x^2 - 1)}{x(3y + 1)}$$

$\boxed{36}$ $y^2 + \ln(x/y) - 4x = -3 \Leftrightarrow y^2 + \ln x - \ln y - 4x = -3 \Rightarrow$

$$2yy' + \tfrac{1}{x} - \tfrac{y'}{y} - 4 = 0 \Rightarrow y'(2y - \tfrac{1}{y}) = 4 - \tfrac{1}{x} \Rightarrow y' = \frac{y(4x - 1)}{x(2y^2 - 1)}$$

$\boxed{37}$ $x \ln y - y \ln x = 1 \Rightarrow \left(x \cdot \tfrac{y'}{y} + 1 \cdot \ln y\right) - \left(\tfrac{y}{x} + y' \ln x\right) = 0 \Rightarrow$

$$y'\left(\tfrac{x}{y} - \ln x\right) = \tfrac{y}{x} - \ln y \Rightarrow y' = \frac{(y/x) - \ln y}{(x/y) - \ln x} = \frac{y(y - x \ln y)}{x(x - y \ln x)}$$

$\boxed{38}$ $y^3 + x^2 \ln y = 5x + 3 \Rightarrow 3y^2 y' + x^2 \cdot \tfrac{y'}{y} + 2x \ln y = 5 \Rightarrow$

$$y'(3y^2 + \tfrac{x^2}{y}) = 5 - 2x \ln y \Rightarrow y' = \frac{y(5 - 2x \ln y)}{3y^3 + x^2}$$

$\boxed{39}$ $\ln y = 3 \ln(5x + 2) + 2 \ln(6x + 1) \Rightarrow \tfrac{y'}{y} = \frac{15}{5x + 2} + \frac{12}{6x + 1} \Rightarrow$

$$y' = \frac{150x + 39}{(5x + 2)(6x + 1)} \cdot y = (150x + 39)(5x + 2)^2(6x + 1)$$

$\boxed{40}$ $\ln y = 2 \ln(x + 1) + 3 \ln(x + 2) + 4 \ln(x + 3) \Rightarrow \tfrac{y'}{y} = \frac{2}{x + 1} + \frac{3}{x + 2} + \frac{4}{x + 3}$

$$\Rightarrow y' = \frac{9x^2 + 34x + 29}{(x + 1)(x + 2)(x + 3)} \cdot y = (9x^2 + 34x + 29)(x + 1)(x + 2)^2(x + 3)^3$$

$\boxed{41}$ $\ln y = \tfrac{1}{2} \ln(4x + 7) + 3 \ln(x - 5) \Rightarrow \tfrac{y'}{y} = \frac{2}{4x + 7} + \frac{3}{x - 5} \Rightarrow$

$$y' = \frac{14x + 11}{(4x + 7)(x - 5)} \cdot y = \frac{(14x + 11)(x - 5)^2}{\sqrt{4x + 7}}$$

$\boxed{42}$ $\ln y = \tfrac{1}{2} \ln(3x^2 + 2) + \tfrac{1}{4} \ln(6x - 7) \Rightarrow \tfrac{y'}{y} = \frac{3x}{3x^2 + 2} + \frac{3}{2(6x - 7)} \Rightarrow$

$$y' = \frac{45x^2 - 42x + 6}{2(3x^2 + 2)(6x - 7)} \cdot y = \frac{3(15x^2 - 14x + 2)}{2(3x^2 + 2)^{1/2}(6x - 7)^{3/4}}$$

$\boxed{43}$ $\ln y = 5 \ln(x^2 + 3) - \tfrac{1}{2} \ln(x + 1) \Rightarrow \tfrac{y'}{y} = \frac{10x}{x^2 + 3} - \frac{1}{2(x + 1)} \Rightarrow$

$$y' = \frac{19x^2 + 20x - 3}{2(x^2 + 3)(x + 1)} \cdot y = \frac{(19x^2 + 20x - 3)(x^2 + 3)^4}{2(x + 1)^{3/2}}$$

$\boxed{44}$ $\ln y = \tfrac{2}{3} \ln(x^2 + 3) + 4 \ln(3x - 4) - \tfrac{1}{2} \ln x \Rightarrow \tfrac{y'}{y} = \frac{4x}{3(x^2 + 3)} + \frac{12}{3x - 4} - \frac{1}{2x} \Rightarrow$

$$y' = \frac{87x^3 - 20x^2 + 189x + 36}{6x(x^2 + 3)(3x - 4)} \cdot y = \frac{(87x^3 - 20x^2 + 189x + 36)(3x - 4)^3}{6x^{3/2}(x^2 + 3)^{1/3}}$$

$\boxed{45}$ $y' = 2x + \frac{2}{2x - 5}$. $x = 3 \Rightarrow y' = m = 8$.

Tangent line: $y - 9 = 8(x - 3)$ or $y = 8x - 15$.

$\boxed{46}$ $2x + 6y = 5 \Leftrightarrow y = -\tfrac{1}{3}x + \tfrac{5}{6}$. The required slope is the negative reciprocal of $-\tfrac{1}{3}$,

or 3. $y = x + \ln x \Rightarrow y' = 1 + \tfrac{1}{x} = 3 \Rightarrow x = \tfrac{1}{2}$.

Tangent line: $y - (\tfrac{1}{2} - \ln 2) = 3(x - \tfrac{1}{2}) \Rightarrow y = 3x - 1 - \ln 2 \approx 3x - 1.69$.

$\boxed{47}$ $y = 5 \ln x - \tfrac{1}{2}x \Rightarrow y' = \frac{5}{x} - \tfrac{1}{2}$. $y' = 0 \Rightarrow x = 10$.

$y'' = -(5/x^2) < 0 \Rightarrow$ the graph is CD for $x > 0$. $x = 10 \Rightarrow y'' = -0.05 < 0 \Rightarrow$

$(10, 5 \ln 10 - 5) \approx (10, 6.51)$ is a maximum on $(0, \infty)$.

48 $y = \ln(x^2 + 1) \Rightarrow y' = \dfrac{2x}{x^2 + 1} \Rightarrow y'' = \dfrac{2(1 - x^2)}{(x^2 + 1)^2}$. On $(-\infty, -1)$, $y'' < 0$.

On $(-1, 1)$, $y'' > 0$. On $(1, \infty)$, $y'' < 0$. Thus, $(\pm 1, \ln 2)$ are *PI*.

49 $T = -2.57\left[\ln(87 - L) - \ln 63\right] \Rightarrow$

$$dT = \frac{-2.57}{87 - L}(-1)\, dL = \frac{2.57}{87 - 80}(\pm 2) \approx \pm 0.73 \text{ yr.}$$

50 $\dfrac{d}{dt}(\ln W = \ln 2.4 + 0.0184h) \Rightarrow \dfrac{1}{W}\cdot\dfrac{dW}{dt} = 0.0184\cdot\dfrac{dh}{dt} \Rightarrow \dfrac{dW}{dt} = (0.0184\,W)\dfrac{dh}{dt}$.

51 (a) The initial velocity and acceleration are given by $s'(0)$ and $s''(0)$, respectively.

$$s(t) = ct + \frac{c}{b}(m_1 + m_2 - bt)\left[\ln(m_1 + m_2 - bt) - \ln(m_1 + m_2)\right] \Rightarrow$$

$$s'(t) = c + \frac{c}{b}(m_1 + m_2 - bt)\cdot\frac{-b}{m_1 + m_2 - bt} +$$

$$\frac{c}{b}(-b)\left[\ln(m_1 + m_2 - bt) - \ln(m_1 + m_2)\right]$$

$$= c + (-c) + (-c)\left[\ln(m_1 + m_2 - bt) - \ln(m_1 + m_2)\right] \Rightarrow$$

$s'(0) = 0$ m/sec. Also, $s''(t) = \dfrac{(-c)(-b)}{m_1 + m_2 - bt} \Rightarrow s''(0) = \dfrac{bc}{m_1 + m_2}$ m/sec^2.

(b) $s'\left(\dfrac{m_2}{b}\right) = (-c)\left[\ln(m_1 + m_2 - m_2) - \ln(m_1 + m_2)\right] = c\ln\left(\dfrac{m_1 + m_2}{m_1}\right)$;

$$s''\left(\frac{m_2}{b}\right) = \frac{bc}{m_1}.$$

52 (a) $\ln\dfrac{I}{I_0} = -\beta T \Leftrightarrow \ln\dfrac{I_0}{I} = \beta T$. $\ln 2.3 = 2.7T \Rightarrow T = \dfrac{\ln 2.3}{2.7} \approx 0.31$ cm.

(b) Let $x = I_0/I$. $\ln x = \beta T \Rightarrow dT = \dfrac{1}{\beta}\cdot\dfrac{1}{x}\, dx = \dfrac{1}{2.7}\cdot\dfrac{1}{2.3}(\pm 0.1) \approx \pm 0.0161$ cm.

53 The graphs coincide if $x > 0$; however,

the graph of $y = \ln(x^2)$ contains points with negative x-coordinates.

54 (a) $y = \ln|x|$ (b) $y = |\ln x|$

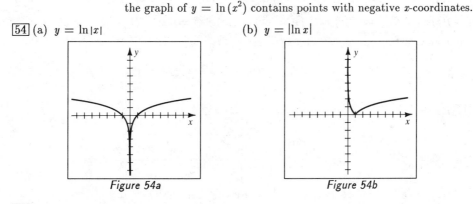

Figure 54a   Figure 54b

55 The root occurs where the graph of $y = \ln x$ intersects that of $y = -x$. This occurs on $(0, 1)$. Letting $x_1 = 0.5$ yields: $x_2 = 0.56438$, $x_3 = 0.56714$, and $x_4 = 0.56714$.

56 If $0 < x \le 1$, then $x > 0$, $\ln x \le 0$, and hence $x > \ln x$. If $x > 1$, let $f(x) = x - \ln x$ and consider $f'(x) = 1 - \dfrac{1}{x} = \dfrac{x - 1}{x} > 0$. Since f' is positive, f is increasing. Now $f(1) = 1 > 0$ implies that $f(x) > 0$ and hence $x - \ln x > 0$, or, equivalently, $x > \ln x$.

57 (a) No, since $f(1) = 0$ and $g(1) = 1$.

(b) Yes. $f(3) \approx 4.39$, $g(3) \approx 1.73$ and

$$f'(x) - g'(x) = \tfrac{4}{x} - \tfrac{1}{2\sqrt{x}} = \frac{8 - \sqrt{x}}{2x} \geq 0 \text{ on } [3, 64] \Rightarrow f(x) \geq g(x).$$

(c) Using large values of x, we conclude that $\lim_{x \to \infty} \left[f(x)/g(x) \right] = 0$.

Hence, $f(x) < g(x)$ for large values of x.   No.

58 (a) Let $f(x) = \ln(x^2)$. $T = \tfrac{2-1}{2(4)} \{ f(1) + 2[f(1.25) + f(1.5) + f(1.75)] + f(2) \} \approx$

$$\tfrac{1}{8}(6.1392) = 0.7674.$$

(b) $f'(x) = 2/x$ and $f''(x) = -2/x^2$. $M \geq |f''(x)|$ on $[1, 2] \Rightarrow M = 2$ when $x = 1$.

$$|\text{Error}| \leq \frac{M(b-a)^3}{12n^2} = \frac{2(2-1)^3}{12(4)^2} = \tfrac{1}{96} \approx 0.0104.$$

Exercises 7.3

1 $f(x) = e^{-5x} \Rightarrow f'(x) = e^{-5x} \cdot D_x(-5x) = e^{-5x} \cdot (-5) = -5e^{-5x}$

2 $f(x) = e^{3x} \Rightarrow f'(x) = e^{3x} \cdot D_x(3x) = e^{3x} \cdot (3) = 3e^{3x}$

3 $f(x) = e^{3x^2} \Rightarrow f'(x) = e^{3x^2} \cdot (6x) = 6xe^{3x^2}$

4 $f(x) = e^{1-x^3} \Rightarrow f'(x) = e^{1-x^3} \cdot (-3x^2) = -3x^2 e^{1-x^3}$

5 $f(x) = \sqrt{1 + e^{2x}} \Rightarrow f'(x) = \tfrac{1}{2}(1 + e^{2x})^{-1/2}(e^{2x})(2) = \dfrac{e^{2x}}{\sqrt{1 + e^{2x}}}$

6 $f(x) = 1/(e^x + 1) = (e^x + 1)^{-1} \Rightarrow f'(x) = (-1)(e^x + 1)^{-2}(e^x) = \dfrac{-e^x}{(e^x + 1)^2}$

7 $f(x) = e^{\sqrt{x+1}} \Rightarrow f'(x) = e^{\sqrt{x+1}} \cdot \tfrac{1}{2}(x+1)^{-1/2} = \dfrac{e^{\sqrt{x+1}}}{2\sqrt{x+1}}$

8 $f(x) = xe^{-x} \Rightarrow f'(x) = (x)(-e^{-x}) + (1)(e^{-x}) = e^{-x}(1 - x)$

9 $f(x) = x^2 e^{-2x} \Rightarrow f'(x) = x^2(-2e^{-2x}) + (2x)e^{-2x} = 2xe^{-2x}(1 - x)$

10 $f(x) = \sqrt{e^{2x} + 2x} = (e^{2x} + 2x)^{1/2} \Rightarrow$

$$f'(x) = \tfrac{1}{2}(e^{2x} + 2x)^{-1/2}(2e^{2x} + 2) = \dfrac{e^{2x} + 1}{\sqrt{e^{2x} + 2x}}$$

11 $f(x) = \dfrac{e^x}{x^2 + 1} \Rightarrow f'(x) = \dfrac{(x^2 + 1)e^x - 2xe^x}{(x^2 + 1)^2} = \dfrac{e^x(x^2 + 1 - 2x)}{(x^2 + 1)^2} = \dfrac{e^x(x - 1)^2}{(x^2 + 1)^2}$

12 $f(x) = x/e^{(x^2)} \Rightarrow f'(x) = \dfrac{e^{(x^2)}(1) - (x)e^{(x^2)}(2x)}{\left[e^{(x^2)} \right]^2} = \dfrac{e^{(x^2)}(1 - 2x^2)}{\left[e^{(x^2)} \right]^2} = \dfrac{1 - 2x^2}{e^{(x^2)}}$

13 $f(x) = (e^{4x} - 5)^3 \Rightarrow f'(x) = 3(e^{4x} - 5)^2 \cdot 4e^{4x} = 12e^{4x}(e^{4x} - 5)^2$

14 $f(x) = (e^{3x} - e^{-3x})^4 \Rightarrow$

$$f'(x) = 4(e^{3x} - e^{-3x})^3(3e^{3x} + 3e^{-3x}) = 12(e^{3x} - e^{-3x})^3(e^{3x} + e^{-3x})$$

15 $f(x) = e^{1/x} + (1/e^x) \Rightarrow f'(x) = e^{1/x} \cdot \left(-\tfrac{1}{x^2} \right) + D_x(e^{-x}) = -\dfrac{e^{1/x}}{x^2} - e^{-x}$

16 $f(x) = e^{\sqrt{x}} + \sqrt{e^x} = e^{x^{1/2}} + (e^x)^{1/2} \Rightarrow$

$$f'(x) = e^{\sqrt{x}} \cdot \tfrac{1}{2}x^{-1/2} + \tfrac{1}{2}(e^x)^{-1/2} \cdot e^x = \dfrac{e^{\sqrt{x}}}{2\sqrt{x}} + \dfrac{\sqrt{e^x}}{2}$$

$\boxed{17}$ $f(x) = \dfrac{e^x - e^{-x}}{e^x + e^{-x}} \Rightarrow f'(x) = \dfrac{(e^x + e^{-x})(e^x - (-e^{-x})) - (e^x - e^{-x})(e^x - e^{-x})}{(e^x + e^{-x})^2} =$

$\dfrac{(e^x + e^{-x})^2 - (e^x - e^{-x})^2}{(e^x + e^{-x})^2} = \dfrac{(e^{2x} + 2 + e^{-2x}) - (e^{2x} - 2 + e^{-2x})}{(e^x + e^{-x})^2} = \dfrac{4}{(e^x + e^{-x})^2}$

$\boxed{18}$ $f(x) = e^{x \ln x} \Rightarrow f'(x) = e^{x \ln x}\left(x \cdot \dfrac{1}{x} + 1 \cdot \ln x\right) = e^{x \ln x}(1 + \ln x)$

$\boxed{19}$ $f(x) = e^{-2x} \ln x \Rightarrow f'(x) = e^{-2x} \cdot \dfrac{1}{x} + (\ln x)(-2e^{-2x}) = e^{-2x}\left(\dfrac{1}{x} - 2\ln x\right)$

$\boxed{20}$ $f(x) = \ln e^x = x \Rightarrow f'(x) = 1$

$\boxed{21}$ $f(x) = \sin e^{5x} \Rightarrow f'(x) = \cos e^{5x} \cdot D_x\left(e^{5x}\right) = 5e^{5x} \cos e^{5x}$

$\boxed{22}$ $f(x) = e^{\sin 5x} \Rightarrow f'(x) = e^{\sin 5x} \cdot D_x(\sin 5x) = (5\cos 5x)e^{\sin 5x}$

$\boxed{23}$ $f(x) = \ln \cos e^{-x} \Rightarrow f'(x) = \dfrac{1}{\cos e^{-x}}(-\sin e^{-x})(-e^{-x}) = \dfrac{e^{-x} \sin e^{-x}}{\cos e^{-x}} = e^{-x} \tan e^{-x}$

$\boxed{24}$ $f(x) = e^{-3x} \cos 3x \Rightarrow$
$$f'(x) = (e^{-3x})(-3\sin 3x) + (\cos 3x)(-3e^{-3x}) = -3e^{-3x}(\sin 3x + \cos 3x)$$

$\boxed{25}$ $f(x) = e^{3x} \tan \sqrt{x} \Rightarrow f'(x) = e^{3x} \cdot \dfrac{\sec^2 \sqrt{x}}{2\sqrt{x}} + 3e^{3x} \tan \sqrt{x} = e^{3x}\left(\dfrac{\sec^2 \sqrt{x}}{2\sqrt{x}} + 3\tan \sqrt{x}\right)$

$\boxed{26}$ $f(x) = \sec e^{-2x} \Rightarrow f'(x) = (\sec e^{-2x} \tan e^{-2x})(-2e^{-2x}) = -2e^{-2x} \sec e^{-2x} \tan e^{-2x}$

$\boxed{27}$ $f(x) = \sec^2(e^{-4x}) = \left[\sec(e^{-4x})\right]^2 \Rightarrow$
$$f'(x) = 2\sec(e^{-4x})\left[\sec(e^{-4x})\tan(e^{-4x})\right](-4e^{-4x}) = -8e^{-4x} \sec^2(e^{-4x})\tan(e^{-4x})$$

$\boxed{28}$ $f(x) = e^{-x} \tan^2 x \Rightarrow$
$$f'(x) = e^{-x}(2\tan x \sec^2 x) + (-e^{-x})\tan^2 x = e^{-x} \tan x(2\sec^2 x - \tan x)$$

$\boxed{29}$ $f(x) = xe^{\cot x} \Rightarrow f'(x) = x\left[e^{\cot x}(-\csc^2 x)\right] + e^{\cot x} \cdot 1 = e^{\cot x}(1 - x\csc^2 x)$

$\boxed{30}$ $f(x) = \ln(\csc e^{3x}) \Rightarrow f'(x) = \dfrac{1}{\csc e^{3x}}(-\csc e^{3x} \cot e^{3x})(3e^{3x}) = -3e^{3x} \cot e^{3x}$

$\boxed{31}$ $e^{xy} - x^3 + 3y^2 = 11 \Rightarrow e^{xy}(xy' + y) - 3x^2 + 6yy' = 0 \Rightarrow$
$$y'(xe^{xy} + 6y) = 3x^2 - ye^{xy} \Rightarrow y' = \dfrac{3x^2 - ye^{xy}}{xe^{xy} + 6y}$$

$\boxed{32}$ $xe^y + 2x - \ln(y + 1) = 3 \Rightarrow (xe^y y' + e^y) + 2 - \dfrac{y'}{y + 1} = 0 \Rightarrow$
$$y'\left(xe^y - \dfrac{1}{y + 1}\right) = -(e^y + 2) \Rightarrow y' = \dfrac{e^y + 2}{\dfrac{1}{y + 1} - xe^y} = \dfrac{(y + 1)(e^y + 2)}{1 - (y + 1)(xe^y)}$$

$\boxed{33}$ $e^x \cot y = xe^{2y} \Rightarrow e^x(-\csc^2 y)y' + e^x \cot y = 2xe^{2y}y' + e^{2y} \Rightarrow$
$$e^x \cot y - e^{2y} = y'(2xe^{2y} + e^x \csc^2 y) \Rightarrow y' = \dfrac{e^x \cot y - e^{2y}}{2xe^{2y} + e^x \csc^2 y}$$

$\boxed{34}$ $e^x \cos y = xe^y \Rightarrow e^x(-\sin y)(y') + e^x \cos y = xe^y y' + e^y \Rightarrow$
$$e^x \cos y - e^y = y'(xe^y + e^x \sin y) \Rightarrow y' = \dfrac{e^x \cos y - e^y}{xe^y + e^x \sin y}$$

$\boxed{35}$ $y = (x - 1)e^x + 3\ln x + 2 \Rightarrow y' = (x - 1)e^x + e^x + \dfrac{3}{x}$. At $x = 1$, $y' = e + 3$.

Tangent line: $y - 2 = (e + 3)(x - 1)$, or $y = (e + 3)x - (e + 1) \approx 5.72x - 3.72$.

36 $6x - 2y = 7 \Leftrightarrow y = 3x - \frac{7}{2}$. The given line has a slope of 3. $y = x - e^{-x} \Rightarrow$

$y' = 1 + e^{-x}$. $y' = 3 \Rightarrow e^{-x} = 2 \Rightarrow x = -\ln 2$. $x = -\ln 2 \Rightarrow$

$y = -\ln 2 - e^{-(-\ln 2)} = -\ln 2 - 2 = -(2 + \ln 2)$. The point $(-\ln 2, -(2 + \ln 2))$

lies on the tangent line. At this point, the tangent line has a slope of 3.

Tangent line: $y + (2 + \ln 2) = 3(x + \ln 2)$, or $y = 3x + (2\ln 2 - 2) \approx 3x - 0.61$.

37 $f(x) = xe^x \Rightarrow f'(x) = e^x(x + 1)$. $f'(x) = 0 \Rightarrow x = -1$. $f'(x) > 0$ if $x > -1 \Rightarrow$

f is ↑ on $[-1, \infty)$. $f'(x) < 0$ if $x < -1 \Rightarrow f$ is ↓ on $(-\infty, -1]$. $f''(x) = e^x(x + 2)$.

$f''(-1) = e^{-1} > 0 \Rightarrow f(-1) = -e^{-1} \approx -0.368$ is a *LMIN*.

$f''(x) > 0$ if $x > -2 \Rightarrow f$ is *CU* on $(-2, \infty)$. $f''(x) < 0$ if $x < -2 \Rightarrow$

           f is *CD* on $(-\infty, -2)$. *PI* is $(-2, -2e^{-2}) \approx (-2, -0.271)$.

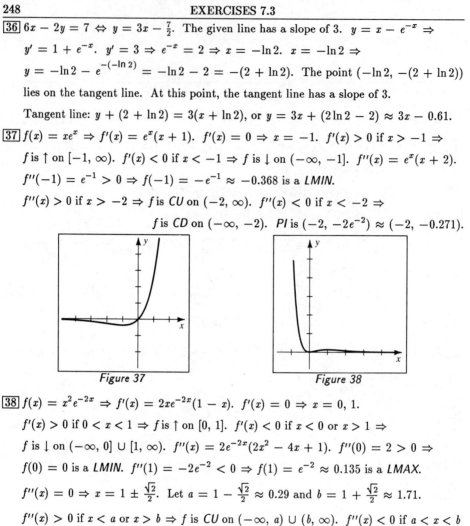

Figure 37   Figure 38

38 $f(x) = x^2 e^{-2x} \Rightarrow f'(x) = 2xe^{-2x}(1 - x)$. $f'(x) = 0 \Rightarrow x = 0, 1$.

$f'(x) > 0$ if $0 < x < 1 \Rightarrow f$ is ↑ on $[0, 1]$. $f'(x) < 0$ if $x < 0$ or $x > 1 \Rightarrow$

f is ↓ on $(-\infty, 0] \cup [1, \infty)$. $f''(x) = 2e^{-2x}(2x^2 - 4x + 1)$. $f''(0) = 2 > 0 \Rightarrow$

$f(0) = 0$ is a *LMIN*. $f''(1) = -2e^{-2} < 0 \Rightarrow f(1) = e^{-2} \approx 0.135$ is a *LMAX*.

$f''(x) = 0 \Rightarrow x = 1 \pm \frac{\sqrt{2}}{2}$. Let $a = 1 - \frac{\sqrt{2}}{2} \approx 0.29$ and $b = 1 + \frac{\sqrt{2}}{2} \approx 1.71$.

$f''(x) > 0$ if $x < a$ or $x > b \Rightarrow f$ is *CU* on $(-\infty, a) \cup (b, \infty)$. $f''(x) < 0$ if $a < x < b$

           $\Rightarrow f$ is *CD* on (a, b). *PI* are approximately $(a, 0.048)$ and $(b, 0.096)$.

39 $f(x) = e^{1/x} \Rightarrow f'(x) = -\dfrac{e^{1/x}}{x^2}$. $f'(x) \neq 0$. f' DNE if $x = 0$. $f'(x) < 0$ if $x \neq 0 \Rightarrow$

f is ↓ on $(-\infty, 0) \cup (0, \infty)$. There are no local extrema. $f''(x) = \dfrac{e^{1/x}(2x + 1)}{x^4}$.

$f''(x) > 0$ if $-\frac{1}{2} < x < 0$ or $x > 0 \Rightarrow f$ is *CU* on $(-\frac{1}{2}, 0) \cup (0, \infty)$.

                $f''(x) < 0$ if $x < -\frac{1}{2} \Rightarrow f$ is *CD* on $(-\infty, -\frac{1}{2})$. *PI* is $(-\frac{1}{2}, e^{-2})$.

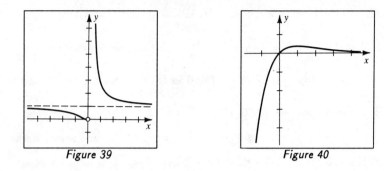

Figure 39   Figure 40

40 $f(x) = xe^{-x} \Rightarrow f'(x) = e^{-x}(1 - x)$. $f'(x) = 0 \Rightarrow x = 1$. $f'(x) > 0$ if $x < 1 \Rightarrow$
f is ↑ on $(-\infty, 1]$. $f'(x) < 0$ if $x > 1 \Rightarrow f$ is ↓ on $[1, \infty)$. $f''(x) = e^{-x}(x - 2)$.
$f''(1) = -e^{-1} < 0 \Rightarrow f(1) = 1/e$ is a *LMAX*. $f''(x) > 0$ if $x > 2 \Rightarrow$
$\quad\quad$ f is *CU* on $(2, \infty)$. $f''(x) < 0$ if $x < 2 \Rightarrow f$ is *CD* on $(-\infty, 2)$. *PI* is $(2, 2e^{-2})$.

41 $f(x) = x \ln x \Rightarrow f'(x) = 1 + \ln x$. $f'(x) = 0 \Rightarrow x = e^{-1}$. $f'(x) > 0$ if $x > e^{-1} \Rightarrow$
f is ↑ on $[e^{-1}, \infty)$. $f'(x) < 0$ if $0 < x < e^{-1} \Rightarrow f$ is ↓ on $(0, e^{-1}]$. $f''(x) = 1/x$.
$f''(e^{-1}) = e > 0 \Rightarrow f(e^{-1}) = -e^{-1}$ is a *LMIN*. $f''(x) > 0$ if $x > 0 \Rightarrow$
f is *CU* on $(0, \infty)$ and there are no *PI*. $\left(\lim_{x \to 0} f(x) = 0\right.$ will be verified later using

$\quad\quad\quad\quad\quad\quad\quad$ L'Hôpital's rule. This is helpful in making the sketch.)

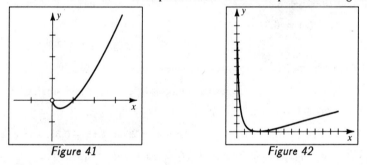

Figure 41   Figure 42

42 $f(x) = (1 - \ln x)^2 \Rightarrow f'(x) = \frac{2}{x}(\ln x - 1)$. $f'(x) = 0 \Rightarrow x = e$.
$f'(x) > 0$ if $x > e \Rightarrow f$ is ↑ on $[e, \infty)$. $f'(x) < 0$ if $0 < x < e \Rightarrow f$ is ↓ on $(0, e]$.
$f''(x) = (2/x^2)(2 - \ln x)$. $f''(e) = 2e^{-2} > 0 \Rightarrow f(e) = 0$ is a *LMIN*.
$f''(x) = 0 \Rightarrow x = e^2$. $f''(x) > 0$ if $0 < x < e^2 \Rightarrow f$ is *CU* on $(0, e^2)$.
$\quad\quad\quad\quad\quad$ $f''(x) < 0$ if $x > e^2 \Rightarrow f$ is *CD* on (e^2, ∞). *PI* is $(e^2, 1)$.

43 The rate r at which a substance decays is obtained by differentiating. Hence,
$\quad\quad\quad$ $r = q'(t) = q_0 e^{-ct} \cdot (-c) = -cq(t)$, where $-c$ is a constant of proportionality.

44 The rate of change of the current, r, is given by
$\quad\quad\quad$ $r = I'(t) = I_0 e^{-Rt/L} \cdot \left(-\frac{R}{L}\right) = -\frac{R}{L} I(t)$, where $-\frac{R}{L}$ is a constant of proportionality.

45 (a) $C(t) = \frac{k}{a-b}(e^{-bt} - e^{-at}) \Rightarrow C'(t) = \frac{k}{a-b}(-be^{-bt} + ae^{-at}) = 0 \Rightarrow$

$ae^{-at} = be^{-bt} \Rightarrow \frac{a}{b} = \frac{e^{-bt}}{e^{-at}} = e^{(a-b)t} \Rightarrow \ln(a/b) = (a-b)t \Rightarrow$

$t = \frac{\ln(a/b)}{a-b} = t_0$. Consider the two cases: (i) $a > b$, and (ii) $a < b$.

(i) If $a > b$, then $\frac{k}{a-b} > 0$, $e^{at} \geq e^{bt}$, and $\frac{a}{e^{at}} - \frac{b}{e^{bt}}$ is positive when

       $t \in [0, t_0)$, zero when $t = t_0$, and negative when $t > t_0$.

(ii) If $a < b$, then $\frac{k}{a-b} < 0$, $e^{at} \leq e^{bt}$, and $\frac{a}{e^{at}} - \frac{b}{e^{bt}}$ is negative when

       $t \in [0, t_0)$, zero when $t = t_0$, and positive when $t > t_0$.

In both cases, $C'(t) > 0$ for $t < t_0$ and $C'(t) < 0$ for $t > t_0 \Rightarrow$

       the maximum concentration occurs at $t = t_0$.

(b) $\lim_{t \to \infty} C(t) = \lim_{t \to \infty} \frac{k}{a-b}(e^{-bt} - e^{-at}) = \frac{k}{a-b}(0 - 0) = 0 \ \{a > 0, b > 0\}$

46 (a) $I(x) = ke^{-1.4x} \Rightarrow I'(x) = -1.4ke^{-1.4x}$. $I'(1) = -1.4ke^{-1.4} \approx -0.345k$.

$I'(5) = -1.4ke^{-1.4(5)} \approx -0.00128k$. $I'(10) = -1.4ke^{-14} \approx -0.00000116k$.

(b) Since $I(0) = k$, we solve $\frac{1}{2}k = ke^{-1.4x}$. Hence, $2 = e^{1.4x} \Rightarrow x = \frac{\ln 2}{1.4} \approx 0.495$ ft.

Similarly, the intensity is one-tenth its surface value if $x = \frac{\ln 10}{1.4} \approx 1.645$ ft.

47 (a) $h(x) = 79.041 + 6.39x - e^{3.261-0.993x} \Rightarrow h(1) = 79.041 + 6.39 - e^{2.268} \approx$

75.8 cm. $h'(x) = 6.39 + 0.993e^{3.261-0.993x} \Rightarrow$

          $h'(1) = 6.39 + 0.993e^{2.268} \approx 15.98$ cm/yr.

(b) The growth rate, $h'(x)$, is decreasing since $h''(x) = -0.986049e^{3.261-0.993x} < 0$.

       Thus, the rate of growth is largest at $x = \frac{1}{4}$ yr and smallest at $x = 6$ yr.

48 Let $W(t) = 2600(1 - 0.51e^{-0.075t})^3 = a(1 + be^{ct})^3$,

       where $a = 2600$, $b = -0.51$, and $c = -0.075$.

(a) $W(0) = a(1 + b)^3 \approx 305.9$ kg. $W'(t) = 3a(1 + be^{ct})^2(bce^{ct}) =$

       $3abce^{ct}(1 + be^{ct})^2$. $W'(0) = 3abc(1 + b)^2 \approx 71.6$ kg/yr.

(b) Let $d = 1800$. $d = a(1 + be^{ct})^3 \Rightarrow t = \frac{1}{c}\ln\left(\frac{\sqrt[3]{d/a} - 1}{b}\right) \approx 19.8$ yr.

$W'\left(\frac{1}{c}\ln\left(\frac{\sqrt[3]{d/a} - 1}{b}\right)\right) = 3ac(\sqrt[3]{d/a} - 1)(\sqrt[3]{d/a})^2 = 3c(d - \sqrt[3]{ad^2}) \approx$

                  52.8 kg/yr.

(c) $\lim_{t \to \infty} W(t) = a(1 + 0)^3 = 2600$ kg. 2600 kg is the maximum attainable weight.

(d) $W''(t) = 3abc(ce^{ct})(1 + be^{ct})^2 + 3abce^{ct}\left[2(1 + be^{ct})(bce^{ct})\right]$

     $= 3abc^2e^{ct}(1 + be^{ct})\left[(1 + be^{ct}) + 2be^{ct}\right]$

     $= 3abc^2e^{ct}(1 + be^{ct})(3be^{ct} + 1)$.

$W''(t) = 0 \Rightarrow t = \frac{1}{c}\ln\left(-\frac{1}{b}\right) = t_1 \approx -8.98$, $t = \frac{1}{c}\ln\left(-\frac{1}{3b}\right) = t_0 \approx 5.67$.

Since $a > 0$ and $b < 0$, $3abc^2 e^{ct} < 0$ for all t. For $t > 0 > t_1$, $(1 + be^{ct}) > 0$.

If $0 < t < t_0$, then $(3be^{ct} + 1) < 0$, and $W''(t) > 0$.

If $t > t_0$, then $(3be^{ct} + 1) > 0$, and $W''(t) < 0$. Thus, t_0 gives a maximum.

49 (a) $f(x) = cx^n e^{-ax} \Rightarrow f'(x) = cx^n e^{-ax}(-a) + cnx^{n-1} e^{-ax} = cx^{n-1} e^{-ax}(n - ax)$.

$f'(x) = 0 \Rightarrow x = \frac{n}{a}$ $\{x = 0$ is an endpoint.$\}$ $f'(x) > 0$ if $0 < x < \frac{n}{a}$ and

$f'(x) < 0$ for $x > \frac{n}{a}$. Thus, f has exactly one $LMAX$. It occurs at $x = \frac{n}{a}$.

(b) When $n = 4$, $f'(x) = cx^3 e^{-ax}(4 - ax)$ and

$f''(x) = 3cx^2 e^{-ax}(4 - ax) + (cx^3 e^{-ax})(-a)(4 - ax) + cx^3 e^{-ax}(-a) = $

$cx^2 e^{-ax}\big[3(4 - ax) - ax(4 - ax) - ax\big] = cx^2 e^{-ax}(ax - 2)(ax - 6)$.

$f''(x) = 0 \Rightarrow x = \frac{2}{a}, \frac{6}{a}$. $f''(x) > 0$ on $(0, \frac{2}{a})$, $f''(x) < 0$ on $(\frac{2}{a}, \frac{6}{a})$, and

$f''(x) > 0$ on $(\frac{6}{a}, \infty)$. This implies a $LMAX$ for f' at $x = \frac{2}{a}$. Since $f'(0) = 0$ and

$$\lim_{x \to \infty} f'(x) = 0,$$ a greater value than $f'(\frac{2}{a}) > 0$ will not be obtained.

50 Let $a = -m/(2kT)$. $F(v) = cv^2 e^{av^2} \Rightarrow F'(v) = cv^2 e^{av^2}(2av) + e^{av^2}(2cv) = $

$2cve^{av^2}(av^2 + 1)$. $F'(v) = 0 \Rightarrow v^2 = -1/a \Rightarrow v = \sqrt{-1/a} = \sqrt{2kT/m}$.

$F'(v) > 0$ on $(0, \sqrt{-1/a})$ and $F'(v) < 0$ on $(\sqrt{-1/a}, \infty)$.

Thus, $F(\sqrt{-1/a}) = -\frac{c}{ae} = \frac{2ckT}{me}$ is a $LMAX$.

51 $D(r) = ae^{-br + cr^2} \Rightarrow D'(r) = ae^{-br + cr^2}(-b + 2cr)$.

$D'(r) = 0 \Rightarrow r = \frac{b}{2c}$.

D is $\downarrow$ on $[0, \frac{b}{2c}]$ and $\uparrow$ on $[\frac{b}{2c}, \infty)$.

$D''(r) = ae^{-br + cr^2}\big[2c + (-b + 2cr)^2\big] > 0 \Rightarrow$

D is always CU. $D(\frac{b}{2c}) = ae^{-b^2/(4c)}$ is a $LMIN$.

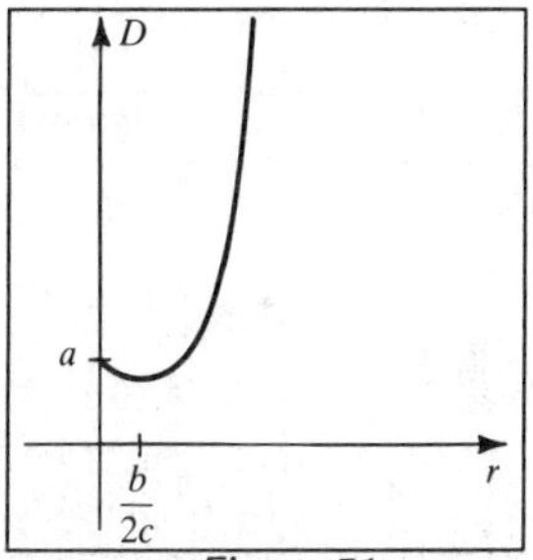

Figure 51

52 (a) $f(x) = x^a e^{(a/b)(1 - x^b)} \Rightarrow f'(x) = x^a e^{(a/b)(1 - x^b)}(-ax^{b-1}) + ax^{a-1} e^{(a/b)(1 - x^b)}$

$= ax^{a-1} e^{(a/b)(1 - x^b)}(-x^b + 1)$. $f'(x) = 0 \Rightarrow x = 1$.

$f'(x) > 0$ on $(0, 1)$ and $f'(x) < 0$ on $(1, \infty) \Rightarrow f(1) = 1$ is a $LMAX$.

(b) Since $y_0 > 0$, $g(x) = y_0 f(x/x_0)$ is maximized when $f(x/x_0)$ is a maximum.

From part (a), the maximum value of f is $f(1)$.

Thus, $x/x_0 = 1 \Rightarrow x = x_0$ and $g(x_0) = y_0 f(1) = y_0$ is a $LMAX$ for $g(x)$.

53 $R(x) = rx \ln(K/x) \Rightarrow R'(x) = r\left[\ln(K/x) + \frac{x}{K/x}(-K/x^2)\right] = r\left[\ln(K/x) - 1\right]$.

$R'(x) = 0 \Rightarrow \ln(K/x) = 1$ $(r > 0) \Rightarrow x = K/e$. $R'(x) > 0$ on $(0, K/e)$ and

$R'(x) < 0$ on $(K/e, \infty)$. Thus, $R(K/e) = rK/e$ is a $LMAX$.

54 $R(x) = xp = 300xe^{-0.02x}$. $R'(x) = 300e^{-0.02x} - 6xe^{-0.02x} = 6e^{-0.02x}(50 - x)$.

$R'(x) = 0 \Rightarrow x = 50$. $R'(x) > 0$ on $(0, 50)$ and $R'(x) < 0$ on $(50, \infty) \Rightarrow$

$$R(\$50) = 15{,}000e^{-1} \approx \$5518.19 \text{ is a } LMAX.$$

55 $f(x) = \frac{1}{\sigma\sqrt{2\pi}}e^{-z^2/2}$ with $z = \frac{x - \mu}{\sigma} \Rightarrow \{$ by the chain rule $\}$

$f'(x) = \frac{1}{\sigma\sqrt{2\pi}}e^{-z^2/2}(-z) D_x(z) = \frac{1}{\sigma\sqrt{2\pi}}e^{-z^2/2}(-z)(\frac{1}{\sigma})$. $f'(x) = 0 \Rightarrow z = 0$, or

equivalently, $x = \mu$. f is $\uparrow$ on $(-\infty, \mu]$ and $\downarrow$ on $[\mu, \infty)$. Thus, $f(\mu) = \frac{1}{\sigma\sqrt{2\pi}}$ is a

$LMAX$. $f''(x) = \frac{1}{\sigma^2\sqrt{2\pi}}\left[e^{-z^2/2}(-1) D_x(z) + (-z)e^{-z^2/2}(-z) D_x(z)\right] =$

$\frac{1}{\sigma^2\sqrt{2\pi}}\left[z^2 e^{-z^2/2}(\frac{1}{\sigma}) - e^{-z^2/2}(\frac{1}{\sigma})\right] = \frac{1}{\sigma^3\sqrt{2\pi}}e^{-z^2/2}(z^2 - 1) = 0 \Rightarrow z = \pm 1$, or

$x = \mu \pm \sigma$. f is CD on $(\mu - \sigma, \mu + \sigma)$ and CU on $(-\infty, \mu - \sigma) \cup (\mu + \sigma, \infty)$.

PI are $\left(\mu \pm \sigma, \frac{1}{\sigma\sqrt{2\pi e}}\right)$. Also, $\lim\limits_{x \to \infty} f(x) = \lim\limits_{x \to -\infty} f(x) = 0$.

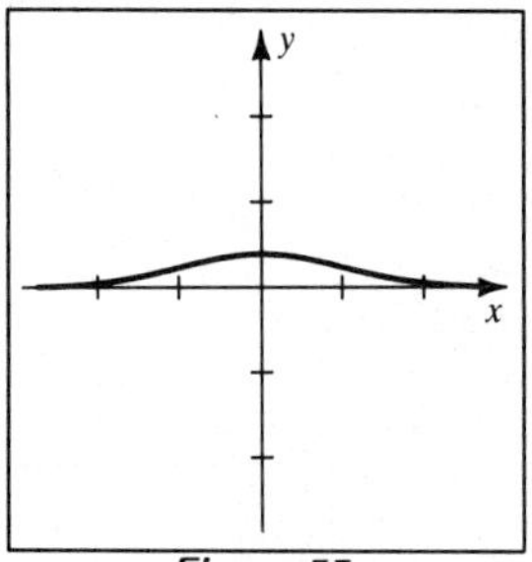

Figure 55 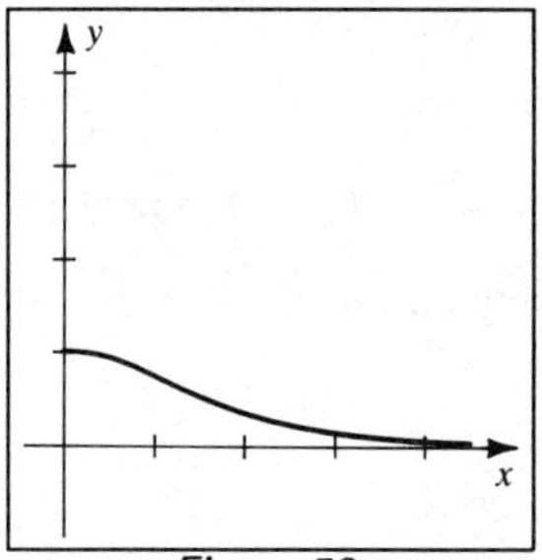   Figure 58

56 Let $f(x) = e^{-x^2}$. $T = \frac{1-0}{2(10)}\{f(0) + 2[f(0.1) + f(0.2) + \cdots + f(0.9)] + f(1)\} \approx$

$\frac{1}{20}[1 + 2(0.990 + 0.961 + \cdots + 0.445) + 0.368] = \frac{1}{20}(14.924) \approx 0.746$.

57 Let $x = r/R > 0$. $v(x) = -kx^2 \ln x \Rightarrow v'(x) = -kx(1 + 2\ln x)$.

$v'(x) = 0 \Rightarrow x = e^{-1/2} \approx 0.607$. $v'(x) > 0$ on $(0, e^{-1/2})$ and

$$v'(x) < 0 \text{ on } (e^{-1/2}, \infty) \Rightarrow v(e^{-1/2}) = k/(2e) \text{ is a } LMAX.$$

58 See *Figure 58*. Since x is the number of damaging events (the *dose*),

restrict x to $[0, \infty)$. $f(x) = 1 - (1 - e^{-x})^3 \Rightarrow f'(x) = -3e^{-x}(1 - e^{-x})^2$.

$f'(x) < 0$ if $x \geq 0 \Rightarrow f$ is $\downarrow$ on $[0, \infty)$.

$f''(x) = -3\left[(-e^{-x})(1 - e^{-x})^2 + e^{-x}(2)(1 - e^{-x})(e^{-x})\right] =$

$3e^{-x}(1 - e^{-x})(1 - 3e^{-x}) = 0 \Rightarrow x = 0, \ln 3$. f is CD on $(0, \ln 3)$ and CU on

$(\ln 3, \infty)$. There is a PI at $(\ln 3, \frac{19}{27}) \approx (1.099, 0.704)$. Also, $\lim\limits_{x \to \infty} f(x) = 0$.

59 This problem is essentially the same as solving $\ln x = -x$ { see §7.2.55 }. The root

occurs where the graph of $y = e^{-x}$ intersects that of $y = x$. This occurs on $(0, 1)$.

Let $f(x) = e^{-x} - x$ and $x_{n+1} = x_n - \frac{e^{-x_n} - x_n}{-e^{-x_n} - 1} = x_n + \frac{e^{-x_n} - x_n}{e^{-x_n} + 1}$.

Letting $x_1 = 0.5$ yields: $x_2 = 0.566$, $x_3 = 0.567$, and $x_4 = 0.567$.

$\boxed{60}$ Let $f(x) = x \ln x - 1$. Since $f(1) = -1 < 0$ and $f(2) = 2 \ln 2 - 1 \approx 0.386 > 0$,

we know by the intermediate value theorem that f has a zero c in $(1, 2)$.

$f(x) < 0$ on $(0, 1)$ and $f'(x) = 1 + \ln x > 0$ on $[1, \infty) \Rightarrow$

f is $\uparrow$ on $[1, \infty)$ and so c is the only zero on $(0, \infty)$. $x_{n+1} = x_n - \dfrac{x_n \ln x_n - 1}{1 + \ln x_n}$.

Letting $x_1 = 1.5$ yields: $x_2 = 1.779$, $x_3 = 1.763$, and $x_4 = 1.763$.

Exercises 7.4

$\boxed{1}$ (a) $u = 2x + 7$, $\frac{1}{2} du = dx \Rightarrow I = \frac{1}{2} \int \frac{1}{u} \, du = \frac{1}{2} \ln |u| + C$

(b) Using the antiderivative from part (a),

$$\left[\tfrac{1}{2} \ln |2x + 7| \right]_{-2}^{1} = \tfrac{1}{2} (\ln 9 - \ln 3) = \tfrac{1}{2} (\ln \tfrac{9}{3}) = \ln (3^{1/2}) = \ln \sqrt{3} \approx 0.55.$$

$\boxed{2}$ (a) $u = 4 - 5x$, $-\frac{1}{5} du = dx \Rightarrow I = -\frac{1}{5} \int \frac{1}{u} \, du = -\frac{1}{5} \ln |u| + C$

(b) $\left[-\tfrac{1}{5} \ln |4 - 5x| \right]_{-1}^{0} = -\tfrac{1}{5} (\ln 4 - \ln 9) = \tfrac{1}{5} (\ln 9 - \ln 4) = \tfrac{1}{5} \ln \tfrac{9}{4} \approx 0.16$

$\boxed{3}$ (a) $u = x^2 - 9$, $\frac{1}{2} du = x \, dx \Rightarrow I = 4 \cdot \frac{1}{2} \int \frac{1}{u} \, du = 2 \ln |u| + C$

(b) $\left[2 \ln |x^2 - 9| \right]_{1}^{2} = 2(\ln |-5| - \ln |-8|) = 2 \ln \tfrac{5}{8} = \ln (\tfrac{5}{8})^2 = \ln \tfrac{25}{64} \approx -0.94$

$\boxed{4}$ (a) $u = x^2 + 4$, $\frac{1}{2} du = x \, dx \Rightarrow I = 3 \cdot \frac{1}{2} \int \frac{1}{u} \, du = \frac{3}{2} \ln |u| + C$

(b) $\left[\tfrac{3}{2} \ln (x^2 + 4) \right]_{1}^{2} = \tfrac{3}{2} (\ln 8 - \ln 5) = \tfrac{3}{2} \ln \tfrac{8}{5} \approx 0.71$

$\boxed{5}$ (a) $u = -4x$, $-\frac{1}{4} du = dx \Rightarrow I = -\frac{1}{4} \int e^u \, du = -\frac{1}{4} e^u + C$

(b) $\left[-\tfrac{1}{4} e^{-4x} \right]_{1}^{3} = -\tfrac{1}{4} (e^{-12} - e^{-4}) \approx 0.0046$

$\boxed{6}$ (a) $u = 3x^3$, $\frac{1}{9} du = x^2 \, dx \Rightarrow I = \frac{1}{9} \int e^u \, du = \frac{1}{9} e^u + C$

(b) $\left[\tfrac{1}{9} e^{3x^3} \right]_{1}^{2} = \tfrac{1}{9} (e^{24} - e^3) \approx 2.94 \times 10^9$

$\boxed{7}$ (a) $u = 2x$, $\frac{1}{2} du = dx \Rightarrow I = \frac{1}{2} \int \tan u \, du = -\frac{1}{2} \ln |\cos u| + C$, by (7.25)(i).

(b) $\left[-\tfrac{1}{2} \ln |\cos 2x| \right]_{0}^{\pi/8} = -\tfrac{1}{2} (\ln \cos \tfrac{\pi}{4} - \ln \cos 0) = -\tfrac{1}{2} (\ln \tfrac{1}{\sqrt{2}} - \ln 1) =$

$$-\tfrac{1}{2} (-\tfrac{1}{2} \ln 2 - 0) = \tfrac{1}{4} \ln 2 \approx 0.17$$

$\boxed{8}$ (a) $u = \frac{1}{3}x$, $3 \, du = dx \Rightarrow I = 3 \int \cot u \, du = 3 \ln |\sin u| + C$, by (7.25)(ii).

(b) $\left[3 \ln |\sin \tfrac{1}{3}x| \right]_{3\pi/2}^{9\pi/4} = 3(\ln \sin \tfrac{3\pi}{4} - \ln \sin \tfrac{\pi}{2}) = 3(\ln \tfrac{1}{\sqrt{2}} - \ln 1) = 3(-\tfrac{1}{2} \ln 2 - 0) =$

$$-\tfrac{3}{2} \ln 2 \approx -1.04$$

$\boxed{9}$ (a) $u = \frac{1}{2}x$, $2 \, du = dx \Rightarrow I = 2 \int \csc u \, du = 2 \ln |\csc u - \cot u| + C$, by (7.25)(iv).

(b) $\left[2 \ln \left| \csc \tfrac{1}{2}x - \cot \tfrac{1}{2}x \right| \right]_{\pi}^{5\pi/3} = 2 \left(\ln \left| \csc \tfrac{5\pi}{6} - \cot \tfrac{5\pi}{6} \right| - \ln \left| \csc \tfrac{\pi}{2} - \cot \tfrac{\pi}{2} \right| \right) =$

$$2 \left[\ln |2 - (-\sqrt{3})| - \ln |1 - 0| \right] = 2 \ln (2 + \sqrt{3}) \approx 2.63$$

$\boxed{10}$ (a) $u = 3x$, $\frac{1}{3} du = dx \Rightarrow I = \frac{1}{3} \int \sec u \, du = \frac{1}{3} \ln|\sec u + \tan u| + C$, by (7.25)(iii).

(b) $\left[\frac{1}{3} \ln|\sec 3x + \tan 3x|\right]_0^{\pi/12} = \frac{1}{3}\left(\ln|\sec\frac{\pi}{4} + \tan\frac{\pi}{4}| - \ln|\sec 0 + \tan 0|\right) =$

$\frac{1}{3}(\ln|\sqrt{2} + 1| - \ln|1 + 0|) = \frac{1}{3}\ln(\sqrt{2} + 1) \approx 0.29$

$\boxed{11}$ $u = x^2 - 4x + 9$, $\frac{1}{2} du = (x - 2) \, dx \Rightarrow I = \frac{1}{2}\int \frac{1}{u} \, du = \frac{1}{2}\ln|u| + C$

$\boxed{12}$ $u = x^4 - 5$, $\frac{1}{4} du = x^3 \, dx \Rightarrow I = \frac{1}{4}\int \frac{1}{u} \, du = \frac{1}{4}\ln|u| + C$ ·

$\boxed{13}$ $\int \frac{(x + 2)^2}{x} \, dx = \int \frac{x^2 + 4x + 4}{x} \, dx = \int \left(x + 4 + \frac{4}{x}\right) dx = \frac{1}{2}x^2 + 4x + 4\ln|x| + C$

$\boxed{14}$ $u = 2 + \ln x$, $du = \frac{1}{x} \, dx \Rightarrow I = \int u^{10} \, du = \frac{1}{11}u^{11} + C$

$\boxed{15}$ $u = \ln x$, $du = \frac{1}{x} \, dx \Rightarrow I = \int u \, du = \frac{1}{2}u^2 + C$

$\boxed{16}$ $u = \ln x$, $du = \frac{1}{x} \, dx \Rightarrow I = \int \frac{1}{u^2} \, du = -\frac{1}{u} + C$

$\boxed{17}$ $\int (x + e^{5x}) \, dx = \frac{1}{2}x^2 + \frac{1}{5}e^{5x} + C$

$\boxed{18}$ $u = \sqrt{x}$, $2 \, du = \frac{1}{\sqrt{x}} \, dx \Rightarrow I = 2\int e^u \, du = 2e^u + C$

$\boxed{19}$ $u = 1 + 2\cos x$, $-\frac{1}{2} du = \sin x \, dx \Rightarrow I = -\frac{1}{2} \cdot 3\int \frac{1}{u} \, du = -\frac{3}{2}\ln|u| + C$

$\boxed{20}$ $u = 1 + \tan x$, $du = \sec^2 x \, dx \Rightarrow I = \int \frac{1}{u} \, du = \ln|u| + C$

$\boxed{21}$ $\int \frac{(e^x + 1)^2}{e^x} \, dx = \int \frac{e^{2x} + 2e^x + 1}{e^x} \, dx = \int (e^x + 2 + e^{-x}) \, dx = e^x + 2x - e^{-x} + C$

$\boxed{22}$ $u = e^x + 1$, $du = e^x \, dx \Rightarrow I = \int \frac{1}{u^2} \, du = -\frac{1}{u} + C$

$\boxed{23}$ $u = e^x + e^{-x}$, $du = (e^x - e^{-x}) \, dx \Rightarrow I = \int \frac{1}{u} \, du = \ln u + C$.

The absolute value is not needed since $u = e^x + e^{-x} > 0$.

$\boxed{24}$ $u = e^x + 1$, $du = e^x \, dx \Rightarrow I = \int \frac{1}{u} \, du = \ln u + C$, since $u = e^x + 1 > 0$.

$\boxed{25}$ $u = x^{1/3}$, $3 \, du = \frac{1}{x^{2/3}} \, dx \Rightarrow I = 3\int \cot u \, du = 3\ln|\sin u| + C$

$\boxed{26}$ $u = e^x$, $du = e^x \, dx \Rightarrow I = \int (1 + \tan u) \, du = u + \ln|\sec u| + C$

$\boxed{27}$ $\int \frac{1}{\cos 2x} \, dx = \int \sec 2x \, dx$.

$u = 2x$, $\frac{1}{2} du = dx \Rightarrow I = \frac{1}{2}\int \sec u \, du = \frac{1}{2}\ln|\sec u + \tan u| + C$.

$\boxed{28}$ $\int (x + \csc 8x) \, dx = \int x \, dx + \int \csc 8x \, dx$.

$u = 8x$, $\frac{1}{8} du = dx \Rightarrow I = \int x \, dx + \frac{1}{8}\int \csc u \, du = \frac{1}{2}x^2 + \frac{1}{8}\ln|\csc u - \cot u| + C$.

$\boxed{29}$ $u = e^{-3x}$, $-\frac{1}{3} du = e^{-3x} \, dx \Rightarrow$

$I = \int (\tan e^{-3x}) e^{-3x} \, dx = -\frac{1}{3}\int \tan u \, du = -\frac{1}{3}\ln|\sec u| + C$

$\boxed{30}$ $u = \cos x$, $-du = \sin x \, dx \Rightarrow I = -\int e^u \, du = -e^u + C$

$\boxed{31}$ $\int \frac{\cos^2 x}{\sin x} \, dx = \int \frac{1 - \sin^2 x}{\sin x} \, dx = \int (\csc x - \sin x) \, dx = \ln|\csc x - \cot x| + \cos x + C$

32 $\int \dfrac{\tan^2 2x}{\sec 2x}\,dx = \int \dfrac{\sec^2 2x - 1}{\sec 2x}\,dx =$

$$\int (\sec 2x - \cos 2x)\,dx = \tfrac{1}{2}\ln|\sec 2x + \tan 2x| - \tfrac{1}{2}\sin 2x + C$$

33 $\int \dfrac{\cos x \sin x}{\cos^2 x - 1}\,dx = \int \dfrac{\cos x \sin x}{-\sin^2 x}\,dx =$

$$-\int \cot x\,dx = -\ln|\sin x| + C = \ln|\sin x|^{-1} + C = \ln|\csc x| + C$$

34 $\int (\tan 3x + \sec 3x)\,dx = \tfrac{1}{3}\ln|\sec 3x| + \tfrac{1}{3}\ln|\sec 3x + \tan 3x| + C$

35 $\int (1 + \sec x)^2\,dx = \int (1 + 2\sec x + \sec^2 x)\,dx = x + 2\ln|\sec x + \tan x| + \tan x + C$

36 $\int \csc x(1 - \csc x)\,dx = \int (\csc x - \csc^2 x)\,dx = \ln|\csc x - \cot x| + \cot x + C$

37 $A = \displaystyle\int_0^{\ln 3} e^{2x}\,dx = \left[\tfrac{1}{2}e^{2x}\right]_0^{\ln 3} = \tfrac{1}{2}\left[(e^{\ln 3})^2 - e^0\right] = \tfrac{1}{2}(3^2 - 1) = 4$

38 $A = \displaystyle\int_0^{\pi/4} 2\tan x\,dx = 2\left[\ln|\sec x|\right]_0^{\pi/4} = 2(\ln\sqrt 2 - \ln 1) = 2(\tfrac{1}{2}\ln 2 - 0) = \ln 2.$

39 Using shells, $V = 2\pi\displaystyle\int_0^1 xe^{-x^2}\,dx\ \{u = -x^2,\ -\tfrac{1}{2}du = x\,dx\} =$

$$2\pi \cdot (-\tfrac{1}{2})\int_0^{-1} e^u\,du = -\pi\left[e^u\right]_0^{-1} = -\pi(e^{-1} - e^0) = \pi(1 - e^{-1}) \approx 1.99.$$

40 Using disks, $V = \pi\displaystyle\int_{-\pi/3}^{\pi/3} (\sec x)^2\,dx = 2\pi\int_0^{\pi/3} \sec^2 x\,dx\ \{\text{even integrand}\} =$

$$2\pi\left[\tan x\right]_0^{\pi/3} = 2\pi\sqrt 3 \approx 10.88.$$

41 $y' = 4e^{2x} + 3e^{-2x} \Rightarrow y = 2e^{2x} - \tfrac{3}{2}e^{-2x} + C.$

$$y = 4 \text{ if } x = 0 \Rightarrow 4 = 2 - \tfrac{3}{2} + C \Rightarrow C = \tfrac{7}{2}.$$

42 $y' = 3e^{4x} - 8e^{-2x} \Rightarrow y = \tfrac{3}{4}e^{4x} + 4e^{-2x} + C.$

$$y = -2 \text{ if } x = 0 \Rightarrow -2 = \tfrac{3}{4} + 4 + C \Rightarrow C = -\tfrac{27}{4}.$$

43 $y'' = 3e^{-x} \Rightarrow y' = -3e^{-x} + C.$ $y' = 1$ if $x = 0 \Rightarrow 1 = -3 + C \Rightarrow C = 4.$

$y' = -3e^{-x} + 4 \Rightarrow y = 3e^{-x} + 4x + C.$

$$y = -1 \text{ if } x = 0 \Rightarrow -1 = 3 + C \Rightarrow C = -4.$$

44 $y'' = 6e^{2x} \Rightarrow y' = 3e^{2x} + C.$ $y' = 2$ if $x = 0 \Rightarrow 2 = 3 + C \Rightarrow C = -1.$

$y' = 3e^{2x} - 1 \Rightarrow y = \tfrac{3}{2}e^{2x} - x + C.$

$$y = -3 \text{ if } x = 0 \Rightarrow -3 = \tfrac{3}{2} + C \Rightarrow C = -\tfrac{9}{2}.$$

45 $1 = \displaystyle\int_0^3 \dfrac{cx}{x^2 + 4}\,dx = c\left[\tfrac{1}{2}\ln(x^2 + 4)\right]_0^3 = \tfrac{1}{2}c(\ln 13 - \ln 4) \Rightarrow c = \dfrac{2}{\ln\frac{13}{4}} \approx 1.697$

46 $1 = \displaystyle\int_0^{10} cxe^{-x^2}\,dx = c\left[-\tfrac{1}{2}e^{-x^2}\right]_0^{10} = -\tfrac{1}{2}c(e^{-100} - 1) \Rightarrow c = \dfrac{2}{1 - e^{-100}} \approx 2$

47 (a) $\displaystyle\int_0^5 3e^{0.2t}\,dt = 3\left[5e^{0.2t}\right]_0^5 = 15(e - 1) \approx 25.77$, round down to 25.

(b) The sixth through fourteenth hours correspond with $t = 5$ to $t = 14$.

$$\int_5^{14} 3e^{0.2t}\,dt = 3\left[5e^{0.2t}\right]_5^{14} = 15(e^{2.8} - e) \approx 205.9$$

(c) $150 = \int_0^x 3e^{0.2t}\, dt \Rightarrow 150 = 15\left[e^{0.2t}\right]_0^x \Rightarrow 10 = e^{0.2x} - 1 \Rightarrow 11 = e^{0.2x} \Rightarrow$

$$\ln 11 = 0.2x \Rightarrow x = 5\ln 11 \approx 11.99,\ \text{or } 12,\ \text{hours}$$

48 (a) $1000 = 500e^{0.07t} \Rightarrow 2 = e^{0.07t} \Rightarrow \ln 2 = 0.07t \Rightarrow t = \frac{100}{7}\ln 2 \approx 9.9 \text{ yr}$

(b) The value of the bond, A, is given by $A = 500e^{0.07t}$. The growth rate of the bond is $A' = 500(0.07)e^{0.07t}$. $A' = 50 \Rightarrow 500(0.07)e^{0.07t} = 50 \Rightarrow$

$$e^{0.07t} = \frac{10}{7} \Rightarrow 0.07t = \ln\frac{10}{7} \Rightarrow t = \frac{100}{7}\ln\frac{10}{7} \approx 5.1 \text{ yr.}$$

49 $\Delta S = \int_{T_1}^{T_2} \frac{c}{T}\, dT = c\left[\ln T\right]_{T_1}^{T_2} = c(\ln T_2 - \ln T_1) = c\ln\frac{T_2}{T_1}.$

Note that T_1 and T_2 are positive when using °K.

50 $R = 8 \Rightarrow E = 9.13 \times 10^{12} \int_0^8 e^{1.25x}\, dx = 9.13 \times 10^{12}\left[0.8e^{1.25x}\right]_0^8 =$

$$7.304 \times 10^{12}(e^{10} - 1) \approx 1.6 \times 10^{17} \text{ J.}$$

51 (a) $Q(t) = Q(t) - Q(0) = \int_0^t 10e^{-4x}\, dx = 10\left[-\frac{1}{4}e^{-4x}\right]_0^t = \frac{5}{2}(1 - e^{-4t})$

(b) $\lim_{t \to \infty} Q(t) = \lim_{t \to \infty} \frac{5}{2}(1 - e^{-4t}) = \frac{5}{2}(1 - 0) = \frac{5}{2}$ coulombs.

52 We would like to find the number of years x such that

$$50 = \int_0^x 6.5e^{0.02t}\, dt = 6.5\left[50e^{0.02t}\right]_0^x = 6.5(50)(e^{0.02x} - 1) \Rightarrow$$

$$50 = 6.5(50)(e^{0.02x} - 1) \Rightarrow \ln\left(\frac{1}{6.5} + 1\right) = 0.02x \Rightarrow x = 50\ln\frac{15}{13} \approx 7.155 \text{ yr}$$

53 (a) $s(t) = \int_0^t v_0 e^{-x/k}\, dx = v_0\left[-ke^{-x/k}\right]_0^t = kv_0(1 - e^{-t/k})$

(b) $\lim_{t \to \infty} s(t) = \lim_{t \to \infty}\left[kv_0(1 - e^{-t/k})\right] = kv_0(1 - 0) = kv_0$

54 $W = \int_{v_0}^{v_1} p\, dv = \int_{v_0}^{v_1} \frac{k}{v}\, dv = k\left[\ln v\right]_{v_0}^{v_1} = k(\ln v_1 - \ln v_0) = k\ln\frac{v_1}{v_0}$

55 Let $f(x) = e^{-x^2}$. $T_2 = \frac{1-0}{2(2)}\left[f(0) + 2f(0.5) + f(1)\right] \approx 0.731370.$

$T_4 = \frac{1-0}{2(4)}\left\{f(0) + 2\left[f(0.25) + f(0.5) + f(0.75)\right] + f(1)\right\} \approx 0.742984.$

$T_{10} = \frac{1-0}{2(10)}\left\{f(0) + 2\left[f(0.1) + f(0.2) + \cdots + f(0.9)\right] + f(1)\right\} \approx 0.746211.$

$R = \frac{1}{3}(4T_4 - T_2) \approx \frac{1}{3}\left[4(0.742984) - (0.731370)\right] \approx 0.746855.$

R is more accurate than T_{10}.

56 Let $f(x) = (\ln x)^2$. $T_2 = \frac{2-1}{2(2)}\left[f(1) + 2f(1.5) + f(2)\right] \approx 0.202314.$

$T_4 = \frac{2-1}{2(4)}\left\{f(1) + 2\left[f(1.25) + f(1.5) + f(1.75)\right] + f(2)\right\} \approx 0.191898.$

$T_{10} = \frac{2-1}{2(10)}\left\{f(1) + 2\left[f(1.1) + f(1.2) + \cdots + f(1.9)\right] + f(2)\right\} \approx 0.188894.$

$R = \frac{1}{3}(4T_4 - T_2) \approx \frac{1}{3}\left[4(0.191898) - (0.202314)\right] \approx 0.188426.$

R is more accurate than T_{10}.

Exercises 7.5

1 $f(x) = 7^x \Rightarrow f'(x) = 7^x \ln 7$, by (7.28)(i).

2 $f(x) = 5^{-x} \Rightarrow f'(x) = (5^{-x} \ln 5) D_x (-x) = -5^{-x} \ln 5$, by (7.28)(ii).

3 $f(x) = 8^{x^2+1} \Rightarrow f'(x) = (8^{x^2+1} \ln 8) D_x (x^2 + 1) = 8^{x^2+1}(2x \ln 8)$

4 $f(x) = 9^{\sqrt{x}} \Rightarrow f'(x) = (9^{\sqrt{x}} \ln 9) D_x \sqrt{x} = \dfrac{9^{\sqrt{x}} \ln 9}{2\sqrt{x}}$

5 $f(x) = \log (x^4 + 3x^2 + 1) \Rightarrow f'(x) = D_x \left[\dfrac{\ln (x^4 + 3x^2 + 1)}{\ln 10} \right] =$

$$\frac{1}{\ln 10} \cdot \frac{1}{x^4 + 3x^2 + 1} \cdot D_x (x^4 + 3x^2 + 1) = \frac{4x^3 + 6x}{(x^4 + 3x^2 + 1)\ln 10}, \text{ by (7.31)(ii).}$$

6 $f(x) = \log_3 |6x - 7| \Rightarrow f'(x) = D_x \left(\dfrac{\ln |6x - 7|}{\ln 3} \right) = \dfrac{6}{(6x - 7)\ln 3}$

7 $f(x) = 5^{3x-4} \Rightarrow f'(x) = (5^{3x-4} \ln 5) D_x (3x - 4) = 5^{3x-4}(3\ln 5)$

8 $f(x) = 3^{2-x^2} \Rightarrow f'(x) = (3^{2-x^2} \ln 3) D_x (2 - x^2) = 3^{2-x^2}(-2x\ln 3)$

9 $f(x) = (x^2 + 1)10^{1/x} \Rightarrow f'(x) = (x^2 + 1)(10^{1/x} \ln 10)(-1/x^2) + (2x) 10^{1/x} =$

$$\frac{-(x^2 + 1) 10^{1/x}(\ln 10)}{x^2} + (2x) 10^{1/x}$$

10 $f(x) = (10^x + 10^{-x})^{10} \Rightarrow f'(x) = 10(10^x + 10^{-x})^9 \left[10^x \ln 10 + 10^{-x} \ln 10 \cdot (-1) \right]$

$$= 10(10^x + 10^{-x})^9 (10^x - 10^{-x})\ln 10$$

11 $f(x) = \log (3x^2 + 2)^5 = 5\log (3x^2 + 2) \Rightarrow$

$$f'(x) = 5 D_x \left[\frac{\ln (3x^2 + 2)}{\ln 10} \right] = 5 \cdot \frac{6x}{(3x^2 + 2)\ln 10} = \frac{30x}{(3x^2 + 2)\ln 10}$$

12 $f(x) = \log \sqrt{x^2 + 1} = \frac{1}{2}\log (x^2 + 1) \Rightarrow f'(x) = \frac{1}{2} D_x \left[\dfrac{\ln (x^2 + 1)}{\ln 10} \right] = \dfrac{x}{(x^2 + 1)\ln 10}$

13 $f(x) = \log_5 \left| \dfrac{6x + 4}{2x - 3} \right| = \log_5 |6x + 4| - \log_5 |2x - 3| \Rightarrow$

$$f'(x) = D_x \left(\frac{\ln |6x + 4|}{\ln 5} - \frac{\ln |2x - 3|}{\ln 5} \right) = \left(\frac{6}{6x + 4} - \frac{2}{2x - 3} \right) \frac{1}{\ln 5}$$

14 $f(x) = \log \left| \dfrac{1 - x^2}{2 - 5x^3} \right| = \log |1 - x^2| - \log |2 - 5x^3| \Rightarrow$

$$f'(x) = D_x \left(\frac{\ln |1 - x^2|}{\ln 10} - \frac{\ln |2 - 5x^3|}{\ln 10} \right) = \left(\frac{2x}{x^2 - 1} + \frac{15x^2}{2 - 5x^3} \right) \frac{1}{\ln 10}$$

15 $f(x) = \log \ln x \Rightarrow f'(x) = D_x \left(\dfrac{\ln \ln x}{\ln 10} \right) = \dfrac{1}{\ln 10} \cdot \dfrac{1}{\ln x} \cdot \dfrac{1}{x} = \dfrac{1}{x \ln x \ln 10}$

16 $f(x) = \ln \log x \Rightarrow f'(x) = \dfrac{1}{\log x} \cdot D_x (\log x) = \dfrac{1}{\log x} \cdot D_x \left(\dfrac{\ln x}{\ln 10} \right) = \dfrac{1}{x \log x \ln 10}$

17 $f(x) = x^e + e^x \Rightarrow f'(x) = ex^{e-1} + e^x$

18 $f(x) = x^\pi \pi^x \Rightarrow f'(x) = x^\pi \pi^x \ln \pi + \pi x^{\pi-1} \pi^x$

19 $f(x) = (x + 1)^x \Rightarrow f'(x) = D_x \left[e^{x \ln (x+1)} \right] =$

$$e^{x \ln (x+1)} \left[x \cdot \frac{1}{x + 1} + 1 \cdot \ln (x + 1) \right] = (x + 1)^x \left[\frac{x}{x + 1} + \ln (x + 1) \right]$$

$\boxed{20}$ $f(x) = x^{4+x^2} \Rightarrow f'(x) = D_x\left[e^{(4+x^2)\ln x}\right] =$

$$e^{(4+x^2)\ln x}\left[(4 + x^2)\cdot\frac{1}{x} + 2x\ln x\right] = x^{4+x^2}\left(\frac{4 + x^2}{x} + 2x\ln x\right)$$

$\boxed{21}$ $f(x) = 2^{\sin^2 x} \Rightarrow f'(x) = 2^{\sin^2 x}(\ln 2)(2\sin x\cos x) = 2^{\sin^2 x}(\sin 2x)\ln 2$

$\boxed{22}$ $f(x) = 4^{\sec 3x} \Rightarrow f'(x) = 4^{\sec 3x}(\ln 4)(3\sec 3x\tan 3x) = 4^{\sec 3x}(3\sec 3x\tan 3x)\ln 4$

$\boxed{23}$ $f(x) = x^{\tan x} \Rightarrow f'(x) = D_x\left[e^{\tan x\ln x}\right] =$

$$e^{\tan x\ln x}\left(\tan x\cdot\frac{1}{x} + \sec^2 x\ln x\right) = x^{\tan x}\left(\frac{\tan x}{x} + \sec^2 x\ln x\right)$$

$\boxed{24}$ $f(x) = (\cos 2x)^x \Rightarrow f'(x) = D_x\left[e^{x\ln(\cos 2x)}\right] =$

$$e^{x\ln(\cos 2x)}\left[x\cdot\frac{1}{\cos 2x}\cdot(-2\sin 2x) + 1\cdot\ln(\cos 2x)\right] = (\cos 2x)^x(\ln\cos 2x - 2x\tan 2x)$$

$\boxed{25}$ (a) $f(x) = e^e$ is of the form (constant base)$^{\text{constant exponent}}$.

This expression is a constant and $f'(x) = 0$.

(b) $f(x) = x^5$ is of the form (variable base)$^{\text{constant exponent}}$.

Invoking the power rule, $f'(x) = 5x^{5-1} = 5x^4$.

(c) $f(x) = x^{\sqrt5}$ is of the form (variable base)$^{\text{constant exponent}}$.

Invoking the power rule, $f'(x) = \sqrt5\,x^{\sqrt5-1}$.

(d) $f(x) = (\sqrt5)^x$ is of the form (constant base)$^{\text{variable exponent}}$.

Invoking (7.28)(i), $f'(x) = (\sqrt5)^x\ln\sqrt5$.

(e) $f(x) = x^{(x^2)}$ is of the form (variable base)$^{\text{variable exponent}}$.

Changing to a natural exponential form (or using logarithmic differentiation),

$$f(x) = e^{x^2\ln x} \Rightarrow f'(x) = e^{x^2\ln x}\left(x^2\cdot\frac{1}{x} + 2x\ln x\right) = x^{(x^2)}(x + 2x\ln x) =$$

$$x^{(x^2)}(x^1)(1 + 2\ln x) = x^{1+x^2}(1 + 2\ln x).$$

$\boxed{26}$ (a)–(d) The forms are similar to those in Exercise 25.

The answers are: (a) 0   (b) $4x^3$ (c) $\pi x^{\pi-1}$ (d) $\pi^x\ln\pi$.

(e) $f(x) = x^{2x} = e^{2x\ln x} \Rightarrow f'(x) = e^{2x\ln x}(2)(x\cdot\frac{1}{x} + 1\cdot\ln x) = 2(x^{2x})(1 + \ln x)$

$\boxed{27}$ (a) $\int 7^x\,dx = \frac{1}{\ln 7}(7^x) + C\,\{\text{by }(7.29)(i)\} = \frac{7^x}{\ln 7} + C$

(b) Using part (a), $\int_{-2}^1 7^x\,dx = \frac{1}{\ln 7}\left[7^x\right]_{-2}^1 = \frac{1}{\ln 7}\left(7 - \frac{1}{49}\right) = \frac{342}{49\ln 7} \approx 3.59$

$\boxed{28}$ (a) $\int 3^x\,dx = \frac{1}{\ln 3}(3^x) + C\,\{\text{by }(7.29)(i)\} = \frac{3^x}{\ln 3} + C$

(b) $\int_{-1}^0 3^x\,dx = \frac{1}{\ln 3}\left[3^x\right]_{-1}^0 = \frac{1}{\ln 3}\left(1 - \frac{1}{3}\right) = \frac{2}{3\ln 3} \approx 0.61$

$\boxed{29}$ (a) $u = -2x$, $-\frac{1}{2}\,du = dx \Rightarrow \int 5^{-2x}\,dx = -\frac{1}{2}\int 5^u\,du = -\frac{5^u}{2\ln 5} + C$

(b) $\displaystyle\int_1^2 5^{-2x}\,dx = -\frac{1}{2\ln 5}\Big[5^{-2x}\Big]_1^2 =$

$$-\frac{1}{2\ln 5}\Big(\frac{1}{625} - \frac{1}{25}\Big) = -\frac{1}{2\ln 5}\Big(-\frac{24}{625}\Big) = \frac{12}{625\ln 5} \approx 0.012$$

$\boxed{30}$ (a) $u = 3x - 1,\ \frac{1}{3}du = dx \Rightarrow \displaystyle\int 2^{3x-1}\,dx = \frac{1}{3}\int 2^u\,du = \frac{2^u}{3\ln 2} + C$

(b) $\displaystyle\int_{-1}^1 2^{3x-1}\,dx = \frac{1}{3\ln 2}\Big[2^{3x-1}\Big]_{-1}^1 = \frac{1}{3\ln 2}\Big(4 - \frac{1}{16}\Big) = \frac{1}{3\ln 2}\Big(\frac{63}{16}\Big) = \frac{21}{16\ln 2} \approx 1.89$

$\boxed{31}$ $u = 3x,\ \frac{1}{3}du = dx \Rightarrow \displaystyle\int 10^{3x}\,dx = \frac{1}{3}\int 10^u\,du = \frac{10^u}{3\ln 10} + C$

$\boxed{32}$ $u = -5x,\ -\frac{1}{5}du = dx \Rightarrow \displaystyle\int 5^{-5x}\,dx = -\frac{1}{5}\int 5^u\,du = \frac{-5^u}{5\ln 5} + C$

$\boxed{33}$ $u = -x^2,\ -\frac{1}{2}du = x\,dx \Rightarrow \displaystyle\int x(3^{-x^2})\,dx = -\frac{1}{2}\int 3^u\,du = \frac{-3^u}{2\ln 3} + C$

$\boxed{34}$ $\displaystyle\int \frac{(2^x + 1)^2}{2^x}\,dx = \int \frac{2^{2x} + 2(2^x) + 1}{2^x}\,dx = \int (2^x + 2 + 2^{-x})\,dx =$

$$\frac{2^x}{\ln 2} + 2x - \frac{2^{-x}}{\ln 2} + C = \frac{2^x - 2^{-x}}{\ln 2} + 2x + C$$

$\boxed{35}$ $u = 2^x + 1,\ du = 2^x \ln 2\,dx \Rightarrow \displaystyle\int \frac{2^x}{2^x + 1}\,dx = \frac{1}{\ln 2}\int \frac{1}{u}\,du = \frac{1}{\ln 2}\ln u + C,\ u > 0$

$\boxed{36}$ $u = 3^x + 4,\ du = 3^x \ln 3\,dx \Rightarrow \displaystyle\int \frac{3^x}{\sqrt{3^x + 4}}\,dx = \frac{1}{\ln 3}\int u^{-1/2}\,du = \frac{2\sqrt{u}}{\ln 3} + C$

$\boxed{37}$ $u = \log x,\ du = \frac{dx}{x\ln 10} \Rightarrow \displaystyle\int \frac{1}{x\log x}\,dx = \ln 10\int \frac{1}{u}\,du = (\ln 10)\ln|u| + C$

$\boxed{38}$ $u = \sqrt{x},\ du = \frac{dx}{2\sqrt{x}} \Rightarrow \displaystyle\int \frac{10^{\sqrt{x}}}{\sqrt{x}}\,dx = 2\int 10^u\,du = \frac{(2)10^u}{\ln 10} + C$

$\boxed{39}$ $u = \cos x,\ -du = \sin x\,dx \Rightarrow \displaystyle\int 3^{\cos x}\sin x\,dx = -\int 3^u\,du = -\frac{3^u}{\ln 3} + C$

$\boxed{40}$ $u = \tan x,\ du = \sec^2 x\,dx \Rightarrow \displaystyle\int \frac{5^{\tan x}}{\cos^2 x}\,dx = \int 5^{\tan x}\sec^2 x\,dx = \int 5^u\,du = \frac{5^u}{\ln 5} + C$

$\boxed{41}$ (a) π^π is of the form (constant base)$^{\text{constant exponent}}$. Thus, $\displaystyle\int \pi^\pi\,dx = \pi^\pi x + C$.

(b) x^4 is of the form (variable base)$^{\text{constant exponent}}$.

$$\text{Thus, } \int x^4\,dx = \frac{x^{4+1}}{4+1} + C = \tfrac{1}{5}x^5 + C.$$

(c) x^π is of the form (variable base)$^{\text{constant exponent}}$. Thus, $\displaystyle\int x^\pi\,dx = \frac{x^{\pi+1}}{\pi+1} + C.$

(d) π^x is of the form (constant base)$^{\text{variable exponent}}$. Thus, $\displaystyle\int \pi^x\,dx = \frac{\pi^x}{\ln \pi} + C.$

$\boxed{42}$ (a)–(d) The forms are similar to those in Exercise 41. The answers are:

(a) $e^e x + C$ (b) $\tfrac{1}{6}x^6 + C$ (c) $\dfrac{x^{\sqrt{5}+1}}{\sqrt{5}+1} + C$ (d) $\dfrac{(\sqrt{5})^x}{\ln\sqrt{5}} + C.$

43 The graphs intersect when $x = 0$. On $[0, 1]$, $2^x \geq 1 - x$. $A = \int_0^1 \left[2^x - (1 - x)\right] dx$

$$= \left[\frac{2^x}{\ln 2} - x + \tfrac{1}{2}x^2\right]_0^1 = \left(\frac{2}{\ln 2} - 1 + \tfrac{1}{2}\right) - \left(\frac{1}{\ln 2}\right) = \frac{1}{\ln 2} - \tfrac{1}{2} \approx 0.94.$$

44 Using disks, $V = \pi \int_1^2 (3^{-x})^2 \, dx = \pi \int_1^2 3^{-2x} \, dx = \pi\left[-\frac{1}{2\ln 3} 3^{-2x}\right]_1^2 =$

$$-\frac{\pi}{2\ln 3}(3^{-4} - 3^{-2}) = -\frac{\pi}{2\ln 3}\left(-\frac{8}{81}\right) = \frac{4\pi}{81\ln 3} \approx 0.14.$$

45 (a) $B'(t) = (0.95)^t \ln(0.95)$. $B'(2) \approx -0.046 \approx \$0.05/\text{yr}$ (decreasing).

(b) $B_{av} = \frac{1}{2 - 0} \int_0^2 (0.95)^t \, dt = \tfrac{1}{2}\left[\frac{(0.95)^t}{\ln(0.95)}\right]_0^2 = \frac{1}{2\ln(0.95)}\left[(0.95)^2 - 1\right] \approx \$0.95.$

46 We need to determine T so that $50 = \int_0^T 5(0.95)^t \, dt$. Thus, $10 = \int_0^T (0.95)^t \, dt =$

$$\left[\frac{(0.95)^t}{\ln(0.95)}\right]_0^T = \frac{1}{\ln(0.95)}\left[(0.95)^T - 1\right] \Rightarrow T = \frac{\ln\left[10\ln(0.95) + 1\right]}{\ln(0.95)} \approx 14 \text{ min.}$$

47 (a) $N(t) = 1000(0.9)^t \Rightarrow dN/dt = N'(t) = 1000(0.9)^t \ln(0.9)$.

$N'(1) = 1000(0.9)^1 \ln(0.9) \approx -95$ trout/yr (a decrease of 95 trout).

$N'(5) = 1000(0.9)^5 \ln(0.9) \approx -62$ trout/yr. $N = 500 \Rightarrow 1000(0.9)^t = 500 \Rightarrow$

$$\tfrac{1}{2} = (0.9)^t \Rightarrow N'(t) = 1000(\tfrac{1}{2})\ln(0.9) \approx -53 \text{ trout/yr.}$$

(b) The total weight of trout in the pond is given by $T(t) = N(t) \cdot W(t) =$

$1000(0.9)^t (0.2 + 1.5t)$. $T'(t) = 1000(0.9)^t\left[1.5 + \ln(0.9)(0.2 + 1.5t)\right] = 0 \Rightarrow$

$0.2\ln(0.9) + 1.5\ln(0.9)t = -1.5 \{1000(0.9)^t \neq 0\} \Rightarrow$

$t = t_0 = \dfrac{-1.5 - 0.2\ln(0.9)}{1.5\ln(0.9)} \approx 9.36$ yr. Since $T'(t) > 0$ on $[0, t_0)$ and

$T'(t) < 0$ on (t_0, ∞), $T(t_0) \approx 5311.53$ is a maximum value.

48 P will be an increasing function of the temperature T if $P' > 0$. Differentiating

implicitly, we have $\log P = a + \dfrac{b}{c + T} \Rightarrow \dfrac{1}{(\ln 10)P}(P') = \dfrac{-b}{(c + T)^2}.$

Since $P > 0$, the sign of P' is determined by $(-b)$. $P' > 0 \Leftrightarrow b < 0$.

49 $\text{pH} = -\log[\text{H}^+] = -\log\left[6.3 \times 10^{-3}\right] \approx 2.201.$

$$\frac{d(\text{pH})}{\text{pH}} = \frac{-\dfrac{d(\text{H}^+)}{(\ln 10)\,\text{H}^+}}{-\log[\text{H}^+]} = \frac{d(\text{H}^+)/\text{H}^+}{(\ln 10)\log[\text{H}^+]} = \frac{\pm 0.5\%}{\ln 10 \, \log(6.3 \times 10^{-3})} \approx \pm 0.1\%.$$

50 $R = \log(I/I_0) \Rightarrow \dfrac{dR}{R} = \dfrac{\dfrac{1}{(\ln 10)(I/I_0)(I_0)}(dI)}{\log(I/I_0)} = \dfrac{\dfrac{1}{(\ln 10)I}(dI)}{\log(100\,I_0/I_0)} =$

$$\frac{dI/I}{\ln 10 \, \log 100} = \frac{\pm 1\%}{(\ln 10)(2)} \approx \pm 0.22\%.$$

51 (a) When $x = x_0$, $R = a\log(x/x_0) = a\log(x_0/x_0) = a\log 1 = a(0) = 0$.

(b) $S = \dfrac{dR}{dx} = \dfrac{a}{(x/x_0)\ln 10\,(x_0)} = \dfrac{k}{x}$, where $k = a/\ln 10$ is the constant of

proportionality, implies that S is inversely proportional to x.

Since $S(x) = \dfrac{k}{x}$ and $S(2x) = \dfrac{k}{2x}$, $S(x) = 2\,S(2x)$, twice as sensitive.

52 The rate of change is given by $\dfrac{d\alpha}{dI} = 10 \cdot \dfrac{1}{(\ln 10)(I/I_0)(I_0)} = \dfrac{10}{I(\ln 10)}$.

(a) $I = 10\,I_0 \Rightarrow \dfrac{d\alpha}{dI} = \dfrac{1}{I_0(\ln 10)} \approx (4.34 \times 10^{-1})/I_0$

(b) $I = 1000\,I_0 \Rightarrow \dfrac{d\alpha}{dI} = \dfrac{1}{100\,I_0(\ln 10)} \approx (4.34 \times 10^{-3})/I_0$

(c) $I = 10{,}000\,I_0 \Rightarrow \dfrac{d\alpha}{dI} = \dfrac{1}{1000\,I_0(\ln 10)} \approx (4.34 \times 10^{-4})/I_0$

53 (a) If $h = r/n$, then $n = r/h$ and $A = P\big[1 + (r/n)\big]^{nt} \Leftrightarrow A = P\big[1 + h\big]^{rt/h}$.

Thus, $\ln A = \ln\Big[P(1 + h)^{rt/h}\Big] = \ln P + rt\ln(1 + h)^{1/h}$.

(b) Since $h = r/n$, $n \to \infty$ if and only if $h \to 0^+$. Thus,

$$\ln A = \lim_{h \to 0^+}\Big[\ln P + rt\ln(1 + h)^{1/h}\Big] = \ln P + rt \lim_{h \to 0^+}\Big[\ln(1 + h)^{1/h}\Big] =$$
$$\ln P + rt\ln e = \ln P + \ln e^{rt} = \ln(Pe^{rt}) \text{ and } A = Pe^{rt}.$$

54 Since $n = 1/h$, $n \to \infty$ if and only if $h \to 0^+$.

Thus, $\displaystyle\lim_{n \to \infty}(1 + \tfrac{1}{n})^n = \lim_{h \to 0^+}(1 + h)^{1/h} = e$.

55 Let $h = \tfrac{x}{n}$. Then $\displaystyle\lim_{n \to \infty}(1 + \tfrac{x}{n})^n = \lim_{h \to 0^+}(1 + h)^{x/h} = \lim_{h \to 0^+}\Big[(1 + h)^{1/h}\Big]^x = e^x$.

56 Using $(1 + h)^{1/h}$, we obtain 2.593742, 2.704814, and 2.716924.

Using $(1 + h + h^2)^{1/h}$, we obtain 2.839421, 2.731726, and 2.719639.

Using $(1 + h + \tfrac{1}{2}h^2)^{1/h}$, we obtain 2.714081, 2.718237, and 2.718281.

Since $e \approx 2.718282$, the third expression, $(1 + h + \tfrac{1}{2}h^2)^{1/h}$,

seems to give the best approximation.

57 (a) They intersect at $x \approx 1.32$.

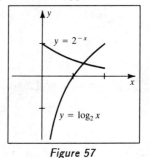

Figure 57

(b) $\pi\displaystyle\int_{1}^{1.32}\Big[(2^{-x})^2 - (\log_2 x)^2\Big]\,dx$

(c) Let $f(x) = (2^{-x})^2 - (\log_2 x)^2$.

$S = (\pi)\dfrac{1.32 - 1}{3(4)} \cdot$

$[f(1) + 4f(1.08) + 2f(1.16) + 4f(1.24) + f(1.32)]$

$\approx \dfrac{0.32\pi}{12}(1.7363) \approx 0.14546$.

Exercises 7.6

1. $q(t) = ke^{ct}$ and $q(0) = 5000 \Rightarrow k = 5000$.

   $q(t) = 5000e^{ct}$ and $q(10) = 5000e^{c(10)} = 15,000 \Rightarrow e^c = 3^{1/10}$.

   Thus, $q(t) = 5000(3^{1/10})^t = 5000(3)^{t/10}$. $q(20) = 5000(3)^2 = 45,000$.

   Also, $q(t) = 50,000 \Rightarrow 3^{t/10} = 10 \Rightarrow (t/10)\ln 3 = \ln 10 \Rightarrow t = \dfrac{10\ln 10}{\ln 3} \approx 20.96$ hr.

2. $q(t) = 20e^{ct}$ and a half-life of 140 days $\Rightarrow 10 = 20e^{c(140)} \Rightarrow e^c = (\tfrac{1}{2})^{1/140}$.

   Thus, $q(t) = 20(\tfrac{1}{2})^{t/140}$. $q(14) = 20(\tfrac{1}{2})^{1/10} \approx 18.66$ mg.

3. $dp/dh = cp \Rightarrow p(h) = ke^{ch}$, by (7.33).

   $p(0) = 30 \Rightarrow k = 30$ and $p(1000) = 30e^{c(1000)} = 29 \Rightarrow e^c = (\tfrac{29}{30})^{1/1000}$.

   Thus, $p(h) = 30(\tfrac{29}{30})^{t/1000}$. $p(5000) = 30(\tfrac{29}{30})^5 \approx 25.32$ in.

4. $dP/dt = 0.05P \Rightarrow P(t) = ke^{0.05t}$, by (7.33).

   $P(0) = 500,000 \Rightarrow P(t) = 500,000e^{0.05t}$. $P(10) = 500,000e^{0.5} \approx 824,361$.

5. Let $t = 0$ correspond to Jan. 1, 1980. $dP/dt = 0.02P \Rightarrow P(t) = ke^{0.02t}$.

   Since $P(0) = 4.5 \times 10^9$, the population (in billions) is given by $P(t) = 4.5e^{0.02t}$.

   $$P(t) = 40 \Rightarrow t = \frac{\ln(40/4.5)}{0.02} \approx 109.24 \text{ yr (March 29, 2089)}.$$

6. $T(t) = (180 - 60)e^{ct} + 60 = 120e^{ct} + 60$. $T(20) = 150 \Rightarrow e^{c(20)} = \tfrac{150-60}{120} \Rightarrow$

   $e^c = (\tfrac{3}{4})^{1/20} \Rightarrow T(t) = 120(\tfrac{3}{4})^{t/20} + 60$. After one hour,

   $T(60) = 120(\tfrac{3}{4})^3 + 60 = 110.625°$. $T(t) = 100 \Rightarrow (\tfrac{3}{4})^{t/20} = \tfrac{100-60}{120} \Rightarrow$

   $$(t/20)\ln\tfrac{3}{4} = \ln\tfrac{1}{3} \Rightarrow t = \frac{20\ln(1/3)}{\ln(3/4)} \approx 76 \text{ min} \approx 1.27 \text{ hr.}$$

7. $T(t) = (40 - 70)e^{ct} + 70 = -30e^{ct} + 70$.

   $T(5) = 60 \Rightarrow e^{c(5)} = \tfrac{60-70}{-30} \Rightarrow e^c = (\tfrac{1}{3})^{1/5}$. Thus, $T(t) = -30(\tfrac{1}{3})^{t/5} + 70$.

   $$T(t) = 65 \Rightarrow (\tfrac{1}{3})^{t/5} = \tfrac{65-70}{-30} \Rightarrow (t/5)\ln\tfrac{1}{3} = \ln\tfrac{1}{6} \Rightarrow t = \frac{5\ln(1/6)}{\ln(1/3)} \approx 8.15 \text{ min.}$$

8. The rate at which salt *does not dissolve* is also directly proportional to the amount
   that does not dissolve. Thus, $q(t) = q_0 e^{ct}$, where q represents the amount of salt
   that remains undissolved. $q(0) = 10 \Rightarrow q_0 = 10$. $q(20) = 6 \Rightarrow 6 = 10e^{c(20)} \Rightarrow$

   $e^c = (\tfrac{3}{5})^{1/20}$. Thus, $q(t) = 10(\tfrac{3}{5})^{t/20}$. If 2 more pounds dissolve, 4 pounds will

   remain. $q(t) = 4 \Rightarrow (\tfrac{3}{5})^{t/20} = \tfrac{4}{10} \Rightarrow t = \dfrac{20\ln(4/10)}{\ln(3/5)} \approx 35.87$ min or

   15.87 additional min.

9. At $t = 0$, $V = 0$, and $0 = RI + L\dfrac{dI}{dt} \Rightarrow \dfrac{dI}{dt} = -\dfrac{R}{L}I$. Proceed as in the solution to

   Example 1, with $c = -R/L$ and $y = I$, to show that $I(t) = ke^{-Rt/L}$.

   $$I(0) = I_0 \Rightarrow I(t) = I_0 e^{-Rt/L}.$$

10. Let $N(t)$ denote the number of counts on the Geiger counter.

    $N(t)$ is directly proportional to the amount of the substance present $\Rightarrow N(t) = ke^{ct}$.

$N(0) = 2000 \Rightarrow k = 2000$ and $N(10) = 1500 \Rightarrow e^c = \left(\frac{1500}{2000}\right)^{1/10}$.

Thus, $N(t) = 2000(\frac{3}{4})^{t/10}$. $N(t) = \frac{1}{2}(2000) \Rightarrow t = \dfrac{10\ln(1/2)}{\ln(3/4)} \approx 24$ days.

11 $\dfrac{dP}{dz} = \dfrac{-0.0342\,P}{T} = \dfrac{-0.0342\,P}{288 - 0.01z} \Rightarrow \dfrac{dP}{P} = (-0.0342)\dfrac{dz}{288 - 0.01z} \Rightarrow$

$\ln P = \frac{-0.0342}{-0.01}\ln(288 - 0.01z) + C \Rightarrow P(z) = e^C(2.88 - 0.01z)^{3.42}$.

$P(0) = 1 \Rightarrow e^C = 288^{-3.42} \Rightarrow P(z) = \left[(288 - 0.01z)/288\right]^{3.42}$.

12 $\dfrac{dW}{dt} = 0.21\,W \Rightarrow W(t) = ke^{0.21t}$. $W(0) = 70 \Rightarrow k = 70$.

$W(30) = 70e^{0.21(30)} \approx 38{,}120$ mg $= 38.12$ g.

13 $q(t) = ke^{ct}$ and $q(0) = 2.5S \Rightarrow k = 2.5S$. A half-life of 29 years $\Rightarrow e^{c(29)} = \frac{1}{2} \Rightarrow$

$e^c = (\frac{1}{2})^{1/29}$. Thus, $q(t) = 2.5S(\frac{1}{2})^{t/29}$. The safe level occurs when $q(t) = S$, i.e.,

$S = 2.5S(\frac{1}{2})^{t/29} \Rightarrow (\frac{1}{2})^{t/29} = \dfrac{1}{2.5} \Rightarrow t = \dfrac{29\ln(2/5)}{\ln(1/2)} \approx 38.34$ yr.

14 $q(t) = ke^{ct}$. A half-life of 27.8 days $\Rightarrow e^{c(27.8)} = \frac{1}{2} \Rightarrow e^c = (\frac{1}{2})^{1/27.8}$.

Thus, $q(t) = k(\frac{1}{2})^{t/27.8}$. We desire $q(2) = 35$, so $k = 35(\frac{1}{2})^{-2/27.8} \approx 36.79$ units.

15 $q(t) = ke^{ct}$. A half-life of 4 hours $\Rightarrow e^{c(4)} = \frac{1}{2} \Rightarrow e^c = (\frac{1}{2})^{1/4}$.

Thus, $q(t) = k(\frac{1}{2})^{t/4}$. We desire $q(\frac{45}{60}) = 20(30) = 600$ mg,

so $k = 600(\frac{1}{2})^{-(45/60)/4} = 600(\frac{1}{2})^{-3/16} \approx 683.27$ mg.

16 $\dfrac{dh}{dt} = -\dfrac{V}{Q}\left(\dfrac{h}{k+h}\right) \Rightarrow \left(\dfrac{k}{h} + 1\right)dh = -\dfrac{V}{Q}\,dt \Rightarrow k\ln h + h = -\dfrac{V}{Q}t + C$.

17 $v\dfrac{dv}{dy} = -\dfrac{k}{y^2} \Rightarrow v\,dv = -k\dfrac{dy}{y^2} \Rightarrow \frac{1}{2}v^2 = \dfrac{k}{y} + C_1 \Rightarrow v = \sqrt{\dfrac{2k}{y} + C_2}$.

$v(y_0) = v_0 = \sqrt{\dfrac{2k}{y_0} + C_2} \Rightarrow C_2 = v_0^2 - \dfrac{2k}{y_0}$. Thus, $v(y) = \sqrt{2k\left(\dfrac{1}{y} - \dfrac{1}{y_0}\right) + v_0^2}$.

18 $\dfrac{dy}{dt} = -0.05y^2 \Rightarrow \dfrac{dy}{y^2} = -0.05\,dt \Rightarrow -\dfrac{1}{y} = -0.05t + C \Rightarrow y(t) = \dfrac{1}{0.05t - C}$.

$y(0) = y_0 \Rightarrow C = -\dfrac{1}{y_0}$. Thus, $y(t) = \dfrac{1}{0.05t + (1/y_0)} = \dfrac{y_0}{0.05\,y_0\,t + 1}$.

19 $q(t) = q_0e^{ct}$. A half-life of 5700 yr $\Rightarrow e^{c(5700)} = \frac{1}{2} \Rightarrow e^c = (\frac{1}{2})^{1/5700}$.

Thus, $q(t) = q_0(\frac{1}{2})^{t/5700}$.

$q(t) = 20\%\,q_0 \Rightarrow 0.2q_0 = q_0(\frac{1}{2})^{t/5700} \Rightarrow t = \dfrac{5700\ln(0.2)}{\ln(1/2)} \approx 13{,}235$ yr.

20 $q(t) = q_0e^{ct}$. A half-life of 12.3 yr $\Rightarrow e^{c(12.3)} = \frac{1}{2} \Rightarrow e^c = (\frac{1}{2})^{1/12.3}$.

Thus, $q(t) = q_0(\frac{1}{2})^{t/12.3}$.

$q(t) = 10\%\,q_0 \Rightarrow 0.1q_0 = q_0(\frac{1}{2})^{t/12.3} \Rightarrow t = \dfrac{12.3\ln(0.1)}{\ln(1/2)} \approx 41$ yr.

21 $dI/dx = I_0e^{-f(x)} \cdot D_x[-f(x)] = I_0e^{-f(x)} \cdot D_x\left[-k\int_0^x \rho(h)\,dh\right] =$

$I_0e^{-f(x)} \cdot \left[-k\rho(x)\right] = -k\rho(x)I_0e^{-f(x)} = -k\rho(x)I$.

22 (a) $f(5) = 3 + 20\left[1 - e^{-0.1(5)}\right] \approx 11$;

$f(9) \approx 15$; $f(24) \approx 21$; $f(30) \approx 22$.

(b) $f(n) = 3 + 20(1 - e^{-0.1n}) \Rightarrow$

$f'(n) = 2e^{-0.1n} > 0$ and $f''(n) = -0.2e^{-0.1n} < 0$.

Hence, f is $\uparrow$ and CD.

(c) $\lim\limits_{n \to \infty} f(n) = \lim\limits_{n \to \infty} (3 + 20 - 20e^{-0.1n}) =$

$23 - 20 \lim\limits_{n \to \infty} e^{-0.1n} = 23 - 20(0) = 23$ days.

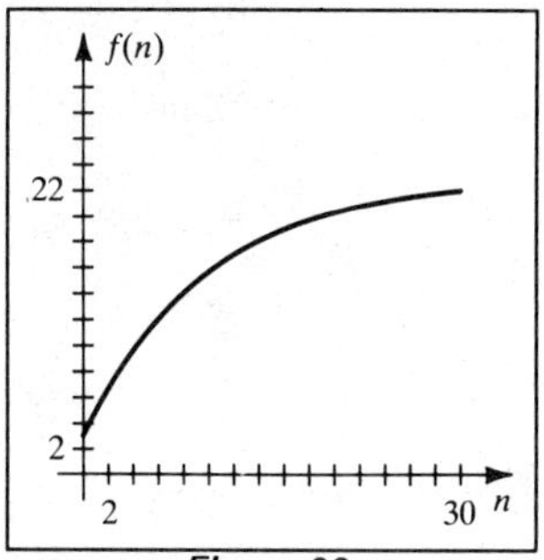

Figure 22

23 $V = \frac{4}{3}\pi r^3 \Rightarrow r = \left(\frac{3}{4\pi}V\right)^{1/3}$. Thus, $S = 4\pi r^2 = 4\pi\left(\frac{3}{4\pi}V\right)^{2/3} = k_1 V^{2/3}$,

for a constant k_1. $\dfrac{dV}{dt}$ is proportional to the surface area of the cell $\Rightarrow$

$\dfrac{dV}{dt} = k_2 S = k_2 k_1 V^{2/3} = kV^{2/3}$, where k_2 and k are constants.

$k > 0$ since the rate of growth, $\dfrac{dV}{dt}$, increases as the surface area S increases.

Solving for V: $V^{-2/3} dV = k\, dt \Rightarrow 3V^{1/3} = kt + C \Rightarrow V(t) = \frac{1}{27}(kt + C)^3$.

24 $\dfrac{dq}{dt} = kq^2 \Rightarrow q^{-2} dq = k\, dt \Rightarrow -\frac{1}{q} = kt + C \Rightarrow q(t) = \dfrac{-1}{kt + C}$.

25 (a) Writing G' as $G'(t) = ABke^{-Bt}e^{-Ae^{-Bt}}$, we see that if $t = t_0 = \dfrac{\ln A}{B}$,

then $G'\left(\dfrac{\ln A}{B}\right) = \dfrac{ABk}{A} e^{-A/A} = Bk/e$. To show that this is a maximum for G',

we use the first derivative test with $G''(t) = AB^2 k(-1 + Ae^{-Bt})e^{-Bt}e^{-Ae^{-Bt}}$.

All factors of G'' are always positive except $(-1 + Ae^{-Bt})$,

which is positive if $t < t_0$, and negative if $t > t_0$.

(b) $B > 0 \Rightarrow e^{-Bt} \to 0$ and $e^{-Ae^{-Bt}} \to e^0 = 1$ as $t \to \infty$. Thus,

$\lim\limits_{t \to \infty} G'(t) = ABk(0)(1) = 0$. Also, $\lim\limits_{t \to \infty} G(t) = \lim\limits_{t \to \infty} ke^{-Ae^{-Bt}} = k(1) = k$.

(c) $G(t) = 10e^{-2e^{-t}}$. The y-intercept is $G(0) = 10e^{-2} \approx 1.35$.

The horizontal asymptote is $\lim\limits_{t \to \infty} G(t) = 10$.

The PI occurs at $x = (1/B)\ln A = \ln 2$. $G' = 20e^{-t} e^{-2e^{-t}} > 0 \Rightarrow G$ is $\uparrow$.

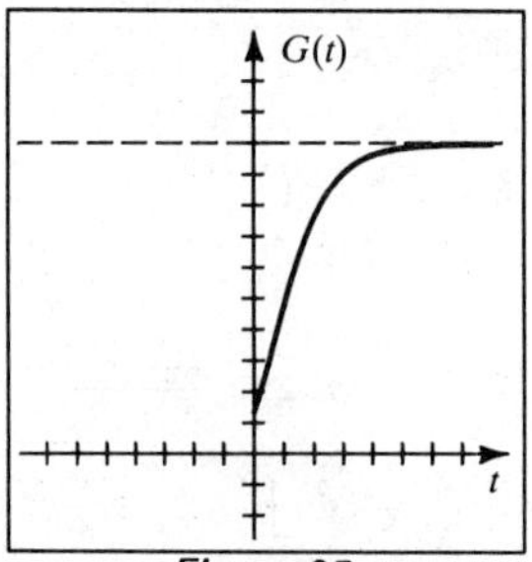

Figure 25

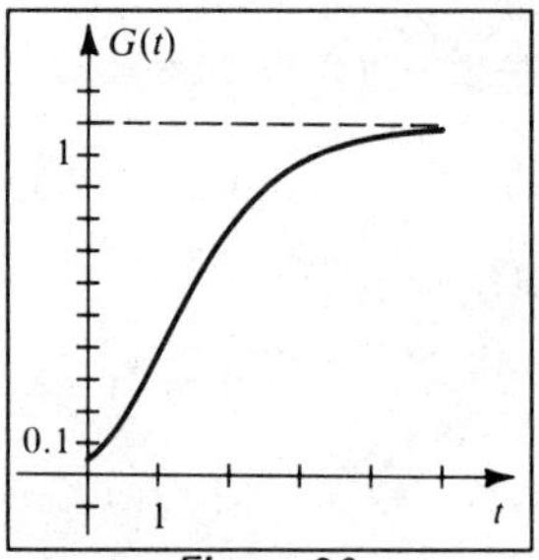

Figure 26

26 $G(t) = 1.1e^{-3.2e^{-1.1t}}$. The y-intercept is $G(0) = 1.1e^{-3.2} \approx 0.045$.

The endpoint value is $G(5) \approx 1.09$. The horizontal asymptote is $\lim\limits_{t \to \infty} G(t) = 1.1$.

The *PI* occurs at $x = \dfrac{\ln 3.2}{1.1} \approx 1.057$. $G' > 0 \Rightarrow G$ is ↑. See *Figure 26*.

7.7 Review Exercises

1 $y = 10 - 15x \Rightarrow 15x = 10 - y \Rightarrow x = \dfrac{10 - y}{15} \Rightarrow f^{-1}(x) = \dfrac{10 - x}{15}$

2 $y = 9 - 2x^2,\ x \le 0 \Rightarrow 2x^2 = 9 - y \Rightarrow x^2 = \dfrac{9 - y}{2} \Rightarrow x = \pm\frac{1}{2}\sqrt{18 - 2y}$

$\{\text{Choose the "}-\text{" since } x \le 0\} \Rightarrow f^{-1}(x) = -\frac{1}{2}\sqrt{18 - 2x}$

3 $f'(x) = 6x^2 - 8 < 0$ for $-1 \le x \le 1 \Rightarrow f$ is ↓ $\Rightarrow f^{-1}$ exists.

Since $f(0) = 5,\ f^{-1}(5) = 0$. $\ D_x f^{-1}(5) = \dfrac{1}{f'(f^{-1}(5))} = \dfrac{1}{f'(0)} = \dfrac{1}{-8} = -\frac{1}{8}$.

4 $f'(x) = 3e^{3x} + 2e^x > 0$ for $x \ge 0 \Rightarrow f$ is ↑ $\Rightarrow f^{-1}$ exists.

Since $f(0) = -2,\ f^{-1}(-2) = 0$. $\ D_x f^{-1}(-2) = \dfrac{1}{f'(f^{-1}(-2))} = \dfrac{1}{f'(0)} = \frac{1}{5}$.

5 $f(x) = \ln|4 - 5x^3|^5 = 5\ln|4 - 5x^3| \Rightarrow f'(x) = 5 \cdot \dfrac{1}{4 - 5x^3} \cdot (-15x^2) = \dfrac{75x^2}{5x^3 - 4}$

6 $f(x) = \ln|x^2 - 7|^3 = 3\ln|x^2 - 7| \Rightarrow f'(x) = 3 \cdot \dfrac{1}{x^2 - 7} \cdot 2x = \dfrac{6x}{x^2 - 7}$

7 $f(x) = (1 - 2x)\ln|1 - 2x| \Rightarrow$

$$f'(x) = \dfrac{(1 - 2x)(-2)}{1 - 2x} + (-2)\ln|1 - 2x| = -2(1 + \ln|1 - 2x|)$$

8 $f(x) = \log\left|\dfrac{2 - 9x}{1 - x^2}\right| = \log|2 - 9x| - \log|1 - x^2| \Rightarrow$

$$f'(x) = D_x\left(\dfrac{\ln|2 - 9x|}{\ln 10} - \dfrac{\ln|1 - x^2|}{\ln 10}\right) = \left(\dfrac{9}{9x - 2} + \dfrac{2x}{1 - x^2}\right)\dfrac{1}{\ln 10}$$

9 $f(x) = \ln\dfrac{(3x + 2)^4\sqrt{6x - 5}}{8x - 7} = 4\ln(3x + 2) + \frac{1}{2}\ln(6x - 5) - \ln(8x - 7) \Rightarrow$

$$f'(x) = \dfrac{12}{3x + 2} + \dfrac{3}{6x - 5} - \dfrac{8}{8x - 7}$$

10 $f(x) = \ln\sqrt[4]{\dfrac{x}{3x + 5}} = \frac{1}{4}\left[\ln x - \ln(3x + 5)\right] \Rightarrow$

$$f'(x) = \frac{1}{4}\left(\dfrac{1}{x} - \dfrac{3}{3x + 5}\right) = \dfrac{5}{4x(3x + 5)}$$

11 $f(x) = \dfrac{1}{\ln(2x^2 + 3)} \Rightarrow f'(x) = -\dfrac{\left[1/(2x^2 + 3)\right] \cdot 4x}{\left[\ln(2x^2 + 3)\right]^2} = \dfrac{-4x}{(2x^2 + 3)\left[\ln(2x^2 + 3)\right]^2}$

12 $f(x) = \dfrac{\ln x}{e^{2x} + 1} \Rightarrow f'(x) = \dfrac{(e^{2x} + 1)(1/x) - (\ln x)(2e^{2x})}{(e^{2x} + 1)^2}$

13 $f(x) = \dfrac{x}{\ln x} \Rightarrow f'(x) = \dfrac{(\ln x) \cdot 1 - x \cdot (1/x)}{(\ln x)^2} = \dfrac{\ln x - 1}{(\ln x)^2}$

14 $f(x) = \dfrac{\ln x}{x} \Rightarrow f'(x) = \dfrac{x \cdot (1/x) - (\ln x) \cdot 1}{x^2} = \dfrac{1 - \ln x}{x^2}$

15 $f(x) = e^{\ln(x^2+1)} = x^2 + 1 \Rightarrow f'(x) = 2x$

$\boxed{16}\ f(x) = \ln e^{\sqrt{x}} = \sqrt{x} \Rightarrow f'(x) = \dfrac{1}{2\sqrt{x}}$

$\boxed{17}\ f(x) = \ln(e^{4x} + 9) \Rightarrow f'(x) = \dfrac{1}{e^{4x} + 9} \cdot 4e^{4x} = \dfrac{4e^{4x}}{e^{4x} + 9}$

$\boxed{18}\ f(x) = 4^{\sqrt{2x+3}} \Rightarrow f'(x) = (4^{\sqrt{2x+3}}\ln 4)\cdot\frac{1}{2}(2x + 3)^{-1/2}(2) = \dfrac{4^{\sqrt{2x+3}}\ln 4}{\sqrt{2x + 3}}$

$\boxed{19}\ f(x) = 10^x \log x \Rightarrow f'(x) = \dfrac{10^x}{x\ln 10} + 10^x(\ln 10)\log x$

$\boxed{20}\ f(x) = 5^{3x} + (3x)^5 \Rightarrow f'(x) = 5^{3x}(\ln 5)(3) + 5(3x)^4(3) = (3\ln 5)5^{3x} + 15(3x)^4$

$\boxed{21}\ f(x) = \sqrt{\ln\sqrt{x}} = (\ln\sqrt{x})^{1/2} \Rightarrow f'(x) = \frac{1}{2}(\ln\sqrt{x})^{-1/2}\left(\dfrac{1}{\sqrt{x}}\cdot\dfrac{1}{2\sqrt{x}}\right) = \dfrac{1}{4x\sqrt{\ln\sqrt{x}}}$

$\boxed{22}\ f(x) = (1 + \sqrt{x})^e \Rightarrow f'(x) = e(1 + \sqrt{x})^{e-1}\cdot\dfrac{1}{2\sqrt{x}} = \dfrac{e(1 + \sqrt{x})^{e-1}}{2\sqrt{x}}$

$\boxed{23}\ f(x) = x^2 e^{-x^2} \Rightarrow f'(x) = x^2 e^{-x^2}(-2x) + e^{-x^2}(2x) = 2xe^{-x^2}(1 - x^2)$

$\boxed{24}\ f(x) = \dfrac{2^{-3x}}{x^3 + 4} \Rightarrow$

$$f'(x) = \dfrac{(x^3 + 4)(2^{-3x})(\ln 2)(-3) - 2^{-3x}(3x^2)}{(x^3 + 4)^2} = \dfrac{(-3)\,2^{-3x}\left[(x^3 + 4)\ln 2 + x^2\right]}{(x^3 + 4)^2}$$

$\boxed{25}\ f(x) = \sqrt{e^{3x} + e^{-3x}} \Rightarrow$

$$f'(x) = \tfrac{1}{2}(e^{3x} + e^{-3x})^{-1/2}(3e^{3x} - 3e^{-3x}) = \dfrac{3(e^{3x} - e^{-3x})}{2\sqrt{e^{3x} + e^{-3x}}}$$

$\boxed{26}\ f(x) = (x^2 + 1)^{2x} = e^{2x\ln(x^2+1)} \Rightarrow f'(x) =$

$$e^{2x\ln(x^2+1)}\left[2x\cdot\dfrac{2x}{x^2 + 1} + 2\ln(x^2 + 1)\right] = (x^2 + 1)^{2x}\left[\dfrac{4x^2}{x^2 + 1} + 2\ln(x^2 + 1)\right]$$

$\boxed{27}\ f(x) = 10^{\ln x} \Rightarrow f'(x) = (10^{\ln x}\ln 10)\cdot\dfrac{1}{x} = \dfrac{10^{\ln x}\ln 10}{x}$

$\boxed{28}\ f(x) = 7^{\ln|x|} \Rightarrow f'(x) = (7^{\ln|x|}\ln 7)\cdot\dfrac{1}{x} = \dfrac{7^{\ln|x|}\ln 7}{x}$

$\boxed{29}\ y = x^{\ln x} \Rightarrow \ln y = \ln x\,(\ln x) = (\ln x)^2 \Rightarrow \dfrac{y'}{y} = 2(\ln x)^1\cdot\dfrac{1}{x} \Rightarrow y' = \dfrac{2\ln x\,(x^{\ln x})}{x}$

$\boxed{30}\ y = (\ln x)^{\ln x} \Rightarrow \ln y = (\ln x)\ln(\ln x) \Rightarrow$

$$\dfrac{y'}{y} = \ln x\cdot\dfrac{1}{x\ln x} + \dfrac{1}{x}\cdot\ln(\ln x) = \dfrac{\ln(\ln x) + 1}{x} \Rightarrow y' = (\ln x)^{\ln x}\left[\dfrac{\ln(\ln x) + 1}{x}\right]$$

$\boxed{31}\ f(x) = \ln|\tan x - \sec x| \Rightarrow$

$$f'(x) = \dfrac{\sec^2 x - \sec x\tan x}{\tan x - \sec x} = \dfrac{\sec x(\sec x - \tan x)}{\tan x - \sec x} = -\sec x$$

$\boxed{32}\ f(x) = \ln\csc\sqrt{x} \Rightarrow f'(x) = \dfrac{1}{\csc\sqrt{x}}\cdot(-\csc\sqrt{x}\cot\sqrt{x})\cdot\dfrac{1}{2\sqrt{x}} = -\dfrac{\cot\sqrt{x}}{2\sqrt{x}}$

$\boxed{33}\ f(x) = \csc e^{-2x}\cot e^{-2x} \Rightarrow$

$$f'(x) = \csc e^{-2x}\left[(-\csc^2 e^{-2x})(-2e^{-2x})\right] + \cot e^{-2x}\left[(-\csc e^{-2x}\cot e^{-2x})(-2e^{-2x})\right]$$
$$= 2e^{-2x}\csc e^{-2x}(\csc^2 e^{-2x} + \cot^2 e^{-2x})$$

$\boxed{34}\ f(x) = x^2 e^{\tan 2x} \Rightarrow$

$$f'(x) = x^2 e^{\tan 2x}(\sec^2 2x)(2) + 2x e^{\tan 2x} = 2x e^{\tan 2x}(x\sec^2 2x + 1)$$

$\boxed{35}$ $f(x) = \ln \cos^4 4x = 4 \ln \cos 4x \Rightarrow f'(x) = 4 \cdot \dfrac{1}{\cos 4x} \cdot (-4 \sin 4x) = -16 \tan 4x$

$\boxed{36}$ $f(x) = 3^{\sin 3x} \Rightarrow f'(x) = (3^{\sin 3x} \ln 3)(3 \cos 3x) = (3 \ln 3 \, \cos 3x) 3^{\sin 3x}$

$\boxed{37}$ $f(x) = (\sin x)^{\cos x} = e^{\cos x \ln \sin x} \Rightarrow f'(x) =$

$\quad e^{\cos x \ln \sin x} \left[\cos x \cdot \dfrac{\cos x}{\sin x} + (-\sin x) \ln \sin x \right] = (\sin x)^{\cos x} (\cos x \cot x - \sin x \ln \sin x)$

$\boxed{38}$ $f(x) = \dfrac{1}{\sin^2 e^{-3x}} \Rightarrow f'(x) = -\dfrac{2 \sin e^{-3x} \cos e^{-3x} (-3e^{-3x})}{(\sin^2 e^{-3x})^2} = \dfrac{6 e^{-3x} \cos e^{-3x}}{\sin^3 e^{-3x}}$

$\boxed{39}$ $1 + xy = e^{xy} \Rightarrow xy' + y = e^{xy}(xy' + y) \Rightarrow$

$$y'(x - xe^{xy}) = ye^{xy} - y \Rightarrow y' = \dfrac{y(e^{xy} - 1)}{x(1 - e^{xy})} = -\dfrac{y}{x}.$$

$\boxed{40}$ $\ln(x + y) + x^2 - 2y^3 = 1 \Rightarrow \dfrac{1}{x+y} \cdot (1 + y') + 2x - 6y^2 y' = 0 \Rightarrow$

$\quad 1 + y' + 2x(x + y) - 6y^2 y'(x + y) = 0 \Rightarrow$

$$y' \left[1 - 6y^2(x + y) \right] = -1 - 2x(x + y) \Rightarrow y' = \dfrac{2x(x + y) + 1}{6y^2(x + y) - 1}$$

$\boxed{41}$ $y = (x + 2)^{4/3}(x - 3)^{3/2} \Rightarrow \ln y = \frac{4}{3} \ln(x + 2) + \frac{3}{2} \ln(x - 3) \Rightarrow$

$\quad \dfrac{y'}{y} = \dfrac{4}{3(x + 2)} + \dfrac{3}{2(x - 3)} \Rightarrow y' = \left[\dfrac{4}{3(x + 2)} + \dfrac{3}{2(x - 3)} \right] (x + 2)^{4/3}(x - 3)^{3/2}$

$\boxed{42}$ $y = \sqrt[3]{(3x - 1) \sqrt{2x + 5}} \Rightarrow \ln y = \frac{1}{3} \ln(3x - 1) + \frac{1}{6} \ln(2x + 5) \Rightarrow$

$\quad \dfrac{y'}{y} = \dfrac{3}{3(3x - 1)} + \dfrac{2}{6(2x + 5)} \Rightarrow y' = \left[\dfrac{1}{3x - 1} + \dfrac{1}{3(2x + 5)} \right] \sqrt[3]{(3x - 1) \sqrt{2x + 5}}$

$\boxed{43}$ (a) $u = \sqrt{x},\ 2\, du = \frac{1}{\sqrt{x}}\, dx \Rightarrow \displaystyle\int \dfrac{1}{\sqrt{x}\, e^{\sqrt{x}}}\, dx = 2 \int e^{-u}\, du = -2e^{-u} + C$

$\quad$ (b) $\displaystyle\int_1^4 \dfrac{1}{\sqrt{x}\, e^{\sqrt{x}}}\, dx = -2 \left[e^{-\sqrt{x}} \right]_1^4 = -2(e^{-2} - e^{-1}) \approx 0.465$

$\boxed{44}$ (a) $u = -3x + 2,\ -\frac{1}{3}\, du = dx \Rightarrow \displaystyle\int e^{-3x+2}\, dx = -\frac{1}{3} \int e^u\, du = -\frac{1}{3} e^u + C$

$\quad$ (b) $\displaystyle\int_0^1 e^{-3x+2}\, dx = -\frac{1}{3} \left[e^{-3x+2} \right]_0^1 = -\frac{1}{3}(e^{-1} - e^2) \approx 2.340$

$\boxed{45}$ (a) $u = -x^2,\ -\frac{1}{2}\, du = x\, dx \Rightarrow \displaystyle\int x\, 4^{-x^2}\, dx = -\frac{1}{2} \int 4^u\, du = -\dfrac{4^u}{2 \ln 4} + C$

$\quad$ (b) $\displaystyle\int_0^1 x\, 4^{-x^2}\, dx = -\dfrac{1}{2 \ln 4} \left[4^{-x^2} \right]_0^1 = -\dfrac{1}{2 \ln 4}\left(\frac{1}{4} - 1 \right) = \dfrac{3}{8 \ln 4} \approx 0.271$

$\boxed{46}$ (a) $u = x^3 + 3x,\ \frac{1}{3}\, du = (x^2 + 1)\, dx \Rightarrow \displaystyle\int \dfrac{x^2 + 1}{x^3 + 3x}\, dx = \frac{1}{3} \int \frac{1}{u}\, du = \frac{1}{3} \ln |u| + C$

$\quad$ (b) $\displaystyle\int_1^2 \dfrac{x^2 + 1}{x^3 + 3x}\, dx = \frac{1}{3} \left[\ln |x^3 + 3x| \right]_1^2 = \frac{1}{3}(\ln 14 - \ln 4) = \frac{1}{3} \ln \frac{7}{2} \approx 0.418$

$\boxed{47}$ $u = x^2,\ \frac{1}{2}\, du = x\, dx \Rightarrow \int x \tan x^2\, dx = \frac{1}{2} \int \tan u\, du = -\frac{1}{2} \ln |\cos u| + C$

$\boxed{48}$ $u = x + \frac{\pi}{6},\ du = dx \Rightarrow \int \cot(x + \frac{\pi}{6})\, dx = \int \cot u\, du = \ln |\sin u| + C$

$\boxed{49}$ $\displaystyle\int x^e\, dx = \dfrac{x^{e+1}}{e + 1} + C$

$\boxed{50}$ $u = 7 - 5x$, $-\frac{1}{5} du = dx \Rightarrow \int \frac{1}{7 - 5x} dx = -\frac{1}{5} \int \frac{1}{u} du = -\frac{1}{5} \ln |u| + C$

$\boxed{51}$ $u = 1 - \ln x$, $-du = \frac{dx}{x} \Rightarrow$

$$\int \frac{1}{x - x \ln x} dx = \int \frac{1}{x(1 - \ln x)} dx = -\int \frac{1}{u} du = -\ln |u| + C$$

$\boxed{52}$ $u = \ln x$, $du = \frac{dx}{x} \Rightarrow \int \frac{1}{x \ln x} dx = \int \frac{1}{u} du = \ln |u| + C$

$\boxed{53}$ $\int \frac{(1 + e^x)^2}{e^{2x}} dx = \int \frac{1 + 2e^x + e^{2x}}{e^{2x}} dx = \int (e^{-2x} + 2e^{-x} + 1) dx =$

$$-\frac{1}{2} e^{-2x} - 2e^{-x} + x + C$$

$\boxed{54}$ $\int \frac{(e^{2x} + e^{3x})^2}{e^{5x}} dx = \int \frac{e^{4x} + 2e^{5x} + e^{6x}}{e^{5x}} dx = \int (e^{-x} + 2 + e^x) dx =$

$$-e^{-x} + 2x + e^x + C$$

$\boxed{55}$ Using long division,

$$\int \frac{x^2}{x + 2} dx = \int \left(x - 2 + \frac{4}{x + 2} \right) dx = \frac{1}{2} x^2 - 2x + 4 \ln |x + 2| + C$$

$\boxed{56}$ Using long division,

$$\int \frac{x^2 + 1}{x + 1} dx = \int \left(x - 1 + \frac{2}{x + 1} \right) dx = \frac{1}{2} x^2 - x + 2 \ln |x + 1| + C$$

$\boxed{57}$ $u = 4/x^2$, $-\frac{1}{8} du = (1/x^3) dx \Rightarrow \int \frac{e^{4/x^2}}{x^3} dx = -\frac{1}{8} \int e^u du = -\frac{1}{8} e^u + C$

$\boxed{58}$ $u = 1/x$, $-du = (1/x^2) dx \Rightarrow \int \frac{e^{1/x}}{x^2} dx = -\int e^u du = -e^u + C$

$\boxed{59}$ $u = x^2 + 1$, $\frac{1}{2} du = x dx \Rightarrow$

$$\int \frac{x}{x^4 + 2x^2 + 1} dx = \int \frac{x}{(x^2 + 1)^2} dx = \frac{1}{2} \int \frac{1}{u^2} du = -\frac{1}{2u} + C$$

$\boxed{60}$ $u = x^4 + 1$, $\frac{1}{4} du = x^3 dx \Rightarrow \int \frac{5x^3}{x^4 + 1} dx = 5 \cdot \frac{1}{4} \int \frac{1}{u} du = \frac{5}{4} \ln u + C$

$\boxed{61}$ $u = 1 + e^x$, $du = e^x dx \Rightarrow \int \frac{e^x}{1 + e^x} dx = \int \frac{1}{u} du = \ln u + C$

$\boxed{62}$ $\int (1 + e^{-3x})^2 dx = \int (1 + 2e^{-3x} + e^{-6x}) dx = x - \frac{2}{3} e^{-3x} - \frac{1}{6} e^{-6x} + C$

$\boxed{63}$ $\int 5^x e^x dx = \int (5e)^x dx$ { treat $5e$ as a constant } $= \frac{(5e)^x}{\ln (5e)} + C$

$\boxed{64}$ $u = x^2$, $\frac{1}{2} du = x dx \Rightarrow \int x \, 10^{(x^2)} dx = \frac{1}{2} \int 10^u du = \frac{10^u}{2 \ln 10} + C$

$\boxed{65}$ $u = \log x$, $du = \frac{1}{x \ln 10} dx \Rightarrow \int \frac{1}{x \sqrt{\log x}} dx = \ln 10 \int u^{-1/2} du = 2 \ln 10 \sqrt{u} + C$

$\boxed{66}$ $u = 1 + 7^x$, $du = (7^x \ln 7) dx \Rightarrow \int 7^x \sqrt{1 + 7^x} dx = \frac{1}{\ln 7} \int u^{1/2} du = \frac{2 u^{3/2}}{3 \ln 7} + C$

$\boxed{67}$ $u = e^{-x}$, $-du = e^{-x} dx \Rightarrow \int e^{-x} \sin e^{-x} dx = -\int \sin u \, du = \cos u + C$

$\boxed{68}$ $u = \sec x$, $du = \sec x \tan x \, dx \Rightarrow \int \tan x \, e^{\sec x} \sec x \, dx = \int e^u du = e^u + C$

$\boxed{69}$ $u = 1 + \cot x,\ -du = \csc^2 x\,dx \Rightarrow \int \dfrac{\csc^2 x}{1 + \cot x}\,dx = -\int \dfrac{1}{u}\,du = -\ln|u| + C$

$\boxed{70}$ $u = \sin x - \cos x,\ du = (\cos x + \sin x)\,dx \Rightarrow$

$$\int \dfrac{\cos x + \sin x}{\sin x - \cos x}\,dx = \int \dfrac{1}{u}\,du = \ln|u| + C$$

$\boxed{71}$ $u = 1 - 2\sin 2x,\ -\frac{1}{4}\,du = \cos 2x\,dx \Rightarrow$

$$\int \dfrac{\cos 2x}{1 - 2\sin 2x}\,dx = -\tfrac{1}{4}\int \dfrac{1}{u}\,du = -\tfrac{1}{4}\ln|u| + C$$

$\boxed{72}$ $u = 3^x,\ du = (3^x \ln 3)\,dx \Rightarrow \int 3^x(3 + \sin 3^x)\,dx = \dfrac{1}{\ln 3}\int (3 + \sin u)\,du =$

$$\dfrac{1}{\ln 3}(3u - \cos u) + C = \dfrac{1}{\ln 3}(3^{x+1} - \cos 3^x) + C$$

$\boxed{73}$ $u = e^x,\ du = e^x\,dx \Rightarrow \int e^x \tan e^x\,dx = \int \tan u\,du = -\ln|\cos u| + C$

$\boxed{74}$ $u = 1/x,\ -du = (1/x^2)\,dx \Rightarrow \int \dfrac{\sec(1/x)}{x^2}\,dx = -\int \sec u\,du = -\ln|\sec u + \tan u| + C$

$\boxed{75}$ $u = 3x,\ \frac{1}{3}\,du = dx \Rightarrow \int (\csc 3x + 1)^2\,dx = \tfrac{1}{3}\int (\csc^2 u + 2\csc u + 1)\,du =$

$$\tfrac{1}{3}(-\cot u + 2\ln|\csc u - \cot u| + u) + C$$

$\boxed{76}$ $\int \cos 2x \csc 2x\,dx = \int \dfrac{\cos 2x}{\sin 2x}\,dx = \int \cot 2x\,dx = \tfrac{1}{2}\ln|\sin 2x| + C$

$\boxed{77}$ $u = 9x,\ \frac{1}{9}\,du = dx \Rightarrow \int (\cot 9x + \csc 9x)\,dx = \tfrac{1}{9}\int (\cot u + \csc u)\,du =$

$$\tfrac{1}{9}\ln|\sin u| + \tfrac{1}{9}\ln|\csc u - \cot u| + C$$

$\boxed{78}$ $\int \dfrac{\sin x + 1}{\cos x}\,dx = \int (\tan x + \sec x)\,dx = -\ln|\cos x| + \ln|\sec x + \tan x| + C$

$\boxed{79}$ $y'' = -e^{-3x} \Rightarrow y' = \tfrac{1}{3}e^{-3x} + C.\ \ y' = 2$ if $x = 0 \Rightarrow 2 = \tfrac{1}{3} + C \Rightarrow C = \tfrac{5}{3}.$

$y' = \tfrac{1}{3}e^{-3x} + \tfrac{5}{3} \Rightarrow y = -\tfrac{1}{9}e^{-3x} + \tfrac{5}{3}x + C.$

$$y = -1 \text{ if } x = 0 \Rightarrow -\tfrac{1}{9} + C = -1 \Rightarrow C = -\tfrac{8}{9}.$$

$\boxed{80}$ (a) $q'(t) = q(t)\,k\sin 2\pi t.$ Since $q(t) > 0\ \forall t$ and $k > 0$, the sign of $q'(t)$ is determined

by the sign of $\sin 2\pi t.$ $\sin 2\pi t > 0$ if $0 < 2\pi t < \pi,\ 2\pi < 2\pi t < 3\pi,$ etc.

Thus, $q'(t) > 0$ on $(n,\ n + \tfrac{1}{2})$ and $q'(t) < 0$ on $(n + \tfrac{1}{2},\ n + 1)$, where n is a

nonnegative integer. Hence, $q(t)$ increases during spring and summer

$(t = 0$ to $t = \tfrac{1}{2})$ and decreases during fall and winter $(t = \tfrac{1}{2}$ to $t = 1).$

(b) $\dfrac{q'(t)}{q(t)} = k\sin 2\pi t \Rightarrow \ln q(t) = -\dfrac{k}{2\pi}\cos 2\pi t + c \Rightarrow q(t) = e^c e^{-\frac{k}{2\pi}\cos 2\pi t}.$

$q(0) = e^c e^{-\frac{k}{2\pi}} = q_0 \Rightarrow e^c = q_0 e^{\frac{k}{2\pi}} \Rightarrow$

$$q(t) = q_0 e^{\frac{k}{2\pi}} e^{-\frac{k}{2\pi}\cos 2\pi t} = q_0 e^{\frac{k}{2\pi}(1-\cos 2\pi t)}.$$

$\boxed{81}$ $a(t) = e^{t/2} \Rightarrow v(t) = 2e^{t/2} + C.\ \ v(0) = 6 \Rightarrow C = 4$ and $v(t) = 2e^{t/2} + 4.$

Since $v(t) > 0$, the distance traveled from $t = 0$ to $t = 4$ is

$$s(4) - s(0) = \int_0^4 v(t)\,dt = \left[4e^{t/2} + 4t\right]_0^4 = 4e^2 + 12 \approx 41.56 \text{ cm.}$$

[82] $f(x) = x^2 \ln x \Rightarrow f'(x) = x(1 + 2\ln x)$.

$f'(x) = 0 \Rightarrow x = e^{-1/2} \approx 0.607$.

$f''(x) = 3 + 2\ln x$. $f''(e^{-1/2}) = 2 > 0 \Rightarrow$

$f(e^{-1/2}) = -1/(2e) \approx -0.184$ is a *LMIN*.

$f''(x) = 0 \Rightarrow x = e^{-3/2} \approx 0.223$.

$f''(x) < 0$ on $(0, e^{-3/2})$ and f is *CD*.

$f''(x) > 0$ on $(e^{-3/2}, \infty)$ and f is *CU*. *PI* at $x = e^{-3/2}$.

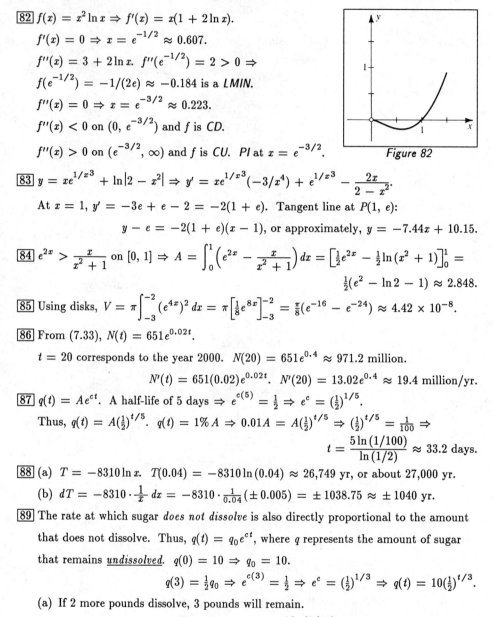
Figure 82

[83] $y = xe^{1/x^3} + \ln|2 - x^2| \Rightarrow y' = xe^{1/x^3}(-3/x^4) + e^{1/x^3} - \dfrac{2x}{2 - x^2}$.

At $x = 1$, $y' = -3e + e - 2 = -2(1 + e)$. Tangent line at $P(1, e)$:

$$y - e = -2(1 + e)(x - 1), \text{ or approximately, } y = -7.44x + 10.15.$$

[84] $e^{2x} > \dfrac{x}{x^2 + 1}$ on $[0, 1] \Rightarrow A = \displaystyle\int_0^1 \left(e^{2x} - \dfrac{x}{x^2 + 1}\right) dx = \left[\tfrac{1}{2}e^{2x} - \tfrac{1}{2}\ln(x^2 + 1)\right]_0^1 =$

$$\tfrac{1}{2}(e^2 - \ln 2 - 1) \approx 2.848.$$

[85] Using disks, $V = \pi \displaystyle\int_{-3}^{-2} (e^{4x})^2\, dx = \pi\left[\tfrac{1}{8}e^{8x}\right]_{-3}^{-2} = \tfrac{\pi}{8}(e^{-16} - e^{-24}) \approx 4.42 \times 10^{-8}$.

[86] From (7.33), $N(t) = 651e^{0.02t}$.

$t = 20$ corresponds to the year 2000. $N(20) = 651e^{0.4} \approx 971.2$ million.

$$N'(t) = 651(0.02)e^{0.02t}. \quad N'(20) = 13.02e^{0.4} \approx 19.4 \text{ million/yr}.$$

[87] $q(t) = Ae^{ct}$. A half-life of 5 days $\Rightarrow e^{c(5)} = \tfrac{1}{2} \Rightarrow e^c = \left(\tfrac{1}{2}\right)^{1/5}$.

Thus, $q(t) = A\left(\tfrac{1}{2}\right)^{t/5}$. $q(t) = 1\% A \Rightarrow 0.01A = A\left(\tfrac{1}{2}\right)^{t/5} \Rightarrow \left(\tfrac{1}{2}\right)^{t/5} = \tfrac{1}{100} \Rightarrow$

$$t = \frac{5\ln(1/100)}{\ln(1/2)} \approx 33.2 \text{ days}.$$

[88] (a) $T = -8310 \ln x$. $T(0.04) = -8310 \ln(0.04) \approx 26{,}749$ yr, or about 27,000 yr.

(b) $dT = -8310 \cdot \tfrac{1}{x}\, dx = -8310 \cdot \tfrac{1}{0.04}(\pm 0.005) = \pm 1038.75 \approx \pm 1040$ yr.

[89] The rate at which sugar *does not dissolve* is also directly proportional to the amount
that does not dissolve. Thus, $q(t) = q_0 e^{ct}$, where q represents the amount of sugar
that remains *undissolved*. $q(0) = 10 \Rightarrow q_0 = 10$.

$$q(3) = \tfrac{1}{2}q_0 \Rightarrow e^{c(3)} = \tfrac{1}{2} \Rightarrow e^c = \left(\tfrac{1}{2}\right)^{1/3} \Rightarrow q(t) = 10\left(\tfrac{1}{2}\right)^{t/3}.$$

(a) If 2 more pounds dissolve, 3 pounds will remain.

$$q(t) = 3 \Rightarrow \left(\tfrac{1}{2}\right)^{t/3} = \tfrac{3}{10} \Rightarrow t = \frac{3\ln(3/10)}{\ln(1/2)} \approx 5.2 \text{ or } 2.2 \text{ additional hr}.$$

(b) $t = 7$ for 8:00 P.M. $10 - q(7) = 10 - 10\left(\tfrac{1}{2}\right)^{7/3} = 10\left[1 - \left(\tfrac{1}{2}\right)^{7/3}\right] \approx 8.016$ lb.

$\boxed{90}$ If the object is cooling, then, $f'(t) < 0$ and $f(t) - T > 0$, $\forall t$. Since the rate is directly proportional to the difference of temperatures, $f'(t) = -k\big[f(t) - T\big]$.

Note that $f'(t) < 0$ and $f(t) - T > 0 \Rightarrow -k < 0$ and k is a positive constant.

$\dfrac{f'(t)}{f(t) - T} = -k \Rightarrow \ln\big[f(t) - T\big] = -kt + c \Rightarrow f(t) = T + e^{-kt}e^{c}$.

At $t = 0$, $f(0) = T + e^{c} \Rightarrow e^{c} = f(0) - T$. Thus, $f(t) = T + \big[f(0) - T\big]e^{-kt}$.

If the object is warming, then $f'(t) > 0$ and $f(t) - T < 0$, $\forall t$.

The same result follows after a similar analysis.

$\boxed{91}$ $q(t) = 100{,}000\,e^{ct}$. $q(20) = 2(100{,}000) \Rightarrow e^{c(20)} = 2 \Rightarrow e^{c} = 2^{1/20}$.

Thus, $q(t) = 100{,}000(2)^{t/20}$, where t is time in minutes.

$q(120) = 100{,}000(2)^{6} = 6{,}400{,}000$ bacteria.

$\boxed{92}$ $p\,dv + cv\,dp = 0 \Rightarrow cv\,dp = -p\,dv \Rightarrow \dfrac{dp}{p} = -\dfrac{1}{c}\dfrac{dv}{v} \Rightarrow$

$\ln p = -\dfrac{1}{c}\ln v + d = d + \ln v^{-1/c} \Rightarrow p = e^{d + \ln v^{-1/c}} = e^{d}e^{\ln v^{-1/c}} \Rightarrow$

$p = e^{d}v^{-1/c} \Rightarrow p(v) = kv^{-1/c}$, where c, d, and k are constants.

Chapter 8: Inverse Trigonometric and Hyperbolic Functions

Exercises 8.1

$\boxed{1}$ (a) $\sin^{-1}(-\frac{\sqrt{2}}{2}) = -\frac{\pi}{4}$ (b) $\cos^{-1}(-\frac{1}{2}) = \frac{2\pi}{3}$ (c) $\tan^{-1}(-\sqrt{3}) = -\frac{\pi}{3}$

$\boxed{2}$ (a) $\sin^{-1}(-\frac{1}{2}) = -\frac{\pi}{6}$ (b) $\cos^{-1}(-\frac{\sqrt{2}}{2}) = \frac{3\pi}{4}$ (c) $\tan^{-1}(-1) = -\frac{\pi}{4}$

$\boxed{3}$ (a) $\arcsin\frac{\sqrt{3}}{2} = \frac{\pi}{3}$ (b) $\arccos\frac{\sqrt{2}}{2} = \frac{\pi}{4}$ (c) $\arctan\frac{1}{\sqrt{3}} = \frac{\pi}{6}$

$\boxed{4}$ (a) $\arcsin 0 = 0$ (b) $\arccos(-1) = \pi$ (c) $\arctan 0 = 0$

$\boxed{5}$ (a) $\sin^{-1}\frac{\pi}{3}$ is <u>not defined</u> since $\frac{\pi}{3} > 1$, i.e., $\frac{\pi}{3} \notin [-1, 1]$

    (b) $\cos^{-1}\frac{\pi}{2}$ is <u>not defined</u> since $\frac{\pi}{2} > 1$, i.e., $\frac{\pi}{2} \notin [-1, 1]$ (c) $\tan^{-1}1 = \frac{\pi}{4}$

$\boxed{6}$ (a) $\arcsin\frac{\pi}{2}$ is <u>not defined</u> since $\frac{\pi}{2} > 1$, i.e., $\frac{\pi}{2} \notin [-1, 1]$

    (b) $\arccos\frac{\pi}{3}$ is <u>not defined</u> since $\frac{\pi}{3} > 1$, i.e., $\frac{\pi}{3} \notin [-1, 1]$ (c) $\arctan(-\frac{\sqrt{3}}{3}) = -\frac{\pi}{6}$

Note: Exercises 7–10 refer to the properties of

$$\sin^{-1}, \cos^{-1}, \text{ and } \tan^{-1} \text{ in (8.2), (8.4), and (8.6), respectively.}$$

$\boxed{7}$ (a) $\sin[\arcsin(-\frac{3}{10})] = -\frac{3}{10}$ since $-1 \le -\frac{3}{10} \le 1$

    (b) $\cos(\arccos\frac{1}{2}) = \frac{1}{2}$ since $-1 \le \frac{1}{2} \le 1$

    (c) $\tan(\arctan 14) = 14$ since 14 is a real number

$\boxed{8}$ (a) $\sin(\sin^{-1}\frac{2}{3}) = \frac{2}{3}$ since $-1 \le \frac{2}{3} \le 1$

    (b) $\cos[\cos^{-1}(-\frac{1}{5})] = -\frac{1}{5}$ since $-1 \le -\frac{1}{5} \le 1$

    (c) $\tan[\tan^{-1}(-9)] = -9$ since -9 is a real number

$\boxed{9}$ (a) $\sin^{-1}(\sin\frac{\pi}{3}) = \frac{\pi}{3}$ since $-\frac{\pi}{2} \le \frac{\pi}{3} \le \frac{\pi}{2}$

    (b) $\cos^{-1}\left[\cos\left(\frac{5\pi}{6}\right)\right] = \frac{5\pi}{6}$ since $0 \le \frac{5\pi}{6} \le \pi$

    (c) $\tan^{-1}\left[\tan\left(-\frac{\pi}{6}\right)\right] = -\frac{\pi}{6}$ since $-\frac{\pi}{2} < -\frac{\pi}{6} < \frac{\pi}{2}$

$\boxed{10}$ (a) $\arcsin\left[\sin\left(-\frac{\pi}{2}\right)\right] = -\frac{\pi}{2}$ since $-\frac{\pi}{2} \le -\frac{\pi}{2} \le \frac{\pi}{2}$

    (b) $\arccos(\cos 0) = 0$ since $0 \le 0 \le \pi$ (c) $\arctan(\tan\frac{\pi}{4}) = \frac{\pi}{4}$ since $-\frac{\pi}{2} < \frac{\pi}{4} < \frac{\pi}{2}$

$\boxed{11}$ (a) $\arcsin(\sin\frac{5\pi}{4}) = \arcsin(-\frac{\sqrt{2}}{2}) = -\frac{\pi}{4}$

    (b) $\arccos(\cos\frac{5\pi}{4}) = \arccos(-\frac{\sqrt{2}}{2}) = \frac{3\pi}{4}$ (c) $\arctan(\tan\frac{7\pi}{4}) = \arctan(-1) = -\frac{\pi}{4}$

$\boxed{12}$ (a) $\sin^{-1}(\sin\frac{2\pi}{3}) = \sin^{-1}\frac{\sqrt{3}}{2} = \frac{\pi}{3}$ (b) $\cos^{-1}(\cos\frac{4\pi}{3}) = \cos^{-1}(-\frac{1}{2}) = \frac{2\pi}{3}$

    (c) $\tan^{-1}(\tan\frac{7\pi}{6}) = \tan^{-1}\frac{\sqrt{3}}{3} = \frac{\pi}{6}$

$\boxed{13}$ (a) $\sin[\cos^{-1}(-\frac{1}{2})] = \sin\frac{2\pi}{3} = \frac{\sqrt{3}}{2}$ (b) $\cos(\tan^{-1}1) = \cos\frac{\pi}{4} = \frac{\sqrt{2}}{2}$

    (c) $\tan[\sin^{-1}(-1)] = \tan(-\frac{\pi}{2})$, which is <u>not defined</u>.

$\boxed{14}$ (a) $\sin(\tan^{-1}\sqrt{3}) = \sin\frac{\pi}{3} = \frac{\sqrt{3}}{2}$ (b) $\cos(\sin^{-1}1) = \cos\frac{\pi}{2} = 0$

    (c) $\tan(\cos^{-1}0) = \tan\frac{\pi}{2}$, which is <u>not defined</u>.

15 (a) Let $\theta = \sin^{-1}\frac{2}{3}$. From *Figure 15a*, $\cot(\sin^{-1}\frac{2}{3}) = \cot\theta = \frac{x}{y} = \frac{\sqrt{5}}{2}$.

(b) Let $\theta = \tan^{-1}(-\frac{3}{5})$. From *Figure 15b*, $\sec[\tan^{-1}(-\frac{3}{5})] = \sec\theta = \frac{r}{x} = \frac{\sqrt{34}}{5}$.

(c) Let $\theta = \cos^{-1}(-\frac{1}{4})$. From *Figure 15c*, $\csc[\cos^{-1}(-\frac{1}{4})] = \csc\theta = \frac{r}{y} = \frac{4}{\sqrt{15}}$.

Note: Triangles could be used for the figures, and may be easier to work with in class.

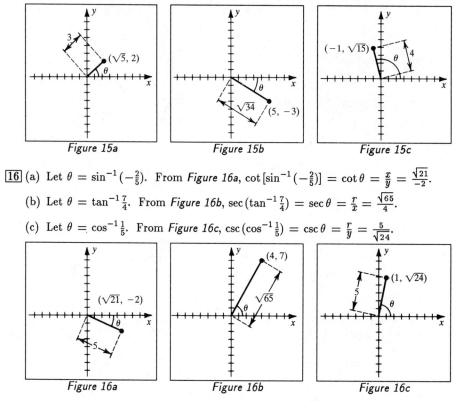

Figure 15a   Figure 15b   Figure 15c

16 (a) Let $\theta = \sin^{-1}(-\frac{2}{5})$. From *Figure 16a*, $\cot[\sin^{-1}(-\frac{2}{5})] = \cot\theta = \frac{x}{y} = \frac{\sqrt{21}}{-2}$.

(b) Let $\theta = \tan^{-1}\frac{7}{4}$. From *Figure 16b*, $\sec(\tan^{-1}\frac{7}{4}) = \sec\theta = \frac{r}{x} = \frac{\sqrt{65}}{4}$.

(c) Let $\theta = \cos^{-1}\frac{1}{5}$. From *Figure 16c*, $\csc(\cos^{-1}\frac{1}{5}) = \csc\theta = \frac{r}{y} = \frac{5}{\sqrt{24}}$.

Figure 16a   Figure 16b   Figure 16c

17 (a) $\text{Sin}(\arcsin\frac{1}{2} + \arccos 0) = \sin(\frac{\pi}{6} + \frac{\pi}{2}) = \sin\frac{2\pi}{3} = \frac{\sqrt{3}}{2}$.

(b) Let $\alpha = \arctan(-\frac{3}{4})$ and $\beta = \arcsin\frac{4}{5}$. Using the difference identity for the cosine and figures as in Exercises 15 and 16, we have $\cos[\arctan(-\frac{3}{4}) - \arcsin\frac{4}{5}]$

$$= \cos(\alpha - \beta) = \cos\alpha\cos\beta + \sin\alpha\sin\beta = \frac{4}{5}\cdot\frac{3}{5} + (-\frac{3}{5})\cdot\frac{4}{5} = 0.$$

(c) Let $\alpha = \arctan\frac{4}{3}$ and $\beta = \arccos\frac{8}{17}$. $\text{Tan}(\arctan\frac{4}{3} + \arccos\frac{8}{17}) =$

$$\tan(\alpha + \beta) = \frac{\tan\alpha + \tan\beta}{1 - \tan\alpha\tan\beta} = \frac{\frac{4}{3} + \frac{15}{8}}{1 - \frac{4}{3}\cdot\frac{15}{8}}\cdot\frac{24}{24} = \frac{32 + 45}{24 - 60} = -\frac{77}{36}.$$

18 (a) Let $\alpha = \sin^{-1}\frac{5}{13}$ and $\beta = \cos^{-1}(-\frac{3}{5})$. $\text{Sin}[\sin^{-1}\frac{5}{13} - \cos^{-1}(-\frac{3}{5})] =$

$$\sin(\alpha - \beta) = \sin\alpha\cos\beta - \cos\alpha\sin\beta = \frac{5}{13}\cdot(-\frac{3}{5}) - \frac{12}{13}\cdot\frac{4}{5} = -\frac{63}{65}.$$

(b) Let $\alpha = \sin^{-1}\frac{4}{5}$ and $\beta = \tan^{-1}\frac{3}{4}$. $\text{Cos}(\sin^{-1}\frac{4}{5} + \tan^{-1}\frac{3}{4}) =$

$$\cos(\alpha + \beta) = \cos\alpha\cos\beta - \sin\alpha\sin\beta = \frac{3}{5}\cdot\frac{4}{5} - \frac{4}{5}\cdot\frac{3}{5} = 0.$$

(c) $\text{Tan}[\cos^{-1}\frac{1}{2} - \sin^{-1}(-\frac{1}{2})] = \tan[\frac{\pi}{3} - (-\frac{\pi}{6})] = \tan\frac{\pi}{2}$, which is <u>not defined</u>.

19 Let $\alpha = \tan^{-1} x$. From *Figure 19*, $\sin(\tan^{-1} x) = \sin \alpha = \dfrac{x}{\sqrt{x^2 + 1}}$.

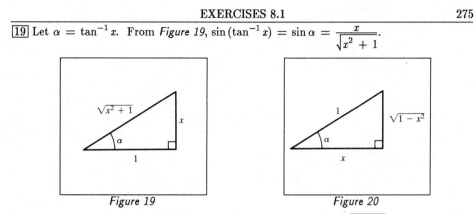

Figure 19   Figure 20

20 Let $\alpha = \arccos x$. From *Figure 20*, $\tan(\arccos x) = \tan \alpha = \dfrac{\sqrt{1 - x^2}}{x}$.

21 Let $\alpha = \sin^{-1} \frac{x}{3}$. From *Figure 21*, $\sec(\sin^{-1} \frac{x}{3}) = \sec \alpha = \dfrac{3}{\sqrt{9 - x^2}}$.

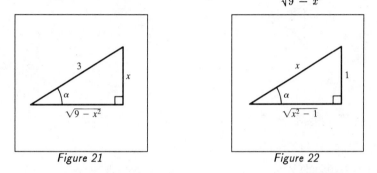

Figure 21   Figure 22

22 Let $\alpha = \sin^{-1} \frac{1}{x}$. From *Figure 22*, $\cot\left(\sin^{-1} \frac{1}{x}\right) = \cot \alpha = \dfrac{\sqrt{x^2 - 1}}{1} = \sqrt{x^2 - 1}$.

Note: If $x < 0$, then $\cot \alpha = -\sqrt{x^2 - 1}$.

23 $y = \sin^{-1} 2x$ ● horizontally compress $y = \sin^{-1} x$ by a factor of 2

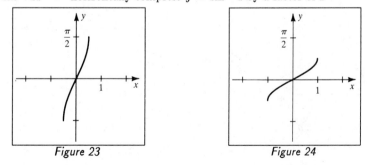

Figure 23   Figure 24

24 $y = \frac{1}{2} \sin^{-1} x$ ● vertically compress $y = \sin^{-1} x$ by a factor of 2

$\boxed{25}$ $y = \cos^{-1} \frac{1}{2} x$ • horizontally stretch $y = \cos^{-1} x$ by a factor of 2

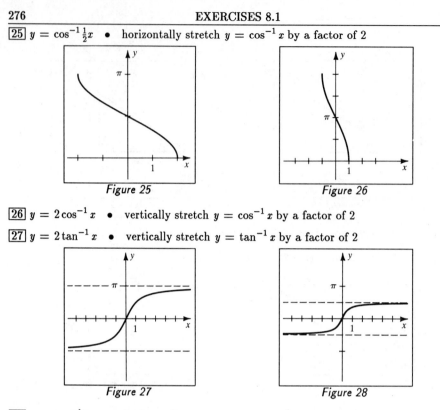

Figure 25   Figure 26

$\boxed{26}$ $y = 2\cos^{-1} x$ • vertically stretch $y = \cos^{-1} x$ by a factor of 2

$\boxed{27}$ $y = 2\tan^{-1} x$ • vertically stretch $y = \tan^{-1} x$ by a factor of 2

Figure 27   Figure 28

$\boxed{28}$ $y = \tan^{-1} 2x$ • horizontally compress $y = \tan^{-1} x$ by a factor of 2

$\boxed{29}$ Sketching a triangle as in Exercises 19–22, we see that $\sin(\arccos x) = \sqrt{1 - x^2}$.

Thus, we have the graph of the semicircle $y = \sqrt{1 - x^2}$ on the interval $[-1, 1]$.

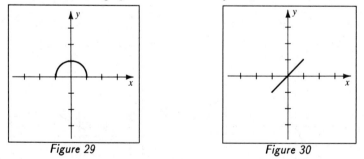

Figure 29   Figure 30

$\boxed{30}$ By a property of $\sin^{-1}$, $\sin(\sin^{-1} x) = x$ for $-1 \le x \le 1$.

Thus, we have the graph of the line $y = x$ on the interval $[-1, 1]$.

$\boxed{31}$ (a) The **inverse cotangent function**, or **arccotangent function**,

denoted by $\cot^{-1}$ or arccot, is defined by

$$y = \cot^{-1} x = \operatorname{arccot} x \quad \text{if and only if} \quad x = \cot y$$

for any real number x and $0 < y < \pi$.

(b) Reflect the graph of $y = \cot x$ on $(0, \pi)$ through the line $y = x$.

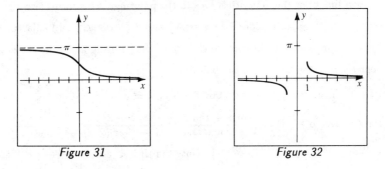

Figure 31   Figure 32

32 (a) The inverse cosecant function, or arccosecant function,

denoted by $\csc^{-1}$ or arccsc, is defined by

$$y = \csc^{-1} x = \text{arccsc } x \quad \text{if and only if} \quad x = \csc y$$

for $|x| \geq 1$ and y in $[-\frac{\pi}{2}, 0)$ or in $(0, \frac{\pi}{2}]$.

(b) Reflect the graph of $y = \csc x$ on $[-\frac{\pi}{2}, 0) \cup (0, \frac{\pi}{2}]$ through the line $y = x$.

33 (a) $2\tan^2 t + 9\tan t + 3 = 0 \Rightarrow$

$$\tan t = \frac{-9 \pm \sqrt{81 - 24}}{4} \Rightarrow t = \arctan\tfrac{1}{4}(-9 \pm \sqrt{57})$$

(b) $\arctan\tfrac{1}{4}(-9 - \sqrt{57}) \approx -1.3337$, $\arctan\tfrac{1}{4}(-9 + \sqrt{57}) \approx -0.3478$

34 (a) $3\sin^2 t + 7\sin t + 3 = 0 \Rightarrow \sin t = \dfrac{-7 \pm \sqrt{49 - 36}}{6} \Rightarrow$

$$t = \arcsin\tfrac{1}{6}(-7 + \sqrt{13}) \ \{\sin t \neq \tfrac{1}{6}(-7 - \sqrt{13}) < -1\}$$

(b) $\arcsin\tfrac{1}{6}(-7 + \sqrt{13}) \approx -0.6013$

35 (a) $15\cos^4 x - 14\cos^2 x + 3 = 0 \Rightarrow (5\cos^2 x - 3)(3\cos^2 x - 1) = 0 \Rightarrow$

$$\cos^2 x = \tfrac{3}{5}, \tfrac{1}{3} \Rightarrow \cos x = \pm\tfrac{1}{5}\sqrt{15}, \pm\tfrac{1}{3}\sqrt{3} \Rightarrow x = \arccos(\pm\tfrac{1}{5}\sqrt{15}), \arccos(\pm\tfrac{1}{3}\sqrt{3})$$

(b) $\arccos\tfrac{1}{5}\sqrt{15} \approx 0.6847$, $\arccos(-\tfrac{1}{5}\sqrt{15}) \approx 2.4569$,

$$\arccos\tfrac{1}{3}\sqrt{3} \approx 0.9553, \ \arccos(-\tfrac{1}{3}\sqrt{3}) \approx 2.1863$$

36 (a) $3\tan^4\theta - 19\tan^2\theta + 2 = 0 \Rightarrow$

$$\tan^2\theta = \frac{19 \pm \sqrt{361 - 24}}{6} \Rightarrow \theta = \arctan\left(\pm\sqrt{\tfrac{1}{6}(19 \pm \sqrt{337})}\right)$$

(b) $\arctan\left(\pm\sqrt{\tfrac{1}{6}(19 - \sqrt{337})}\right) \approx \pm 0.3162$, $\arctan\left(\pm\sqrt{\tfrac{1}{6}(19 + \sqrt{337})}\right) \approx \pm 1.1896$

37 (a) Let β denote the angle by the sailboat with opposite side d and hypotenuse k.

Now $\sin\beta = \frac{d}{k} \Rightarrow \beta = \sin^{-1}\frac{d}{k}$. Using alternate interior angles,

we see that $\alpha + \beta = \theta$. Thus, $\alpha = \theta - \beta = \theta - \sin^{-1}\frac{d}{k}$.

(b) $\alpha = 53.4° - \sin^{-1}\frac{50}{210} \approx 39.63°$ or $40°$.

38 (a) Draw a line from the art critic's eyes to the painting. This forms two right triangles with opposite sides 8 {upper $\triangle$} and 2 {lower $\triangle$} and adjacent side x. Let α be the angle of elevation to the top of the painting and β be the angle of depression of the bottom of the painting.

$$\text{Since } \tan\alpha = \frac{8}{x} \text{ and } \tan\beta = \frac{2}{x}, \theta = \alpha + \beta = \tan^{-1}\frac{8}{x} + \tan^{-1}\frac{2}{x}.$$

(b) $\tan\theta = \tan(\alpha + \beta) = \dfrac{\tan\alpha + \tan\beta}{1 - \tan\alpha\tan\beta} = \dfrac{8/x + 2/x}{1 - (8/x)(2/x)} \cdot \dfrac{x^2}{x^2} = \dfrac{8x + 2x}{x^2 - 16} =$

$\dfrac{10x}{x^2 - 16} \Rightarrow \theta = \tan^{-1}\left(\dfrac{10x}{x^2 - 16}\right)$. Note that if $0 < x < 4$, $\dfrac{10x}{x^2 - 16} < 0$ and $90° < \theta < 180°$, <u>not</u> $-90° < \theta < 0°$ since $0° < \theta < 180°$ in any triangle.

If $x = 4$, $\dfrac{10x}{x^2 - 16}$ is undefined and $\theta = 90°$.

If $x > 4$, $\dfrac{10x}{x^2 - 16} > 0$ and $0 < \theta < 90°$.

(c) $45° = \tan^{-1}\left(\dfrac{10x}{x^2 - 16}\right) \Rightarrow \tan 45° = \dfrac{10x}{x^2 - 16} \Rightarrow (1)(x^2 - 16) = 10x \Rightarrow$

$x^2 - 10x - 16 = 0 \Rightarrow x = \dfrac{10 \pm \sqrt{164}}{2} = \{x > 0\}\ x = 5 + \sqrt{41} \approx 11.4$ ft.

39 (a) The angle whose sine is x ($\sin^{-1}x$) is the same as the angle whose tangent is

$\dfrac{x}{\sqrt{1-x^2}}\left(\tan^{-1}\dfrac{x}{\sqrt{1-x^2}}\right)$. To help understand this statement, draw a triangle with angle α that has opposite side x and hypotenuse 1 (similar to *Figure 21*). The adjacent side is $\sqrt{1-x^2}$. If $-1 < x < 1$, the range of $\sin^{-1}x$ is $-\frac{\pi}{2} < y < \frac{\pi}{2}$, which is the same as $\tan^{-1}\dfrac{x}{\sqrt{1-x^2}}$.

(b) From *Figure 20*, $\cos^{-1}x = \tan^{-1}\dfrac{\sqrt{1-x^2}}{x}$. If $0 < x < 1$, the ranges of $\cos^{-1}x$ and $\tan^{-1}\dfrac{\sqrt{1-x^2}}{x}$ are both $0 < y < \frac{\pi}{2}$. However, if $-1 < x < 0$, the range of $\cos^{-1}x$ is $\frac{\pi}{2} < y < \pi$, and the range of $\tan^{-1}\dfrac{\sqrt{1-x^2}}{x}$ is $-\frac{\pi}{2} < y < 0$. Therefore, we must add π to the $\tan^{-1}$ value and $\cos^{-1}x = \tan^{-1}\dfrac{\sqrt{1-x^2}}{x} + \pi$ if $-1 < x < 0$.

40 To find $\sin^{-1}(\sin^{-1}x)$, $\sin^{-1}x$ must be in the domain of $\sin^{-1}$, that is, $-1 \le \sin^{-1}x \le 1$. Thus $\sin(-1) \le \sin(\sin^{-1}x) \le \sin(1)$,

or approximately $-0.84147 \le x \le 0.84147$.

Exercises 8.2

1   $f(x) = \sin^{-1}\sqrt{x} \Rightarrow f'(x) = \dfrac{1}{\sqrt{1 - (\sqrt{x})^2}} \cdot D_x(\sqrt{x}) = \dfrac{1}{\sqrt{1-x}} \cdot \dfrac{1}{2\sqrt{x}} = \dfrac{1}{2\sqrt{x}\sqrt{1-x}}$

2   $f(x) = \sin^{-1}\frac{1}{3}x \Rightarrow f'(x) = \dfrac{1}{\sqrt{1 - (\frac{1}{3}x)^2}} \cdot \dfrac{1}{3} = \dfrac{1}{3\sqrt{\dfrac{9-x^2}{9}}} = \dfrac{1}{\sqrt{9-x^2}}$

3   $f(x) = \tan^{-1}(3x - 5) \Rightarrow f'(x) = \dfrac{1}{1 + (3x - 5)^2} \cdot 3 = \dfrac{3}{9x^2 - 30x + 26}$

$\boxed{4}$ $f(x) = \tan^{-1}(x^2) \Rightarrow f'(x) = \dfrac{1}{1 + (x^2)^2} \cdot 2x = \dfrac{2x}{1 + x^4}$

$\boxed{5}$ $f(x) = e^{-x}\operatorname{arcsec} e^{-x} \Rightarrow f'(x) =$

$e^{-x}\left[\dfrac{1}{e^{-x}\sqrt{(e^{-x})^2 - 1}} \cdot (-e^{-x})\right] + (-e^{-x})\operatorname{arcsec} e^{-x} = \dfrac{-e^{-x}}{\sqrt{e^{-2x} - 1}} - e^{-x}\operatorname{arcsec} e^{-x}$

$\boxed{6}$ $f(x) = \sqrt{\operatorname{arcsec} 3x} \Rightarrow$

$$f'(x) = \tfrac{1}{2}(\operatorname{arcsec} 3x)^{-1/2} \dfrac{1}{(3x)\sqrt{(3x)^2 - 1}} \cdot 3 = \dfrac{1}{2x\sqrt{\operatorname{arcsec} 3x}\sqrt{9x^2 - 1}}$$

$\boxed{7}$ $f(x) = x^2 \arctan(x^2) \Rightarrow$

$$f'(x) = x^2\left[\dfrac{1}{1 + (x^2)^2}\right](2x) + (2x)\arctan(x^2) = \dfrac{2x^3}{1 + x^4} + 2x\arctan(x^2)$$

$\boxed{8}$ $f(x) = \tan^{-1}\sin 2x \Rightarrow f'(x) = \dfrac{1}{1 + (\sin 2x)^2} \cdot 2\cos 2x = \dfrac{2\cos 2x}{1 + \sin^2 2x}$

$\boxed{9}$ $f(x) = \sec^{-1}\sqrt{x^2 - 1} \Rightarrow$

$$f'(x) = \dfrac{1}{\sqrt{x^2 - 1}\sqrt{(\sqrt{x^2 - 1})^2 - 1}}\left[\tfrac{1}{2}(x^2 - 1)^{-1/2}(2x)\right] = \dfrac{x}{(x^2 - 1)\sqrt{x^2 - 2}}$$

$\boxed{10}$ $f(x) = x^2\sec^{-1}5x \Rightarrow$

$$f'(x) = x^2\left(\dfrac{1}{(5x)\sqrt{(5x)^2 - 1}} \cdot 5\right) + (2x)\sec^{-1}5x = \dfrac{x}{\sqrt{25x^2 - 1}} + 2x\sec^{-1}5x$$

$\boxed{11}$ $f(x) = \dfrac{1}{\sin^{-1}x} \Rightarrow f'(x) = -\dfrac{1/\sqrt{1 - x^2}}{(\sin^{-1}x)^2} = -\dfrac{1}{\sqrt{1 - x^2}(\sin^{-1}x)^2}$

$\boxed{12}$ $f(x) = \arcsin \ln x \Rightarrow f'(x) = \dfrac{1}{\sqrt{1 - (\ln x)^2}} \cdot \dfrac{1}{x} = \dfrac{1}{x\sqrt{1 - (\ln x)^2}}$

$\boxed{13}$ $f(x) = (1 + \cos^{-1}3x)^3 \Rightarrow$

$$f'(x) = 3(1 + \cos^{-1}3x)^2\left(-\dfrac{1}{\sqrt{1 - (3x)^2}} \cdot 3\right) = -\dfrac{9(1 + \cos^{-1}3x)^2}{\sqrt{1 - 9x^2}}$$

$\boxed{14}$ $f(x) = \cos^{-1}\cos e^x \Rightarrow f'(x) = -\dfrac{1}{\sqrt{1 - (\cos e^x)^2}}(-\sin e^x \cdot e^x) = \dfrac{e^x\sin e^x}{\sqrt{\sin^2 e^x}} =$

$$\dfrac{e^x\sin e^x}{|\sin e^x|} \text{ equals } e^x \text{ if } \sin e^x > 0 \text{ or } -e^x \text{ if } \sin e^x < 0$$

$\boxed{15}$ $f(x) = \ln\arctan(x^2) \Rightarrow f'(x) = \dfrac{1}{\arctan(x^2)}\left(\dfrac{1}{1 + (x^2)^2} \cdot 2x\right) = \dfrac{2x}{(1 + x^4)\arctan(x^2)}$

$\boxed{16}$ $f(x) = \arctan\dfrac{x + 1}{x - 1} \Rightarrow f'(x) = \dfrac{1}{1 + \left(\dfrac{x + 1}{x - 1}\right)^2}\left[\dfrac{(x - 1)(1) - (x + 1)(1)}{(x - 1)^2}\right] =$

$$\dfrac{(x - 1)^2}{(x - 1)^2 + (x + 1)^2} \cdot \dfrac{-2}{(x - 1)^2} = \dfrac{-2}{2x^2 + 2} = -\dfrac{1}{x^2 + 1}$$

$\boxed{17}$ $f(x) = \cos(x^{-1}) + (\cos x)^{-1} + \cos^{-1}x \Rightarrow$

$$f'(x) = -\sin\left(\tfrac{1}{x}\right)\left(-\tfrac{1}{x^2}\right) + \left[-(\cos x)^{-2}(-\sin x)\right] + \left(-\dfrac{1}{\sqrt{1 - x^2}}\right) =$$

$$(1/x^2)\sin(1/x) + \dfrac{\sin x}{\cos x} \cdot \dfrac{1}{\cos x} - \dfrac{1}{\sqrt{1 - x^2}} = (1/x^2)\sin(1/x) + \tan x\sec x - \dfrac{1}{\sqrt{1 - x^2}}$$

$\boxed{18}$ $f(x) = x\arccos\sqrt{4x+1} \Rightarrow$

$$f'(x) = x\left(-\frac{1}{\sqrt{1-(\sqrt{4x+1})^2}}\right)\left[\frac{1}{2}(4x+1)^{-1/2}(4)\right] + (1)\cdot\arccos\sqrt{4x+1}$$

$$= -\frac{2x}{\sqrt{-4x}\sqrt{4x+1}} + \arccos\sqrt{4x+1}$$

$\boxed{19}$ $f(x) = 3^{\arcsin(x^3)} \Rightarrow$

$$f'(x) = (3^{\arcsin(x^3)}\ln 3)\cdot\frac{1}{\sqrt{1-(x^3)^2}}\cdot(3x^2) = 3^{\arcsin(x^3)}\frac{(3\ln 3)\,x^2}{\sqrt{1-x^6}}$$

$\boxed{20}$ $f(x) = \left(\frac{1}{x} - \arcsin\frac{1}{x}\right)^4 \Rightarrow$

$$f'(x) = 4\left(\frac{1}{x} - \arcsin\frac{1}{x}\right)^3\left[-\frac{1}{x^2} - \frac{1}{\sqrt{1-(1/x)^2}}\left(-\frac{1}{x^2}\right)\right] =$$

$$-\frac{4}{x^2}\left(\frac{1}{x} - \arcsin\frac{1}{x}\right)^3\left(1 - \frac{1}{\sqrt{(x^2-1)/x^2}}\right) = \frac{4}{x^2}\left(\frac{1}{x} - \arcsin\frac{1}{x}\right)^3\left(\sqrt{\frac{x^2}{x^2-1}} - 1\right)$$

$\boxed{21}$ $f(x) = \frac{\arctan x}{x^2+1} \Rightarrow f'(x) = \frac{(x^2+1)\left[1/(x^2+1)\right] - (\arctan x)(2x)}{(x^2+1)^2} = \frac{1 - 2x\arctan x}{(x^2+1)^2}$

$\boxed{22}$ $f(x) = \frac{e^{2x}}{\sin^{-1}5x} \Rightarrow$

$$f'(x) = \frac{(\sin^{-1}5x)(2e^{2x}) - (e^{2x})\left[5/\sqrt{1-(5x)^2}\right]}{(\sin^{-1}5x)^2} = (e^{2x})\frac{2\sin^{-1}5x - 5/\sqrt{1-25x^2}}{(\sin^{-1}5x)^2}$$

$\boxed{23}$ $f(x) = \sqrt{x}\sec^{-1}\sqrt{x} \Rightarrow$

$$f'(x) = \sqrt{x}\cdot\frac{1}{\sqrt{x}\sqrt{(\sqrt{x})^2-1}}\left(\frac{1}{2\sqrt{x}}\right) + \frac{1}{2\sqrt{x}}\cdot\sec^{-1}\sqrt{x} = \frac{1}{2\sqrt{x}}\left(\frac{1}{\sqrt{x-1}} + \sec^{-1}\sqrt{x}\right)$$

$\boxed{24}$ $f(x) = (\sin 2x)(\sin^{-1}2x) \Rightarrow$

$$f'(x) = (\sin 2x)\frac{1}{\sqrt{1-(2x)^2}}\cdot 2 + (2\cos 2x)\sin^{-1}2x = \frac{2\sin 2x}{\sqrt{1-4x^2}} + 2\cos 2x\sin^{-1}2x$$

$\boxed{25}$ $f(x) = (\tan x)^{\arctan x} = e^{\arctan x\ln(\tan x)} \Rightarrow$

$$f'(x) = e^{\arctan x\ln(\tan x)}\left(\arctan x\cdot\frac{1}{\tan x}\cdot\sec^2 x + \frac{1}{1+x^2}\cdot\ln\tan x\right)$$

$$= (\tan x)^{\arctan x}\left(\arctan x\cot x\sec^2 x + \frac{\ln\tan x}{1+x^2}\right)$$

$\boxed{26}$ $f(x) = (\tan^{-1}4x)e^{\tan^{-1}4x} \Rightarrow$

$$f'(x) = (\tan^{-1}4x)e^{\tan^{-1}4x}\left[\frac{1}{1+(4x)^2}\cdot 4\right] + \left[\frac{1}{1+(4x)^2}\cdot 4\right]e^{\tan^{-1}4x}$$

$$= \frac{4e^{\tan^{-1}4x}}{1+16x^2}(\tan^{-1}4x+1)$$

$\boxed{27}$ $x^2 + x\sin^{-1}y = ye^x \Rightarrow 2x + x\cdot\frac{1}{\sqrt{1-y^2}}\cdot y' + 1\cdot\sin^{-1}y = ye^x + y'e^x \Rightarrow$

$$y'\left(\frac{x}{\sqrt{1-y^2}} - e^x\right) = ye^x - 2x - \sin^{-1}y \Rightarrow y' = \frac{ye^x - 2x - \sin^{-1}y}{\frac{x}{\sqrt{1-y^2}} - e^x}$$

$\boxed{28}$ $\ln(x+y) = \tan^{-1}xy \Rightarrow \frac{1}{x+y}\cdot(1+y') = \frac{1}{1+(xy)^2}\cdot(xy'+y) \Rightarrow$

$$y'\left(\frac{1}{x+y} - \frac{x}{1+x^2y^2}\right) = \frac{y}{1+x^2y^2} - \frac{1}{x+y} \Rightarrow y' = \frac{y(x+y) - (1+x^2y^2)}{(1+x^2y^2) - x(x+y)}$$

29 (a) Using (8.9)(ii), $\displaystyle\int \frac{1}{x^2+16}\,dx = \int \frac{1}{4^2+x^2}\,dx = \frac{1}{4}\tan^{-1}\frac{x}{4} + C$

(b) $\displaystyle\int_0^4 \frac{1}{x^2+16}\,dx = \left[\frac{1}{4}\tan^{-1}\frac{x}{4}\right]_0^4 = \frac{1}{4}(\tan^{-1}1 - \tan^{-1}0) = \frac{1}{4}\left(\frac{\pi}{4} - 0\right) = \frac{\pi}{16}$

30 (a) $u = e^x,\ du = e^x\,dx \Rightarrow \displaystyle\int \frac{e^x}{1+(e^x)^2}\,dx = \int \frac{1}{1^2+u^2}\,du = \tan^{-1}u + C$

(a) $\displaystyle\int_0^1 \frac{e^x}{1+e^{2x}}\,dx = \left[\tan^{-1}(e^x)\right]_0^1 = \tan^{-1}e - \tan^{-1}1 = \tan^{-1}e - \frac{\pi}{4} \approx 0.43$

31 (a) $u = x^2,\ \frac{1}{2}du = x\,dx \Rightarrow \displaystyle\int \frac{x}{\sqrt{1-(x^2)^2}}\,dx = \frac{1}{2}\int \frac{1}{\sqrt{1-u^2}}\,du = \frac{1}{2}\sin^{-1}u + C$

(b) $\displaystyle\int_0^{\sqrt{2}/2} \frac{x}{\sqrt{1-x^4}}\,dx = \left[\frac{1}{2}\sin^{-1}(x^2)\right]_0^{\sqrt{2}/2} = \frac{1}{2}(\sin^{-1}\frac{1}{2} - \sin^{-1}0) = \frac{1}{2}(\frac{\pi}{6} - 0) = \frac{\pi}{12}$

32 (a) $\displaystyle\int \frac{1}{x\sqrt{x^2-1}}\,dx = \int \frac{1}{x\sqrt{(x)^2-1}}\,dx = \sec^{-1}x + C$

(b) $\displaystyle\int_{2/\sqrt{3}}^2 \frac{1}{x\sqrt{x^2-1}}\,dx = \left[\sec^{-1}x\right]_{2/\sqrt{3}}^2 = \sec^{-1}2 - \sec^{-1}\frac{2}{\sqrt{3}} = \frac{\pi}{3} - \frac{\pi}{6} = \frac{\pi}{6}$

33 $u = \cos x,\ -du = \sin x\,dx \Rightarrow \displaystyle\int \frac{\sin x}{\cos^2 x + 1}\,dx = -\int \frac{1}{u^2+1}\,du = -\tan^{-1}u + C$

34 $u = \sin x,\ du = \cos x\,dx \Rightarrow \displaystyle\int \frac{\cos x}{\sqrt{9-\sin^2 x}}\,dx = \int \frac{1}{\sqrt{3^2-u^2}}\,du = \sin^{-1}\frac{u}{3} + C$

35 $u = \sqrt{x},\ 2\,du = \frac{1}{\sqrt{x}}\,dx \Rightarrow \displaystyle\int \frac{1}{\sqrt{x}(1+x)}\,dx = 2\int \frac{1}{1+u^2}\,du = 2\tan^{-1}u + C$

36 $u = e^{-x},\ -du = e^{-x}\,dx \Rightarrow \displaystyle\int \frac{1}{e^x\sqrt{1-e^{-2x}}}\,dx = -\int \frac{1}{\sqrt{1-u^2}}\,du = -\sin^{-1}u + C$

37 $u = e^x,\ du = e^x\,dx \Rightarrow \displaystyle\int \frac{e^x}{\sqrt{16-e^{2x}}}\,dx = \int \frac{1}{\sqrt{16-u^2}}\,du = \sin^{-1}\frac{u}{4} + C$

38 $u = \sec x,\ du = \sec x \tan x\,dx \Rightarrow \displaystyle\int \frac{\sec x \tan x}{1+\sec^2 x}\,dx = \int \frac{1}{1+u^2}\,du = \tan^{-1}u + C$

39 $u = x^3,\ \frac{1}{3}du = x^2\,dx \Rightarrow \displaystyle\int \frac{1}{x\sqrt{x^6-4}}\,dx = \frac{1}{3}\int \frac{x^2}{x\cdot x^2\sqrt{(x^3)^2-2^2}}\,dx =$

$\quad\quad \frac{1}{3}\displaystyle\int \frac{1}{u\sqrt{u^2-2^2}}\,du = \frac{1}{3}\cdot\frac{1}{2}\sec^{-1}\frac{u}{2} + C = \frac{1}{6}\sec^{-1}(x^3/2) + C$

40 $u = 36 - x^2,\ -\frac{1}{2}du = x\,dx \Rightarrow$

$\quad\quad \displaystyle\int \frac{x}{\sqrt{36-x^2}}\,dx = -\frac{1}{2}\int u^{-1/2}\,du = -\frac{1}{2}(2\sqrt{u}) + C = -\sqrt{u} + C$

41 $u = x^2 + 9,\ \frac{1}{2}du = x\,dx \Rightarrow \displaystyle\int \frac{x}{x^2+9}\,dx = \frac{1}{2}\int \frac{1}{u}\,du = \frac{1}{2}\ln u + C,\ u > 0$

42 $u = \sqrt{x} \Rightarrow u^2 = x$ and $2u\,du = dx.$

$\quad\quad \displaystyle\int \frac{1}{x\sqrt{x-1}}\,dx = \int \frac{2u\,du}{u^2\sqrt{u^2-1}} = 2\int \frac{1}{u\sqrt{u^2-1}}\,du = 2\sec^{-1}u + C$

[43] $u = e^x$, $du = e^x\, dx$ and $dx = \frac{1}{u}\, du$.

$$\int \frac{1}{\sqrt{e^{2x} - 25}}\, dx = \int \frac{1}{u\sqrt{u^2 - 5^2}}\, du = \frac{1}{5}\sec^{-1}\frac{u}{5} + C$$

[44] $u = 4 - e^x$, $-du = e^x\, dx \Rightarrow \int \frac{e^x}{\sqrt{4 - e^x}}\, dx = -\int u^{-1/2}\, du = -2u^{1/2} + C$

[45] Let x denote the length of the side opposite angle θ. $\tan\theta = \frac{x}{7} \Rightarrow \theta = \tan^{-1}\frac{x}{7}$ and

$$d\theta = \left[\frac{1}{1 + (x/7)^2} \cdot \frac{1}{7}\right] dx = \frac{1}{7\left[1 + \left(\frac{10}{7}\right)^2\right]}\left(\pm 0.5 \cdot \frac{1}{12}\right) = \pm\frac{49}{7 \cdot 149 \cdot 24} = \pm\frac{7}{3576}\ \text{rad}.$$

[46] $y = \tan^{-1} x \Rightarrow y' = \frac{1}{1 + x^2}$. Let s be the arc length of the graph.

$$\text{At } x = 0,\ ds = \sqrt{1 + (y')^2}\, dx = \sqrt{1 + (1)^2}\,(0.1) = \sqrt{2}/10 \approx 0.1414.$$

[47] From *Figure 47*, $\tan\theta = \frac{5}{x} \Rightarrow \theta = \tan^{-1}\frac{5}{x}$.

By the chain rule, $\dfrac{d\theta}{dt} = \dfrac{d\theta}{dx} \cdot \dfrac{dx}{dt} = \dfrac{-5/x^2}{1 + (5/x)^2}(500) = \dfrac{-5}{x^2 + 25}(500)$.

At $x = 2$, $\dfrac{d\theta}{dt} = -\dfrac{5}{29}(500)\ \text{rad/hr} = -\dfrac{25}{1044}\ \text{rad/sec}$ (negative since θ is decreasing).

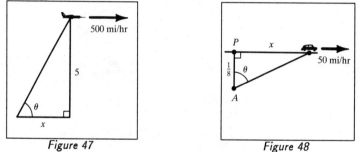

Figure 47   Figure 48

[48] From *Figure 48*, $\tan\theta = \frac{x}{1/8} \Rightarrow \theta = \tan^{-1} 8x$. By the chain rule,

$$\frac{d\theta}{dt} = \frac{d\theta}{dx} \cdot \frac{dx}{dt} = \frac{8}{1 + (8x)^2}(50).\ \text{At } x = \tfrac{1}{4},\ \frac{d\theta}{dt} = 80\ \text{rad/hr} = \frac{1}{45}\ \text{rad/sec}.$$

[49] From *Figure 49*, $\theta = \alpha - \beta = \tan^{-1}(80/x) - \tan^{-1}(60/x)$ is to be maximized.

$$\frac{d\theta}{dx} = \frac{-80/x^2}{1 + (80/x)^2} - \frac{-60/x^2}{1 + (60/x)^2} = \frac{60}{x^2 + 3600} - \frac{80}{x^2 + 6400}.\ \frac{d\theta}{dx} = 0 \Rightarrow$$

$$60(x^2 + 6400) - 80(x^2 + 3600) = 0 \Rightarrow 20x^2 = 96{,}000 \Rightarrow x = \sqrt{4800} \approx 69.3\ \text{ft}.$$

This is a maximum since $\dfrac{d\theta}{dx} > 0$ on $(0, \sqrt{4800})$ and $\dfrac{d\theta}{dx} < 0$ on $(\sqrt{4800}, \infty)$.

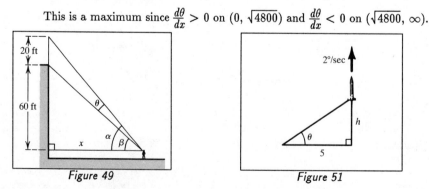

Figure 49   Figure 51

$\boxed{50}$ $v(t) = (1 + t^2)^{-1} \Rightarrow a(t) = v'(t) = \dfrac{-2t}{(1 + t^2)^2}$.

Since $t \geq 0$, $|a(t)| = |v(t)| \Rightarrow \dfrac{2t}{(1 + t^2)^2} = \dfrac{1}{1 + t^2} \Rightarrow 2t = 1 + t^2 \Rightarrow t = 1$.

Also, $v(t) = s'(t) = \dfrac{1}{1 + t^2} \Rightarrow s(t) = \tan^{-1} t + C$. $s(0) = 0 \Rightarrow C = 0$.

Thus, $s(1) = \tan^{-1} 1 = \frac{\pi}{4}$ ft to the right of the origin.

$\boxed{51}$ From *Figure 51*, $\tan\theta = \frac{h}{5}$ and $\theta = \tan^{-1}\frac{h}{5}$. At $\theta = 30°$,

$h = 5\tan\theta = 5 \cdot \dfrac{\sqrt{3}}{3}$ and $\dfrac{d\theta}{dh} = \dfrac{1}{1 + (h/5)^2} \cdot \dfrac{1}{5} = \dfrac{1}{5(1 + \frac{1}{3})} = \dfrac{3}{20}$. By the chain rule,

$$\dfrac{dh}{dt} = \dfrac{dh}{d\theta} \cdot \dfrac{d\theta}{dt} = \dfrac{1}{d\theta/dh} \cdot \dfrac{d\theta}{dt} \{(7.8)\} = \dfrac{20}{3}(2 \cdot \dfrac{\pi}{180}) = \dfrac{2\pi}{27} \approx 0.233 \text{ mi/sec.}$$

$\boxed{52}$ From the figure, $\sin\theta = \dfrac{b}{l_2} \Rightarrow l_2 = b\csc\theta$ and $\cos\theta = \dfrac{a - l_1}{l_2} \Rightarrow l_2 = (a - l_1)\sec\theta$.

Eliminating l_2 yields $b\csc\theta = (a - l_1)\sec\theta \Rightarrow b\cot\theta = a - l_1 \Rightarrow l_1 = a - b\cot\theta$.

$E = k\left(\dfrac{a - b\cot\theta}{r_1^4} + \dfrac{b\csc\theta}{r_2^4}\right) \Rightarrow \dfrac{dE}{d\theta} = k\left(\dfrac{b\csc^2\theta}{r_1^4} - \dfrac{b\csc\theta\cot\theta}{r_2^4}\right)$.

$\dfrac{dE}{d\theta} = 0 \Rightarrow b\csc^2\theta\, r_2^4 = b\csc\theta\cot\theta\, r_1^4 \Rightarrow \dfrac{\cot\theta}{\csc\theta} = \dfrac{r_2^4}{r_1^4} \{\csc\theta \neq 0\} \Rightarrow$

$$\cos\theta = \left(\dfrac{r_2}{r_1}\right)^4 \Rightarrow \theta = \cos^{-1}\left(\dfrac{r_2}{r_1}\right)^4.$$

$\boxed{53}$ $f(x) = \arcsin x \Rightarrow f'(x) = \dfrac{1}{\sqrt{1 - x^2}} \Rightarrow 1 + [f'(x)]^2 = 1 + \dfrac{1}{1 - x^2} = \dfrac{2 - x^2}{1 - x^2}$

Let $F(x) = \sqrt{\dfrac{2 - x^2}{1 - x^2}}$. Then $L = \displaystyle\int_0^{1/2} F(x)\, dx$. $S =$

$\dfrac{0.5 - 0}{3(4)}\left[F(0) + 4F(0.125) + 2F(0.25) + 4F(0.375) + F(0.5)\right] \approx \frac{1}{24}(17.3798) \approx 0.72$.

$\boxed{54}$ $f(x) = 4\arctan(x^2) \Rightarrow f'(x) = \dfrac{4(2x)}{1 + (x^2)^2} \Rightarrow 1 + [f'(x)]^2 = 1 + \dfrac{64x^2}{(1 + x^4)^2}$

Let $F(x) = 4\arctan(x^2)\sqrt{1 + \dfrac{64x^2}{(1 + x^4)^2}}$. Then, by (6.19), $S = 2\pi\displaystyle\int_0^1 F(x)\, dx$.

$T = (2\pi)\dfrac{1 - 0}{2(8)}\{F(0) + 2\left[F(0.125) + F(0.250) + \cdots + F(0.875)\right] + F(1)\} \approx$

$$\frac{\pi}{8}(81.3942) \approx 31.96.$$

Exercises 8.3

$\boxed{1}$ (a) $\sinh 4 = \dfrac{e^4 - e^{-4}}{2} \approx 27.2899$

(b) $\cosh\ln 4 = \dfrac{e^{\ln 4} + e^{-\ln 4}}{2} = \dfrac{4 + (e^{\ln 4})^{-1}}{2} = \dfrac{4 + 4^{-1}}{2} = \dfrac{17}{8} = 2.1250$

Note: Cosh and sech are even functions, whereas sinh, tanh, coth, and csch are odd.

(c) $\tanh(-3) = -\tanh 3 = -\dfrac{e^3 - e^{-3}}{e^3 + e^{-3}} \approx -0.9951$

(d) $\coth 10 = \dfrac{e^{10} + e^{-10}}{e^{10} - e^{-10}} \approx 1.0000$ (e) $\operatorname{sech} 2 = \dfrac{2}{e^2 + e^{-2}} \approx 0.2658$

(f) $\operatorname{csch}(-1) = -\operatorname{csch} 1 = -\dfrac{2}{e^1 - e^{-1}} \approx -0.8509$

$\boxed{2}$ (a) $\sinh \ln 4 = \dfrac{e^{\ln 4} - e^{-\ln 4}}{2} = \dfrac{4 - (e^{\ln 4})^{-1}}{2} = \dfrac{4 - 4^{-1}}{2} = \dfrac{15}{8} = 1.8750$

(b) $\cosh 4 = \dfrac{e^4 + e^{-4}}{2} \approx 27.3082$

(c) Using the result in Exercise 1, $\tanh 3 = -\tanh(-3) \approx -(-0.9951) = 0.9951.$

(d) $\coth(-10) = -\coth 10 \approx -1.0000$ (e) $\operatorname{sech}(-2) = \operatorname{sech} 2 \approx 0.2658$

(f) $\operatorname{csch} 1 = -\operatorname{csch}(-1) \approx -(-0.8509) = 0.8509$

$\boxed{3}$ $f(x) = \sinh 5x \Rightarrow f'(x) = \cosh 5x \cdot 5 = 5 \cosh 5x$

$\boxed{4}$ $f(x) = \sinh(x^2 + 1) \Rightarrow f'(x) = \left[\cosh(x^2 + 1)\right] \cdot 2x = 2x \cosh(x^2 + 1)$

$\boxed{5}$ $f(x) = \cosh(x^3) \Rightarrow f'(x) = \left[\sinh(x^3)\right] \cdot 3x^2 = 3x^2 \sinh(x^3)$

$\boxed{6}$ $f(x) = \cosh^3 x = (\cosh x)^3 \Rightarrow f'(x) = 3(\cosh x)^2 \cdot \sinh x = 3 \cosh^2 x \sinh x$

$\boxed{7}$ $f(x) = \sqrt{x} \tanh \sqrt{x} \Rightarrow$

$$f'(x) = \sqrt{x} \operatorname{sech}^2 \sqrt{x} \left(\dfrac{1}{2\sqrt{x}}\right) + \left(\dfrac{1}{2\sqrt{x}}\right) \tanh \sqrt{x} = \dfrac{1}{2\sqrt{x}}\left(\sqrt{x} \operatorname{sech}^2 \sqrt{x} + \tanh \sqrt{x}\right)$$

$\boxed{8}$ $f(x) = \arctan \tanh x \Rightarrow f'(x) = \dfrac{1}{1 + (\tanh x)^2} \cdot \operatorname{sech}^2 x = \dfrac{\operatorname{sech}^2 x}{1 + \tanh^2 x}$

$\boxed{9}$ $f(x) = \coth(1/x) \Rightarrow f'(x) = -\operatorname{csch}^2(1/x) \cdot (-1/x^2) = (1/x^2) \operatorname{csch}^2(1/x)$

$\boxed{10}$ $f(x) = \dfrac{\coth x}{\cot x} \Rightarrow$

$$f'(x) = \dfrac{(\cot x)(-\operatorname{csch}^2 x) - (\coth x)(-\csc^2 x)}{(\cot x)^2} = \dfrac{-\cot x \operatorname{csch}^2 x + \csc^2 x \coth x}{\cot^2 x}$$

$\boxed{11}$ $f(x) = \dfrac{\operatorname{sech}(x^2)}{x^2 + 1} \Rightarrow f'(x) = \dfrac{(x^2 + 1)\left[-\operatorname{sech}(x^2) \tanh(x^2) \cdot 2x\right] - \operatorname{sech}(x^2) \cdot 2x}{(x^2 + 1)^2}$

$$= \dfrac{-2x \operatorname{sech}(x^2)\left[(x^2 + 1) \tanh(x^2) + 1\right]}{(x^2 + 1)^2}$$

$\boxed{12}$ $f(x) = \sqrt{\operatorname{sech} 5x} \Rightarrow$

$$f'(x) = \tfrac{1}{2}(\operatorname{sech} 5x)^{-1/2}(-\operatorname{sech} 5x \tanh 5x) \cdot 5 = -\tfrac{5}{2}\sqrt{\operatorname{sech} 5x} \tanh 5x$$

$\boxed{13}$ $f(x) = \operatorname{csch}^2 6x \Rightarrow f'(x) = 2\operatorname{csch} 6x \cdot (-\operatorname{csch} 6x \coth 6x) \cdot 6 = -12 \operatorname{csch}^2 6x \coth 6x$

$\boxed{14}$ $f(x) = x \operatorname{csch} e^{4x} \Rightarrow$

$$f'(x) = x(-\operatorname{csch} e^{4x} \coth e^{4x} \cdot 4e^{4x}) + 1 \cdot \operatorname{csch} e^{4x} = \operatorname{csch} e^{4x}(1 - 4x\, e^{4x} \coth e^{4x})$$

$\boxed{15}$ $f(x) = \ln \sinh 2x \Rightarrow f'(x) = \dfrac{1}{\sinh 2x} \cdot 2\cosh 2x = 2 \cdot \dfrac{\cosh x}{\sinh x} = 2\coth 2x$

$\boxed{16}$ $f(x) = \sinh^2 3x \Rightarrow f'(x) = 2\sinh 3x \cdot \cosh 3x \cdot 3 = 6\sinh 3x \cosh 3x$

$\boxed{17}$ $f(x) = \cosh\sqrt{4x^2 + 3} \Rightarrow$

$$f'(x) = \sinh\sqrt{4x^2 + 3} \cdot \tfrac{1}{2}(4x^2 + 3)^{-1/2}(8x) = \dfrac{4x \sinh\sqrt{4x^2 + 3}}{\sqrt{4x^2 + 3}}$$

$\boxed{18}$ $f(x) = \dfrac{1 + \cosh x}{1 - \cosh x} \Rightarrow$

$$f'(x) = \dfrac{(1 - \cosh x)(\sinh x) - (1 + \cosh x)(-\sinh x)}{(1 - \cosh x)^2} = \dfrac{2\sinh x}{(1 - \cosh x)^2}$$

$\boxed{19}$ $f(x) = \dfrac{1}{\tanh x + 1} \Rightarrow f'(x) = -\dfrac{\operatorname{sech}^2 x}{(\tanh x + 1)^2}$ { reciprocal rule }

20 $f(x) = \ln|\tanh x| \Rightarrow$

$$f'(x) = \frac{1}{\tanh x} \cdot \operatorname{sech}^2 x = \frac{\cosh x}{\sinh x} \cdot \frac{1}{\cosh^2 x} = \frac{1}{\sinh x} \cdot \frac{1}{\cosh x} = \operatorname{csch} x \operatorname{sech} x$$

21 $f(x) = \coth \ln x \Rightarrow f'(x) = -\operatorname{csch}^2 \ln x \cdot \frac{1}{x} =$

$$-\frac{1}{x}\left(\frac{2}{e^{\ln x} - e^{-\ln x}}\right)^2 = -\frac{1}{x}\left[\frac{2}{x - (1/x)}\right]^2 = -\frac{1}{x} \cdot \frac{4x^2}{(x^2 - 1)^2} = -\frac{4x}{(x^2 - 1)^2}$$

Note: $f(x)$ could be written as $\dfrac{x^2 + 1}{x^2 - 1}$, and then differentiated.

22 $f(x) = \coth^3 2x \Rightarrow f'(x) = 3\coth^2 2x \cdot (-\operatorname{csch}^2 2x) \cdot 2 = -6\coth^2 2x \operatorname{csch}^2 2x$

23 $f(x) = e^{3x} \operatorname{sech} x \Rightarrow$

$$f'(x) = e^{3x}(-\operatorname{sech} x \tanh x) + 3e^{3x} \operatorname{sech} x = e^{3x} \operatorname{sech} x(3 - \tanh x)$$

24 $f(x) = \frac{1}{2}\operatorname{sech}(x^2 + 1) \Rightarrow$

$$f'(x) = \frac{1}{2}\left[-\operatorname{sech}(x^2 + 1)\tanh(x^2 + 1) \cdot 2x\right] = -x\operatorname{sech}(x^2 + 1)\tanh(x^2 + 1)$$

25 $f(x) = \tan^{-1}(\operatorname{csch} x) \Rightarrow f'(x) = \dfrac{1}{1 + (\operatorname{csch} x)^2}(-\operatorname{csch} x \coth x) = -\dfrac{\operatorname{csch} x \coth x}{1 + (\coth^2 x - 1)}$

$$= \frac{-\operatorname{csch} x}{\coth x} = -\frac{1}{\sinh x} \cdot \frac{\sinh x}{\cosh x} = -\operatorname{sech} x$$

26 $f(x) = \operatorname{csch} \ln x \Rightarrow f'(x) = -\operatorname{csch} \ln x \coth \ln x \cdot \frac{1}{x}$

$$= -\frac{1}{x}\left(\frac{2}{e^{\ln x} - e^{-\ln x}}\right)\left(\frac{e^{\ln x} + e^{-\ln x}}{e^{\ln x} - e^{-\ln x}}\right) = -\frac{1}{x}\left[\frac{2}{x - (1/x)}\right]\left[\frac{x + (1/x)}{x - (1/x)}\right]$$

$$= -\frac{1}{x}\left(\frac{2x}{x^2 - 1}\right)\left(\frac{x^2 + 1}{x^2 - 1}\right) = -\frac{2(x^2 + 1)}{(x^2 - 1)^2}$$

Note: $f(x)$ could be written as $\dfrac{2x}{x^2 - 1}$, and then differentiated.

27 $u = x^3$, $\frac{1}{3} du = x^2 dx \Rightarrow \int x^2 \cosh(x^3)\, dx = \frac{1}{3}\int \cosh u\, du = \frac{1}{3}\sinh u + C$

28 $\displaystyle\int \frac{1}{\operatorname{sech} 7x}\, dx = \int \cosh 7x\, dx.\;\; u = 7x,\; \frac{1}{7} du = dx \Rightarrow I = \frac{1}{7}\int \cosh u\, du = \frac{1}{7}\sinh u + C$

29 $u = \sqrt{x},\; 2\, du = \dfrac{dx}{\sqrt{x}} \Rightarrow \displaystyle\int \frac{\sinh \sqrt{x}}{\sqrt{x}}\, dx = 2\int \sinh u\, du = 2\cosh u + C$

30 $u = 2x^2,\; \frac{1}{4} du = x\, dx \Rightarrow \int x\sinh(2x^2)\, dx = \frac{1}{4}\int \sinh u\, du = \frac{1}{4}\cosh u + C$

31 $\displaystyle\int \frac{1}{\cosh^2 3x}\, dx = \int \operatorname{sech}^2 3x\, dx.\;\; u = 3x,\; \frac{1}{3} du = dx \Rightarrow I = \frac{1}{3}\int \operatorname{sech}^2 u\, du = \frac{1}{3}\tanh u + C$

32 $u = 5x,\; \frac{1}{5} du = dx \Rightarrow \int \operatorname{sech}^2 5x\, dx = \frac{1}{5}\int \operatorname{sech}^2 u\, du = \frac{1}{5}\tanh u + C$

33 $u = \frac{1}{2}x,\; 2\, du = dx \Rightarrow$

$$\int \operatorname{csch}^2\left(\tfrac{1}{2}x\right) dx = 2\int \operatorname{csch}^2 u\, du = -2\int -\operatorname{csch}^2 u\, du = -2\coth u + C$$

34 $\displaystyle\int (\sinh 4x)^{-2}\, dx = \int \frac{1}{(\sinh 4x)^2}\, dx = \int \operatorname{csch}^2 4x\, dx.$

$$u = 4x,\; \tfrac{1}{4} du = dx \Rightarrow I = -\tfrac{1}{4}\int -\operatorname{csch}^2 u\, du = -\tfrac{1}{4}\coth u + C$$

35 $u = 3x,\; \frac{1}{3} du = dx \Rightarrow \int \tanh 3x \operatorname{sech} 3x\, dx = -\frac{1}{3}\int -\operatorname{sech} u \tanh u\, du = -\frac{1}{3}\operatorname{sech} u + C$

36 $\displaystyle\int \sinh x \operatorname{sech}^2 x\, dx = \int \sinh x \cdot \frac{1}{\cosh^2 x}\, dx = \int \frac{\sinh x}{\cosh x} \cdot \frac{1}{\cosh x}\, dx =$

$$-\int -\tanh x \operatorname{sech} x\, dx = -\operatorname{sech} x + C$$

$\boxed{37}$ $\displaystyle \int \cosh x \operatorname{csch}^2 x \, dx = \int \cosh x \cdot \frac{1}{\sinh^2 x} \, dx = \int \frac{\cosh x}{\sinh x} \cdot \frac{1}{\sinh x} \, dx =$

$$-\int -\coth x \operatorname{csch} x \, dx = -\operatorname{csch} x + C$$

$\boxed{38}$ $u = 6x, \; \frac{1}{6} \, du = dx \Rightarrow \int \coth 6x \operatorname{csch} 6x \, dx = -\frac{1}{6} \int -\coth u \operatorname{csch} u \, du = -\frac{1}{6} \operatorname{csch} u + C$

$\boxed{39}$ $\displaystyle \int \coth x \, dx = \int \frac{\cosh x}{\sinh x} \, dx. \quad u = \sinh x, \; du = \cosh x \, dx \Rightarrow I = \int \frac{1}{u} \, du = \ln|u| + C$

$\boxed{40}$ $\displaystyle \int \tanh x \, dx = \int \frac{\sinh x}{\cosh x} \, dx. \quad u = \cosh x, \; du = \sinh x \, dx \Rightarrow I = \int \frac{1}{u} \, du =$

$$\ln u + C, \; u > 0$$

$\boxed{41}$ $u = \sinh x, \; du = \cosh x \, dx \Rightarrow \int \sinh x \cosh x \, dx = \int u \, du = \frac{1}{2} u^2 + C$

$\boxed{42}$ $\displaystyle \int \operatorname{sech} x \, dx = \int \frac{1}{\cosh x} \, dx = \int \frac{\cosh x}{\cosh^2 x} \, dx = \int \frac{\cosh x}{1 + \sinh^2 x} \, dx = \int \frac{1}{1 + u^2} \, du$

$$\{ u = \sinh x \} = \tan^{-1} u + C$$

$\boxed{43}$ $A = \displaystyle \int_0^1 \sinh 3x \, dx = \left[\frac{1}{3} \cosh 3x \right]_0^1 = \frac{1}{3} (\cosh 3 - 1) \approx 3.023$

$\boxed{44}$ $L = \displaystyle \int_0^1 \sqrt{1 + \sinh^2 x} \, dx = \int_0^1 \cosh x \, dx = \Big[\sinh x \Big]_0^1 = \sinh 1 \approx 1.175$

$\boxed{45}$ $y' = \cosh x = 2 \Rightarrow e^x + e^{-x} = 4 \Rightarrow e^{2x} + 1 = 4e^x \Rightarrow (e^x)^2 - 4e^x + 1 = 0 \Rightarrow$

$e^x = 2 \pm \sqrt{3} \; \{ \text{quadratic in } e^x \} \Rightarrow x = \ln(2 \pm \sqrt{3})$. At $x = \ln(2 + \sqrt{3}), \; y = \sqrt{3}$.

Similarly, at $x = \ln(2 - \sqrt{3}), \; y = -\sqrt{3}$. Thus, the points are $(\ln(2 \pm \sqrt{3}), \pm \sqrt{3})$.

$\boxed{46}$ Using disks, $V = \pi \displaystyle \int_{-1}^1 (\cosh x)^2 \, dx = 2\pi \int_0^1 \left[\frac{1}{2} (\cosh 2x + 1) \right] dx \; \{ \text{see Exercise 68} \} =$

$$\pi \int_0^1 (\cosh 2x + 1) \, dx = \pi \left[\frac{1}{2} \sinh 2x + x \right]_0^1 = \pi \left(\frac{1}{2} \sinh 2 + 1 \right) \approx 8.839.$$

$\boxed{47}$ From *Figure 47*, $\triangle ODQ$ is a right triangle with base

cosh t and height sinh t. Its area is

$A_1 = \frac{1}{2}(\cosh t)(\sinh t)$. The area of the nonshaded part

of the triangle is the area bounded by the curve

$y = \sqrt{x^2 - 1}$, the x-axis, and the vertical line $x = \cosh t$.

This area is $A_2 = \displaystyle \int_1^{\cosh t} \sqrt{x^2 - 1} \, dx$. The area of the

shaded region is $A = A_1 - A_2$. It follows that

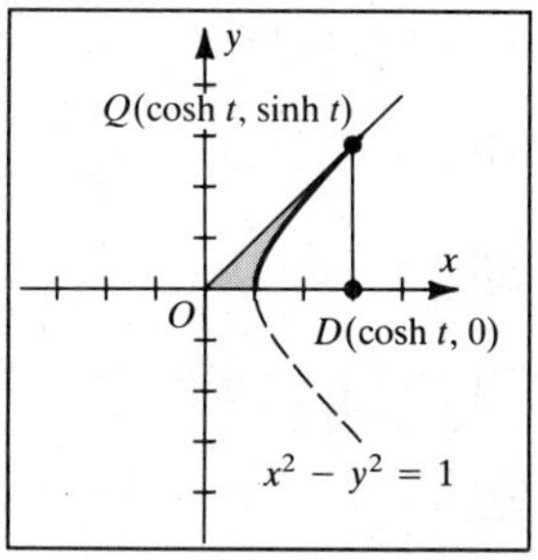

Figure 47

$\frac{dA}{dt} = \frac{1}{2}(\cosh^2 t + \sinh^2 t) - \sqrt{\cosh^2 t - 1} (\sinh t) \; \{ \text{Exercise 51, §5.6} \}$

$\quad = \frac{1}{2}(\cosh^2 t + \sinh^2 t) - \sinh^2 t = \frac{1}{2}(\cosh^2 t - \sinh^2 t) = \frac{1}{2}(1) = \frac{1}{2}$.

Therefore, $A = \frac{1}{2} t + C$ and $C = 0$ since $A = 0$ if $t = 0$. Thus, $t = 2A$.

$\boxed{48}$ Since $\cosh^2 t - \sinh^2 t = 1$, the point $P(\cosh t, \sinh t)$ lies on the hyperbola

$x^2 - y^2 = 1$. In quadrants I and IV, $x \geq 1$. Since the range of $\cosh t$ is $[1, \infty)$,

there exists a t such that $x = \cosh t$. $x^2 - y^2 = 1 \Rightarrow y = \pm \sqrt{x^2 - 1} =$

$\pm \sqrt{\cosh^2 t - 1} = \pm \sqrt{\sinh^2 t} = \pm \sinh t$ for all t. If t is positive, both $\cosh t$ and

$\sinh t$ are positive, and P is in the first quadrant. If t is negative, $\cosh t$ is positive

and $\sinh t$ is negative, and P is in the fourth quadrant.

Thus, each (x, y) on the graph can be expressed as $(\cosh t, \sinh t)$. See Figure 8.17.

49 (a) By symmetry, $A = 2 \displaystyle\int_0^{315} \left(-127.7 \cosh \frac{x}{127.7} + 757.7\right) dx =$

$$2 \left[-(127.7)^2 \sinh \frac{x}{127.7} + (757.7)x \right]_0^{315} \approx 286{,}574 \text{ ft}^2.$$

(b) $y' = -\sinh \frac{x}{127.7} \Rightarrow 1 + (y')^2 = 1 + \sinh^2 \frac{x}{127.7} = \cosh^2 \frac{x}{127.7} \Rightarrow L =$

$$2 \int_0^{315} \sqrt{\cosh^2 \frac{x}{127.7}}\, dx = 2 \int_0^{315} \cosh \frac{x}{127.7}\, dx = 2 \left[127.7 \sinh \frac{x}{127.7}\right]_0^{315} \approx 1494 \text{ ft}.$$

50 Let $c = \sqrt{\frac{g}{km}}$. $y = km \ln \cosh ct \Rightarrow y' = km \cdot \frac{1}{\cosh ct} \cdot \sinh ct \cdot c = ckm \tanh ct$.

$y'' = ckm \operatorname{sech}^2 ct \cdot c = c^2 km \operatorname{sech}^2 ct$. Thus, $m \dfrac{d^2 y}{dt^2} + \dfrac{1}{k}\left(\dfrac{dy}{dt}\right)^2$

$= m(c^2 km \operatorname{sech}^2 ct) + \frac{1}{k}(ckm \tanh ct)^2 = c^2 km^2 \operatorname{sech}^2 ct + c^2 km^2 \tanh^2 ct$

$= c^2 km^2 (\operatorname{sech}^2 ct + \tanh^2 ct) = c^2 km^2 (1) = c^2 km^2 = \frac{g}{km} \cdot km^2 = mg$.

51 (a) $\displaystyle\lim_{h \to \infty} v^2 = \lim_{h \to \infty} \frac{gL}{2\pi} \tanh \frac{2\pi h}{L} = \frac{gL}{2\pi} \lim_{h \to \infty} \tanh \frac{2\pi h}{L} = \frac{gL}{2\pi}(1) = \frac{gL}{2\pi}$

Note: $\displaystyle\lim_{x \to \infty} \tanh x = \lim_{x \to \infty} \frac{e^x - e^{-x}}{e^x + e^{-x}} = \lim_{x \to \infty} \frac{1 - e^{-2x}}{1 + e^{-2x}} = 1$. See Figure 8.18.

(b) Let L be arbitrary and define $f(h) = [v(h)]^2$.

Then, $f(0) = 0$, $f'(h) = \frac{gL}{2\pi} \operatorname{sech}^2 \frac{2\pi h}{L} \cdot \frac{2\pi}{L} = g \operatorname{sech}^2 \frac{2\pi h}{L}$ and $f'(0) = g$.

Now for small enough h, and hence, small $\frac{h}{L}$ we have, $f(h) - f(0) \approx f'(0)(h) \Rightarrow$

$v^2 - 0 \approx (g)(h) \Rightarrow v \approx \sqrt{gh}$. Thus, the rate of change in the position of the

wave with respect to the depth is independent of its length.

Alternate solution: Let $f(x) = \tanh x$. Then $f(x) - f(0) \approx f'(0)x \Rightarrow$

$\tanh x - 0 \approx \operatorname{sech}^2(0)x \Rightarrow \tanh x \approx x$ when $x \approx 0$. Let $x = \frac{2\pi h}{L}$.

Then, if $x \approx 0$ and hence $\frac{h}{L} \approx 0$, $v^2 = \frac{gL}{2\pi} \tanh\left(\frac{2\pi h}{L}\right) \approx \left(\frac{gL}{2\pi}\right)\left(\frac{2\pi h}{L}\right) = gh \Rightarrow$

$$v \approx \sqrt{gh} \text{ for } x \approx 0.$$

52 If $y = A \cosh Bx$, then $y' = AB \sinh Bx$ and $y'' = AB^2 \cosh Bx$. Thus,

$y y'' = A^2 B^2 \cosh^2 Bx = A^2 B^2 (1 + \sinh^2 Bx) = A^2 B^2 + A^2 B^2 \sinh^2 Bx =$

$A^2 B^2 + (y')^2$. Now $A^2 B^2 + (y')^2 = 1 + (y')^2$ if and only if $A^2 B^2 = 1$, or,

equivalently, $AB = 1$, since $A, B > 0$.

53 (a) From *Figure 53*, $a \approx 0.7$.

(b) Let $f(x) = \text{sech}^2 x - \tanh x$. Thus $f'(x) = -2\,\text{sech}^2 x \tanh x - \text{sech}^2 x$.

$$x_{n+1} = x_n - \frac{\text{sech}^2 x_n - \tanh x_n}{-2\,\text{sech}^2 x_n \tanh x_n - \text{sech}^2 x_n} \text{ and } x_1 = 0.7 \text{ yield:}$$

$x_2 = 0.721664$, $x_3 = 0.721818$. Hence, $x \approx 0.722$.

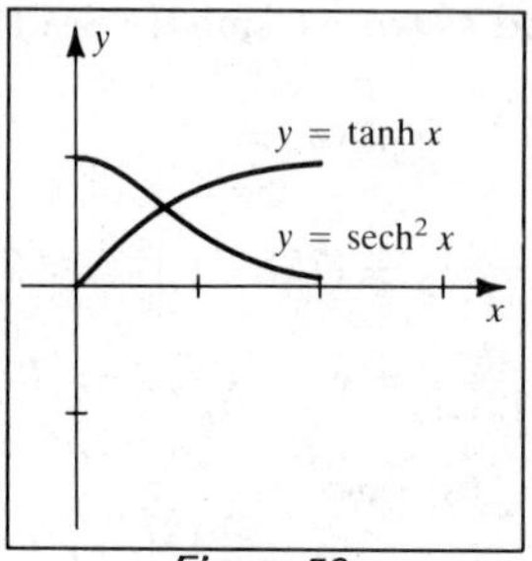

Figure 53

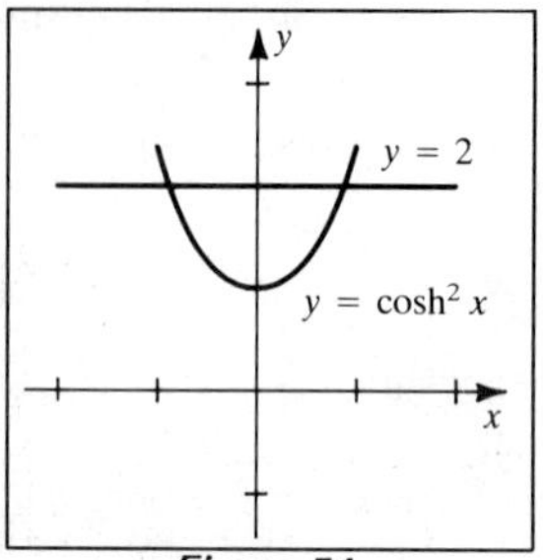

Figure 54

[54] (a) $m = \displaystyle\int_{-0.88}^{0.88} (2 - \cosh^2 x)\,dx$; $M_x = \dfrac{1}{2}\displaystyle\int_{-0.88}^{0.88} \left[2^2 - (\cosh^2 x)^2 \right] dx$;

$M_y = 0$ by symmetry

(b) Let $F(x) = 2 - \cosh^2 x$. $m \approx$

$$S = \frac{0.88 - (-0.88)}{3(4)}\left[F(-0.88) + 4F(-0.44) + 2F(0) + 4F(0.44) + F(0.88) \right]$$

$\approx \frac{1.76}{12}(8.3564) \approx 1.2256$. Similarly, $M_x \approx \frac{1.76}{12}(13.1937) \approx 1.9351$.

Thus, $\bar{x} = \dfrac{M_y}{m} = 0$ and $\bar{y} = \dfrac{M_x}{m} \approx 1.58$.

[55] $\cosh x + \sinh x = \dfrac{e^x + e^{-x}}{2} + \dfrac{e^x - e^{-x}}{2} = \dfrac{2e^x}{2} = e^x$

[56] $\cosh x - \sinh x = \dfrac{e^x + e^{-x}}{2} - \dfrac{e^x - e^{-x}}{2} = \dfrac{2e^{-x}}{2} = e^{-x}$

[57] $\sinh(-x) = \dfrac{e^{-x} - e^{-(-x)}}{2} = \dfrac{e^{-x} - e^x}{2} = \dfrac{-(e^x - e^{-x})}{2} = -\sinh x$

[58] $\cosh(-x) = \dfrac{e^{-x} + e^{-(-x)}}{2} = \dfrac{e^{-x} + e^x}{2} = \cosh x$

[59] $\sinh x \cosh y + \cosh x \sinh y = \dfrac{(e^x - e^{-x})(e^y + e^{-y})}{4} + \dfrac{(e^x + e^{-x})(e^y - e^{-y})}{4} =$

$\dfrac{(e^{x+y} + e^{x-y} - e^{-x+y} - e^{-x-y}) + (e^{x+y} - e^{x-y} + e^{-x+y} - e^{-x-y})}{4} =$

$\dfrac{2e^{x+y} - 2e^{-x-y}}{4} = \dfrac{e^{x+y} - e^{-(x+y)}}{2} = \sinh(x + y)$

[60] $\cosh x \cosh y + \sinh x \sinh y = \dfrac{(e^x + e^{-x})(e^y + e^{-y})}{4} + \dfrac{(e^x - e^{-x})(e^y - e^{-y})}{4} =$

$\dfrac{(e^{x+y} + e^{x-y} + e^{-x+y} + e^{-x-y}) + (e^{x+y} - e^{x-y} - e^{-x+y} + e^{-x-y})}{4} =$

$\dfrac{2e^{x+y} + 2e^{-x-y}}{4} = \dfrac{e^{x+y} + e^{-(x+y)}}{2} = \cosh(x + y)$

$\boxed{61}$ $\sinh(x - y) = \sinh(x + (-y))$

$$= \sinh x \cosh(-y) + \cosh x \sinh(-y) \text{ (Exercise 59)}$$

$$= \sinh x \cosh y - \cosh x \sinh y \text{ (Exercises 57 and 58)}$$

$\boxed{62}$ $\cosh(x - y) = \cosh(x + (-y))$

$$= \cosh x \cosh(-y) + \sinh x \sinh(-y) \text{ (Exercise 60)}$$

$$= \cosh x \cosh y - \sinh x \sinh y \text{ (Exercises 57 and 58)}$$

$\boxed{63}$ $\tanh(x + y) = \dfrac{\sinh(x + y)}{\cosh(x + y)} = \dfrac{\sinh x \cosh y + \cosh x \sinh y}{\cosh x \cosh y + \sinh x \sinh y}$ (Exercises 59 and 60).

Divide the numerator and denominator by the product $\cosh x \cosh y$ to obtain

$$\frac{\tanh x + \tanh y}{1 + \tanh x \tanh y}.$$

$\boxed{64}$ Verify in a manner similar to that used in Exercise 63 or

establish the fact that $\tanh(-x) = -\tanh x$ and verify as in Exercises 61 and 62.

$\boxed{65}$ Let $y = x$ in Exercise 59. $\boxed{66}$ Let $y = x$ in Exercise 60.

$\boxed{67}$ From Exercise 66, $\cosh 2y = \cosh^2 y + \sinh^2 y = (1 + \sinh^2 y) + \sinh^2 y =$

$1 + 2\sinh^2 y$, and hence $\sinh^2 y = \dfrac{\cosh 2y - 1}{2}$. Let $y = \frac{x}{2}$ to obtain the identity.

$\boxed{68}$ From Exercise 66, $\cosh 2y = \cosh^2 y + \sinh^2 y = \cosh^2 y + (\cosh^2 y - 1) =$

$2\cosh^2 y - 1$, and hence $\cosh^2 y = \dfrac{\cosh 2y + 1}{2}$. Let $y = \frac{x}{2}$ to obtain the identity.

$\boxed{69}$ Let $y = x$ in Exercise 63.

$\boxed{70}$ $\dfrac{\sinh x}{1 + \cosh x} = \dfrac{2\sinh \frac{x}{2} \cosh \frac{x}{2}}{1 + \left(\cosh^2 \frac{x}{2} + \sinh^2 \frac{x}{2}\right)}$ (Exercises 65 and 66)

$$= \frac{2\sinh \frac{x}{2} \cosh \frac{x}{2}}{2\cosh^2 \frac{x}{2}} = \frac{\sinh \frac{x}{2}}{\cosh \frac{x}{2}} = \tanh \frac{x}{2}$$

$\boxed{71}$ $\cosh nx + \sinh nx = \dfrac{e^{nx} + e^{-nx}}{2} + \dfrac{e^{nx} - e^{-nx}}{2} = e^{nx} = (e^x)^n = (\cosh x + \sinh x)^n$

$\boxed{72}$ $\cosh nx - \sinh nx = \dfrac{e^{nx} + e^{-nx}}{2} - \dfrac{e^{nx} - e^{-nx}}{2} = e^{-nx} = (e^{-x})^n =$

$$(\cosh x - \sinh x)^n \text{ (Exercise 56)}$$

Exercises 8.4

$\boxed{1}$ (a) Using (8.16), $\sinh^{-1} 1 = \ln\left[(1) + \sqrt{(1)^2 + 1}\right] = \ln(1 + \sqrt{2}) \approx 0.8814.$

(b) $\cosh^{-1} 2 = \ln\left[(2) + \sqrt{(2)^2 - 1}\right] = \ln(2 + \sqrt{3}) \approx 1.3170$

(c) $\tanh^{-1}\left(-\frac{1}{2}\right) = \frac{1}{2}\ln\left[\dfrac{1 + (-1/2)}{1 - (-1/2)}\right] = \frac{1}{2}\ln\dfrac{1/2}{3/2} = \frac{1}{2}\ln\frac{1}{3} \approx -0.5493$

(d) $\text{sech}^{-1}\frac{1}{2} = \ln\dfrac{1 + \sqrt{1 - (1/2)^2}}{1/2} = \ln\dfrac{1 + (\sqrt{3}/2)}{1/2} = \ln(2 + \sqrt{3}) \approx 1.3170.$

Some calculators have a $\cosh^{-1}$ function, but not a sech^{-1} function.

Use the relationship $\text{sech}^{-1}(x) = \cosh^{-1}(1/x)$ to compute values of sech^{-1}.

Note that parts (b) and (d) are equal.

2 (a) $\sinh^{-1}(-2) = \ln\left[(-2) + \sqrt{(-2)^2 + 1}\right] = \ln(-2 + \sqrt{5}) \approx -1.4436$

   (b) $\cosh^{-1} 5 = \ln\left[(5) + \sqrt{(5)^2 - 1}\right] = \ln(5 + \sqrt{24}) \approx 2.2924$

   (c) $\tanh^{-1}\frac{1}{3} = \frac{1}{2}\ln\left[\dfrac{1 + (1/3)}{1 - (1/3)}\right] = \frac{1}{2}\ln\dfrac{4/3}{2/3} = \frac{1}{2}\ln 2 \approx 0.3466$

   (d) $\operatorname{sech}^{-1}\frac{3}{5} = \ln\dfrac{1 + \sqrt{1 - (3/5)^2}}{3/5} = \ln\dfrac{1 + (4/5)}{3/5} = \ln 3 \approx 1.0986$

3 $f(x) = \sinh^{-1} 5x \Rightarrow f'(x) = \dfrac{1}{\sqrt{(5x)^2 + 1}} \cdot 5 = \dfrac{5}{\sqrt{25x^2 + 1}}$

4 $f(x) = \sinh^{-1} e^x \Rightarrow f'(x) = \dfrac{1}{\sqrt{(e^x)^2 + 1}} \cdot e^x = \dfrac{e^x}{\sqrt{e^{2x} + 1}}$

5 $f(x) = \cosh^{-1}\sqrt{x} \Rightarrow f'(x) = \dfrac{1}{\sqrt{(\sqrt{x})^2 - 1}} \cdot \frac{1}{2}x^{-1/2} = \dfrac{1}{2\sqrt{x}\sqrt{x - 1}}$

6 $f(x) = \sqrt{\cosh^{-1} x} \Rightarrow f'(x) = \frac{1}{2}(\cosh^{-1} x)^{-1/2} \cdot \dfrac{1}{\sqrt{(x)^2 - 1}} \cdot 1 = \dfrac{1}{2\sqrt{\cosh^{-1} x}\sqrt{x^2 - 1}}$

7 $f(x) = \tanh^{-1}(-4x) \Rightarrow f'(x) = \dfrac{1}{1 - (-4x)^2} \cdot (-4) = -\dfrac{4}{1 - 16x^2} = \dfrac{4}{16x^2 - 1}$

8 $f(x) = \tanh^{-1}\sin 3x \Rightarrow f'(x) = \dfrac{1}{1 - (\sin 3x)^2} \cdot 3\cos 3x = \dfrac{3\cos 3x}{\cos^2 3x} = 3\sec 3x$

9 $f(x) = \operatorname{sech}^{-1} x^2 \Rightarrow f'(x) = \dfrac{-1}{x^2\sqrt{1 - (x^2)^2}} \cdot 2x = -\dfrac{2}{x\sqrt{1 - x^4}}$

10 $f(x) = \operatorname{sech}^{-1}\sqrt{1 - x} \Rightarrow$

$$f'(x) = \dfrac{-1}{\sqrt{1 - x}\sqrt{1 - (\sqrt{1 - x})^2}} \cdot \frac{1}{2}(1 - x)^{-1/2} \cdot (-1) = \dfrac{1}{2(1 - x)\sqrt{x}}$$

11 $f(x) = x\sinh^{-1}(1/x) \Rightarrow f'(x) = x \cdot \dfrac{1}{\sqrt{(1/x)^2 + 1}} \cdot \left(-\dfrac{1}{x^2}\right) + 1 \cdot \sinh^{-1}(1/x) =$

$$-\dfrac{\sqrt{x^2}}{x\sqrt{1 + x^2}} + \sinh^{-1}(1/x) = -\dfrac{|x|}{x\sqrt{1 + x^2}} + \sinh^{-1}(1/x)$$

12 $f(x) = \dfrac{1}{\sinh^{-1} x^2} \Rightarrow \{\text{using the reciprocal rule}\}$

$$f'(x) = -\dfrac{D_x \sinh^{-1} x^2}{(\sinh^{-1} x^2)^2} = -\dfrac{2x}{(\sinh^{-1} x^2)^2 \sqrt{(x^2)^2 + 1}} = -\dfrac{2x}{(\sinh^{-1} x^2)^2 \sqrt{x^4 + 1}}$$

13 $f(x) = \ln\cosh^{-1} 4x \Rightarrow f'(x) = \dfrac{1}{\cosh^{-1} 4x} \cdot \dfrac{1}{\sqrt{(4x)^2 - 1}} \cdot 4 = \dfrac{4}{\sqrt{16x^2 - 1}\,\cosh^{-1} 4x}$

14 $f(x) = \cosh^{-1}\ln 4x \Rightarrow f'(x) = \dfrac{1}{\sqrt{(\ln 4x)^2 - 1}} \cdot \dfrac{1}{4x} \cdot 4 = \dfrac{1}{x\sqrt{(\ln 4x)^2 - 1}}$

15 $f(x) = \tanh^{-1}(x + 1) \Rightarrow f'(x) = \dfrac{1}{1 - (x + 1)^2} \cdot 1 = \dfrac{1}{-x^2 - 2x} = -\dfrac{1}{x^2 + 2x}$

16 $f(x) = \tanh^{-1} x^3 \Rightarrow f'(x) = \dfrac{1}{1 - (x^3)^2} \cdot 3x^2 = \dfrac{3x^2}{1 - x^6}$

17 $f(x) = \operatorname{sech}^{-1}\sqrt{x} \Rightarrow f'(x) = \dfrac{-1}{\sqrt{x}\sqrt{1 - (\sqrt{x})^2}} \cdot \frac{1}{2}x^{-1/2} = -\dfrac{1}{2x\sqrt{1 - x}}$

$\boxed{18}\ f(x) = (\text{sech}^{-1} x)^{-1} \Rightarrow$

$$f'(x) = -1(\text{sech}^{-1} x)^{-2} \cdot \frac{-1}{x\sqrt{1-(x)^2}} \cdot 1 = \frac{1}{x\sqrt{1-x^2}\,(\text{sech}^{-1} x)^2}$$

$\boxed{19}\ u = 4x,\ \frac{1}{4} du = dx \Rightarrow \int \frac{1}{\sqrt{81+16x^2}}\, dx = \frac{1}{4}\int \frac{1}{\sqrt{9^2+u^2}}\, du = \frac{1}{4}\sinh^{-1}\frac{u}{9} + C$

$\boxed{20}\ u = 4x,\ \frac{1}{4} du = dx \Rightarrow \int \frac{1}{\sqrt{16x^2-9}}\, dx = \frac{1}{4}\int \frac{1}{\sqrt{u^2-3^2}}\, du = \frac{1}{4}\cosh^{-1}\frac{u}{3} + C$

$\boxed{21}\ u = 2x,\ \frac{1}{2} du = dx \Rightarrow \int \frac{1}{49-4x^2}\, dx = \frac{1}{2}\int \frac{1}{7^2-u^2}\, du = \frac{1}{2}\cdot\frac{1}{7}\tanh^{-1}\frac{u}{7} + C$

$\boxed{22}\ u = \cos x,\ -du = \sin x\, dx \Rightarrow \int \frac{\sin x}{\sqrt{1+\cos^2 x}}\, dx = -\int \frac{1}{\sqrt{1+u^2}}\, du = -\sinh^{-1} u + C$

$\boxed{23}\ u = e^x,\ du = e^x\, dx \Rightarrow \int \frac{e^x}{\sqrt{e^{2x}-16}}\, dx = \int \frac{1}{\sqrt{u^2-4^2}}\, du = \cosh^{-1}\frac{u}{4} + C$

$\boxed{24}$ Dividing the numerator and the denominator by 3, $\int \frac{2}{5-3x^2}\, dx = \frac{2}{3}\int \frac{1}{\frac{5}{3}-x^2}\, dx =$

$$\frac{2}{3}\int \frac{1}{(\sqrt{5/3})^2-x^2}\, dx = \frac{2}{3}\cdot\sqrt{\frac{3}{5}}\tanh^{-1}\!\left(\sqrt{\frac{3}{5}}x\right) + C = \frac{2}{\sqrt{15}}\tanh^{-1}\!\left(\sqrt{\frac{3}{5}}x\right) + C$$

$\boxed{25}\ u = x^2,\ \frac{1}{2} du = x\, dx \Rightarrow \int \frac{1}{x\sqrt{9-x^4}}\, dx = \int \frac{x}{x\cdot x\sqrt{9-(x^2)^2}}\, dx = \frac{1}{2}\int \frac{1}{u\sqrt{3^2-u^2}}\, du =$

$$-\frac{1}{2}\cdot\frac{1}{3}\text{sech}^{-1}\frac{|u|}{3} + C = -\frac{1}{6}\text{sech}^{-1}\frac{x^2}{3} + C$$

$\boxed{26}\ u = e^x,\ du = e^x\, dx \Rightarrow \int \frac{1}{\sqrt{5-e^{2x}}}\, dx = \int \frac{e^x}{e^x\sqrt{5-(e^x)^2}}\, dx = \int \frac{1}{u\sqrt{(\sqrt{5})^2-u^2}}\, du =$

$$-\frac{1}{\sqrt{5}}\text{sech}^{-1}\frac{|u|}{\sqrt{5}} + C = -\frac{1}{\sqrt{5}}\text{sech}^{-1}\frac{e^x}{\sqrt{5}} + C$$

$\boxed{27}$ Let the particle have coordinates $P(1, y)$. Its distance from the origin is $\sqrt{1+y^2}$ and its velocity is given by $\frac{dy}{dt} = k\sqrt{1+y^2}$, where k is a constant of proportionality.

$\frac{dy}{dt} = 3$ at $y = 0 \Rightarrow k = 3$. Then, $\frac{dy}{\sqrt{1+y^2}} = 3\, dt \Rightarrow \sinh^{-1} y = 3t + C \Rightarrow$

$y = \sinh(3t + C)$. At $t = 0$, $y = \sinh C = 0 \Rightarrow C = 0$. Thus, $y = \sinh 3t$.

$\boxed{28}$ Let $z = y' = \frac{dy}{dx}$. Then, for $x > 0$, $2x\frac{dz}{dx} = \sqrt{1+z^2} \Rightarrow \frac{dz}{\sqrt{1+z^2}} = \frac{1}{2}\cdot\frac{dx}{x} \Rightarrow$

$\sinh^{-1} z = \frac{1}{2}\ln x + C \Rightarrow z = \sinh(\ln\sqrt{x} + C)$. The speed of the dog is z. Since the dog is initially at $(1, 0)$ and heads directly towards its master at $(0, 0)$, the dog's direction of movement is "horizontal" and $y' = z = \sinh C = 0 \Rightarrow C = 0$ at $x = 1$.

Thus, $z = \sinh(\ln\sqrt{x}) = \frac{1}{2}\!\left(\sqrt{x} - \frac{1}{\sqrt{x}}\right)$. Letting $z = \frac{dy}{dx} = \frac{1}{2}\!\left(\sqrt{x} - \frac{1}{\sqrt{x}}\right) \Rightarrow$

$y = \frac{1}{3}x^{3/2} - x^{1/2} + C$. Since the dog starts at $(1, 0)$,

$$y = 0 \text{ when } x = 1 \Rightarrow 0 = \frac{1}{3} - 1 + C \Rightarrow C = \frac{2}{3}.$$

29 $y = \sinh^{-1} x = \ln\left(x + \sqrt{x^2 + 1}\right)$ is an odd function with domain D = range R = $\mathbb{R}$.

Since $\lim\limits_{x \to \infty} \sqrt{x^2 + 1} = x$, $y = \sinh^{-1} x$ is asymptotic to $y = \ln x + \ln 2$ for positive x.

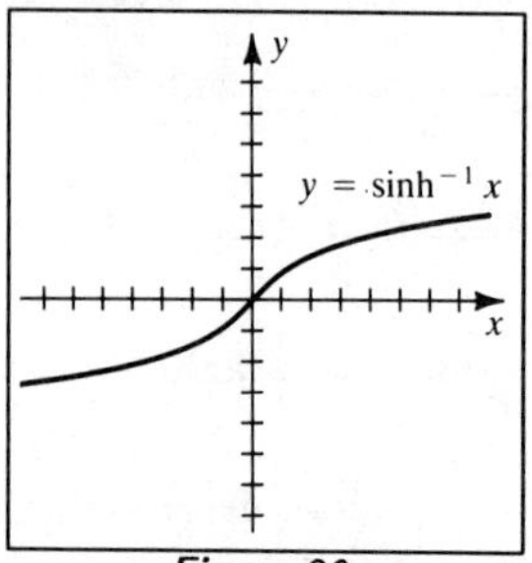

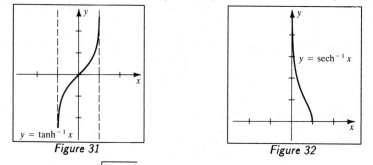

Figure 29 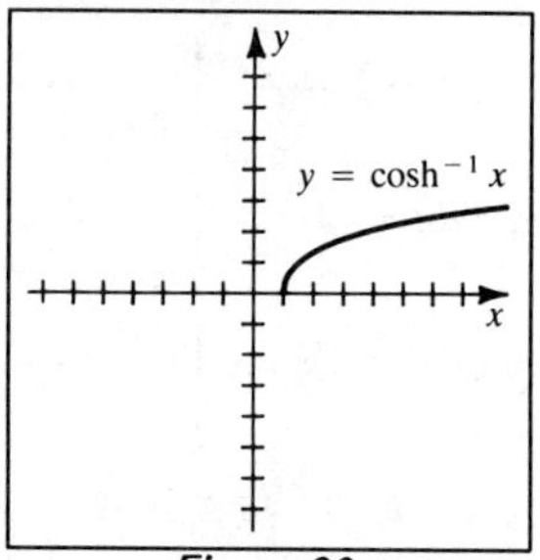   Figure 30

30 $y = \cosh^{-1} x = \ln\left(x + \sqrt{x^2 - 1}\right)$ has domain D: $x \geq 1$ and range R: $y \geq 0$.

Since $\lim\limits_{x \to \infty} \sqrt{x^2 - 1} = x$, $y = \cosh^{-1} x$ is asymptotic to $y = \ln x + \ln 2$ for positive x.

Its values are just slightly less than those of $\sinh^{-1} x$.

31 $y = \tanh^{-1} x = \frac{1}{2}\ln\dfrac{1 + x}{1 - x}$ is an odd function with domain D: $|x| < 1$ and range

R = $\mathbb{R}$. The graph has vertical asymptotes at $x = \pm 1$. The graph is similar to that

of $y = \tan x$, but $\left|\tanh^{-1} x\right| > |\tan x|$ for $0 < |x| < 1$.

Figure 31   Figure 32

32 $y = \text{sech}^{-1} x = \ln\dfrac{1 + \sqrt{1 - x^2}}{x}$ has domain D: $0 < x \leq 1$ and range R: $y \geq 0$.

The graph has a vertical asymptote at $x = 0$.

33 $D_x \cosh^{-1} u = D_x \ln\left(u + \sqrt{u^2 - 1}\right) = \dfrac{1 + u/\sqrt{u^2 - 1}}{u + \sqrt{u^2 - 1}} D_x u =$

$$\dfrac{\sqrt{u^2 - 1} + u}{\sqrt{u^2 - 1}\left(u + \sqrt{u^2 - 1}\right)} D_x u = \dfrac{1}{\sqrt{u^2 - 1}} D_x u, \; u > 1$$

34 $D_x \tanh^{-1} u = \frac{1}{2} D_x\left[\ln(1 + u) - \ln(1 - u)\right] = \frac{1}{2}\left(\dfrac{1}{1 + u} + \dfrac{1}{1 - u}\right) D_x u =$

$$\dfrac{1}{1 - u^2} D_x u, \; |u| < 1$$

$\boxed{35}$ $D_x \operatorname{sech}^{-1} u = D_x \left[\ln\left(1 + \sqrt{1 - u^2}\right) - \ln u \right]$

$$= \left[\frac{-u/\sqrt{1 - u^2}}{1 + \sqrt{1 - u^2}} - \frac{1}{u} \right] D_x u = \left[\frac{-u^2 - \sqrt{1 - u^2}\left(1 + \sqrt{1 - u^2}\right)}{u\sqrt{1 - u^2}\left(1 + \sqrt{1 - u^2}\right)} \right] D_x u$$

$$= \left[-\frac{u^2 + \sqrt{1 - u^2} + 1 - u^2}{u\sqrt{1 - u^2}\left(1 + \sqrt{1 - u^2}\right)} \right] D_x u = -\frac{1}{u\sqrt{1 - u^2}} D_x u, \; 0 < u < 1$$

$\boxed{36}$ $D_u\left(\cosh^{-1}\frac{u}{a}\right) = \dfrac{1}{\sqrt{(u/a)^2 - 1}} \cdot \dfrac{1}{a} = \dfrac{a}{\sqrt{u^2 - a^2}} \cdot \dfrac{1}{a} = \dfrac{1}{\sqrt{u^2 - a^2}}$

$\boxed{37}$ $D_u\left(\frac{1}{a}\tanh^{-1}\frac{u}{a}\right) = \frac{1}{a}\left[\dfrac{1}{1 - (u/a)^2} \cdot \dfrac{1}{a} \right] = \frac{1}{a}\left(\dfrac{a^2}{a^2 - u^2} \cdot \dfrac{1}{a} \right) = \dfrac{1}{a^2 - u^2}$

$\boxed{38}$ If $u > 0$, then $|u| = u$. Thus, $D_u\left(-\frac{1}{a}\operatorname{sech}^{-1}\frac{|u|}{a}\right) = D_u\left(-\frac{1}{a}\operatorname{sech}^{-1}\frac{u}{a}\right) =$

$$-\frac{1}{a}\left[\dfrac{-1}{(u/a)\sqrt{1 - (u/a)^2}} \cdot \dfrac{1}{a} \right] = -\frac{1}{a}\left(\dfrac{-a^2}{u\sqrt{a^2 - u^2}} \cdot \dfrac{1}{a} \right) = \dfrac{1}{u\sqrt{a^2 - u^2}}. \;\text{If } u < 0,$$

then $|u| = -u$, and differentiating the right-hand side yields the same result.

$\boxed{39}$ $y = \cosh^{-1}x \Rightarrow x = \cosh y = \frac{1}{2}(e^y + e^{-y}) \; (x \geq 1) \Rightarrow 2x = e^y + e^{-y} \Rightarrow$

$e^{2y} - 2xe^y + 1 = 0 \Rightarrow e^y = \frac{1}{2}\left(2x \pm \sqrt{4x^2 - 4}\right) = x \pm \sqrt{x^2 - 1}$.

The $+$ sign must be chosen since $y \geq 0 \Rightarrow e^y \geq 1$, and $x - \sqrt{x^2 - 1} < 1$ if $x > 1$.

Hence, $y = \ln\left(x + \sqrt{x^2 - 1}\right), \; x \geq 1$.

$\boxed{40}$ $y = \tanh^{-1}x \Rightarrow x = \tanh y = \dfrac{e^y - e^{-y}}{e^y + e^{-y}} \Rightarrow xe^y + xe^{-y} = e^y - e^{-y} \Rightarrow$

$xe^{2y} + x = e^{2y} - 1 \Rightarrow x + 1 = e^{2y}(1 - x) \Rightarrow e^{2y} = \dfrac{1 + x}{1 - x} \Rightarrow 2y = \ln\dfrac{1 + x}{1 - x} \Rightarrow$

$$y = \frac{1}{2}\ln\frac{1 + x}{1 - x}, \; |x| < 1.$$

$\boxed{41}$ $y = \operatorname{sech}^{-1}x \Rightarrow x = \operatorname{sech} y = \dfrac{2}{e^y + e^{-y}} \Rightarrow xe^y + xe^{-y} = 2 \Rightarrow$

$xe^{2y} - 2e^y + x = 0 \Rightarrow e^y = \dfrac{2 \pm \sqrt{4 - 4x^2}}{2x} = \dfrac{1 \pm \sqrt{1 - x^2}}{x}$. The $+$ sign must be

chosen since $y \geq 0 \Rightarrow e^y \geq 1$. Hence, $y = \ln\dfrac{1 + \sqrt{1 - x^2}}{x}, \; 0 < x \leq 1$.

$\boxed{\text{8.5 Review Exercises}}$

$\boxed{1}$ $f(x) = \arctan\sqrt{x - 1} \Rightarrow f'(x) = \dfrac{1}{1 + (\sqrt{x - 1})^2} \cdot \frac{1}{2}(x - 1)^{-1/2} = \dfrac{1}{2x\sqrt{x - 1}}$

$\boxed{2}$ $f(x) = \tan^{-1}(\ln 3x) \Rightarrow f'(x) = \dfrac{1}{1 + (\ln 3x)^2} \cdot \dfrac{1}{3x} \cdot 3 = \dfrac{1}{x\left[1 + (\ln 3x)^2\right]}$

$\boxed{3}$ $f(x) = x^2 \operatorname{arcsec}(x^2) \Rightarrow$

$$f'(x) = x^2 \cdot \dfrac{1}{x^2\sqrt{(x^2)^2 - 1}} \cdot 2x + (2x)\cdot \operatorname{arcsec}(x^2) = \dfrac{2x}{\sqrt{x^4 - 1}} + 2x\operatorname{arcsec}(x^2)$$

$\boxed{4}$ $f(x) = \dfrac{1}{\cos^{-1} x} \Rightarrow f'(x) = -1(\cos^{-1} x)^{-2} \cdot \dfrac{-1}{\sqrt{1 - (x)^2}} = \dfrac{1}{\sqrt{1 - x^2}\,(\cos^{-1}x)^2}$

$\boxed{5}$ $f(x) = 2^{\arctan 2x} \Rightarrow f'(x) = (2^{\arctan 2x} \ln 2) \cdot \dfrac{1}{1 + (2x)^2} \cdot 2 = 2^{\arctan 2x}\left(\dfrac{2\ln 2}{1 + 4x^2}\right)$

$\boxed{6}$ $f(x) = (1 + \operatorname{arcsec} 2x)^{\sqrt{2}} \Rightarrow$

$$f'(x) = \sqrt{2}\,(1 + \operatorname{arcsec} 2x)^{\sqrt{2}-1} \cdot \dfrac{1}{2x\sqrt{(2x)^2 - 1}} \cdot 2 = \dfrac{\sqrt{2}\,(1 + \operatorname{arcsec} 2x)^{\sqrt{2}-1}}{x\sqrt{4x^2 - 1}}$$

$\boxed{7}$ $f(x) = \ln \tan^{-1}(x^2) \Rightarrow f'(x) = \dfrac{1}{\tan^{-1}(x^2)} \cdot \dfrac{1}{1 + (x^2)^2} \cdot 2x = \dfrac{2x}{(1 + x^4)\tan^{-1}(x^2)}$

$\boxed{8}$ $f(x) = \dfrac{1 - x^2}{\arccos x} \Rightarrow$

$$f'(x) = \dfrac{(\arccos x)(-2x) - (1 - x^2)(-1/\sqrt{1 - x^2})}{(\arccos x)^2} = \dfrac{-2x \arccos x + \sqrt{1 - x^2}}{(\arccos x)^2}$$

$\boxed{9}$ $f(x) = \sin^{-1}\sqrt{1 - x^2} \Rightarrow$

$$f'(x) = \dfrac{1}{\sqrt{1 - (\sqrt{1 - x^2})^2}} \cdot \dfrac{1}{2}(1 - x^2)^{-1/2}(-2x) = \dfrac{1}{\sqrt{x^2}} \cdot \dfrac{-x}{\sqrt{1 - x^2}} = \dfrac{-x}{\sqrt{x^2(1 - x^2)}}$$

$\boxed{10}$ $f(x) = \sqrt{\sin^{-1}(1 - x^2)} \Rightarrow$

$$f'(x) = \dfrac{1}{2}\left[\sin^{-1}(1 - x^2)\right]^{-1/2} \cdot \dfrac{1}{\sqrt{1 - (1 - x^2)^2}} \cdot (-2x) = \dfrac{-x}{\sqrt{\sin^{-1}(1 - x^2)}\sqrt{2x^2 - x^4}}$$

$\boxed{11}$ $f(x) = (\tan x + \tan^{-1} x)^4 \Rightarrow f'(x) = 4(\tan x + \tan^{-1} x)^3\left(\sec^2 x + \dfrac{1}{1 + x^2}\right)$

$\boxed{12}$ $f(x) = \tan^{-1}\sqrt{\tan 2x} \Rightarrow$

$$f'(x) = \dfrac{1}{1 + (\sqrt{\tan 2x})^2} \cdot \dfrac{1}{2}(\tan 2x)^{-1/2}(2\sec^2 2x) = \dfrac{\sec^2 2x}{(1 + \tan 2x)\sqrt{\tan 2x}}$$

$\boxed{13}$ $f(x) = \tan^{-1}(\tan^{-1} x) \Rightarrow f'(x) = \dfrac{1}{1 + (\tan^{-1}x)^2} \cdot \dfrac{1}{1 + x^2} = \dfrac{1}{(1 + x^2)\left[1 + (\tan^{-1}x)^2\right]}$

$\boxed{14}$ $f(x) = e^{4x}\sec^{-1} e^{4x} \Rightarrow f'(x) = e^{4x} \cdot \dfrac{1}{e^{4x}\sqrt{(e^{4x})^2 - 1}} \cdot 4e^{4x} + 4e^{4x} \cdot \sec^{-1} e^{4x} =$

$$4e^{4x}\left(\dfrac{1}{\sqrt{e^{8x} - 1}} + \sec^{-1} e^{4x}\right)$$

$\boxed{15}$ $f(x) = \cosh e^{-5x} \Rightarrow f'(x) = \sinh e^{-5x} \cdot e^{-5x} \cdot (-5) = -5e^{-5x}\sinh e^{-5x}$

$\boxed{16}$ $f(x) = \dfrac{\ln \sinh x}{x} \Rightarrow f'(x) = \dfrac{x\left(\dfrac{1}{\sinh x} \cdot \cosh x\right) - (\ln \sinh x)(1)}{(x)^2} = \dfrac{x \coth x - \ln \sinh x}{x^2}$

$\boxed{17}$ $f(x) = e^{-x}\sinh e^{-x} \Rightarrow$

$$f'(x) = e^{-x}\cosh e^{-x} \cdot (-e^{-x}) + (-e^{-x})\sinh e^{-x} = -e^{-x}(e^{-x}\cosh e^{-x} + \sinh e^{-x})$$

$\boxed{18}$ $f(x) = e^{x \cosh x} \Rightarrow f'(x) = e^{x \cosh x}(x \sinh x + \cosh x)$

$\boxed{19}$ $f(x) = \dfrac{\sinh x}{\cosh x - \sinh x} \Rightarrow f'(x) = \dfrac{(\cosh x - \sinh x)\cosh x - \sinh x(\sinh x - \cosh x)}{(\cosh x - \sinh x)^2}$

$$= \dfrac{\cosh^2 x - \sinh^2 x}{(\cosh x - \sinh x)^2} = \dfrac{1}{(e^{-x})^2} \,\{\text{see } 8.3.56\} = e^{2x}$$

20 $f(x) = \ln \tanh(5x + 1) \Rightarrow$

$$f'(x) = \frac{1}{\tanh(5x+1)} \cdot \text{sech}^2(5x+1) \cdot 5 = 5 \coth(5x+1) \, \text{sech}^2(5x+1)$$

21 $f(x) = \sinh^{-1}(x^2) \Rightarrow f'(x) = \dfrac{1}{\sqrt{(x^2)^2 + 1}} \cdot 2x = \dfrac{2x}{\sqrt{x^4 + 1}}$

22 $f(x) = \cosh^{-1} \tan x \Rightarrow f'(x) = \dfrac{1}{\sqrt{(\tan x)^2 - 1}} \cdot \sec^2 x = \dfrac{\sec^2 x}{\sqrt{\tan^2 x - 1}}$

23 $f(x) = \tanh^{-1}(\tanh \sqrt[3]{x}) = \sqrt[3]{x} \Rightarrow f'(x) = \frac{1}{3}x^{-2/3} = \dfrac{1}{3x^{2/3}}$

24 $f(x) = (1/x) \tanh(1/x) \Rightarrow f'(x) = (1/x) \, \text{sech}^2(1/x) \cdot (-1/x^2) + (-1/x^2) \tanh(1/x)$

$$= (-1/x^2)\Big[(1/x) \, \text{sech}^2(1/x) + \tanh(1/x)\Big]$$

25 $\displaystyle\int \frac{1}{4 + 9x^2} \, dx = \frac{1}{9}\int \frac{1}{\left(\frac{2}{3}\right)^2 + x^2} \, dx = \frac{1}{9} \cdot \frac{1}{\frac{2}{3}} \tan^{-1}\frac{x}{\frac{2}{3}} + C = \frac{1}{6}\tan^{-1}\frac{3x}{2} + C$

26 $u = 4 + 9x^2, \ \frac{1}{18}\, du = x \, dx \Rightarrow \displaystyle\int \frac{x}{4 + 9x^2} \, dx = \frac{1}{18}\int \frac{1}{u} \, du = \frac{1}{18}\ln u + C, \ u > 0$

27 $u = 1 - e^{2x}, \ -\frac{1}{2}\, du = e^{2x} \, dx \Rightarrow$

$$\int \frac{e^{2x}}{\sqrt{1 - e^{2x}}} \, dx = -\frac{1}{2}\int u^{-1/2} \, du = -\frac{1}{2}(2u^{1/2}) + C = -\sqrt{u} + C$$

28 $u = e^x, \ du = e^x \, dx \Rightarrow \displaystyle\int \frac{e^x}{\sqrt{1 - e^{2x}}} \, dx = \int \frac{1}{\sqrt{1 - u^2}} \, du = \sin^{-1}u + C$

29 $u = x^2, \ \frac{1}{2}\, du = x \, dx \Rightarrow \displaystyle\int \frac{x}{\text{sech}(x^2)} \, dx = \frac{1}{2}\int \cosh u \, du = \frac{1}{2}\sinh u + C$

30 $u = x^2, \ \frac{1}{2}\, du = x \, dx \Rightarrow$

$$\int \frac{1}{x\sqrt{x^4 - 1}} \, dx = \int \frac{x}{x \cdot x \sqrt{(x^2)^2 - 1}} \, dx = \frac{1}{2}\int \frac{1}{u\sqrt{u^2 - 1}} \, du = \frac{1}{2}\sec^{-1}u + C$$

31 $\displaystyle\int_{-1/2}^{1/2} \frac{1}{\sqrt{1 - x^2}} \, dx = 2\Big[\sin^{-1}x\Big]_0^{1/2} = 2(\sin^{-1}\tfrac{1}{2} - \sin^{-1}0) = 2(\tfrac{\pi}{6} - 0) = \tfrac{\pi}{3}$

32 $u = \sin x \Rightarrow du = \cos x \, dx. \ x = 0, \frac{\pi}{2} \Rightarrow u = 0, 1.$

$$\int_0^{\pi/2} \frac{\cos x}{1 + \sin^2 x} \, dx = \int_0^1 \frac{1}{1 + u^2} \, du = \Big[\tan^{-1}u\Big]_0^1 = \tan^{-1}1 - \tan^{-1}0 = \tfrac{\pi}{4} - 0 = \tfrac{\pi}{4}.$$

33 $u = \ln x, \ du = \frac{1}{x}\, dx \Rightarrow \displaystyle\int \frac{\sinh(\ln x)}{x} \, dx = \int \sinh u \, du = \cosh u + C$

34 $u = 1 - 2x, \ -\frac{1}{2}\, du = dx \Rightarrow \int \text{sech}^2(1 - 2x) \, dx = -\frac{1}{2}\int \text{sech}^2 u \, du = -\frac{1}{2}\tanh u + C$

35 $u = 2x, \ \frac{1}{2}\, du = dx \Rightarrow \displaystyle\int \frac{1}{\sqrt{9 - 4x^2}} \, dx = \frac{1}{2}\int \frac{1}{\sqrt{3^2 - u^2}} \, du = \frac{1}{2}\sin^{-1}\frac{u}{3} + C$

36 $u = 9 - 4x^2, \ -\frac{1}{8}\, du = x \, dx \Rightarrow$

$$\int \frac{x}{\sqrt{9 - 4x^2}} \, dx = -\frac{1}{8}\int u^{-1/2} \, du = -\frac{1}{8}(2u^{1/2}) + C = -\frac{1}{4}\sqrt{u} + C$$

37 $u = 2x, \ \frac{1}{2}\, du = dx \Rightarrow \displaystyle\int \frac{1}{x\sqrt{9 - 4x^2}} \, dx = \frac{1}{2}\int \frac{1}{(\frac{1}{2}u)\sqrt{3^2 - u^2}} \, du = -\frac{1}{3}\text{sech}^{-1}\frac{|u|}{3} + C$

$\boxed{38}$ $u = 2x,\ \frac{1}{2}\,du = dx \Rightarrow \int \dfrac{1}{x\sqrt{4x^2 - 9}}\,dx = \frac{1}{2}\int \dfrac{1}{(\frac{1}{2}u)\sqrt{u^2 - 3^2}}\,du = \frac{1}{3}\sec^{-1}\frac{u}{3} + C$

$\boxed{39}$ $u = 25x^2 + 36,\ \frac{1}{50}\,du = x\,dx \Rightarrow$

$$\int \dfrac{x}{\sqrt{25x^2 + 36}}\,dx = \frac{1}{50}\int u^{-1/2}\,du = \frac{1}{50}(2u^{1/2}) + C = \frac{1}{25}\sqrt{u} + C$$

$\boxed{40}$ $u = 5x,\ \frac{1}{5}\,du = dx \Rightarrow \int \dfrac{1}{\sqrt{25x^2 + 36}}\,dx = \frac{1}{5}\int \dfrac{1}{\sqrt{u^2 + 6^2}}\,du = \frac{1}{5}\sinh^{-1}\frac{u}{6} + C$

$\boxed{41}$ $m_{AB} = \dfrac{7 - (-3)}{4 - 2} = 5.$ $y' = \dfrac{3}{\sqrt{1 - 9x^2}} = 5 \Rightarrow \frac{9}{25} = 1 - 9x^2 \Rightarrow 9x^2 = \frac{16}{25} \Rightarrow$

$$x^2 = \frac{16}{9 \cdot 25} \Rightarrow x = \pm\frac{4}{15}. \text{ The points are } (\pm\frac{4}{15},\ \sin^{-1}(\pm\frac{4}{5})).$$

$\boxed{42}$ $y' = \dfrac{x}{\sqrt{1 - x^2}} + \sin^{-1}x$ and $y'' = \dfrac{\sqrt{1 - x^2} + x^2/\sqrt{1 - x^2}}{1 - x^2} + \dfrac{1}{\sqrt{1 - x^2}} =$

$$\dfrac{2 - x^2}{(1 - x^2)^{3/2}} > 0 \text{ on } (-1, 1). \text{ The graph is } CU \text{ on } (-1, 1). \text{ No } PI.$$

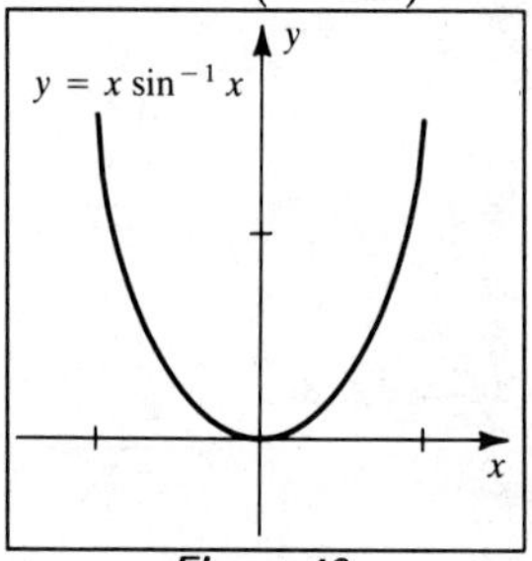

Figure 42

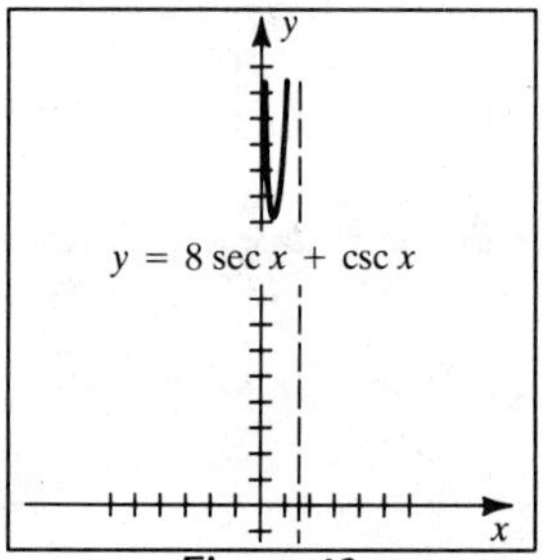

Figure 43

$\boxed{43}$ $f(x) = 8\sec x + \csc x \Rightarrow f'(x) = 8\sec x\tan x - \csc x\cot x = \dfrac{8\sin^3 x - \cos^3 x}{\sin^2 x\cos^2 x}.$

$f'(x) = 0 \Rightarrow 8\sin^3 x = \cos^3 x \Rightarrow 2\sin x = \cos x \Rightarrow \tan x = \frac{1}{2} \Rightarrow x = c = \tan^{-1}\frac{1}{2}.$

$f'(x) < 0$ on $(0, c)$ and $f'(x) > 0$ on $(c, \frac{\pi}{2})$. Hence, $f \downarrow$ on $(0, c]$ and $\uparrow$ on $[c, \frac{\pi}{2})$.

f has a *LMIN* of $f(c) = 5\sqrt{5}.$

$\boxed{44}$ $A = \displaystyle\int_0^1 \dfrac{x}{1 + x^4}\,dx.$ $u = x^2 \Rightarrow \frac{1}{2}\,du = x\,dx.$ $x = 0, 1 \Rightarrow u = 0, 1.$

$$A = \frac{1}{2}\int_0^1 \dfrac{1}{1 + u^2}\,du = \frac{1}{2}\Big[\tan^{-1}u\Big]_0^1 = \frac{1}{2}(\frac{\pi}{4} - 0) = \frac{\pi}{8}.$$

$\boxed{45}$ (a) $f(x) = e^{-x/2}\sin 2x \Rightarrow f'(x) = -\frac{1}{2}e^{-x/2}\sin 2x + 2e^{-x/2}\cos 2x =$

$e^{-x/2}(2\cos 2x - \frac{1}{2}\sin 2x).$ $f'(x) = 0 \Rightarrow \dfrac{\sin 2x}{\cos 2x} = \tan 2x = 4 \Rightarrow$

$2x = \tan^{-1}4 + \pi n \Rightarrow x = \frac{1}{2}\tan^{-1}4 + \frac{\pi}{2}n,\ n = 0, 1, 2, 3.$ These will all be

x-coordinates of local extrema since the derivative changes sign at each value.

(b) $x \approx 0.66, 2.23, 3.80, 5.38$ for $n = 0, 1, 2, 3.$

$\boxed{46}$ $y' = \dfrac{\operatorname{sech}^2\left(\frac{1}{2}x\right)}{2\tanh\left(\frac{1}{2}x\right)} = \dfrac{1}{2\sinh\left(\frac{1}{2}x\right)\cosh\left(\frac{1}{2}x\right)} = \dfrac{1}{\sinh\left(2\cdot\frac{1}{2}x\right)}$ { see 8.3.65 } $= \operatorname{csch} x.$

$$L = \int_1^2 \sqrt{1 + (\operatorname{csch} x)^2}\,dx = \int_1^2 \sqrt{\coth^2 x}\,dx = \int_1^2 \coth x\,dx\ (\coth x > 0 \text{ for } x > 0) =$$

$$\int_1^2 \frac{\cosh x}{\sinh x}\,dx = \Big[\ln|\sinh x|\Big]_1^2 = \ln\frac{\sinh 2}{\sinh 1} \approx 1.13.$$

$\boxed{47}$ From *Figure 47*, $\tan\theta = \dfrac{h}{500} \Rightarrow \theta = \tan^{-1}\dfrac{h}{500}.$ $\dfrac{d\theta}{dt} = \dfrac{d\theta}{dh}\cdot\dfrac{dh}{dt} = \dfrac{500}{500^2 + h^2}\cdot\dfrac{dh}{dt}.$

When $h = 100$ and $\dfrac{dh}{dt} = 2$, $\dfrac{d\theta}{dt} = \dfrac{1}{260}$ rad/sec $\approx 0.22°$/sec.

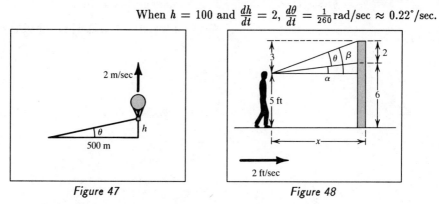

Figure 47   Figure 48

$\boxed{48}$ From *Figure 48*, $\theta = \beta - \alpha$, $\tan\beta = (3/x)$, and $\tan\alpha = (1/x)$.

$$\tan\theta = \tan(\beta - \alpha) = \frac{\tan\beta - \tan\alpha}{1 + \tan\beta\tan\alpha} = \frac{(3/x) - (1/x)}{1 + (3/x)(1/x)}\cdot\frac{x^2}{x^2} = \frac{2x}{x^2 + 3}. \text{ Thus,}$$

$$\theta = \tan^{-1}\left(\frac{2x}{x^2 + 3}\right) \text{ and } \frac{d\theta}{dx} = \frac{1}{1 + \left[2x/(x^2+3)\right]^2}\cdot\frac{6 - 2x^2}{(x^2+3)^2} = \frac{6 - 2x^2}{x^4 + 10x^2 + 9}.$$

(a) $x = 8$ and $\dfrac{dx}{dt} = -2$ { decreasing } $\Rightarrow$

$$\frac{d\theta}{dt} = \frac{d\theta}{dx}\cdot\frac{dx}{dt} = \frac{-122}{4745}\cdot(-2) = \frac{244}{4745} \approx 0.0514\,\text{rad/sec.}$$

(b) $\dfrac{d\theta}{dx} = 0 \Rightarrow 6 - 2x^2 = 0 \Rightarrow x = \sqrt{3}$ ft.

Since $\dfrac{d\theta}{dx} > 0$ for $0 < x < \sqrt{3}$ and $\dfrac{d\theta}{dx} < 0$ for $x > \sqrt{3}$, this gives a maximum.

$\boxed{49}$ Let s denote the altitude of the stunt man. Then $s(t) = -\frac{1}{2}gt^2 + v_0 t + s_0 =$

$-16t^2 + 100.$ Now, $\tan\theta = \dfrac{s}{200} = \dfrac{100 - 16t^2}{200} \Rightarrow \theta = \tan^{-1}\left(\dfrac{25 - 4t^2}{50}\right).$

Thus, $\dfrac{d\theta}{dt} = \dfrac{1}{1 + \left[\frac{1}{50}(25 - 4t^2)\right]^2}\cdot\left(-\frac{8}{50}t\right).$ At $t = 2$, $\dfrac{d\theta}{dt} = -\dfrac{800}{2581} \approx -0.31$ rad/sec.

$\boxed{50}$ (a) Let s denote the swimming distance from I to P, w the walking distance from P to the camp, and $\theta = \angle AIP$. The total energy spent is given by $c = c_1 s + c_2 w$. Thus, $\cos\theta = \frac{k}{s}$ and $\sin\theta = \frac{d-w}{s} \Rightarrow s = k\sec\theta$ and $w = d - s\sin\theta = d - (k\sec\theta)\sin\theta = d - k\tan\theta$. Hence, $c = c_1 k\sec\theta + c_2(d - k\tan\theta)$.

(b) $\frac{dc}{d\theta} = c_1 k\sec\theta\,\tan\theta - c_2 k\sec^2\theta$. $\frac{dc}{d\theta} = 0 \Rightarrow c_1 k\sec\theta\,\tan\theta = c_2 k\sec^2\theta \Rightarrow$ $c_1\tan\theta = c_2\sec\theta\,\{\sec\theta \neq 0\} \Rightarrow c_1\sin\theta = c_2\,\{\cos\theta \neq 0 \text{ since } \theta \in [0, \frac{\pi}{2})\} \Rightarrow$ $\theta = \theta_0 = \arcsin(c_2/c_1)$, which will be a minimum value since

$$\frac{dc}{d\theta} < 0 \text{ if } 0 \le \theta < \theta_0 \text{ and } \frac{dc}{d\theta} > 0 \text{ if } \theta_0 < \theta < \frac{\pi}{2}.$$